Programmer's Guide
to Presentation Manager

Programmer's Guide to Presentation Manager

Alan Southerton

Addison-Wesley Publishing Company, Inc.

Reading, Massachusetts Menlo Park, California New York
Don Mills, Ontario Wokingham, England Amsterdam Bonn Sydney
Singapore Tokyo Madrid San Juan

Many of the designations used by manufacturers and sellers to distinguish their products are claimed as trademarks. Where those designations appear in this book and Addison-Wesley was aware of a trademark claim, the designations have been printed in initial capital letters.

The opinions expressed are solely those of the author and do not necessarily reflect the views of the publisher or any other organization.

Library of Congress Cataloging-in-Publication Data
Southerton, Alan.
    Programmer's guide to presentation manager

    Includes index.
    1. OS/2 (Computer operating systems)
2.   Presentation manager (Computer program)
I.   Title.
 QA76.76.063S655   1989   005.4'469   88-34997
 ISBN 0-201-19440-6

Production Editor: Amorette Pedersen
Cover Design by: Doliber Skeffington Design
Set in 11 New Century Schoolbook

ABCDEFGHIJ-AL-89
First Printing, May, 1989

I am honored to dedicate
this book to my parents,
Albert Southerton,
and Kathleen Floyd Southerton,
to whom I am deeply indebted
for their encouragement.

CONTENTS

INTRODUCTION

The Presentation Manager marks a new era in the computer industry. It has an excellent chance of becoming the standard user-interface for the next 5 to 10 years, if not longer.

The support behind the Presentation Manager is the support of every MS-DOS user, whether they know it or not. The reason: the Presentation Manager is the most logical upgrade to the MS-DOS environment, because it alone promises to maintain ties with MS-DOS. For example, it is likely that Borland will continue to port new versions of Sidekick to the Presentation Manager, long before it even considers a port to another graphical user-interface.

Indeed, even the graphical user-interfaces that have surfaced in the UNIX community have their ties to the Presentation Manager. *Motif*, for one, uses an interface based on the Presentation Manager. It is also said that for the rival *Open Look* to succeed, it will have to resemble the Presentation Manager as well. And meanwhile, the Presentation Manager itself continues to make inroads into the UNIX environment, via the work at Hewlett-Packard and Santa Cruz Operation.

Why do users need a graphical user-interface? They seem to be happy enough using their character-based applications. The answer is once you begin using a product with a graphical interface, you will never want to use anything else. It enhances the speed with which you can perform tasks as well as gives you a real-time view of your product — whether it be a memo in a word processor, an illustration in a graphics package, or a book in a desktop publisher.

The last example is not merely a whimsical allusion. This book stands as a testament to the graphical user-interface. It was entirely written and produced using the IBM Interleaf Publisher on a PS/2 Model 70. Interleaf is a desktop publishing package produced by Interleaf Corp. of Cambridge, Mass., and licensed by IBM. Its UNIX versions are used widely by corporations and the IBM version, while relatively new, promises to become just as popular.

Although Interleaf Publisher runs under the DOS environment, it foretells things to come under OS/2 and the Presentation Manager. Because of Interleaf, this book was produced in a shorter amount of time than if I had written it in a word processor and then submitted the files to my publisher. Some of Interleaf's features such as automatic vertical justification and its unrivaled illustration tools also made the production of this book much easier. Now the only question is how long will it take for software companies such as Interleaf to embrace the Presentation Manager?

My feeling is that it won't be long. From talking to companies such as Ashton-Tate and WordPerfect Corp., it is clear that they are committed to the Presentation Manager. Numerous other companies have also announced support for the Presentation Manager. Still others have already released OS/2 kernel-based programs and intend to upgrade these with Presentation Manager versions. The popular belief is that once you develop an application for OS/2 and the Presentation Manager, you can port that application to other environments, including ones based on IBM's SAA architecture. The future of the Presentation Manager indeed looks good.

The goal of this book is two-fold: one, to provide introductory material and examples, so you can begin programming the Presentation Manager; and two, to serve as a reference after you have become familiar with the Presentation Manager. Although it is more than likely that you have to refer to other books and manuals, this book will reduce the number of books that you are forced to have within reach of your keyboard. Whenever possible, it lists critical functions, messages, and identifiers that are everyday fare in the Presentation Manager. Unfortunately, because the Presentation Manager is such a large environment, this book could not fully address the Graphics Programming Interface. It does, however, provide an introduction to graphics programming, as well as attempts to provide a comprehensive look at the Win library functions as well as the Presentation Manager's extensive message library. The one prerequisite for using this book — as well as the Presentation Manager — is you have a knowledge of the C programming language.

Needless to say, I could not have written this book without help from many corners. First and foremost, I would like to acknowledge my wife, Cameron, and my son, Thomas, for their endurance while I worked around the clock in the final months of the book. I would also like to acknowledge my young niece, Katie, because I was unable to give her the computer support to which she had become accustomed.

Additionally, I would like to acknowledge numerous persons and companies throughout the industry. Microsoft, especially, was extremely helpful in supplying software, support, and technical advice. It is impossible to name everyone at Microsoft who lent assistance, but I would like to acknowledge Marty Taucher, Cathryn Hinsch, Tanya van Dam, Byron Dazey, Lionel Job, and Michael Hyman. I would also like to thank Scott Brooks and Kevin Allen at IBM for their assistance. Also deserving acknowledgment for their assistance are Nan Borreson of Borland and Amy Pedersen of Benchmark Productions.

Because of the nature of this book and the Presentation Manager itself, I fully anticipate a thorough re-examination of its contents before any second printing. As a result, if you have comments, clarifications, or corrections, I would appreciate hearing about them. You can reach me through my publisher, or via CompuServe or MCI mail. My CompuServe ID is 76530,1233 and I can be reached via MCI by typing my name, or alternatively, by my ID, 339-7921.

I truly hope you enjoy working with the Presentation Manager and that this book is helpful. Good luck in this new world. — *Alan Southerton*

CHAPTER 1

FROM THE OUTSIDE IN

The PMAPI (Presentation Manager Application Program Interface) is the official name given the programmer-to-user OS/2 windowing interface that is the Presentation Manager. The PMAPI, as you will see, results as much from user interface issues as it does from programming issues. These two components are inextricably linked. Both are object oriented in nature: the Presentation Manager programming interface relies heavily on object oriented programming methods and structure; its user interface presents data in the form of onscreen objects.

The user interface for the Presentation Manager predates the beginning of Presentation Manager development. Of course, the explanation for this is Microsoft *Windows*, which served as the windowing model for the Presentation Manager. Some user interface differences do exist between the two environments. The most notable is the Presentation Manager's support for true multitasking, which essentially asks the user to adopt a new way of thinking about running windowed applications. Some enhancements do show up in the Presentation Manager user interface, including its advanced set of system utilities as well as the use of a proportionally spaced font in system windows, menus, and dialog boxes. In general, however, the Presentation Manager user interface is strikingly similar to the *Windows* user interface.

Understanding the nooks and crannies of the Presentation Manager is vital to programmers. If you do not have *Windows* experience, you should take some time to study the Presentation Manager from the user's viewpoint. You should also study one or two commercial applications — either one that runs under *Windows*, or one that runs under the Presentation Manager. Even if you are experienced with the Presentation Manager, you should read this chapter: in addition to describing the interface, it provides an overview of the individual components of the Presentation Manager. Further, the chapter describes the various system utilities that play an intricate role in the Presentation Manager interface, including the *Task Manager* and *Start Programs* utilities.

The Presentation Manager also can window non-Presentation Manager programs. For example, it is possible for the user to execute any OS/2 kernel-based program from the *Start Programs* utility. More important, the Presentation Manager supports OS/2 kernel-based programs written using the advanced Vio (video input/output) library functions. Advanced Vio programs can be displayed in a Presentation Manager window, yet retain the character I/O format of kernel-based programs. The advanced Vio interface is described in this chapter.

Interface Issues

To be well versed in the Presentation Manager's user interface is the first step in being a Presentation Manager programmer. True, a skilled programmer can learn the fundamentals of the Presentation Manager toolkit and stir-fry a program; but the result, even though the fast food approach might look good, would likely be far from standard Presentation Manager fare. This is because Presentation Manager applications generally adhere to the programming style set forth by Microsoft's *Presentation Manager Application Style Guide*.

The style guide is not a fascist document. It merely describes the agreed upon interface techniques used for the Presentation Manager. To be sure, Microsoft dictated many of these tenets, but as one well known law suit has underscored, the same interface fundamentals exist in other windowing environments. In fact, the more that window environments appear on the scene, the more it appears that there are precious few alternatives to manipulating menus, dialog boxes, mouse pointers, and windows. The *SunView* window interface that Sun Microsystems uses on its 32-bit UNIX workstations is similar in many ways to the Presentation Manager. Indeed, although various interface differences exist between the *SunView* interface and the Presentation Manager, a user from either environment can quickly comprehend the subtleties of the other environment. To Microsoft's credit, the combined keyboard/mouse interface of the Presentation Manager is the most thorough of any commercially available windowing package.

On a more parochial level, it is important that all Presentation Manager applications present users with the interface tools to which they have become accustomed. This is to your benefit as much as to the user's, because it ensures that, in the least, your application's interface will be successful. On the other hand, omitting an interface component such as a scrollbar or clipboard access is a sure way to anger users. What is more, by adhering to the spirit of the *Application Style Guide*, you ultimately participate in a larger force that enables more and more people to attain a certain level of computer literacy. (While it might be a lofty forecast, persons at Microsoft have predicted that the Presentation Manager interface will be as common as microwave ovens one day.)

Mouse Versus Keyboard

The Presentation Manager is heavily biased in favor of the mouse. And this is quite understandable. The mouse lends a certain fluidity to the on-screen manipulation of objects that the keyboard cannot even begin to approximate. For example, it is much easier to resize a window with the mouse than with the cursor keys, which do the deed, but much more slowly. Similarly, the mouse outmaneuvers the keyboard inside many applications that require the user to select a given item.

Some users, particularly skilled typists, balk at using a device that causes them to lift their fingers from the keyboard. Usually, even these users change their tune after becoming accustomed to a mouse, but in the event they cannot adapt to the mouse, the Presentation Manager provides a keyboard interface through the use of keyboard accelerators. A keyboard accelerator lets the user select a menu item by pressing a predefined key sequence. For example, the keyboard accelerator to close a window is always Alt-F4. The user does not have to display the menu in order to use a keyboard accelerator. Additionally, mouse devotees should note that some keyboard accelerators actually perform some tasks better than the mouse. A case in point involves traversing multiple windows: the Alt-Esc key sequence performs this with ease, while the mouse method — which can entail moving windows to access a hidden window — pales in comparison.

The Presentation Manager supports one-, two-, and three-button mice. From left to right, the mouse buttons are referred to as button 1, button 2, and button 3, respectively. On a one-button mouse, the button is referred to as button 1; on a two-button mouse, the left button is button 1 and the right button is button 2; and on a three-button mouse, the left button is button 1, the center button is button 2, and the right button is button 3. Visually, the mouse is represented by the mouse pointer. A pointer is a bit-mapped icon that moves across the screen and between windows. Its logical position corresponds to the direction in which the user moves the mouse on the desktop. In your application, you can program custom pointers that have a specific meaning for a given window. Alternatively, you can rely on the Presentation Manager's system-defined pointers. In either case, you should use the system pointers for the explicit purposes they serve. Table 1-1 lists some of the more common system pointers and describes the purpose of each one.

Table 1-1: Selected System Pointers

BITMAP	DESCRIPTION
Arrow	The default system pointer. Used to move across the screen and between windows. The user selects items from menus and other controls with this pointer.
Hourglass	Indicates that some operation is occurring and the user must wait until it is completed. Should be used sparingly because of the Presentation Manager's multitasking capability.
I-beam	Used in dialog boxes, listboxes, and anywhere else that requires text insertion. The user begins entering text immediately after the I-beam pointer.
Hand	Used to indicate that an onscreen object should be moved. The user simply places the hand pointer on the object and drags it with the mouse.
Sizing Arrow	A double-headed, slanted arrow used to indicate that an onscreen object should be resized. The Presentation Manager uses this arrow to indicate that the user can resize a window.
Moving Arrow	A doubled-headed, straight arrow used to indicate that an onscreen object can be moved. The Presentation Manager uses this arrow to indicate that the user can move a window.

The mouse is used extensively to select items. For example, to select a menu item, the user moves the mouse until the pointer lies on the item. Pressing button 1 causes the item to appear in reverse video. Releasing the button completes the selection process, and the menu command or action takes effect immediately. The user can also select multiple items by simultaneously pressing the Shift key and button 1. In some cases, it is necessary to double click button 1 in order to execute a selection. Double clicking is the act of pressing a mouse button twice in quick succession. Table 1-2 summarizes the default uses for mouse buttons 1 and 3; note that button 2 is entirely reserved for use by an application.

Table 1-2: Mouse Button Default Functionality

BUTTON	ACTION	DESCRIPTION
Button 1	Click	Selects the item beneath the pointer. Allows extended selection when pressed along with the Shift key.
Button 1	Double Click	Selects item beneath the pointer and executes the item in most cases. Allows extended selection/execution when pressed simultaneously with the Shift key.
Button 1	Hold	Anchors a range to the beginning pointer coordinate and defines the range as the user moves the mouse. Purpose is application dependent.
Button 3	Click	Jumps to the *Task Manager*, which becomes the active window and displays a list of available programs.
Button 3	Double Click	Jumps to the next task specified by the *Task Manager*, including programs in OS/2 or the MS-DOS box.

Using the keyboard maintains much of the logic of the mouse. The keyboard devotee must use the arrow keys to move across the screen and between windows. In a menu, dialog box, or other control, the arrow keys again duplicate the functionality of the mouse. For example, using the Up or Down arrow key to highlight a menu item automatically selects the item. Using the Shift key in combination with the Up or Down arrow key lets the user select multiple items. To move from one menu to the next, or from one area of a dialog box to the next, the Tab key is employed. Instead of double clicking on an item to execute it, the user merely presses the Enter key. To toggle between selected items, the user presses the Spacebar.

The Presentation Manager's keyboard interface offers all users convenient methods to move between windows and perform other actions. Table 1-3 lists common key sequences that the Presentation Manager uses for interface operations. Do not redefine these keys if you want your application to be consistent with other Presentation Manager applications.

Table 1-3: Presentation Manager Keyboard Interface

KEY(S)	DESCRIPTION
Alt-Esc	Jumps to the next task specified by the *Task Manager*, including programs concurrently running in OS/2 or the MS-DOS box.
Ctrl-Esc	Jumps to the *Task Manager*, which becomes the active window and displays a lists of running programs.
Enter	Enters data specified in an input window, including any default action. In an application, produces a line feed/carriage return.
Cursor keys	Advances highlight bar to the next available selection. In an application, traditional compass-based cursor movement.
Shift-Cursor	Allows extended selection in the input field.
Ctrl-Arrow	Advances the cursor to the beginning/end of fields.
Spacebar	Toggles selection status. Works as normal in an application.
Tab	Advances cursor between groups of controls.
F1	Invokes a help screen.
F10	Toggles between the application and the application's action bar.
Alt	Toggles between the application and application's action bar. Note that the user must both depress and release Alt.
Shift-Esc	Invokes system menu.
Alt-F4	Closes active window if close is included in the system menu.
Alt-F5	Restores currently specified window.
Alt-F7	Moves currently specified window.
Alt-F8	Resizes currently specified window.
Alt-F9	Minimizes currently specified window.
Alt-F10	Maximizes currently specified window.

Besides the key sequences listed in Table 1-3, Microsoft recommends that applications such as word processors and graphics programs use a small set of keys to perform editing functions. These keys, which are listed in Tables 1-4 and 1-5, should be referenced as keyboard accelerators in any menus that contain the corresponding function.

Table 1-4: General Purpose Editing Keys

KEY(S)	SUGGESTED FUNCTION
Alt-Backspace	Invokes undo function.
Del	Cuts a single character or highlighted text to the clipboard.
Ctrl-Ins	Copies the contents of the clipboard to the application.
Shift-Ins	Inserts the contents of the clipboard to the application.
Shift-Del	Clears the contents of the clipboard.

Table 1-5: General Purpose Movement/Selection Keys

KEY(S)	SUGGESTED FUNCTION
Tab	Advances right by one field.
Shift-Tab	Advances left by one field
Enter	Enters data for processing.
Cursor keys	Advances in the given direction by one field.
Ctrl-Cursor	Advances in the given direction to the beginning or end of a field, group, or section.
Shift-Ctrl-Cursor	Resets the input focus and extends the current selection to the beginning or end of a field, group, or section.
PageUp	Scrolls up one screen.
PageDown	Scrolls down one screen.
Ctrl-PageUp	Scrolls left one screen.

(continued)

Table 1-5: Continued

KEY(S)	SUGGESTED FUNCTION
Ctrl-PageDown	Scrolls right one screen.
Shift-PageUp	Scrolls up one screen, extending the selection.
Shift-PageDown	Scrolls down one screen, extending the selection.
Shift-Cursor	Moves the input focus and extends the selection on unit in the given direction.
Insert	Toggles the insert and replace modes.
Ctrl-Insert	Copies current selection to the clipboard.
Shift-Insert	Pastes the contents of the clipboard.
Delete	Deletes the current selection.
Ctrl-Delete	Deletes to the end of the line.
Shift-Delete	Cuts current selection to the clipboard.
Backspace	Deletes one character to the left of the current position.
Alt-Backspace	Cancels the previous editing command.
Home	Moves to the beginning of a line.
Ctrl-Home	Moves to the top of the file.
Shift-Home	Moves to the beginning of a line and extends the current selection.
Shift-Ctrl-Home	Moves to the top of the file and extends the current selection.
End	Moves to the end of a line.
Ctrl-End	Moves to the end of the file.
Shift-End	Moves to the end of a line and extends the current selection.
Shift-Ctrl-End	Moves to the end of the file and extends the current selection.
Ctrl-Spacebar	Adds an item to the current selection.
Shift-Spacebar	Extends the selection to the current position from the previous end point.

The *Application Style Guide* strongly recommends a consistent keyboard interface. As a result, you can expect a majority of Presentation Manager applications will adhere to the recommendations put forth in the guide. This being the case, it is to your advantage to adopt the conventions as well.

The Desktop

The desktop is the first screen that appears in the Presentation Manager. When you boot OS/2 with the Presentation Manager correctly installed, the desktop displays an open version of the *Start Programs* window. It also displays an iconized version of the *Task Manager*. If the *Spooler Queue Manager* and the MS-DOS 3.3 environment were selected during installation, the desktop shows these in iconized form as well.

With the exception of the so-called DOS box, the system utilities have the capability to interact directly with any Presentation Manager program. For example, an application can add itself as an entry in the *Task Manager*'s list of programs that it executes. Similarly, program entries can be added to the *Start Programs* utility. The *Spooler Queue Manager*, meanwhile, sits waiting for the user to execute a print job, at which point it assumes control of the job and gives the user various printing options.

When the user invokes a Presentation Manager application — either from the *Task Manager*, *Start Programs*, or the OS/2 command prompt — the frame window associated with the application appears on the desktop. The positioning of the frame window depends on the application. If the application does not set the position, the frame window appears near the center of the desktop. This pattern is repeated for as many applications that the user executes, with each application frame window slightly offset from the previously displayed frame window.

Even with several applications running concurrently, part of the desktop usually remains visible to the user. This is convenient if the user wants to access an application represented by an icon (see the next section). Typically, the only time the desktop is not visible is when the user maximizes the display of an application window — that is, the user explicitly issues a maximize command to convert the application window into a full-screen display.

Microsoft is fond of describing the desktop as having a "messy desk" appearance. This is most evident when the user executes and overlaps numerous applications. The application with the input focus — namely, the application ready to receive mouse and/or keyboard input — is distinguished among the various windows by different colors and shading.

Another important desktop concept is z-order. When more than one application window sits on the desktop, an inherent three-dimensional order, or z-order, is in effect. This is especially applicable when several overlapped windows appear on the desktop. The desktop itself has no ranking in the z-order, but acts as the reference point for the z-order. The topmost window on an overlapped stack of windows always has the highest z-order ranking, while the window at the bottom of the stack has the lowest ranking. Z-order is an especially useful concept for the programmer who must determine which frame window amongst several frame windows is activated in a given circumstance. Frequently, z-order is also referred to as the jump order of applications.

The last significant component of the desktop is the parking lot, the term given the invisible grid that spans the desktop screen. The parking lot feature is like a "snap to grid" feature found in popular graphics programs. In the desktop, it lets the user align icons that represent Presentation Manager applications. This is simply accomplished by dragging the icon — clicking and holding down on the mouse and then moving the mouse so that the icon moves on the screen. The parking lot is an aesthetic feature that might be lost in the lengthy list of Presentation Manager features; without the parking lot, however, many users would complain.

The Frame Window

Knowing the components of the frame window — the main window in any Presentation Manager application — is the best place to begin learning the Presentation Manager interface. The frame window is a child of the desktop window. The consequence of this is its screen positioning is always relative to the desktop screen.

The main window area in the frame window is called the *client area* — the area that the user can access, and where an application displays its screen output. Indeed, because of the importance of the client area, the frame window is often referred to as the client window. Additionally, you will see references to the standard window in some Microsoft manuals; again, this is another name for the frame window. This book, in perhaps a masochistic attempt at consistency, uses the terms frame window and client area (or client window), but rarely uses standard window.

Numerous components can be incorporated into a frame window. These components — which are actually a form of windows themselves, as explained in Chapter 4 — imbue the Presentation Manager with a set of powerful user control devices. These window controls include the titlebar, menubar, system menu, borders, scrollbars, minimize and maximize controls, and system icon. The following sections describe each control.

Titlebar — The titlebar contains the current window name, which is usually the application name. A highlighted titlebar indicates that the associated window has the input focus — that is, it is ready to receive keyboard and/or mouse input. In many applications, the titlebar text is obtained from the application description that the user enters in the *Start Programs* utility.

Menubar — The menubar is located underneath the titlebar. It contains an application's main menu items, which themselves can invoke pulldown menus. Typically, the menubar also contains an item to invoke user help. This is located to the extreme right of the menubar and is labeled F1 = Help.

System Menu — The system menu is located in the upper left-hand side of the window. It incorporates system controls in an application, including controls to resize, move, restore, and minimize and maximize the window; close the application, and call the *Task Manager*. The system menu is independent of any menu structure that you build into an application.

Borders — Window borders range in size from 1 to 50 units, and are selected from the *Control Panel* system utility. In addition to enhancing the appearance of a window, borders let the user resize a window by clicking the mouse on any area of a border and then dragging the border to its new size.

Scrollbars — Vertical and/or horizontal scrollbars allow the user to scroll the contents of the frame window's client area. Scrollbars span the width and/or height of the client area. They let the user scroll the client area line-by-line, or screen-by-screen. Additionally, scrollbars can be used elsewhere in the Presentation Manager as an incremental control mechanism.

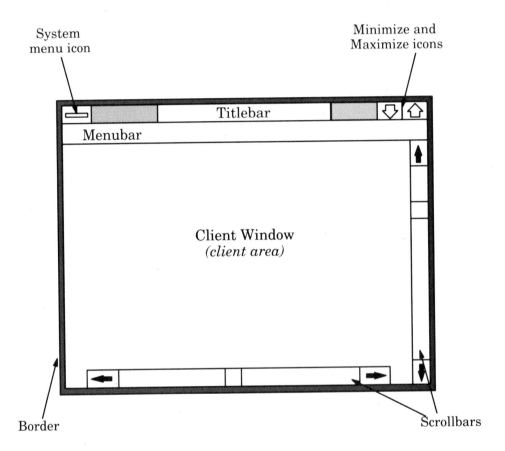

Figure 1-1: Typical frame window and controls

Most applications use all of the various optional controls in their frame windows. If any single control is omitted, it is usually the scrollbar controls. Figure 1-1 illustrates a typical frame window and all possible components that you can program into it.

Minimize and Maximize Controls — These controls give the user a quick way to change the size of a window. Minimize and maximize controls occur in three places in the frame window: as items on the system menu; as icons located in the upper right-hand section of the window; and as part of the titlebar. The latter requires the user to double click on the titlebar to toggle a window's restore and maximize state.

System Icon — The system icon represents an application when its display size is reduced to approximately one-inch by one-inch. The application continues running, but typically the user is unaware of this, and instead simply sees the icon. To restore the application, the user can double click the mouse on the icon.

An application can have multiple frame windows. In such an implementation, each frame window is a child of the desktop. More commonly, an application only has one frame window. When an application requires additional windows, control windows are typically used. In turn, these control windows are considered child windows of the frame window.

The client area of the frame window varies in size and shape. Moving and resizing windows usually depends on the whim of the user. An application must be able to resize or *clip* any display output contained in the client area. From a programming viewpoint, you will find that you can often perform resizing and clipping operations automatically, as long as you do not hard-code screen coordinate values. A typical resizing operation is when a window adjusts its contents after being maximized.

Clipping is a slightly different story. When the Presentation Manager clips a text line or graphic, it does not display the part that extends beyond the visible client area. The key word here is visible. For example, if another window covered part of the client area, the Presentation Manager would not display the output in the hidden part of the client area.

Clipping also occurs because a frame window can logically exceed the dimensions of the desktop screen. This can be a programmed effect or occur as a result of the user moving and resizing the frame window. An intentional use of this effect occurs in applications that need to show a window display for a graphic requiring landscape printing. Of course, if you do program this type of clipping, you should include scrollbar controls so the user can view all of the client area.

STYLE TIP: FRAME WINDOW NECESSITIES

First and foremost, applications should have at least one frame window. As explained, this is the primary interface for the user. It contains the client area and various controls to assist the user. Minimally, the controls that you should incorporate into the frame window are a titlebar, system menu, minimize and maximize controls, window border, and a system icon. If clipping is likely to be an issue, the application should also contain scrollbars. And, of course, for applications that use a command structure, as most do, a menubar should be used to organize the commands into logical pulldown menu selections.

Control Windows

The Presentation Manager uses a predefined set of control windows to obtain user input associated with system and application functions. Besides being an excellent programming tool, control windows offer the user a consistent way to perform actions. An example of a control window is the simple "About Box," which summarizes the purpose of an application.

Control windows underscore the important concept of window relationships. A control window is always a descendent of a frame window. It can either be a direct descendent (a child) of the frame window, or a descendent of another control window, which itself must be a descendent of the frame window. Control windows are always positioned relative to the frame window, not the desktop, meaning a control window remains within the boundaries of the frame window. To describe this relationship, the control window is said to be clipped on the surface of its parent. Additionally, a control window moves and resizes itself when the frame window moves.

These concepts are of general interest to the user, but not necessary for correct use of the Presentation Manager. The one exception is the user who employs the system-defined key sequences to move between control windows within a larger window. On the other hand, control windows are of prime importance to the programmer and they are described in detail throughout this book.

Control windows are often responsible for performing system-oriented tasks. When this is true, control windows should use a standard keyboard interface for these tasks. In fact, some control windows such as entry field controls recognize special interface keys, even when they no longer can accept regular text input. Table 1-6 lists and describes the key sequences used for system-oriented tasks performed from control windows.

Table 1-6: Control Window Keyboard Interface

KEY(S)	DESCRIPTION
Alt, Minus	Selects the system menu for the active window.
Ctrl-F4	Closes the active window.
Ctrl-F5	Restores the active window to its previous size.
Ctrl-F6	Advances to the next window, making it the active window.
Ctrl-F7	Moves the active window.
Ctrl-F8	Resizes the active window.
Ctrl-F9	Decreases the size of the active window.
Ctrl-F10	Increases the size of the active window.

Menus

While they might not look like windows, all menus created by an application are, in fact, control windows. The *Application Style Guide* dictates that any command-oriented application must make its commands available through a menu structure. Minimally, the items contained in the frame window's menubar can comprise the entire menu structure. More often, each menubar item invokes a pulldown menu.

Each item in a pulldown menu has three fields associated with it. The first field contains a check mark if the item has been previously selected and the selection remained in force. The second field contains a short description of the command. In this field, one letter is underscored, indicating that the user can select the desired item by pressing the appropriate mnemonic. No two items in the same pulldown menu can use the same letter as their mnemonic. The last field, which is right justified, contains an accelerator key associated with the command.

Often, menu items are divided into categories by a horizontal bar called a *separator*. This is a technique used to group different types of items together. In all, menu items fall into the three categories described in Table 1-7.

Table 1-7: The Three Types of Menu Items

ITEM	DESCRIPTION
Command	Performs some action without requiring additional information from the user. Examples of this type of command are the minimize, maximize, and close items from the system menu.
State setter	Sets the state of a given attribute by toggling the attribute on and off. A menu containing various font selections uses this type of menu item. State setters are the only menu items that use check marks.
Dialog box	Dialog box commands simply invoke a dialog box, which requests additional information from the user before the command can be executed. Dialog box commands are always denoted by an ellipses.

Dialog Boxes

Dialog boxes are the most flexible controls available in the Presentation Manager. They display information about an application and provide the user with a convenient method of supplying input. For example, a word processor can use a dialog box to let the user set all attributes for a given font, including point size, style, and type. Alternatively, you can use a dialog box to complement the functionality of an application. A relevant example of this would be an entry field dialog box that served as a note pad in a spreadsheet or accounting program.

Dialog boxes and the controls they use vary according to the application. The type of controls that a dialog box uses depends on its relationship to the application. Generally, a dialog box should offer the user the choice of selecting a displayed value, or entering a new value. Dialog boxes also include a host of automatic attribute features that indicate the current selection state, among other things.

Dialog boxes fall into three categories: modal, modeless, and system modal. The category to which a dialog box belongs is dependent on its relationship to its frame window. The modal dialog box is perhaps the most common of the three, but both modeless and system modal dialog boxes are usedful in given situations. Table 1-8 describes the three dialog box types.

Table 1-8: The Three Categories of Dialog Boxes

CATEGORY	DESCRIPTION
Modal	A modal dialog box forces the user to enter input data or exit before the input focus returns to the frame window or any currently available child windows. The user is free to shift input focus to a concurrently running application.
Modeless	A modeless dialog box lets the user switch input focus between the dialog box and the frame window or any currently available child window. A modeless dialog box also has its own control menu, with options to move and close.
System modal	A system modal dialog box has the same characteristics as a modal dialog box, but additionally prevents the user from shifting input focus to any other window. A system modal dialog box should only be used to warn the user of an impending system error from which it is unlikely that the application will recover.

In addition to the standard mouse interface, dialog boxes use a mnemonic interface when applicable. The user can also control some dialog box controls by pressing certain system default keys. The following descriptions summarize each type of dialog box.

Pushbutton — Command-oriented buttons that contain labels indicating the command they perform. To select a pushbutton, the user clicks on it with the mouse, or selects the current pushbutton by pressing the Spacebar. Pushbuttons can be used alone in a dialog box, or used as OK and Cancel buttons to accept the contents of a dialog box. In most cases, pushbuttons appear centered at the bottom of a dialog box.

Radio Button — Option-oriented buttons with labels placed on the right side of the button. To select a radio button, the user clicks on it, or uses the Tab key to move between groups of radio buttons and the cursor keys to move between radio buttons in one group.

Checkbox — Option-oriented box that lets the user specify multiple options. To select a checkbox, the user clicks on it with the mouse, or uses the Tab key to move between groups of checkboxes and the cursor keys to move between checkboxes in the same group.

Listbox — Choice-oriented box that presents a list of available items such as disk files or help screens. To select a listbox item, the user double-clicks on it with the mouse, or uses the cursor to move to an item and presses the Return key.

Edit Control — Data entry control that lets the user enter text and numeric data. To select an edit control, the user clicks on it with the mouse, or uses the Tab key to move between edit controls. Note that the user does not have to press the Enter key after typing in the data.

Message Boxes

A message box is a special purpose dialog box. Its capabilities are limited compared to a dialog box, but it is an important device to warn users of a program error, or when the application requires additional information to process a command.

When a message box appears, it is automatically centered on the display screen. The size of the message box is fixed. The actual box is 46 characters wide. The text within the box spans up to 33 characters in width. Minimally, a message box is three lines deep, but its depth can range up to two-thirds of the display screen. In addition to programmer-defined message boxes, the Presentation Manager uses four types of system message boxes. These are distinguished by the icon that accompanies the message. Table 1-9 lists the various icons and describes each message box type.

Table 1-9: Message Box Types

ICON	DESCRIPTION
Status	Tells the user that a task is currently being performed. Alternatively, it can request the user to perform a required action.
Note	Asks the user to confirm an action that is about to be performed. A note message box can also offer the user several actions from which to choose.
Warning	Warns the user that an impending action can result in a loss of data or other undesirable situation. Usually, a message box containing a warning gives the user a chance to cancel the operation.
Stop	Tells the user that a system error needs to be corrected before processing can continue. Note that the stop message box is system-modal.

System Utilities

The system utilities that come with the Presentation Manager provide the user convenient methods of manipulating windows, files, system defaults, and print jobs. As a user yourself, it is a good idea to become familiar with how the system utilities work. The utilities described in this section are:

- *Start Programs* utility
- *Control Panel* utility
- *Task Manager*
- *Spooler Queue Manager*
- *File System* utility
- *Help* facility

These utilities represent some very serious work on the part of IBM and Microsoft to integrate useful tools directly into the Presentation Manager interface. As a programmer, you have the option of directly linking a program to some of these utilities. For example, you can have an application add its name to the list of programs supported by the *Task Manager*. Additionally, the Presentation Manager provides several functions to access the *Spooler Queue Manager* from an application.

CONFIGURATION TIP: THE OS2.INI FILE

Don't try to edit the OS2.INI file. It is not a text file as Microsoft *Windows* pros might expect, being that the Window's equivalent, WIN.INI, is a text file. Instead, OS2.INI is a binary file. The user can make changes to the system settings that it contains through the *Start Programs* and *Control Panel* utilities. As a Presentation Manager programmer, you can also use one of several Win functions to directly modify OS2.INI.

Start Programs

The *Start Programs* utility provides a standard Presentation Manager window that lets the user start any application listed in the OS2.INI file. If an application is not listed in OS2.INI, the user can add an application to the file by using *Start Programs*. You should note that the OS2.INI file is a binary file and cannot be edited in a word processor or other editor.

Start Programs functions like any other window, with one exception: the user cannot close Start Programs. Additionally, if its Minimize on run option is set, *Start Programs* becomes an icon after the user invokes an application from it.

By default, *Start Programs* appears on the desktop when the user boots the Presentation Manager. Program titles are arranged into groups. In a new installation, the group that appears includes entries to invoke the *File System* utility, an OS/2 windowed command prompt, or a full-screen version of the OS/2 command line environment. The user can change the group by accessing the Group menu item from the window's menubar and clicking on the Utility Programs option. This redraws the window and displays entries to invoke the *Control Panel*, CHKDSK, and FORMAT. The IBM version of OS/2, by default, includes an entry for the OS/2 System Editor.

To create a new group, the user simply chooses the Add option from the Group menu, and then fills out the information requested by the dialog box that appears. To add programs to the new group, the Add option is selected from the Programs menu.

The Add program dialog box is simple enough. The title that the user enters becomes the working title in the application's titlebar (if you code it that way). The Path and filename field requires that the user enter the drive, path and full filename of the application. (Note that this includes the .EXE extension for the application filename.) The Parameters field takes any arguments that the user needs to supply the program. The Working directory field specifies the drive, path, and directory for ancillary files used by the application.

The *Start Programs* window also provides options to delete, change, and copy program information. The Change option works identically to the Add option. Interestingly, it is through the Change option that the user can specify an OS2INIT.CMD file for the two OS/2 command environments invoked from Start Programs. This file, which serves the same purpose as the AUTOEXEC.BAT file in DOS, must be specified for both the windowed and full-screen OS/2 environments; otherwise, neither environment will invoke the file. To specify OS2INIT.CMD, the user must add the following line to the Parameters field after invoking the Change option:

```
/K C:\OS2INIT.CMD
```

This assumes that OS2INIT.CMD is located in the root directory. If it located elsewhere, its correct path should also be specified. Note, however, that the user can set system paths and environment variables in the CONFIG.SYS file — a significant change compared to DOS 3.3 and OS/2 version 1.0.

Control Panel Utility

The *Control Panel* utility is an essential ingredient in the Presentation Manager user interface. The *Control Panel* provides a way to change such system settings as time, date, mouse speed, window colors, border size, communications settings, printer settings, and print spooler options. Like *Start Programs*, the *Control Panel* makes changes to the OS2.INI file.

Much of the *Control Panel* is self explanatory; the user simply observes the standard interface logic of the Presentation Manager.

Task Manager

The *Task Manager* provides the user a convenient way to organize and arrange running applications. The *Task Manager* appears as an icon on the desktop when the system is first started. It remains as such until the user specifically invokes it. Like *Start Programs*, it cannot be closed.

The handiest feature of the *Task Manager* is it lets the user quickly change the input focus. Often, if numerous applications are on the desktop, it is difficult to access an application's window, without moving or resizing other windows higher up in the z-order. By clicking on the application's title in the *Task Manager*, the user can avoid reordering windows. After the user jumps to an application, the *Task Manager* becomes an icon if its Minimize after use option is set; otherwise, it remains an open window on the desktop.

Another nifty feature of the *Task Manager* is it lets the user tile or cascade any number of windows that are open on the desktop. Tiling windows aligns them vertically and horizontally like squares in a checkerboard.

Cascading windows aligns them diagonally from the top to the bottom of the screen. Each cascaded window overlaps the previous window so the user has mouse access to all windows on the desktop.

Spooler Queue Manager

The *Spooler Queue Manager* lets the user manipulate print jobs and queues. It remains active throughout a Presentation Manager session, either in window or icon format. It runs concurrently with other programs and maintains an up-to-the-minute listing of print queues and their contents.

No matter where the user prints a file, the *Spooler Queue Manager* is able to track it and display an appropriate listing. This applies to files printed from applications in the DOS compatibility box as well. When a job changes status, the *Spooler Queue Manager* immediately updates the screen if its Auto refresh option is set.

The *Spooler Queue Manager* gives the user the ability to cancel, hold, reprint, and set priorities for print jobs. To set a priority, the user invokes the Job option, which displays the Job Details dialog box. The normal priority for a print job is 50. The allowable priority range is 1 to 99.

In addition to the priority level, the Job Details dialog box displays various other printer and print file information. Note, however, that this information is set by the system. The user can only change the priority level.

File System Utility

The *File System* utility is the most comprehensive application included with the Presentation Manager. Its capabilities mirror most of the directory and file manipulation features offered in the OS/2 command environment. It is also one of the best examples of a full-fledged Presentation Manager application.

Microsoft itself touts the *File System* utility for its object oriented appearance. Some of its more distinctive features are:

- Displays directory and file listings
- Traverses directories
- Copies and deletes files and directories

- Moves and renames files and directories

- Creates directories

- Alters directory and file attributes

- Executes one or more applications

The File option on the main menu of the *File System* utility provides access to command-oriented options. Each time the user views a directory in the *File System* utility, it opens a new child window to hold the directory display. Many of the menu options in the *File System* utility invoke a dialog box for the user to make selections and provide information. Additionally, the utility provides submenu options to select and deselect multiple files.

Other options on the *File System* utility's main menu let the user organize the directory displays in different ways. For example, the Full file details selection in Options item toggles the display between verbose and brief listings. The Tree menu controls the display of the directory hierarchy. The Arrange menu provides options to cascade and tile windows that contain various directories. The Window option lists the opened directories and lets the user quickly move between the corresponding windows.

Help Facility

The Presentation Manager's Help facility is omnipresent. All applications should have a help facility that is available to the user in the same uniform way typified by the Presentation Manager utilities. The user should be able to get help by:

- Pressing F1, which displays a help window related to the current subject matter such as a dialog box or menu item.

- Clicking on the F1 = Help area in the frame window's menubar. This also displays a help window related to the current subject matter.

- Clicking on a help button in a dialog box, which displays a help window related to the current field in the dialog box.

After the user selects Help, a child window of the current window is displayed. This window summarizes the current subject matter and provides buttons to cancel, display an index of help topics, or display a listing of keyboard accelerators and the function associated with each one. A help window also contains a vertical scrollbar to scroll through the help text when it exceeds the help window's default size.

Advanced Vio Interface

The advanced Video Input/Output (Vio) interface allows monospaced character-oriented applications to run in a Presentation Manager window. These applications behave identically to applications that run under the OS/2 kernel API.

An advanced Vio application has a system menu like Presentation Manager applications. This means the user can move, resize, and minimize and maximize the window, but the similarity to a standard Presentation Manager window ends there. No additional built-in Presentation Manager features such as pulldown menus and other control windows are supported. The advanced Vio function library can be used for graphics output, however, and it does access some of the Presentation Manager's internal mechanisms for this purpose. Applications also can make use of extended font sets available through the advanced Vio library.

CHAPTER 2

FROM THE INSIDE OUT

From the programmer's viewpoint, the PMAPI (Presentation Manager Application Program Interface) resembles the user's perspective of the Presentation Manager — with some important additions. For one thing, the user doesn't care about the method used to display data onscreen, but you, the programmer, need to embrace the concepts of *presentation spaces* and *device contexts* to display text strings as well as graphics. Nor does the user care that the Presentation Manager transforms mouse and keyboard input into *messages*, but messages are the foundation of Presentation Manager programming and you want to learn everything you can about them.

Understanding the user interface, however, is the best conceptual introduction to the Presentation Manager. Beyond that, you need to understand some basic OS/2 concepts, presentation spaces, device contexts, messages, and a little about object oriented programming. This chapter, as well as the next two chapters, interweaves this conceptual material along with the nuts and bolts. For example, it is extremely important that you understand the basic structure of the PMAPI Toolkit, including header files, data types, function libraries, naming conventions, and function declarations. This basic information is presented in this chapter, following a summary of OS/2 multitasking and the Presentation Manager's input and output mechanisms.

Although the Presentation Manager runs under OS/2, and OS/2 in turn is designed for 80286-based PCs, the Presentation Manager transcends most of its environment. You do need to understand the OS/2 kernel programming techniques as far as multitasking and memory management are concerned, but little more. Figure 2-1 generalizes the components of OS/2 and the Presentation Manager.

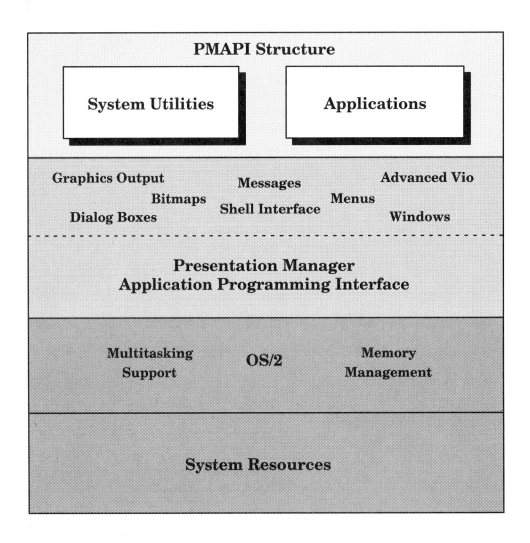

Figure 2-1: OS/2 and Presentation Manager Components

Some OS/2 Details

Where it counts, OS/2 is a world apart from MS-DOS. For one thing, it supports multitasking via its time-sliced, priority-based *preemptive task scheduler*. This sounds like a mouthful, but it says it all about the way OS/2 multitasks: It means OS/2 has the capability to discriminate between important and less important tasks and appropriately process their requests for CPU time. Included in its approach to multitasking are such features as separate execution of *processes* within the same program; separate execution of *threads*; and interprocess and inter-thread communication via *semaphores*, *pipes*, and *queues*. Additionally, OS/2 implements a *file locking* scheme to prevent applications from simultaneously accessing the same file.

Another major advance in OS/2 is *virtual memory management*, which allows an application to use more memory space than available RAM would allow. When an application requests more memory than is available, OS/2 *swaps* processes or segments within processes to disk. When it needs to retrieve the code associated with these processes or segments, it typically reloads it from the application's .EXE file or *dynamic link library* (DLL). The term used to describe the OS/2 swapping process is *memory overcommit*, which means OS/2 always ensures that it has enough swap space on disk as well as enough RAM to restore swapped out processes and segments.

At the heart of OS/2 is *protected mode*. This is the multitasking mode of the 80286 chip. In contrast, *real mode* is the single-tasking, interrupt-driven mode of the 80286 chip, the mode that MS-DOS programs use. Of course, as you have undoubtedly heard, never these two modes shall meet. (Microsoft, however, accomplished the next best thing by providing the DOS compatibility box in which the user can run most existing DOS applications, even while OS/2 applications continue to run.)

Protected mode does exactly what its name says: it protects applications from one another as well as protecting the operating system itself from unruly applications. Because of this, a system crash is a much rarer event under OS/2 than it is under DOS. The mechanism that OS/2 uses to implement its protection scheme is called *ring protection*.

CONFIGURATION TIP: WHERE 'DAT SWAPPER.DAT

The file SWAPPER.DAT is where OS/2 places most of the code its swaps out of memory (some available RAM is also used as an intermediate swap space). The file is controlled with the SWAPPATH statement in CONFIG.SYS. With SWAPPATH, you can specify how much disk space SWAPPER.DAT must leave for application use. You can specify from 512K to approximately 32MB. As the need arises, OS/2 increases the size of the file, but it always leaves the amount you specify free. You can also specify the location of the swap file with the SWAPPATH command. The following example specifies E:\KEEPSWAP as location of SWAPPER.DAT and tells OS/2 to reserve 896K for application use: SWAPPATH = E:\KEEPSWAP 896

Multitasking

OS/2 uses several structural elements to control multitasking. The way in which we think about the relationship between these elements is critical to understanding OS/2 multitasking. Basically, the structure of OS/2 is hierarchical and comprises screen groups, processes, and threads. The Presentation Manager runs as a single screen group. From a PMAPI perspective, this means you only need to be concerned with processes and threads, which are summarized as:

- A *process* can be equivalent to a program, or it can be fully owned by a program. A process is always activated by loading an .EXE file. It is said to own the system resources associated with the program. A process also contains environment related data such as current drive, path and environment strings. A process can create a subprocess, known familiarly as a child process.

- A *thread* belongs to a process and performs its instructions such as accessing the CPU or a disk drive. It is said to be the basic unit of execution in OS/2. A thread cannot own systems resources; rather, it shares those of the process that spawned it. A thread, however, can create another thread, which then assumes a life of its own and does not necessarily terminate when its progenitor terminates.

When you begin programming the Presentation Manager, you will likely think of processes and threads as *parents* and *children*. The CPU itself does not address the concept of a process; rather, it strictly deals with threads in allotting slices of its time. The following sections look at the behavior of threads and processes.

Threads

OS/2 manages multitasking by dishing out a *time slice* of CPU time to a thread. Unlike some UNIX environments, OS/2 does not merely poll the currently active tasks. Instead, it assigns a time slice according to a task's priority. In applications, the programmer ultimately assigns a priority level to a task. In other situations, such as when a user designates a task to run in the background, the operating system assigns the priority.

OS/2 does not treat all threads the same way. Each thread has a task level, or category, assigned to it. The three task levels are: *time critical*, *general priority*, and *idle time*. Figure 2-2 illustrates OS/2's priority-based approach to handling threads.

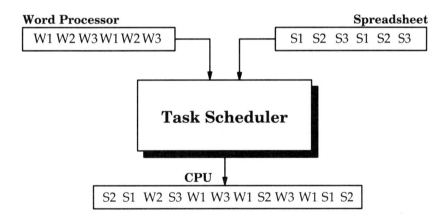

Figure 2-2: OS/2 Task Scheduling

Because threads fall into three time sensitive categories, the OS/2 task scheduler can discriminate between tasks when it receives a request to process a thread. In addition, each of these three categories has 32 possible priority levels. If more than one thread has the same priority level, the task scheduler services the thread on a first-come, first-serve basis.

Time critical threads receive the highest priority from the task scheduler. Once a thread receives time critical status, the scheduler does not attempt to modify it, even when CPU resources begin to diminish. As a programmer in a multi-application environment, you should exercise restraint in assigning time critical status to a thread. Typically, only threads that need rapid response time should be given time critical status. When a time critical thread begins to consume more than 20 percent of the CPU's time, overall system response time slows noticeably.

The next scheduler category, general priority, is the most common processing level. If a general priority thread has the same priority level as another general priority thread, the task scheduler allots CPU time to the thread with the greater I/O and CPU requirements. Or if one of the two threads of equal priority can be performed in the background, the task scheduler gives priority to the foreground thread. Additionally, the task scheduler can arbitrarily limit a general priority thread's access to the CPU when the CPU is in high demand.

Threads in the idle time category receive the lowest priority from the task scheduler. The task scheduler only allots time to a thread in this category when no other time critical or general priority threads require CPU time. In general, the idle time category is of little use — it is included in this system because it is the mirror image of the time critical category.

Altogether, OS/2 is capable of handling 255 threads. The operating system itself, including the Presentation Manager, uses a fair number of these threads. The Presentation Manager administers most of its threads internally. When the Presentation Manager is first initialized by OS/2, its screen group threads receive time critical status. When a window receives the input focus, the Presentation Manager notifies the task scheduler that its time critical status should be shifted to this window.

As application-generated process should not use too many threads. Failing to adhere to this advice is a sure way to cause problems, likely resulting in degraded system performance. Ideally, a process should have a primary thread and a limited number of secondary threads. The primary thread is important. For one thing, a primary thread's ID is always 1. This distinguishes it from its secondary threads. Thread 1 is also special because it is the thread that is interrupted when a process receives a system signal.

CONFIGURATION TIP: DIG THOSE THREADS

Adjusting the THREAD command in the CONFIG.SYS file gives the user the ability to change the number of threads that applications can use. On most systems, the default is 64 threads reserved for applications. The user can adjust this number upward, taking into consideration that the kernel itself uses 14 threads and the Presentation Manager uses about 15 threads. Note that increasing the number of threads decreases the amount of RAM available to the system.

Processes

A process is a collection of system resources, including threads, physical memory, file handles, and semaphores. Creating a process is the first order of business for OS/2 when a program is loaded. This initial process owns the system resources that the program requires, both at startup and throughout the life of the program. This process is the parent of any subsequent, or child processes that the program creates.

Child processes inherit many of the system resources from the parent. Combined with its primary thread, which OS/2 automatically creates, this is all the child process needs to perform its instructions. Typically, a child process performs a single task and returns control to the parent. Sound familiar? Yes, you can think of child processes as functions, but they are more than that. A single child process is likely to be tied to a function, and that function may call other functions, or create other child processes. Similarly, when control returns from the function that created the child process, it is a good bet that the lifetime of the child process ends.

The major difference between a function and a child process is the inheritance factor. You need not take any special steps to set up the child process' environment, but you can't say the same about a function, unless the function is fully dependent on global variables. Indeed, the child process typically needs no additional information about its parent in order for it to perform its instructions and return a value (so to speak) to the parent.

The Presentation Manager handles process management for you when you initialize a window, pop up a dialog box, or have your code perform some other Presentation Manager function. Times will arise, however, when you want your Presentation Manager application to perform some operation not necessarily within the bounds of the Presentation Manager code. At these times, as with threads, you use the Dos library functions to create independent processes.

Application Model

What is important to keep in mind from a Presentation Manager perspective is not so much the internal OS/2 mechanisms, but the fact that the Presentation Manager can orchestrate multitasking procedures. After this, just think of the Presentation Manager as building its own environment — an environment full of interesting life forms such as dialog boxes, message queues, and presentation spaces.

You should have a good idea about the internal mechanisms of the Presentation Manager from reading about its user interface. Figure 2-3, which illustrates the Presentation Manager in terms of input and output, puts the various components in perspective from the programmer's viewpoint.

Input Mechanisms

The Presentation Manager gets input from the user in two basic ways: standard keyboard/mouse input and dialog boxes. Additionally, the Presentation Manager processes system-related input, timer messages, and inter-application input.

Keyboard and mouse input is asynchronous. It is processed through the system message queue, which transforms it into messages that an application can recognize (see Chapter 3). Once keyboard/mouse messages leave the system input queue, they proceed to the programmer-designed function that handles messages generated by the associated window. In order for this function to handle the messages, a program must install an application message queue. Every instance of a frame window must have an application message queue associated with it. Typically, the code for the application message queue is placed in **main()**. Alternatively, you can call a custom function that sets up message queue.

Input obtained from the user through dialog boxes is also processed by the system input queue, but it is rerouted to the function that handles the dialog box. The dialog box window procedure is an internally subclassed

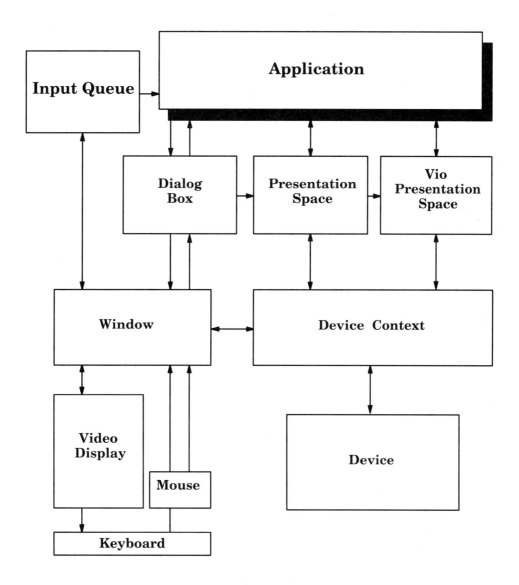

Figure 2-3: PMAPI Application Model

procedure, but only processes input that can be interpreted by various dialog box controls such as pushbuttons, listboxes, and entry fields. Subclassing, which is a technique that diverts messages initially targeted for a different procedure, allows an unrelated procedure to process these messages. When a dialog box procedure successfully processes a message, the system passes a resultant message to the application message queue, where it is can be processed by the client window procedure or handled by the frame window's default processing loop.

Output Mechanisms

A presentation space is the Presentation Manager's canvas. On it, you draw both text and graphics using functions from the window management (Win) library, but mostly functions from the Graphics Programming Interface (Gpi) library. The Presentation Manager itself uses presentation spaces when it needs to draw a window, dialog box, or other control on the screen.

In most cases, you can think of a presentation space as operating independently of a given device, including the screen. Via a presentation space, you can specify text and objects in terms of *world coordinates*, which the Presentation Manager converts for devices attached to the system. This approach, while it might represent a new way of thinking for many programmers, relieves you of having to understand how the actual device handles output from your application. Presentation spaces are responsible for the following:

- Defining color attributes

- Providing default attributes

- Restoring clipped regions

- Converting world coordinates

- Defining fonts and logical symbols

- Handling user-defined line types

- Storing segments of graphic data

Presentation spaces do not entirely liberate you from devices. In order for a presentation space to focus output to a device such as the screen or a laser printer, it must be associated with a device context. A device context contains the low-level information about the hardware device. Using this information, the Presentation Manager is able to map the world coordinate description of an object into a device-specific description. Device contexts are responsible for the following:

- Accessing devices
- Communicating with devices
- Conveying user-defined line types
- Providing device information on request

Device contexts themselves are based on device drivers that the system knows about. This includes device drivers for monitors. In order to support a non-standard device, the application developer must create a driver using a device driver kit available from Microsoft.

Function Libraries

By reading about the Presentation Manager from the user's viewpoint (see Chapter 1), you know that windows are responsible for displaying output. Generally speaking, you can map the various Presentation Manager components directly to a function library. Most of the components are contained in the function library denoted by the prefix Win (for Window). Graphics output and bitmaps are handled by the library denoted by Gpi (Graphics Program Interface). Here's the complete list of function libraries with which a Presentation Manager programmer need be concerned:

- Dev — device output functions.
- Dos — kernel library calls.
- Gpi — graphics and bitmap functions.
- Spl — print spooler functions.
- Vio — advanced video I/O functions.
- Win — window and user interface functions.

Each prefix has its first letter uppercased and the next two letters lowercased. Additionally, IBM and Microsoft have also attempted to standardize the logic used in deriving function names. Most function names observe the following order:

```
[prefix] + [verb] + [object]
```

As with the prefix, both the verb and object in a function name have their first letter uppercased. For example, WinDrawPointer is an eminently readable function that does what it says: it draws a mouse pointer. Table 2-1 lists and describes some of the more common verbs used in the Win and Gpi libraries.

Table 2-1: Common Verbs Used in Win and Gpi Libraries

VERB	LIBRARY	DESCRIPTION
Create	Both	Creates an object such as a menu or message queue.
Delete	Both	Removes access to an object such as atom table, bitmap, or graphic data segment.
Destroy	Both	Removes an object from memory, typically as a shutdown procedure. Windows and presentation spaces are good examples.
Draw	Both	Draws specified components such as text and bitmaps.
Enable	Win	Enables a process such as window updating.
End	Both	Terminates a given process such as window painting or the definition of a graphic path.
Get	Both	Retrieves an object or an attribute of an object. Not to be confused with the query verb, which retrieves data about a specified object or process.
Load	Both	Loads an object (typically a resource such as a menu or font) and implements it in an application.
Lock	Win	Prevents access to the specified object. For example, Win-LockWindow locks a window.
Query	Both	Returns information about a specified object or process. Unlike the Get verb, functions with the Query verb have no side effects.
Set	Both	Sets the state or attributes for an object or process such as window position or a graphic segment priority.

As you might expect, the Win and Gpi libraries do not have as much in common when it comes to the objects that the verbs affect. When the two libraries do share a common object, the name of the object is usually abbreviated in the Win library and spelled out in the Gpi library. For example, Rect is the Win representation of rectangle, while Rectangle is the Gpi representation.

For the most part — especially as you learn how to program the Presentation Manager — you will be concerned with the approximately 235 Win functions and 225 Gpi functions. The other libraries, with the exception of the Dos library, have highly specialized roles. The Dos functions handle many basic system chores for both kernel and Presentation Manager programming. In particular, you need to use the Dos calls to open and read ASCII files.

You can also use the Dos calls for memory management and creating multitasking routines, but the Win library also offers a selection of calls for both these purposes. If you are familiar with the Dos functions, and feel that you can use them in Presentation Manager programs, go ahead and do so. As the need arises throughout this book, relevant Dos calls are explained. For a complete reference, refer to either a book or manual dedicated to OS/2 kernel programming.

Header Files

Each function library is associated with a particular header file in the PMAPI. Table 2-2 lists the header files that contain function definitions affecting the Presentation Manager.

Table 2-2: Header Files with PMAPI Function Declarations

LIBRARY	HEADER FILE	DESCRIPTION
Dos	BSEDOS.H	Dos functions.
Dev	PMDEV.H	All device output functions.
Gpi	PMGPI.H	All graphics/bitmap functions.
Spl	PMSPL.H	All print spooling functions.

(continued)

Table 2-2: Continued

LIBRARY	HEADER FILE	DESCRIPTION
Vio	BSESUB.H	General Vio functions.
Vio	PMAVIO.H	Advanced Vio functions.
Win	PMWIN.H	Most Window functions.
Win	PMSPL.H	Window shell functions.
Win	PMORD.H	Win advanced Vio functions.

In some cases, such as with the Win library, function definitions are contained in more than one header file. Naturally, the header files contain definitions for data types, structures, and system-wide constants as well as functions.

It is handy to know in which header file a function definition resides, but you don't include the header files from Table 2-2 directly into your C program. Instead, you include the general purpose header file OS2.H, which includes all other headers files. The critical lines from OS2.H are the following:

```
#include <os2def.h>
#include <bse.h>
#include <pm.h>
```

As is apparent, OS2.H includes three other header files. The OS2DEF.H header file contains critical **define**s for both kernel and Presentation Manager programming. The BSE.H and PM.H files, like the OS2.H file itself, are primarily responsible for including more header files in what is a rather large hierarchy of header files (see Figure 2-4). BSE.H includes kernel-specific header files, and PM.H includes Presentation Manager-specific header files.

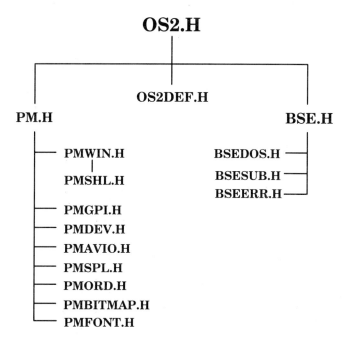

Figure 2-4: Presentation Manager Header Files

What if you don't want to include every line of every header file in your application? Actually, this doesn't happen unless you explicitly specify it by defining two constants before including OS2.H. The constants — or symbols, which is the term preferred by the designers of the Presentation Manager — are INCL_BASE and INCL_PM. Thus, if you want to include every line of every header file in your application, use the following code:

```
#define INCL_BASE
#define INCL_PM
#include <os2.h>
```

The INCL_BASE and INCL_PM symbols are recognized by the BSE.H and PM.H header files, respectively. Each header file tests for these symbols using the preprocessor's **ifdef** key word. When a given symbol is TRUE, additional symbols are defined and the same process occurs in subsequently included header files. Here are the relevant lines from PM.H:

```
#ifdef INCL_PM
    #define INCL_WIN
    #define INCL_GPI
    #define INCL_DEV
    #define INCL_AVIO
    #define INCL_SPL
    #define INCL_PIC
    #define INCL_ORDERS
    #define INCL_BITMAPFILEFORMAT
    #define INCL_FONTFILEFORMAT
    #define INCL_ERRORS
#endif /* INCL_PM */

#include <pmwin.h>       /* Window Manager definitions */
#include <pmgpi.h>       /* GPI definitions */
#include <pmdev.h>       /* Device Context definitions */
```

When PM.H finds that INCL_PM is TRUE, several more symbols become valid as well. These symbols are typically referred to as subcomponents of INCL_PM and essentially include all parts of all the Presentation Manager header files. (Header files not listed in the excerpt are loaded later on in PM.H.) Table 2-3 gives the meanings of the various subcomponents included by defining INCL_PM.

Table 2-3: INCL_PM Subcomponents

SUBCOMPONENT	LOADS ALL OF...
INCL_WIN	Window management
INCL_GPI	Gpi
INCL_DEV	Device support
INCL_AVIO	Advanced Vio
INCL_SPL	Spooler
INCL_ORDERS	Graphical order formats
INCL_BITMAPFILEFORMAT	Bitmap file format
INCL_FONTFILEFORMAT	Font file format
INCL_ERRORS	OS/2 errors

The BSE.H header file works the same pattern as PM.H. If it finds that INCL_BASE is valid, it defines INCL_DOS (the Dos kernel functions), INCL_SUB (the Vio, Kbd, and Mou functions, and INCL_DOSERRORS (the OS/2 error constants). Again, even if INCL_BASE has not been defined by your application, BSE.H goes ahead and includes BSEDOS.H, BSESUB.H, and BSEERR.H.

A more selective way of including header file data is by defining the subcomponents directly, instead of using the base symbol. Many simple programs don't require the amount of definition derived from using the base symbols. This technique can also reduce the compiled size of your application. The following three lines of code will give you access to most of the header file data that you need:

```
#define INCL_WIN
#define INCL_GPI
#include <os2.h>
```

Even this level of definition can be unnecessary. As it turns out, INCL_WIN and INCL_GPI are base types themselves. Their subcomponents virtually split up the Win and Gpi libraries by functional category. Tables 2-4 and 2-5 list these additional subcomponents. Examine the tables closely: they not only describe the subcomponents, they comprise a virtual road map to the Presentation Manager.

Table 2-4: INCL_WIN Subcomponents

SUBCOMPONENT	LOADS ALL OF...
INCL_WINWINDOWMGR	General window management
INCL_WINMESSAGEMGR	Message management
INCL_WININPUT	Mouse and keyboard input
INCL_WINDIALOGS	Dialog boxes
INCL_WINSTATICS	Static controls
INCL_WINBUTTONS	Button controls

(continued)

Table 2-4: Continued

SUBCOMPONENT	LOADS ALL OF...
INCL_WINENTRYFIELDS	Entry Fields
INCL_WINLISTBOXES	List box controls
INCL_WINMENUS	Menu controls
INCL_WINSCROLLBARS	Scroll bar controls
INCL_WINFRAMEMGR	Frame manager
INCL_WINFRAMECTLS	Frame controls (titlebars & size border)
INCL_WINRECTANGLES	Rectangle routines
INCL_WINSYS	System values (and colors)
INCL_WINTIMER	Timer routines
INCL_WINACCELERATORS	Keyboard accelerators
INCL_WINTRACKRECT	WinTrackRect() function
INCL_WINCLIPBOARD	Clipboard manager
INCL_WINCURSORS	Text cursors
INCL_WINPOINTERS	Mouse pointers
INCL_WINHOOKS	Hook manager
INCL_WINSWITCHLIST	Shell Switch List API
INCL_WINPROGRAMLIST	Shell Program List API
INCL_WINSHELLDATA	Shell data
INCL_WINCOUNTRY	Country support
INCL_WINHEAP	Heap Manager
INCL_WINATOM	Atom Manager
INCL_WINCATCHTHROW	WinCatch/WinThrow support
INCL_WINERRORS	Error code definitions

Table 2-5: INCL_GPI Subcomponents

SUBCOMPONENT	LOADS ALL OF...
INCL_GPICONTROL	Basic PS control
INCL_GPICORRELATION	Picking, Boundary and Correlation
INCL_GPISEGMENTS	Segment Control and Drawing
INCL_GPISÉGEDITING	Segment Editing via Elements
INCL_GPITRANSFORMS	Transform and Transform Conversion
INCL_GPIPATHS	Paths and Clipping with Paths
INCL_GPILOGCOLORTABLE	Logical Color Tables
INCL_GPIPRIMITIVES	Drawing Primitives and Primitive Attributes
INCL_GPILCIDS	Physical and Logical Fonts with Lcids
INCL_GPIBITMAPS	Bitmaps and Pel Operations
INCL_GPIREGIONS	Regions and Clipping with Regions
INCL_GPIMETAFILES	Metafiles
INCL_GPIERRORS	defined if INCL_ERRORS defined

Data Types and Structures

Before you can make sense of its header files — including the function definitions contained in them — you need to understand the scheme the Presentation Manager uses for its data types. The Presentation Manager does
not use standard C data types. Instead, it creates its own set of data types
using the C **define** and **typedef** statements.

The reason for this is portability. During development of the Presentation Manager, Microsoft had envisioned porting it to different operating
systems — not the least of which is the 80386 version of OS/2. Even as
Microsoft released version 1.1 of the Presentation Manager, it was also
working on a project with Hewlett-Packard to port the Presentation Man-

ager to an H-P version of the X Windows environment. The universality of data types between versions of the Presentation Manager ensures that applications will run under different operating environments, with a minimum of change to an application's code.

The OS2DEF.H header file contains most of the **define**s and **typedef**s that create the Presentation Manager's data types — all of which appear in uppercase characters. The underscore character is not used in data types, thus distinguishing them from system-defined constants. Additionally, you can broadly categorize the Presentation Manager's data types into five groups:

- Data types that correspond to the standard C data types.

- Data types that are used as handles, which are internally assigned values for referencing various objects.

- Data types associated with the various structures used by OS/2 and the Presentation Manager.

- Data types that are mostly special to the Presentation Manager (that is, OS/2 does not use them) and serve a narrow purpose.

- Data types that use far pointers in order to accommodate the 80286's segmented memory architecture.

When you become familiar with the first four groups, you will have learned the fifth group as well. The reason for this is most data types in the Presentation Manager have a corresponding far pointer data type. A far pointer contains both the segment and offset address and allows you to access any memory segment in the 80286.

Standard Data Types

The practice of redefining standard C data types is fairly common. The names that IBM and Microsoft chose for the new types are as close to an industry standard as possible. For example, some multi-environment programmers might recognize the Presentation Manager's USHORT data type sooner than they would recognize **unsigned short**, its standard C counterpart.

Table 2-6 lists and defines the data types that the Presentation Manager uses to represent the standard C data types. The actual **define**s and **typedef**s for these types are in OS2DEF.H.

Table 2-6: Presentation Manager's Version of Standard C Data Types

DATA TYPE	BITS	C EQUIVALENT
CHAR	8	char
UCHAR	8	unsigned char
BYTE	8	unsigned char
SHORT	16	short
USHORT	16	unsigned short
BOOL	16	unsigned short
INT	16	int
UINT	16	unsigned int
LONG	32	long
ULONG	32	unsigned long

Handle Data Types

The second group of data types represents handles. Presentation Manager handles are similar to file handles used in MS-DOS. Handles are obtained by calling various Presentation Manager functions. You store the handle in a variable of the data type for the handle. In turn, you supply the handle to other Presentation Manager functions. In this way, the Presentation Manager can reference large objects with a minimum of overhead (see Chapter 3).

Most handles are **typedef**ed as one of two previously defined data types: SHANDLE, which is an unsigned short; and LHANDLE, which is a generic far pointer (a 32-bit quantity). Table 2-7 lists the data types used for handles and indicates whether they are a SHANDLE or LHANDLE. Note that all handle data types begin with the letter H.

Table 2-7: Presentation Manager Handle Data Types

HANDLE	OF TYPE	OBJECT
HACCEL	LHANDLE	Accelerator table
HATOMTABL	LHANDLE	Atom table
HAB	LHANDLE	Anchor block
HBITMAP	LHANDLE	Bitmap
HDC	LHANDLE	Device context
HENUM	LHANDLE	Enumerated windows list
HMODULE	USHORT	DLL Module
HRGN	LHANDLE	Graphics region
HMQ	LHANDLE	Message queue
HMF	LHANDLE	Metafile
HFILE	SHANDLE	Open file
HHEAP	LHANDLE	Heap
HPIPE	SHANDLE	Named pipe
HPOINTER	LHANDLE	Mouse pointer
HPROGRAM	LHANDLE	Switch-list entry
HPS	LHANDLE	Presentation space
HSEM	VOID FAR *	System semaphore
HSPL	LHANDLE	Spooler
HSWITCH	LHANDLE	Switch entry
HVPS	USHORT	Vio presentation space
HWND	LHANDLE	Window

Structures and Their Pointers

The Presentation Manager is heavily reliant on structures. Quite often, accessing a structure is the most convenient way — and sometimes the only way — to obtain system-related information. Just as often, you have to use one or more pointers to a structure as arguments in a function call. The latter case is more salient in regard to data types, but here's a look at a commonly used structure that illustrates both practices:

```
typedef struct _FATTRS {
    USHORT     usRecordLength;
    USHORT     fsSelection;
    LONG       lMatch;
    CHAR       szFacename[FACESIZE];
    USHORT     idRegistry;
    USHORT     usCodePage;
    LONG       lMaxBaselineExt;
    LONG       lAveCharWidth;
    USHORT     fsType;
    USHORT     fsFontUse;
} FATTRS;
```

As you probably guessed, the FATTRS structure is used to specify font information. To specify a font change — say, one that results from a user selection — you typically use a second copy of FATTRS and place the new font information in this copy. Then you set the fields from the system-active copy of FATTRS equal to the application's copy. Many times, you do not need to change every field. With FATTRS, for instance, you might not want to change the character width and height, so you do not make any changes to the *lMaxBaselineExt* and *lAveCharWidth* fields.

When the new font information has been transferred, you need to call the GpiCreateLogFonts function to initiate the font change. This requirement exemplifies the structure reference in a function. The following code changes the field values of the system-active copy of FATTRS and then calls GpiCreateLogFonts:

```
fatSystem.usRecordLength      = sizeof(FATTRS) ;
fatSystem.lMatch              = fatLocal->lMatch;
fatSystem.fsSelection         = fatLocal->fsSelection;
strcpy(fatSystem.szFacename, fatLocal->szFacename) ;
fatSystem.idRegistry          = fatLocal->idRegistry ;
```

```
fatSystem.usCodePage        = 850;
fatSystem.lMaxBaselineExt   = fatLocal->lMaxBaselineExt;
fatSystem.lAveCharWidth     = fatLocal->lAveCharWidth;
fatSystem.fsType            = FATTR_TYPE_FIXED;
fatSystem.fsFontUse         = 0;

GpiCreateLogFont(hps, pchname, lcid, &fatSystem);
```

Some additional calls are required to complete the font change, but this code serves the purpose at hand. Fortunately, many of the structures in the Presentation Manager are not as long as FATTRS. For example, you frequently need to obtain screen coordinates via the POINTL structure. This structure is tailored to this purpose, containing only *x* and *y* fields that correspond to the horizontal and vertical screen coordinates. Similarly, the RECTL structure is frequently used to obtain screen dimension information. This structure contains only four fields: *xLeft*, *yBottom*, *xRight*, and *yTop*.

To create a copy of a structure in your application, you have the choice of using the structure tag name or the data type associated with the structure. The more common method is to reference the data type, as in:

```
FATTRS fatSystem;
```

When you use a structure, you should try to retain some form of the suggested variable name for the structure. The suggested variable name for FATTRS is *fat*. Thus, because the example used two copies of FATTRS, *fatSystem* and *fatLocal* were used. The suggested variable names for POINTL and RECTL are *ptl* and *rcl*, respectively.

Special Types

The Presentation Manager uses several data types for narrow purposes as well as a few specialized data types used by OS/2. The most obvious of these data types is one already used by Microsoft C — namely, the PASCAL data type, which can be used to define a function that uses the Pascal calling sequence. This is important to note because all Presentation Manager functions use the Pascal calling sequence — that is, they push their arguments onto the stack from left to tright, rather than from right to left as C functions are wont to do. In addition to the PASCAL data type, the

Presentation Manager uses several other special data types, which are described in Table 2-8.

Table 2-8: Presentation Manager Special Data Types

ITEM	TYPE	DESCRIPTION
ATOM	USHORT	Numeric representation of a character string.
COLOR	LONG	Color type for constants such as CLR_BLUE. These can be ORed together for a unique 32-bit value.
FIXED	LONG	Fixed point number containing an implicit binary point between the second and third hexadecimal digits. Used to extract 16-bit integer and a 16-bit fraction from a 32-bit value.
FIXED88	USHORT	Contains an implicit binary point between the second and third hexadecimal digits.
FIXED114	USHORT	Fixed point signed number containing an implicit binary point between bits 13 and 14. Bit 15 holds the sign. Positive 1.0 is equal to 16384 (0x4000). Negative 1.0 is equal to 16384 (0xC000).
MPARAM	VOID FAR *	Message parameter 32 bits in length that contains one or more other data types used in message decoding.
MRESULT	VOID FAR *	Message result returned by several Win message functions and application window procedures. It is 32 bits and contains one or more data types.
PFNWP	MRESULT	The Presentation Manager's most powerful data type. It is a far pointer to a far pointer that references the four values used in window message passing.
PID	USHORT	Process identifier.
TID	TID	Thread identifier.
SEL	USHORT	Memory segment selector.
STR[8]	CHAR	Fixed length character string.
STR[16]	CHAR	Fixed length character string.
STR[32]	CHAR	Fixed length character string.
STR[64]	CHAR	Fixed length character string

Pointers

Most data types, including structure data types, can be referenced using pointers. OS/2 and the Presentation Manager **typedef** a pointer data type for most every other data type supported. This represents an effort on the part of IBM and Microsoft to make the Presentation Manager easily portable to other environments.

Using the predefined pointer types also keeps your code consistent when you program using different Microsoft C 5.1 compiler models. The primary benefit here is you do not have to explicitly declare far pointers. This means you do not have to change your code if you decide to recompile a compact or large model program as a small or medium model program. For example, because PUSHORT is **typedef**ed as a far pointer to a USHORT in OS2DEF.H, you do not have to explicitly declare this in your code. Instead, you simply declare a pointer variable as follows:

```
PUSHORT pusPtr;
```

The Presentation Manager also makes use of generic far pointers. A generic far pointer delays specification of the data type until the compiler references it. A generic far pointer is **typedef**ed in OS2DEF.H as follows:

```
typedef VOID FAR *PVOID;
```

It is your responsibility to cast the pointer when you later reference it. You can also use the macros described in Chapter 3 to extract data from a generic far pointer.

Naming Conventions

IBM and Microsoft recommend that you follow a strict set of naming conventions when writing OS/2 and Presentation Manager applications. The conventions apply to structures, structure fields, constants, message parameters, and function arguments. (This book uses the convention of referring to function parameters as arguments in order to distinguish them from message parameters.)

Because the definitions contained in the OS/2 and Presentation Manager header files use these conventions, it is to your advantage to know them well — whether or not you use them in your own code!

The conventions are known as Hungarian notation and were developed by Microsoft programmer, Charles Simonoyi. The stated purpose of Hungarian notation is to make code more readable. The following rules summarize the use of Hungarian notation:

1. All arguments, parameters, and fields can consist of three elements — a prefix, base type, and qualifier.
2. The base type identifies the data type of the variable. All letters in the base type are lowercased.
3. The prefix supplies additional information about the base type. For example, it could specify that the variable is a pointer. All letters in the prefix are lowercased.
4. The qualifier indicates the purpose of the variable. The qualifier can consist of one or more words, with the first letter of each word uppercased.

Hungarian notation does make code more readable, but it also makes it longer (a bothersome feature, to say the least). As a result, you will likely run across programs that omit variable prefixes and make the qualifier as short as possible. On the other hand, many of the field names of OS/2 and Presentation Manager structures use some very long names. For instance, you probably noticed *lMaxBaselineExt* in the FATTRS structure.

Nonetheless, Hungarian notation is useful. For example, *fQueue* immediately tells you that it is a flag for a queue. If you add the word *Object* to it (so you have *fQueueObject*), you can probably deduce that the queue is related to an object window. Whether you want to go all the way and make it *fQueueObjectWindow* is up to you. Table 2-9 lists the base conventions.

Table 2-9: Hungarian Notation Base Types

DATA TYPE	BASE	DESCRIPTION
BOOL	f	Denotes a flag or boolean variable. TRUE flags represent an active status. Zero values indicate FALSE. All others values imply TRUE.
BYTE	b	Denotes any unsigned 8-bit value.
CHAR	ch	Denotes a signed 8-bit value.

(continued)

Table 2-9: Continued

DATA TYPE	BASE	DESCRIPTION
CHAR[]	sz	Denotes a null-terminated character array.
LONG	l	Denotes a signed 32-bit value.
SHORT	s	Denotes a signed 16-bit value.
SEL	sel	Denotes a segment selector.
UCHAR	uch	Denotes an unsigned 8-bit value.
UCHAR	fb	Denotes an array of flags if more than one flag is packed in an 8-bit value.
ULONG	ul	Denotes an unsigned 32-bit value.
ULONG	fl	Denotes an array of flags if more than one flag is packed in a 32-bit value.
USHORT	us	Denotes an unsigned 16-bit value.
USHORT	fs	Denotes an array of flags if more than one flag is packed in a 16-bit value.

The prefix convention can be extremely helpful in reading Presentation Manager code. Commonly used prefixes are *id* for identifier and *a* for array. Table 2–10 lists all the prefix conventions.

Table 2-10: Hungarian Notation Prefixes

PREFIX	DESCRIPTION
a	Denotes an array and is combined with the base type and optionally a qualifier. A typical example is *achCustomer*, which represents an array of customer names.
c	Denotes a count of items and is combined with the base type to form the variable name. Often, a qualifier is not necessary. A typical example is *cch*, which represents a count of characters.
h	Denotes a handle. For example, *hwnd* represents a handle to a window. (See Chapter 3 for a list of common handle names.)
i	Denotes an array index.

(continued)

Table 2-10: Continued

PREFIX	DESCRIPTION
id	Denotes an identifier. For example, *idWindow* represents the ID for some window and *idFrameWindow* represents the ID for the frame window.
np	Denotes a near pointer. For example, *nps* means a near pointer to a SHORT.
off	Denotes an offset and is used for values that are offsets from the beginning of a buffer or structure.
p	Denotes a far pointer. For example, *pch* represents a far pointer to a character, and *psz* represents a far pointer to a null terminate character string.

Constants

The wild and wonderful world of Presentation Manager constants might make you catch your breath at first sight. In all, there are more than 1,000 constants defined in the OS/2 and Presentation Manager header files. You have already gotten a whiff of them from the INCL identifiers.

Like variables, constants follow a strict Hungarian notation. Constants are always uppercased and contain two parts: a prefix and qualifier. A prefix is always followed by an underscore character, but its length varies. Most important system constants for the Presentation Manager have prefixes of two or three letters, but others range up to nine letters in length. Typically, prefix names are derived from an associated function, object, or process. The association is not always clear, however. The rest of the constant, the qualifier, is more straightforward. It usually indicates an action or state connected to an associated function, object, or process.

Constants are defined as 16- or 32-bit numbers. When you use constants in function calls, you can often OR them together to produce different results. (Constants that you can OR usually have three-letter prefixes.) Quite frequently, it is easier to set a variable equal to an ORed string of constants. Alternatively, by studying the values from a series of constants that you want to specify, you might find that the complement of one constant equals the series you want to OR together. This is a convenient trick, but has the drawback of not explicitly stating what constants are in effect.

Another approach is to define frequently used series of constants in a separate header file, and then use your custom identifiers. For your convenience, this book lists the numeric values associated with constants so you can choose the manner in which you manipulate them. Here's a look at one commonly used set of constants:

```
#define SWP_SIZE              0x0001
#define SWP_MOVE              0x0002
#define SWP_ZORDER            0x0004
#define SWP_SHOW              0x0008
#define SWP_HIDE              0x0010
#define SWP_NOREDRAW          0x0020
#define SWP_NOADJUST          0x0040
#define SWP_ACTIVATE          0x0080
#define SWP_DEACTIVATE        0x0100
#define SWP_EXTSTATECHANGE    0x0200
#define SWP_MINIMIZE          0x0400
#define SWP_MAXIMIZE          0x0800
#define SWP_RESTORE           0x1000
#define SWP_FOCUSACTIVATE     0x2000
#define SWP_FOCUSDEACTIVATE   0x4000
```

These constants define window positioning characteristics. They are used with three functions from the Win library: WinSetWindowPos, WinSetMultWinPos, and WinQueryWindowPos. From the earlier description of the Set and Query verbs, it should be obvious that the WinSetWindowPos and WinSetMultWinPos functions are used to establish the screen position of one or more windows. The WinQueryWindowPos returns positioning information about an already established window. The following call to WinSetWindowPos shows how the SWP constants are ORed together. (More information on this subject appears in Chapter 4).

```
WinSetWindowPos(
            hwndFrame,       /* Frame window handle. */
            HWND_TOP,        /* Specifies topmost position. */
            60,              /* Horizontal base coordinate. */
            60,              /* Vertical base coordinate. */
            250,             /* Horizontal size. */
            250,             /* Vertical size. */
            SWP_ACTIVATE     /* Activate when topmost. */
            | SWP_SIZE       /* Changes size. */
            | SWP_MOVE       /* Moves window. */
            | SWP_SHOW);     /* Shows window.  */
```

Getting used to Presentation Manager constants is a tiresome task. When you find a series of constants that works a particular effect, you should make notes on it, or paste it into a file devoted to information on constants.

Function Declarations

Having seen an actual function call in the last section, it is now time to take a look at how the Presentation Manager declares functions. It might seem a little unfamiliar if you're a C programmer with a standard DOS background. But once you know the purpose of the Presentation Manager's unusual function declarations, they will become a fact of life. Without further ado, here's the function declaration for the WinSetWindowPos function as it appears in the PMWIN.H header file:

```
BOOL APIENTRY WinSetWindowPos(HWND hwnd,
            HWND hwndInsertBehind,SHORT x,
            SHORT y, SHORT cx, SHORT cy, USHORT fs)
```

In this book, functions are listed in more traditional format. All data information is replicated in this format, with the one exception of the APIENTRY identifier. The following is the typical representation:

```
BOOL WinSetWindowPos(hwnd, hwndInsertBehind, x, y, cx, cy, fs)
HWND    hwnd;
HWND    hwndInsertBehind;
SHORT   x;
SHORT   y;
SHORT   cx;
SHORT   cy;
USHORT  fs;
```

The comments in the WinSetWindowPos call in the previous section tell you the purpose of the seven arguments in WinSetWindowPos. You should also be able to discern some information about the data types and variables from reading the section on naming conventions. As it turns out, the SWP constants are contained in an array of flags — which you know because *fs* is the standard way to name an array of flags. But what about the

APIENTRY identifier? Here's how APIENTRY (read API entry) is defined in the OSDEF.H header file:

```
#define APIENTRY pascal far
```

What this seeminglessly uneventful **define** statement does is make APIENTRY an identifier that transforms a standard C function call into a Pascal function call.

The significance of transforming a standard C function call into a Pascal function call is the function's arguments are pushed onto the stack from left to right, not from right to left as is the case with a standard C function call. It also means the function performs its own stack housekeeping — in that it removes its own arguments from the stack when the call terminates.

The reason behind this approach is speed: the Pascal method is simply faster on 80286 and 80386 machines. As a result, all OS/2 and Presentation Manager functions use the APIENTRY identifier.

You probably also noted that WinSetWindowPos returns a BOOL value. About 120, or just about half of the Win functions, return TRUE or FALSE values. For the most part, you need not be concerned with retaining the return value of a Win function typed as BOOL.

Some other Win functions do return useful information. As a matter of interest, Table 2-11 lists the number of Win functions that return a given data type. You should note the various returns types in the table, but you should also remember that it is somewhat an intuitive process to attempt to categorize the Presentation Manager functions in this manner. Yet using your intuition is not meaningless — the Presentation Manager embraces a broad rangle of data types. And, remember, its developers not only had the current implementation in mind when they made the golden sample of the Presentation Manager, they also had the 80386 version in mind. This said, it is still just a good idea to become intimately familiar with the data types and return values of the Presentation Manager (although it is somewhat safe to say that you do not need to be as familiar with the return types as the data types).

Another interesting fact about the Win functions is that most of them take either a window handle (HWND) or an anchor block handle (HAB) as their first argument. About 120 take window handles and another 70 or so take anchor block handles. Another nine functions take a handle to a presentation space (HPS) and six others take a handle to a message queue (HMQ). About 10 other functions take some form of a handle to an object, leaving only 7 or so Win functions that do not require a handle as their first argument.

The Gpi functions are easier to categorize. All but a handful of Gpi functions take a handle to a presentation space as their first argument. The remaining eight or so functions take either an anchor block handle or a metafile handle.

The return values for the Gpi functions are also more uniform that the Win functions. Again, all but a handful of Gpi functions return a value of type BOOL or LONG. About 125 return a BOOL and another 85 or so return a LONG. The remaining functions return bitmap, metafile and device context handles.

Table 2-11: Win Function Return Types

TYPE	#	TYPE	#
ATOM	3	HPS	4
BOOL	120	HSWITCH	21
HAB	1	HWND	21
HACCEL	3	LONG	2
HATOMTBL	3	MRESULT	7
HBITMAP	1	PFNWP	1
HDC	2	PSZ	2
HENUM	1	PVOID	2
HHEAP	3	SHORT	17
HMQ	1	ULONG	6
HPOINTER	4	USHORT	26
HPROGRAM	2		

CHAPTER 3

GETTING THE MESSAGE

Learning the Presentation Manager can be a difficult undertaking for someone who has had little experience with object oriented programming or a message-based architecture. The good news is you can still program the Presentation Manager without being proficient in either of these environments: while the Presentation Manager uses techniques from object oriented programming, it does not rely on them fully.

In most respects, the Presentation Manager is its own environment. Once you initialize a window, just about all of the programming tools that you need are available through one of the Presentation Manager's function libraries. Because of this comprehensive structure, it is not a bad idea to divide the Presentation Manager into conceptual sections and explore a single section at a time (even though you might later recognize subtleties between different sections). Accordingly, this chapter is devoted to messages and how you process them.

Understanding the Presentation Manager's message-based architecture is a necessary prerequisite to creating your first program. Even so, it is difficult, if not impossible, to delineate Presentation Manager messages without describing the program structure through which messages flow. Thus, this chapter focuses on messages, but also presents example material that includes code to initialize, register, and create a standard window. For the time being, accept these calls on face value. Chapter 4 explores them in depth; their detailed explanation here would merely serve to cloud the issue of messages. By the time you finish reading Chapter 4, you should have a decent grounding in both messages and windows — the duo that drives all Presentation Manager programming.

Object Oriented

Development of the Presentation Manager was strongly influenced by existing object oriented environments, including the work already accomplished in Microsoft *Windows* and *Smalltalk-80* by Xerox. Principally, these and other object oriented environments use a message-based architecture that conveys data to predefined objects used by the environment.

What exactly is an object? An object is an internal structure that contains its own set of operations, which it executes on itself. Different external events cause an object to execute different operations or the same operations in different ways. A real life example of an object is a police department. Different external events — the calls it receives via its emergency switchboard — cause it to respond in predefined ways. A call alerting it of a suspicious person in the neighborhood causes it to dispatch a squad car to quietly cruise the neighborhood streets. A call alerting it of a serious car accident causes it to dispatch multiple cruisers with their lights flashing and sirens wailing.

In the Presentation Manager, windows are the primary objects. Windows fit the previous description of objects with one exception: the programmer is responsible for writing the window procedure, which becomes part of the window object. Like other object oriented environments, Presentation Manager objects are distinguished by the the handles that you use to reference them. A handle is a system-defined 32-bit value that identifies the object. You supply the variable name for the handle; the Presentation Manager supplies the arbitrary system value. Table 3-1 lists the various Presentation Manager objects, their data type, and the variable name usually used to reference the handle.

Table 3-1: Presentation Manager Objects

OBJECT	DATA TYPE	HANDLE
Accelerator table	HACCEL	*haccel*
Anchor block	HAB	*hab*
Atom table	HATOMTBL	*hatomtbl*
Bitmap	HBITMAP	*hbm*

(continued)

Table 3-1: Continued

OBJECT	DATA TYPE	HANDLE
Device context	HDC	*hdc*
DLL Module	HMODULE	*hmod*
Graphics region	HRGN	*hrgn*
Heap	HHEAP	*hheap*
Message queue	HMQ	*hmq*
Metafile	HMF	*hmf*
Mouse pointer	HPOINTER	*hptr*
Named pipe	HPIPE	*hpipe*
Open file	HFILE	*hf*
Presentation Space	HPS	*hps*
Program	HPROGRAM	*hprog*
System semaphore	HSYSSEM	*hsem*
Switch entry	HSWITCH	*hsw*
VIO presentation space	HVPS	*hvps*
Window	HWND	*hwnd*
Window enumeration	HENUM	*henum*

As a programmer at the toolkit level, you are rarely privy to the internal workings of an object — to you, it is a black box, a mysterious device that can render impressive results through an instance of itself, but does so only when prompted by predefined stimuli. Messages are the stimuli. In a sense, a message is like a standard function call. Not only is it the entity that travels through an application and yields results, it also carries arguments and returns values just as a function does. Additionally, message data is saved on a stack, as is function data. With both messages and functions, flow of control is blocked until the message or function returns.

Figure 3-1 illustrates the conceptual relationship between a message and an object.

Messages do have unique characteristics. One key difference to a function is a message always carries at least one argument; a function can be devoid of arguments. The one argument that a message always carries is the selection mechanism — namely, the parameter that distinguishes it from other messages and consequently tells the object what operation to perform. Another way messages and functions differ is a function always references a definite address in memory where the code for the function resides. A message does not reference memory at all; instead, it tells the current instance of the object what memory address to reference. And as alluded to already, another difference is a function not only specifies an operation, it carries the information on how to perform the operation. Messages simply specify the operation.

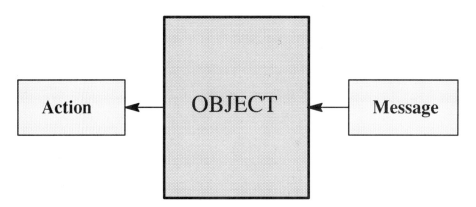

Figure 3-1: Message/Object Relationship

Message System

The Presentation Manager itself is responsible for generating most of the more than 100 general purpose messages that you will come to know. In addition to these, there are more than 150 special purpose messages that service such controls as dialog box windows and scrollbars. Not to stop here, the Presentation Manager also lets you create your own messages. In all, there are four categories of messages in the Presentation Manager:

- *Input messages* are generated by the Presentation Manager in response to keyboard and mouse input.

- *System messages* are generated by the Presentation Manager in response to a programmed event or a system interrupt.

- *Control messages* provide two-way communication with a child window, including menus, scrollbars, titlebars, listboxes, entry fields, pushbuttons, and display objects.

- *User messages* are defined by the programmer and are used within an application to convey data after a predefined event occurs.

Each category of general purpose messages is handled differently by the Presentation Manager. Ultimately, messages from each category are processed through the application message queue (also referred to as the window message queue when more than one queue is in effect). At this point, you, the programmer, take an interest in messages by anticipating which ones will emerge from the application message queue. The routines you code are based on this process of anticipation. Ultimately, however, many messages are processed in a default way by the Presentation Manager itself.

Before keyboard and mouse messages enter the application message queue, the Presentation Manager converts raw input into message form. Upon doing this, it places an input message into the system message queue. The system message queue stores approximately 60 keystrokes and/or mouse clicks. An input message proceeds to the *input router*, which selects the application to receive the message. Its selection is based on the current state of the input focus. The Presentation Manager establishes the input focus as a result of user actions such as a mouse click in a window. It can also set input focus as the result of a programmed event such as a function call. Figure 3-2 illustrates the flow of an input message.

The next message category is system messages. These are not as straightforward as input messages, because some system messages require processing through the Presentation Manager's system message queue, while others do not. One example of a system message that the

Presentation Manager slots into the system message queue is the system timer message. Another is any dynamic data exchange (DDE) message. Other systems messages go directly to the application message queue, including messages that create and destroy windows, clipboard messages, and more. In a sense, the Presentation Manager acts as its own clearinghouse for many system messages; others it sends through the system message queue. This duality of processing method points out a consequential point: it is more important to know that a message is processed through the application message queue than how it arrived there. You should note, however, that various Microsoft reference materials do mention the system message queue.

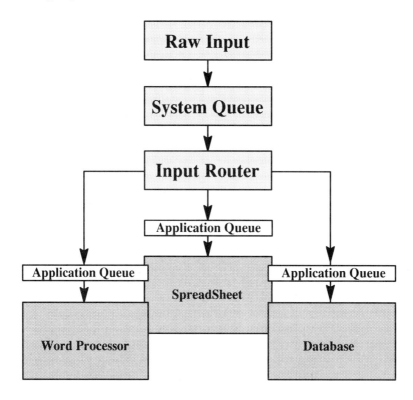

Figure 3-2: Input Message Flow

The third category of messages acts as the interface to the Presentation Manager's special control objects: dialog boxes, listboxes, pushbuttons, and a host of others. Some of these messages you might never have a need to use. For example, it is entirely possible to write an application that does not include a listbox. On the other hand, you will use some controls quite frequently. A typical use of control messages is to carry messages back to a control object from a window procedure. For example, you can send a menu a message to deemphasize a previously selected menu item.

The fourth category of messages falls under the heading of user messages, but these are more aptly described as programmer-defined messages. You create these messages by defining them either at the top of your program or in a separate header file. In general, these messages never leave the application: you post them to the application message queue from one part of the program so that they are processed by another part. User messages are particularly worthy for multiple thread applications, because in most instances, they are an efficient way of passing data between threads. Perhaps the most common use of user messages involves processing menu selections — in that, you can associate user messages with menu items and then process the user message after it emerges from the application queue.

The Messages

Up until now, there has been no mention of a message by name. From here on, the story is quite the opposite. Message names permeate every part of the Presentation Manager. By extension, any book on the Presentation Manager must also carry the weight of the Presentation Manager's extensive message base.

There are eight sets of messages defined by the Presentation Manager. The most frequently used types of messages are those prefixed with WM. For example, the message WM_PAINT tells your application to repaint a window. Note that messages always appear in uppercase letters. This style, combined with the prefix and underscore, help to distinguish messages from the hundreds of other identifiers used in the Presentation Manager. Table 3-2 lists and describes the various types of messages by their prefix.

Table 3-2: Presentation Manager Message Types

PREFIX(S)	DESCRIPTION
WM	General window messages used for standard processing such as keyboard input, window creation and validation, and tracking mouse movement and select/deselect actions.
BM, EM	Messages dedicated to system status information for control windows such as pushbuttons used in dialog box windows.
LM	Listbox control processing.
MM	Menu control window processing.
SBM	Scrollbar control window processing.
SM	Display object processing.
TBM	Titlebar processing.

For the time being, you need not concern yourself with any of the message types other than the WM type. Now, however, is the time to get acquainted with the WM messages, which will be part of the first Presentation Manager program that you write — and part of every program thereafter. Table 3-3 presents some of the more commonly used WM messages.

Table 3-3: The WM Messages

MESSAGE	DESCRIPTION
WM_CHAR	Contains the most recent key press in the queue.
WM_CLOSE	Announces that a window is about to close.
WM_COMMAND	Carries data from child windows and accelerators.
WM_CONTROL	Carries control data for child windows.
WM_CREATE	Announces that a window has just been created.
WM_DESTROY	Announces that a window is about to be destroyed.

(continued)

Table 3-3: Continued

MESSAGE	DESCRIPTION
WM_ERASEBACKGROUND	Tells the frame window to redraw itself.
WM_FOCUSCHANGE	Announces that the focus window is changing.
WM_HELP	Announces request from user for help.
WM_HSCROLL	Announces request to scroll window.
WM_INITDLG	Occurs when a dialog box window is created.
WM_INITMENU	Occurs when a menu is being initialized.
WM_PAINT	Announces that a window needs to be repainted.
WM_QUIT	Announces that application is terminating.
WM_SETFOCUS	Announces a change of input focus.
WM_SIZE	Occurs when size of window changes.
WM_SYSCOMMAND	Contains command message from a control window.
WM_TIMER	Occurs when the timer has timed out.
WM_USER	Defines beginning of user messages.
WM_VSCROLL	Announces request to scroll window.

Even this abridged list of message seems large in number. The complete list is contained in the reference section of this book (Chapter 18). In the meantime, take heart: you will be relieved to know that the Presentation Manager automatically processes most of the WM messages, if you let it. The WM messages that it doesn't process are only there for your convenience: you don't have to process them if you have no need to do so. The WM_CREATE message is a perfect example of this. It essentially has no purpose as far as the Presentation Manager is concerned. You can use it, however, to perform window initialization routines — such as to obtain the coordinates of the new window. For the moment, this is getting ahead of the game: you need to know the internal elements of a message before you can obtain the window coordinates in the WM_CREATE message.

Inside The Message

For the most part, when you process any Presentation Manager message, you want to obtain the data inside the message. True, sometimes you do not need to extract any data from a message, and instead merely process the message so you can execute a routine at a given point in time. This is not an infrequent practice, but more frequently, you will concern yourself with the data contained inside a message.

A message contains four basic values. First, it contains a handle to the window to which the message is addressed. The handle is referred to as *hwnd* of type HWND. The next value in a message is the message name itself. This is referred to as *msg* of type USHORT. The next two values are a message's real muscle. Known as message parameters, these values are 32-bits long and are referred to as *mp1* and *mp2* of type MPARAM. Figure 3-3 shows the data layout of a Presentation Manager message.

A message is always defined by the current value of the QMSG structure. You can actually derive a message's values from the QMSG structure — as you do when dealing with hook functions — but this generally rails against the Presentation Manager's messaging scheme. Here's what the QMSG structure looks like:

```
typedef struct _QMSG { /* qmsg */
            HWND        hwnd;
            USHORT      msg;
            MPARAM      mp1;
            MPARAM      mp2;
            ULONG       time;
            POINTL      ptl;
} QMSG;
```

The two additional fields in QMSG provide some handy information. The *time* field contains the time that the message originated. This is useful in developing journal routines that, among other things, can record a keyboard session and later replay the keystrokes, much like macro-recorders found in some popular word processors. The *ptl* field has a much wider application: it tells you the position of the mouse when the message originated. The *ptl* field references the POINTL structure, which stores the actual *x* and *y* coordinates for the mouse pointer.

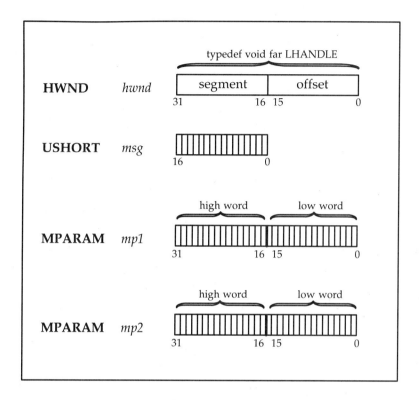

Figure 3-3: Data Layout of a Message.

There is still much more inside a message — specifically inside the *mp1* and *mp2* parameters, the two most important variables in the Presentation Manager. You probably have already guessed these message parameters are 32 bits long for a good reason. The reason is they contain more than one value. In some cases, both *mp1* and *mp2* can contain two distinct 16-bit values: high and low word values of type USHORT, but they can also contain other values, ranging from pointers to four values of type UCHAR per parameter. Frequently, the *mp1* parameter contains a command associated with the current message, or it identifies a window or other object on which some action should be performed. The *mp2* parameter, as an inexact rule, contains information that further describes the data contained in *mp1*.

The Presentation Manager makes several macros available to extract as well as create message parameter values. The latter are useful when it comes time to modify the contents of a message, send a message to a control window, or define values for a user message. Alternatively, you can use some of the macros from the OS/2 kernel programmer's toolkit. Tables 3-4 and 3-5 list the Presentation Manager macros for extracting and creating message parameter values.

Table 3-4: Macros for Extracting Message Parameter Values

MACRO	DEFINED AS
PVOIDFROMMP(mp)	((VOID FAR *)(mp))
HWNDFROMMP(mp)	((HWND)(mp))
CHAR1FROMMP(mp)	((UCHAR)(mp))
CHAR2FROMMP(mp)	((UCHAR)((ULONG)mp >> 8))
CHAR3FROMMP(mp)	((UCHAR)((ULONG)mp >> 16))
CHAR4FROMMP(mp)	((UCHAR)((ULONG)mp >> 24))
SHORT1FROMMP(mp)	((USHORT)(ULONG)(mp))
SHORT2FROMMP(mp)	((USHORT)((ULONG)mp >> 16))
LONGFROMMP(mp)	((ULONG)(mp))

Table 3-5: Macros for Creating Message Parameter Values

MACRO	DEFINED AS
MPFROMP(p)	((MPARAM)(VOID FAR *)(p))
MPFROMHWND(hwnd)	((MPARAM)(HWND)(hwnd))
MPFROMCHAR(ch)	((MPARAM)(USHORT)(ch))
MPFROMSHORT(s)	((MPARAM)(USHORT)(s))

(continued)

Table 3-5: Continued

MACRO	DEFINED AS
MPFROM2SHORT(s1, s2)	((MPARAM)MAKELONG(s1, s2))
MPFROMSH2CH(s, uch1, ch2)	((MPARAM)MAKELONG(s, MAKESHORT(uch1,uch2)))
MPFROMLONG(l)	((MPARAM)(ULONG)(l))

Using the macros is straightforward. To extract a value from a message parameter, you can either use the macros in Table 3-4 in standalone fashion, or use them inside a function call. The following examples show how to do this. The second example includes a call to the much-used WinPostMsg function.

```
/* Set variable to extract USHORT from low word
   of message parameter contained in mp1. */

   usValue = SHORT1FROMMP(mp1);

/* Use macro inside with WinPostMsg function. */
   WinPostMsg(hwnd, WM_USR1,

   MPFROM2SHORT(usLength,usBytes),0L);
```

The first example simply sets *usValue* to the USHORT contained in the lower byte of *mp1*. (Note that *usValue* is prefixed with *us*, the naming convention that denotes a USHORT.) The second example is not as obvious. The purpose of WinPostMsg is to post, not send, a message. In doing so, it passes the four message values: *hwnd*, *msg*, *mp1*, and *mp2*. The third argument, *mp1*, is satisfied by using the MPFROM2SHORT macro; it simply creates a ULONG value from the two USHORTs, *usLength* and *usBytes*. The function call could be rewritten like this:

```
/* Verbose way of satisfying WinPostMsg. */

   hwnd = currenthwnd;
   msg = USR1;
```

```
mp1 = MPFROM2SHORT(usLength, usBytes);
mp2 = OL;
WinPostMsg(hwnd, msg, mp1, mp2);
```

The Presentation Manger also offers three stack macros to extract message data. These are designed for extracting keyboard, mouse, and command data only. Table 3-6 lists the stack macros.

Table 3-6: Command-Oriented Message Macros

MACRO	DEFINED AS
CHARMSG(pmsg)	((struct _CHARMSG FAR *) ((PBYTE)pmsg - sizeof(MPARAM) * 2))
COMMANDMSG(pmsg)	((struct _COMMANDMSG FAR*) ((PBYTE)pmsg - sizeof(MPARAM) * 2))
MOUSEMSG(pmsg)	((struct _MOUSEMSG FAR *) ((PBYTE)pmsg - sizeof(MPARAM) * 2))

As Table 3-6 indicates, the stack macros are limited to processing the WM_CHAR, WM_MOUSEMOVE, WM_BUTTON*, WM_COMMAND, WM_SYSCOMMAND, and WM_HELP messages. These macros work by using the address of the message to reference the special message structure available on the stack.

The message structure that each macro references is fully accessible to you. Although it is not common practice, you can obtain values from each of these structures, which are defined as follows:

```
/* Message structure for WM_CHAR message data. */

struct _CHARMSG {
        USHORT chr;             /* mp2 low word */
        USHORT vkey;            /* mp2 high word */
        USHORT fs;              /* mp1 low word */
        UCHAR cRepeat;          /* mp1 bits 16 - 23 */
        UCHAR scancode;         /* mp1 bits 24 - 31 */
    };
```

```
/* Message structure for WM_COMMAND, WM_HELP,
and WM_SYSCOMMAND message data. */

    struct _COMMANDMSG {
            USHORT source;          /* mp2 low word */
            BOOL  fMouse;
            USHORT cmd;             /* mp1 low word */
            USHORT unused;
    };



/* Message structure for WM_MOUSEMOVE and
WM_BUTTON* message data. */

    struct _MOUSEMSG {
            USHORT codeHitTest;     /* mp2 low word */
            USHORT unused;          /* mp2 high word */
            SHORT  x;               /* mp1 low word */
            SHORT  y;               /* mp1 high word */
    };
```

To use a stack macro, you must use the structure pointer operator (->) when referencing a field. The following examples show various ways of using the stack macros:

```
/* Set local variable equal to cmd field from the
   _COMMANDMSG structure. */

    usCommand = COMMANDMSG(&msg)-> cmd;



/* Obtain mouse coordinates from the x and y fields
   in the _MOUSEMSG structure. */

    usXpos = MOUSEMSG(&msg)-> x;
    usYpos = MOUSEMSG(&msg)-> y;



/* Test for the KC_CHAR flag contained in low word of
mp1, and then process the character code contained
in low word of mp2.*/

    if(CHARMSG(&msg)-> fs & KC_CHAR)
    {
```

```
switch(CHARMSG(&msg)-> chr)
{
   case '\r':
            .
            .
            break;
   case 't':
            .
            break;
   }
}
```

You will find that using these macros saves you a significant amount of coding. Many of the examples in this book make use of the stack macros. Figure 3-4 shows the orientation of the various message values on the stack.

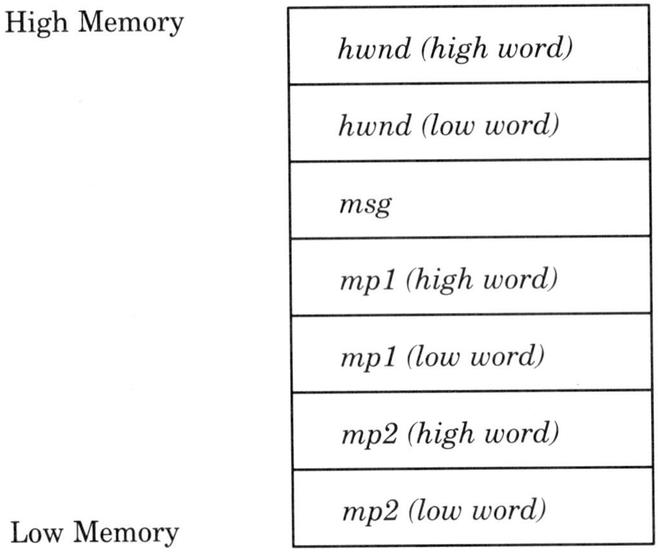

High Memory

hwnd (high word)
hwnd (low word)
msg
mp1 (high word)
mp1 (low word)
mp2 (high word)
mp2 (low word)

Low Memory

Figure 3-4: Message Parameter Stack Orientation

Although the stack macros are handy, in many cases you will find that the other Presentation Manager macros are just as handy. Feel free to use either type of macro. Additionally, you can use the OS/2 macros if you pefer these.

The Message Queue

So far, you have been looking at messages in a vacuum. If you closely followed the previous section, the description of the application message queue in this section will be more pertinent. But what is the application message queue?

The application message queue comes into existence when you call the WinCreateMsgQueue function. WinCreateMsgQueue sets asides a block of memory to store messages (various copies of the QMSG structure) that your application processes. You call WinCreateMsgQueue once, and only once, for each program thread associated with a window.

Many small Presentation Manager programs only require a single message queue (and this is where the term application message queue is most appropriate). Larger applications use additional message queues for such purposes as running child windows and displaying messages boxes. You can also create object windows by using a secondary thread. Object windows are used for multitasking procedures and incorporating custom objects into a Presentation Manager application. When you create separate threads of execution without creating a message queue for them, these threads are called queueless threads.

Before you can call WinCreateMsgQueue, you need an *anchor block handle*. An anchor block handle identifies the message queue. You obtain the anchor block handle by calling the WinInitialize function (explained in Chapter 4). You must then call WinCreateMsgQueue immediately. Here's the definition for WinCreateMsgQueue:

```
HMQ WinCreateMsgQueue(HAB, cmsg)
HAB hab;
SHORT cmsg;
```

In addition to the anchor block handle, WinCreateMsgQueue needs to know the size of the message queue. You can set *cmsg* to a custom number of events or messages. You might need to increase the queue size if your program includes dynamic data exchange (DDE) routines; needs to perform a task that causes it to ignore the message queue for a considerable amount of time; or handles a lot of graphics commands. For example, a setting of 80 messages would handle an extremely large graphics program. Most programs can use the default size of 10 messages. You can accept the default size by simply setting *csmg* to zero. Here's the most common form of the WinCreateMsgQueue call:

```
hmq = WinCreateMsgQueue(hab, 0);
```

The call to WinCreateMsgQueue returns a value of *hmq*, which contains the message queue handle. You need this variable in order to remove the application message queue when you close out your program. The Win-DestroyMsgQueue function accomplishes this. Here's the typical call:

```
WinDestroyMsgQueue(hmq);
```

You also need *hmq* to dispatch messages throughout your program. The actual dispatching occurs from a **while** loop that is typically set up in **main()**. Figure 3-5 shows the message flow from program initialization to an application's primary function, the client window procedure.

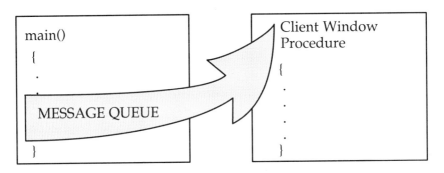

Figure 3-5: Presentation Manager Message Flow

Think of the message queue as a black box. Like windows, message queues are objects and therefore have the black box quality described earlier. Messages enter the queue sequentially, based on their time of occurrence, and emerge from the queue in the same order. The beauty of the message queue is it sends the messages directly to the associated window procedure. By looking at the message loop, you might wonder how this is possible:

```
while(WinGetMsg(hab, &qsmg, NULL, 0, 0))
        WinDispatchMsg(hab, &qmsg);
```

Obviously, the WinDispatchMsg must have something to do with slot-ting messages to the application window procedure. It does, but only be-cause it passes the buck to the Presentation Manager, which sends all messages to the function that you specify when you create the applica-tion's standard window. This function is generally referred to as the client window procedure (but this is getting ahead of the game). For now, take a look at the definition for WinGetMsg:

```
BOOL WinGetMsg(hab, pqmsg, hwndFilter, msgFirst, msgLast)
HAB hab;
PQMSG pqmsg;
HWND hwndFilter;
USHORT msgFirst, msgLast;
```

By now, you should be familiar with the *hab* (handle anchor block) argu-ment. The second argument is also familiar, but somewhat disguised: *pqmsg* is a far pointer to the QMSG structure (which, as you recall, always contains the current message and the data it carries).

The next three arguments to WinGetMsg provide the framework for cre-ating a message filter. Essentially, filtering allows you to process mes-sages in a different order than they exist in the queue. For example, you can structure a filter so it waits for a WM_BUTTONCLICKLAST message after receiving a WM_BUTTONCLICKFIRST message. Normally, if you do not care what messages your application procedure receives, you set these arguments to NULL, 0, and 0. If you use the filter arguments, you can:

- Specify a value for *hwndFilter* and limit the message to a specific win-dow or child of that window.

- Specify values for *msgFirst* and *msgLast* and establish a range of allow-able messages.

- Combine the two approaches and limit the range of messages for a spe-cific window or its children.

The one hitch to filtering messages is you have to ensure that some al-lowable message can occur. If this is not the case, WinGetMsg doesn't know any better and just continues to sit there waiting for the message that isn't going to come. In other words, your application hangs.

The second part of the message loop is the WinDispatchMsg function. WinDispatchMsg simply calls the Presentation Manager to dispatch the current message to the programmer-defined function that it associates with the message queue. How does the Presentation Manager know which window to send the message to? The definition of WinDispatchMsg contains the answer:

```
ULONG WinDispatchMsg(hab, pqmsg)
HAB     hab;
PQMSG   pqmsg;
```

Where is the answer? In the *pqmsg* argument, which references the QMSG structure. The QMSG structure contains a *hwnd* field that tells the Presentation Manager where to send the message. It is that simple: you do not have to worry about calling functions from **main()**; the Presentation Manager calls them for you.

When the window procedure associated with the message queue finishes processing the current message, control always returns to the message loop. WinGetMsg continues to work until no further messages exist in the queue. This situation only occurs if a WM_QUIT message has been issued by the Presentation Manager.

Message Processing

Window functions are passive animals. They lie in wait for messages sent to them by the Presentation Manager. It is your job as programmer to put as much life into the application window as possible. Your primary tool to do so is the **switch-case** construction. Each **case** statement in the construction handles a specific message. The associated block of code is said to be the *message handler*.

Here is a sample program that shows you some basic message processing. The program creates a standard window and prints a line of text for every message processed by the client window procedure, which is called AppWndProc in the example. Pay particular attention to the processing of the WM_DESTROY message. It is fuel for further fodder.

```
/* MSGPRINT.C (prints acknowledgment of messages) */

#include <os2.h>
```

```
MRESULT EXPENTRY AppWndProc(HWND, USHORT, MPARAM, MPARAM);

int main (void)
{
HMQ     hmq;
HWND    hwndFrame, hwndClient;
QMSG    qmsg;
static CHAR   szTitleBar[40];
static CHAR   szClass[] = "Message Print";
ULONG   ctlData = FCF_STANDARD
                     & ~FCF_MENU ~FCF_ACCELTABLE;

    hab = WinInitialize(0);
    hmq = WinCreateMsgQueue(hab, 0);
    WinRegisterClass(hab, szClass, ClientWndProc,
                  CS_SIZEREDRAW, 0);

    hwndFrame = WinCreateStdWindow(HWND_DESKTOP,
                  WS_VISIBLE | FS_ICON,
                  &ctlData, szClass,
                  szTitleBar,0L, NULL,
                  ID_RESOURCE,
                  &hwndClient);

    while(WinGetMsg(hab, &qmsg, NULL, 0, 0))
            WinDispatchMsg(hab, &qmsg);

    WinDestroyWindow(hwndFrame);
    WinDestroyMsgQueue(hmq);
    WinTerminate(hab);

    return(0);

}
MRESULT EXPENTRY MainAppProc(hwnd, msg, mp1, mp2)
HWND    hwnd;
USHORT msg;
MPARAM mp1, mp2;
{
static SHORT usXsize, usYsize;

switch (msg)
    {
    case WM_CREATE:
            WriteMessageText(hwnd);
            return(FALSE);
```

```
        case WM_ACTIVATE:
                WriteMessageText(hwnd);
                return(TRUE);

        case WM_SIZE:
                usXsize = SHORT1FROMMP(mp2);
                usYsize = SHORT2FROMMP(mp2);
                return(FALSE);

        case WM_DESTROY:
                WriteMessageText(hwnd);
                return(NULL);

        case WM_CLOSE:
                WriteMessageText(hwnd);
                WinDefWindowProc(hwnd, msg, mp1, mp2);

        default:
                return(WinDefWindowProc(hwnd, msg, mp1, mp2));
        }
        return(0);
}

VOID WriteMessageText(hwnd)
HWND  hwnd;
{
CHAR  szString[] = 'Message now has been processed.'
static RECTL  rcl;
static BOOL    bFlag = TRUE;

        hps = WinGetPS(hwnd, NULL, NULL);
        if(bFlag) {
                WinQueryWindowRect(hwnd, &rcl);
                bFlag = FALSE;
        }
        else
                rcl.yBottom += 20;

        WinDrawText(hps, -1, szString,
                        &rcl, CLR_NEUTRAL,
                        CLR_BACKGROUND,
                        DT_CENTER | DT_VCENTER
                        | DT_ERASERECT);

        WinEndPaint(hps);
}
```

As you can see from the example, you do not have to write a **switch** statement that anticipates every conceivable message. Most unanticipated messages — or messages you simply do not care to anticipate — are processed by the WinDefWindowProc function. In essence, this function shovels most unprocessed messages back to the Presentation Manager, which then processes the message.

You can place WinDefWindowProc at the end of the client window function, or alternatively, you can place it in the default section of the **switch** statement, supplying it the same arguments that the Presentation Manager originally passed to the application window. Here's the code:

```
default:
        return(WinDefWindowProc(hwnd, msg, mp1, mp2));
```

The arguments to WinDefWindowProc are the same as those passed to the client window procedure itself (MainAppProc in the example). This circumstance should give you a clear perspective on the client window procedure. In point of fact, the client window procedure is a staging ground for messages: you can do with them whatever you want in this staging ground, or let them roll in and out, comfortable in the notion that the Presentation Manager will perform default message processing when necessary.

What about the messages processed in the client window procedure? You simply place these in various **case** statements inside the **switch** statement. In the example, the client window procedure handles the WM_CREATE, WM_ACTIVATE, and WM_DESTROY messages by calling the WriteMessage function and then passing a message return value back to the Presentation Manager. With WM_CREATE, for example, the window procedure returns a FALSE value, because no problem developed during the message processing. If a problem had developed — say, a memory check revealed that not enough memory existed to run the application — you could return a TRUE value, which would cause the Presentation Manager to abort its attempt to create the program's window.

Each message that you process has its own set of requirements. The WM_PAINT message, for example, requires that you call the WinBeginPaint function at the start of the **case** statement; and the WinEndPaint function before closing the **case** statement. Generally, what you do after you meet these type of requirements is your own business — as long as you do not do it for too long a period of time. That is, whatever processing you perform inside a message loop should take no longer than 1/10 of a second. This is a stylistic suggestion by Microsoft. If you know processing is going to exceed the 1/10 limit, you should perform it in a separate thread of execution.

One other message from the example offers an interesting twist; the WM_CLOSE message is processed by the window procedure, but then returned to the Presentation Manager for default processing. This is necessary because the WM_CLOSE message internally generates a WM_QUIT message, which must be processed in order for the Presentation Manager to close the specified window. (Instead of using WinDefWindowProc here, you could use the WinPostMsg function and actually post the WM_QUIT message.)

Finally, you probably noticed the use of the message macros in the WM_SIZE message block in the example. The WM_SIZE message occurs when a window changes it size. The horizontal size is stored in the low word of *mp2*; the vertical size is stored in the high word of *mp2*. Extracting these values into static SHORTs gives you continuous access to the window size — not just access during the WM_SIZE message. This is a technique that you will employ time and again in your Presentation Manager programs.

Message Management

The Presentation Manager supports several message functions to give you latitude in the way messages are passed. In this regard, two important distinctions exist: some functions directly *send* messages to windows, while others *post* messages to the window's message queue. The WinDispatchMsg function, for example, sends messages because it forwards messages from the message queue, but the WinPostMsg function posts messages to the message queue.

One message function that deserves immediate scrutiny is the WinSendMsg function. As its name says, WinSendMsg sends a message. The destination of the message is another window's message queue — unless, of course, you send it to the current message queue (a state of affairs that amounts to recursion). WinSendMsg is truly one of the most powerful functions in the Presentation Manager, and it is your primary way of communicating with control windows. Here's its definition:

```
MRESULT WinSendMsg(hwnd, msg, mp1, mp2)
HWND hwnd;
USHORT msg;
MPARAM mp1, mp2;
```

As you can see, the arguments to WinSendMsg are identical to those received by the client window procedure. You'll also note that WinSendMsg is declared as the same type as the client window procedure. And more often than not, you will find yourself using the message construction macros with WinSenfMsg. The following code, which sends a message to a radio button control, represents a typical way of using WinSendMsg:

```
WinSendMsg(hwndRadio[sEvent],
          BM_SETCHECK,
          MPFROMSHORT(TRUE),
          NULL);
```

Here, this code simply tells a radio button to display a check mark, indicating that it was the previously used control. The first argument, *hwndRadio*, identifies the radio button. This argument is indexed by *sEvent*, which is a handy way of distinguishing button controls. The second argument, BM_SETCHECK, corresponds to *msg*. This particular message is one of several predefined button messages (hence, the BM prefix). The third argument constructs the value for BM_SETCHECK. In this case, the value is TRUE, which tells the radio button to check itself. The last argument is NULL because BM_SETCHECK does not use its *mp2* parameter.

An additional set of macros — known as message result macros — play a role in using the WinSendMsg function. These macros are somewhat similar to those used for extracting data from messages. The difference is you use them to extract data from the value returned by WinSendMsg.

Instead of referring to *mp1* or *mp2*, the message result macros refer to *mr*. You use them in almost an identical manner as other data extraction macros. The following fragment gives you the flavor of an MRESULT macro, but don't be concerned with the parameters it uses. For now, be satisfied to know that you use a message result macro to extract data from a function such as WinSendMsg.

```
id = SHORT1FROMMR(WinSendMsg(
                        hwndList1,
                        LM_QUERYSELECTION,
                          MPFROMSHORT(LIT_FIRST),
                          NULL));
          .
          .
          .
          .

WinSendMsg(hwndList1,
          LM_QUERYITEMTEXT,
          MPFROM2SHORT(id, sizeof(szItem)),
          MPFROMP(szItem));
```

The important point to note in these calls to WinSendMsg is that you can obtain the *id* value from the first call by using the message result macro. In turn, you need to use this value in the second call to WinSendMsg, which in the example obtains a text string from a listbox. Table 3-7 lists the message result macros.

Table 3-7: Message Result Macros

FUNCTION	DESCRIPTION
PVOIDFROMMR(mr)	((VOID FAR *)(mr))
SHORT1FROMMR(mr)	((USHORT)((ULONG)mr))
SHORT2FROMMR(mr)	((USHORT)((ULONG)mr >> 16))
LONGFROMMR(mr)	((ULONG)(mr))

The MRESULT macros come in two flavors. In addition to the macros to extract data from a return value, there is a less frequently used set of macros to construct a return value. In certain circumstances, you might want to use these macros, in lieu of default processing, to pass a return value from one window procedure to another. Table 3-8 lists these macros.

84

Table 3-8: Return Value Macros

FUNCTION	DESCRIPTION
MRFROMP(p)	((MRESULT)(VOID FAR *)(p))
MRFROMSHORT(s)	((MRESULT)(USHORT)(s))
MRFROM2SHORT(s1, s2)	(MRESULT)MAKELONG(s1, s2))
MRFROMLONG(l)	((MRESULT)(ULONG)(l))

Message Functions

As you will come to learn, message passing is truly the heart of the Presentation Manager, which features a hefty set of functions used to enhance message handling. As you have already seen, the WinSendMsg function is vital to message processing. As with WinSendMsg, a message is sent to a window owned by the current thread of execution — namely, the thread that you create with the call to WinCreateMsgQueue. In this case, the window procedure is called recursively as a subroutine.

The message model changes a little when you use the message functions with multiple threads of execution. For messages sent to another thread, the Presentation Manager switches to the appropriate thread. At this point, the message is either posted to the message queue of the associated window, or sent directly to the window procedure itself. For example, the WinPostQueueMsg function posts a message to a separate thread, but the WinSendMsg and WinPostMsg send messages to window procedures associated with the separate thread. Additional aspects of threads and multitasking are described in Chapter 16. For now, review Table 3-9, which lists and describes the various message functions.

Table 3-9: Presentation Manager Message Functions

FUNCTION	DESCRIPTION
WinBroadcastMsg	Broadcasts a messages to multiple child windows. The function sends or posts messages, depending on its orientation to the message queue.
WinCreateMsgQueue	Creates a message queue for a window and is always associated with only one thread of execution.
WinCallMsgFilter	Calls a specially-designed hook function. Can be used to bypass a filter installed in a public control window.
WinDdePostMsg	Uses shared memory to post a message to a window owned by a concurrently running application.
WinDestroyMsgQueue	Destroys the specified message queue.
WinDispatchMsg	Calls the window procedure and sends it a message from the message queue.
WinGetMsg	Gets a message from a specified message queue and provides message filtering capabilities.
WinPeekMsg	Examines the message queue and optionally removes a message from the queue for processing. The function also supports filtering.
WinPostMsg	Posts a message to the message queue associated with the specified window. Convenient for multiple thread processing.
WinPostQueueMsg	Posts a message to the message queue identified by its message queue handle.
WinQueryMsgPos	Returns the mouse pointer position associated with the last message obtained from the message queue.
WinQueryMsgTime	Returns the time associated with the last message obtained from the message queue.
WinQueryQueueInfo	Obtains information on the specified message queue, including the maximum number of messages the queue can hold.
WinQueryQueueStatus	Obtains the type of messages currently in the specified message queue.
WinSendDlgItemMsg	Sends a message to the specified item belonging to a dialog box.

(continued)

Table 3-9: Continued

FUNCTION	DESCRIPTION
WinSendMsg	Sends a message to the specified window function. Amounts to a recursive call if used for the current window procedure.
WinWaitMsg	Waits for the next message that coincides with the filter set up by WinGetMsg or WinPeekMsg.

Querying The Queue

If you do use various techniques to modify the queue such as message filtering, you can use the WinQueryQueueInfo function to provide your application with queue data. Among other things, WinQueryQueueInfo tells
you the number of messages the queue can hold — a consideration that
affects the type of filters you construct. (If you find that you need to increase the number of messages a queue can hold, increase the size when
you create the queue with WinCreateMsgQueue.) Here's the definition for
WinQueryQueueInfo:

```
BOOL WinQueryQueueInfo(hmq, pmqi, cbCopy)
HMQ hmq;
PMQINFO pmqi;
USHORT cbCopy;
```

The *hmq* argument is the handle to the message queue. The *pmqi* and
cbCopy arguments are used in referencing the MQINFO structure, which
contains queue information. The *cbCopy* argument simply specifies the
size of the copy of the structure that is created with the call to WinQuery-
QueueInfo. The *pmqi* argument references the copy of the structure, which
is defined as follows:

```
typedef struct _MQINFO {
    USHORT    cb;
    PID       pid;
    TID       tid;
    USHORT    cmsgs;
    PVOID     pReserved;
} MQINFO;
```

The fields in MQINFO are straightforward. The *cb* field contains the size of the structure. The *pid* and *tid* field contains the process and thread IDs, respectively. The last field, *cmsgs*, contains the maximum number of messages that the queue can hold.

The WinQueryQueueStatus function is also useful in obtaining queue information. Specifically, it allows you to determine whether a given type of message exists in the queue. Here's some typical code to handle the call to WinQueryQueueStatus:

```
VOID QueueChecker(usCurrent, usAdded)
USHORT *usCurrent, *usAdded;
{
    ULONG  ulMessage;
    ulMessage = WinQueryQueueStatus(HWND_DESKTOP);
    *usCurrent = HIUSHORT(ulMessage);
    *usAdded = LUUSHORT(ulMessage);
}
```

In the example, the actual call to WinQueryQueueStatus requires the handle to the desktop as its only argument. The values returned in *ulMessage* contain the messages currently in the queue as well as those added to the queue since the previous call to WinQueryQueueStatus. The example uses the OS/2 kernel macros to extract the values, which you can manipulate by using the predefined queue status (QS) identifiers. Table 3-10 lists these identifiers.

Table 3-10: Queue Status Identifiers

IDENTIFIER	BIT	MESSAGE TYPE
QS_KEY	0x0001	Character message.
QS_MOUSEBUTTON	0x0002	Mouse button message.
QS_MOUSEMOVE	0x0004	Mouse position message.
QS_MOUSE	0x0006	Mouse button or position message.
QS_TIMER	0x0008	Timer message.

(continued)

Table 3-10: Continued

IDENTIFIER	BIT	MESSAGE TYPE
QS_PAINT	0x0010	Paint message.
QS_POSTMSG	0x0020	Posted message.
QS_SEM1	0x0040	Semaphore message.
QS_SEM2	0x0080	Semaphore message.
QS_SEM3	0x0100	Semaphore message.
QS_SEM4	0x0200	Semaphore message.
QS_SENDMSG	0x0400	Sent message.

CHAPTER 4

CREATING WINDOWS

There is one Presentation Manager function you won't see documented: the Presentation Manager itself. This is an exaggeration, but it is helpful to think of the Presentation Manager as nothing more than another function — albeit, an extremely large function, one capable of performing so many system-oriented tasks that it takes on a life of its own. As you seek to understand program flow in Presentation Manager code, it is often useful to view some steps as a *function of the Presentation Manager*. If you are writing pseudo code, it might be helpful to borrow from mathematical notation and write:

$$\Sigma\ (Presentation\ Manager) = Some\ Event$$

This is mainly a learning technique. The Presentation Manger is really a rich and powerful interface to OS/2 and it qualifies as an operating system in its own right. When you suddenly realize that the window functions you create are never directly called by your programs, thinking of the Presentation Manager as a function might ease the culture shock.

The business of this chapter is to show you — on a function-by-function basis — how to produce simple Presentation Manger windows. Some of the more interesting functions covered in this chapter are WinRegisterClass, WinCreateStdWindow, WinSetWindowPos, and WinAddSwitchEntry. Although these functions don't embody everything you need to know about windows, they give you a good start. Generally, they behave as good C functions are wont — and their arguments provide a comfortable introduction to several window concepts. And as you begin to program the Presentation Manager, you will become more familiar with these functions than any others.

A First Template

Probably the most efficient way to create a Presentation Manager program is to have a template that you can use time and again as a launching pad. A good template incorporates the fundamental steps that should be addressed in an introductory description of creating a Presentation Manager program. The following template serves both purposes and the rest of this chapter is devoted to explaining what is actually going on in the template (in case you ever need to build an application with your eyes closed). Throughout the book, specific code examples are denoted as additions to the template — so that by the end of the book, you will have a template that you can use repeatedly.

```
/* TEMPLATE.C (Standard template program) */

#define INCL_PM

#include <os2.h>
#include <string.h>

MRESULT EXPENTRY TemplateWndProc(HWND,USHORT,MPARAM,MPARAM);

HAB     hab;
HMQ     hmq;
HWND    hwndFrame, hwndTemplate;

int main(void)
{

static CHAR szClass[] = "Template";
static CHAR szTitleBar[15] = "Blank Template";
ULONG ctlData = FCF_TITLEBAR | FCF_SYSMENU | FCF_SIZEBORDER
                    | FCF_MINMAX;

USHORT fSwp = SWP_ACTIVATE | SWP_SIZE | SWP_MOVE | SWP_SHOW;
PID     pid;
TID     tid;
QMSG    qmsg;
SWCNTRL swctl;


hab = WinInitialize(NULL);
hmq = WinCreateMsgQueue(hab, 0);
```

```
WinRegisterClass(
        hab,                    /* Anchor block handle. */
        szClass,                /* Registered class name. */
        TemplateWndProc,        /* Message queue function. */
        CS_SIZEREDRAW,          /* Class style */
        0);                     /* NULL */

hwndFrame = WinCreateStdWindow(
        HWND_DESKTOP,             /* Desktop is parent. */
        WS_VISIBLE,             /* Window style. */
        &ctlData,               /* Frame creation flags. */
        szClass,                /* Window class name. */
        szTitleBar,             /* Title is program filename. */
        0L,                     /* Client area style. */
        NULL,                   /* Handle to module resources. */
        0,                      /* Custom resource ID. */
        &hwndTemplate);         /* Client window handle. */

WinSetWindowPos(
        hwndFrame,              /* Handle to frame window. */
        HWND_TOP,               /* Place at top of the z-order. */
        50,                     /* Horizontal base position. */
        50,                     /* Vertical base position. */
        250,                    /* Width from base position. */
        250,                    /* Height from base position. */
        fSwp);                  /* Positioning control flags. */

WinQueryWindowProcess(hwndFrame, &pid, &tid);

swctl.hwnd = hwndFrame;              /* Window handle. */
swctl.hwndIcon = NULL;               /* Icon handle. */
swctl.hprog = NULL;                  /* Program handle. */
swctl.idProcess = pid;               /* Process ID. */
swctl.idSession = NULL;              /* Session ID. */
swctl.uchVisibility = SWL_VISIBLE;        /* Vis indicator. */
swctl.fbJump = SWL_JUMPABLE;              /* Jump indicator. */
strcpy(swctl.szSwtitle, "Template Demo");  /* Task Manager. */

WinAddSwitchEntry(&swctl);

while(WinGetMsg(hab, &qmsg, NULL, 0, 0))
            WinDispatchMsg(hab, &qmsg);

WinDestroyWindow(hwndFrame);
WinDestroyMsgQueue(hmq);
WinTerminate(hab);
}
```

```
MRESULT EXPENTRY TemplateWndProc(hwnd, msg, mp1, mp2)
HWND   hwnd;
USHORT msg;
MPARAM mp1, mp2;
{
HPS hps;

switch (msg)
  {
   case WM_ERASEBACKGROUND:
        return(TRUE);
  }
  return WinDefWindowProc(hwnd, msg, mp1, mp2);
}
```

What does this rigidly structured, function-laden program buy you? A lot, really. Accomplishing the same thing without Presentation Manager functions would require an immense amount of code. Yet through the nine functions contained in the template you get a full-blown Presentation Manager window, frame controls, and an entry into the Task Manager switchlist. And if you do not want to use the *Task Manager* interface, you can write a similar template, leaving out two function calls and a total of 10 lines of code. Before delving into the functions in detail, Table 4-1 provides a quick review of them.

Table 4-1: Preliminary Setup Functions

FUNCTION	RETURNS	DESCRIPTION
WinInitialize	Handle	Initializes the Presentation Manager.
WinCreateMsgQueue	Handle	Creates message queue for current thread.
WinRegisterClass	Boolean	Registers a class name for a window.
WinCreateStdWindow	Handle	Creates the frame window and its controls.
WinSetWindowPos	Boolean	Sets the window position.
WinQueryWindowProcess	Boolean	Obtains process and thread IDs.
WinAddSwitchEntry	Handle	Modifies switchlist data.

As you can see, the function names closely match their descriptions. For the time being, don't be concerned with the return values. You'll see other tables such as this one throughout the book. Typically, they appear at the beginning of a section and explain several functions.

The next question is how to get this program running. For the sake of beginners, the template example uses a minimum number of Presentation Manager components. For example, it uses neither an icon, nor an accelerator table. Thus, compiling the program means all you need besides the source code is a make file and a module definition file.

The module definition file is a file that the LINK program uses when it makes the application's .EXE file. In practice, it usually has the same filename as the application's source code file, but has a .DEF filename extension. Most simple Presentation Manager programs can make use of the same module definition file, with some minor changes from program to program, if you change the names of message queue functions. Here's a module definition file that works for the template example as well as for most of the programs in this book:

```
; TEMPLATE.DEF (Module Definition File)

NAME          TEMPLATE

DESCRIPTION   'Template Example'

PROTMODE
CODE          LOADONCALL
DATA          LOADONCALL
HEAPSIZE      1024
STACKSIZE     8192

EXPORTS       TemplateWndProc
```

The first line of this module definition file is a comment and the semicolon serves as the comment character. The next line uses the NAME statement, which lets you specify the name of the program and differentiate it from a dynamic link library, which also uses the module definition file.

The PROTMODE statement simply specifies that the program only runs in protected mode. The CODE statement specifies that the application's code segment is not loaded until accessed (the default, if this line is not specified). The DATA statement specifies the identical loading characteristic for the application's data segment. The HEAPSIZE specifies the size, in bytes, of the application's local heap. Similarly, the STACKSIZE statement specifies the size, in bytes, of the application's stack. A minimum size of 8,192 bytes, or 4K, is recommended. Of course, you can increase the stack size as your needs dictate. It is very common for Presentation Manager programmers to make 8K their personal minimum stack size.

The last statement, EXPORTS, is perhaps the most critical one in regard to the architecture of the Presentation Manager. The EXPORTS statement specifies the name of any function that requires exporting to another module. In the present case, the TemplateWndProc function — the function that handles the client window's message queue — is exported to the Presentation Manager's run-time module. You reference multiple functions and dynamic link libraries using the same EXPORTS statement. In fact, up to 3,072 export definitions can be referenced, each on a separate line. The LINK program also provides an IMPORTS statement, which you use when you want to access code contained in a dynamic link library.

Now for the make file. As with the module definition file, you can use the same make file for many Presentation Manager programs. And as with the definition file, the make file used for the template example works with all other programs in this book, unless otherwise noted. Here's what it looks like:

```
# TEMPLATE (Make File)

template.obj : template.c
    cl -c -W3 -As -G2sw -Oas -Zpei template.c

template.exe : template.obj template.def
    link template, /align:16, NUL, os2, template
```

Again, the first line is a comment, using the number (pound) sign as the comment character. The next line tells the LINK program to construct an object module from the source code. The subsequent line is the critical line, the one that invokes the CL compiler and specifies the appropriate switches. Table 4-2 lists and defines the switches used.

Table 4-2: Switches Used to Construct Object Module

SWITCH	ACTION
-c	Instructs the CL compiler to compile, but not link, the program.
-W3	Sets the warning level at three.
-As	Specifies a small memory model.
-G2sw	Specifies the 80286 instruction set, turns off stack checking, and specifies Presentation Manager window processing.
-0as	Controls optimization by relaxing alias checking and favoring code size.
-Zpei	Packs structure members on the specified byte boundary, enables extensions specific to Microsoft C, and generates debugging data for Microsoft CodeView.

Window Initialization

Before you do anything else, you must initialize the Presentation Manager. Even though it sets in motion a host of complex code, initializing the Presentation Manager is the most straightforward step you'll encounter. The call is this simple:

```
hab = WinInitialize();
```

WinInitialize is a 32-bit anchor block handle. Most Presentation Manager functions require a handle of one sort or another. In the early steps of a program, you supply the anchor block handle to functions such as WinCreateMsgQueue — because, quite simply, it is the only handle you have going for you.

Many Presentation Manager functions can be paired with a function that performs a similar, but opposite, task. As you would expect, such is the case for WinInitialize. To end a Presentation Manager program properly (a politeness that OS/2 generally appreciates), your code should call WinTerminate, which takes *hab* as its only argument:

```
WinTerminate(hab);
return(0);
```

WinTerminate is of type BOOL and returns a boolean verifier. Any resources allocated to the program thread are deallocated when you call WinTerminate. If, for some reason, you did not call WinTerminate at the end of the program, the Presentation Manager deallocates the resources itself. The example also includes the C **return** function. It is always good programming practice to use the **return** function at the end of **main()**, although OS/2 suffers no side effects if you omit it.

The Message Queue

The message queue is the most vital and dynamic aspect of the Presentation Manager. On one hand, it saves enormous amounts of programming labor; on the other, it makes Presentation Manager code difficult to follow. The WinCreateMsgQueue function is the first message-related function you need to call in your Presentation Manager program. As an initialization function, WinCreateMsgQueue carries out the straightforward task of creating the message queue (see Chapter 3).

Window Class Registration

If you owned several cars and intended to use them all from time to time, but never all at once, it would be convenient if you could switch license plates when necessary. Well, the real word doesn't work like this, and neither does the Presentation Manger. If you intend on creating a window (even a second and third standard window), you must register its class in advance. Here's a closer look at the function that registers a window class:

```
BOOL WinRegisterClass(hab, pszClass, pfnWndProc,
                      flStyle, cbWinData)
HAB hab;
PSZ pszClass,
PFNWP pfnWndProc;
ULONG flStyle;
USHORT cbWindowData;
```

The first argument to WinRegisterClass requires an anchor block handle. As with WinCreateMsgQueue, you supply the *hab* value returned from the call to WinInitialize. The next argument, *pszClass*, is an integral part of setting the stage for the creation of subsequent windows. The naming conventions tell you that *pszClass* is a pointer to a null-terminated character string. Its purpose here is to identify the class of the window. Because you want to create your own windows, the class falls into the general category of a private class. Typically, it is a good idea to extract the class name from your program name. Alternatively, you might derive a name based on your own class naming conventions.

The third argument, *pfnWndProc*, is set to the name of the function that you create to process client window messages. You must predeclare the function name at the top of your source code file. You should also give the function a name that tips off anyone reading the program that the function is, indeed, the function that handles client window messages. Some of the more common names are ClientWndProc, ClientAreaProc, and AppWndProc.

The *pfnWndProc* argument is of type PFNWP, which was briefly summarized in Chapter 2. A PFNWP data type is a far pointer to a far pointer that references the four arguments passed to the frame window procedure. Here's how PFNWP is **typedef**ed:

```
typedef MRESULT (PASCAL FAR *PFNWP)
                        (HWND, USHORT, MPARAM, MPARAM);
```

As you can see, the four data types referenced through the PFNWP data types represent the arguments passed to the client window function and returned to the Presentation Manager via WinDefWindowProc.

For the most part, you need not worry about manipulating *pfnWndProc* yourself; the Presentation Manager does it for you. If you need to subclass a window, however, you must retain the address in *pfnWndProc* before passing it to the subclassed window function. You can use the WinQueryClassInfo to obtain the address for a given window.

The next argument to WinRegisterClass is the *flStyle*. The *flStyle argument* determines the class style of the window you are registering. Specifying the CS identifier tells the Presentation Manager what characteristics you want the window to have. If you set *flStyle* to 0L, the Presentation Manager registers the window with the default class style, which does not afford you much in the way of features. For example, the window neither repaints itself nor clips any sibling windows. To set the class style, you use the CS constants, which represent 32-bit numbers that you can OR together. Table 4-3 lists the identifiers that you can use to satisfy the *flStyle* argument.

Table 4-3: Class Style Constants

STYLE	BIT	DESCRIPTION
CS_MOVENOTIFY	0x00000001L	Causes a WM_MOVE message to be sent to the frame window's control procedure whenever the user moves the window.
CS_SIZEREDRAW	0x00000004L	Causes the Presentation Manager to invalidate a resized window and consequently send a WM_PAINT message to the frame window procedure.
CS_HITTEST	0x00000008L	Lays the ground work for graphics hit testing (clicking on an object area so that the area can be selected).
CS_PUBLIC	0x00000010L	Allows creation of public window controls that can be used among different applications just as frame windows and control windows are used.
CS_FRAME	0x00000020L	Specifies that the class style enforces frame window behavior.
CS_CLIPCHILDREN	0x20000000L	Restricts the clipping area — the area of the window that is redrawn — to the area not occupied by one or more child windows.
CS_PARENTCLIP	0x08000000L	Restricts the clipping area — the area of the window that is redrawn — to the clipping area defined by the parent window. Not applicable to frame windows.
CS_CLIPSIBLINGS	0x10000000L	Restricts the clipping area — the area of the window that is redrawn — to the area not occupied by one or more sibling windows. (Should not be used with the frame window.)

(continued)

Table 4-3: Continued

STYLE	BIT	DESCRIPTION
CS_SAVEBITS	0x04000000L	Allows the Presentation Manager to redraw a window without WM_PAINT message processing.
CS_SYNCPAINT	0x02000000L	Makes WM_PAINT a non-queued message, meaning it is sent directly to the associated window procedure. Not generally applicable to frame windows.

For the time being — and for many Presentation Manager applications — all you need concern yourself with is the CS_SIZEREDRAW constant. The Presentation Manager looks to the bit manipulated by CS_SIZEREDRAW to find out whether it should resize and redraw the window. If the bit is on, the Presentation Manager generates a WM_PAINT message after the window has been moved or resized.

CODE TIP: PUBLIC WINDOWS

The Presentation Manager uses predefined control windows that allow you to construct a common user interface. Another way of looking at these control windows — which include scrollbars, listboxes, and radio-buttons — is as public class styles available for use in other windows. Generally, these public controls offer enough diversity to manage most situations, but you can complement them with your own public controls when necessary. Public controls are registered through WinRegisterClass. They have window procedures just like private window and they handle messages in the same way. In order to create public controls, you must locate the WinRegisterWindow code as well as the associated window procedure in a dynamic link library. You must also specify the CS_PUBLIC constant when you call WinRegisterWindow. Additionally, the DLL must be loaded by the Presentation Manager shell when the shell itself is loaded. In order for this to happen, the DLL must export an initialization function with an ordinal value of one. You define this as the associated .DEF file. The initialization function invokes WinRegisterClass as well as any other code necessary to initialize your very own public control.

The final argument to WinRegisterClass lets you specify the location of the window you are registering. If the window is within the program itself, set *cbWindow* to NULL. If it is located in a dynamic link library that you created, specify the name of the library. In order to do this, you must call DosLoadModule to get a handle to the module.

The Frame Window

The call to the WinCreateStdWindow function creates an application's frame window. The frame window — or standard window, as the function calls it — contains the client area, which can be used as either the main workspace for your application and/or as a staging ground for child windows. The Presentation Manager's *File System* utility is a good example of an application that uses the client area for both purposes.

Because the frame window is one of the Presentation Manager's primary objects, you can create widely diverse types of frame windows with the call to WinCreateStdWindow. Initially, you should be concerned with the different types of child windows that you can implement through WinCreateStdWindow. The child windows, which are called *frame controls*, include the following components:

- Border controls
- Title bar
- System menu
- Application menu
- Minimize and maximize controls
- Scrollbar controls

The frame controls –– and even the frame window itself — are created with preregistered window classes provided by the system. The frame window is the glue that holds together the frame controls as well as the client area. The frame window internally manages the frame controls and client area in response to user requests such as those requiring window resizing or repositioning. Additionally, it also routes system and application-generated messages to the proper frame control, or to the client window procedure (in order to handle activities in the client window). To keep things straight, the Presentation Manager provides a set of frame IDs (denoted by the FID prefix) that can be used to identify a frame control, or even the client area. Table 4-4 lists the frame control IDs.

Table 4-4: Frame Control IDs

IDENTIFIER	BIT	FRAME CONTROL
FID_SYSMENU	0x8002	System menu.
FID_TITLEBAR	0x8003	Application titlebar.
FID_MINMAX	0x8004	Minimize/maximize box.
FID_MENU	0x8005	Application menu.
FID_VERTSCROLL	0x8006	Vertical scrollbar.
FID_HORZSCROLL	0x8007	Horizontal scrollbar.
FID_CLIENT	0x8008	Client area.

Now it is time to take a closer look at the actual call to the WinCreateStdWindow function. Like so much in the Presentation Manager, it might seem interminable at first glance, but learn the details of WinCreateStdWindow, and you will have progressed a long way on the road to Presentation Manager programming.

```
HWND WinCreateStdWindow(hwndParent, flStyle, pCtlData,
                pszClass, pszTitle, styleClient, hmod,
                idResources, phwndClient)
HWND hwndParent;
ULONG flStyle;
PVOID pCtlData;
PSZ pszClass, pszTitle;
ULONG styleClient;
HMODULE hmod;
USHORT idResources;
PHWND phwndClient;
```

The first step in using the WinCreateStdWindow is to supply it a parent window handle. Although relatively simple to satisfy, the *hwndparent* argument is critical in setting up more than one level of window. It allows you to track multiple levels of windows.

The first window created in the Presentation Manager is called a top-level window and it is the child of the desktop window. The desktop window itself is automatically created when you enter the Presentation Manager environment and is the patriarch of all windows (except object windows, which do not require a screen display).

To specify the desktop as the parent in the WinCreateStdWindow call, you can either specify HWND_DESKTOP, which is system-defined as NULL, or specify NULL.

Alternatively, if you wanted an existing frame window to spawn a second frame window (which is not necessarily a standard technique), you would specify the handle of the existing window in *hwndParent*. To specify an object window, you supply *hwndParent* the predefined constant of HWND_OBJECT, or the handle of an existing object window. If necessary, you can use either of two functions to obtain a handle for WinCreateStdWindow — namely, the WinQueryDesktopWindow or WinQueryObjectWindow function. In most cases, however, you can simply supply HWND_DESKTOP, and you are on your way.

The next order of business is the window style. Satisfying the style argument is not as clear cut as specifying a handle. The reason for this is *flStyle* does more than its name implies: it not only establishes the style of the window, it tells the Presentation Manager to create the frame window controls mentioned earlier. As with the WinRegisterClass function and its CS constants, you do this by ORing together various 32-bit style identifiers. The constants for *flStyle* are denoted by a WS prefix.

What gets tricky with *flStyle* is not all of the WS constants have a direct effect on the style of the window.

Some of the constants specifically apply to control windows (see Chapter 7); others specify the size of the standard window; and still others flip a couple of bits to establish the style of future generations of windows. Table 4-5 lists and describes the WS constants.

Table 4-5: Window Style Constants

STYLE	BIT	DESCRIPTION
WS_VISIBLE	0x80000000L	Makes the window visible. By default, the window is invisible.
WS_DISABLED	0x40000000L	Disables the window. By default, the window is enabled.
WS_CLIPCHILDREN	0x20000000L	Excludes child windows when drawing occurs in the window.
WS_CLIPSIBLINGS	0x10000000L	Excludes siblings when drawing occurs in the window.
WS_PARENTCLIP	0x08000000L	Controls window clipping when drawing occurs in the window.
WS_SAVEBITS	0x04000000L	Saves screen image under the window when the window becomes visible.
WS_SYSMODAL	0x02000000L	Makes the window dominant, in that all keyboard and mouse input is automatically routed to it.
WS_MINIMIZED	0x01000000L	Causes the window to appear as an icon when first invoked.
WS_MAXIMIZED	0x00800000L	Causes the window to occupy the full screen when first invoked.
WS_GROUP	0x00400000L	Not relevant to WinCreateStdWindow. Used when creating dialog boxes.
WS_TABSTOP	0x0020000L	Not relevant to WinCreateStdWindow. Used when creating dialog boxes.

For most frame windows, you are likely only to specify WS_VISIBLE. This constant tells the Presentation Manager to make the frame window visible. If you do not specify it, the Presentation Manager leaves the frame window invisible, which is its default state. If you do not specify WS_VISIBLE when creating a frame window, you can call WinSetWindowPos and WinShowWindow at a later time to make the window visible. You should also note that when you create a dialog box window, two other style constants are available. These are the FS identifiers, which you can OR with the WS identifiers.

The next step in satisfying the WinCreateStdWindow call is to satisfy the *pCtlData* argument. The *pCtlData* argument is slightly different to *flStyle*, in that *pCtlData* is a pointer to a ULONG value that specifies the frame controls (versus the operating styles). To create a frame control, you specify any of the *frame creation flags*, which are denoted by an FCF prefix. Again, you can OR these identifiers to produce combined effects. Table 4-6 lists and describes the FCF constants.

Table 4-6: Frame Creation Flags

IDENTIFIER	BIT	DESCRIPTION
FCF_TITLEBAR	0x00000001L	Creates a titlebar.
FCF_SYSMENU	0x00000002L	Creates a system menu.
FCF_MENU	0x00000004L	Permits the implementation of application-specific menu.
FCF_SIZEBORDER	0x00000008L	Creates a wide sizing border.
FCF_MINBUTTON	0x00000010L	Creates a minimize box.
FCF_MAXBUTTON	0x00000020L	Creates a maximize box.
FCF_MINMAX	0x00000030L	Creates maximize and minimize boxes.
FCF_VERTSCROLL	0x00000040L	Creates a vertical scrollbar.
FCF_HORZSCROLL	0x00000080L	Creates a horizontal scrollbar.
FCF_DLGBORDER	0x00000100L	Draws window with standard dialog border.
FCF_BORDER	0x00000200L	Draws a thin window border.
FCF_SHELLPOSITION	0x00000400L	Specifies that the Presentation Manager shell should size and position the window it is created.

(continued)

Table 4-6: Continued

IDENTIFIER	BIT	DESCRIPTION
FCF_TASKLIST	0x00000800L	Specifies that the program title is added to the frame window title. Both are displayed in the titlebar as well as in the application's task manager entry.
FCF_NOBYTEALIGN	0x00001000L	Specifies that window moving and resizing occur on a coordinate-by-coordinate basis. When not in effect, moving and resizing occurs in multiples of coordinates. The exact number is device dependent.
FCF_NOMOVEWITHOWNER	0x00002000L	Specifies that window should not move with its owner window. (Not relevant for a top-level frame window.)
FCF_ICON	0x00004000L	Permits an icon to be created when the window is created. The icon is specified by *idResources* and is used to represent the window when minimized.
FCF_ACCELTABLE	0x00008000L	Permits the loading of a keyboard accelerator table as specified in *idResources*.
FCF_SYSMODAL	0x00010000L	Specifies that the frame window is a system modal window.

For straightforward applications, you won't be interested in all the tricks that the *flStyle* and *pCtlData* arguments can perform. Instead, you'll probably want something more mundane like a system menu, minimum and maximum buttons, scroll bars, sizing border, and a visible window. The following statement does the trick.

```
    WS_VISIBLE              /* Make window visible. */
        | FS_SIZEBORDER     /* Attach sizing border. */
```

```
| FS_TITLEBAR         /* Attach titlebar. */
| FS_SYSMENU         /* Attach system menu. */
| FS_MINMAX          /* Activate min/max buttons. */
| FS_HORZSCROLL      /* Attach horiz. scrollbar. */
| FS_VERTSCROLL      /* Attach vertical scrollbar. */
```

Once you become familiar with the meanings of the constants, the comments become superfluous. Even so, it is still somewhat of a laborious task to type all these constants every time you create a window. As an alternative, you can initialize *pCtlData* to the value of the FCF identifiers that you want to use:

```
pCtlData = FCF_TITLEBAR | FCF_SYSMENU | FCF_MINMAX
           | FCF_SIZEBORDER | FCF_TASKLIST
           | FCF_MENU | FCF_ACCELTABLE
           | FCF_SHELLPOSITION | FCF_ICON
```

Study the previous example closely. The FCF values represented are considered the standard set of identifiers for use with most frame windows. In fact, they are so standard that yet another FCF identifier is defined to make it easier for you to specify them:

```
FCF_STANDARD    0x0000CC3FL
```

Alternatively, you can define your own FCF identifier. For example, you might want to use all the identifiers embraced by FCF_STANDARD, with the exception of one or two. You also might want to use your own standard on more than one occasion, so you could place it in a custom header file. The following example uses the FCF_STANDARD identifier, but excludes the FCF_SHELLPOSITION identifier:

```
#define FCF_MYSTANDARD FCF_STANDARD & ~FCF_SHELLPOSITION
```

Not all combinations of frame creation flags produce desirable results. For example, when FCF_SYSMENU, FCF_MINBUTTON, FCF_MAX-BUTTON, or FCF_MINMAX are used, you should also specify FCF_TIT-LEBAR. If you do not, the area normally occupied by the titlebar is not properly drawn by the frame control procedure.

The next argument to WinCreateStdWindow is less complex, in that it does not require a selection of identifiers. The key word here is require, because *pszClass* can be a pointer referencing the WC_FRAME identifier, which belongs to a small group of window class identifiers that are used for creating child windows. Normally, you specify the window class when you call the WinRegisterClass function, and then reference the same variable in WinCreateStdWindow. In the template example, the window class was set equal to "Template" and declared as a static CHAR. If you set *pszClass* to NULL, no client area is created. You might want to do this if your application used a series of child windows, but did not require a client area.

The next argument, *pszTitle*, is a pointer to the titlebar text. You can satisfy this argument in several ways. The easiest way is to enclose the program name in quotes right in the function call. You can also initialize a CHAR variable to do the job. Or, as the template example does, you can set *pszTitle* to NULL, which tells the Presentation Manager to use the program filename as the titlebar text. If you want the program filename to be displayed by the Task Manager, you must specify FCF_TASKLIST in *pCtlData* and set *pszTitle* to NULL.

If you want you own titlebar name, but do not want a Task Manager entry, omit FCF_TASKLIST from *pCtlData*, specify FCF_TITLEBAR instead, and specify a string for *pszTitle*. To gain even greater control, you can use the WinAddSwitchEntry function to place any string you want in the Task Manager (as you will see shortly).

The final four arguments can be summarized briefly. The sixth argument to WinCreateStdWindow is simple. You practically always set *styleClient* to 0L, which specifies the default window style for the client area of the frame window. The only time you would have to specify a window style here — that is, one of the WS identifiers — is if you set *pszClass* to a zero-length string.

The seventh and eighth arguments reference resources. In the template example, *hmod* and *idResources* have been set to NULL and 0, respectively. You will see how these have an effect on window initialization in later chapters. The final argument, *phwndClient*, is of type PHWND, the far pointer that references the handle to the procedure that processes the frame window's messages that are associated with the client area (in other words, the client window procedure). To satisfy this argument, declare a handle and then supply WinCreateStdWindow the handle.

Window Position

To make your application's frame window appear on a certain part of the desktop, or to make it larger or smaller than the default size, you must call WinSetWindowPos when you initialize the window. Figure 4-1 shows the frame window's coordinate system.

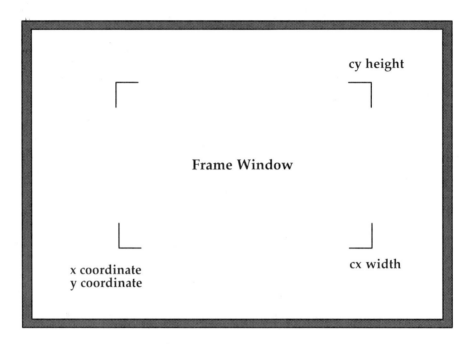

Figure 4-1: Frame window coordinate system

The alternative is accepting the size and position specified through the FCF_SHELLPOSITION identifier. The template example omits the identifier in its call to the WinCreateStdWindow function. If you neither specify the FCF_SHELLPOSITION identifier, nor use the WinSetWindowPos function, the Presentation Manager sizes a window to zero dimensions.

Most of the definition for WinSetWindowPos is straightforward. Because it can be called from almost anywhere, it includes a system of checks and balances that can get complex. Here's the definition of WinSetWindowPos:

```
BOOL WinSetWindowPos(hwnd, hwndInsBehind, x, y, cx, cy, fs)
HWND hwnd, hwndInsBehind;
SHORT x, y, cx, cy;
USHORT fs;
```

The first two arguments, *hwnd* and *hwndInsBehind*, identify the window you want to position and where you want to position it relative to other windows. To satisfy *hwndInsBehind*, you can either specify HWND_TOP, HWND_BOTTOM, or a particular sibling window already in existence. The HWND_TOP option places the specified window on top of all sibling windows, making it the topmost window in sibling z-order. The HWND_BOTTOM places the window at the bottom of the sibling z-order. Naming a sibling window places the specified window behind the sibling.

The next four arguments — *x*, *y*, *cx*, and *cy* — specify the space on the desktop that the window occupies (*cx* and *cy* are common Presentation Manager designations for width and height variables). This is a fairly simple idea, but you must remember that the Presentation Manager begins its coordinate system at the bottom left-hand side of the desktop.

In order for you to coordinate settings to take full effect, you must specify the SWP_MOVE and SWP_SIZE constants when satisfying the next argument, *fs*. This argument is responsible for describing the positioning characteristics of the your window. Table 4-7 lists and describes the SWP constants.

Table 4-7: Window Positioning Options

IDENTIFIER	BIT	DESCRIPTION
SWP_SIZE	0x0001	Allows the window to change size.
SWP_MOVE	0x0002	Allows the window to change position.
SWP_ZORDER	0x0004	Allows the window to move in the z-order.
SWP_SHOW	0x0008	Specifies that the window is immediately displayed when created.
SWP_HIDE	0x0010	Specifies that the window is hidden when created.

(continued)

Table 4-7: Continued

IDENTIFIER	BIT	DESCRIPTION
SWP_NOREDRAW	0x0020	Disallows redraw upon change in size or position.
SWP_NOADJUST	0x0040	Inhibits WM_ADJUSTWINDOWPOS before a change in size or position.
SWP_ACTIVATE	0x0080	Activates the window when it becomes the topmost window in the z-order. If *hwnd* is the frame window, and SWP_ZORDER is specified, this option also activates *hwndInsBehind* when it is topmost.
SWP_DEACTIVATE	0x0100	Deactivates the window when it is the active window.
SWP_MINIMIZE	0x0400	Minimizes the window if SWP_MOVE and SWP_SIZE are specified. This option is mutually exclusive with SWP_MAXIMIZE and SWP_RESTORE.
SWP_MAXIMIZE	0x0800	Maximizes the window if SWP_MOVE and SWP_SIZE are specified. This option is mutually exclusive with SWP_MINIMIZE and SWP_RESTORE.
SWP_RESTORE	0x1000	Restores the window if SWP_MOVE and SWP_SIZE are specified. This option is mutually exclusive with SWP_MAXIMIZE and SWP_MINIMIZE.

The Switchlist

A descriptive text string that appears in the *Task Manager* is called a switchlist entry. The user selects a switchlist entry by double clicking on it with the mouse, or by highlighting it and using *Task Manager* menu options. The cleanest approach to add a switchlist entry is to use the WinAddSwitchEntry function. With WinAddSwitchEntry, you can overcome the restrictions of FCF_TASKLIST and FCF_TITLEBAR, which otherwise control the switchlist and titlebar text.

The optimum situation is to have a descriptive text string represent an application in the *Task Manager's* roll of programs. In the application's frame window titlebar, you will likely want a similar, but more concise, text string. Alternatively, you might like the program filename to appear in the titlebar (the method used in the template example). With either combination, you need to use WinAddSwitchEntry. And to do so means following a relatively simple, but lengthy, process. The following steps describe how to set up and call WinAddSwitchEntry:

1. Create a local copy of the SWCNTRL structure to reference switchlist data items. Additionally, declare variables to hold the current process and thread IDs.

2. Obtain the process ID associated with *hwndFrame* by calling the Win-QueryWindowProcess function.

3. Define the fields of the local copy of the SWCNTRL structure.

4. Call WinAddSwitchEntry, supplying it the address of the local copy of the SWCNTRL structure.

The WinQueryWindowProcess function is vital to this sequence because it is the most convenient way to obtain the application's process ID. It can be used in many different situations throughout an application, but is required here because the SWCNTRL structure makes use of the process ID. Here is the definition for WinQueryWindowProcess:

```
BOOL WinQueryWindowProcess(hwnd, ppid, ptid)
HWND hwnd;
PPID ppid;
PTID ptid;
```

Whenever you use WinQueryWindowProcess in connection with the switchlist entry, the first argument is always a handle to the frame window. The next two arguments are pointers to the process and thread IDs, respectively. All you need to do is declare local variables for these pointers and supply their addresses when calling WinQueryWindowProcess.

The next step is to fill in the various fields of the SWCNTRL structure. Unfortunately, even though you might not need to fill in a field, you still must set it equal to NULL. Here is the definition for SWCNTRL:

```
typedef struct _SWCNTRL {
        HWND        hwnd;
        HWND        hwndIcon;
        HPROGRAM    hprog;
        USHORT      idProcess;
        USHORT      idSession;
        UCHAR       uchVisibility;
        UCHAR       fbJump;
        CHAR        szSwtitle[MAXNAMEL+1];
        BYTE        fReserved;
} SWCNTRL;
```

Now here is the code that sets the local copy of SWCNTRL in the template example.

```
swctl.hwnd = hwndFrame;
swctl.hwndIcon = NULL;
swctl.hprog = NULL;
swctl.idProcess = pid;
swctl.idSession = NULL;
swctl.uchVisibility = SWL_VISIBLE;
swctl.fbJump = SWL_JUMPABLE;
strcpy(swctl.szSwtitle, "Template Demo")
```

As with many functions, the first field in SWCNTRL is the handle to the associated window. In the case of the template example, this represents the handle to the frame window. Two of the fields in SWCNTRL can be set to NULL without a second thought. These are *hprog*, and *idSession*, which represent the program handle and session ID, respectively. You can also set *hwndIcon* to NULL if your application does not use a minimize icon.

The remaining fields in SWCNTRL must be set. The process ID, represented by *pid*, is required so the *Task Manager* can interact with your application, including terminating it upon user request. Two more arguments that deserve consideration are *uchVisbility* and *fbJump*. Satisfy these fields with the SWL (switch list) identifiers. Tables 4-8 and 4-9 list and describe these identifiers.

114

Table 4-8: SWL Visibility Identifiers

IDENTIFIER	VALUE	DESCRIPTION
SWL_VISIBLE	(BYTE)0x04	Enters the program in the task list.
SWL_INVISIBLE	(BYTE)0x01	Omits the program from the task list.
SWL_GRAYED	(BYTE)0x02	Enters the program in the task list, but the user cannot switch to it.

Table 4-9: SWL Jump Identifiers

IDENTIFIER	VALUE	DESCRIPTION
SWL_JUMPABLE	(BYTE)0x02	Enables the jump sequence.
SWL_NOTJUMPABLE	(BYTE)0x01	Does not enable the jump sequence.

The next to last field in SWCNTRL sets the actual title that appears in the Task Manager. To actually insert a different string in the Task Manager listing, you must use *strcpy* to copy the string to the *szSwtitle* field. If you want to have the Task Manager use the same string that appears in the titlebar, specify both FCF_TASKLIST and FCF_TITLEBAR in the *pCtlData* argument of WinCreateStdWindow, and set *szSwtitle* to NULL.

Once you have filled in all the fields of the SWCNTRL structure, all you need to do is call WinAddSwitchEntry, which requires the address of the local copy of SWCNTRL as its only argument. The common reference to SWCNTRL is *swctl*, although some programmers prefer *sw*.

The Rest of the Story

For the time being, the rest of the story involves what happens in the client area of the frame window. The TemplateWndProc function in the template example processes but a single message: WM_ERASEBACKGROUND, which fills the client area with the system default background color. Try removing the message processing block from the TemplateWndProc. You'll see a strange looking frame window — one that looks like a see-through frame, with the client area colored the same as the desktop.

Indeed, the template example does not do much beyond setting up the frame window and the environment in which your application can process messages. What is needed is an example that does something such as deliver the traditional C greeting to the world. The following example does the trick. You can link and compile it by using the same module definition and make file that you used for the template example — just change the filenames and the name of the client window procedure.

```
/* HELLO.C (Simple greeting program) */

#define INCL_PM

#include <os2.h>

MRESULT EXPENTRY ClientAreaProc(HWND,USHORT,MPARAM,MPARAM);

HAB     hab;
HMQ     hmq;
HWND    hwndFrame, hwndGreeting;

int main(void)
{
static CHAR szClass[] = "Greeting";
ULONG  ctlData = FCF_TITLEBAR | FCF_SYSMENU | FCF_SIZEBORDER
                 | FCF_MINMAX | FCF_TASKLIST
                 | FCF_SHELLPOSITION;
USHORT fSwp = SWP_ACTIVATE | SWP_SIZE | SWP_MOVE | SWP_SHOW;
QMSG   qmsg;


hab = WinInitialize(NULL);
hmq = WinCreateMsgQueue(hab, 0);
WinRegisterClass(hab, szClass, FrameWndProc,
                 CS_SIZEREDRAW, 0);

hwndFrame = WinCreateStdWindow(
                 HWND_DESKTOP,
                 WS_VISIBLE,
                 &ctlData,
```

```
                    szClass,
                    NULL,
                    0L,
                    NULL,
                    0,
                    &hwndGreeting);

while(WinGetMsg(hab, &qmsg, NULL, 0, 0))
          WinDispatchMsg(hab, &qmsg);

WinDestroyWindow(hwndFrame);
WinDestroyMsgQueue(hmq);
WinTerminate(hab);
}


MRESULT EXPENTRY ClientAreaProc(hwnd, msg, mp1, mp2)
HWND    hwnd;
USHORT  msg;
MPARAM  mp1, mp2;
{

HPS hps;
RECTL rcl, rclBox;
static SHORT i = 1;
static CHAR szGreeting[13] = "Hello World!";

switch (msg)
  {
    case WM_PAINT:
        hps = WinBeginPaint(hwnd, NULL, NULL);
        WinQueryWindowRect(hwnd, &rcl);
        rclBox.xLeft = rcl.xRight / 4;
        rclBox.yBottom = rcl.yTop / 4;
        rclBox.xRight = rcl.xRight / 4 * 3;
        rclBox.yTop = rcl.yTop / 4 * 3;
        WinFillRect(hps, &rcl, CLR_YELLOW);

        WinDrawBorder(hps, &rclBox, i, i, CLR_RED,
                   CLR_BACKGROUND, DB_STANDARD) ;

        if(i <= (SHORT)rclBox.xRight
                   && i <= (SHORT)rclBox.yTop)
            i+=5;
        else
            i = 1;
```

```
WinDrawText (hps, -1, szGreeting, &rclBox,
             CLR_NEUTRAL,CLR_BACKGROUND,
             DT_CENTER | DT_VCENTER) ;

WinEndPaint (hps) ;
return (NULL) ;
}

return WinDefWindowProc (hwnd, msg, mp1, mp2) ;
}
```

This program slightly modifies the template example in respect to creating the frame window. For one thing, it uses the FCF_SHELLPOSITION identifier in satisfying the *pCtlData* argument of WinCreateStdWindow. This relieves you of positioning the window and adding an entry to the *Task Manager* — FCF_SHELLPOSITION handles it for you. Additionally, a NULL value is specified in the *pszTitle* argument to WinCreateStd-Window. This technique automatically places the program filename in the titlebar of the frame window as well as in the *Task Manager* switchlist. Some new functions are also used in the program. These are summarized in Table 4-10.

Table 4-10: New Functions Used in HELLO.C Example

FUNCTION	RETURNS	DESCRIPTION
WinBeginPaint	Handle	Obtains a presentation space and allows you to draw in the client area of a frame window.
WinQueryWindowRect	Boolean	Obtains the dimensions of the client area rectangle.
WinFillRect	Boolean	Fills the client window rectangle with a specified color.
WinDrawBorder	Boolean	Draws a border around the specified rectangle.
WinDrawText	String length	Writes a single line of text within the specified rectangle.

As you can see from Table 4-10, much of the code in the client area procedure of HELLO.C deals with manipulating the rectangle that is the client area. It is worth mentioning that the client area is itself a window, but one that you cannot create without also creating a frame window. (To achieve independent window-like control in the client area, you must create a child control window and size it exactly to the dimensions of the client area rectangle.)

The WM_PAINT message is the workhorse message in the example program. The client window procedure receives a WM_PAINT message whenever the client area needs repainting. This includes when the window is maximized, restored, moved, resized, or when it regains focus after another window such as the *Task Manager* window has occupied part of the client area. In a more extensive program — in which message processing time becomes a factor — you can split up the message processing duty between WM_PAINT, WM_SIZE, and various focus messages. In this way, the WM_PAINT message is relieved somewhat of its processing chores and the program only obtains the client area dimensions when necessary.

Drawing in the Client Window

The HELLO.C example uses WinBeginPaint to obtain the handle to a presentation space. A presentation space is an internal interface that talks to the Presentation Manager's *device context* for a given device.

WinBeginPaint always returns the Presentation Manager's default presentation space, called the *cached micro-PS*, which is designed to draw on the display monitor. This includes handling the Presentation Manager's own drawing needs as well as drawing to windows that you create. Most importantly, it represents a quick and efficient way to draw to the client area. The call to WinEndPaint restores the presentation space.

Using WinBeginPaint is the most concise way to draw text and simple graphics on the display monitor. (For more complex graphics, you must create more advanced presentation spaces, which are described in Chapter 9.) For the time being, here's a quick look at the WM_PAINT handler:

```
case WM_PAINT:
        hps = WinBeginPaint (hwnd, NULL, NULL);
```

```
WinEndPaint(hps);
return(NULL);
```

The first argument to WinBeginPaint is the familiar application window handle. The next argument specifies the type of presentation space. Setting this argument to NULL specifies the cached micro-PS presentation space. The last argument can also be set to NULL, which is often the case. If you do supply a value of type RECTL in this argument, the function returns a pointer to the smallest rectangle bounding the update region in the client window. Most importantly, as shown in the example code, WinBeginPaint returns a handle to a presentation space (denoted by *hps*).

When you call WinBeginPaint, you must call WinEndPaint within the same message block. The WinEndPaint function simply takes *hps* as its only argument and immediately closes access to the presentation space. You should also note that invoking WinBeginPaint hides the desktop pointer when it is within the current window and WinEndPaint restores the pointer.

The next step in the WM_PAINT message block is to find out the dimensions of the client area rectangle. One way to accomplish this is by calling WinQueryWindowRect. This function fills a copy of the RECTL structure with the current coordinates of the specified window. Here's the definition of the RECTL structure:

```
typedef struct {
    LONG xLeft;              /* Bottom left horizontal pixel.*/
    LONG yBottom;           /* Bottom left vertical pixel.*/
    LONG xRight;            /* Top right horizontal pixel.*/
    LONG yTop;              /* Top right vertical pixel. */
} RECTL;
```

To use the WinQueryWindowRect function, you must declare a variable that references a RECTL structure. The variable is usually *rcl*. Additionally, you might want to define variables corresponding to the fields in the structure, if you want to retain the previous values of the individual fields.

Another way to obtain the dimensions of the client window is through the WM_SIZE message. The Presentation Manager performs no default processing on this message, but the WM_SIZE message is quite powerful when you choose to process it. The message allows you to obtain the previous and current dimensions of the client window each time the window is resized. Values corresponding to the previous width and height of the client window are contained in *mp1*. Typically, you use variable names that contain *cx* and *cy* (representing width and height). The following code extracts both the previous and current dimensions of the client window:

```
case WM_SIZE:
    cxPrevious = SHORT1FROMMP(mp1);
    cyPrevious = SHORT2FROMMP(mp1);
    cxCurrent = SHORT1FROMMP(mp2);
    cyCurrent = SHORT2FROMMP(mp2);

    return(NULL);
```

The previous program example did not handle the WM_SIZE message because it was convenient to perform all processing in the WM_PAINT message block. Many of the program examples in this book do use the WM_SIZE message, however.

Back to the current program: after it obtains the size of the client area rectangle, it creates a new set of dimensions that define a rectangle that is 1/4 the size of the client area. Next, the WinFillRect function paints the full dimensions of the client area. Here's the definition for WillFillRect:

```
BOOL WinFillRect(hps, prcl, clr)
HPS hps;
PRECTL prcl;
LONG clr;
```

As with all functions that draw in the client area, the first argument to WinFillRect is the handle to the active presentation space. Internally, *hps* identifies the target rectangle for WinFillRect. The next argument simply takes a pointer to the local copy of the RECTL structure. The last argument takes an identifier corresponding to a system-defined color or a system RGB color, which is device dependent. Table 4-11 lists the system-defined colors.

Table 4-11: System-Defined Colors

COLOR	VALUE
CLR_DEFAULT	(-3L)
CLR_WHITE	(-2L)
CLR_BLACK	(-1L)
CLR_BACKGROUND	0L
CLR_BLUE	1L
CLR_RED	2L
CLR_PINK	3L
CLR_GREEN	4L
CLR_CYAN	5L
CLR_YELLOW	6L
CLR_NEUTRAL	7L
CLR_DARKGRAY	8L
CLR_DARKBLUE	9L
CLR_DARKRED	10L
CLR_DARKPINK	11L
CLR_DARKGREEN	12L
CLR_DARKCYAN	13L
CLR_BROWN	14L
CLR_PALEGRAY	15L

After the full client area has been painted in the example, the WinDraw-Border isolates a rectangle defined by the *rclBox*. WinDrawBorder creates a red border line that increases in size each time the user resizes or moves the frame window. Here's the definition for WinDrawBorder:

```
BOOL WinDrawBorder(hps, prcl, cx, cy, clrFore,
                      clrBack, rgfCmd)
HPS hps;
PRECTL prcl;
SHORT cx, cy;
LONG clrFore, clrBack;
USHORT rgfCmd;
```

The first argument to WinDrawBorder is a handle to the active presentation space. The second argument, *prcl*, is a pointer to the RECTL structure. WinDrawBorder uses *prcl* to calculate the next two arguments, *cx* and *cy*. For these arguments, the values are obtained from the *xLeft*, *xRight*, *yBottom*, and *yTop* fields of RECTL. The third and fourth arguments to WinDrawBorder establish the thickness of the border. The next two arguments take system-defined colors as listed in Table 4-11. The final argument sets the style of the actual border. You fill this argument with any of the DB identifiers. As with other style identifiers, you can OR these to produce a particular result. Table 4-12 lists the DB identifiers.

Table 4-12: Border Style Settings

FLAG	BIT	DESCRIPTION
DB_PATCOPY	0x0000	Causes a system-defined raster operation (ROP_PATCOPY) to draw the border.
DB_PATINVERT	0x0001	Causes a system-defined raster operation (ROP_PATINVERT) to draw the border.
DB_DESTINVERT	0x0002	Causes a system-defined raster operation (ROP_DESTINVERT) to draw the border.
DB_AREAMIXMODE	0x0003	Maps the foreground mix attribute into a Bitblt raster operation.
DB_ROP	0x0007	Specifies an ROP identifier.
DB_INTERIOR	0x0008	Draws the interior in the current background color.
DB_AREAATTRS	0x0010	Draws the border and interior in the color set by surrounding color attributes.

(continued)

Table 4-12: Continued

FLAG	BIT	DESCRIPTION
DB_STANDARD	0x0100	Causes the *cx* and *cy* arguments to be multiplied by the system SV_CXBORDER and SV_CYBORDER constants.
DB_DLGBORDER	0x0200	Draws a standard dialog box border. Specifying DB_PATCOPY creates an active dialog box border. Specifying DB_PATINVERT creates an inactive dialog box border.

The WinDrawText function is similar to WinDrawBorder. The two functions require many of the same arguments and fulfill the same basic purpose: to place output on a given area of the display monitor. You would not use WinDrawText for extensive text output, because it is designed to display only one line of text per call and it always uses the currently valid font. When you require extensive text handling capabilities, you should use the text functions in the Gpi function set. In this book, however, WinDrawText is used somewhat frequently until the Gpi text functions are detailed in Chapter 11. For now, here's how WinDrawText is defined:

```
SHORT WinDrawText (hps, cchText, pchText, prcl,
                   clrFore, clrBack, rgfCmd)
HPS hps;
SHORT cchText;
PSZ pchText;
PRECTL prcl;
LONG clrFore, clrBack;
USHORT rgfCmd;
```

Again, the first argument to WinDrawText is a handle to the active presentation space. The next argument, *cchText*, simply tells the Presentation Manager the length of the string, so it can handle it appropriately. If you set *cchText* to -1, as the example did, the Presentation Manager assumes the string is zero-terminated and calculates the length of the string for you. The *pchText* argument is simply the string to display. If you want, you can hard code the string in the function call, or set a variable to contain the string. Including a carriage return or line feed character in the string terminates the string, even if more text occurs after either of these characters.

The *rgfCmd* argument specifies how you want the text displayed. This includes both physical positioning and character attributes. Fill this argument with any of the DT identifiers, which can be ORed to produce a particular result. The DT_CENTER and DT_CENTER constants used in the example cause the Presentation Manager to center the text, both horizontally and vertically. Table 4-13 lists and describes the text display constants.

Some of the DT text control constants are mutually exclusive. Combining mutually exclusive constants can lead to unpredictable results. Ensure that you do not specify the following combinations:

- DT_LEFT, DT_CENTER, and DT_RIGHT.

- DT_TOP, DT_VCENTER, and DT_BOTTOM.

Additionally, DT_WORDBREAK can only be specified with DT_TOP and DT_LEFT. You should also note that WinDrawText can alter your original text string. You can find out how many characters have been omitted from the string by using the return value from WinDrawText, which is a SHORT containing the current length of the string.

Table 4-13: Text Control Identifiers

IDENTIFIER	BIT	DESCRIPTION
DT_LEFT	0x0000	Left justifies the text.
DT_EXTERNALLEADING	0x0080	Adds the external leading value to the bottom of the bounding rectangle. This constant only has an effect if the DT_TOP and DT_QUERY-EXTENT constants are also used.
DT_CENTER	0x0100	Centers the text horizontally on the currently valid line.
DT_RIGHT	0x0200	Right justifies the text.

(continued)

Table 4-13: Continued

IDENTIFIER	BIT	DESCRIPTION
DT_TOP	0x0000	Justifies the text at the top of the active window.
DT_VCENTER	0x0400	Vertically centers the text in the active window.
DT_BOTTOM	0x0800	Justifies the text at the bottom of the active window.
DT_HALFTONE	0x1000	Displays the text in halftone format.
DT_MNEMONIC	0x2000	If a mnemonic prefix character is encountered, the next character is drawn with mnemonic emphasis.
DT_WORDBREAK	0x4000	Only complete words are displayed. If a word does not completely fit on the line, the entire word is omitted.
DT_ERASERECT	0x8000	Erases rectangle before drawing text.
DT_QUERYEXTENT	0x0002	No text is displayed. Instead, rcl is redefined to the coordinates of the rectangle that bounds the string.
DT_TEXTATTRS	0x0040	Draws the text using the foreground and background colors of the presentation space.

Summary

The method that the Presentation Manager uses to call the function controlling the client window (or client area, if you prefer) is inextricably tied to the method it uses to manage the frame window. You need to understand the various initialization processes that lead up to the creation of the standard window. For your convenience, the following checklist summarizes some key points.

1. Predeclare your application window function. You must do this before **main()** using the new ANSI standard format for predeclaring a function.

2. Create a static CHAR variable and set it equal to the window class for your client window function.

3. Create a HWND variable for your client window. For example, some appropriate names are ClientAreProc and ClientWndProc. Alternatively, many programmers use some name derived from the program name.

4. Place your window class variable in the second argument position in the WinRegisterClass function.

5. Place the name of your client window function in the third argument position of the WinRegisterClass function.

6. Place your window class variable in the second argument position in the WinCreateStdWindow function.

7. Place your HWND variable for your client window in the last argument position of the WinCreateStdWindow function.

8. Before compiling the program, ensure that you have referenced the name of the client window function in the EXPORTS statement in your module definition file.

By all means, you can create a separate file for **main()** and use standard naming conventions, so you do not have to repeat this sequence each time you create a new Presentation Manager program. As a learning aid, this is a sanity saver. For a finished application program, you might want to incorporate both **main()** and your application window function into the same file. As is traditional, you would then place groups of related functions in separate files and link these files at compile time. Throughout most of this book, however, example code is incorporated into the same file as **main()**.

CHAPTER 5

WINDOW MANAGEMENT

The previous chapter told a blatant lie: somewhere in its pages fell the phrase "the rest of the story." By no means is it ever wise to use this phrase in the context of the Presentation Manager. The feats you can accomplish and the applications that you can develop with the Presentation Manager are only limited by the amount of available creativity. Accordingly, this chapter takes a look at some of the key concepts involved in window management. Understanding how to manage the relationships between windows is key to creating an effective Presentation Manager program.

The Frame Window Revisited

Earlier, the frame window was described in some detail, but not enough. Most of the attention in earlier chapters was placed on the client area (or client window, whichever you prefer), and its associated message queue. Indeed, this is a valid introductory approach — but to get the full picture, you have to begin thinking of the frame window as an entity unto itself, something quite distinct from the client window and its message queue. The reason is the frame window has its own internal message processing procedure. Through this procedure, which will be called the *frame control procedure*, travel all of the WM messages in one form or another. In essence, when you invoke the WinDefWindowProc, you are asking the frame control procedure to process the specified message.

The frame control procedure also serves as a conduit for other internal procedures that administer the components of the frame window — with the major exception of the client window, which the application itself must administer. You are already familiar with the components that the frame control procedure administers. They include the titlebar, menus, minimize and maximize icons, and the system scrollbars. Each of these components has its own internal Presentation Manager procedure (residing in one of the system's dynamic link libraries). The frame control procedure actually processes all messages before any other procedure. For the most part, this initial processing consists of routing a message to the control procedure for which the message was designed — including the frame control procedure itself.

In most cases, the frame control procedure gives the client window procedure first dibs on a message. In any given application, the majority of these messages just fall through the message handlers in the client window procedure and are processed by the WinDefWindowProc function. This function routes the message to the default window procedure. Ironically, for most messages, the default window procedure is the frame control procedure — from whence the message got its first push, so to speak.

In highly specific instances, you might want to process a message designed specifically for the frame window. In order to do this, you have to subclass the frame procedure. All this means is you incorporate a procedure into your application to process frame control messages. The procedure, in turn, acts as a frontend to the internal frame control procedure, because you still want the internal version to handle the workhorse processing necessary to manage the frame window. In some cases, you will modify the values contained in a message such as with the WM_UPDATE-FRAME message. In other cases, the presence of a message in your subclassed frame control procedure signals the application to perform some action related to the message. This is the case with the WM_FORMAT-FRAME message, which the following program example uses as a signal to adjust the state of the system menu.

```
#define INCL_PM
#include <os2.h>

MRESULT EXPENTRY ApplicationProc(HWND,USHORT,MPARAM,MPARAM);
MRESULT EXPENTRY FrameSubclass(HWND,USHORT,MPARAM,MPARAM);

HAB hab;
HMQ hmq;
HWND hwndMaximum;
HWND hwndFrame;
HWND hwndMenu;
```

```
PFNWP FrameControlProc;

SHORT cdecl main()
{

QMSG qmsg;
HWND hwndSystemMenu;
SHORT idSystemMenu;
MENUITEM mi;
static CHAR szClass[] = "MaxWindow";

ULONG ctldata = FCF_TITLEBAR | FCF_SYSMENU | FCF_MINMAX
                | FCF_SIZEBORDER | FCF_SHELLPOSITION
                | FCF_TASKLIST;


hab = WinInitialize(NULL);
hmq = WinCreateMsgQueue(hab, 0);
WinRegisterClass(
                hab,
                szClass,
                ApplicationProc,
                CS_SIZEREDRAW, 0);

hwndFrame = WinCreateStdWindow(
                HWND_DESKTOP,
                0L,
                &ctldata,
                szClass,
                NULL,
                0L,
                NULL,
                0,
                &hwndMaximum);

hwndSystemMenu = WinWindowFromID(hwndFrame, FID_SYSMENU);

idSystemMenu = (SHORT)WinSendMsg(hwndSystemMenu,
                MM_ITEMIDFROMPOSITION, 0L, 0L);

WinSendMsg(hwndSystemMenu,
                MM_QUERYITEM,
                MPFROM2SHORT(idSystemMenu, FALSE),
                (MPARAM)(PMENUITEM)&mi);

hwndMenu = mi.hwndSubMenu;
```

```
FrameControlProc = WinSubclassWindow(hwndFrame,
                                        FrameSubclass);


WinSetWindowPos(hwndFrame, NULL, 50, 50, 50, 50,
            SWP_SIZE | SWP_MOVE | SWP_SHOW | SWP_MAXIMIZE);

while(WinGetMsg(hab, &qmsg, NULL, 0, 0))
        WinDispatchMsg(hab, &qmsg);

WinDestroyWindow(hwndFrame);
WinDestroyMsgQueue(hmq);
WinTerminate(hab);
}

MRESULT EXPENTRY ApplicationProc(hwnd, msg, mp1, mp2)
HWND   hwnd;
USHORT msg;
MPARAM mp1;
MPARAM mp2;
{
    HPS   hps;
    RECTL rcl;
    static CHAR szMessage[16] = "Meet Max Window";

    switch(msg)
      {
        case WM_CLOSE:
            WinPostMsg(hwnd, WM_QUIT, 0L, 0L);
            break;

        case WM_PAINT:
            hps = WinBeginPaint(hwnd, NULL, NULL);
            WinQueryWindowRect(hwnd, &rcl);
            WinFillRect(hps, &rcl, CLR_YELLOW);

            WinDrawText(hps, -1, szMessage, &rcl,
                    CLR_NEUTRAL, CLR_BACKGROUND,
                    DT_CENTER | DT_VCENTER);
            WinEndPaint(hps);
            break;

        case WM_ERASEBACKGROUND:
            return(TRUE);
            break;
```

```
        default:
            return(WinDefWindowProc(hwnd, msg, mp1, mp2));
    break;
    }
  return(0L);
}

MRESULT EXPENTRY FrameSubclass(hwnd, msg, mp1, mp2)
HWND hwnd;
USHORT msg;
MPARAM mp1, mp2;
{

    switch(msg)
      {
        case WM_FORMATFRAME:
            WinSendMsg(WinWindowFromID
                    (hwndFrame,FID_MINMAX),
                    MM_SETITEMATTR,
                    MPFROM2SHORT(SC_RESTORE, FALSE),
                    MPFROM2SHORT(
                        MIA_DISABLED,MIA_DISABLED));

        case WM_INITMENU:
            WinSendMsg(hwndMenu,
                    MM_SETITEMATTR,
                    MPFROM2SHORT(SC_RESTORE,TRUE),
                    MPFROM2SHORT(
                        MIA_DISABLED, MIA_DISABLED));

        default:
            return((*FrameControlProc)(hwnd,msg,mp1,mp2));
      }
    return(FALSE);
}
```

When you run this program, it immediately displays a maximized window. If you try to resize it, you can't: the resize option has been shut off in the system menu. All you can do is minimize the window so it is in icon format. While this type of application is somewhat against the style conventions of Presentation Manager applications, it can be convenient to enforce a maximized window for some applications such as ones that display image data and require a full screen to do so.

The manner in which the program stifles the system menu won't be discussed until the next chapter. Suffice it to say that menu-oriented messages are *sent* to the internal frame control procedure and the result is the deactivated menu options as well as a deactivated window resizing icon (the double arrow version).

The important concept embodied in the example program is the subclassing of the frame control procedure and the application-based use of WM messages designed for frame use. The following summary describes the important points of the program:

1. The program registers and creates a frame window as normal, with one exception: the call to WinCreateStdWindow specifies 0L instead of WS_VISIBLE in the window style argument. This prevents the frame window from displaying immediately upon execution.

2. After some menu initialization code, the program subclasses the frame control procedure by calling the WinSubclassWindow function. The address for the frame control procedure is stored in a variable called *FrameControlProc*, which is of type PFNWP.

3. The program calls the WinSetWindowPos to maximize the window and make it visible at the same time. This is accomplished by ORing the SWP_SHOW and SWP_MAXIMIZE positioning flags in the last argument to the function. Note that because WinSetWindowPos requires horizontal and vertical values in arguments three through six, this call filled the arguments with meaningless values. As a result of the window being maximized, and kept that way, these values are never used.

4. Most importantly, the program incorporates a frontend to the frame control procedure. The frontend is the *FrameSubclassProc*. It looks and acts like a client window procedure, but it gives you control over frame-oriented messages. When it returns a value to the internal frame control procedure, it passes the address stored in *FrameControlProc* (obtained as the return value from the WinSubclassWindow function).

The WinSubclassWindow window function is critical to the entire program. It not only gives you the ability to incorporate a frontend to the frame control procedure, but it establishes the flow of control for the program (see Figure 5-1).

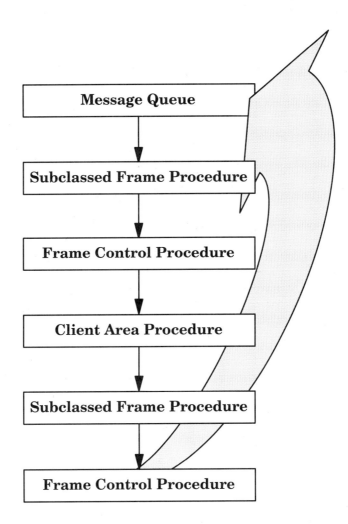

Figure 5-1: Control flow with a subclassed frame procedure

The primary control flow mechanism that you, the programmer, have at your disposal is the ability to specify the address of the frame control procedure. Here's a closer look at the WinSubclassWindow function:

```
PFNWP WinSubclassWindow (hwnd, pfnwp)
HWND hwnd;
PFNWP pfnwp;
```

The first argument to WinSubclassWindow is the handle to the window procedure that you want to subclass. You should note you can subclass any window procedure, not just the frame control procedure as in the previous program. The second argument to WinSubclassWindow holds the critical PFNWP address of the subclassed procedure. The Presentation Manager automatically associates the PFNWP address with the window specified by *hwnd*. It's that easy to redirect control flow.

The return value from WinSubclassWindow is also an important component of subclassing a window procedure. To efficiently subclass another procedure, you should call the old window procedure by returning its address. This effectively replaces the WinDefWindowProc call used in the client window procedure. Here's the salient line from the program example:

```
return ((*FrameControlProc) (hwnd,msg,mp1,mp2));
```

By returning a pointer in this statement, you redirect the Presentation Manager's attention to the internal frame control procedure — which is exactly where you want control flow to be at this point in the program. If and when you need to end the subclassing process, supply the the address of the subclassed procedure, not the frontend procedure. For example, the following call restores full control to the Presentation Manager's frame control procedure:

```
WinSubclassWindow (hwndFrame, &FrameControlProc);
```

One other point must be mentioned about subclassing: you cannot subclass a window created by another thread. This is a logical limitation, because a window created by another thread does not have its own message queue — unless, of course, it is an object window, which you probably wouldn't want to subclass anyway.

Frame Window Messages

By now you have likely gotten the message: there are window messages and then there are window messages. The circumstances, whatever they may be, dictate the meaning and accessibility of the WM messages. Some of them are designed primarily for use by the client window procedure. A lesser number are designed primarily for the frame control procedure. Most, however, can be accessed regardless of the window procedure. Table 5-1 lists the WM messages designed for the frame control procedure.

If you closely examine the frame control message, you will notice that few of them have anything to do with the so-called frame. This is not surprising because the frame is but a collection of other Presentation Manager control windows.

Recall the FID identifiers from Chapter 4. These identifiers represent control windows, each of which has several messages designed to cause the frame control procedure to initiate an action on its behalf. Inside the Presentation Manager, these earmarked messages are actually telling the frame control procedure to invoke the procedure that internally administers the control. Note, too, that an FID identifier is internally associated — or *preregistered* — for each of the frame window's control components. (You can also use the FID identifiers to specify control windows by using the WinCreateWindow function. This use is explained in Chapter 8.)

Table 5-1: Frame Window Messages

MESSAGE	DESCRIPTION
WM_ACTIVATE	Toggles a window's active state.
WM_BUTTON1DBLCLK	Indicates a click on the left mouse button.
WM_BUTTON1DOWN	Indicates the left mouse button is depressed.
WM_BUTTON1UP	Indicates the left mouse button is released.
WM_BUTTON2DBLCLK	Indicates a click on the center mouse button.
WM_BUTTON2DOWN	Indicates the center mouse button is depressed.

(continued)

Table 5-1: Continued

MESSAGE	DESCRIPTION
WM_BUTTON2UP	Indicates the center mouse button is released.
WM_BUTTON3DBLCLK	Indicates a click on the right mouse button.
WM_BUTTON3DOWN	Indicates the right mouse button is depressed.
WM_BUTTON3UP	Indicates the right mouse button is released.
WM_CALCFRAMERECT	Allows preservation of resized window areas.
WM_CHAR	Contains the most recent key press in the queue.
WM_CLOSE	Announces that a window is about to close.
WM_DRAWITEM	Tells owners that a listbox item needs redrawing.
WM_ERASEBACKGROUND	Tells the frame window to redraw itself.
WM_FLASHWINDOW	Tells the current window to flash.
WM_FOCUSCHANGE	Announces that the focus window is changing.
WM_FORMATFRAME	Tells frame window to recalculate the controls.
WM_INITMENU	Occurs when a menu is being initialized.
WM_MEASUREITEM	Command to calculate height of items.
WM_MENUSELECT	Announces a menu item has been selected by user.
WM_MINMAXFRAME	Announces minimize, maximize, or restore operation.
WM_NEXTMENU	Allows you to obtain next/previous menu handle.
WM_PAINT	Announces that a window needs to be repainted.
WM_QUERYBORDERSIZE	Contains the window border dimensions.
WM_QUERYFOCUSCHAIN	Queries the current input focus chain.
WM_QUERYFRAMECTLCOUNT	Allows you to obtain the count of frame controls.
WM_QUERYICON	Retrieves icon handle from frame window.
WM_QUERYWINDOWPARAMS	Retrieves parameters from window data structure.

(continued)

Table 5-1: Continued

MESSAGE	DESCRIPTION
WM_SETICON	Contains icon handle to set application icon.
WM_SETWINDOWPARAMS	Occurs when window configuration changes.
WM_SIZE	Occurs when size of window changes.
WM_SYSCOMMAND	Contains command message from a control window.
WM_TRACKFRAME	Notification that tracking operation is beginning.
WM_TRANSLATEACCEL	Allows accelerator translation of WM_CHAR.
WM_UPDATEFRAME	Occurs after format change to window.

Window Relationships

As if you had dropped in on a family, you probably have realized that Presentation Manager windows have a parent-to-child relationship. When you create a parent, or frame window, almost any window created in that same program is a descendent of the frame window. This includes the frame controls — titlebar, sizing border, system menu, and minimize and maximize controls — as well as the client area window. Altogether, this nuclear family of windows is called the *standard window*, which explains how WinCreateStdWindow got its name: it's a family name.

The desktop window sits at the head of this family. The standard window — or to be consistent, the frame window (which also is called a top-level window) — is the first born son of the desktop window. In turn, any child windows of the frame window are the grandchildren of the desktop; any grandchildren of the frame window are great-grandchildren of the desktop, *ad infinitum*. In other words, the desktop window is the patriarch of all windows created in the Presentation Manager (except for object windows, which are invisible rogues as far as the rules of window breeding are concerned). Internally, the desktop window has a window procedure just like all other windows. Paying homage to the desktop is obvious through the WinCreateStdWindow function. What does this function require you to do? Supply HWND_DESKTOP as the parent window, of course. Take a look at Figure 5-2: it is a typical family portrait.

By the way, what is a child window of the frame? It is any window, be it a control window such as an application menu or dialog box, that is created within the application. And of course, during its creation, it informed the Presentation Manager that its parent was the frame window. The family of Presentation Manager windows is not hard to get along with. As you might guess, child windows can experience some difficulty living up to the expectation of their parents. For example, a child window must always be displayed within the confines of its parent window — that is, the child window is always clipped to its parent window.

Child windows must also tow the same line as their parent. This means a child window position on the desktop is always relative to its position to its parent. Test this out! Load the *File Manager* utility and move and resize its various child windows. You will see that whenever you move the frame window, the child window moves along with it. Its position relative to the frame window remains unchanged, even though its position relative to the desktop has changed. And speaking of relativity, when a parent window is minimized or destroyed, the same fate befalls the child window.

As for *sibling* relationships, the rules are not as clear cut (yes, you have to worry about children bickering with one another). Generally, siblings can overlap each other as long as they stay in the dimensions of the parent window. You can think of sibling windows as a microcosm of top-level windows: as with top-level windows, the Presentation Manager automatically overlaps siblings windows. Additionally, all sibling windows are linked together. In other words, sibling windows constitute their own personal z-order. Of course, the z-order of the desktop subordinates the z-order of several siblings.

Despite the Presentation Manager's family rules, you can exercise some control over the way child windows act. Do this either when you register a child window, or when you actually create it. For example, you can specify style bits when you call WinCreateWindow (note that the *Std* is missing from this function name), or when you create a dialog box using the resource template. The mechanics of both WinCreateWindow and resource templates are explained in subsequent chapters. For now, suffice it to say

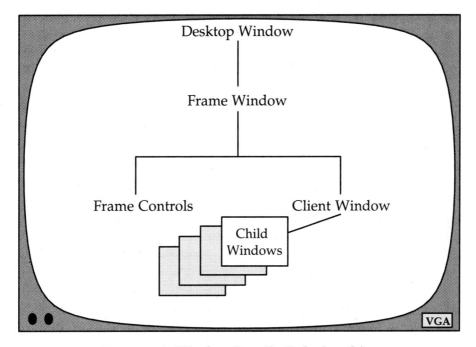

Figure 5-2: Window Family Relationships

that the Presentation Manager supports several window styles and classes that modify window behavior such as:

- Any window's ability to exclude the area of its children.
- A child window's ability to exclude the area of its siblings.
- A window's ability to be clipped to its default rectangle or to the visible region of its parent.

To implement a behavior pattern when you register a child window, you must specify the CS style bit. To implement the same pattern when you create a child window, you can specify the WS class bit. The following styles and classes are applicable:

- WS_CLIPCHILDREN — Excludes child windows.
- WS_CLIPSIBLINGS — Excludes sibling windows.

- CS_PARENTCLIP — Maps visible region to the parent window.

- CS_CLIPCHILDREN — Excludes the specified child window.

- CS_CLIPSIBLINGS — Excludes the specified sibling window.

You should not attempt to use the WinCreateStdWindow call to specify class and style bits that affect child and sibling windows. Doing so causes the Presentation Manager to apply these bits against the frame controls and client window. This is an undesirable situation because it contradicts the default behavior of the frame window.

The Presentation Manager allows you to vary from the rules of the family because of speed considerations: performing clipping calculations can be time consuming, so you are allowed to deactivate clipping if you want. When you want to prevent a parent window from drawing on its children, use WS_CLIPCHILDREN or CS_CLIPCHIDREN. The way these bits work is if both the parent and child are *invalidated* at the same time, the system redraws the parent first. The system then redraws first generation child windows and continues down the lineage until its has redrawn all child windows. When a child window becomes invalid on its own, the system redraws it without redrawing the parent window. To enhance this redrawing method, you can specify WS_CLIPSIBLINGS or CS_CLIPSI-BLINGS, both of which ensure that the system redraws sibling windows in front to back order. This is the normal pattern, anyway, but specifying these bits enforces the rule when the screen arrangement of sibling windows may not be readily apparent to the system.

The CS_PARENTCLIP class allows you to specify the same visible region for non-overlapping windows that have the same parent. This relieves the system of having to perform multiple calculations to establish the visible region. When you use this class, however, do not use the other four styles and classes that modify child and sibling window behavior: they merely serve to contradict the purpose of CS_PARENTCLIP.

Owner Windows

Another important relationship exists between a frame window and its subordinate windows — namely, the relationship of an owner window to an owned-window (any other control or child window within its sphere of influence). Unlike the parent-child relationship, the owner relationship has nothing to do with a window's display behavior. Instead, it dictates how the Presentation Manager passes messages between windows.

A window does not need an owner window. Establishing an owner, however, ensures that notification messages go into the queue associated with the window intended to process them. The most common notification messages are WM_COMMAND, WM_SYSCOMMAND, and WM_CONTROL, but several other WM messages notify a window of an impending event as well. The WM_MEASUREITEM, for example, notifies a listbox owner that the listbox has been created and it needs information about the font size of the characters that the owner wants it to display.

When you don't know the owner of a window — or the parent of a child for that matter — the WinQueryWindow function can come in handy. WinQueryWindow returns the handle to a window based on the relationship you specify. Here's the definition for WinQueryWindow:

```
HWND WinQueryWindow(hwnd, cmd, fLock)
HWND hwnd;
SHORT cmd;
BOOL fLock;
```

The first argument to WinQueryWindow is a handle to a window. The window that you specify is the one you know something about — the one whose owner or parent is in question. The next argument, *cmd*, specifies the relationship of *bwnd* that you want to satisfy. The Presentation Manager supports a set of identifiers denoted by a QW prefix that covers just about every relationship imaginable, not that there are that many. The identifier for an owner relationship is QW_OWNER; for a parent-child relationship, it is QW_PARENT. Table 5-2 lists and describes all the QW identifiers. The final argument to WinQueryWindow simply specifies whether to lock the window. You should also note that when using WinQueryWindow to enumerate windows of other threads, the z-ordering of the windows can change, meaning the function might not enumerate all current windows. If you do need to enumerate windows in different threads, you should use the WinGetNextWindow function.

Table 5-2: Window Relationship Identifiers

IDENTIFIER	DESCRIPTION
QW_NEXT	Next window in z-order (window below).
QW_PREV	Previous window in z-order (window above).
QW_TOP	Child window topmost in the lineage.
QW_BOTTOM	Child window at the bottom of the lineage.
QW_OWNER	Owner of window.
QW_PARENT	Parent of window (HWND_OBJECT if object window).
QW_NEXTTOP	Next enumerated main window. This is the order the Alt-Esc key sequence follows in jumping between windows.
QW_PREVTOP	Previous enumerated window. This is the order the Alt-Esc key sequence follows in jumping between windows.

Window Painting

The last section broached the topic of repainting. To understate the issue, there is slightly more to repainting than the familial relationships between windows. In fact, the Presentation Manager supports dual approaches to repainting windows — that is, it supports both *asynchronous* and *synchronous* repainting.

The default method used by the Presentation Manager is asynchronous repainting, which simply means the window is not repainted until the system has the resources to do so. For example, if a window contained a heavily detailed graphic that took up to 10 seconds to compose, asynchronous repainting would be appropriate. The reason is the system could continue to collect user keyboard and mouse input, instead of immediately devoting a large piece of CPU time to repainting the window. Additionally, for systems not laden with RAM, asynchronous repainting obviates the need for the system to swap large sections of application code to disk. For most applications, it is good practice to leave the system default of asynchronous repainting alone.

Synchronous repainting is a different story. Synchronous repainting causes a window to be drawn immediately. It is especially useful if a window has a parent that does not have the WS_CLIPCHILDREN style bit set, yet both need repainting simultaneously. You must explicitly tell the Presentation Manager that you want the system to synchronously repaint a window. You do this by specifying the CS_SYNCPAINT class style when you register the frame window, or WS_SYNCPAINT when you create it.

The WM_PAINT Message

Internally, the system generates a WM_PAINT message whenever a window becomes invalid. For instance, a window is invalid when it is created, so one of the first messages out of the message queue is the WM_PAINT message. A window is also invalidated when it is moved, resized, when another window overlaps it, or when it is minimized, maximized, and restored. Again, all of these circumstances result in a WM_PAINT message.

This methodology, while it might seem a little maze-like, obviates the need for the system to save the bitmap associated with a window, and then restore the bitmap later. The Presentation Manager's simple solution is to have the application redraw its window contents. Thus, you should structure your code so that every time a window receives a WM_PAINT message, any routines that draw text or graphics in a window are accessed during the WM_PAINT message handler.

The first item of business for a WM_PAINT message handle is to call the WinBeginPaint function. This call returns a handle to a presentation space, which is necessary for any drawing to occur in a window. Here's a closer look at WinBeginPaint:

```
HPS WinBeginPaint (hwnd, hps, prclPaint)
HWND hwnd;
HPS hps;
PRECTL prclPaint;
```

The first argument to WinBeginPaint is the familiar client window handle. The next argument, *hps*, specifies the type of presentation space. Setting this argument to NULL specifies the cached micro-PS, which is the presentation space that the Presentation Manager itself uses to draw windows and other items on the desktop. The last argument, *prclPaint*, can also be set to NULL, which is most often the case. If you do supply a value a pointer to a RECTL structure in this argument, *prclPaint* is set to the smallest rectangle bounding the update region in the application window.

Remember that when you call WinBeginPaint, you must call WinEnd-Paint before control leaves the WM_PAINT handler. The WinEndPaint function takes *hps* as its only argument and immediately closes access to the cached micro-PS. You should also note that invoking WinBeginPaint hides the desktop pointer when it is within the current window and WinEndPaint restores the pointer. Similarly, WinBeginPaint hides the tracking rectangle if it is active and WinEndPaint restores it.

Between WinBeginPaint and WinEndPaint, you place the code that draws to the window. In previous examples, the code has always been a Win function primarily designed for quick drawing needs. You can also access a full-blown text display or graphics routine from the the WM_PAINT message handle. For example, you can invoke programmer-defined functions from WM_PAINT to draw whatever you want. The only stipulation, as mentioned earlier, is the routine should not exceed the 1/10 second rule. If it takes longer than that, consider placing the routine in a separate thread of execution.

The WinInvalidateRect function is a handy way to make your code more structured, but not free you from the 1/10 second rule. WinInvalidateRect obtains a presentation space handle, erases the contents of the client window, and then causes the WM_PAINT handler to repaint the screen — without having the WM_PAINT handle specifically call the drawing routine. Here's the definition for WinInvalidateRect:

```
BOOL WinInvalidateRect(hwnd, prcl, fInclChildren)
HWND hwnd;
PRECTL prcl;
BOOL fInclChildren
```

A simple enough looking function — you have seen two of the three arguments before: *hwnd* is the handle to the window that interests you and *prcl* is the pointer to the rectangle corresponding to the window. The third argument, *fInclChildren*, specifies the window lineage affected by the call. Specifying TRUE for *fInclChildren* causes the descendants of *hwnd* to be included in the invalid rectangle. Specifying FALSE causes the descendants to be included only if the style of the parent is not WS_CLIPCH-ILDREN.

The important point about WinInvalidateRect is it generates a WM_PAINT message. If you have placed WinInvalidateRect in a drawing routine, it causes the WM_PAINT message to be processed immediately after the routine releases control to the system. The following program example uses WinInvalidateRect to generate a WM_PAINT message whenever a WM_TIMER message is processed. Two different beeps — one long, one short — keep track of the messages when you run the program.

```
#define INCL_PM
#define INCL_DOSMEMMGR
#include <os2.h>
#include <stdio.h>
#include <math.h>
#include <string.h>
#include "memwatch.h"

MRESULT EXPENTRY MemoryWndProc(HWND,USHORT,MPARAM,MPARAM);

HAB    hab;
HMQ    hmq;
HWND   hwndFrame, hwndMemory;

SHORT cdecl main()
{
static CHAR szClass[7] = "Memory";
static CHAR szTitle[13] = "Memory Watch";
ULONG ctlData = FCF_TITLEBAR | FCF_SYSMENU | FCF_SIZEBORDER
                | FCF_MINMAX;

USHORT fSwp = SWP_ACTIVATE | SWP_SIZE | SWP_MOVE | SWP_SHOW;
QMSG   qmsg;

hab = WinInitialize(NULL);
hmq = WinCreateMsgQueue(hab, 0);
WinRegisterClass(
            hab,
            szClass,
            TemplateWndProc,
            CS_SIZEREDRAW, 0);

hwndFrame = WinCreateStdWindow(
            HWND_DESKTOP,
            WS_VISIBLE,
```

```
                   &ctlData,
                   szClass,
                   szTitle,
                   OL, NULL, 0,
                   &hwndMemory);

WinSetWindowPos(hwndFrame, HWND_TOP, 275, 10, 300, 50, fSwp);

WinStartTimer(hab, hwndMemory, ID_TIMER, 1000);

while(WinGetMsg(hab, &qmsg, NULL, 0, 0))
               WinDispatchMsg(hab, &qmsg);

WinDestroyWindow(hwndFrame);
WinDestroyMsgQueue(hmq);
WinTerminate(hab);
return(0);
}

MRESULT EXPENTRY TemplateWndProc(hwnd, msg, mp1, mp2)
HWND   hwnd;
USHORT msg;
MPARAM mp1, mp2;
{
  HPS   hps;
  RECTL rcl;
  CHAR  szMessage[50];
  static ULONG ulMemBlock, ulOldBlock;

  switch (msg)
    {
      case WM_TIMER:
        DosBeep(200,100);
        DosMemAvail(&ulMemBlock);
        if(ulMemBlock != ulOldBlock)
          {
              ulOldBlock = ulMemBlock;
              WinInvalidateRect(hwnd, NULL, FALSE);
          }
        return(0);

      case WM_PAINT:
        hps = WinBeginPaint(hwnd, NULL, NULL);
        WinQueryWindowRect(hwnd, &rcl);
        sprintf(szMessage,
                "Largest memory block: %.f K",
                (double)ulMemBlock/1024);
```

```
        WinDrawText(hps, -1, szMessage, &rcl,
              CLR_NEUTRAL, CLR_BACKGROUND,
              DT_CENTER | DT_VCENTER | DT_ERASERECT);
        DosBeep(110,500);
        WinEndPaint( hps);
        return(NULL);


    }
  return WinDefWindowProc(hwnd, msg, mp1, mp2);
}
```

This program starts a timer using the WinStartTimer function and periodically checks the largest available memory block, using the Dos-MemAvail function. To control window repainting, it calls the WinInvalidateRect function each time the client window procedure handles a WM_TIMER message. The remainder of the work is performed in the WM_PAINT handler, where WinDrawText erases the background using the DT_ERASERECT option in its *rgfCmd* argument.

The WM_PAINT handler also uses **sprintf**, a standard C function that stores formatted text to a buffer. You can't use the old reliable **printf** function in Presentation Manager programs, but you can format most output using **sprintf**. In addition to using it to format output for WinDrawText, you can also use it with GpiCharStringAt, a Gpi library function that is used for most text output (see Chapter 11).

Erasing the Background

As you have seen, erasing the background is an important precursor to drawing in a window. By using the WM_ERASEBACKGROUND message, you can enhance the speed at which the system repaints windows. The client window receives the WM_ERASEBACKGROUND message before receiving the WM_PAINT message. This gives you an opportunity to tell the Presentation Manager — or more specifically, the frame control procedure — the opportunity to repaint the background of the client window.

Primarily, the WM_ERASEBACKGROUND message allows you to have the screen cleared and painted with the currently specified system color, which by default is off-white. The WM_ERASEBACKGROUND message is generated by the frame window. The frame window sends the WM_ERASEBACKGROUND message to the client window each time the frame window receives a WM_PAINT message. If there is no client window, the frame window sends this message to itself.

The normal way to handle WM_ERASEBACKGROUND is to trap it in the client window procedure and immediately return a value of TRUE to the frame control procedure. Here's the appropriate code:

```
case WM_ERASEBAVKGROUND:
     return(TRUE);
```

This instructs the frame window procedure to erase the background of the client window. In effect, this invalidates the client window as much as a call to the WinInvalidateRect does. The default processing of the WM_ERASEBACKGROUND message is for WinDefWindowProc to return FALSE to the frame control procedure. If this is the case, the frame control procedure performs no action.

Interestingly, you can obtain the handle to the frame window's presentation space from WM_ERASEBACKGROUND. This presentation space is a cached-PS and it is defined in frame coordinates, not client window coordinates. The handle is contained in *mp1* of the message. You can also obtain a pointer to the frame window's rectangle structure (RECTL), which is contained in *mp2*. By using these two points of reference, you can selectively erase parts of the client window procedure without obtaining you own presentation. If you use this technique, the message handler for WM_ERASEBACKGROUND should return a value of FALSE to the frame control procedure.

Client Window Setup

There is a special place in Presentation Manager windows where you can perform initialization or setup chores specifically geared toward your program. This place is the WM_CREATE message handler. The WM_CREATE message is the first message that a client window receives. It is a direct result of the call to WinCreateStdWindow, which generates it.

The most common use of WM_CREATE is to intercept it as a signal that a window is being created. Once you do this, you can perform some operation that you only need to perform a single time for the window. For example, the previous program called the WinSetTimer function in **main()**. You could also make this same call in the WM_CREATE handler. By placing the call in a test statement, you can determine whether the system can support another timer. If it can, you return FALSE from the WM_CRE-ATE handler. This tells the frame control procedure to go ahead and create the window — everything is okay from the client window perspective. If the system could not create a timer, you would return TRUE from the WM_CREATE handler, telling the frame control procedure not to create the window.

In addition to acting as a signal, the WM_CREATE message also allows you to access the master window structure, CREATESTRUCT. When you create a window, the system places all information about that window in CREATESTRUCT. Here's a look at the CREATESTRUCT structure:

```
typedef struct _CREATESTRUCT {
            PVOID pPresParams;
            PVOID pCtlData;
            USHORT id;
            HWND  hwndInsBehind;
            HWND  hwndOwner;
            SHORT cy;
            SHORT cx;
            SHORT y;
            SHORT x;
            ULONG flStyle;
            PSZ   pszText;
            PSZ   pszClass;
            HWND  hwndParent;
} CREATESTRUCT;
```

The fields in CREATESTRUCT should be familiar to you from using the WinCreateStdWindow and WinSetWindowPos functions. Review the descriptions of these functions in Chapter 4 if you are still uncomfortable with the variable names used in the function calls (the same names are used to identify the fields in CREATESTRUCT).

You can access the CREATESTRUCT structure through the WM_CRE-ATE message. The client window procedure receives this message when a window is created. You can extract either a pointer to the *pCtlData* field of CREATESTRUCT, which is contained in *mp1* parameter of WM_CRE-ATE; or you can retain a pointer to the entire structure by extracting it from the *mp2* parameter.

Again, the most common use of WM_CREATE is to perform some initialization operation. Take a look at the following program example,
which creates a timer in the WM_CREATE handler. The program also
does some non-standard things to the frame window.

```c
#define INCL_PM
#define INCL_DOSMEMMGR
#include <os2.h>
#include <stdio.h>
#include <math.h>
#include <string.h>

#define ID_TIMER 1

MRESULT EXPENTRY Mem2WndProc(HWND, USHORT, MPARAM, MPARAM) ;

HAB     hab;
HMQ     hmq;
HWND    hwndFrame, hwndMemory;

int main(void)
{
static CHAR szClass[] = "Memory2";
ULONG ctlData = FCF_SYSMENU | FCF_BORDER
                | FCF_TASKLIST | FCF_TITLEBAR;
USHORT fSwp = SWP_SIZE | SWP_MOVE;
QMSG qmsg;

hab = WinInitialize(NULL) ;
hmq = WinCreateMsgQueue(hab, 0) ;

WinRegisterClass(hab, szClass, Mem2WndProc, 0L, 0) ;

hwndFrame = WinCreateStdWindow(HWND_DESKTOP,
                    WS_VISIBLE,
                    &ctlData,
                    szClass,
                    NULL,
                    0L,
                    NULL,
                    0, &hwndMemory) ;

WinSetWindowPos(hwndFrame, HWND_TOP, 300, 10, 250, 50, fSwp) ;

while(WinGetMsg(hab, &qmsg, NULL, 0, 0))
```

```
                    WinDispatchMsg(hab, &qmsg);

WinDestroyWindow(hwndFrame);
WinDestroyMsgQueue(hmq);
WinTerminate(hab);

return(0);
}

MRESULT EXPENTRY Mem2WndProc(hwnd, msg, mp1, mp2)
HWND   hwnd;
USHORT msg;
MPARAM mp1, mp2;
{

  HPS  hps;
  RECTL rcl;
  CHAR  szMessage[50];
  static ULONG ulMemBlock, ulOldBlock;

  switch (msg)
    {
      case WM_CREATE:
         if(WinStartTimer(hab, hwnd, ID_TIMER, 1000))
               return(FALSE);
         else
               return(TRUE);

      case WM_TIMER:
         DosMemAvail(&ulMemBlock);
         if(ulMemBlock != ulOldBlock)
           {
               ulOldBlock = ulMemBlock;
               WinInvalidateRect(hwnd, NULL, FALSE);
           }
         return(FALSE);

      case WM_PAINT:
         hps = WinBeginPaint(hwnd, NULL, NULL);
         WinQueryWindowRect(hwnd, &rcl);

         sprintf(szMessage,
               "Largest memory block: %.f K",
               (double)ulMemBlock/1024);
         WinDrawText(hps, -1, szMessage, &rcl,
               CLR_NEUTRAL, CLR_YELLOW,
               DT_CENTER | DT_VCENTER | DT_ERASERECT);
```

```
            WinEndPaint ( hps ) ;
            return ( NULL ) ;
    }
   return WinDefWindowProc ( hwnd, msg, mp1, mp2 ) ;
}
```

In addition to making the point that you can call WinSetTimer from the WM_CREATE handler, this program adapts the frame window to its purpose at hand — namely, to sit on the desktop and give the user an indication of memory usage. The frame window is now similar to the frame window used by the *Control Panel* utility, which allows the user to resize and close the window, but nothing else. The key to this modified frame window is the fewer number of FCF identifiers used in the WinCreate-StdWindow call. You have to trim down the number of identifiers supplied to WinSetWindowPos as well.

Scrollbar Control

Until now, two extremely important FCF identifiers have been ignored: FCF_HSCROLL and FCF_VSCROLL. From their names, you can guess that these are the identifiers you use when you want to create scrollbars for your program. The reason they have not been described until now is that they require extensive logic to implement — unlike most of the other standard frame window controls.

Scrollbars are an important component in a windowing environment. They allow the user to display sections of text and graphics that exceed the current dimensions of the window. Additionally, they can be used in a standard application such as a text editor or spreadsheet as an alternative method of moving through the document or worksheet. You should note, too, that the Microsoft *Application Style Guide* recommends the use of scrollbars for most programs.

A scrollbar consists of five distinct parts. On either end of a scrollbar is an arrow contained in a small box. Clicking on this area with the mouse causes the contents of the window to scroll incrementally in the direction of the arrow. Bordering each arrow area is a halftone area. Clicking in this area cases the contents of the window to scroll one page in the direction of the bordering arrow. The last component of a scrollbar is the scrollbar slider, which is the small, lightly colored box. The position of the slider varies according to the relative position of the current window contents to the file that it belongs. By dragging the slider with the mouse you can quickly move through an entire document using the horizontal scrollbar, or just as quickly move from side to side using the vertical scrollbar. Figure 5-3 shows the various parts of a horizontal scrollbar.

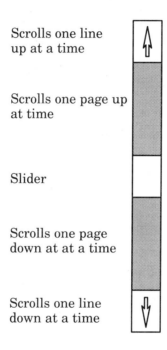

Scrolls one line up at a time

Scrolls one page up at time

Slider

Scrolls one page down at at a time

Scrolls one line down at a time

Figure 5-3: Scrollbar Components

Internally, a scrollbar is similar to other system control windows. They send and receive messages like other controls and you can process these messages in the client window procedure. The two scrollbar messages that you handle in the client window procedure are WM_HSCROLL and WM_VSCROLL. In and of themselves, these messages do not signal the application to scroll a window's contents in a certain direction. Rather, movement commands are contained in the parameters of these messages:

- *mp1* — The scrollbar window ID, which is a USHORT value used for targeting a given scrollbar.

- *mp2 (low)* — The current slider position associated with the scrollbar identified by *mp1*. When this SHORT value is FALSE, it means the slider is not being moved.

- *mp2 (high)* — One of several system-defined scrollbar command identifiers constants (denoted by an SB prefix) that tell an application in which direction to move the contents of a window.

Once you extract the *mp1* and *mp2 (high)* data from a scrollbar message, you need to extract the directional information. Depending on the extent of your scrollbar logic, you might want to use a series of **if** statements or build a **switch-case** handler to respond to the various SB constants. Tables 5-3 and 5-4 list the SB command identifiers.

Table 5-3: WM_HSCROLL Command Identifiers

COMMAND	VALUE	DESCRIPTION
SB_LINELEFT	1	Indicates a mouse click on the scrollbar's left arrow, or a VK_LEFT key press.
SB_LINERIGHT	2	Indicates a mouse click on the scrollbar's right arrow, or a VK_RIGHT key press.
SB_PAGELEFT	3	Indicates a mouse click to the left of the slider, or a VK_PAGELEFT key press.
SB_PAGERIGHT	4	Indicates a mouse click to the right of the slider, or a VK_PAGERIGHT key press.
SB_SLIDERTRACK	5	Indicates the user has changed the slider position with the mouse.
SB_SLIDERPOSITION	6	Contains the slider's final position.
SB_ENDSCROLL	7	Indicates the user has finished scrolling. Not applicable for absolute slider positioning.

Table 5-4: WM_VSCROLL Command Identifiers

COMMAND	VALUE	DESCRIPTION
SB_LINEUP	1	Indicates a mouse click on the scrollbar's up arrow, or a VK_UP key press.
SB_LINEDOWN	2	Indicates a mouse click on the scrollbar's down arrow, or a VK_DOWN key press.
SB_PAGEUP	3	Indicates a mouse click above the slider, or a VK_PAGEUP key press.
SB_PAGEDOWN	4	Indicates a mouse click below the slider, or a VK_PAGEDOWN key press.
SB_SLIDERTRACK	5	Indicates the user has changed the slider position with the mouse.
SB_SLIDERPOSITION	6	Contains the slider's final position.
SB_ENDSCROLL	7	Indicates the user has finished scrolling. Not applicable for absolute slider positioning.

The WM_CREATE message handler is a vital part of scrollbar processing. In the WM_CREATE handler, you need to obtain the handle of the scrollbar as well as send it initialization data. The following routine serves these purposes:

```
case WM_CREATE:

    hwndVscroll = WinWindowFromID(
                    WinQueryWindow(hwnd,
                            QW_PARENT, FALSE),
                    FID_VERTSCROLL);

    WinSendMsg(hwndVscroll,
                SBM_SETSCROLLBAR,
                MPFROM2SHORT(sVscroll, 0),
                MPFROM2SHORT(0, TotalLines - 1));
    return(FALSE);
```

You obtain the handle to a scrollbar by using the WinWindowFromID function in tandem with the WinQueryWindow function. Note that the return value from WinWindowFromID must be a static variable (of type HWND). Ascribe this to the one-shot nature of the WM_CREATE message: if you don't store the return value as a static, you have to make repeated calls to WinWindowFromID, which is defined as follows:

```
HWND WinWindowFromID(hwndParent, id)
HWND hwndParent;
USHORT id;
```

The WinWindowFromID simply obtains a handle to a child window. The first argument, *hwndParent*, is the handle to the parent window. The second argument, *id*, is another value that you probably don't have readily available, so use the WinQueryWindow function to satisfy the argument. If WinWindowFromID discovers that no scrollbar window — or any child window, for that matter — exists with the named ID, it returns NULL.

After you initialize a scrollbar, you are ready to begin processing its messages. At this point, your major concern is communicating with the scrollbar. As shown in the previous WM_CREATE handler, you use the WinSendMsg function along with a predefined set of scrollbar messages. These messages are denoted with the SBM prefix and basically are designed to tell the scrollbar what to do. Table 5-5 lists these messages.

Table 5-5: Scrollbar Control Messages

MESSAGE	BIT	DESCRIPTION
SBM_SETSCROLLBAR	0x01a0	Sets slider range.
SBM_SETPOS	0x01a1	Sets slider position.
SBM_QUERYPOS	0x01a2	Retrieves slider position.
SBM_QUERYRANGE	0x01a3	Retrieves slider's boundary values.
SBM_SETHILITE	0x01a4	Sets highlight state of scrollbar.
SBM_QUERYHILITE	0x01a5	Obtains highlight state of scrollbar.

When you include scrollbars in a program, you must implement your own logic to position text and graphics in the window area dictated by the scrollbar commands. The most common way to do this is to incorporate one or more program-wide counters into your drawing routines. The following example program uses this method.

```
#define INCL_DOS
#define INCL_WIN

#include <os2.h>
#include <stdio.h>
#include <stdlib.h>
#include "scroll.h"

MRESULT EXPENTRY ScrollWndProc(HWND, USHORT, MPARAM, MPARAM);
VOID  ReadTextFile(VOID);
CHAR szDisplay[50][81];
SHORT TotalLines = 0;

int main()
{
static CHAR szClass [] = "Scroll";
HAB      hab;
HMQ      hmq;
HWND     hwndClientArea, hwndFrame;
QMSG     qmsg;
ULONG    ctlData = FCF_TITLEBAR | FCF_SYSMENU
                 | FCF_SIZEBORDER | FCF_MINMAX | FCF_VERTSCROLL
                 | FCF_SHELLPOSITION;


hab = WinInitialize(NULL);
hmq = WinCreateMsgQueue(hab, 0);

WinRegisterClass(hab, szClass,
             ScrollWndProc, CS_SIZEREDRAW, 0);

hwndFrame = WinCreateStdWindow(
             HWND_DESKTOP, WS_VISIBLE,
             &ctlData, szClass, NULL, 0L,
             NULL, 0, &hwndClientArea);

while(WinGetMsg(hab, &qmsg, NULL, 0, 0))
             WinDispatchMsg(hab, &qmsg);

WinDestroyWindow(hwndFrame);
WinDestroyMsgQueue(hmq);
WinTerminate(hab);
```

```
return 0;
}

MRESULT EXPENTRY ScrollWndProc(hwnd, msg, mp1, mp2)
HWND hwnd;
USHORT msg;
MPARAM mp1, mp2;
   {
     static HWND hwndVscroll;
     static SHORT sVscroll=0, cxClient, cyClient;
     static SHORT sVsave;
     CHAR szBuffer[80];
     HPS hps;
     SHORT i=0;
     RECTL rcl, rclDraw;

     switch(msg)
        {
         case WM_CREATE:
               ReadTextFile();
               hwndVscroll = WinWindowFromID(
                                   WinQueryWindow(hwnd,
                                   QW_PARENT, FALSE),
                                   FID_VERTSCROLL);

               WinSendMsg(hwndVscroll, SBM_SETSCROLLBAR,
                       MPFROM2SHORT(sVscroll, 0),
                       MPFROM2SHORT(0, TotalLines - 1));

         return(FALSE);

         case WM_SIZE:
               cxClient = SHORT1FROMMP(mp2);
               cyClient = SHORT2FROMMP(mp2);
               return(FALSE);

         case WM_VSCROLL:
               switch(SHORT2FROMMP(mp2))
                  {
                   case SB_LINEUP:
                         sVscroll--;
                         break;

                   case SB_LINEDOWN:
                         sVscroll++;
                         break;
                  }
```

```
                    WinSendMsg(hwndVscroll, SBM_SETPOS,
                            MPFROM2SHORT(sVscroll, 0), NULL);
                    WinInvalidateRect(hwnd, NULL, FALSE);
                    return(FALSE);

            case WM_ERASEBACKGROUND:
                    return(TRUE);

            case WM_PAINT:
                    hps = WinBeginPaint(hwnd, NULL, NULL);
                    WinQueryWindowRect(hwnd, &rcl);
                    WinFillRect(hps, &rcl, CLR_YELLOW);

                    rclDraw.xLeft = rcl.xLeft;
                    rclDraw.yBottom = rcl.yBottom;
                    rclDraw.xRight = rcl.xRight;

                    sVsave = sVscroll;
                    for(i=0; i < TotalLines; i++)
                        {
                            if(sVscroll > sVsave)
                              rclDraw.yTop = rcl.yTop -
                                        ((i + sVscroll) * 12);
                            else
                              rclDraw.yTop = rcl.yTop -
                                        ((i - sVscroll) * 12);

                            sprintf(szBuffer, "%s", szDisplay[i]);

                            WinDrawText(hps, -1, szBuffer,
                                        &rclDraw,CLR_BLACK,
                                        CLR_YELLOW, DT_TOP);
                        }

                    WinEndPaint(hps);
                    return(NULL);
        }

    return(WinDefWindowProc(hwnd, msg, mp1, mp2));
}

VOID ReadTextFile()
{
CHAR    szText[50][BUFLENGTH+1];
USHORT usAction, usBytes;
HFILE   hf;
ULONG   ulSize = 0;
```

```
SHORT   i=0, j=0, k=0, n=0;


DosOpen("TESTFILE", &hf, &usAction, ulSize,
             ATTRIBUTE, OPENFLAG, OPENMODE, 0L);

do {
    DosRead(hf, szText[i], BUFLENGTH, &usBytes);
    szText[i][usBytes] = 0;
    i++;
} while(usBytes == BUFLENGTH);

TotalLines = i;
i=0;

while(j <= TotalLines)
    switch(szText[j][i])
       {
        case 10:
             szDisplay[k][n] = 0;
             k++;
             n=0;
             i++;
             break;

        case 13:
             i++;
             break;

        case 0:
             j++;
             i=0;
             break;

        default:
             szDisplay[k][n] = szText[j][i];
             i++;
             n++;
       }

    TotalLines = k;
    DosClose(hf);
}
```

The program, titled SCROLL.C, reads an ASCII file from disk and displays the contents in the client window. As written, the program only reads a file called TESTFILE, which must be located in the current directory. You can easily enhance this by using the command line arguments recognized by **main()**. In its present form, the program is also limited to reading a 50-line file. Additionally, the program uses a two-dimensional string array so you can immediately see how displaying a line of text relates to the scrollbar WM_VSCROLL message and its SB_LINEUP and SB_LINEDOWN commands. For each of these commands, the text is repositioned accordingly.

The WinDrawText function is used in the program to display the text, with its *rgfCmd* argument set to DT_TOP, which causes the line of text to be displayed at the top of the specified rectangle. Because of this limitation of WinDrawText, the program always adjusts the current rectangle so the next line of text is placed appropriately. Once you become familiar with the GpiCharStringAt function (explained in Chapter 11), you will likely never think of using WinDrawText to display more than 10 to 20 lines of text at a time. The program, however, does show that WinDrawText can save you some overhead for simple text applications. In fact, maybe someone should write an EDLIN for the Presentation Manager? (There must be someone out there who would appreciate such a contradiction!)

Speaking of Scrolling

In addition to message-based window scrolling, the Presentation Manager supports a function that lets you scroll the contents of a window. The function in question is named WinScrollWindow, which not only scrolls a window's contents, but also maintains the relative position of the current cursor or tracking rectangle. Here's the definition for WinScrollWindow:

```
SHORT WinScrollWindow(hwnd, dx, dy, prclScroll, prclClip,
                      hrgnUpdate, prclUpdate, rgfsw)
HWND hwnd;
SHORT dx, dy;
PRECTL prclScroll, prclClip;
HRGN hrgnUpdate;
PRECTL prclUpdate;
USHORT rgfsw;
```

As usual, the first argument is a handle to a window. The second and the third arguments — *dx* and *dy* — specify the scrolling distance. You specify these values in device units (that is, pixel coordinates as used to locate an item on the desktop window). The *prclScroll* argument references a structure that specifies the rectangle to scroll. Setting *prclScroll* to NULL scrolls the entire window. The next argument, *prclClip*, specifies the clipping rectangle. The *hrgnUpdate* argument specifies the update region in the rectangle. If you set this to NULL, *hrgnUpdate* is modified to hold the region uncovered by the scroll. Setting it to a non-NULL value causes it to fill the specified region with the bounding region of the invalid bits uncovered by the scroll. The next to last argument, *prclUpdate*, returns the boundaries of the rectangle invalidated as a result of the scrolling operation. And the last argument, *rgfsw*, specifies how WinScrollWindow should handle child windows in the scroll area. You can specify one, or both, of the following:

- SW_SCROLLCHILDREN — Specifying this identifier causes all child windows within the intersection of *prclScroll* and *prclClip* to be scrolled by *dx* and *dy* units.

- SW_INVALIDATERGN — Specifying this identifier causes the invalid region that results from the scroll to be added to the update regions of all affected windows. If any of these windows are of style WS_SYNCPAINT, a WM_PAINT message might result from specifying SW_INVALIDATERGN. If one did result, it would occur before WinScrollWindow returned.

Using WinScrollWindow without setting SW_SCROLLCHILDREN results in the fastest possible use. When *hwnd* is anything but a child window that is clipped, child windows that lie within the scrolling area are also scrolled.

If this is the case, you should call the WinScrollWindow function using the SW_SCROLLCHILDREN option. The fastest method, however, is not to specify the SW_SCROLLCHILDREN and SW_INVALIDATERGN options. To quickly repeat a scroll, leave out the the SW_INVALIDATERGN flag and just repaint the invalid area if the invalid region is rectangular; otherwise, invalidate the area and update it. If the scrolling does not happen often, include the SW_INVALIDATERGN flag, and WinScrollWindow will invalidate and update synchronous paint windows automatically before returning.

Closing a Window

The topic of window management is an open-ended one. In fact, it could comprise a book unto itself, but for the time being, one other topic should be described in this chapter: closing a window.

The Microsoft *Application Style Guide* suggests that you develop your own closing routines for an application. Minimally, it suggests that you include a menu (available from the top-level menubar) that lets the user terminate the application. Alternatively, this menu usually offers the user a chance to resume the application, although just moving the mouse pointer away from the menu accomplishes the same thing. Even if you don't include a special menu option to close an application, you can still manage the way an application terminates. If there is no special menu option, the user can close an application in one of three ways:

- By selecting the close option from the system menu.

- By double-clicking on the system menu icon.

- By pressing Alt-F4.

As a result of any of these actions, the system menu's frame window receives a WM_SYSCOMMAND message carrying an SC_CLOSE constant. The frame control procedure processes this message by sending the client window a WM_CLOSE message. If you choose not to handle this message in the client window procedure, the WinDefWindowProc function handles it by posting a WM_QUIT message to the message queue associated with the current window. If you do handle the message, you must similarly post a WM_QUIT message, or redirect program flow to WinDefWindowProc. Here's what a the relevant call to WinPostMsg looks like:

```
WinPostMsg(hwnd, WM_QUIT, 0L, 0L);
```

Usually, it is only necessary to post a WM_QUIT message from subclassed procedures. In the client window procedure, you can handle the WM_CLOSE message and rely on some variation of default processing. For example, if you handle WM_CLOSE, perform some action, and include an option that aborts the close operation, you can return NULL to the frame control procedure. This negates the WM_CLOSE message. The following program examples uses this technique.

```
/* CLOSER.C (Demonstrates WM_CLOSE and WM_DESTROY messages)

#define INCL_PM
#include <os2.h>

MRESULT EXPENTRY CloserWndProc(HWND, USHORT, MPARAM, MPARAM);

HAB    hab;
HMQ    hmq;
HWND   hwndFrame, hwndCloser;

int main (void)
{
static CHAR szClass[7] = "Closer";
static CHAR szTitle[16] = "Closing Example";
ULONG ctlData = FCF_TITLEBAR | FCF_SYSMENU | FCF_SIZEBORDER
                | FCF_MINMAX | FCF_SHELLPOSITION;
QMSG   qmsg;


hab = WinInitialize(NULL);
hmq = WinCreateMsgQueue(hab, 0);
WinRegisterClass(hab, szClass, CloseWndProc,
                CS_SIZEREDRAW, 0);

hwndFrame = WinCreateStdWindow(
                              HWND_DESKTOP,
                              WS_VISIBLE,
                              &ctlData,
                              szClass,
                              szTitle,
                              0L,
                              NULL,
                              0,
                              &hwndCloser);

while(WinGetMsg(hab, &qmsg, NULL, 0, 0))
               WinDispatchMsg(hab, &qmsg);

WinDestroyWindow(hwndFrame);
WinDestroyMsgQueue(hmq);
WinTerminate(hab);
return(0);
}
```

```
MRESULT EXPENTRY CloserWndProc(hwnd, msg, mp1, mp2)
HWND   hwnd;
USHORT msg;
MPARAM mp1, mp2;
  {
   SHORT i;

   switch (msg)
      {

      case WM_DESTROY:
            for(i=0; i<10; i++)
              DosBeep(100,100+i);

            if(
              MBID_YES == WinMessageBox(
              HWND_DESKTOP, hwnd,
              "You are in the WM_DESTROY handler.\n"
              "Clean up operations should occur here.",
              "Closing Message",
              0, MB_OKAY| MB_NOICON
              | MB_MOVEABLE))
            break;

      case WM_CLOSE:
            for(i=0; i<10; i++)
              DosBeep(100,100+i);

            if(
              MBID_YES == WinMessageBox(
              HWND_DESKTOP, hwnd,
              "You are about to quit the program.\n"
              "Are you sure you want to do this?",
              "Closing Message",
              0, MB_YESNOCANCEL | MB_DEFBUTTON3
              | MB_ICONQUESTION | MB_MOVEABLE))

            break;

            return(0);

      case WM_ERASEBACKGROUND:
            return(TRUE);
      }

   return(WinDefWindowProc(hwnd, msg, mp1, mp2));
  }
```

In addition to demonstrating the WM_CLOSE message, this program example introduces you to the WM_DESTROY message. The system generates this message whenever a window is about to be destroyed. The primary purpose of the message is to allow you to perform any necessary housekeeping activities, although you can abort the destroy sequence if you desire.

CHAPTER 6

RESOURCES AND MENUS

What is an application without a menu? Not much, perhaps, but probably it's much easier to write than a typical menu-driven program that demands numerous kludges in otherwise robust code. Many times, you have likely wanted to dispense with the tedious work of creating menus — of meandering menu paths you've created in order to debug them — and instead concentrate solely on fine-tuning the code that drives your application.

Although Presentation Manager programs use numerous menus, the menu structure already exists for you. As you've seen, you need not concern yourself with the system menu: the Presentation Manager creates it automatically when it finds the FCF_SYSMENU identifier in the call to WinCreateStdWindow. Wouldn't it be nice if the Presentation Manager created all your menus?

In a way, it does. Of course, you have to help a little. For instance, you must specify FCF_MENU when calling WinCreateStdWindow. Additionally, you must track the messages associated with various menu items. And if you want to supercharge your menus, you have to master a special set of messages dedicated to enhancing the actual menu display.

For the most part, creating and implementing menus in the Presentation Manager is much easier than doing the same from scratch. The user also benefits from the Presentation Manager's standardized menu system, because menu logic is consistent between applications.

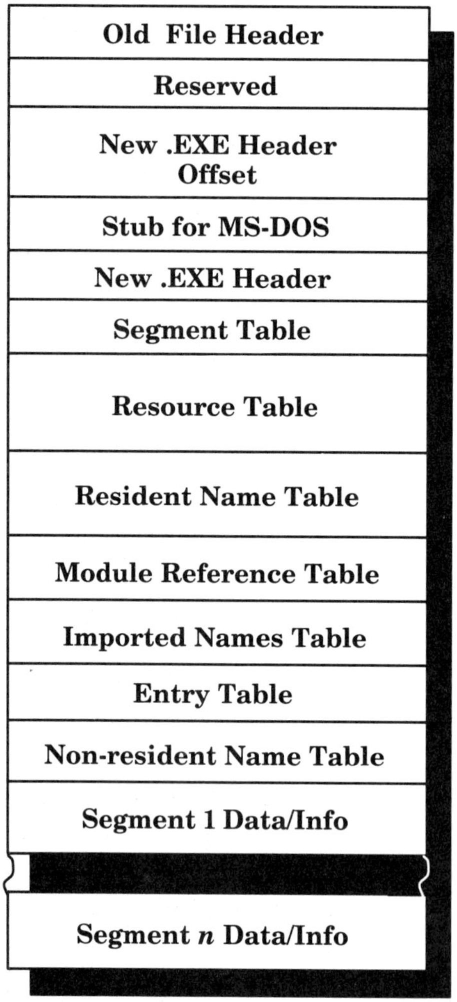

Old File Header
Reserved
New .EXE Header Offset
Stub for MS-DOS
New .EXE Header
Segment Table
Resource Table
Resident Name Table
Module Reference Table
Imported Names Table
Entry Table
Non-resident Name Table
Segment 1 Data/Info
Segment *n* Data/Info

Figure 6-1: The OS/2 .EXE File, which represents a new format compared to its MS-DOS format, but still supports a header for MS-DOS programs.

Menus Are Resources

Resources are a new concept for programmers coming from the MS-DOS world (unless you are a *Windows* programmer). You can store resources such as icons, bitmaps, strings and menu information in an .EXE file without interfering with the file's normal code and data segments. Figure 6-1 illustrates the various parts of an OS/2 .EXE file.

Besides the OS/2 specific header information, what's important in an OS/2 header file is its resource segment. The Presentation Manager uses 14 different resource types and stores them in the .EXE file's resource segment. Table 6-1 lists the Presentation Manager's resource types.

Table 6-1: Presentation Manager Resource Type

IDENTIFIER	ID	DESCRIPTION
RT_POINTER	1	Mouse pointer shape
RT_BITMAP	2	Bitmap
RT_MENU	3	Menu resource
RT_DIALOG	4	Dialog respirce
RT_STRING	5	String tables
RT_FONTDIR	6	Font directory
RT_FONT	7	Font
RT_ACCELTABLE	8	Accelerator tables
RT_RCDATA	9	Binary data
RT_MESSAGE	10	Error message tables
RT_DLGINCLUDE	11	Dialog include filename
RT_VKEYTBL	12	Key to vkey tables
RT_KEYTBL	13	Key to UGL tables
RT_CHARTBL	14	Glyph to character tables

An .EXE file can contain multiple resource segments, corresponding to the different RT resources that your program requires. In other words, each resource receives its own resource segment. The exceptions are string and text message resources. With these, you can store multiple instances of each in the resource segment's string table. Figure 6-2 takes a closer look at the resource table.

As illustrated in Figure 6-2, the resource segment consists of the alignment shift count, which is a 32-bit integer based on an exponent of 2. The alignment shift count specifies the total bytes in each alignment sector. A resource is located in .EXE file based on the multiplicative product of its alignment offset and alignment sector size.

The next item in the resource table is the resource type header, which consists of two active fields and one reserved field for system use. The first active field (0x0000) is the type ID, which contains a positive value corresponding to the RT identifier, or is set to zero to indicate the end of the resource. This also tells the Presentation Manager to shift its attention to the string table and deal with its contents, if any.

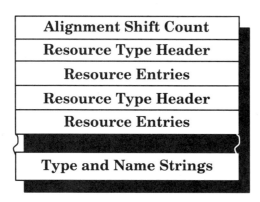

Figure 6-2: The Resource Table, which specifies the location, size, type, and name of resources.

The resource type header is followed by the specified number of resource entries. Table 6-2 lists the fields common to all resource entries.

Table 6-2: Resource Entry Field

FIELD	DESCRIPTION
0x000	Offset to the resource data. The offset is the value in alignment units, relative to the beginning of the file.
0x0002	Length in bytes of the resource.
0x0004	Resource status flag. A value of 0x0010 specifies the resource can be moved; 0x0020 specifies the resource can be shared; and 0x0040 specifies the resource is not demand loaded.
0x0006	Specifies the resource name ID, or is an offset to the resource string relative to the beginning of the resource table.

The last component of the resource table is the string table. The first byte in each string specifies the length of the string in bytes. If the first byte is zero, the Presentation Manager knows it has reached the end of the resource table. Note that these strings are not null-terminated.

Resources can also be stored in a dynamic link library. The resource table format is identical in a DLL to that in the application program's .EXE file. You might want to use the DLL approach when several programs draw upon the same resources, although OS/2 does make local .EXE file resources available to concurrently running programs.

In order for the Presentation Manager to recognize different resources — and subcategories within a resource — each type of resource has a 16-bit identifier. This identifier is usually referred to as a type ID. The Presentation Manager reserves integers 1 through 255 for system-related type IDs. If you need to use custom resources, these must be numbered beginning with a number greater than 255 as unique type IDs.

There are three ways to load a resource: use the DosLoadModule function to load a resource from a DLL; use the DosGetResource function to load a resource from the program's .EXE file; or, simplest of all, do it through Presentation Manager functions. You should note, however, that if you create custom resources, you must use DosLoadModule and/or DosGetResource.

Standard Resources

The Presentation Manager loads a resource as either the result of a function call such as GpiLoadBitMap, which loads a bitmap based on the RT_BITMAP resource identifier; or when it finds a valid FCF identifier in the style argument to the WinCreateStdWindow function.

Recall from Chapter 4 that three of the FCF identifiers received cursory treatment: FCF_MENU, FCF_ICON, and FCF_ACCELTABLE. If any of these FCF identifiers are included in the style argument to the WinCreateStdWindow function, the Presentation Manager attempts to load the corresponding resource.

To allow the Presentation Manager to access a resource, you must define a unique ID number for the resource. How you define this ID number depends on the type of resource. When you create a menu resource, you define the menu resource ID in a custom header file included by both the menu script and the application program. For example, assuming you defined a resource identifier of ID_TOPLEVEL, the following call to WinCreateStdWindow would load the resource.

```
ctlData = FCF_TITLEBAR | FCF_SYSMENU | FCF_SIZEBORDER
          | FCF_MINMAX | FCF_MENU;

hwndFrame = WinCreateStdWindow(
                        HWND_DESKTOP,
                        WS_VISIBLE,
                        &ctlData,
                        szClass,
                        szTitleBar,
                        0L,
                        NULL,
                        ID_TOPLEVEL,    /* Resource ID. */
                        &hwndTemplate);
```

Two changes have occurred in this call to WinCreateStdWindow, compared to previous versions. In the second argument, FCF_MENU is now included in the ORed constants that comprise the frame window style. And in the eighth argument, the ID_TOPLEVEL resource identifier has been specified. This is all it takes to incorporate your menu resource in your application program's .EXE file.

How do you create a resource? Different resources are created different ways. To create an icon resource, for example, you use the Microsoft *Icon Editor*. Similarly, to create a dialog box, you use the Microsoft *Dialog Box Editor*. To create a menu resource, all you need is your usual editor and the Microsoft *Resource Compiler*, which compiles all resources so they can be linked into an application program's .EXE file. The next section explains how to write a menu resource script and compile it with the Resource Compiler.

Creating A Menu Resource

You create a menu resource script in an ASCII editor, then compile it with the Resource Compiler. This produces a file with a .RES extension, which you then link to your program's .EXE file. The following make file will serve to compile and link most Presentation Manager programs that use menu resources:

```
# MENU (Example Make File)

menu.obj : menu.c
    cl -c -W3 -AS -G2sw -Oas -Zpei menu.c

menu.res : menu.rc menu.h
    rc -r menu

menu.exe : menu.obj menu.res menu.def
    link menu, /align:16, NUL, os2, menu
    rc menu.res
```

When you create a menu resource script, you also need a header file. The latter defines the constants that you use in the resource script. As a result, it is more orderly to create the header file first. Both the menu resource script and the application program **include** the header file. Here's an example header file used by subsequent code examples in this chapter:

```
/* GRAPHICS.H — Header file for example
graphics display program. */

#define ID_TOPLEVEL    1          ./* Menu resource ID. */
```

```
#define IDM_SERVICE      -1          /* Service submenu ID. */

#define IDM_ERASE         0
#define IDM_QUIT          1

#define IDM_DRAW         -1          /* Draw submenu ID. */
#define IDM_BOX           2
#define IDM_ARC           3
#define IDM_LINE          4
#define IDM_PARC          5
#define IDM_XARC          6
#define IDM_PLINE         7
#define IDM_FILLET        8
#define IDM_SPLINE        9
```

You'll recognize the first defined statement as the menu resource ID used in the previous WinCreateStdWindow example. The next two sets of identifiers correspond to a submenu and the items contained in the submenu. For example, IDM_SERVICES identifies the Service submenu, while IDM_ERASE and IDM_QUIT identify selections on the Services submenu. By convention, the prefix IDM denotes submenu names and submenu items.

Both the menu resource script and application program use these IDM identifiers. You can define an IDM identifier as any integer number, but you can't assign the same number to two IDM identifiers. Note that IDM identifiers for the menu (or submenu, if you considered the menubar to be the top-level menu) are defined as -1. This approach allows you to consecutively number all menu item IDs, which can come in handy in the source code — that is, you can test for ID values based on known ranges. You can assign values other than -1 to the submenu names, but you should still consecutively number all menu items. The template upgrade program at the end of this chapter uses this alternative approach.

Before you create a menu resource script, you must be familiar with the language statements recognized by the Resource Compiler. Some statements are the same as those used by the C preprocessor such as **define** and **ifdef**. Others are unique to the Resource Compiler. Tables 6-3 through 6-5 describe the statements that you need to know to write a menu resource script.

Table 6-3: Menu Resource Script Statements

STATEMENT	SYNTAX
MENU	<menuID> <load option> <mem-option> <codepageID>
SUBMENU	<string> <cmd> <flags>
MENUITEM	<string> <cmd> <flags>

Table 6-4: Options to the MENU Statement

OPTION	DESCRIPTION	
<menuID>	The menu resource ID.	
<load option>	One of the following key words specifying load time:	
	PRELOAD	Loaded immediately.
	LOADONCALL	Loaded when called.
<mem-option>	One of the following key words specifying resource status:	
	FIXED	Attaches resource to single memory location.
	MOVEABLE	Allows movement of resource to compact memory when necessary.
	DISCARDABLE	Allows discarding of resource when it is no longer needed.
<codepageID>	Name or number that identifies a code page.	

The first step in creating a menu resource script is to include the header file that contains your menu identifiers. Additionally, you must include OS2.H, which contains definitions for some system menu identifiers. After this, use the Resource Compiler statements to set up your menu structure. You can scope items using either C-style French brackets or the Pascal **begin** and **end** statements. Use the MENU key word to set up the top-level menu. Then use the SUBMENU and MENUITEM statements to structure the submenus.

Table 6-5: Options to the SUBMENU and MENUITEM Statements

OPTION	DESCRIPTION
\<string\>	An ASCII string enclosed in quotation marks. The escape characters \t (tab) and \a (right justify text) are permitted. Quotation marks are inserted by prefixing a quotation mark with a quotation mark.
\<cmd\>	The IDM identifier, which is used as the command value in the WM_COMMAND message, and in the WM_SYSCOMMAND message when flags is set to MIS_SYSCOMMAND. The cmd value should be unique for each SUBMENU or MENUITEM key words.
\<flags\>	Menu options defined by the MIS_ and MIA_ identifiers. For information on these identifiers, refer to Tables 6-6 and 6-7.

The following example creates two submenus in keeping with those defined in the GRAPHICS.H header file:

```
/* GRAPHICS.RC — Menu resource script for

example graphics display program. */

#include <os2.h>
#include "graphics.h"

MENU ID_MAINMENU, PRELOAD
{
    SUBMENU "~Service", -1
    {
            MENUITEM "~Erase",IDM_ERASE, MIA_CHECKED
            MENUITEM "~Quit",SC_CLOSE, MIS_SYSCOMMAND
            MENUITEM "~Help",IDM_HELP, MIS_HELP
    }
    SUBMENU "~Draw", -1
    {
            MENUITEM "Gpi~Box",IDM_BOX, MIA_CHECKED
            MENUITEM "GpiFull~Arc",IDM_ARC
            MENUITEM "Gpi~Line",IDM_LINE
            MENUITEM "Gpi~PartialArc",IDM_PARC, MIS_BREAK
            MENUITEM "GpiPoin~tArc",   IDM_XARC
            MENUITEM "GpiPoll~yLine",  IDM_PLINE
            MENUITEM "GpiPollyFille~t",IDM_FILLET
            MENUITEM "GpiPoly~Spline",IDM_SPLINE
    }
}
```

This script creates a top-level menu and two submenus. From the user's viewpoint, the top-level menu itself does not have a name. It simply fills the action bar with the submenu names, Service and Draw. To select a submenu, the user either moves the cursor to the submenu name, or types the underscored character in the submenu name. The Presentation Manager handles the selection mechanics internally, but lets you specify the underscore character for a menu item. You do so by placing the tilde character (~) before the letter you want underscored.

When the user selects the Service submenu, a simple pop-up window appears. It consists of the MENUITEM strings, Erase and Help. The Presentation Manager automatically sizes the pop-up window based on the number of menu items.

The display for the Draw submenu is a little different than the Service submenu. For one thing, it has more menu items. But more importantly, it is divided into two boxes, each containing four menu items. The MIS_BREAK constant following the fourth MENUITEM statement in the Draw submenu code is responsible for this. MIS_BREAK identifies a menu item style. Table 6-6 describes the MIS style bits.

Table 6-6: Menu Item Style Bits

IDENTIFIER	BIT	DESCRIPTION
MIS_TEXT	0x0001	Text string.
MIS_BITMAP	0x0002	Bitmap.
MIS_SEPARATOR	0x0004	Includes separator bar.
MIS_OWNERDRAW	0x0008	Object drawn by program.
MIS_SUBMENU	0x0010	Invokes a submenu.
MIS_SYSCOMMAND	0x0040	Generates WM_SYSCOMMAND.
MIS_HELP	0x0080	Generates WM_HELP.
MIS_STATIC	0x0100	Disallows access to item.
MIS_BUTTONSEPARATOR	0x0200	Separator bar restricting cursor.
MIS_BREAK	0x0400	Starts another menu window.
MIS_BREAKSEPARATOR	0x0800	Draws separator for another menu.

To achieve combined effects using the MIS identifiers, you can OR them together. You cannot, however, combine MIS identifiers that fulfill the same type of function. The best way to learn about the combined effects of MIS identifiers is to experiment with them.

By default, the only MIS identifier that the Resource Compiler uses is MIS_STRING. Accordingly, you do not have to specify MIS_STRING. Of the other three identifiers, you might often resort to MIS_SEPARATOR, which draws a horizontal bar under the associated menu item. This is a useful tool when you want to separate a group of items, without displaying a second column. The MIS_BITMAP identifier lets you replace a pop-up menu with a bitmap denoting a menu item. Similarly, you can use the MIS_OWNERDRAW identifier to draw a custom graphic-style menu. If you use MIS_OWNERDRAW, you need to write handlers for the WM_MEASUREITEM and WM_DRAWITEM messages.

The identifiers that control column and row organization are straightforward. The MIS_BREAK and MIS_BREAKSEPARATOR identifiers simply break the current column or row. The difference between the two identifiers is the latter draws a bar before the new column or row.

The MIS_BUTTONSEPARATOR also draws a separator bar, but does not start a new row or column. Instead, it right justifies the associated menu item and prevents the user from selecting an item via the highlight bar. The user must press the underscored letter to select an item in the separated area. This is useful when you want to separate an item that has a different stature than other items on the same menu. For example, you can use this technique to isolate the help option on the main menu.

The message-oriented identifiers change the default message type. Normally, menus generate WM_COMMAND messages — and, for the most part, most of your code will be oriented toward WM_COMMAND messages. Specifying the MIS_SYSCOMMAND identifier, however, forces a WM_SYSCOMMAND message, instead of a WM_COMMAND message. As a result, you can allow the Presentation Manager to process the WM_SYSCOMMAND message automatically. In the previous menu resource script, the Quit option on the Service menu uses the MIS_SYSCOMMAND identifier to let the user exit the program without returning to the system menu. The MIS_HELP identifier simply changes the WM_COMMAND message to a WM_HELP message.

The system-oriented identifiers put diverse tasks in motion. The MIS_SUBMENU identifier simply invokes another submenu. This is the default action when you use the SUBMENU key word in the resource script. The MIS_STATIC identifier prohibits the user from accessing a menu item. This is handy if you're creating a demo program and want to limit access to parts of the program. The MIS_NODISMISS identifier causes the current menu to stay on-screen after the user selects the associated menu item. This is a useful tool when the selection of one menu item requires the immediate selection of another. MIS_NODISMISS also gives you the capability of customizing your menu system so that menus remain active an item has been selected.

One other set of identifiers gives assistance to the flags argument in the SUBMENU and MENUITEM statements. These are the MIA identifiers, which further enhance your control over the display characteristics of a menu. The MIA identifiers occupy the upper four positions in the 32-bit memory location (otherwise occupied by the MIS identifiers).

The MIA identifiers allow you to manipulate the attributes associated with each menu item. Table 6-7 lists and describes the MIA identifiers.

Table 6-7: Menu Item Attribute Bits

IDENTIFIER	BIT	DESCRIPTION
MIA_FRAMED	0x1000	Encloses a menu item in a box. Limited to top-level menus.
MIA_CHECKED	0x2000	Places a check at the left of a menu item. Limited to submenus.
MIA_DISABLED	0x4000	Disables a menu item and displays it in gray text.
MIA_HILITED	0x8000	Highlights a menu item in reverse video.

The MIA identifiers are handy interface tools. The MIA_FRAMED and MIA_HILITED identifiers draw the user's attention to the currently selected menu item. This is only possible when the menu remains onscreen. The Presentation Manager itself uses these formats.

The MIA_CHECKED identifier does what its name implies: places a check next to the currently active item. Conversely, the MIA_DISABLED identifier changes the text color of the menu item to gray when the item cannot possibly be accessed. The effects of both the MIA_CHECKED and MIA_DISABLED identifiers can be changed in the application program.

Handling Menu Messages

Each time the user selects a menu item, the Presentation Manager processes the action by converting it into a message. Internally, the Presentation Manager processes the message by sending it to the frame control procedure. From there, it follows the route common to all frame window messages: it is routed to the application message queue, and ultimately to the client window procedure.

Menu Messages Types

By default, a menu action produces a WM_COMMAND message. As noted in the previous section, you can specify that a menu action produce a WM_SYSCOMMAND or WM_HELP message instead of a WM_COM-MAND message. As a rule, most of the coding logic used for WM_COM-MAND messages also applies to these two other types.

Menus produce some specialized messages that you can use with the WM_COMMAND message. Three of these messages are WM_INIT-MENU, WM_MENUSELECT, and WM_MENUEND. It is not absolutely necessary for you to trap these messages, although they do supply helpful information on a pending WM_COMMAND menu message. One use of WM_MENUSELECT is to trigger some action associated with the user moving the highlight bar. Another is to preempt a WM_COMMAND message as demonstrated later in this section. More often than not, however, you will let the WinDefWindowProc function route the WM_INITMENU, WM_MENUSELECT, and WM_MENUEND for default processing.

Another set of messages devoted to menus are those prefixed with MM. Generally, these messages let you control menus dynamically. They work with the MIS and MIA identifiers and must be issued to the Presentation Manager by using the WinSendMsg and WinPostMsg functions.

With the MM messages, you can tailor your menu system so it constantly readjusts itself, based on previous menu selections. If your needs are not that great, you can delete and insert menu items, based on some event in the application program. Table 6-8 lists and describes the MM messages.

Table 6-8: Menu Messages

MESSAGE	VALUE	DESCRIPTION
MM_INSERTITEM	0x0180	Inserts a menu item.
MM_DELETEITEM	0x0181	Deletes a menu item.
MM_QUERYITEM	0x0182	Retrieves data about a menu item.
MM_SETITEM	0x0183	Sets item definition.
MM_QUERYITEMCOUNT	0x0184	Retrieves the number of menu items.
MM_STARTMENUMODE	0x0185	Starts menu selection.
MM_ENDMENUMODE	0x0186	Terminates menu selection.
MM_DISMISSMENU	0x0187	Removes the menu display.
MM_REMOVEITEM	0x0188	Removes a menu item.
MM_SELECTITEM	0x0189	Selects a menu item.
MM_QUERYSELITEMID	0x018A	Retrieves the ID of the selected item.
MM_QUERYITEMTEXT	0x018B	Copies menu string to a buffer.
MM_QUERYITEMTEXTLENGTH	0x018C	Retrieves the text length of an item.
MM_SETITEMHANDLE	0x018D	Sets the menu item handle.
MM_SETITEMTEXT	0x018E	Sets the menu item text.
MM_ITEMPOSITIONFROMID	0x018F	Retrieves position of menu item.
MM_ITEMIDFROMPOSITION	0x0190	Retrieves a menu item's ID.
MM_QUERYITEMATTR	0x0191	Retrieves attributes and style bits.
MM_SETITEMATTR	0x0192	Sets a menu item's attributes.
MM_ISITEMVALID	0x0193	Queries validity of a menu item.

Message Handling

Because the Presentation Manager uses WM_COMMAND messages for internal processing, you cannot rely merely on a **case** statement to trap a menu message in the application window. Instead, you must add a second **switch-case** block to your code, or simply use an **if** statement to complete the trap.

Before you reach this point, you must write some perfunctory code to obtain handles for both the frame and menu windows. Then, when you finish processing menu messages, you must do some extra preparatory work to set up the WM_PAINT message. These steps are not complex, just detailed. Here's a complete description of processing menu messages:

1. Set up a **switch-case** block to trap the WM_COMMAND message.

2. Obtain the frame window handle using WinQueryWindow.

3. Obtain the menu window handle using WinWindowFromID.

4. If necessary, include code to modify the menu. For example, you could signal the menu to relocate the check mark that denotes the active menu item.

5. Set up a **switch-case** block or **if** statement to trap only menu-related WM_COMMAND messages.

6. Optionally, you can store the menu ID in a local static variable. You will likely need this in later processing, such as in the WM_PAINT message.

7. Optionally, invalidate the application window, so you force a WM_PAINT message. This ensures that the results of the user's menu selection are displayed (if the item was display-oriented).

Most, if not all, of your menu code should be scoped inside the WM_COMMAND **case** statement. This is especially true if your menu messages can originate from menus with different parent windows. Alternatively, you can place code within a WM_MENUINIT handler to disable or enable menu items. Even with this technique, you must place the WinQueryWindow and WinWindowFromID functions inside the WM_COMMAND handler.

The only reason you need to obtain the parent window handle from WinQueryWindow is to use the handle as an argument in WinWindowFromID. You use this handle later to set up the WM_PAINT message. Here's the shorthand way to get the handle:

```
hwndMenu=WinWindowFromID(
          WinQueryWindow(hwnd,QW_PARENT,FALSE));
```

This code returns the handle to the menu window. The QW_PARENT constant specifies that you want the call to WinQueryWindow to return the parent window handle. As an aside, you can use similarly prefixed constants, such as QW_OWNER, to return the owner window handles, and QW_TOP to return the top-most child window handle.

After you obtain the menu window handle, it is time to start dissecting the WM_COMMAND message. You can use the SHORT1FROMMP and SHORT2FROMMP messages to obtain the parameter values contained in WM_COMMAND. To merely obtain the *cmd* value in *mp1 (low)*, you can use the COMMANDMSG macro (as described in Chapter 3). The COMMANDMSG macro requires the address of the currently active message, usually denoted as *msg*. The code looks like this:

```
COMMANDMSG(&msg)->cmd;
```

Armed with the COMMANDMSG macro, you can set up a secondary test of the WM_COMMAND message. If your menu does not retain profile characteristics — meaning a check mark and shaded options — you can immediately begin a series of **if** statements or an inner **switch-case** construction. If you want to alter the profile characteristics, now is the time to do it. The following code fragment relocates the check mark in the selected menu. The fragment is based on the GRAPHICS.RC menu script and assumes some static SHORT variables, including *sItemID*, *sCurrentID1*, and *sCurrentID2*.

```
sItemID = COMMANDMSG(&msg) -> cmd;
if(sItemID >= IDM_ERASE && sItemID <= IDM_QUIT)
{
   WinSendMsg(hwndMenu,MM_SETITEMATTR,
           MPFROM2SHORT(sCurrentID1,TRUE),
           MPFROM2SHORT(MIA_CHECKED,0));

   sCurrentID1=COMMANDMSG(&msg)->cmd;
```

```
WinSendMsg(hwndMenu,MM_SETITEMATTR,
        MPFROM2SHORT(sCurrentID1,TRUE),
        MPFROM2SHORT(MIA_CHECKED,MIA_CHECKED));
}

else if(sItemID >= IDM_BOX && sItemID <= IDM_SPLINE)
{
        WinSendMsg(hwndMenu,MM_SETITEMATTR,
                MPFROM2SHORT(sCurrentID2,TRUE),
                MPFROM2SHORT(MIA_CHECKED,0));

sCurrentID2=COMMANDMSG(&msg)->cmd;

WinSendMsg(hwndMenu,MM_SETITEMATTR,
        MPFROM2SHORT(sCurrentID2,TRUE),
        MPFROM2SHORT(MIA_CHECKED,MIA_CHECKED));
}
```

This code dissects the *mp1* and *mp2* values of the WM_COMMAND message and uses the WinSendMsg function to reset these values. (The second argument to the WinSendMsg function lets you return a message to the Presentation Manager). The previous example sends an MM_SET-ITEMATTR message to the menu control. This message dictates the contents of the USHORTs that you obtain by using the MPFROM2SHORT macro.

The USHORTs you must supply for *mp1* are the menu item ID (which is the equivalent of the *cmd* argument in the menu resource script), and a boolean flag. Setting the flag to TRUE tells the Presentation Manager to search for the menu item specified in the first part of *mp1*.

The USHORTs for *mp2* consist of the attribute mask and attribute data, both of which must be one of the MIA identifiers listed in Table 6-7. If you set the lower USHORT of *mp2* to 0, this instructs the internal menu code to remove the attribute specified in the upper USHORT of *mp2*. Setting both USHORTs to the same MIA identifier activates the specified attribute.

Ensure that you set the static variables corresponding to the current IDs of menu items (*sCurrentID1* and *sCurrentID2* in the example) to the IDs associated with the MIA_CHECKED identifier in the menu resource script. If you do not, this default check mark litters your menu for as long as it is displayed.

A NOTE ON SENDING MESSAGES

The WinSendMsg function does not return until the message contained in *msg* has been processed. Usually, this means the Presentation Manager processes the message by default, but you could set up your own code to handle the message. In cases where the window receiving the message belongs to the same thread, the window function is called immediately as a subroutine. If the window is of another thread or process, the Presentation Manager switches to the appropriate thread and calls the appropriate window function, passing the message to the window function. The message is not placed in the destination thread's queue.

Once you have singled out a menu item, you can process it using **if** statements or a **switch-case** construction. The following code fragment tests for some of the menu items from the GRAPHICS.RC code:

```
switch (COMMANDMSG (&msg) ->cmd)
{
    case IDM_ERASE:      /* Erase menu item. */
            .
            .

            break;

    case IDM_QUIT:       /* Quit menu item. */
            .
            .

            break;

    case IDM_LINE:       /* GpiLine menu item. */
            .
            .
            break;

        case IDM_SPLINE:      /* GpiPolySpline item. */
            .
            break;
}
```

If the actual execution of a menu item is going to exceed 1/10 of a second, you should not base all your processing in the handler for the menu command. Instead, you can create one or more threads to process the menu item action. Using multiple threads is explained in Chapter 16.

Menu Dedicated Messages

Using any of the three menu dedicated messages — WM_MENUSELECT, WM_INITMENU, and WM_MENUEND — gives you an added layer of control over the menu interface. Each time the user accesses the menu window and selects a menu item, the Presentation Manager generates these messages along with the standard WM_COMMAND message.

The WM_INITMENU and WM_MENUSELECT messages afford you an opportunity to make changes in the menu window before the WM_COMMAND message arrives in the message queue. The WM_INIT-MENU message arrives in the message queue the instant that the user invokes a menu. The WM_MENUSELECT message, on the other hand, only occurs if the user moves the highlight bar through the list of menu items.

The WM_INITMENU message is an imminently practical message, letting you tailor a menu based on previous events. For example, if a modem option on a menu cannot be used because the modem is busy, you can disable the option using WM_INITMENU. The Presentation Manager alerts the user of this by graying out the modem menu item. Here's the code to accomplish this:

```
case WM_INITMENU:

    sItemID = COMMANDMSG(&msg) -> cmd;
    if(sItemID = IDM_MODEM && modemFlag = TRUE)
    WinSendMsg(hwndMenu,MM_SETITEMATTR,
            MPFROM2SHORT(sItemID,TRUE),
            MPFROM2SHORT(MIA_DISABLED, MIA_DISABLED));
```

The practicality of the WM_MENUSELECT message is not immediately apparent. By convention, the user can select a menu item by moving the highlight bar and pressing Return, or by pressing the underscored character in the menu item. One obvious way to use WM_MENUSELECT is to incorporate it in a routine to display a help message associated with each menu item. Of course, if the user selects the menu item by pressing the underscored character, there is precious little time for displaying the help message.

A less obvious use of WM_MENUSELECT is to intercept a message for a menu item that is not available. Instead of graying out the modem option, as WM_INITMENU did in the previous example, you can intercept the message associated with the modem, then display a status box as shown in the following code:

```
case WM_MENUSELECT:

    sItemID = COMMANDMSG(&msg) -> cmd;
    if(sItemID = IDM_MODEM && modemFlag = TRUE)
            WinMessageBox(HWND_DESKTOP,hwnd,
                "Modem busy. Start monitor thread?",
                szCap,
                0, MB_OKCANCEL | MB_ICONQUESTION);
    else
    {
            /* Start modem thread (not implemented). */
    }

    WinSendMsg(hwndMenu,MM_ENDMENUMODE,
            MPFROM2SHORT(MIT_END,NULL),
            MPFROM2SHORT(NULL, NULL));
    break;
```

This code is only the tip of a multithread iceberg, but it demonstrates an important use of WM_MENUSELECT. By intercepting an otherwise invalid menu selection, the code lets the user start a monitor to signal when the modem becomes available. But what happens to the menu after this?

Sending the MM_ENDMENUMODE message to the Presentation Manager aborts the entire menu process. The MM_ENDMENUMODE message requires the menu item ID in the first USHORT of *mp1*. The remainder of the USHORTs for both *mp1* and *mp2* must be set to NULL.

The last menu dedicated message, WM_MENUEND, simply alerts you of the pending termination of the menu. Uses for this message are limited. One possible implementation is to trap the WM_MENUEND message, then restart the menu using MM_STARTMENUMODE. This message must be posted, not sent. The following code takes cares of posting the MM_STARTMENUMODE message:

```
WinPostMessage(hwnd, MM_STARTMENUMODE,
            MPFROM2SHORT(IDM_DRAW,MIS_NODISMISS),NULL));
```

Here, the first USHORT of *mp1* is set to IDM_DRAW, a valid submenu ID from the previous examples. The second USHORT of *mp1* is set to the MIS_NODISMISS identifier, which instructs the Presentation Manager to resume the menu display. You might want to use this type of code if some event related to a previous menu blocked the selected menu item. In such a case, you would likely display a message box before routing the user back to the menu.

System Messages

At times, you might want to integrate a WM_SYSCOMMAND message into your menu system. For example, if maximizing the current window happened to be important to a given window routine, you could integrate a system message to do this. An even more convenient use of WM_SYSCOM-MAND is to give the user a way to quit the application from a submenu. In the previous menu resource script, this was accomplished with the following line:

```
MENUITEM "~Quit", SC_CLOSE, MIS_SYSCOMMAND
```

Here, the MIS_SYSCOMMAND style bit tells the Presentation Manager to treat the Quit menu item as a WM_SYSCOMMAND message, instead of a WM_COMMAND message. This is fairly obvious. But what about this SC_CLOSE identifier?

The SC_CLOSE identifier is used internally by the Presentation Manager, which handles SC_CLOSE in much the same manner that the client window procedure handles the WM_CLOSE message. As you probably guessed, there are several SC identifiers that correspond to other Presentation Manager command messages. Table 6-9 lists and describes the SC identifiers.

Table 6-9: WM_SYSCOMMAND Values

IDENTIFIER	VALUE	DESCRIPTION
SC_SIZE	0x8000	Sends a message to the control registered as FID_SIZEBORDER.
SC_MOVE	0x8001	Sends a TBM_TRACKMOVE message to the control registered as FID_TITLEBAR.
SC_MINIMIZE	0x8002	Causes a FID_MINMAX control to minimize the frame window.
SC_MAXIMIZE	0x8003	Causes a FID_MINMAX control to maximize the frame window.
SC_CLOSE	0x8004	Causes the frame control procedure to issue a WM_CLOSE message (if the Close option is enabled on the system menu).
SC_NEXT	0x8005	Causes the active window status to cyle to the next window in the z-order.
SC_APPMENU	0x8006	Sends a MM_STARTMENUMODE message to the control registered as FID_APPMENU.
SC_SYSMENU	0x8007	Sends a MM_STARTMENUMODE message to the control registered as FID_SYSMENU.
SC_RESTORE	0x8008	Causes a FID_MINMAX control to restore the frame window to its previous state (if the Restore option is enabled on the system menu).
SC_NEXTFRAME	0x8009	Activates the next frame window in the z-order (if the frame window is a child of the desktop window).
SC_NEXTWINDOW	0x8010	Activates the next window that has the same order as the current window.
SC_TASKMANAGER	0x8011	Activates the Task Manager.

When you specify MIS_SYSCOMMAND for a menu item, the upper USHORT of *mp1* in the associated WM_SYSCOMMAND message contains the actual reference to the SC identifier. If necessary, you can trap an

SC identifier. Doing so, however, defeats the purpose of using it in the first place — that is, to allow the Presentation Manager to process the message by default, via the WinDefWindowProc function.

Help Messages

Help messages are handled identically to command messages. The only difference is that WM_HELP is the message identifier, instead of WM_COMMAND. In the previous menu resource script, the Help menu item was specified with the following code:

```
MENUITEM "~Help", IDM_HELP, MIS_HELP
```

The MIS_HELP style bit tells the Presentation Manager that this menu item must be treated as a WM_HELP message, instead of a WM_COM-MAND message.

When you trap a WM_HELP message, you need only extract the low USHORT from *mp1*, although both USHORTS in *mp2* contain useful information for receiving pushbutton and mouse related events. You should also note that a WM_HELP message occurs whenever the user presses the F1 key.

Menu Control

Control over menus does not end with the menu resource script. Instead, you can use the WinSendMsg function and several of the MM menu messages to modify menus on-the-fly. Using this technique, you can create new menus, add or delete items to existing menus, or add and delete items from the system menu. If your application calls for it — and if you are willing to build the support code — you can give users the capability to modify menus.

Dynamic Menus

Dynamically manipulating a menu is similar to controlling other windows in the Presentation Manager. The techniques used with WinSendMessage are also similar to those used to relocate check marks and gray out menu items. First you must obtain the handle for the menu you want to modify.

As already explained, this is accomplished using the WinWindowFromID function as in the following call:

```
hwndSubMenu=WinWindowFromID(
              WinQueryWindow(hwnd,QW_PARENT,FALSE));
```

After you obtain the menu window handle, you can use the Win-SendMessage function to add or delete items — that is, if you know about and have accessed the MENUITEM structure. The MENUITEM structure is defined as follows:

```
typedef struct _MENUITEM
{
    SHORT      iPosition;
    USHORT     afStyle;
    USHORT     id;
    HWND       hwndSubMenu;
    ULONG      item;
} MENUITEM
```

The *iPosition* field in the MENUITEM structure contains the position of an item in the menu. The first position is 0. The next field, *afStyle*, contains the menu item style, which corresponds to one of the MIS identifiers (see Table 6-6). The *id* field contains the menu item ID that you specify in the menu resource header file. The *hwndSubMenu* field, simply enough, contains the submenu handle, if any. And the *item* field, just as simply, identifies the menu item.

One interesting aspect of the MENUITEM structure is that it gives you a dynamic method of changing the data associated with a menu. This is especially useful if you want to give users the ability to tailor the format of an application's menus.

More to the point, you can reference the MENUITEM structure to insert and remove menu items. Again, this is accomplished using the Win-SendMessage function. When you specify MM_INSERTITEM in Win-SendMessage, however, you must use the MPFROMP macro instead of the MPFROM2SHORT macro.

The MPFROMP lets you fill the entire MENUITEM structure. The way you construct *p* is up to you. Usually, it is given a variable name of *mi* of type MENUITEM. The following code defines a new menu item ID, specifies text for a menu item, declares a variable associated with MENUITEM, and calls WinSendMessage to create a menu item called Copy on the Service submenu from the previous examples.

```
#define IDM_COPY
    .
    .
    .
static CHAR        *szMenuText = "Copy";
static MENUITEM    mi = {
            MIT_END,MIS_TEXT,IDM_COPY,NULL,NULL }
    .
    .
    .

    WinSendMessage(hwndSubMenu, MM_INSERTITEM,
            MPFROMP(mi);
            MPFROMP(szMenuText);
```

This call to WinSendMessage is clear-cut. It uses the data from *mi* to fill the MENUITEM structure. The only new element is the MIT_END identifier. This specifies that the new menu item is inserted at the end of the menu. The MIT_END flag is one of three MIT values. The other two flags specify errors. Table 6-10 lists these flags.

Table 6-10: Menu Item Flags

IDENTIFIER	DESCRIPTION
MIT_END	Tells menu control to add string to the end of the menu.
MIT_MEMERROR	Informs calling function of memory allocation error.
MID_ERROR	Informs calling function of error (other than MIT_MEMERROR).

Not So Dynamic Menus

In some applications, you might not want to load your entire menu system upon execution of the program. Perhaps your application invokes a series of modules, not all of which need to reside in memory. Or perhaps you merely want to let the user decide upon a given menu system.

You can have this type of flexibility if your application loads and creates it menus on a runtime basis. The functions that you use to do this are Win-LoadMenu and WinCreateMenu.

The WinLoadMenu function loads a menu either from an application program's .EXE file or a dynamic link library. If the latter is the case, Win-LoadMenu calls DosLoadResource to obtain a module handle to the resource. WinLoadMenu is defined as follows:

```
HWND WinLoadMenu(hwndFrame, hmod, idMenu)
HWND    hwndFrame;
HMODULE hmod
USHORT  idMenu
```

The first argument to WinLoadMenu is the owner and parent window handle — which, in the case of most menus you will create, is the frame window. The next argument is the menu resource id. Specifying NULL here tells WinLoadMenu that you want to load a menu resource from the application program's .EXE file. If you want to load the menu resource from a dynamic link library, you must specify the module handle to the DLL. The last argument to WinLoadMenu is the ID associated with the menu resource. You can either define this in the application program or in a header file included in the program.

Once you load a menu resource, you can use the WinCreateMenu function to activate your menus. WinCreateMenu is defined as follows:

```
HWND WinCreateMenu(hwndParent, lpmt)
HWND    hwndParent
PVOID   lpmt
```

As usual, the first argument to WinCreateMenu is the owner and parent window handle, which again is the frame window. The second argument, *lpmt*, names the menu resource in its binary format.

Keyboard Accelerators

Some users like the mouse. Other users hover above the keyboard whenever possible. For these folks, the Presentation Manager — as *Windows* did before it — offers a keyboard interface for most system related commands. What is more, the Presentation Manager's keyboard interface lets the user work in one window, yet issue keyboard-based commands to move the current focus to other windows in the z-order. You can even program key sequences that exist in their own right, unrelated to any given menu item.

The Presentation Manager lets you incorporate a keyboard interface into your application programs by using a keyboard accelerator table. A keyboard accelerator table is usually included in the same resource script in which you define your menus. It is automatically compiled by the Resource Compiler when you compile the menu resource.

Internally, the WinGetMsg function automatically translates keyboard accelerators. When WinGetMsg retrieves a message associated with a accelerator key, it converts the message into either a WM_COMMAND, WM_SYSCOMMAND, or WM_HELP message.

The *Application Style Guide* recommends that each menu item have a corresponding keyboard accelerator. Microsoft does not dissuade you from programming keyboard accelerators unrelated to menu items, although it does discourage any large scale use of this technique. Additionally, Microsoft recommends that you extend the use of system-dedicated key sequences to your application program. Refer to Chapter 1 for a complete listings of these sequences.

Creating an Accelerator Table

Creating a keyboard accelerator table is similar to defining menus in the resource script. By convention, the keyboard accelerator definitions occur after the menu definitions in the resource script. Note that you don't have to include any keyboard accelerator **define** statements in your header file.

The Resource Compiler recognizes a keyboard accelerator by the ACCELTABLE statement. The complete format used with the ACCELTABLE statement is as follows:

```
ACCELTABLE <id> <memory mgr flags> <codepageid>
{
    <keyval>, <cmd>, <acceloption, acceloption>
    .
    .
    .
}
```

In many applications, you need only specify the *id* argument for the ACCELTABLE statement. The *id* argument is simply the resource ID that you choose to give the accelerator table. The *memory mgr flags* argument specifies one of the following memory options:

- FIXED

- MOVEABLE

- DISCARDABLE

The last argument to the ACCELTABLE statement is *codepageid*. This argument simply specifies the name or number that identifies the associated code page.

For the actual key defintions, the arguments are similar in form to those used to define menu items. Table 6-11 defines each argument.

Table 6-11: Key Value Definition Options

FIELD	DESCRIPTION
keyval	A constant or quoted character representing the keyboard accelerator. The CHAR *acceloption* is assumed for quoted characters. A control character is specified for quoted character prefixed with the control character symbol ($\wedge$).
cmd	An identifier for use with the WM_COMMAND, WM_SYSCOMMAND, and WM_HELP messages. For menu item matching accelerators, the IDM identifier for the menu item should be specified here.
acceloption	A Resource Compiler key word defining the type of accelerator option. The VIRTUALKEY, SCANCODE, and CHAR key words denote the message type for the accelerator. The SHIFT, CONTROL, and ALT key words specify a shift state match.

Specifying different *acceloption* key words with one another can get tricky when the same key is referenced twice. The general rule is the more restrictive accelerator option should appear first in the accelerator table. For example, the definition for Ctrl-F11 should appear before the definition for F11.

Unlike menu resource statements, you do not have to block keyboard accelerators according to their corresponding menu. For readability's

sake, however, you should define accelerators in the order that corresponding menu items appear. Here's the keyboard accelerator version of
the GRAPHICS.RC example:

```
/* GRAPHICS.RC — Menu resource script with keyboard
accelerator for example program GRAPHICS.C. */
#include <os2.h>
#include "graphics.h"

MENU ID_MAINMENU, PRELOAD
{
    SUBMENU "~Service", -1
    {
        MENUITEM "~Erase\t^E",      IDM_ERASE, MIA_CHECKED
        MENUITEM "~Quit\tALT+F4", SC_CLOSE, MIS_SYSCOMMAND
        MENUITEM "~Help\tF1",         IDM_HELP, MIS_HELP
    }

    SUBMENU "~Draw", -1
    {
        MENUITEM "Gpi~Box\t^B",          IDM_BOX, MIA_CHECKED
        MENUITEM "GpiFull~Arc\t^A",      IDM_ARC
        MENUITEM "Gpi~Line\t^L",         IDM_LINE
        MENUITEM "Gpi~PartialArc\t^P", IDM_PARC, MIS_BREAK
        MENUITEM "GpiPoin~tArc\t^T",     IDM_XARC
        MENUITEM "GpiPoll~yLine\t^Y",    IDM_PLINE
        MENUITEM "GpiPolly~Fillet\t^F",     IDM_FILLET
        MENUITEM "GpiPoly~Spline\t^S", IDM_SPLINE
    }
}

ACCELTABLE ID_RESOURCE
{
    "^E",        IDM_ERASE
    VK_F4        SC_CLOSE   VIRTUALKEY, ALT
    VK_F1        IDM_HELP   VIRTUALKEY
    "^B"         IDM_BOX
    "^A"         IDM_ARC
    "^L"         IDM_LINE
    "^P"         IDM_PARC
    "^T"         IDM_XAR
    "^Y"         IDM_PLINE
    "^F"         IDM_FILLET
    "^S"         IDM_SPLINE
}
```

No additional steps are required to compile a resource script that has a keyboard accelerator table. For your application program to recognize the table, you must include the FCF_ACCELTABLE frame style identifier in the second argument to WinCreateStdWindow. This is required even though you have already specified the FCF_MENU identifier. Recall that menus and keyboard accelerators are, in fact, different resources — thus, the necessity for specifying separate frame style identifiers.

Template Upgrade

Menus are an important part of any template. The following upgrade to the template program begun in Chapter 4 includes three menus that provide the framework for file management, editing, and system-related routines. Because the routines are not implemented for the File and Edit menus, the program displays a message box to inform you of this. The Resume and Close options on the Exit menu are functional, however.

```
/* TMPL2.C  (Upgrade to Template Program in Chapter 4) */

#define INCL_PM

#include <os2.h>
#include <string.h>
#include "tmpl2.h"


MRESULT EXPENTRY TemplateWndProc(HWND,USHORT,MPARAM,MPARAM);
VOID DisplayMsg(HWND,SHORT);

HAB     hab;
HMQ     hmq;
HWND    hwndFrame, hwndTemplate;

int main(void)
{

static CHAR szClass[9] = "Template";
static CHAR szTitleBar[15] = "Blank Template";
ULONG ctlData = FCF_TITLEBAR | FCF_SYSMENU | FCF_SIZEBORDER
                | FCF_MINMAX | FCF_MENU | FCF_ACCELTABLE;

USHORT  fSwap = SWP_ACTIVATE | SWP_SIZE | SWP_MOVE | SWP_SHOW;
PID     pid;
```

```
TID       tid;
QMSG      qmsg;
SWCNTRL swctl;


hab = WinInitialize(NULL);
hmq = WinCreateMsgQueue(hab, 0);
WinRegisterClass(hab, szClass,
                    TemplateWndProc, CS_SIZEREDRAW, 0L);

hwndFrame = WinCreateStdWindow(
                            HWND_DESKTOP,
                            WS_VISIBLE,
                            &ctlData,
                            szClass,
                            szTitleBar,
                            0L,
                            NULL,
                            ID_MENURES,
                            &hwndTemplate);

WinSetWindowPos(hwndFrame, HWND_TOP, 50, 50,
                250, 250, fSwap);

WinQueryWindowProcess(hwndFrame, &pid, &tid);

swctl.hwnd = hwndFrame;
swctl.hwndIcon = NULL;
swctl.hprog = NULL;
swctl.idProcess = pid;
swctl.idSession = NULL;
swctl.uchVisibility = SWL_VISIBLE;
swctl.fbJump = SWL_JUMPABLE;
strcpy(swctl.szSwtitle, "Template Demo 2");

WinAddSwitchEntry(&swctl);

while(WinGetMsg(hab, &qmsg, NULL, 0, 0))
            WinDispatchMsg(hab,&qmsg);

WinDestroyWindow(hwndFrame);
WinDestroyMsgQueue(hmq);
WinTerminate(hab);

return(0);
}
```

```
MRESULT EXPENTRY TemplateWndProc(hwnd, msg, mp1, mp2)
HWND   hwnd;
USHORT msg;
MPARAM mp1, mp2;
{
    HPS hps;

    switch (msg)
        {
        case WM_ERASEBACKGROUND:
            return(TRUE);

        /* case WM_PAINT:
            hps = WinBeginPaint(hwnd, NULL, NULL);
            WinEndPaint(hps) ;
            return(NULL);  */

        case WM_COMMAND:
            switch((COMMANDMSG(&msg)->cmd))
                {
                case IDM_FILENEW:
                    DisplayMsg(hwnd, IDM_FILENEW - 410);
                    return(NULL);

                case IDM_FILEOPEN:
                    DisplayMsg(hwnd, IDM_FILEOPEN - 410);
                    return(NULL);

                case IDM_FILESAVE:
                    DisplayMsg(hwnd, IDM_FILESAVE - 410);
                    return(NULL);

                case IDM_FILESAVEAS:
                    DisplayMsg(hwnd,
                             IDM_FILESAVEAS - 410);
                    return(NULL);

                case IDM_FILEDIRECTORY:
                    DisplayMsg(hwnd,
                             IDM_FILEDIRECTORY - 410);
                    return(NULL);

                case IDM_EDITRESTORE:
                    DisplayMsg(hwnd,
                             IDM_EDITRESTORE - 410);
                    return(NULL);
```

```
                  case IDM_EDITCUT:
                        DisplayMsg(hwnd, IDM_EDITCUT - 410);
                        return(NULL);

                  case IDM_EDITCOPY:
                        DisplayMsg(hwnd, IDM_EDITCOPY - 410);
                        return(NULL);

                  case IDM_EDITPASTE:
                        DisplayMsg(hwnd, IDM_EDITPASTE - 410);
                        return(NULL);

                  case IDM_EDITCLEAR:
                        DisplayMsg(hwnd, IDM_EDITCLEAR - 410);
                        return(NULL);

                  case IDM_EXITRESUME:
                        return(NULL);

                  case IDM_EXITEXIT:
                        if(MBID_YES == WinMessageBox(
                           HWND_DESKTOP, hwnd,
                           "You are about to quit the program. \n"
                           "Are you sure you want to do this?",
                           "Closing Message",
                           0, MB_YESNOCANCEL | MB_DEFBUTTON3
                           | MB_ICONQUESTION | MB_MOVEABLE))
                        {
                           WinPostMsg(
                                    hwndFrame, WM_QUIT, 0L, 0L);
                           break;
                        }
                        else
                           return(NULL);

                  }
            }

      return WinDefWindowProc(hwnd, msg, mp1, mp2);
}


VOID DisplayMsg(hwnd, sMenuValue)
HWND hwnd;
SHORT sMenuValue;
{
```

```
    static char *szMenu[] = { "File", "Open", "Save", "Save as",
                                "Directory", "Restore", "Cut",
                                "Copy", "Paste", "Clear" };

    WinMessageBox(HWND_DESKTOP, hwnd,
                "This menu item is not yet implemented.",
                szMenu[sMenuValue],
                0, MB_YESNOCANCEL | MB_DEFBUTTON3
                | MB_ICONQUESTION | MB_MOVEABLE);
}
```

CHAPTER 7

CONTROL WINDOWS

You've already seen how to create the frame window. Creating a control window is not much different. In fact, the frame window is considered a control window in its own right (or slight, if you happen to favor the frame window), so you're already accustomed to control windows. The message system used by control windows is also similar in methodology to that used by the frame control procedure.

Actually, your familiarity with control windows doesn't end with the frame window. That is, whenever the Presentation Manager creates the frame window, you can have it create its usual set of support windows — the border size window, titlebar, system menu, scrollbars, and minimize and maximize icons. All of these are also considered control windows. And by the way, the menus that you create specifically for an application also get the rubric of control windows.

This is only the tip of the control window iceberg. In addition to these system-oriented controls, the Presentation Manager lets you create control windows that display inside the client area window, including such windows as pushbuttons, listboxes and entry-field controls. Then, to tie a neat knot on the subject of control windows, the Presentation Manager gives you an automatic form of a control window with its own special procedure — namely, the dialog box, which is described in Chapter 8.

One of the major differences between dialog boxes and the control windows discussed in this chapter is dialog boxes require an application-based window procedure. Whether you think this is a benefit, or a detriment, depends on how you feel about subclassing window procedures yourself. Needless to say, the automatic window procedures associated with the control windows described in this chapter make programming them a little bit easier. On the other hand, dialog boxes provide extensive capabilities, without which you might have a much harder time programming the Presentation Manager.

Control Window Basics

Although programming the Presentation Manager is often an exercise in conformity, control windows give you a way to personalize your programs. By placing one or more control windows directly in your application's main screen, you can make your program stand out, yet still observe the tenets of the *Application Style Guide*.

Internally, an event such as clicking the mouse on an pushbutton control window produces one of several messages, including instances of the WM_COMMAND message. As usual, the application window function processes the message with a **switch-case** construction, or with some well-placed **if** statements. As with other messages, you can choose to ignore the messages generated by a control window. You guessed it: the WinDefWindowProc procedure handles any unprocessed messages.

As was the case with menus, the Presentation Manager provides a set of messages that you can send to a control window with the WinSendMsg function. You can use these messages to set control window attributes, or even to adjust a scrollbar that you can optionally designate for a control window. The Presentation Manager also lets you redefine the screen position and dimensions of a control window. This is accomplished using the WinSetWindowPosition function.

The WinCreateWindow Function

The process of creating a control window is similar to that used to create the frame window. The major difference is that the control window inherits properties of the frame window, such as the space it occupies on the screen. Because of this relationship — and because you need to pay more attention to detail such as window positioning — the control window is really the archetypal child window.

How does the Presentation Manager give birth to this special child? Not surprisingly, the seed is planted in the WinCreateStdWindow call when you create the frame window. The frame window, after all, is usually both the parent and owner of a control window. The actual function you use to create a control window is WinCreateWindow, which looks a lot like WinCreateStdWindow, both at first glance and when you get to know it well. Without further ado, here's the definition for WinCreateWindow:

```
HWND WinCreateWindow(hwndParent, pszClass, pszName,
                     flStyle, x, y, cx, cy,
                     hwndOwner,hwndInsBehind,
                     id, pCtlData, pPresParams)
HWND hwndParent;
PSZ pszClass, pszName;
ULONG flStyle;
SHORT x, y, cx, cy;
HWND hwndOwner, hwndInsBehind;
USHORT id;
PVOID pCtlData, pPresParams;
```

As you can see, the WinCreateWindow function takes several more arguments than the WinCreateStdWindow function. The first argument, as usual, is the parent window handle. The difference is that while the frame window's parent is the desktop, a control window's parent is the window in which it is created. In most cases, this is the client window, which is returned in the last argument to WinCreateStdWindow.

The second argument to WinCreateWindow specifies the class type for the control window. Here, you have the option of creating your own class of control window by pre-registering a private class type through the WinRegisterClass function. To do this, you can declare a character string as a global variable, then reference the string in both the second argument to WinRegisterClass and also in the second argument to WinCreateWindow. Alternatively, you can specify one of several predefined window classes. These classes are denoted by a WC prefix and defined in Table 7-1. Although you might develop special reasons for using any or all of the window classes in Table 7-1, only five of the class types are commonly used in Presentation Manager programs. These types are:

- WC_BUTTON

- WC_ENTRYFIELD

- WC_LISTBOX

- WC_SCROLLBAR

- WC_STATIC

Unlike many other identifiers used in the Presentation Manager, you can't combine window class identifiers — the reason being that the identifier specifies a unique type of window, usually dedicated to a given situation. Note also that the Presentation Manager casts the ULONG value of each window class to type PSZ.

Table 7-1: Predefined Window Classes

CLASS	BIT	DESCRIPTION
WC_FRAME	(PSZ) 0xFFFF0001L	Standard frame controls.
WC_BUTTON	(PSZ) 0xFFFF0003L	Pushbutton window.
WC_MENU	(PSZ) 0xFFFF0004L	System and custom menus.
WC_STATIC	(PSZ) 0xFFFF0005L	Static text and rectangle.
WC_ENTRYFIELD	(PSZ) 0xFFFF0006L	Text entry window.
WC_LISTBOX	(PSZ) 0xFFFF0007L	Data listbox window.
WC_SCROLLBAR	(PSZ) 0xFFFF0008L	Scrollbar controls.
WC_TITLEBAR	(PSZ) 0xfFFFF00009L	Titlebar (window).

The next argument, *pszName*, specifies a name for the control window. You declare *pszName* as a character string in the application function that contains WinCreateWindow. Unless you plan on having varying names, you can define the string at the same time you declare it. The Presentation Manager automatically displays the text inside the control window. If you do not want a name for the control window, set the *pszName* argument to NULL.

The *flStyle* argument is the heart of the WinCreateWindow function. It specifies the style of the control window and informs the Presentation

Manager as to exactly how the control window should appear. Whatever style you select, it must be ORed with the WS_VISIBLE style bit. If you neglect to do this, the Presentation Manager still creates the control window. The only problem is you won't be able to see it.

The style of control window that you select depends on the window class you specify in the second argument to WinCreateWindow. For example, to create a button control window, you must specify the WC_BUTTON window style. In the same manner, to create a scrollbar control, you must select the WC_SCROLLBAR style; and to create a listbox control, you must select the WC_LISTBOX style. To give a control window combined features, you can OR any of the following styles:

- WS_VISIBLE
- WS_BUTTON
- WS_STATIC
- WS_ENTRYFIELD
- WS_LISTBOX
- WS_SCROLLBAR
- WS_TITLEBAR

This technique lets you combine window appearance controls, such as a titlebar or sizing borders. More importantly, it lets you combine text controls with buttons and listboxes. To get formatted text controls with automatic radio buttons, for example, you must first include WC_STATIC and WC_BUTTON in the second argument to WinCreateWindow, then specify the style constant for radio buttons in the third argument of WinCreate-Window. (Style constants are explained in subsequent sections of this chapter.)

The next four arguments to the WinCreateWindow function — x, y, cx, and cy — specify the dimensions. The default x and y coordinates are zero (corresponding to the lower left-hand corner of the parent window). The cx and cy arguments specify the width and height of the control box, respectively.

The *hwndOwner* argument (the eighth argument to WinCreateWindow), specifies which window processes control messages from the control window. This window is referred to as the owner window. It is usually the same window as the parent window, which is to say, the client area window. You can, however, reroute control window messages to a different window merely by specifying that window's handle in *hwndOwner*.

The *hwndInsBehind* argument physically associates the control window with other control windows (or sibling windows). If you specify HWND_TOP, the Presentation Manager places the control window on top of all its sibling windows. If you specify HWND_BOTTOM, the control window appears behind all its sibling windows.

You can specify a handle to a sibling window, in which case the Presentation Manager places the control window directly behind the sibling. One predefined constant you never want to specify is HWND_DESKTOP. This would place the control window behind the frame window, rendering it useless.

The next argument, *id*, assigns an ID to the control window. It is used to identify the control when you handle the WM message related to the control. A typical handler — at least for the WM_CONTROL message — looks like this:

```
case WM_CONTROL:
        id = SHORT1FROMMP(mp1);
        if(id >= 0 || id <= 52)

        .
        .
        .

        return(NULL);
```

You can use any number between 0 and 32,768 for control window IDs, but it's good practice to consecutively number control windows beginning with 0. You can either predefine control window IDs as is necessary for menu windows, or dynamically assign a value to a control window.

The last two arguments to WinCreateWindow are system oriented. The *pCtlData* passes data derived from the WM_CREATE message, but is typically set to NULL. On the other hand, you must set the *pPresParams* to NULL because it is a reserved field.

Button Controls

The logic behind button control windows is ubiquitous to Presentation Manager applications. Simply put, the user accepts or rejects some action presented on the screen by pressing the correct button.

What happens next depends on the type of button control window in use. The Presentation Manager makes eight basic button styles available to you. Some, in fact, do not produce different types of buttons, although they do specify variations in the user interface. Table 7-2 describes the various button styles. As with other Presentation Manager controls, button controls communicate with the application function via messages. Only BS_PUSHBUTTON generates a WM_COMMAND message, however.

Table 7-2: Button Control Window Styles

STYLE	VALUE	DESCRIPTION
BS_PUSHBUTTON	0x0000L	Standard pushbutton control containing an identifying string. Generates a WM_COMMAND message.
BS_CHECKBOX	0x0001L	Tells if the current item is selected with check mark. Generates a WM_CONTROL message.
BS_AUTOCHECKBOX	0x0002L	Automatically toggles state of check box when user clicks on it. Generates a WM_CONTROL message.
BS_RADIOBUTTON	0x0003L	Displays selected and unselected buttons. The owner must update check marks. Generates a WM_CONTROL message.
BS_AUTORADIOBUTTON	0x0004L	Automatically displays selection state of buttons in a group. Generates a WM_CONTROL message.
BS_3STATE	0x0005L	Allows three button types: selected, unselected, and indeterminate. Generates a WM_CONTROL message.
BS_AUTO3STATE	0x0006L	Automatically toggles selected, unselected, and indeterminate buttons. Generates a WM_CONTROL message.
BS_USERBUTTON	0x0007L	Generates a WM_CONTROL message.

Pushbutton Controls

Trapping the WM_COMMAND message generated by a BS_PUSHBUTTON control can involve an additional, albeit simple, layer of processing. This additional layer, which stems from the necessity to distinguish the BS_PUSHBUTTON source, simply means extracting *mp2 (low)* in the WM_COMMAND message. The following line of code accomplishes this.

```
cmdsrc=SHORT1FROMMP(mp2);
```

The *cmdsrc* variable gets its name from the identifier that the macro extracts, namely, one of the four command source (CMDSRC) identifiers used to distinguish WM_COMMAND messages. Table 7-3 lists these identifiers which, for pushbutton controls, are always contained in the low word of *mp2*.

Table 7-3: Command Source Identifiers

IDENTIFIER	VALUE	DESCRIPTION
CMDSRC_PUSHBUTTON	1	Pushbutton control source.
CMDSRC_MENU	2	Menu control source.
CMDSRC_ACCELERATOR	3	Accelerator control source.
CMDSRC_OTHER	0	Additional command source.

Depending on how you structure your code, you might not have to trap the CMDSRC identifier. If, for example, you assign unique IDs to each pushbutton control — that is, unique even among IDs for menus, keyboard accelerators and any IDs associated with the CMDSRC_OTHER source — you could process pushbutton WM_COMMAND messages with a single-layered, **switch-case** construction.

Ultimately, the low word of *mp1* lets you identify the currently active pushbutton. The low word of *mp1* contains the button control ID. You can use either the COMMANDMSG macro or the SHORT1FROMMP macro to trap the ID. The following example shows the appropriate message processing structure (assuming the need to trap the CMDSRC source).

```
case WM_COMMAND:
    if((cmdsrc=SHORT1FROMMP(mp2))==CMDSRC_PUSHBUTTON)
            switch(COMMANDMSG(&msg) -> cmd)
    {
            case BUTTON_1:
                    break;
                    .
            case BUTTON_2;
                    break;
    }
```

The other *mp1* parameter, the high word, is set to 0 and has no function related to processing the WM_COMMAND message. The parameters in *mp2* do contain additional information. The low word of *mp2* indicates whether the user selected the button via the mouse or the keyboard. If the keyboard was used, *mp2 (low)* is set to 0. All other values indicate the mouse was used. With the BS_PUSHBUTTON style, you can use complementary styles to create the pushbutton. You do this by ORing any of five possible styles when you specify BS_PUSHBUTTON in the fourth argument to WinCreateWindow. Table 7-4 lists these styles.

Table 7-4: Complimentary Pushbutton Styles

STYLE	BIT	DESCRIPTION
BS_HELP	0x0100L	Posts a WM_HELP message instead of either a WM_COMMAND message or a WM_SYS-COMMAND message.
BS_SYSCOMMAND	0x0200L	Posts a WM_SYSCOMMAND message instead of a WM_COMMAND message.
BS_DEFAULT	0x0400L	Draws a default pushbutton.
BS_NOMOUSEFOCUS	0x0800L	Does not set the mouse (pointer) focus when the user clicks the mouse button.
BS_NOBORDER	0x1000L	Draws button without frame, giving the impression of static text.

Obviously, some of these complimentary styles are mutually exclusive. For example, you cannot (nor would you want to) OR a BS_HELP message with a BS_SYSCOMMAND; nor can you OR a BS_DEFAULT message with a BS_NOBORDER message (attempting to OR either of these combinations could produce unpredictable results). In most cases, you will find that the BS_PUSHBUTTON style serves the purpose. The following example creates four BS_PUSHBUTTON controls to change window color.

```
/* PUSHBUTN.C (Example pushbutton program) */

#define INCL_WIN
#include <os2.h>
#include <stddef.h>

MRESULT EXPENTRY ButtonWndProc(HWND, USHORT, MPARAM, MPARAM);

int main(void)
{
static CHAR szClass[] = "pushbutn";
HAB     hab;
HMQ     hmq;
HWND    hwndFrame, hwndClient;
QMSG    qmsg;
ULONG   ctlData = FCF_TITLEBAR | FCF_SYSMENU | FCF_MINMAX
                | FCF_SIZEBORDER | FCF_SHELLPOSITION
                | FCF_TASKLIST;


hab = WinInitialize(NULL);
hmq = WinCreateMsgQueue(hab, 0);

WinRegisterClass(hab, szClass,
                        ButtonWndProc, CS_SIZEREDRAW, 0);

hwndFrame = WinCreateStdWindow(
                HWND_DESKTOP,
                WS_VISIBLE,
                &ctlData,
                szClass,
                NULL,
                0L,
                NULL,
                0,
                &hwndClient);
```

```
while(WinGetMsg(hab, &qmsg, NULL, 0, 0))
WinDispatchMsg(hab, &qmsg);

WinDestroyWindow(hwndFrame);
WinDestroyMsgQueue(hmq);
WinTerminate(hab);

return(0);
}

MRESULT EXPENTRY ButtonWndProc(hwnd, msg, mp1, mp2)
HWND hwnd;
USHORT msg;
MPARAM mp1, mp2;
   {
   SHORT        i, xPos;
   RECTL        rcl;
   HPS          hps;
   static CHAR  *szLabel[] =
                   { "Red", "Blue", "Green", "Yellow" };
   static HWND  hwndPush[4];
   static LONG  lColor = CLR_DEFAULT;

   switch(msg)
      {
      case WM_CREATE :

             xPos = -88;      /* arbitrary offset */

             for(i=0; i<4; i++)
                 hwndPush[i] = WinCreateWindow(
                    hwnd,            /* Parent window. */
                    WC_BUTTON,       /* Class identifier. */
                    szLabel[i],      /* Button label. */
                    WS_VISIBLE       /* Window style. */
                    | BS_PUSHBUTTON,
                    xPos += 110,     /* Horizontal position. */
                    10,              /* Vertical position. */
                    100,             /* Width . */
                    40,              /* Height. */
                    hwnd,            /* Owner window. */
                    HWND_TOP,        /* Z-order placement. */
                    i,               /* Button ID. */
                    NULL,            /* Control data. */
                    NULL);           /* Reserved. */
             return(FALSE);
```

```
case WM_COMMAND:

    WinInvalidateRect(hwnd, NULL, TRUE);

    switch(COMMANDMSG(&msg)->cmd)
      {
        case 0:
          lColor = CLR_RED;
          break;

        case 1:
          lColor = CLR_BLUE;
          break;

        case 2:
          lColor = CLR_GREEN;
          break;

        case 3:
          lColor = CLR_YELLOW;
          break;
      }

    return(NULL);

case WM_PAINT:
    hps = WinBeginPaint(hwnd, NULL, NULL);
    WinQueryWindowRect(hwnd, &rcl);
    WinFillRect(hps, &rcl, lColor);
    WinEndPaint(hps);
    return(NULL);

case WM_ERASEBACKGROUND:
    return(TRUE);
  }
return WinDefWindowProc(hwnd, msg, mp1, mp2);
}
```

Radio Button Controls

A radio button gets its name from old-fashioned car radios that used mechanical pushbuttons for station selection. Selecting a radio button — be it in the Presentation Manager or a '57 Chevy — makes the chosen button the active button until another button is selected. In other words, if you like the station, leave the button selected.

To create radio buttons in a child window, you must specify the BS_RADIOBUTTON style in the fourth argument to WinCreateWindow. Although the Presentation Manager makes another radio button style available, BS_AUTORADIOBUTTON, it is reserved for use with dialog boxes (see Chapter 8). The BS_RADIOBUTTON style cannot be ORed with any other button styles.

Not only do radio buttons have a different interface style than do push-buttons, the BS_RADIOBUTTON style also requires different handling than the BS_PUSHBUTTON style. The reason for this is BS_RADIOBUT-TON generates a WM_CONTROL message instead of a WM_COMMAND message. The effect of this is minimal: you lose the capability of default WM_COMMAND processing, but are still able to trap, process, and perform some action based on a radio button message.

Unlike pushbutton controls, radio buttons have no command source parameter (removing one layer of code from the trapping mechanism). To process a BS_RADIOBUTTON, you need only trap the low word from *mp1*. The extracted value, of course, is the radio button ID. Note, however, that you cannot use the COMMANDMSG macro to extract the ID. You must instead use the SHORT1FROMMP macro as in the following:

```
id=SHORT1FROMMP(mp1);
```

Once you have identified the radio button, you might want to determine how the user selected the radio button. This is especially useful if you have implemented special routines for radio button actions that result from double-clicking the mouse. The information is stored in the high word of *mp1*. Extracting the high word results in either a value of BN_CLICKED or BN_DBLCLICKED. The BN prefix stands for button notification, while the messages themselves are self-explanatory.

The *mp2* parameter to BS_RADIOBUTTON contains the control window handle in the high word. This represents an alternative way to identify a given radio button, but the contents of *mp2 (high)* in the WM_CONTROL message vary, depending on the source. As a result, for purposes of code standardization, it is better to identify a radio button through *mp1 (low)*. Note also that the low word of *mp2* does not contain any useful information for radio button processing.

Button Messages

As with menus, processing button controls can be a two-way conversation. Many times you will want to effect some change to the button interface. For example, you might want to highlight the previously selected button. To do this, you use the WinSendMsg function to send a BM message to the button control window. Quite simply, the BM prefix stands for button message. Table 7-5 describes the BM messages.

Table 7-5: Application Generated Button Messages

STYLE	BIT	DESCRIPTION
BM_CLICK	0x0120	Simulates a mouse click on the specified button.
BM_QUERYCHECKINDEX	0x0121	Determines the zero-based index of a checked radio button.
BM_QUERYHILITE	0x0122	Determines whether a button is highlighted.
BM_SETHILITE	0x0123	Highlights the specified button.
BM_QUERYCHECK	0x0124	Determines whether a button is checked.
BM_SETCHECK	0x0125	Associates a check with the specified button.
BM_SETDEFAULT	0x0126	Sets the default state of the specified button.

Using WinSendMsg to process BM messages is much more concise than using it to send menu messages. Refer to Chapter 3 for a lengthy explanation of WinSendMsg. To supply WinSendMsg with a handle to the button control window, you can either save the handle when you create the button control, or use the WinWindowFromID function. If you are using several button controls, which is probably the case, the easiest way to maintain their handles is in an array of type HWND. The following code represents a call to WinSendMsg for the purpose of sending a BM message.

```
WinSendMsg(hwndRadio[sValue],
        BM_SETCHECK, MPFROMSHORT(1), NULL);
```

The following program example uses WinSendMsg at several key points in its handling of radio button controls. The program, which creates some 52 radio buttons, displays a system value based on the radio button chosen.

```
/* RADIOBUT.C (Example radio button program) */
#define INCL_PM
#include <os2.h>
#include <stdio.h>

MRESULT EXPENTRY RadioWndProc(HWND,USHORT,MPARAM,MPARAM);
MRESULT EXPENTRY FrameSubProc(HWND,USHORT,MPARAM,MPARAM);

HAB hab;
HMQ hmq;
HWND hwndMaximum;
HWND hwndFrame;
HWND hwndMenu;
PFNWP FrameControlProc;

int main(void)
{

QMSG qmsg;
HWND hwndSystemMenu;
SHORT idSystemMenu;
MENUITEM mi;
static CHAR szClass[] = "Radio";

ULONG ctldata = FCF_TITLEBAR | FCF_SYSMENU | FCF_MINMAX
                | FCF_SIZEBORDER | FCF_SHELLPOSITION
                | FCF_TASKLIST;

hab = WinInitialize(NULL);
hmq = WinCreateMsgQueue(hab, 0);
WinRegisterClass(hab, szClass, RadioWndProc,
                 CS_SIZEREDRAW, 0);

hwndFrame = WinCreateStdWindow(
                     HWND_DESKTOP,
                     0L,
                     &ctldata,
                     szClass,
                     NULL,
                     0L,
                     NULL,
```

```
                                        0,
                                        &hwndMaximum);

       hwndSystemMenu = WinWindowFromID(hwndFrame, FID_SYSMENU);
       idSystemMenu = (SHORT)WinSendMsg(hwndSystemMenu,
                               MM_ITEMIDFROMPOSITION, 0L, 0L);
       WinSendMsg(hwndSystemMenu, MM_QUERYITEM,
                               MPFROM2SHORT(idSystemMenu, FALSE),
                               (MPARAM)(PMENUITEM)&mi);
       hwndMenu = mi.hwndSubMenu;
       FrameControlProc = WinSubclassWindow(
                               hwndFrame, FrameSubProc);
       WinSetWindowPos(hwndFrame, NULL, 50, 50, 50, 50,
                               SWP_SIZE | SWP_MOVE
                               | SWP_SHOW | SWP_MAXIMIZE);

       while(WinGetMsg(hab, &qmsg, NULL, 0, 0))
                       WinDispatchMsg(hab, &qmsg);

       WinDestroyWindow(hwndFrame);
       WinDestroyMsgQueue(hmq);
       WinTerminate(hab);
       }

       MRESULT EXPENTRY RadioWndProc(hwnd, msg, mp1, mp2)
       HWND  hwnd;
       USHORT msg;
       MPARAM mp1;
       MPARAM mp2;
       {

         SHORT i, j=1, xPos, yPos, id;
         static SHORT sValue = 0;
         RECTL rcl, rclBox;
         HPS hps;
         CHAR szBuffer[80];
         static HWND hwndRadio[52];

         static CHAR *szLabel[] = {
           "SV_SWAPBUTTON", "SV_DBLCLKTIME", "SV_CXDBLCLK",
           "SV_CYDBLCLK", "SV_CXSIZEBORDER", "SV_CYSIZEBORDER",
           "SV_ALARM", "SV_RESERVED*", "SV_RESERVED*",
           "SV_CURSORRATE", "SV_FIRSTSCROLLRATE", "SV_SCROLLRATE",
           "SV_NUMBEREDLISTS", "SV_WARNINGFREQ", "SV_NOTEFREQ",
           "SV_ERRORFREQ", "SV_WARNINGDURATION", "SV_NOTEDURATION",
           "SV_ERRORDURATION", "SV_RESERVED*", "SV_CXSCREEN",
           "SV_CYSCREEN", "SV_CXVSCROLL", "SV_CYHSCROLL",
```

```
"SV_CYVSCROLLARROW", "SV_CXHSCROLLARROW", "SV_CXBORDER",
"SV_CYBORDER", "SV_CXDLGFRAME", "SV_CYDLGFRAME",
"SV_CYTITLEBAR", "SV_CYVSLIDER", "SV_CXHSLIDER",
"SV_CXMINMAXBUTTON", "SV_CYMINMAXBUTTON", "SV_CYMENU",
"SV_CXFULLSCREEN", "SV_CYFULLSCREEN", "SV_CXICON",
"SV_CYICON", "SV_CXPOINTER", "SV_CYPOINTER",
"SV_DEBUG", "SV_CMOUSEBUTTONS", "SV_POINTERLEVEL",
"SV_CURSORLEVEL", "SV_TRACKRECTLEVEL", "SV_CTIMERS",
"SV_MOUSEPRESENT", "SV_CXBYTEALIGN", "SV_CYBYTEALIGN",
"SV_CSYSVALUES" };


switch(msg)
  {
    case WM_CREATE:
      yPos = 420;
      xPos = -170;

      for(i=0; i<52; i++)
        {
            hwndRadio[i] = WinCreateWindow(
                            hwnd,
                            WC_BUTTON,
                            szLabel[i],
                            WS_VISIBLE | BS_RADIOBUTTON,
                            xPos += 200,
                            yPos,
                            200,
                            28,
                            hwnd,
                            HWND_BOTTOM,
                            i,
                            NULL,
                            NULL);

            if(j==3)
              {
                  j=1;
                  xPos = -170;
                  yPos -= 20;
              }
            else
                  j++;
        }

      WinSendMsg(hwndRadio[sValue],
                BM_SETCHECK, MPFROMSHORT(1), NULL);
```

```
            return(FALSE);

        case WM_CONTROL:
            id = SHORT1FROMMP(mp1);
            if(id >= 0 || id <= 52)
              {
                  WinSendMsg(hwndRadio[sValue],
                          BM_SETCHECK, MPFROMSHORT(0), NULL);
                  sValue = id;
                  WinSendMsg(hwndRadio[sValue],
                          BM_SETCHECK, MPFROMSHORT(1), NULL);

                  WinInvalidateRect(hwnd, NULL, TRUE);
              }

            return(NULL);

        case WM_PAINT:
            hps = WinBeginPaint(hwnd, NULL, NULL);
            WinQueryWindowRect(hwnd, &rcl);
            rclBox.xLeft = (rcl.xRight / 4);
            rclBox.yBottom = 5;
            rclBox.xRight = rcl.xRight / 4 * 3;
            rclBox.yTop = 65;
            WinFillRect(hps, &rclBox, CLR_BACKGROUND);
            WinDrawBorder(hps, &rclBox, 5, 5, CLR_RED,
                          CLR_BACKGROUND, DB_STANDARD);

            sprintf(szBuffer,
                    "%s = %d",
                    szLabel[sValue],
                    WinQuerySysValue(HWND_DESKTOP, sValue));

            WinDrawText(hps, -1, szBuffer, &rclBox,
                        CLR_NEUTRAL, CLR_BACKGROUND,
                        DT_CENTER | DT_VCENTER);

            WinEndPaint(hps);
            return(NULL);

        case WM_ERASEBACKGROUND:
            return(TRUE);

    }
  return(WinDefWindowProc(hwnd, msg, mp1, mp2));
}
```

```
MRESULT EXPENTRY FrameSubProc(hwnd, msg, mp1, mp2)
HWND hwnd;
USHORT msg;
MPARAM mp1, mp2;
{

  switch(msg)
    {

      case WM_FORMATFRAME:
        WinSendMsg(WinWindowFromID(hwndFrame, FID_MINMAX),
                   MM_SETITEMATTR,
                   MPFROM2SHORT(SC_RESTORE, FALSE),
                   MPFROM2SHORT(MIA_DISABLED,
                                MIA_DISABLED));

      case WM_INITMENU:
                   WinSendMsg(hwndMenu,
                   MM_SETITEMATTR,
                   MPFROM2SHORT(SC_RESTORE, TRUE),
                   MPFROM2SHORT(MIA_DISABLED,
                                MIA_DISABLED));

      default:
        return((*FrameControlProc)(hwnd, msg, mp1, mp2));
    }

  return FALSE;

}
```

Listbox Controls

A listbox control window is a window that presents the user with a list of items from which to choose. The Presentation Manager automatically includes a horizontal scrollbar in a listbox and enables it when the number of items exceeds the height of the listbox. The user can scroll through the list of items using an associated scrollbar. The only sizing considerations that you should have when you create a listbox are aesthetic ones.

Each item in the listbox is uniquely identified by an index constant such as LIT_FIRST. A listbox item comprises both a text string, which can be zero or more characters, and a handle. You can use the handle to refer to application data that you associate with a given item. The maximum number of items in a listbox can range up to 32,767 items. Ensure, however, that enough memory exists for the number of items.

As with other control windows, listboxes have distinct styles. These styles allow you to specify positioning and behavior characteristics of each listbox that you create. Table 7-6 describes the available listbox control window styles.

Table 7-6: Listbox Control Window Styles

STYLE	BIT	DESCRIPTION
LS_MULTIPLESEL	0x00000001L	Allows the user to select more than one item at a time. Uses additional identifiers prefixed with LDBI.
LS_OWNERDRAW	0x00000002L	Specifies that one or more items can be drawn by the owner. These items are usually bitmaps, not strings.
LS_NOADJUSTPOS	0x00000004L	Specifies that the listbox be drawn to the already supplied size. Using this style can obscure sections of some items.

Listbox controls generate a WM_CONTROL message (another instance in which the WM_COMMAND route is bypassed). To process a listbox-generated WM_CONTROL message, you must extract the low word from *mp1* using the SHORT1FROMMP macro. The extracted value is the listbox ID. After you get the ID, you can use SHORT2FROMMPto extract the LN notification code from the high word of *mp1*. Table 7-7 lists the codes.

Table 7-7: Message Notification Codes

CODE	VALUE	DESCRIPTION
LN_SELECT	1	Signifies an item has been selected.
LN_SETFOCUS	2	The listbox received the focus.

(continued)

Table 7-7: Continued

CODE	VALUE	DESCRIPTION
LN_KILLFOCUS	3	The listbox relinquished the focus.
LN_SCROLL	4	Signifies that the listbox will scroll horizontally (if scrollbar is present).
LN_ENTER	5	Return or Enter key has been pressed or mouse has been double-clicked.

As with radio buttons, it is better to identify a listbox through the low word of *mp1* in the WM_CONTROL message. The *mp2* parameter does not contain any useful information for listbox processing.

In addition to the WM_CONTROL message, listboxes of style LS_OWN-ERDRAW also cause two more messages to be generated: WM_DRAW-ITEM and WM_MEASUREITEM. If you use the default listbox format, you don't need to process these messages. On the other hand, if you need to perform some special processing related to the contents of a listbox, these messages prove invaluable. Here's a description of each message:

- WM_DRAWITEM — Occurs when a listbox requires redrawing. You can take advantage of this message if you need to modify the listbox contents before they are redrawn. For example, you could change text fonts during the processing of this message. The low word of *mp1* for WM_DRAWITEM contains the ID for the listbox. The *mp2* parameter is a pointer to the OWNERITEM structure.

- WM_MEASUREITEM — Occurs when a listbox is created. It gives you an opportunity to specify the height of items that the control uses. The low word of *mp1* for WM_MEASUREITEM contains the ID of the listbox. The *mp2* parameter is a pointer to a text item.

Listbox Messages

The Presentation Manager also provides a set of messages that you can send to listboxes. You send these messages with WinSendMsg, using the same techniques described for button controls. Typically, you use the various MPFROM* macros to construct a message for a listbox. To obtain data from a listbox, you use the SHORT1 FROMMR macro. Table 7-8 details the listbox messages.

Table 7-8: Listbox Messages

MESSAGE	VALUE	DESCRIPTION
LM_QUERYITEMCOUNT	0x0160	Returns the number of listbox items.
LM_INSERTITEM	0x0161	Inserts a listbox item.
LM_SETTOPINDEX	0x0162	Scrolls an item to the top of the listbox.
LM_DELETEITEM	0x0163	Deletes a listbox item.
LM_SELECTITEM	0x0164	Sets the selection state of the item. TRUE in *mp2* selects the item. FALSE deselects it.
LM_QUERYSELECTION	0x0165	Enumerates the selected items in the listbox.
LM_SETITEMTEXT	0x0166	Causes the listbox to copy a text string into the specified listbox item.
LM_QUERYITEMTEXTLENGTH	0x0167	Returns the length of the string associated with the specified item.
LM_QUERYITEMTEXT	0x0168	Returns the text string associated with the specified listbox item.
LM_SETITEMHANDLE	0x0169	Sets item handle in mp1 to that specified in *mp2*.
LM_QUERYITEMHANDLE	0x016A	Returns the handle of the specified listbox item.
LM_SEARCHSTRING	0x016B	Allows various text string searches, including case-sensitive searches.
LM_SETITEMHEIGHT	0x016C	Sets the height of the items in the listbox.
LM_QUERYTOPINDEX	0x016D	Returns the index value of the top item of the listbox.
LM_DELETEALL	0x016E	Deletes the specified item from a listbox.

As with the other control windows, it is often more convenient to use a listbox within a dialog box. At times, legitimate reasons do arise that make it attractive to implement some control windows by using the WinCreate-StdWindow function. This is perhaps most true when it comes to listboxes and entry-field controls (see the next section), both of which provide convenient access to string data.

When you do use one or more listboxes that are a child of the client window, you must consider how you will go about repainting the client window. One way technique involves specifying the CS_CLIPCHILDREN identifier in the call to WinRegisterClass when you create the frame window. This automatically excludes child windows from the window repainting process. But what happens when you want to exclude one child window, yet temporarily remove another child window? The following program, which displays two listboxes (one by default and the other as a result of a menu selection) hides and displays a second listbox at will.

```
/* LISTBOX.H (Header file) */

#define LB_1  255
#define LB_2  256

#define ID_MENURES 1

#define IDM_LISTBOXMENU 500
#define IDM_LISTBOXTEXT 501
#define IDM_LISTBOXSHOW 502
#define IDM_LISTBOXHIDE 503


/* LISTBOX.RC (Resource script) */

#include <os2.h>
#include "listbox.h"

MENU ID_MENURES
{
SUBMENU "~Listbox", IDM_LISTBOXMENU
  {
     MENUITEM "~Display text",  IDM_LISTBOXTEXT
     MENUITEM "~Show listbox",  IDM_LISTBOXSHOW
     MENUITEM "~Hide listbox",  IDM_LISTBOXHIDE
  }
}
```

```
/* LISTBOX.C  (Listbox example program) */


#define INCL_PM
#include <os2.h>
#include <string.h>
#include "listbox.h"

MRESULT EXPENTRY ClientAreaProc(HWND,USHORT,MPARAM,MPARAM);

HAB    hab;
HMQ    hmq;

int main(void)
{
QMSG qmsg;
HWND hwndFrame, hwndClient;

static CHAR szClass[] = "List";
ULONG ctldata = FCF_TITLEBAR | FCF_SYSMENU | FCF_MINMAX
               | FCF_SIZEBORDER | FCF_SHELLPOSITION
               | FCF_TASKLIST | FCF_MENU;


hab = WinInitialize(NULL);
hmq = WinCreateMsgQueue(hab, 0);
WinRegisterClass(
               hab,
               szClass,
               ClientAreaProc,
               CS_SIZEREDRAW | CS_CLIPCHILDREN,
               0);

hwndFrame = WinCreateStdWindow(
                    HWND_DESKTOP,
                    WS_VISIBLE,
                    &ctldata,
                    szClass,
                    NULL,
                    0L,
                    NULL,
                    ID_MENURES,
                    &hwndClient);

while(WinGetMsg(hab, &qmsg, NULL, 0, 0))
          WinDispatchMsg(hab, &qmsg);
```

```
WinDestroyWindow(hwndFrame);
WinDestroyMsgQueue(hmq);
WinTerminate(hab);

return(0);
}


MRESULT EXPENTRY ClientAreaProc(hwnd, msg, mp1, mp2)
HWND  hwnd;
USHORT msg;
MPARAM mp1;
MPARAM mp2;
{

    RECTL rcl, rclClip;
    HPS  hps;
    SHORT i, id, sIndex;
    CHAR szItem[80];
    static HWND hwndList1, hwndList2;
    static CHAR *szStates[] = { "Alabama", "Alaska", "Arizona",
                "Arkansas", "California", "Colorado",
                "Connecticut", "Delaware", "Florida",
                "Hawaii", "Idaho", "Illinois", "Indiana",
                "Iowa", "Kansas", "Kentucky", "Louisiana",
                "Maine", "Maryland", "Massachusetts",
                "Michigan", "Minnesota", "Mississippi",
                "Missouri", "Montana", "Nebraska", "Nevada",
                "New Hampshire", "New Jersey", "New Mexico",
                "New York", "North Carolina", "North Dakota",
                "Ohio", "Oklahoma", "Oregon", "Pennsylvania",
                "Rhode Island", "South Carolina",
                "South Dakota", "Tennessee", "Texas", "Utah",
                "Vermont", "Virginia", "Washington",
                "West Virginia", "Wisconsin", "Wyoming" };

    switch(msg)
       {
         case WM_CREATE:

               hwndList1 = WinCreateWindow(hwnd, WC_LISTBOX,
                           NULL, WS_VISIBLE
                           | LS_NOADJUSTPOS,
                           50, 50, 150, 200,
                           hwnd, HWND_BOTTOM,
                           LB_1, NULL, NULL);
```

```
                    hwndList2 = WinCreateWindow(hwnd, WC_LISTBOX,
                                       NULL, LS_NOADJUSTPOS,
                                       300, 50, 150, 200, hwnd,
                                       HWND_BOTTOM, LB_2, NULL,
                                       NULL);

          return(FALSE);

               case WM_COMMAND:
                    switch((COMMANDMSG(&msg)->cmd))
                       {
                          case IDM_LISTBOXTEXT:
                             for(i=0; i<50; i++)
                                {
                                   sIndex = strlen(szStates[i]);
                                   strncpy(szItem, szStates[i],
                                          sIndex);
                                   szItem[sIndex] = '\0';

                                   WinSendMsg(hwndList1,
                                          LM_INSERTITEM,
                                          MPFROM2SHORT(LIT_END, 0),
                                          MPFROMP(szItem));
                                }
                          break;

                          case IDM_LISTBOXSHOW:
                             WinShowWindow(hwndList2, TRUE);
                             break;

                          case IDM_LISTBOXHIDE:
                             WinShowWindow(hwndList2, FALSE);
                             WinInvalidateRect(hwnd, NULL, NULL);
                             break;

                       }
               break;


               case WM_CONTROL:
                    id = SHORT1FROMMP(mp1);
                    if(id == LB_1 && SHORT2FROMMP(mp1) == LN_ENTER)
                       {
                          id = SHORT1FROMMR(WinSendMsg(
                                       hwndList1,
                                       LM_QUERYSELECTION,
                                       MPFROMSHORT(LIT_FIRST),
```

```
                                NULL));

                if( id == LIT_NONE )
                    break;
            else
                WinSendMsg(hwndList1, LM_QUERYITEMTEXT,
                        MPFROM2SHORT(id, sizeof(szItem)),
                        MPFROMP(szItem));

            WinSendMsg(hwndList2, LM_INSERTITEM,
                    MPFROM2SHORT(LIT_END, 0),
                    MPFROMP(szItem));


            }
            return(NULL);

        case WM_PAINT:
            WinQueryWindowRect(hwndList1, &rclClip);
            hps = WinBeginPaint(hwnd, NULL, &rclClip);
            WinQueryWindowRect(hwnd, &rcl);
            WinFillRect(hps, &rcl, CLR_BACKGROUND);
            WinEndPaint(hps);
            return(NULL);

        case WM_ERASEBACKGROUND:
            return(TRUE);

        default:
            return(WinDefWindowProc(hwnd, msg, mp1, mp2));


    }
    return(0L);


}
```

When you run this program, it displays a listbox (*hwndList1*) in the left side of the client window. Selecting the text display option from the menu fills the listbox with the names of the 50 states. Selecting the show listbox option displays a second listbox (*hwndList2*) in the window. This listbox is created at the same time as the *hwndList1*, but without the WS_VISIBLE bit specified. As a result, *hwndList2* is not displayed until you select the appropriate menu option, which causes the program to invoke the Win-ShowWindow function.

After both listboxes are displayed, you can copy a text item from *hwndList1* to *hwndList2* by double-clicking on the item, or by pressing the Return key when an item is selected. The following line of code is responsible for this behavior:

```
if(id == LB_1 && SHORT2FROMMP(mp1) == LN_ENTER)
```

Although this statement tests for the listbox ID (a key concern), it also tests for the LN_ENTER notification code, which ensures that control flow only progresses when the user double-clicks or presses Return. If you omitted the test for LN_ENTER, and merely tested for the ID, control flow would also fall through the **if** statement when the user clicked on the listbox's scrollbar.

Finally, the way in which the example program hides *hwndList2* deserves illumination. First, note that the CS_CLIPCHILDREN bit is set in the call to WinRegisterClass. Still, the Presentation Manager needs to know the rectangle to exclude from painting after the WinInvalidateRect call forces a WM_PAINT message. This information is obtained by calling the WinQueryWindowRect function to get the coordinates of *hwndList1*. In turn, *rclClip* is specified in the call to WinBeginPaint, which excludes *hwndList1* from the repainting process.

Entry-Field Controls

Entry-field controls share a resemblance to listbox controls, but they also allow the user to enter and edit text. Implemented correctly, you could create a full-fledged text editor using edit-field controls (which often also are known as entry-box).

Onscreen, an entry-field control appears as a rectangular window sized to the text dimensions that you specify. You can display an entry-field with or without text, depending on the application. In a file loading utility, for example, you might want to display a suggested filename when the user first invokes the utility. Conversely, you could display an empty entry-field and simply have the user enter the filename from scratch.

When an entry-field has the input focus, it displays a thin cursor, which indicates that the user can begin editing the displayed text, if it exists; or begin inserting new text. How the text is actually arranged inside the entry-field's rectangle depends on the style assigned to the entry-field. Extensive use of entry-field controls means you must reference the ENTRYFDATA structure. By doing so, you can make alterations to text or simply discover whether an associated message has had a certain effect on the currently referenced text. Here's the definition of the ENTRYFDATA:

```
typedef struct _ENTRYFDATA {
            USHORT cb;
            USHORT cchEditLimit;
            USHORT ichMinSel;
            USHORT ichMaxSel;
} ENTRYFDATA;
```

The *cb* field in the ENTRYFDATA field structure represents the length of the control data in bytes. The second field, *cchEditLimit*, specifies the maximum number of characters that can be entered into the entry-field. Related to this field is an interesting user interface measure — interesting, in that the Presentation Manager sounds an alarm if the user attempts to enter a text string that is longer than that specified (see the EM_SETTEXTLIMIT message, which is explained shortly in Table 7-11).

The third field, *ichMinSel,* is used in combination with the fourth field, *ichMaxSel*. Together, these fields allow you to identify the current selection within the entry-field. This occurs because characters within the text that have byte offsets less than *ichMaxSel* and greater than *ichMinSel* represent the current selection. When *ichMinSel* equals *ichMaxSel*, the Presentation Manager places the insert point and cursor in the rectangle belonging to the current selection. When *ichMinSel* equals zero and *ichMaxSel* is greater than or equal to the text limit prescribed by EM_SETTEXTLIMIT, the entire text is selected.

After gaining an awareness of the ENTRYFDATA structure, the first step in creating an entry-field control is to decide what style of control you want. Style for entry-fields means text positioning. The system-defined style allows you to place text in several ways. Table 7-9 describes the different entry-field styles, which are denoted by an ES prefix.

Table 7-9: Entry-Field Styles

MESSAGE	BIT	DESCRIPTION
ES_LEFT	0x00000000L	Left justifies the text in the entry-field rectangle. The system uses this as the default style when ES_RIGHT or ES_CENTER is not specified.
ES_RIGHT	0x00000001L	Right justifies the text in the entry-field rectangle. This is mutually exclusive with the ES_RIGHT and ES_CENTER values.
ES_CENTER	0x00000004L	Centers the text in the entry-field rectangle. This is mutually exclusive with the ES_RIGHT and ES_LEFT values.
ES_MARGIN	0x00000008L	Draws a frame around the entry-field rectangle and incorporates a margin around the text. The size of the margin is half the width and height of the current character size.

From the client window point of view, you need to handle the WM_CONTROL message when you work with entry-fields. The WM_CONTROL message contains a notification code in *mp1* and a handle to the current entry-field in *mp2*. As usual, the return value for WM_CONTROL is NULL. Thus, your major concern is the notification code that WM_CONTROL passes to the client window. Notification codes are denoted by an EN prefix. Here's a typical code fragment that tests for an entry-field notification code:

```
if(id == EF_1 && SHORT2FROMMP(mp1) == EN_MEMERROR)
    return(NULL);
```

As with listboxes, you need to test for both the control ID and the particular notification code. In this fragment, the **if** statement tests for an error generated by the listbox associated with *id*. If an error occurs, control passes back to the window procedure and a value of NULL is returned to immediately abort processing of the message. Table 7-10 details all the entry-field notification codes, which are denoted by an EN prefix.

Table 7-10: Entry-Field Notification Codes

MESSAGE	BIT	DESCRIPTION
EN_SETFOCUS	0x0001	Indicates the entry-field is receiving the input focus.
EN_KILLFOCUS	0x0002	Indicates the entry-field is losing the input focus.
EN_CHANGE	0x0004	Indicates a modified entry-field has been displayed.
EN_SCROLL	0x0008	Indicates the entry-field is going to scroll in the horizontal direction. This code results from: a call to WinScrollWindow; a change to the content of the entry-field; or repositioning of the entry-field cursor.
EN_MEMERROR	0x0010	Indicates that not enough memory is available to display the text string prescribed by EM_SETTEXTLIMIT. If you obtain this error, ensure that enough memory is allocated for the text strings associated with the entry-field control.

There is another WM message that plays a role in entry-field processing — namely, the WM_CHAR message. The WM_CHAR message is explained in Chapter 11, so there is no need to go into a full description of it here. Concern for the WM_CHAR message arises when an entry-field is already filled with text. If this occurs, then the entry-field passes the WM_CHAR messages to the client window (or the current owner window). In some cases, the entry-field control does not pass along the message. The reason for this is some key sequences continue to be meaningful to an entry-field control, even after they have been filled with text. These sequences are generated by virtual keys. After trapping the WM_CHAR message, you can test for a virtual key with the following code:

```
if(SHORT1FROMMP == KC_VIRTUALKEY)
```

If this test is TRUE, you need to extract additional values from the WM_CHAR message to affect entry-field processing. Refer to Chapter 11 for additional information. For now, Table 7-11 lists the key sequences that survive a full entry-field control.

Table 7-11: WM_CHAR Values Affecting Entry-Fields

KEY SEQUENCE	ACTION
Left cursor	Moves the cursor to the left one character.
Right cursor	Moves the cursor to the right one character.
Shift-right cursor	Extends the selection right one character.
Shift-left cursor	Extends the selection left one character.
Home	Moves the cursor to the beginning of the entry-field.
End	Moves the cursor to the end of the text in an entry-field.
Backspace	Deletes one character left of the cursor.
Delete	Deletes the current character, or the character to the right.
Shift-Delete	Cuts the selection to the clipboard.
Shift-Insert	Copies the selection from the clipboard.
Ctrl-Delete	Deletes text to the end of the current line.
Shift-Insert	Copies the selection to the clipboard.

Entry-Field Messages

The entry-field messages allow you insert and delete text in an entry-field as well as affect other changes. For example, you can set the selection state of an entry-field by sending the EM_SETSEL message. You can also obtain the return values from some of the EM messages by using the SHORT1FROMMR macro. Table 7-12 lists the entry-field messages.

In addition to using the EM messages, you can use the WinQueryWindowText function when working with entry-field controls. This function obtains a text string from a window and copies it into a buffer. If the string is longer than *cchBufferMax*, the function truncates it. Here's the definition for WinQueryWindowText.

```
SHORT WinQueryWindowText (hwnd, cchBufferMax, pszBuffer)
HWND hwnd;
SHORT cchBufferMax;
PSZ pszBuffer;
```

The *hwnd* argument is a handle to an entry-field control (or other window, such as the frame window when you use this function to query the titlebar text). The *cchBufferMax* argument specifies the length of the text buffer, into which you copy the window text. The *pszBuffer* argument is the actual pointer to the buffer.

Table 7-12: Entry-Field Messages

MESSAGE	VALUE	DESCRIPTION
EM_QUERYCHANGED	0x0140	Checks if contents have changed.
EM_QUERYSEL	0x0142	Retrieves offsets of first and last character.
EM_SETSEL	0x0142	Sets selection range.
EM_SETTEXTLIMIT	0x0143	Sets maximum characters in entry-field.
EM_CUT	0x0144	Deletes selection in entry-field control.
EM_COPY	0x0145	Pastes selection in entry-field control.
EM_CLEAR	0x0146	Deletes selection in entry-field control.
EM_PASTE	0x0147	Pastes from the clipboard.
EM_QUERYFIRSTCHAR	0x0148	Retrieves offset of first visible character.
EM_SETFIRSTCHAR	0x0149	Sets first character on left.

The WinQueryWindowText function can prove quite useful when dealing with entry field data. In a program, a typical call to WinQueryWindowText looks like this:

```
for(i=0; i < 10; i++)
   WinQueryWindowText(hwndEntry[i],
            sizeof(szField[i]),szField[i]);
```

This is a convenient way to quickly collect the text contained in a series of entry-field controls. Recall that if you have no other way of identifying the handle to the entry-field, you could use the WinWindowFromID function to do so.

Static Controls

Static controls simply allow you to display text and boxes in order to enhance a control window. Static controls accept no input, nor do they send any notification messages to the parent window. Static controls are important, however, because they give you precise control over text labels for button controls as well as over text fields in listbox controls.

Static controls also allow you to spruce up child windows (as well as dialog boxes) with custom-made bitmaps. In connection to this, static controls use the following two messages:

- SM_QUERYHANDLE — Returns the bitmap handle. A NULL value indicates an error occurred, or no bitmap handle existed.

- SM_SETHANDLE — Sets the bitmap handle. Applies only to static control styles of SS_ICON, SS_SYSICON, and SS_BITMAP.

Static controls also support three WM messages. These give you an opportunity to modify an event before it occurs. Here are the supported WM messages:

- WM_MATCHMNEMONIC — Occurs when it is necessary to determine if a typed character matches a mnemonic in a control's window text. The system assumes that the character does not match and returns FALSE. You can assert that the character does match by returning a TRUE.

- WM_QUERYWINDOWPARAMS — Occurs as a result of querying the static control parameters.

- WM_SETWINDOWPARAMS — Occurs as a result of changing the static control parameters.

You can create a static control with WinCreateWindow function by specifying the WM_STATIC identifier. Generally, you can process static controls similarly to other control windows. For its style, you must specify an SS identifier. Table 7-13 lists the style identifiers associated with static controls.

7-13: Static Control Style Constants

IDENTIFIER	BIT	DESCRIPTION
SS_TEXT	0x0001L	Creates a text field, using DT identifiers for formatting.
SS_GROUPBOX	0x0002L	Places left justified title in box usually containing radio buttons.
SS_ICON	0x0003L	Specifies that an icon is to be drawn. The static control text string contains the resource ID with which to load the icon. The byte format of the string is: 0xFF, low byte of the resource ID, and the high byte of the resource ID. In the actual string, the first character must be a pound (#) sign. The remainder of the string consists of the decimal representation of the resource ID.
SS_BITMAP	0x0004L	Specifies that a bitmap is to be drawn. The static control text string contains the resource ID with which to the load the bitmap. The byte and text format for the string is the same as it is for the SS_ICON style.
SS_FGNDRECT	0x0005L	Specifies that the foreground color fills the associated rectangle.
SS_HALFTONERECT	0x0007L	Specifies that a rectangle be created with a halftone fill.
SS_BKGNDRECT	0x0007L	Specifies that the background color fills the associated rectangle.
SS_FGNDFRAME	0x0008L	Specifies that a box is to be created with a foreground colored frame.
SS_HALFTONEFRAME	0x0009L	Specifies that a framed rectangle be created with a halftone fill.
SS_BKGNDFRAME	0x000AL	Specifies that a box is to be created with a background colored frame.
SS_SYSICON	0x000BL	Specifies that a system icon is to be drawn. The system SPRT value replaces the icon resource ID; otherwise, this operates identically to the SS_ICON style.

Scrollbar Controls

Scrollbars give you a way to let the user know that more information exists than displayed onscreen. At the same time, they also give the user a handy way of displaying this information — by moving the mouse pointer and clicking on the scrollbar, the user can quickly scroll new data into the window.

You can also implement scrollbars to give the user a visual method of increasing or decreasing a current value. For example, an interface for scaling bit-mapped images can include a scrollbar to let the user adjust the gray level of an image. By clicking the mouse pointer one unit to the right or left of the scrollbar's thumb, the user can increase or decrease the gray level.

Do not confuse scrollbar controls in a child window with those used for the frame window's sizing border (which are specified by the FCF_VERT-SCROLL and FCF_HORZSCROLL style identifiers in the WinCreate-StdWindow call). Child window scrollbars are created by specifying the WC_SCROLLBAR class identifier in the second argument to WinCreate-Window. The following scrollbar styles control the vertical and horizontal placement of scrollbars.

- SBS_HORZ — Creates a horizontal scrollbar. Its bit value is 0x0000L.

- SBS_VERT — Creates a vertical scrollbar. Its bit value is 0x0001L.

You specify one of the SBS styles in the fourth argument to WinCreateWindow. Additionally, you can organize text in a scrollbar control window by ORing the SS_TEXT control style used by static control windows. Along with the SS_TEXT style, you must OR one of the following DT identifiers:

- DT_LEFT — Left justifies text.

- DT_CENTER — Centers text.

- DT_RIGHT — Right justifies text.

Scrollbar controls generate either a WM_HSCROLL or WM_VSCROLL message, depending on the physical orientation of the scrollbar. Processing these messages is identical to scrollbar processing that you use in the client window procedure. Refer to Chapter 5 for additional information on this aspect of scrollbar processing, including the messages an application sends to the scrollbar controls.

Control Window Queries

At times, you will need to obtain data related to control windows. The Presentation Manager provides several functions for this purpose. Table 7-14 lists a selected group of these functions.

Table 7-14: Control Window Query Functions

FUNCTION	DESCRIPTION
WinIsChild	Determines if one window is descended from another window.
WinIsOwner	Determines if one window is the owner of another window.
WinQueryWindow	Returns the handle of a window with the relationship to the window specified by the function arguments.
WinQueryWindowPos	Allows you to manipulate the dimensions of a window, using the SWP structure.
WinQueryWindowProcess	Obtains the process and thread IDs of the thread that created the window.
WinQueryWindowRect	References the RECT structure, giving you the window dimensions.
WinQueryWindowText	Obtains a text string from the specified window.
WinQueryWindowULong	Obtains the unsigned long integer value at a specified offset into the reserved window words memory of a given window.
WinQueryWindowUShort	Obtains the unsigned short value at a specified offset into the reserved window words memory of a given window.
WinSetOwner	Lets you change the owner window of the specified window.

Table 7-14: Continued

FUNCTION	DESCRIPTION
WinSetWindowPos	Provides a way to reposition the specified window, using SWP window constants.
WinUpdateWindow	Lets you update the specified window and all associated child windows.
WinWindowFromID	Returns a child window handle.
WinWindowFromPoint	Locates the descendent of the specified window from among a series of windows.

CHAPTER 8

DIALOG BOXES

Dialog boxes provide the user with a convenient way to enter control data in an application. Usually, the user pops up a dialog box while working in the client window. Then, because of the capabilities offered by the dialog box, the user can set a control, select a filename, or perform any of several other types of operations. In general, a dialog box allows the user to turn on some function associated with an activity in the client window.

A dialog box goes beyond the mere selection of a menu item. Because it allows the user to specify arguments for a current activity, it is necessarily capable of making discrete adjustments to system and program data. Dialog boxes also maintain a record of previously used arguments and automatically prompt the user to accept or reject them. By convention, the user invokes a dialog box from a menu item that has a *trailing ellipsis*.

To the Presentation Manager, a dialog box is a collection of control windows. You can combine various types of control windows in a dialog box to produce meaningful interface styles for various functions. The Presentation Manager provides a default keyboard interface that enables the user to move between control windows using the Tab and cursor keys, among others.

Dialog boxes can be *modal*, *modeless*, or *system-modal*. Modal dialog boxes limit the input focus to the current dialog box, effectively blocking the user from moving between the application and the dialog box. Conversely, a modeless dialog box lets the user move freely between the main application and the dialog box. For example, with a modeless dialog box, the user can access the system menu, enter data into the frame window, or perform any other system or application function. Both types of dialog boxes are usually invoked from a menu. The third type of dialog box is a system-modal dialog box, which serves to alert the user of an impending system error. The system-modal dialog box gives the user a chance to correct the error, or minimally, save the application's data to disk.

The Dialog Box Editor

As with menus, you create a dialog box by using a resource template and the RC resource compiler. To create dialog boxes, you have the choice of using the dialog box editor, which gives you a *wysiwyg* display as you work, or entering a series of statements and arguments in a resource file.

An application's dialog boxes are defined in a text file with a .DLG extension. You include this file in the resource definition file using the **rcinclude** directive. As you saw in Chapter 6, a resource definition file is denoted by the .RC extension. Ultimately, the resource compiler produces a binary form of the resource definition file. The binary file is denoted by a .RES extension. Figure 8-1 shows the relationship between these files.

When you use the *Dialog Box Editor*, you can create a new .RES file or read an existing one and its associated header file if it exists. The *Dialog Box Editor* then performs the following steps:

1. Modifies the dialog box resources in the .RES file and saves it to disk.

2. Creates a .DLG file, which contains the test resource definition of the dialog boxes in the .RES file.

3. Modifies the header file, which contains constant definitions. The editor uses the #define C preprocessor directive to define the constants.

The *Dialog Box Editor* only modifies resources associated with dialog boxes. It ignores all other resources in a .RES file. Because the *Dialog Box Editor* does not read the .DLG file, any prior contents of a .DLG file are lost once the editor accesses and saves it. When the editor reads an include file, it only reads and writes constant declarations. Thus, any other recent changes to the include file are lost.

When you run the *Dialog Box Editor*, it produces a large-window display consisting of three main sections: the editing area, status window, and panel title. Also included in the *Dialog Box Editor* is an extensive help system, which is sufficient enough to learn the various commands to create, size and specify attributes for dialog boxes.

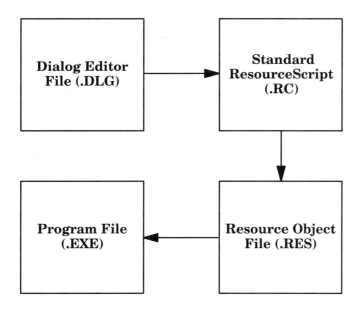

Figure 8-1: Resource Compiler Files

Dialog Box Resource File

Another way to create a dialog box resource is by writing the resource script file yourself. Because the *Dialog Box Editor* can sometimes be tedious — if not time consuming — you might want to do all your dialog box scripts in an ASCII editor, and then run them through the resource compiler. If you know what different types of dialog boxes you want, you can streamline this approach by making templates.

You can also use the *Dialog Box Editor* to create your initial script, then modify the resulting .DLG file in an ASCII editor. Whichever method you choose, you should be familiar with resource compiler statements. Coding a dialog box resource file is similar to creating a menu resource file — the key words are different, but the logic is the same. Moreover, you know most of the controls common to dialog boxes such as checkboxes and pushbuttons

To begin a dialog resource script, you must specify a DLGTEMPLATE statement. This informs the resource compiler that it is about to process a dialog script. The DLGTEMPLATE statement defines the identifier, load and memory options, dialog dimensions, and controls associated with the dialog box. You can specify multiple DLGTEMPLATE statements in a single resource script, but each template must have a unique ID. The DLGTEMPLATE statement has the following form:

```
DLGTEMPLATE dialog-id [load-option] [mem-option]
```

The only required argument to the DLGTEMPLATE is *dialog-id*. This specifies the dialog box's unique ID, which you use as a reference in the application source code. The *load-option* argument tells the Presentation Manager when to load the dialog box from disk. The available options are:

- PRELOAD — The dialog box is loaded upon execution of the application program.

- LOADONCALL — The dialog box is loaded when the application invokes the WinLoadDlg function. This is the default option.

The *mem-option* argument to DLGTEMPLATE tells the Presentation Manager how to handle the dialog box once it has been loaded into system memory. The available options are:

- FIXED — The dialog box remains at a defined memory location.

- MOVEABLE — The dialog box is moved from one memory location to another location in order to accommodate system needs.

- DISCARDABLE — The dialog box is discarded after the user exits from it.

You can specify more than one *mem-option* argument. The default is MOVEABLE and DISCARDABLE. Additionally, you must follow DLG-TEMPLATE with either a left French bracket, or the key word BEGIN. The *Dialog Box Editor* uses the key word approach. Similarly, you must use a right French bracket, or the key word END to indicate the end of the dialog box script.

To create a specific dialog box, you use a DIALOG resource statement. The key words that satisfy this statement resemble the standard name for the control. For example, the key word for a pushbutton is DEFPUSH-BUTTON (for default pushbutton), and even more simply, the key word for a checkbox is CHECKBOX. The DIALOG statement has the following form:

```
DIALOG text, id, x, y, width, height, [, style] [, framectl]
```

The DIALOG statement defines the actual window for the dialog box. The statement specifies the position of the dialog box relative to the frame window; the dimensions of the dialog box; and the style of the dialog box. A DIALOG statement is typically paired with a DLGTEMPLATE statement and must contain at least one control definition that is denoted by CON-TROL, DEFPUSHBUTTON, CHECKBOX, or some other valid key word. Table 8-1 lists the statements and key words for dialog box scripts.

Table 8-1: Resource Compiler Statements and Key Words

SCRIPT ITEM	DESCRIPTION
AUTORADIOBUTTON	Creates an automatic radio button control. If no style is specified, the style is BS_AUTORADIOBUTTON.
CHECKBOX	Creates a checkbox control. If no style is specified, the style is the ORed value of BS_CHECKBOX and WS_TABSTOP.
CTLDATA	Defines control data for the dialog box.
DEFPUSHBUTTON	Creates a default pushbutton control. If no style is specified, the style is the ORed value of BS_PUSHBUTTON, BS_DE-FAULT, and WS_TABSTOP.
DIALOG	Defines the window for the dialog box, including its position and dimensions. Usually, only one instance of the DIALOG key word is associated with the DLGTEMPLATE statement.
DLGINCLUDE	Specifies a file to be included in the dialog box template. This file contains dialog box IDs used in both the template and application program.
DLGTEMPLATE	Tells the resource compiler to create a dialog box template. Each dialog box template must have a unique ID value.

(continued)

Table 8-1: Continued

SCRIPT ITEM	DESCRIPTION
EDITTEXT	Creates an entry field control into which the user supplies input data. If no style is specified, the style is the ORed value of ES_AUTOSCROLL and WS_TABSTOP.
GROUPBOX	Creates a group box control that groups other controls together. If no style is specified, the style is the ORed value of SS_GROUPBOX and WS_TABSTOP.
ICON	Creates an icon-based control that is displayed in the dialog box. (Do not confuse this key word with its use in specifying an icon resource for the main application.) If no style is specified, the style is SS_ICON.
LISTBOX	Creates a listbox control that displays predefined data from which the user makes a selection. If no style is specified, the style is WS_TABSTOP.
LTEXT	Creates a left-aligned text control. If no style is specified, the style is the ORed value of SS_TEXT, DT_LEFT, and WS_GROUP.
PRESPARAMS	Defines presentation arguments for a dialog box.
PUSHBUTTON	Creates a pushbutton control. If no style is specified, the styles of BS_PUSHBUTTON and WS_TABSTOP are ORed.
RADIOBUTTON	Creates a radiobutton control. If no style is specified, the style is BS_RADIOBUTTON.
RTEXT	Creates a right-aligned text control. If no style is specified, the style is the ORed value of SS_TEXT, DT_RIGHT, and WS_GROUP.

If applicable, the *text* argument in the DIALOG statement specifies a title for the dialog box. The *id* argument specifies a unique ID. In most cases, you can merely specify an integer ID versus a constant (as is the case with IDs for dialog box controls). As with menus, you specify an integer ID. Put some thought into the numbering scheme, so you can take advantage of the relationships between IDs in your application source code.

The next four arguments — *x, y, width*, and *height* — specify the dimensions of the dialog box. The *x* and *y* arguments specify the horizontal and vertical coordinates, beginning at the lower left-hand corner of the dialog box. The *width* and *height* arguments specify the dimensions of the dialog box. The units of measure for these arguments are dialog units. A dialog unit is 1/4 the value of the current character value (see box).

DIALOG UNITS

Dialog units are a unique measurement in the Presentation Manager. They allow you to create dialog boxes that retain the same relative dimensions, regardless of the type of display monitor. Horizontal (x) units equal 1/4 the width of the system font character. Vertical (y) units equal 1/8 the height of the system font character. The valid integer range is 1 through 65,535. A typical dialog box can range anywhere from 100 units by 80 units to 130 units by 170 units. The specified dialog box style affects the way you calculate the width and height of a dialog box. It is important to note that the FS_SCREENALIGN style orients a dialog box relative to the display screen. And the FS_MOUSEALIGN style orients a dialog box relative to the current position of the mouse pointer. All other dialog boxes are oriented relative to the parent window.

The last two arguments — *style* and *framectl* — designate the style and frame style of the dialog box. Typically, all you need do is specify FS_DLGBORDER to create a standard dialog box. To enhance the dialog box display, you can OR any of several other FS and WS identifiers for the style argument; and you can specify FCF_TITLEBAR for the *framectl* argument. Of course, some identifiers from the FS and WS styles are incompatible with each other. Table 8-2 lists some of the more common styles that satisfy the style arguments.

The WS_VISIBLE style, as it pertains to dialog boxes, differs from its use with a frame window. In many cases, if you do not specify WS_VISIBLE, the Presentation Manager still displays the dialog box. If the user types ahead, selects an item, and presses the Enter key, the dialog box might not display — depending on how fast the user typed. Without WS_VISIBLE specified, the Presentation Manager will not display the dialog box until all WM_CHAR messages have been cleared from the keyboard input queue. Thus, if the input queue contains instructions for the dialog box, the Presentation Manager processes the instructions without displaying the dialog box. Because this is a handy feature, you will likely want to make use of it in your final product. While you are developing your application, it is a good idea to specify WS_VISIBLE.

Table 8-2: Common Dialog Box Styles

STYLE	BIT	DESCRIPTION
FS_DLGBORDER	0x00000080L	Specifies dialog border.
FS_BORDER	0x00000100L	Specifies standard border.
FS_SCREENALIGN	0x00000200L	Aligns dialog box to the origin of the screen.
FS_MOUSEALIGN	0x00000400L	Aligns dialog box to current pointer position.
WS_TABSTOP	0x00020000L	Allows tabbing between controls.
WS_SAVEBITS	0x04000000L	Saves display under dialog box.
WS_VISIBLE	0x80000000L	Makes dialog box visible.

Dialog Box Controls

The DIALOG statement is followed by one or more CONTROL statements, or predefined qualifiers (key words) such as DEFPUSHBUTTON or CHECKBOX. If you want, you can nest CONTROL statements. Note that if a nested statement creates a child window or control, its parent and owner is the window created by the previous CONTROL statement. Ordinarily, you will not find it necessary to nest CONTROL statements.

Both CONTROL statements and predefined key words such as CHECKBOX and DEFPUSHBUTTON use a series of arguments to specify position, dimensions, style, and associated information such as the text string that the user sees inside the control. The CONTROL, which also specifies the class of the control window, has the following form:

```
CONTROL text, id, x, y, width, height, class [style...]
```

Note the similarities between the CONTROL and DIALOG statements. The *text* argument in the CONTROL statement specifies the control label if the control requires one. This label must be enclosed in quotation marks. The *id* argument is a given ID for the control. You can assign *id* an integer value in the range 0 to 65,535, or use IDs defined in an include file.

The *x* and *y* arguments in the CONTROL statement specify the horizontal and vertical coordinates of the control relative to the dialog box, which is the parent window. The *width* and *height* arguments specify the dimensions of the control itself. Thus, if you are locating a control such as an AUTORADIOBUTTON inside a GROUPBOX control, the *x*, *y*, *width*, and *height* arguments for the innermost control should be within the range set by the outermost control.

The *class* argument is where the CONTROL statement differs from the DIALOG statement. For dialog boxes, you select a class type from a subset of the system window class identifiers. Table 8-3 lists the valid identifiers, which are mutually exclusive.

Table 8-3: Dialog Box Classes

CLASS	VALUE	DESCRIPTION
WC_STATIC	0xffff0005L	Static text field, box, or rectangle.
WC_BUTTON	0xffff0003L	Button control.
WC_ENTRYFIELD	0xffff0006L	Rectangular entry field.
WC_LISTBOX	0xffff0007L	Character string list.
WC_SCROLLBAR	0xffff0008L	Scrollbar control.

Each class has it own subset of style identifiers to satisfy the optional style argument in the CONTROL statement. In some cases, you can OR styles from the same subset, but you cannot mix styles from different subsets. You can also OR the WS_VISIBLE, WS_GROUP, and WS_TABSTOP styles for all classes. Similarly, you can OR the text display identifiers such as DT_LEFT, DT_CENTER, and DT_RIGHT with style identifiers in all classes. You can also use WC_STATIC styles to enhance various controls. (Refer to Chapter 7 for a complete description of the styles used by each class of dialog boxes. In this respect, there is no difference between dialog boxes and control windows, which is subject of Chapter 7.) For convenience, here's a summary of the styles that each class uses:

- WC_BUTTON — Style identifiers for this class are prefixed with BS. When used in the CONTROL statement, most of these identifiers have the same effect as the various button statements that the resource compiler recognizes. See Table 7-2 in Chapter 7.

- WC_LISTBOX — Style identifiers for this class are prefixed with LS. The equivalent resource compiler statement is LISTBOX. The different listbox styles allow you to specify positioning and behavior characteristics of each listbox that you create. See Table 7-6 in Chapter 7.

- WC_ENTRYFIELD — Style identifiers for this class are prefixed with ES. The equivalent resource compiler statement is EDITTEXT. The single purpose of the ES styles is to format text. See Table 7-9 in Chapter 7.

- WC_STATIC — Style identifiers for this class are prefixed with SS. These style types allow you to manipulate static text. By combining these style types with the DT identifiers, you can many different custom styles. See Table 7-13 in Chapter 7.

- WC_SCROLLBAR — Style identifiers for this class are prefixed with SBS. The SBS set of identifiers is limited to SBS_VERT and SBS_HORZ, both of which are widely used in the Presentation Manager. See the section titled "Scrollbar Controls" in Chapter 7.

This wraps up the CONTROL statement. Finishing the rest of the resource script merely requires adding two instances of the END key word (or two right curly brackets). The following example — which is anything but a real life example — creates a dialog box with several different kinds of controls.

```
DLGTEMPLATE 257 LOADONCALL MOVEABLE DISCARDABLE
{

    DIALOG "", 257, 3, 35, 201, 417, FS_NOBYTEALIGN
            |FS_DLGBORDER | WS_VISIBLE
            | WS_CLIPSIBLINGS | WS_SAVEBITS

        {
            CONTROL "PushButton", 256, 40, 370, 103, 17,
                    WC_BUTTON, BS_PUSHBUTTON | WS_TABSTOP
```

```
                    | WS_VISIBLE
        CONTROL "Checkbox", 257, 40, 335, 99, 12,
                WC_BUTTON,BS_CHECKBOX | WS_TABSTOP
                | WS_VISIBLE
        CONTROL "Radiobutton", 258, 40, 300, 85, 15,
                WC_BUTTON,BS_RADIOBUTTON | WS_TABSTOP
                | WS_VISIBLE
        CONTROL "Text", 262, 50, 240, 32, 12,
                WC_ENTRYFIELD, ES_LEFT | ES_MARGIN
                | WS_TABSTOP | WS_VISIBLE

        CONTROL "GroupBox", 263, 135, 170, 44, 64,
                WC_STATIC,SS_GROUPBOX | WS_GROUP
                | WS_VISIBLE
        CONTROL "StaticText", 264, 36, 190, 62, 11,
                WC_STATIC,SS_TEXT | DT_LEFT | DT_TOP
                | WS_GROUP| WS_VISIBLE
    }
}
```

Predefined Controls

Generally, predefined control statements such as DEFPUSHBUTTON and CHECKBOX have the same basic syntax as the CONTROL statement. The one exception is the ICON statement, which ignores the width and height arguments because it sizes itself. (You must, however, place some arbitrary value in these arguments for the ICON statement.)

Naturally, predefined control statements do not require a class argument. You can also omit the title string and the resource compiler recognizes the omission. The basic form for predefined control statements is:

```
STATEMENT text, id, x, y, width, height, [, style]
```

The following examples show a valid use of the various predefined control statements. Each example uses the default for the control.

```
/* Automatic Radio button using BS_AUTORADIOBUTTON
as the default. */

    AUTORADIOBUTTON "Button 1", 256, 40, 300, 85, 15

/* Checkbox using BS_CHECKBOX and WS_TABSTOP defaults. */
```

```
    CHECKBOX "Checkbox 1", 257, 40, 300, 100, 100

/* Default Pushbutton (BS_PUSHBUTTON | BS_DEFAULT). */
    DEFPUSHBUTTON "Pushbutton 1", 258, 15, 15, 25, 50

/* Groupbox using SS_GROUPBOX and WS_TABSTOP default. */
    GROUPBOX "Group Title", 259, 100, 100, 500, 100
/* Icon control using SS_ICON default. */
    ICON 260, 265, 145, 0, 0
/* Listbox using WS_TABSTOP default. */
    LISTBOX 261, 10, 10, 100, 100
/* Pushbutton using BS_PUSHBUTTON default. */
    PUSHBUTTON "Cancel", 262, 40, 40, 300, 75
/* Radio-button using BS_RADIOBUTTON default. */
    RADIOBUTTON "Button 1", 40, 300, 85, 15
```

Whether you use predefined control statements or the CONTROL state-ment is purely a matter of personal preference. Because the Dialog Box Editor uses CONTROL statements, this is one argument for using the CONTROL statement method. On the other hand, if you find the *Dialog Box Editor* cumbersome to use, you might opt for the predefined state-ments because of greater readability.

Dialog Box Processing

It might come as a relief to know that you don't have to process dialog mes-sages along with messages for your main application window. In fact, for every different style of dialog box in your application, it is good practice to have a separate function process the associated dialog messages. Gener-ally speaking, processing messages in a dialog box function is more straightforward than processing messages in the main application function — primarily because you don't have to worry about repainting the current window or filtering keyboard and mouse input.

As with the main application function, control passes to a dialog box function via an intermediate function. For modeless dialog boxes, the intermediate function is WinDlgBox. You call WinDlgBox and specify, among other items, the name of dialog box function that you want to invoke. WinDlgBox is defined as follows:

```
USHORT WinDlgBox(hwndParent, hwndOwner, pfnDlgProc,
                   hmod, idDlg, pCreateParams)
HWND hwndParent hwndOwner;
PFNWP pfnDlgProc;
HMODULE hmod;
USHORT idDlg;
PVOID pCreateParams;
```

The first two arguments in WinDlgBox should be familiar to you: *hwndparent* specifies the parent window handle (which is HWND_DESKTOP more often than not); and *hwndOwner* specifies the owner window handle. The next argument, *DlgProc*, holds the name of the dialog box procedure. The *hmod* argument then identifies the resource for the dialog box. Setting *hmod* to NULL tells the Presentation Manager that the resource is part of the application's .EXE file. If you do not set *hmod* to NULL, you must specify the module handle returned by the DosLoadModule function. The *idDig* argument specifies the ID for the dialog box. This is the integer or constant you assigned in the second argument of the DIALOG statement value in the corresponding resource script. The last argument, *pCreateParams*, points to any initialization data that you have specified in the resource script. If you have no initialization data, set this argument to NULL.

WinDlgBox also returns a useful boolean value, *usResult*, which represents the exit status of the dialog box. If *usResult* is true, the user exited the dialog box by pressing either the Enter key or clicking on the "Okay" button. If *usResult* is false, the user exited by pressing the Escape key or clicking on the "Cancel" button. Additionally, *usResult* can contain an error code if the dialog box was abnormally terminated. The error code is equivalent to DID_ERROR, a system constant defined in PMWIN.H. The Presentation Manager also uses two other system constants for dialog boxes — DID_OK and DID_CANCEL. Both of these are detailed later in this section.

For modal dialog boxes, you can efficiently make the call to WinDlgBox within your menu-handling function. (On the other hand, modeless dialog boxes require more overhead, meaning you should dedicate a function to creating them.) To invoke a dialog box linked to a menu item, simply trap the appropriate menu message, then call WinDlgBox.

Processing a modeless dialog box is simple enough. The primary message with which you must be concerned is WM_COMMAND. The *mp1* parameter of WM_COMMAND contains the command value that the user enters via the dialog box; the *mp2* parameter contains the source of the command. You can also process WM_CONTROL messages generated by a dialog box control. With WM_CONTROL messages, the *mp1* parameter contains the ID of the control that originates the message; the *mp2* parameter identifies the event such as button click, which is represented by the BN_CLICK message.

The third kind of message generated by dialog box controls is WM_INITDLG. This message is sent to the dialog box function before the dialog box appears on the screen. The *mp1* parameter of WM_INITDLG identifies the dialog box control with the pending input focus. The *mp2* parameter points to the CREATEPARAMS structure used by the WinLoadDlg, WinCreateDlg, and WinProcessDlg functions.

The following example shows how to process the WM_INITDLG messages, as well as the WM_COMMAND and WM_CONTROL messages. The example is intended for use in a program that changes the background colors of the frame window from red to green. The example assumes two checkbox controls — one labeled red and the other labeled green. (If both colors are checked, the resulting color is blue.) The two colors are associated with control IDs that, in a full program, would be defined in the resource header file. The example also assumes two default pushbuttons — one labeled "OK" and the other labeled "Cancel."

```
MRESULT EXPENTRY CheckBoxDB(hwndDlg, msg, mp1, mp2 )
HWND    hwndDlg;
USHORT  msg;
MPARAM  mp1;
MPARAM  mp2;
```

```
{
    USHORT  i;

    switch (msg)
    {
        case WM_INITDLG:
            WinSendDlgItemMsg(hwndDlg, IDM_RED,
                    BM_SETCHECK, MPFROM2SHORT(TRUE, 0),
                    NULL);
            break;

        case WM_CONTROL:
            if(SHORT2FROMMP(mp1) == BN_CLICKED)
            {
                WinSendDlgItemMsg(hwndDlg, SHORT1FROMMP(mp1),
                    BM_SETCHECK, MPFROM2SHORT(TRUE, 0),
                    NULL);
                WinInvalidateRect(hwndClient, NULL, FALSE);
            }
            break;

        case WM_COMMAND:
            switch(SHORT1FROMMP(mp1))
            {
                case DID_OK:
                    for(i=500;i<300;i+=50)
                            DosBeep(i,100);
                    WinDismissDlg(hwndDlg, TRUE);
                    break;

                case DID_CANCEL:
                    WinDismissDlg(hwndDlg, FALSE);
                    break;

                default:
                    break;
            }

        default:
            return(WinDefDlgProc(hwndDlg, msg, mp1, mp2));
    }
    return(0L);
}
```

In the example, the WM_INITDLG message is trapped in order to place a check mark in the checkbox for the color red, the startup color. This is accomplished through the WinSendDlgMsg function, which parallels the

WinSendMsg function, but conveniently uses the dialog item ID as one of its arguments. IDM_RED is the checkbox ID that should be defined in the resource header file. The control window message responsible for setting the check mark is BM_SETCHECK (see box). Setting the upper word of *mp1* to TRUE — via the MPFROM2SHORT macro — tells the Presentation Manager to set the check mark.

The WM_CONTROL message lets you perform some operation before the checkbox command takes effect. In the example, the SHORT2FROM-MP macro extracts the click status of the WM_CONTROL message from the high word of *mp1*. BN_CLICKED represents a single mouse click. (For the purpose of the example, extracting the click status is unnecessary, but is good practice because most Presentation Manager routines respond to a double-click, which is represented by the BN_DBLCLICKED message.) You will notice in the WinSendDlgItemMsg function that the SHORT1FROMMP and MPFROM2SHORT macros are used in tandem: the former identifies the checkbox control while the latter sets the upper word of *mp1* for the BM_SETCHECK message. The final task in the WM_CONTROL block is to invalidate the client window (using WinInvalidateRect) so it can be repainted with its new color.

BM_SETCHECK

You can change the checked state of a button control — any of BS_CHECKBOX, BS_AUTOCHECKBOX, BS_RADIOBUTTON or BS_AUTORADIOBUTTON — by sending it a BM_SETCHECK message. The checked state changes if *mp1* is TRUE and the control is checked.; or if *mp1* is FALSE and the control is unchecked. For BS_3STATE and BS_AUTO3STATE styles, the button is unchecked if *mp1* equals 0; checked if *mp1* equals 1; and indeterminate if *mp1* equals 2. The *mp2* parameter associated with BM_SETCHECK must be set to NULL. (Refer to Chapter 7 for specific information on various control window messages.)

Processing the WM_COMMAND message requires a minimum of code. In fact, the example could have sufficed with much less code, but the inner case statements point out the use of the DID_OK and DID_CANCEL constants. These constants, which are defined in PMWIN.H, are used to identify the "Okay" and "Cancel" pushbuttons common to most dialog boxes.

(Increasingly, however, many applications use "Enter" instead of "Okay" to denote the pushbutton that accepts the changes made in the dialog box.) As with other identifiers, DID_OK and DID_CANCEL are contained in the lower word of *mp1*.

The WinDismissDlg function is also called during processing of the WM_COMMAND message. Technically, WinDismissDlg hides the current dialog box — but as far as modal dialog boxes are concerned, it destroys them. WinDismissDlg is defined as follows:

```
BOOL WinDismissDlg(hwndDlg, usResult)
HWND hwndDlg;
USHORT usResult;
```

If you have been following closely, you might wonder how you obtain *hwndDlg*. You don't. When you call your dialog box function via WinDlgBox, the Presentation Manager automatically assigns a handle to the dialog box. This is available to you as *hwnd* in the dialog box function, meaning you must physically locate the call to WinDismissDlg within the dialog box function. On the other hand, how you satisfy the *usResult* argument is totally up to you. In the example, a TRUE value indicates that a DID_OK message occurred; a FALSE value indicates a DID_CANCEL message occurred. Both *hwndDlg* and *usResult* are maintained internally by the Presentation Manager.

Before control returns to WinDlgBox — remember, the function that started it all — you should call the WinDefDlgProc function. WinDefDlgProc is similar to the WinDefWindowProc in the main application function. Both perform default message processing. And their arguments are almost identical. Here's how WinDefDlgProc is defined:

```
MRESULT WinDefDlgProc(hwndDlg, msg, mp1, mp2)
HWND hwndDlg;
USHORT msg;
MPARAM mp1, mp2;
```

WinDefDlgProc performs default processing for any message not processed within the dialog box function. WinDefDlgProc also enhances the default keyboard interface by processing the input from the following keys: Esc, which exits the dialog box without accepting changes; and spacebar and Enter, which accept changes and exit the dialog box.

Modeless Dialog Boxes

From the user's perspective, modeless dialog boxes are friendlier than modal dialog boxes, but even so, don't get carried away with them. The *Application Style Guide* advises that modal dialog boxes should be used for requesting input, thus ensuring that the user responds to the input request before continuing to work.

There is only one major difference between a modal and modeless dialog box — namely, the latter lets you shift the input focus away from the open dialog box. This means you can pop-up a dialog box, look at it, and then pop-up another dialog box — or perform some other operation — without closing the original dialog box. This is especially powerful in applications that require the user to go back and forth between the frame window and a dialog box. Accordingly, the *Application Style Guide* strongly suggests that modeless dialog boxes be limited to displaying information that does not require a response from the user. The best example of modeless dialog boxes is the Presentation Manager's help system.

The differences between modal and modeless dialog boxes increase significantly when it comes to coding. Modeless dialog boxes require much more programming overhead. Additionally, there are cosmetic differences. Because a modeless dialog box lets the user shift the input focus, you need to treat it more like a window than a modal dialog box. For one thing, you have to give the user the ability to move a modeless dialog box by including a titlebar with the dialog box. You accomplish this by specifying FCF_TITLEBAR when you define the control window in the resource script. For example, the following resource script fragment sets up an entry field box suitable for a modeless application:

```
DLGTEMPLATE 2 LOADONCALL MOVEABLE DISCARDABLE
{

    DIALOG "Example List Box", 2, 23, 91, 117, 245,
            FS_DLGBORDER | WS_GROUP
            | WS_VISIBLE, FCF_TITLEBAR

        {
            CONTROL "", 1256, 12, 22, 91, 167, WC_LISTBOX,
                WS_VISIBLE
```

```
        CONTROL "Choose an item. Use Scroll.", 3, 5, 196,
                104, 14, WC_STATIC, SS_TEXT | DT_LEFT
                | DT_TOP | WS_GROUP | WS_VISIBLE
    }
}
```

Activating a modeless dialog box is not as streamlined as opening and closing a modal dialog box. You cannot use the WinDlgBox function for modeless dialog boxes. Instead, you must use the WinLoadDlg, which loads the dialog box from its template. Here's the definition for WinLoad-Dlg:

```
HWND WinLoadDlg(hwndParent, hwndOwner, pfnDlgProc,
                    hmod, idDlg, pCreateParams)
HWND hwndParent, hwndOwner;
PFNWP pfnDlgProc;
HMODULE hmod;
USHORT idDlg;
PVOID pCreateParams;
```

If you compare WinDlgBox and WinLoadDlg, you will immediately notice that they take the same arguments. Most important, WinLoadDlg points to a dialog box procedure exactly like WinDlgBox. The major difference between the two functions is WinLoadDlg does not initiate full processing of a dialog box message. It does send WM_INITDLG to the dialog box function, but then returns control to the function that invoked it. The return value for WinLoadDlg is the handle to the dialog box.

Full message processing is handled by the WinProcessDlg function. By design, WinProcessDlg can direct messages to either a dialog box function or a window function. WinProcessDlg is defined as follows:

```
USHORT WinProcessDlg(hwndDlg)
HWND hwndDlg;
```

WinProcessDlg does not return until WinDismissDlg is called. The return value for WinProcessDlg is the value specified to WinDismissDlg.

In addition to using WinDismissDlg to hide a dialog box, you need to call the WinDestroyWindow function to eliminate it altogether. WinDestroyWindow takes the dialog box handle as its only argument and returns a TRUE value upon successfully completing the operation. If you want to guard against inadvertently destroying a dialog box — or any other window, for that matter — you can trap the WM_DESTROY process and include a routine to abort the process when necessary.

Modeless Entry Field Boxes

When you use modal entry field dialog boxes, you can normally access the user-supplied data with the WinQueryDlgItemShort or WinQueryDlg-ItemText function.

A modal dialog box releases its data upon termination. Because a modeless dialog can continue to exist after the user enters data, the data is not necessarily released to the calling function. You can avoid this uncertainty by posting a message after the user enters a data item. Here's an example function to handle modeless entry field data.

```
MRESULT EXPENTRY EntryFieldDlg(hwndDlg, msg, mp1, mp2)
HWND    hwndDlg;
USHORT  msg;
MPARAM mp1, mp2;
{

    switch(msg)
    {
        case WM_COMMAND:
            switch(SHORT1FROMMP( mp1 ))
            {
               case DID_OK:
                    WinPostMsg(hwndClient,
                            WM_USER_EFDONE, 0L, 0L);
               case DID_CANCEL:
                    WinPostMsg(hwndClient,
                            WM_USER_EFDESTROY,
                            0L, 0L);
               default:
                    break;
            }
            break;

        default:
            return(WinDefDlgProc( hwndDlg, msg, mp1, mp2));
        }
    return(FALSE);
    }
}
```

This example activates two programmer-defined messages that you post to the message queue in the main window function. The messages are:

- WM_USER_EFDONE

- WM_USER_EFDESTROY

Ensure that you define these message in a header file by appropriately basing their value on the WM_USER message. To retrieve the actual data in the example function — say, string data from five entry fields — you can use the WinQueryWindowText function from within the client window function. Here is a typical call to WinQueryWindowText:

```
for(i=0;i<=5;i++)
{
    WinQueryWindowText(hwndDlg, i,
            sizeof(szEntry[i]), szEntry[i]);
}
```

The key to using this type of **for** loop is setting your entry field IDs to the range specified in the loop. For example, acceptable IDs defined in a header file would be ENTRY_0 through ENTRY_4. Note that if it is awkward to track *hwndDlg* from within the main window function, you can use a call to WinWindowFromID as your first argument to WinQueryDlgItemText.

Mixing Modality

Another consideration in creating your dialog box template is whether you want a combination of modal and modeless dialog boxes, or just the modeless variety.

Unless you want your dialog boxes to dynamically change modality, you can differentiate dialog box modes in the resource script. To do this, you simply OR the FS_SYSMODAL identifier with the other class identifiers in the DIALOG statement. The resulting dialog box retains all other characteristics of its modeless version, but prohibits the user from shifting the input focus.

An efficient way to load a combination of modal and modeless dialog boxes is to use a global boolean variable to denote the modality of any given dialog box. You can then use the WinDlgBox function to load modal dialog boxes, and the WinLoadDlg function to load modeless dialog boxes. The following code underscores this approach.

```
VOID cdecl LoadDialog(hwndParent, hwndOwner, idDlg,
                        DialogProc, modal)
HWND hwndParent;
HWND hwndOwner;
SHORT idDlg;
PFNWP DialogProc;
BOOL modal;
{

    if(modal)
        WinDlgBox(hwndParent, hwndOwner, DialogProc,
            NULL, idDlg, NULL );
    else
    {
        if(WinIsWindow(hab, hwndDlg))
            WinDestroyWindow(hwndDlg);
            hwndDlg = WinLoadDlg(hwndParent, hwndOwner,
                                    DialogProc,NULL, idDlg,
NULL);
    }
}
```

In the example, modal dialog boxes are loaded using WinDlgBox if *modal* is TRUE. Otherwise, a modeless dialog box is loaded using the WinLoadDlg function. Note that the WinIsWindow function is used to ascertain whether a modeless dialog box is currently active — either in its visible or invisible state. WinIsWindow simply tests whether the *hwndDlg* is valid; if a modeless dialog box does not exist, this handle is invalid. If WinIsWindow returns TRUE, the WinDestroyWindow function terminates the modeless dialog box.

Dialog Box Codes

At times, you might want to know the capabilities of a given dialog box control before invoking it. A dedicated system message — WM_QUERYDLG-CODE — gives you the ability to anticipate dialog box controls via a predefined set of codes.

To use the WM_QUERYDLGCODE message, you must send it directly to the dialog box control. This is accomplished using the WinSendMsg and WinWindowFromID functions. Here is an example call:

```
codeDlg=WinSendMsg(WinWindowFromID(hwndDlg,GB_1),
                   WM_QUERYDLGCODE, 0L, 0L);
```

Note that the second argument to WinWindowFromID is the ID of the control window in the dialog box. This is either an integer or a predefined ID from the resource header file. The returned value is the actual dialog code. Table 8-4 lists the dialog codes.

Table 8-4: Predefined Dialog Box Codes

IDENTIFIER	BIT	DESCRIPTION
DLGC_ENTRYFIELD	0x0001	Entry field item.
DLGC_BUTTON	0x0002	Button item.
DLGC_RADIOBUTTON	0x0004	Radio button.
DLGC_STATIC	0x0008	Static item.
DLGC_DEFAULT	0x0010	Default pushbutton.
DLGC_PUSHBUTTON	0x0020	Normal pushbutton.
DLGC_CHECKBOX	0x0040	Checkbox button control.
DLGC_SCROLLBAR	0x0080	Scroll bar.
DLGC_MENU	0x0100	Menu.

Enumerating Dialog Boxes

The WinEnumDlgItem function returns the window handle of a dialog item within a dialog box. This is a handy function when you need to reference one or more dialog item handles, and you have not maintained their values in static variables. The return value is the window handle of the item. Note that the window is always an immediate child window of the window corresponding to the dialog box handle that you supply the function.

Enumerating dialog box items is also a convenient way of obtaining style information about the items. The WinEnumDlgBox function supports a set of system identifiers explicitly for this purpose. Without further ado, here's the definition for WinEnumDlgItem:

```
HWND WinEnumDlgItem(hwndDlg, hwnd, code, fLock)
HWND hwndDlg, hwnd;
USHORT code;
BOOL fLock;
```

The *hwndDlg* argument to WinEnumDlgItem is a handle to the dialog box window. The second handle, *hwnd*, specifies the child window of the dialog box, which can be an immediate child window or any other window with a lower z-order ranking than *hwndDlg* (as long as *hwnd* is a descendant of *hwndDlg*). The third argument, *code*, specifies the actual dialog box item. This is where special set of identifiers, which are denoted by an EDI prefix, enters the scene. Table 8-5 describes the EDI identifiers.

Table 8-5: Dialog Item Enumeration Identifiers

CODE	VALUE	DESCRIPTION
EDI_FIRSTTABITEM	0	Specifies the first item of the WS_TABSTOP style. The *hwnd* argument is ignored.
EDI_LASTTABITEM	1	Specifies the last item of the WS_TABSTOP style. The *hwnd* argument is ignored.
EDI_NEXTTABITEM	2	Specifies the next item of WS_TABSTOP style and wraps to the beginning of the list.
EDI_PREVTABITEM	3	Specifies the previous of WS_TABSTOP style and wraps at the end of the list.
EDI_FIRSTGROUPITEM	4	Specifies the first item in the same group.
EDI_LASTGROUPITEM	5	Specifies the last item in the same group.
EDI_NEXTGROUPITEM	6	Specifies the next item in the same group. Ensures wrap-around.
EDI_PREVGROUPITEM	7	Specifies the previous item in the same group. Ensures wrap-around.

The final argument to WinEnumDlgItem is *fLock*. You have seen this argument in many previous window related functions. It is especially useful in connection with dialog box items, because it prohibits access to the item under certain conditions. This is especially useful in an multi-application, or multi-threaded environment.

Message Boxes

A message box is another form of a modal dialog box. Although its capabilities are limited compared to a dialog box, message boxes are a convenient way to display error messages and other important data. The *Application Style Guide* suggests that message boxes be used only to notify the user of a program error, or when the application requires additional information to process a command.

When a message box appears, it is automatically centered on the display screen. The actual box is 46 characters wide. The text within the box spans up to 33 characters in width. Minimally, a message box is 3 lines deep, but its depth can range up to two-thirds of the display screen.

In addition to programmer-defined message boxes, the Presentation Manager uses four types of system message boxes. These are distinguished by the icon that accompanies the message. The four types are:

- Status — Informs the user of a task in progress.

- Note — Reminds the user to enter a command.

- Warning — Alerts the user to unpredictable consequences.

- Stop — Informs the user of a system failure.

These four groups are widely accepted and allow you to easily enhance an application. Table 8-6 describes the message box styles that you can use when you implement one of these basic types. Each style is associated with a unique identifier. As with other windows, you can OR different styles together. Note, however, that you can't OR styles within the same group. The label group falls in the range up to 0x0008, and the the icon group continues up to 0x0040. The group that carries the value of the current button press ranges from 0x0000 to 0x0400. Two other MB identifiers, MB_HELP and MB_MOVEABLE, are standalone values and can be ORed with other values.

Table 8-6: Message Box Types

TYPE	BIT	DESCRIPTION
MB_OK	0x0000	Signifies OK pushbutton.
MB_OKCANCEL	0x0001	Signifies OK and Cancel pushbuttons.
MB_RETRYCANCEL	0x0002	Message box has retry and cancel pushbuttons.
MB_ABORTRETRYIGNORE	0x0003	Message box has pushbuttons for abort, retry, or ignore error state.
MB_YESNO	0x0004	Signifies Yes and No pushbuttons.
MB_YESNOCANCEL	0x0005	Message box has pushbuttons for yes, no, and cancel responses.
MB_CANCEL	0x0006	Signifies a Cancel pushbutton.
MB_ENTER	0x0007	Signifies an Enter pushbutton.
MB_ENTERCANCEL	0x0008	Signifies an Enter and a Cancel pushbutton.
MB_NOICON	0x0000	Message box does not contain an icon.
MB_ICONQUESTION	0x0010	Signifies a question mark icon.
MB_ICONEXCLAMATION	0x0020	Signifies an exclamation point icon.
MB_ICONASTERISK	0x0030	Signifies an asterisk icon.
MB_ICONHAND	0x0040	Signifies a hand icon.
MB_DEFBUTTON1	0x0000	Signifies the first button is the default. This is the normal default.
MB_DEFBUTTON2	0x0100	Signifies the second button is the default.

(continued)

Table 8-6: Continued

TYPE	BIT	DESCRIPTION
MB_DEFBUTTON3	0x0200	Signifies the third button is the default.
MB_APPLMODAL	0x0000	Signifies the message box is application modal.
MB_SYSTEMMODAL	0x1000	Signifies the message box is system modal
MB_HELP	0x2000	Signifies a Help pushbutton.
MB_MOVEABLE	0x4000	Signifies the message box is moveable.

To create your own message boxes, use the WinMessageBox function. WinMessageBox takes responsibility for creating, displaying, and driving the message box window. Here's the definition for WinMessageBox:

```
USHORT WinMessageBox(hwndParent, hwndOwner, pszText,
                     pszCaption, idWindow, flStyle)
HWND hwndParent, hwndOwner;
PSZ pszText, pszCaption;
USHORT idWindow, flStyle;
```

The *hwndParent* argument identifies the message box's parent window. Typically, this is HWND_DESKTOP, or NULL if the message box is the only window displayed. The *hwndOwner* argument specifies the message box's owner window, which is often the same window as the parent window. The *pszText* and *pszCaption* arguments point to the box text and title text, respectively. The *idWindow* argument specifies the message box's window ID. When the system receives a WM_HELP message, this ID is passed to the HK_HELP hook. Lastly, *flStyle* specifies one of the MB identifiers.

The WinMessageBox function returns a message identifier associated with the user's action. Table 8-7 lists these messages.

Table 8-7: Message Box Message Identifier Types

IDENTIFIER	VALUE	DESCRIPTION
MBID_OK	1	OK pushbutton selected.
MBID_CANCEL	2	Cancel pushbutton or Escape key selected.
MBID_ABORT	3	Abort pushbutton selected.
MBID_RETRY	4	Retry pushbutton selected.
MBID_IGNORE	5	Ignore pushbutton selected.
MBID_YES	6	Yes pushbutton selected.
MBID_NO	7	No pushbutton selected.
MBID_HELP	8	Help selected.
MBID_ENTER	9	Enter key selected.
MBID_ERROR	0xffff	Message box error.

Template Upgrade

It's time for an upgrade. The following upgrade to the template program (first presented in Chapter 4) now incorporates several dialog boxes, including an About box, a necessity for any program that intends to comply with the *Application Style Guide*. Here's the upgrade:

```
; TMPL3.DEF (Module Definition File)

NAME        TMPL3

DESCRIPTION 'Template 3'
PROTMODE
HEAPSIZE    1024
STACKSIZE   8192
EXPORTS     TemplateWndProc @1
            RadioDlgBoxProc @2
            LBoxDlgBoxProc  @3
            EntryDlgBoxProc @4
            AboutDlgBoxProc @5
```

```
/* TMPL2.H (Header file) */

#define IDD_NULL          -1

#define ID_MENURES        1
#define IDM_HELP          3

#define IDM_FILEMENU      400
#define IDM_FILENEW       410
#define IDM_FILEOPEN      411
#define IDM_FILESAVE      412
#define IDM_FILESAVEAS    413
#define IDM_FILEDIRECTORY 414

#define IDM_EDITMENU      402
#define IDM_EDITRESTORE   415
#define IDM_EDITCUT       416
#define IDM_EDITCOPY      417
#define IDM_EDITPASTE     418
#define IDM_EDITCLEAR     419

#define IDM_EXITMENU      403
#define IDM_EXITRESUME    420
#define IDM_EXITEXIT      421

#define IDM_DIALOGMENU    500     /* Menu numbering changing! */
#define IDM_DIALOGRADIO   501
#define IDM_DIALOGLBOX    502
#define IDM_ENTRYFIELD    503
#define IDM_ABOUT         504     /* From file menu. */

#define IDD_DIALOG1       600
#define IDD_OP0           601
#define IDD_OP1           602
#define IDD_OP2           603
#define IDD_OP4           604
#define IDD_OP5           605
#define IDD_OP6           606
#define IDD_OP7           607
#define IDD_OP8           608
#define IDD_OP9           609

#define IDD_DIALOG2       700
#define IDD_LISTBOX       701

#define IDD_DIALOG3       800
#define IDD_ENTRYFIELD    801
```

```
#define IDD_ABOUT          900


/* TMPL3.RC (Resource Script) */

#include <os2.h>
#include "tmpl3.h"

MENU ID_MENURES
{
  SUBMENU "~File", IDM_FILEMENU
    {
      MENUITEM "~New\t^N", IDM_FILENEW
      MENUITEM "~Open...\t^O", IDM_FILEOPEN, MIA_CHECKED
      MENUITEM "~Save\t^S", IDM_FILESAVE
      MENUITEM "Save as...", IDM_FILESAVEAS, MIS_SEPARATOR
      MENUITEM "~Directory...\t^D", IDM_FILEDIRECTORY
      MENUITEM "~About...\t", IDM_ABOUT
    }

  SUBMENU "~Edit", IDM_EDITMENU
    {
      MENUITEM "Restore", IDM_EDITRESTORE
      MENUITEM "Cut\tSh Del", IDM_EDITCUT
      MENUITEM "Copy\tF2", IDM_EDITCOPY
      MENUITEM "Paste\tSh Ins", IDM_EDITPASTE
      MENUITEM "~Clear\t^C", IDM_EDITCLEAR
    }

  SUBMENU "~Dialogs", IDM_DIALOGMENU
    {
      MENUITEM "~Radiobuttons", IDM_DIALOGRADIO
      MENUITEM "~Listbox", IDM_DIALOGLBOX
      MENUITEM "~Entry-field", IDM_ENTRYFIELD
    }

  SUBMENU "E~xit", IDM_EXITMENU
    {
      MENUITEM "Resume", IDM_EXITRESUME
      MENUITEM "Exit\tF3", IDM_EXITEXIT
    }
```

```
    MENUITEM "F1=Help", IDM_HELP, MIS_HELP | MIS_BUTTONSEPARATOR
}

ACCELTABLE ID_MENURES
  {
   "^F", IDM_FILEMENU
   "^N", IDM_FILENEW
   "^O", IDM_FILEOPEN
   "^S", IDM_FILESAVE
   "^D", IDM_FILEDIRECTORY
   "^E", IDM_EDITMENU
   VK_DELETE, IDM_EDITCUT, VIRTUALKEY, SHIFT
   VK_F2, IDM_EDITCOPY, VIRTUALKEY
   VK_INSERT, IDM_EDITPASTE, VIRTUALKEY, SHIFT
   "^C", IDM_EDITCLEAR
   "^E", IDM_EXITMENU
   VK_F3, IDM_EXITEXIT,   VIRTUALKEY
  }

DLGTEMPLATE IDD_DIALOG1
  {
   DIALOG "", 2, 15, 5, 200, 137, FS_DLGBORDER
    {
       CTEXT "Template Options", IDD_NULL, 20, 127, 160, 8
       GROUPBOX      "Group Box", IDD_NULL,  5, 20, 170, 102
       AUTORADIOBUTTON "Option 1", IDD_OP0, 8, 102, 90, 12,
                               WS_GROUP
       AUTORADIOBUTTON "Option 2", IDD_OP1, 8, 92, 95, 12
       AUTORADIOBUTTON "Option 3", IDD_OP2, 8, 82, 95, 12
       AUTORADIOBUTTON "Option 4", IDD_OP4, 8, 72, 95, 12
       AUTORADIOBUTTON "Option 5", IDD_OP5, 8, 62, 95, 12
       AUTORADIOBUTTON "Option 6", IDD_OP6, 8, 52, 95, 12
       AUTORADIOBUTTON "Option 7", IDD_OP7, 8, 42, 95, 12
       AUTORADIOBUTTON "Option 8", IDD_OP8, 8, 32, 95, 12
       AUTORADIOBUTTON "Option 9", IDD_OP9, 8, 22, 95, 12
       DEFPUSHBUTTON "Ok", MBID_OK, 6, 4, 38, 12,
                               WS_TABSTOP | WS_GROUP
       PUSHBUTTON "Cancel", MBID_CANCEL, 56, 4, 38, 12,
                               WS_TABSTOP | WS_GROUP

    }
  }

DLGTEMPLATE IDD_DIALOG2
  {
   DIALOG "", 2, 15, 5, 200, 137, FS_DLGBORDER
    {
       CTEXT "Template Listbox", IDD_NULL, 20, 127, 160, 8
```

```
            LISTBOX IDD_LISTBOX, 10, 25, 95, 80,
                              WS_TABSTOP | WS_GROUP
            DEFPUSHBUTTON "Ok", MBID_OK, 6, 4, 38, 12,
                              WS_TABSTOP | WS_GROUP
            PUSHBUTTON "Cancel", MBID_CANCEL, 56, 4, 38, 12,
                              WS_TABSTOP | WS_GROUP
        }
    }

DLGTEMPLATE IDD_DIALOG3
  {
    DIALOG "", 2, 15, 5, 200, 70, FS_DLGBORDER
        {
            CTEXT "Template Entry-Field", IDD_NULL, 20, 60, 160, 8
            EDITTEXT "", IDD_ENTRYFIELD, 10, 35, 95, 12, ES_MARGIN
            DEFPUSHBUTTON "Ok", MBID_OK, 6, 4, 38, 12,
                              WS_TABSTOP | WS_GROUP
            PUSHBUTTON "Cancel", MBID_CANCEL, 56, 4, 38, 12,
                              WS_TABSTOP | WS_GROUP
        }
    }

DLGTEMPLATE IDD_ABOUT
  {
    DIALOG "", 1, 20, 20, 150, 130, FS_DLGBORDER
        {
            CTEXT "Template About Box" IDD_NULL 0, 100, 150, 8
            CTEXT "This is a template program," IDD_NULL
                              0, 70, 150, 8
            CTEXT "which you can build on. Right" IDD_NULL,
                              0, 55, 150, 8
            CTEXT "now, you're in the About Box" IDD_NULL,
                              0, 40, 150, 8
            DEFPUSHBUTTON "Ok", DID_OK, 6, 4, 40, 12,
                              WS_TABSTOP | WS_GROUP
        }
    }


/* TMPL3.C (Template upgrade) */

#define INCL_PM

#include <os2.h>
#include <string.h>
#include "tmpl3.h"
```

```
MRESULT EXPENTRY TemplateWndProc(HWND,USHORT,MPARAM,MPARAM);
MRESULT EXPENTRY RadioDlgBoxProc(HWND,USHORT,MPARAM,MPARAM);
MRESULT EXPENTRY LBoxDlgBoxProc(HWND,USHORT,MPARAM,MPARAM);
MRESULT EXPENTRY EntryDlgBoxProc(HWND,USHORT,MPARAM,MPARAM);
MRESULT EXPENTRY AboutDlgBoxProc(HWND,USHORT,MPARAM,MPARAM);
VOID DisplayMessageBox(HWND,SHORT);

HAB hab;
HMQ hmq;
HWND hwndFrame, hwndTemplate;

int main(void)
{

static CHAR szClass[9] = "Template";
static CHAR szTitleBar[15] = "Blank Template";
ULONG ctlData = FCF_TITLEBAR | FCF_SYSMENU | FCF_SIZEBORDER
                | FCF_MINMAX | FCF_MENU | FCF_ACCELTABLE;

USHORT fSwap = SWP_ACTIVATE | SWP_SIZE | SWP_MOVE | SWP_SHOW;
PID pid;
TID tid;
QMSG qmsg;
SWCNTRL swctl;


hab = WinInitialize(NULL);
hmq = WinCreateMsgQueue(hab, 0);
WinRegisterClass(
            hab,
            szClass,
            TemplateWndProc,
            CS_SIZEREDRAW,
            0);

hwndFrame = WinCreateStdWindow(
            HWND_DESKTOP,
            WS_VISIBLE,
            &ctlData,
            szClass,
            szTitleBar,
            0L,
            NULL,
            ID_MENURES,
            &hwndTemplate);

WinSetWindowPos(
```

```
                    hwndFrame,
                    HWND_TOP,
                    50,
                    50,
                    250,
                    250,
                    fSwap);

    WinQueryWindowProcess(hwndFrame, &pid, &tid);

    swctl.hwnd = hwndFrame;
    swctl.hwndIcon = NULL;
    swctl.hprog = NULL;
    swctl.idProcess = pid;
    swctl.idSession = NULL;
    swctl.uchVisibility = SWL_VISIBLE;
    swctl.fbJump = SWL_JUMPABLE;
    strcpy(swctl.szSwtitle, "Template Demo");

    WinAddSwitchEntry(&swctl);

    while(WinGetMsg(hab, &qmsg, NULL, 0, 0))
                WinDispatchMsg(hab, &qmsg);

    WinDestroyWindow(hwndFrame);
    WinDestroyMsgQueue(hmq);
    WinTerminate(hab);

    return(0);
}


MRESULT EXPENTRY TemplateWndProc(hwnd, msg, mp1, mp2)
HWND hwnd;
USHORT msg;
MPARAM mp1, mp2;
{
    HPS hps;

    switch (msg)
       {
          case WM_ERASEBACKGROUND:
              return(TRUE);

/*        case WM_PAINT:
              hps = WinBeginPaint(hwnd, NULL, NULL);
              WinEndPaint(hps);
```

```
        return(NULL);  */

case WM_COMMAND:
      switch((COMMANDMSG(&msg)->cmd))
        {
          case IDM_FILENEW:
            DisplayMessageBox(hwnd,
                        IDM_FILENEW - 410);
            return(NULL);

          case IDM_FILEOPEN:
            DisplayMessageBox(hwnd,
                        IDM_FILEOPEN - 410);
            return(NULL);

          case IDM_FILESAVE:
            DisplayMessageBox(hwnd,
                        IDM_FILESAVE - 410);
            return(NULL);

          case IDM_FILESAVEAS:
            DisplayMessageBox(hwnd,
                        IDM_FILESAVEAS - 410);
            return(NULL);

          case IDM_FILEDIRECTORY:
            DisplayMessageBox(hwnd,
                        IDM_FILEDIRECTORY - 410);
            return(NULL);

          case IDM_EDITRESTORE:
            DisplayMessageBox(hwnd,
                        IDM_EDITRESTORE - 410);
            return(NULL);

          case IDM_EDITCUT:
            DisplayMessageBox(hwnd,
                        IDM_EDITCUT - 410);
            return(NULL);

          case IDM_EDITCOPY:
            DisplayMessageBox(hwnd,
                        IDM_EDITCOPY - 410);
            return(NULL);

          case IDM_EDITPASTE:
            DisplayMessageBox(hwnd,
```

```
                              IDM_EDITPASTE - 410);
            return(NULL);

      case IDM_EDITCLEAR:
        DisplayMessageBox(hwnd,
                          IDM_EDITCLEAR - 410);
        return(NULL);

      case IDM_EXITRESUME:
        return(NULL);

      case IDM_EXITEXIT:
        if(MBID_YES == WinMessageBox(
           HWND_DESKTOP, hwnd,
           "You are about to quit the program.\n"
           "Are you sure you want to do this?",
           "Closing Message",
              0, MB_YESNOCANCEL | MB_DEFBUTTON3
              | MB_ICONQUESTION | MB_MOVEABLE))
           {
           WinPostMsg(hwndFrame,
                      WM_QUIT, 0L, 0L);
           break;
           }
        else
           return(NULL);

      case IDM_DIALOGRADIO:
        WinDlgBox(HWND_DESKTOP,
                  hwnd, RadioDlgBoxProc,
                  NULL, IDD_DIALOG1, NULL);
        break;

      case IDM_DIALOGLBOX:
        WinDlgBox(HWND_DESKTOP,
                  hwnd, LBoxDlgBoxProc,
                  NULL, IDD_DIALOG2, NULL);
        break;

      case IDM_ENTRYFIELD:
        WinDlgBox(HWND_DESKTOP,
                  hwnd, EntryDlgBoxProc,
                  NULL, IDD_DIALOG3, NULL);
        break;

      case IDM_ABOUT:
        WinDlgBox(HWND_DESKTOP,
```

```
                                    hwnd, AboutDlgBoxProc,
                                    NULL, IDD_ABOUT, NULL);
                    break;

            }

    }

    return WinDefWindowProc(hwnd, msg, mp1, mp2);
}

VOID DisplayMessageBox(hwnd, sMenuValue)
HWND hwnd;
SHORT sMenuValue;
{

    static char *szMenu[] = { "File", "Open", "Save", "Save as",
    "Directory", "Restore", "Cut", "Copy",
    "Paste", "Clear" };

    WinMessageBox(HWND_DESKTOP, hwnd,
            "This menu item is not yet implemented.",
            szMenu[sMenuValue],
            0, MB_YESNOCANCEL | MB_DEFBUTTON3
            | MB_ICONQUESTION | MB_MOVEABLE);
}

MRESULT EXPENTRY RadioDlgBoxProc(hwndDlg, msg, mp1, mp2)
HWND hwndDlg;
USHORT msg;
MPARAM mp1, mp2;
{
    SHORT id;

    switch(msg)
        {
        case WM_CONTROL:
            id = SHORT1FROMMP(mp1);
            if(id >= IDD_OP0 && id <= IDD_OP9)
                DosBeep(100,300);
            break;
        }

    return(WinDefDlgProc(hwndDlg, msg, mp1, mp2));
}
```

```
MRESULT EXPENTRY LBoxDlgBoxProc(hwndDlg, msg, mp1, mp2)
HWND hwndDlg;
USHORT msg;
MPARAM mp1, mp2;
{

    SHORT i;
    static CHAR *szString[] = {"one\0", "two\0", "three\0",
                "four\0", "five\0", "six\0", "seven\0",
                "eight\0", "nine\0", "ten\0", "eleven\0",
                "twelve\0", "thirteen\0", "fourteen\0",
                "fifteen\0", "sixteen\0", "seventeen\0",
                "eighteen\0", "nineteen\0", "twenty\0" };

    switch(msg)
        {
        case WM_INITDLG:
                for(i=0; i<20; i++)
                WinSendDlgItemMsg(hwndDlg, IDD_LISTBOX,
                        LM_INSERTITEM,
                        MPFROM2SHORT(LIT_END, 0),
                        MPFROMP(szString[i]));
                break;
        }
    return(WinDefDlgProc(hwndDlg, msg, mp1, mp2));
}


MRESULT EXPENTRY EntryDlgBoxProc(hwndDlg, msg, mp1, mp2)
HWND hwndDlg;
USHORT msg;
MPARAM mp1, mp2;
{

    switch(msg)
        {
        case WM_CONTROL:
                if(SHORT1FROMMP(mp1) == IDD_ENTRYFIELD
                    && SHORT2FROMMP(mp1) == EN_KILLFOCUS)
                DosBeep(100,300);
                break;
        }

    return(WinDefDlgProc(hwndDlg, msg, mp1, mp2));
}
```

```
MRESULT EXPENTRY AboutDlgBoxProc(hwndDlg, msg, mp1, mp2)
HWND hwndDlg;
USHORT msg;
MPARAM mp1, mp2;
{

    return(WinDefDlgProc(hwndDlg, msg, mp1, mp2));
}
```

CHAPTER 9

GRAPHICS PROGRAMMING INTERFACE

The Presentation Manager's graphic environment represents a great stride forward for PC-based graphics. Its major advantage over other systems is it frees the programmer from having to address the issue of device drivers by providing presentation spaces as the intermediate interface to devices. From a capabilities viewpoint, the Presentation Manager not only offers the graphic features of Microsoft *Windows*, it goes beyond this and delivers features typically found only on supermini and mainframe computers — most notably, its large selection of graphics primitives.

In a graphics-based system such as the Presentation Manager, each bit contained in a character is fully addressable — meaning the hardware (be it a printer or monitor) is the only limitation on the amount of data the Presentation Manager can display. Conversely, a character-based system such as MS-DOS only displays a maximum of 2,000 characters per screen (80 characters by 25 lines). The Presentation Manager takes full advantage of a monitor such as a VGA and can address each of its 307,200 pixels (640 by 480 resolution).

Even OS/2 kernel applications make use of the Presentation Manager's graphic capabilities. For an OS/2 application to produce a graphic image, it first builds the image in memory. When the application wants to display the graphic image on screen, it uses advanced Vio calls to invoke the Presentation Manager's Graphic Programming Interface (Gpi). The Presentation Manager then converts the memory image into a command or series of commands that the display uses to produce the image.

The Presentation Manager and the OS/2 kernel serve as the interface between applications and the device drivers for various hardware devices. Applications need not know the details of the hardware. This device independence means that developers can focus on new features and functionality, rather than writing device drivers for different hardware components. This also means hardware can be changed without constantly updating applications. The only remaining third-party requirement falls on the shoulders of the hardware manufacturers — they must ensure that their components provide a Presentation Manager device driver.

This chapter provides an introductory look at the Gpi library. As a result, the description in this chapter is limited to an overview of presentation spaces and devices contexts, and a selected number of Gpi functions, including several that affect default environment conditions such as color and object patterns.

The Presentation Space

A presentation space is the Presentation Manager's device interface. You can think of it as a device driver, if you like, but it is more than that. For one thing, it relieves you from understanding how an actual device — be it a display monitor, printer, or memory bitmap — handles output from your program.

In the Presentation Manger, device interface considerations are relegated to the device context, which contains low-level information about the hardware device. In turn, the device context receives higher level instructions from the presentation space, which itself receives instructions from the Gpi functions. The Presentation Manager offers three types of presentation spaces.

Each type of presentation space offers different capabilities and requires different programming techniques. The general rule to follow in choosing a presentation space is for more complex device needs, you need a more powerful presentation space. The three types of presentation spaces are:

- Cached-PS — The default presentation space created by the Presentation Manager itself. It is only valid for monitor-based graphics and is limited to drawing in the current window.

- Micro-PS — Similar to the cached-PS, but allows you to control the default environment and specify different units of measure. It also provides greater control over updating obscured regions of a window.

- Normal-PS — Most advanced type of presentation space. It supports monitor-based as well as printer/plotter graphics. It lets you create and save metafiles and *function chains*.

The first order of business in using the Gpi library is defining a presentation space, which is an internal data structure containing the necessary information to exchange graphic data with a device context. A device context is also a data structure. It defines a physical output device such as a monitor, printer, or plotter.

The most rudimentary view of a presentation space — but the one to which you will become most accustomed — is that of a geometric plane. This plane can exist in the abstract, although it is still handy to think of it as the display monitor or a printed page.

All *x-y* coordinates in the plane are represented as pixels. The (0, 0) coordinates of the plane begin in its lower left-hand corner. The (*n*-1, *n*-1) coordinates, or the end of the plane, exist in the upper right-hand corner. Obviously, *x*-values increase to the right while *y*-values increase vertically.

Internally, the Presentation Manager maintains the coordinate plane — via the presentation space — as its own data structure. This structure types the overall coordinates of the plane, as well as individual coordinates in it, as unsigned long integers.

The Presentation Manager does not use floating point numbers to describe the presentation space because of the 80286's inherent inability to deal effectively with floats. The structures that you, the programmer, use to define the coordinate plane are RECTL, POINTL, and SIZE.

Two general ways of describing the coordinate system are frequently mentioned in connection to the Gpi functions. These are world coordinates (also known as Cartesian coordinates) and model coordinates (also known as device coordinates).

Figure 9-1 shows the coordinate plane of a presentation space in terms of world coordinates. It uses the ubiquitous *x*, *y*, *cx*, and *cy* variables as points of reference.

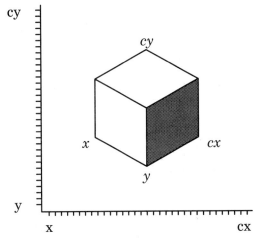

Figure 9-1: World coordinate system used to describe presentation space objects.

Preparing a graphic image for an external device primarily involves converting the image from world to model coordinates. This process is called a normalization transformation, which is traditionally based on the following relationship between world and model coordinates:

```
cxModel = (xWorld - xWorldMin) / (xWorldMax - xWorldMin);
cyModel = (yWorld - yWorldMin) / (yWorldMax - yWorldMin);
```

The Gpi library provides functions to handle transformations for you. When you specify a device context and move graphics into a new device context, transformations occur automatically. The combination of a presentation space and device context is, indeed, a powerful tandem — allowing the Presentation Manager to automatically communicate data to the hardware device drivers and produce images for the new environment, with little programmer overhead. Figure 9-2 shows the relationship between the presentation space, device context, and output devices.

As a Presentation Manager programmer, you do not need to know anything about these device drivers. You simply define a presentation space and device context and then use the Gpi functions to create graphics. In cases when you only need minimum graphics capabilities for the video display, you do not even need to define a device context — instead, the Presentation Manager accesses the default device context, which it uses to draw windows.

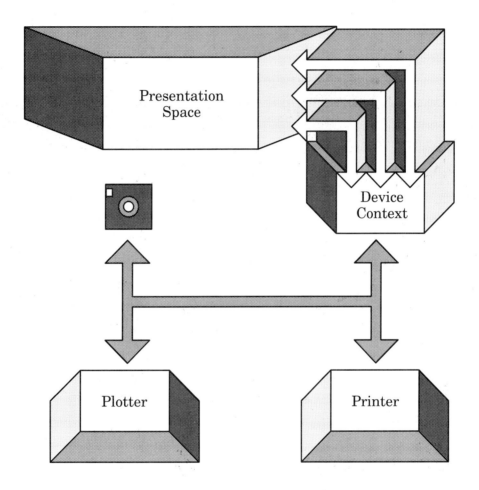

Figure 9-2: Graphic Output System

The Cached-PS

The cached-PS allows you to quickly access a subset of Gpi functions from within any application. In general, the cached-PS operates identically to the micro-PS, but gives you limited control over the default environment of the presentation space. Note, too, that the automatically created device context for a cached-PS accesses only the visible sections of a window. In other words, if you have a graphic that takes a long time to display and decide to hot-key to another window (which overlaps the first window), no drawing will occur in the obscured section of the window. You access a cached-PS by using any of the following Win functions:

- WinGetPS

- WinGetClipPS

- WinGetScreenPS

You must be meticulous in setting up and restoring a presentation space. When you create a cached-PS, adhere to the following steps:

1. Create a frame window as you normally would.

2. Create a presentation space using either the WinGetPS, Win-GetScreenPS, or WinGetClipPS.

3. Draw into the presentation space.

4. Restore the presentation space by using the WinReleasePS function.

Besides the visible region drawback, a cached-PS has other drawbacks compared to a micro- or normal-PS. The most obvious one is a cached-PS requires you to restore, or release, the presentation space immediately after using it. (If you don't, the system will hang!) The reason for this is the Presentation Manager also makes frequent use of the cached-PS. This means a conflict is likely to arise — if not between your application and the Presentation Manager, then between your application and another application.

Another drawback to a cached-PS is the coordinates of the presentation space are always anchored at the lower left corner (0,0) of the window if you use WinGetPS or WinGetClipPS; or the lower left corner of the screen if you use WinGetScreenPS. There is no automatic way to modify this state of affairs. Both micro and normal presentation spaces support the concept of a presentation page, which lets you selectively locate the starting coordinates of the presentation space.

Yet there are advantages to the cached-PS. For one thing, combined with its automatically created screen device context, it uses only about 1.5K of RAM. This is compared to the about 30K to 45K that you can eat up using the more advanced presentation spaces in a full-fledged application. Additionally, using a cached-PS also offers you speed advantages if your application creates and destroys numerous child control windows.

The Presentation Manager internally performs all visible region calculations the first time you invoke WinGetPS. Thereafter, it bases its calculations on the first calculation, allowing for even faster access to the cached presentation space. The only disadvantage here is the redundancy involved in getting and releasing the presentation space.

To create a cached-PS, you need to declare a variable of type HPS, (typically called hps) and call either the WinGetPS, WinGetClipPS, or WinGetScreenPS functions. WinGetPS is the more commonly used function of the two. Here's the typical call:

```
hps = WinGetPS(hwnd)
```

The handle supplied to WinGetPS points to the current window. After you invoke WinGetPS, you can use any of the Gpi functions available to the micro-PS by referencing *hps*.

The drawing area of the presentation space — also referred to as its visible region — is determined by the frame and class styles of *hwnd*. If you set *hwnd* to HWND_DESKTOP, the presentation space encompasses the entire screen, meaning you can draw in any window on the desktop. Otherwise, if you set *hwnd* to a specific window, you can modify its visible region using the various styles described in Table 9-1.

Table 9-1: Window Styles Affecting WinGetPS

STYLE	BIT	EFFECT
WS_CLIPSIBLINGS	0x10000000L	Excludes sibling windows.
WS_CLIPCHILDREN	0x20000000L	Excludes child windows.
CS_PARENTCLIP	0x80000000L	Maps visible region to the scope of the parent window, including child and sibling windows.

When your application completes its graphic routines, you must call the WinReleasePS function to close the presentation space. The Win-ReleasePS function takes *hps* as its only argument.

Basic Drawing

To draw in a presentation space, you must always be aware of the concept of current position. As a rule, Gpi functions reference the current position and a new position through the use of the POINTL structure and the GpiMove function. Basically, the GpiMove function defines the coordinates that shape your object. Here's the definition for GpiMove:

```
BOOL GpiMove(hps, pptl)
HPS hps;
PPOINTL pptl;
```

As with all but a few Gpi functions, the first argument to GpiMove is a handle to the active presentation space. The second argument is a pointer to the POINTL structure. Before calling GpiMove, you must set the current position by referencing POINTL. Then, for a simple object such as a line, you reference POINTL one more time before calling GpiLine function. The following routine draws a horizontal line from left (100, 300) to right (300, 100) in world coordinates, using pixels as the unit of measure (the default unit of measure for the cached-PS).

```
GpiSetColor(hps, CLR_BLUE);
ptl.x = 100;
```

```
ptl.y = 100;
GpiMove (hps, &ptl);
ptl.x = 300;
ptl.y = 100;
GpiLine(hps, &ptl);
```

Notice that GpiLine takes the same arguments as GpiMove. If you like, you can think of GpiMove as drawing the first half of the line and GpiLine as drawing the second half. In reality, however, GpiMove marks the current position so that the Presentation Manager can reference it when it receives a drawing instruction. This becomes even clearer in light of the GpiBeginArea and GpiEndArea functions, which allow you to specify a series of GpiMove calls. Here's the definition for GpiBeginArea:

```
BOOL GpiBeginArea(hps, flOptions)
HPS hps;
ULONG flOptions;
```

Observe that GpiBeginArea does not reference the POINTL structure. The function itself is not responsible for marking the current position; rather it simply tells the Presentation Manager to treat all calls to GpiMove as defining a sequence until it receives a corresponding call to GpiEndArea. Typically, GpiBeginArea is said to be responsible for the *construction* of an area. Its *flOptions* argument specifies how the Presentation Manager should draw the objects in the constructed area. Table 9-2 lists and describes these options, which you can OR to obtain combined effects.

Table 9-2: GpiBeginArea Options

IDENTIFIER	BIT/VALUE	DESCRIPTION
BA_NOBOUNDARY	0L	Omits boundary lines.
BA_BOUNDARY	0x0001L	Draws boundary lines (default).
BA_ALTERNATE	0L	Constructs interior in alternate mode, meaning a point is placed in the interior if the number of boundary crossings (set by extending linear points until they intersect) is odd.

(continued)

Table 9-2: Continued

IDENTIFIER	BIT/VALUE	DESCRIPTION
BA_WINDING	0x0002L	Constructs interior in winding mode, meaning a point is placed in the interior if the number of boundary crossings (set by negating lines each time one exists that goes in the opposite direction) is non-zero.

The constructed area is terminated by a call to GpiEndArea. In between GpiBeginArea and GpiEndArea, you can call such functions as GpiMove, GpiLine, GpiPartialArc, and GpiPolyLine, and more. Most relevant, for the time being, are GpiMove and GpiLine: once you call GpiBeginArea, you can call GpiMove any number of times to mark points in an object. To connect the points in an object, you call a drawing function such as GpiLine. The following program example includes a routine that uses this technique. It also introduces several other drawing functions.

```
/* GPISAMP1.H (Header file) */
#define IDM_MENURES      1
#define IDD_DLGMIX       2
#define IDD_DLGPAT       3
#define IDM_HELP         4

#define IDM_DRAW         100
#define IDM_SCREEN       101
#define IDM_BOXES        102
#define IDM_ARCS         103
#define IDM_CIRCLES      104
#define IDM_LINES        105
#define IDM_TRIANGLES    106

#define IDM_ATTRIBUTES   110
#define IDM_DLGMIX       111
#define IDM_DLGPAT       112

#define IDD_NULL         -1

#define IDD_FM0          200
#define IDD_FM1          201
#define IDD_FM2          202
#define IDD_FM4          204
```

```
#define IDD_FM5          205
#define IDD_FM6          206
#define IDD_FM7          207
#define IDD_FM8          208
#define IDD_FM9          209
#define IDD_FM10         210
#define IDD_FM11         211
#define IDD_FM12         212
#define IDD_FM13         213
#define IDD_FM14         214
#define IDD_FM15         215
#define IDD_FM16         216
#define IDD_FM17         217

#define IDD_PAT0         300
#define IDD_PAT1         301
#define IDD_PAT2         302
#define IDD_PAT3         303
#define IDD_PAT4         304
#define IDD_PAT5         305
#define IDD_PAT6         306
#define IDD_PAT7         307
#define IDD_PAT8         308
#define IDD_PAT9         309
#define IDD_PAT10        310
#define IDD_PAT11        311
#define IDD_PAT12        312
#define IDD_PAT13        313
#define IDD_PAT14        314
#define IDD_PAT15        315
#define IDD_PAT16        316
#define IDD_PAT17        317



/* GPISAMP1.RC (Resource Script) */

#include <os2.h>
#include "gpisamp1.h"

MENU IDM_MENURES
{
SUBMENU "~Draw", IDM_DRAW
{
    MENUITEM "~Clear screen\t^S", IDM_SCREEN
    MENUITEM "~Boxes\t^B", IDM_BOXES, MIA_CHECKED
    MENUITEM "~Arcs\t^A", IDM_ARCS
```

```
    MENUITEM "~Circles\t^C", IDM_CIRCLES
    MENUITEM "~Lines\t^L", IDM_LINES
    MENUITEM "~Triangles\t^B", IDM_TRIANGLES
}
SUBMENU "~Attributes", IDM_ATTRIBUTES
{
    MENUITEM "GpiSetMix\t^M", IDM_DLGMIX
    MENUITEM "GpiSetPattern\t^P", IDM_DLGPAT
}

MENUITEM "F1=Help", IDM_HELP, MIS_HELP | MIS_BUTTONSEPARATOR
}

ACCELTABLE IDM_MENURES
{
    "^S", IDM_SCREEN
    "^B", IDM_BOXES
    "^A", IDM_ARCS
    "^C", IDM_CIRCLES
    "^L", IDM_LINES
    "^T", IDM_TRIANGLES
    "^M", IDM_DLGMIX
"^P", IDM_DLGPAT
}

DLGTEMPLATE IDD_DLGMIX
{
DIALOG "", 2, 15, 5, 270, 137, FS_DLGBORDER
{
CTEXT       "GpiSetMode Options",
IDD_NULL, 30, 127, 160, 8

GROUPBOX "Color modes", IDD_NULL, 5, 20, 245, 102
AUTORADIOBUTTON "FM_DEFAULT", IDD_FM0,8,102, 90, 12, WS_GROUP
AUTORADIOBUTTON "FM_OR", IDD_FM1, 8, 92, 95, 12
AUTORADIOBUTTON "FM_OVERPAINT", IDD_FM2,  8, 82, 95, 12
AUTORADIOBUTTON "FM_XOR", IDD_FM4, 8, 72, 95, 12
AUTORADIOBUTTON "FM_LEAVEALONE", IDD_FM, 5, 8, 62, 95, 12
AUTORADIOBUTTON "FM_AND", IDD_FM6, 8, 52, 95, 12
AUTORADIOBUTTON "FM_SUBTRACT", IDD_FM7, 8, 42, 95, 12
AUTORADIOBUTTON "FM_NOTMASKSRC", IDD_FM8, 8, 32, 95, 12
AUTORADIOBUTTON "FM_ZERO", IDD_FM9, 8, 22, 95, 12
AUTORADIOBUTTON "FM_NOTMERGESRC", IDD_FM10, 123, 102, 102, 12
AUTORADIOBUTTON "FM_NOTXORSRC", IDD_FM11, 123, 92, 102, 12
AUTORADIOBUTTON "FM_INVERT", IDD_FM12, 123, 82, 102, 12
AUTORADIOBUTTON "FM_MERGESRCNOT", IDD_FM13, 123, 72, 102, 12
AUTORADIOBUTTON "FM_NOTCOPYSRC", IDD_FM14, 123, 62, 102, 12
```

```
AUTORADIOBUTTON "FM_MERGENOTSRC", IDD_FM15, 123, 52, 102, 12
AUTORADIOBUTTON "FM_NOTMASKSRC", IDD_FM16, 123, 42, 102, 12
AUTORADIOBUTTON "FM_ONE", IDD_FM17, 123, 32, 102, 12
DEFPUSHBUTTON  "Ok", MBID_OK, 6, 4, 38, 12,
                        WS_TABSTOP | WS_GROUP
PUSHBUTTON "Cancel", MBID_CANCEL, 56, 4, 38, 12,
                        WS_TABSTOP | WS_GROUP

}
}

DLGTEMPLATE IDD_DLGPAT
{
DIALOG "", 3, 15, 5, 270, 137, FS_DLGBORDER
{
CTEXT "GpiSetPattern Options",
IDD_NULL, 30, 127, 160, 8
GROUPBOX "Pattern modes", IDD_NULL, 5, 20, 245, 102
AUTORADIOBUTTON "PATSYM_DEFAULT",  IDD_PAT0, 8, 102, 95,
                        12, WS_GROUP
AUTORADIOBUTTON "PATSYM_DENSE1", IDD_PAT1, 8, 92, 95, 12
AUTORADIOBUTTON "PATSYM_DENSE2", IDD_PAT2, 8, 82, 95, 12
AUTORADIOBUTTON "PATSYM_DENSE3", IDD_PAT3, 8, 72, 95, 12
AUTORADIOBUTTON "PATSYM_DENSE4", IDD_PAT4, 8, 62, 95, 12
AUTORADIOBUTTON "PATSYM_DENSE5", IDD_PAT5, 8, 52, 95, 12
AUTORADIOBUTTON "PATSYM_DENSE6", IDD_PAT6, 8, 42, 95, 12
AUTORADIOBUTTON "PATSYM_DENSE7", IDD_PAT7, 8, 32, 95, 12
AUTORADIOBUTTON "PATSYM_DENSE8", IDD_PAT8, 8, 22, 95, 12
AUTORADIOBUTTON "PATSYM_VERT", IDD_PAT9, 123, 102, 102, 12
AUTORADIOBUTTON "PATSYM_HORIZ", IDD_PAT10 123, 92, 102, 12
AUTORADIOBUTTON "PATSYM_DIAG1", IDD_PAT11, 123, 82, 102, 12
AUTORADIOBUTTON "PATSYM_DIAG2", IDD_PAT12, 123, 72, 102, 12
AUTORADIOBUTTON "PATSYM_DIAG3", IDD_PAT13, 123, 62, 102, 12
AUTORADIOBUTTON "PATSYM_DIAG4", IDD_PAT14, 123, 52, 102, 12
AUTORADIOBUTTON "PATSYM_NOSHADE", IDD_PAT15, 123, 42, 102, 12
AUTORADIOBUTTON "PATSYM_SOLID", IDD_PAT16, 123, 32, 102, 12
AUTORADIOBUTTON "PATSYM_HALFTONE", IDD_PAT17,123, 22, 102, 12
DEFPUSHBUTTON  "Ok", MBID_OK, 6, 4, 38, 12,
                        WS_TABSTOP | WS_GROUP
PUSHBUTTON    "Cancel", MBID_CANCEL, 56, 4, 38, 12,
                        WS_TABSTOP | WS_GROUP

}
}


/* GPISAMP1.C (Graphics sample program) */
#define INCL_WIN
```

```
#define INCL_GPI

#include <os2.h>
#include <stddef.h>
#include <stdlib.h>
#include "gpisamp1.h"

MRESULT EXPENTRY GraphicsWndProc(HWND,USHORT,MPARAM,MPARAM);
MRESULT EXPENTRY ModesDlgBoxProc(HWND,USHORT,MPARAM,MPARAM);

VOID DrawBoxes(HPS,SHORT,SHORT);
VOID DrawCircles(HPS,SHORT,SHORT);
VOID DrawArcs(HPS,SHORT,SHORT);
VOID DrawLines(HPS,SHORT,SHORT);
VOID DrawTriangles(HPS,SHORT,SHORT);
VOID DrawSetup(HPS);

HAB  hab;
LONG lMixMode = FM_OVERPAINT;
LONG lPatMode = PATSYM_SOLID;

int main (void)
{
static CHAR szClass[] = "Gpi Sample";
HMQ   hmq ;
HWND  hwndClient, hwndFrame ;
QMSG  qmsg ;
ULONG ctlData = FCF_TITLEBAR | FCF_SYSMENU | FCF_SIZEBORDER
                | FCF_MINMAX | FCF_TASKLIST | FCF_SHELLPOSITION
                | FCF_MENU | FCF_ACCELTABLE;

hab = WinInitialize(0);
hmq = WinCreateMsgQueue(hab, 0);
WinRegisterClass(hab, szClass, GraphicsWndProc, 0L, 0);

hwndFrame = WinCreateStdWindow(HWND_DESKTOP, WS_VISIBLE,
                &ctlData, szClass, NULL, 0L,
                NULL, IDM_MENURES, &hwndClient);

while (WinGetMsg (hab, &qmsg, NULL, 0, 0))
            WinDispatchMsg (hab, &qmsg);

WinDestroyWindow(hwndFrame);
WinDestroyMsgQueue(hmq);
WinTerminate(hab);
return(0);
}
```

```
MRESULT EXPENTRY GraphicsWndProc(hwnd, msg, mp1, mp2)
HWND hwnd;
USHORT msg;
MPARAM mp1, mp2;
{
HPS  hps;
RECTL rcl;
static SHORT cx, cy;

switch (msg)
   {
    case WM_SIZE:
         cx = SHORT1FROMMP (mp2);
         cy = SHORT2FROMMP (mp2);
         return(NULL);

    case WM_COMMAND:
         switch((COMMANDMSG(&msg)->cmd))
            {
             case IDM_SCREEN:
                   hps = WinGetPS(hwnd);
                   WinQueryWindowRect(hwnd, &rcl);
                   WinFillRect(hps, &rcl, CLR_BACKGROUND);
                   WinReleasePS(hps);
                   return(NULL);

             case IDM_BOXES:
                   hps = WinGetPS(hwnd);
                   DrawBoxes(hps, cx, cy);
                   WinReleasePS(hps);
                   return(NULL);

             case IDM_CIRCLES:
                   hps = WinGetPS(hwnd);
                   DrawCircles(hps, cx, cy);
                   WinReleasePS(hps);
                   return(NULL);

             case IDM_ARCS:
                   hps = WinGetPS(hwnd);
                   DrawArcs(hps, cx, cy);
                   WinReleasePS(hps);
                   return(NULL);

             case IDM_LINES:
                   hps = WinGetPS(hwnd);
```

```
                        DrawLines(hps, cx, cy);
                        WinReleasePS(hps);
                        return(NULL);

                case IDM_TRIANGLES:
                        hps = WinGetPS(hwnd);
                        DrawTriangles(hps, cx, cy);
                        WinReleasePS(hps);
                        return(NULL);

                case IDM_DLGMIX:
                        WinDlgBox(HWND_DESKTOP, hwnd,
                                        ModesDlgBoxProc,
                                        NULL, IDD_DLGMIX, NULL);
                        break;

                case IDM_DLGPAT:
                        WinDlgBox(HWND_DESKTOP, hwnd,
                                        ModesDlgBoxProc,
                                        NULL, IDD_DLGPAT, NULL);
                        break;
                }
        break;

    case WM_ERASEBACKGROUND:
        return(TRUE);

    case WM_HELP:
        WinMessageBox (HWND_DESKTOP, hwnd,
                "Help window would go here",
                "Drawing Examples", 0,
                MB_OK | MB_ICONEXCLAMATION);
        return(0);
    }

  return WinDefWindowProc (hwnd, msg, mp1, mp2) ;
}

MRESULT EXPENTRY ModesDlgBoxProc(hwndDlg, msg, mp1, mp2)
HWND hwndDlg;
USHORT msg;
MPARAM mp1, mp2;
{
SHORT idFM;

  switch(msg)
    {
```

```
        case WM_CONTROL:
            idFM = SHORT1FROMMP (mp1);
            if (idFM >= IDD_FM0 && idFM <= IDD_FM17)
                lMixMode = (LONG) idFM - 200;
                if (idFM >= IDD_PAT0 && idFM <= IDD_PAT17)
                lPatMode = (LONG) idFM - 300;
            break;
    }
  return (WinDefDlgProc (hwndDlg, msg, mp1, mp2));
}

VOID DrawBoxes (hps, cx, cy)
HPS hps;
SHORT cx, cy;
{
SHORT i, n;
LONG c = 1;
POINTL ptl;

    DrawSetup (hps);
    for (i=0; i<10; i++)
        for (n=0; n<10; n++)
            {
                GpiSetColor (hps, (LONG)(rand() % 16));
                ptl.x = ((cx/10) * n + n);
                ptl.y = ((cy - i) - ((cy/10) + ((cy/10) * i)));
                GpiMove (hps, &ptl);
                ptl.x = ptl.x + (cx/10);
                ptl.y = ptl.y + (cy/10);
                GpiBox (hps, DRO_FILL, &ptl, 0L, 0L);
                if (c == 16) c = 1; else c++;
            }
}

VOID DrawCircles (hps, cx, cy)
HPS hps;
SHORT cx, cy;
{
LONG i;
POINTL ptl;

    DrawSetup (hps);
    for (i=10; i<=150; i+=5)
      {
        DosBeep (500, 150);
        GpiSetColor (hps, (LONG)(rand() % 16));
        ptl.x = cx/2;
```

```
            ptl.y = cy/2;
            GpiMove(hps, &ptl);
            GpiFullArc(hps, DRO_OUTLINEFILL, i * 65536L);
        }
}

VOID DrawArcs(hps, cx, cy)
HPS hps;
SHORT cx, cy;
{
LONG i;
POINTL ptl;
POINTL aptl[2];

    DrawSetup(hps);
    for(i=10; i<=250; i+=2)
        {
            GpiSetColor(hps, (LONG) (rand() % 16));
            ptl.x = (cx - (cx/10));
            ptl.y = (cy - (cy/10) - i);
            aptl[0].x = cx/2;
            aptl[0].y = cy/2;
            aptl[1].x = ((cx - cx) + (cx/10));
            aptl[1].y = ((cy - cy) + (cy/10) + i);
            GpiMove(hps, &ptl);
            GpiPointArc(hps, aptl);
        }
}

VOID DrawLines(hps, cx, cy)
HPS hps;
SHORT cx, cy;
{
SHORT i=0;
POINTL ptl;

    DrawSetup(hps);
    for(i=0; i<10; i++)
        {
            GpiSetColor(hps, (LONG) (rand() % 16));
            ptl.x = cx/10;
            ptl.y = cy/(1 + i);
            GpiMove (hps, &ptl);
            ptl.x = cx - cx/10;
            ptl.y = cy/(1 + i);
            GpiLine(hps, &ptl);
        }
```

```
}

VOID DrawTriangles(hps, cx, cy)
HPS hps;
SHORT cx, cy;
{
SHORT i;
POINTL ptl, aptl[5];

    aptl[0].x = cx/4; aptl[0].y = cy/4 * 3;
    aptl[1].x = cx/4; aptl[1].y = cy/4;
    aptl[2].x = cx/4 * 3; aptl[2].y = cy/4;
    aptl[3].x = cx/4 * 3; aptl[3].y = cy/4 * 3;
    aptl[4].x = cx/4; aptl[4].y = cy/4 * 3;

    DrawSetup(hps);
    for(i=0; i<4; i++)
      {
        GpiSetColor(hps, (LONG) i+1);
        GpiBeginArea(hps, BA_BOUNDARY);
        ptl.x = aptl[i].x;
        ptl.y = aptl[i].y;
        GpiMove (hps, &ptl);
        ptl.x = cx/2;
        ptl.y = cy/2;
        GpiLine(hps, &ptl);
        ptl.x = aptl[i+1].x;
        ptl.y = aptl[i+1].y;
        GpiLine (hps, &ptl);
        GpiEndArea(hps);
      }
}

VOID DrawSetup(hps)
HPS hps;
{
    GpiSetBackColor(hps, 1L + CLR_BLUE);
    GpiSetBackMix(hps, BM_OVERPAINT);
    GpiSetPattern(hps, lPatMode);
    GpiSetMix(hps, lMixMode);
}
```

The example program provides five drawing options — boxes, circles, arcs, lines, and triangles. Each of the routines used to draw these shapes requires that you supply environment parameters to the presentation space before using them. The program also makes extensive use of the

POINTL structure in order to establish various drawing coordinates. For example, the box drawing routine divides the current window into 100 squares. Using the POINTL structure, in conjunction with the *cx* and *cy* values obtained from the WM_SIZE message, allows the program to automatically adjust this matrix when the user resizes or maximizes the window. In general, this approach offers more fluid control over window resizing considerations than the techniques used with the RECTL structure. You will see more of the POINTL structure in subsequent chapters.

GpiSetColor is the one function common to all the drawing routines in the program example. It is one of 55 Gpi functions that define drawing attributes for objects drawn before the release of the active presentation space. Most of these functions simply perform their assigned task and return a BOOL value to indicate success or failure. Here's the definition for GpiSetColor:

```
BOOL GpiSetColor(hps, clr)
HPS hps;
LONG clr;
```

The first argument to GpiSetColor is a handle to the active presentation space. The second argument references one of the predefined system colors as described in Chapter 4. The GpiSetBackColor, also used in the program example, operates identically to GpiSetColor, except that it sets the background color. Note that *clr* is of type LONG and that all number values in presentation space require 32-bit LONG typing. Additionally, you should note that other functions — most relevantly, those contained in the Draw-Setup routine in the example — affect the color mix produced by GpiSetColor. Here's the definition for GpiSetMix, which sets the current foreground mix attribute for a drawn object.

```
BOOL GpiSetMix(hps, lMixMode)
HPS hps;
LONG lMixMode;
```

With GpiSetMix, you specify a color mode identifier, instead of a color. The pertinent identifiers are denoted by an FM prefix. The program example includes a dialog box that allows you to select the various modes. Table 9-3 lists and describes the various modes.

Table 9-3: GpiSetMix Modes

IDENTIFIER	VALUE	OBJECT COLOR RESULT
FM_DEFAULT	0L	System default; same as FM_OVERPAINT.
FM_OR	1L	ORs an object's color value.
FM_OVERPAINT	2L	Draws object in current color.
FM_XOR	4L	XORs an object's color value.
FM_LEAVEALONE	5L	Leaves current color intact.
FM_AND	6L	ANDs an object's color value.
FM_SUBTRACT	7L	ANDs inverted source with background.
FM_MASKSRCNOT	8L	ANDs source and inverted background.
FM_ZERO	9L	Sets object color to all zeros.
FM_NOTMERGESRC	10L	Inverts ORed source and background.
FM_NOTXORSRC	11L	Inverts XORed source and background.
FM_INVERT	12L	Inverts background color.
FM_MERGESRCNOT	13L	ORs source with inverted background.
FM_NOTCOPYSRC	14L	Inverts object color.
FM_MERGENOTSRC	15L	ORs inverted source with background.
FM_NOTMASKSRC	16L	Inverts ANDed source and background.
FM_ONE	17L	Sets object color to all ones.

The GpiSetBackMix function operates similarly to GpiSetMix, but does not need to offer as many mix options. It does offer BM_OR, which ORs the background with the object overlapping it; BM_OVERPAINT, which paints the object's background over anything beneath it; BM_XOR, which performs an exclusive OR operation on the background with the object overlapping it; and BM_LEAVEALONE, which prohibits an object's background from affecting anything beneath it. The example uses BM_OVER-

PAINT to prevent the window background from affecting the object's background.

The GpiSetPattern function is another function that you will use frequently. It sets up the shading for an object and offers 17 different default patterns and more than 235 additional patterns based on this default set. GpiSetPattern simply takes a presentation space handle and a pattern value as its only arguments. The allowable values for patterns range from 1L to 255L. The best way to become familiar with the different patterns is by running the example program and using the GpiSetPattern dialog box.

The WinGetClipPS Function

A second method of creating a cached-PS is with the WinGetClipPS function. WinGetClipPS limits the scope of the presentation space to the windows named in the function call. Here's the definition for WinGetClipPS:

```
HPS WinGetClipPS(hwnd, hwndClip, fs)
HWND hwnd, hwndClip;
USHORT fs;
```

As with the WinGetPS function, WinGetClipPS returns a handle to the presentation space created by the function call. The scope of the presentation space is determined by *hwndClip*, which specifies the direction in which the presentation space is clipped; and *fs*, which specifies the extent of the clipping process. Tables 9-4 and 9-5 describe the values that you can specify for *hwndClip* and *fs*.

Table 9-4: WinGetClipPS Clipping Direction

VALUE	DESCRIPTION
NULL	Clips all sibling windows identified by the *hwnd* argument.
HWND_TOP	Clips the first sibling window and all subsequent windows until the window specified by *hwnd*, or until a NULL value is obtained.
HWND_BOTTOM	Clips the final sibling window and all prior windows until the window specified by *hwnd*, or until a NULL value is obtained.

Table 9-5: WinGetClipPS Clipping Extent

IDENTIFIER	BIT	DESCRIPTION
PSF_LOCKWINDOWUPDATE	0x0001	Prevents locking of the presentation space associated with *hwnd*. Overrides any prior call to WinLockWindowUpdate.
PSF_CLIPUPWARDS	0x0002	Clips all sibling windows before window specified by *hwndClip*.
PSF_CLIPDOWNWARDS	0x0004	Clips all sibling windows after window specified by *hwndClip*.
PSF_CLIPSIBLINGS	0x0008	Clips all siblings of *hwndClip*.
PSF_CLIPCHILDREN	0x0010	Clips all children of *hwndClip*.
PSF_PARENTCLIP	0x0020	Sets presentation space of parent to coordinates of *hwnd*.

The WinGetScreenPS Function

The WinGetScreenPS lets you draw anywhere on the desktop window. The motivating factors behind drawing on the desktop are probably best left to message writers and graffiti artists. That said, you should note that you must take special care when drawing on the desktop — because Win-GetScreenPS lets you draw on top of existing windows.

The best way to prevent overwriting other windows is to enumerate all windows on the desktop before executing any drawing functions, establish the position of existing windows, and then establish an unoccupied desktop area where you can draw. Additionally, you should avoid overwriting the icon area of the desktop.

Before you do anything, you need to get the size of the desktop. You can obtain this by querying the system value associated with the monitor. You use either the WinQueryWindowRect or WinQuerySysValue function to get the desktop dimensions. Here's the WinQuerySysValue version:

```
cxDesktop = (SHORT)WinQuerySysValue(
                HWND_DESKTOP, SV_CXSCREEN);
```

```
cyDesktop = (SHORT)WinQuerySysValue(
                    HWND_DESKTOP, SV_CYSCREEN);
```

While you're at the system level, you might as well also get the value needed to avoid the icon area. This value is the combination of SV_CYICON and SV_CYTITLEBAR — the latter being the titlebar space allotted to an icon. The following code gets the necessary value:

```
cyIcon  = (SHORT)WinQuerySysValue(
                    HWND_DESKTOP, SV_CYICON);
cyTitlebar = (SHORT)WinQuerySysValue(
                    HWND_DESKTOP, SV_CYTITLEBAR);
cyIconArea = cyIcon + cyTitlebar;
```

This complete, you can use the WinBeginEnumWindows to enumerate all the frame windows on the desktop. You accomplish this by specifying HWND_DESKTOP as the window for which WinBeginEnumWindows performs its enumeration. After obtaining the frame window handles, you can enumerate the child windows for each window to ensure that you do not overwrite a child window that is not clipped to its parent. Once you are satisfied that you have all the possible window handles, you can call Win-QueryWindowRect to establish the dimensions of any active windows. In turn, you can test whether the desktop location where you want to draw is not occupied by using the WinPtInRect function.

The Micro-PS

The micro-PS is similar to the cached-PS. One difference is you can specify a device context with a micro-PS, but even here the micro-PS remains limited. The reason is you can only use a single device context with a micro-PS. Thus, specifying a device context other than the monitor prohibits you from using the monitor. The one clear advantage of the micro-PS over the cached-PS is the ability that it gives you to control the default drawing environment.

One environmental factor that you can control is the actual size of the presentation space. The micro-PS gives you the capability of addressing what is called a presentation page, or a specified area within the available presentation that defines the visible area of the presentation space. The presentation page also provides a straightforward method of defining the units of measure for the presentation space.

Before you can create a micro-PS, you need to specify a device context. A device context can be specified one of two ways: using the WinOpenWindowDC function, which associates the device context with the specified window; and using the DevOpenDC function, which supports multiple processes, including multi-threaded windows and hardware devices. For most micro-PS needs, you can use WinOpenWindowDC, which takes a handle to the window in which you want to draw as its only argument. It returns a handle to a device context (of type HDC). After this, you call GpiCreatePS, which is defined as follows:

```
HPS GpiCreatePS(hab, hdc, psizl, flOptions)
HAB hab;
HDC hdc;
PSIZEL psizl;
ULONG flOptions;
```

Besides the familiar *hab* argument, GpiCreatePS references the specified device context in the *hdc* argument. The *psizl* argument points to the presentation page by referencing the PSIZEL — which contains the *cx* and *cy* values that specify the dimensions of the page. The *fOptions* specifies optional parameters that can be ORed to produce combined effects. These parameters fall into four categories listed in Table 9-6. Each category contains its own set of identifiers, which are listed in Tables 9-7 through 9-9. Read the tables carefully because they also pertain to the normal-PS, which is described in the next section.

Table 9-6: Option Categories for GpiCreatePS

STYLE	BIT	DESCRIPTION
PS_UNITS	0x00FCL	Specifies units of measure for the presentation space.
PS_FORMAT	0x0F00L	Specifies options for storing coordinates in function chains. Use with a normal-PS only.
PS_TYPE	0x1000L	Specifies the type of presentation space. The default is GPIT_MICRO, which identifies the micro-PS.
PS_ASSOCIATE	0x4000L	Specifies whether the presentation space is associated with the device context.

When you specify the PS_UNITS option, you can choose from seven identifiers that specify the units of measure. The default unit of measure is the pixel (or pel as it is often referred to in the Presentation Manager). Table 9-7 lists the identifiers associated with the various units of measure.

Table 9-7: Units of Measure for GpiCreatePS

STYLE	BIT	DESCRIPTION
PU_ARBITRARY	0x0004L	Dynamic application units.
PU_PELS	0x0008L	Standard pixel measurements.
PU_LOMETRIC	0x000CL	Units of 0.1 mm.
PU_HIMETRIC	0x0010L	Units of 0.01 mm.
PU_LOENGLISH	0x0014L	Units of 0.01 inches.
PU_HIENGLISH	0x0018L	Units of 0.001 inches.
PU_TWIPS	0x001CL	Units of 1/1440 inches.

The PS_FORMAT identifier allows you to select the data format used for storing data related to the presentation space. In most situations, the Gpi function require LONG values. If you decide to use SHORT values, you must properly handle the SHORT values. In particular, you must ensure that coordinate values fall in the range of -32768 through 32767 when you use the following drawing modes (as set by GpiSetDrawingMode):

- DM_RETAIN — Causes an object to be retained instead of immediately drawn. This is not the case with DM_DRAW, which is the default drawing mode.

- DM_DRAWANDRETAIN — Retains an object and then draws it. This is a combination of the DM_DRAW and DM_RETAIN modes.

To change the data format, you must specify a GPIF identifier with the PS_FORMAT option in the call to GpiCreatePS. Table 9-8 lists the GPIF identifiers.

Table 9-8: Format Categories for GpiCreatePS

STYLE	BIT/VALUE	DESCRIPTION
GPIF_DEFAULT	0L	Specifies SHORT data type (default).
GPIF_SHORT	0x0100L	Specifies SHORT data type.
GPIF_LONG	0x0200L	Specifies LONG data type.

The last set of identifiers is actually two sets that work together. The PS_TYPE identifiers specify the type of presentation space. The PS_AS-SOCIATE identifiers tell the Presentation Manager whether to associate the presentation space with a device context. Table 9-9 lists these two set of identifiers.

Table 9-9: Type and Associate Categories for GpiCreatePS

STYLE	BIT/VALUE	DESCRIPTION
GPIT_NORMAL	0L	Specifies normal-PS (default).
GPIT_MICRO	0x1000L	Specifies micro-PS.
GPIA_NOASSOC	0L	Specifies no association.
GPIA_ASSOC	0x4000L	Specifies association with the device context and is required if GPIT_MI-CRO is specified.

When you need to terminate a micro-PS, you can use the GpiDestroyPS function. If you have no special reason for terminating the presentation space, but want to exit the application, you should destroy the presentation space. Although the Presentation Manager is supposed to automatically destroy a presentation space when you issue the WinDestroyWindow call, this is not the case in release 1.1 of the Presentation Manager.

You can also use the WinGetScreenPS function to create a micro-PS. This function creates a presentation space that encompasses the entire screen, which lets you simultaneously update multiple windows. One side effect, however, is WinGetScreenPS has no automatic clipping control. As a result, you need to use the WinLockWindowUpdate function to protect other windows onscreen.

The Normal-PS

As far as presentation spaces go, the normal-PS is the supercharged variety. In addition to providing the capabilities of the micro-PS, the normal-PS lets you chain Gpi functions so that you can execute them as a programmer-defined group. Additionally, a normal-PS gives you the ability to switch between different device contexts, merely by specifying a different device context. And very importantly, the normal-PS gives you a means to store graphic data to disk by using metafiles.

Function chaining is indeed a powerful feature. You define a function chain in what is called a *segment*. This is somewhat of a poor choice of terminology, because the word segment commonly refers to memory segments in Intel processors. A Gpi segment, however, is an arbitrary area in memory that holds a function chain (in essence, the code for the functions themselves). Once you specify a function chain, you can execute it within the current presentation or processing via the WM_PAINT message. In addition to function chains, you can also execute segment chains. Both are accomplished by calling one of several different Gpi functions dedicated to executing a segment such as GpiDrawChain or GpiDrawSegment. Usually, you define a function or segment chain after you process the WM_SIZE message.

Somewhat similar to function chains and segments are metafiles. The number of calls required to create, save, and display a metafile are not as numerous as the functions necessary to manage chains and segments. Additionally, because this is an introductory text, it is more important to describe how to save graphic data than to perform advanced manipulation of that data.

A metafile is a snapshot of a presentation space. Its chief asset to Gpi programming is it allows you to store an image to disk, although you can just as easily store a metafile in a memory buffer to replay it later within the same application. In order to use the Gpi metafile functions, you need to specify a device context for the metafile — in essence, making a metafile the equivalent of a device (and what you learn about device contexts from metafiles, you can generally apply to other devices).

To create a device context for a metafile, you must use the DevOpenDC function. This function lets you establish a special device context for the metafile. Here's the definition for DevOpenDC:

```
HDC DevOpenDC(hab, type, pszToken,
                       count, pbData, hdcComp)
HAB hab;
LONG type;
PSZ pszToken;
LONG count;
PDEVOPENDATA pbData;
HDC hdcComp;
```

The first argument is the anchor block handle. The second argument, *type*, specifies the type of device for which to open the device context. For a metafile, the system identifier is OD_METAFILE. Table 9-10 explains each type of device that you can use with DevOpenDC.

Table 9-10: Supported Devices for DevOpenDC Function

IDENTIFIER	VALUE	DESCRIPTION
OD_QUEUED	2L	Any device that is accessed through the Presentation Manager print queue. Typical examples are printers and plotters.
OD_DIRECT	5L	Any device capable of handling direct output. Again, printers and plotters are typical examples.
OD_INFO	6L	Any device that must supply the Presentation Manager with data describing its formatting characteristics. The OD_INFO identifier causes the function merely to gather this data. Again, printers and plotters are good examples.
OD_METAFILE	7L	A metafile, which requires a corresponding definition of presentation space characteristics (handled by the Gpi metafile functions).
OD_MEMORY	8L	A bitmap that is placed in memory (refer to Chapter 10 for additional information).

The next argument, *pszToken*, points to a *device information token* contained in the OS2.INI file. If you do not intend on using OS2.INI to hold device information related to an application, you can specify a unique name or merely place an asterisk in quotation marks in the argument field. Because Microsoft and IBM have plans to expand the functionality of DevOpenDC, it is recommended that you use a unique name instead of the asterisk. According to Microsoft, this will ensure compatibility with later releases of OS/2.

The next two arguments are also responsible for specifying device information. The *count* argument simply tells DevOpenDC how many data elements are contained in the device information sequence. If you do not specify device information through *pszToken*, you must do so through the *pbData* argument, which contains the data that DevOpenDC requires from the DEVOPENSTRUC. The latter is defined as follows:

```
typedef struct _DEVOPENSTRUC {
PSZ             pszLogAddress;
PSZ             pszDriverName;
PDRIVDATA       pdriv;
PSZ             pszDataType;
PSZ             pszComment;
PSZ             pszQueueProcName;
PSZ             pszQueueProcParams;
PSZ             pszSpoolerParams;
PSZ             pszNetworkParams;
} DEVOPENSTRUC;
```

You can satisfy *pbData* by referencing DEVOPENSTRUC and setting each field either to the value you want to specify or to NULL. Because the structure is somewhat large — and because, more often than not, you will find yourself setting most of the fields to NULL — you can alternatively create an array of type PSZ and then cast it to PDEVOPENDATA in the actual call to DevOpenDC. If you do this, you will probably want to use a global array, but the subsequent examples use a static array for proximity's sake.

The final argument to DevOpenDC is used for loading bitmaps into memory. Other devices merely need this field to be set to NULL. That's it for the arguments to DevOpenDC. Now here's a look at a routine that initializes a device context for a metafile:

```
HDC InitDeviceContext(HAB, HPS)
HAB hab;
HPS hps;
{
HDC hdc;
static PSZ pbData[9] = {0L,"DISPLAY",0L,0L,0L,0L,0L,0L,0L};

    hdc = DevOpenDC(hab, OD_METAFILE, "*", 2L,
    (PDEVOPENDATA) pbData, NULL);
    return(hdc);
}
```

Notice how the *pbData* argument is handled in the DevOpenDC call. For metafiles, the only DEVOPENSTRUC field that needs a value other than NULL is the *pszDriverName* field. The string name that you supply *pszDriverName* must correspond to the filename for the monitor driver, which is contained in OS2.INI — and thus, in a full-scale application, you would likely want to use *pszToken* argument to supply device information to DevOpenDC. (This would eliminate any need for the user to specify a device name when installing the application.)

Armed with a device context — the *hdc* value returned by DevOpenDC — you can create a presentation space in which to store a metafile. To create a normal-PS, which is the only presentation space that can accommodate metafiles, you use GpiCreatePS and associate the presentation space with the previous device context. Here's some typical code that sets the presentation page equal to the client area of the frame window:

```
sizl.x = 0;
sizl.y = 0;
hps = GpiCreatePS(hab, hdc, &sizl,
                    PU_PELS
                    | GPIF_DEFAULT
                    | GPIT_NORMAL
                    | GPIA_ASSOC);
```

Here, the zero settings in the SIZEL structure are mostly responsible for setting the presentation page equal to that of the client area. Additionally, you must ensure that you specify GPIA_ASSOC in the *flOptions* argument to GpiCreatePS.

If you do not want the presentation page equal to the client area, just modify the SIZEL fields and don't bother with GPI_ASSOC. For example, say you want the presentation page to always equal the right third of the client area window. To do this, you would process the WM_SIZE message and set the SIZEL fields this way:

```
sizel.x = cxClient - (cxClient/3);
sizel.y = cyClient;
```

With techniques such as this one, you can establish an area of interest for your presentation space. In a normal-PS, you can establish one presentation space equal to the client area, and overlap a second presentation space with an area of interest that is smaller than the dimensions of the client window. Using metafiles, you can then snap an area of interest and later redisplay it in a full page presentation space, if you like. More to the point, here's a revised version of the previous initialization routine that incorporates the call to GpiCreatePS:

```
VOID InitMetaFilePS (hwnd, hps, hpsMeta, hdcMeta)
HWND hwnd;
HPS hps, *hpsMeta;
HDC *hdcMeta;
{
SIZEL size;
static PSZ aDCdata[9] = {0L,"DISPLAY",0L,0L,0L,0L,0L,0L,0L};

    flOptions = GpiQueryPS(hps, &size);
    *hdcMeta = DevOpenDC(hab, OD_METAFILE, "*", 2L,
                         (PDEVOPENDATA) aDCdata, NULL);
    *hpsMeta = GpiCreatePS(hab, hdcMeta, &size, flOptions);
}
```

Besides the addition of the GpiCreatePS call, this routine differs from the previous one in that it uses the GpiQueryPS function. The Gpi-QueryPS function simply queries the values of a specified presentation space — values, say, that you leave intact for general drawing purposes — and then returns these values in *flOptions*. You can obtain the precise value contained in *flOptions* by ANDing them with any of the subordinate identifiers such as PU_PELS or GPIF_DEFAULT. Note also that Gpi-QueryPS returns the current values of the SIZEL structure. This obviates the need to set the SIZEL fields if you can ensure these values are appropriate. The latter technique is used in the following program example, which creates a presentation space explicitly for initialization purposes.

```
/* ROPETRIK.H (Header file) */

#define IDM_MENURES      1
#define IDM_HELP         2

#define IDM_DRAW         100
#define IDM_SCREEN       101
#define IDM_POLYFILLET   102
#define IDM_SAVEMETAFILE 103
#define IDM_PLAYMETAFILE 104

/* ROPETRIK.RC (Resource Script) */

#include <os2.h>
#include "ropetrik.h"

MENU IDM_MENURES
{
SUBMENU "~Draw",  IDM_DRAW
{
MENUITEM "~Clear screen\t^C", IDM_SCREEN
MENUITEM "Poly~Fillet\t^F",   IDM_POLYFILLET, MIA_CHECKED
MENUITEM "~Save Metafile\t^S", IDM_SAVEMETAFILE
MENUITEM "~Play Metafile\t^P", IDM_PLAYMETAFILE
}

MENUITEM "F1=Help",    IDM_HELP, MIS_HELP
| MIS_BUTTONSEPARATOR
}

ACCELTABLE IDM_MENURES
{
"^C", IDM_SCREEN
"^F", IDM_POLYFILLET
"^S", IDM_SAVEMETAFILE
"^P", IDM_PLAYMETAFILE
}

/* ROPETRIK.C (Program File) */

#define INCL_WIN
#define INCL_GPI
#define METASAMPLE "metatest.xxx"

#include <os2.h>
#include "ropetrik.h"
```

```
MRESULT EXPENTRY GraphicsWndProc(HWND,USHORT,MPARAM,MPARAM);

VOID DrawPolyFillet(HPS);
VOID DrawSetup(HPS);
VOID InitializePS(HWND);
HPS InitializeMetaFile(VOID);
HMF RecordMetaFile(HPS, HMF*);
VOID PlayMetaFile(HWND, HMF);

HAB   hab;
HPS   hpsInit;
HDC   hdcMeta;
ULONG flOptions = PU_PELS | GPIF_DEFAULT
                        | GPIT_NORMAL | GPIA_ASSOC;


int main (void)
{
static CHAR szClass[] = "Gpi Sample";
HMQ   hmq ;
HWND  hwndClient, hwndFrame ;
QMSG  qmsg ;
ULONG ctlData = FCF_TITLEBAR | FCF_SYSMENU | FCF_SIZEBORDER
                | FCF_MINMAX | FCF_TASKLIST | FCF_SHELLPOSITION
                | FCF_MENU | FCF_ACCELTABLE;

hab = WinInitialize (0) ;
hmq = WinCreateMsgQueue (hab, 0) ;
WinRegisterClass (hab, szClass, GraphicsWndProc,
                CS_SYNCPAINT | CS_SIZEREDRAW, 0) ;

hwndFrame = WinCreateStdWindow (HWND_DESKTOP, WS_VISIBLE,
                &ctlData, szClass,
                NULL, 0L, NULL,
                IDM_MENURES, &hwndClient) ;

while (WinGetMsg (hab, &qmsg, NULL, 0, 0))
        WinDispatchMsg (hab, &qmsg) ;

WinDestroyWindow (hwndFrame) ;
WinDestroyMsgQueue (hmq) ;
WinTerminate (hab) ;
return 0 ;
}

MRESULT EXPENTRY GraphicsWndProc(hwnd, msg, mp1, mp2)
HWND hwnd;
```

```
USHORT msg;
MPARAM mp1, mp2;
{
HPS  hpsWin, hpsMeta;
HMF  hmf, hmfTest;

  switch (msg)
    {
        case WM_CREATE:
             InitializePS(hwnd);
             break;

        case WM_COMMAND:
             switch ((COMMANDMSG(&msg)->cmd))
                 {
                     case IDM_SCREEN:
                         hpsWin = WinGetPS(hwnd);
                         GpiErase(hpsInit);
                         WinReleasePS(hpsWin);
                         return(NULL);

                     case IDM_POLYFILLET:
                         hpsWin = WinGetPS(hwnd);
                         DrawSetup(hpsWin);
                         DrawPolyFillet(hpsWin);
                         WinReleasePS(hpsWin);
                         break;

                     case IDM_SAVEMETAFILE:
                         hpsMeta = InitializeMetaFile();
                         RecordMetaFile(hpsMeta, &hmfTest);
                         break;

                     case IDM_PLAYMETAFILE:
                         PlayMetaFile(hwnd, hmfTest);
                         break;
                 }
             break;

        case WM_ERASEBACKGROUND:
             return(TRUE);

        case WM_CLOSE:
             GpiDestroyPS(hpsInit);
             WinPostMsg(hwnd, WM_QUIT, 0L, 0L);
             break;
```

```
             case WM_HELP:
                    WinMessageBox (HWND_DESKTOP, hwnd,
                            "Help window would go here",
                            "Drawing Examples", 0,
                            MB_OK | MB_ICONEXCLAMATION);
                            return(0);
        }

    return WinDefWindowProc (hwnd, msg, mp1, mp2) ;
}

VOID DrawPolyFillet (hps)
HPS hps;
{
LONG i = 17;
POINTL ptl;
static POINTL aptl[17] = { {500,30}, {125,50}, {475,70},
                            {150,90},{450,110},{175,130},
                            {425,150},{200,170},(400,190},
                            {225,210},{375,230},{100,400},
                            {250,250},{350,270},{275,290},
                            {800,400},{275,290} };

    ptl.x = 100;
    ptl.y = 10;
    GpiMove (hps, &ptl);
    GpiPolyFillet (hps, i, aptl);
}

VOID DrawSetup (hps)
HPS hps;
{
LINEBUNDLE lbnd;

    lbnd.lColor = CLR_RED;
    lbnd.usMixMode = FM_OVERPAINT;
    GpiSetAttrs (hps,
                PRIM_LINE,
                LBB_COLOR
                | LBB_WIDTH,
                0L, &lbnd);
}

VOID InitializePS (hwnd)
HWND hwnd;
{
SIZEL size;
```

```
HDC hdcInit;

    hdcInit = WinOpenWindowDC(hwnd);
    size.cx = 0;
    size.cy = 0;
    hpsInit = GpiCreatePS(hab, hdcInit, &size, flOptions);
}

HPS InitializeMetaFile()
{
HPS  hpsMeta;
SIZEL size;
static PSZ aDCdata[9] = {0L,"DISPLAY",0L,0L,0L,0L,0L,0L,0L};

    GpiQueryPS(hpsInit, &size);

    hdcMeta = DevOpenDC(hab,
                        OD_METAFILE,
                        "*",
                        2L,
                        (PDEVOPENDATA) aDCdata,
                        NULL);

    hpsMeta = GpiCreatePS(hab, hdcMeta, &size, flOptions);
    return(hpsMeta);
}

HMF RecordMetaFile(hps, hmfTest)
HPS hps;
HMF *hmfTest;
{
HMF hmf;

    GpiCreateLogColorTable(hps, LCOL_RESET,
    LCOLF_RGB, 0L, 0L, 0L);
    DrawPolyFillet(hps);
    GpiAssociate(hps, NULL);
    hmf = DevCloseDC(hdcMeta);
    GpiDestroyPS(hps);
    DosDelete(METASAMPLE, 0l);
    GpiSaveMetaFile(hmf, METASAMPLE);
    *hmfTest = hmf;
    return(hmf);
}

VOID PlayMetaFile(hwnd, hmf)
HWND hwnd;
```

```
HMF hmf;
{
HPS   hps;
LONG  cSegments;
BYTE  cchDesc[253];
static LONG alOptions[10] = {0L,LT_ORIGINALVIEW,RS_DEFAULT,
              LC_LOADDISC, RES_DEFAULT,SUP_DEFAULT,
              CTAB_DEFAULT, CREA_DEFAULT,0L,RSP_DEFAULT};

    hmf = GpiLoadMetaFile(hab, METASAMPLE);
    hps = WinGetPS(hwnd);
    GpiPlayMetaFile(hps, hmf, 10L, alOptions,
    &cSegments, 253L, cchDesc);
    WinReleasePS(hps);
}
```

The ROPETRIK program should be run in a maximized window. The window coordinates used to create the rope are hard-coded and assume a full-sized client window. To create a metafile, simply click on the Save MetaFile option in the user menu. You do not even have to draw the rope first, although you can if you want. To replay the metafile, click on the Play MetaFile option in the menu.

The actual drawing in the example is performed by GpiPolyFillet, which draws a series of curves based on the points in the *aptl* array. An interesting aspect to GpiPolyFillet (not shown in the example) is its ability to create a curve by supplying it only two points. The way this works is the function draws an imaginary line from the current position to the first *aptl* point, and then draws another imaginary line to the second *aptl* point. The curve is constructed based on the tangent of the first imaginary line. The curve begins at the current position. This is illustrated in Figure 9-3.

Metafile Basics

The power of the normal-PS to create multiple presentation spaces is apparent in the ROPETRIK program — perhaps to much so, because the program could have been structured so it did not rely on as many calls to WinGetPS. (Recall, however, that WinGetPS is a much more efficient call for simple drawing needs.)

In the program example, the presentation manager is initialized similarly to the initialization technique used in the previously listed version of

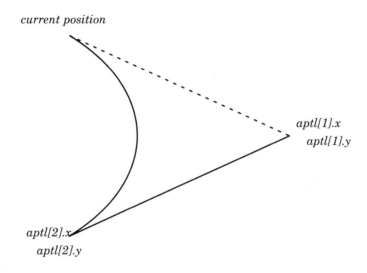

current position

aptl[1].x
aptl[1].y

aptl[2].x
aptl[2].y

Figure 9-3: GpiPolyFillet's Automatic Arc

the InitMetaFilePS routine. Then, after the IDM_SAVEMETAFILE message handler receives the handle to the metafile presentation space (*hpsMeta*), it calls the RecordMetaFile routine, where things start to get interesting. The first thing this routine does is call the GpiCreateColorLogTable function. GpiCreateColorLogTable is a good way to ensure that standard color conventions are used in metafiles, which might be replayed in a presentation space with vastly different color settings than in the space in which they were recorded. Basically, GpiCreateLogColorTable redefines the entries in the system's logical color table. Here's its definition:

```
BOOL GpiCreateLogColorTable (hps, flOptions, lFormat, iStart,
                             clTable, alTable)
HPS hps;
ULONG flOptions;
LONG lFormat;
LONG iStart;
LONG clTable;
PLONG alTable;
```

As usual, the first argument to GpiCreateLogColorTable is the handle to the presentation space. The next argument, *flOptions*, tells the Presentation Manager what color table to use. The identifiers that you can specify for this argument are explained in Table 9-11.

Table 9-11: Color Table Options

IDENTIFIER	BIT	DESCRIPTION
LCOL_RESET	0x0001L	Specifies the default color table.
LCOL_REALIZABLE	0x0002L	Defers color table control to the GpiRealize-ColorTable function.
LCOL_PURECOLOR	0x0004L	Prevents color dithering.

To confuse matters a little, the LCOL identifiers have a closely associated set of identifiers denoted by the LOLF prefix. These identifiers, which satisfy the *lFormat* option, specify the formatting for the entries in the color table. They are described in Table 9-12.

Table 9-12: Color Table Formatting Options

IDENTIFIER	VALUE	DESCRIPTION
LCOLF_INDRGB	1L	Array of RGB index entries. Each index pair comprises a four-byte local format value, and four-byte color value.
LCOLF_CONSECRGB	2L	Array of RGB index entries that correspond to the current value of *iStart* and then increment. Each entry is four bytes in length.
LCOLF_RGB	3L	Specifier that sets the color index to the RGB mode.

The next three argument can be summarized briefly. The *iStart* argument specifies the starting index and is only applicable if you use the

LCOLF_CONSECRGB identifier. In all other cases, you should set this to NULL. The *clTable* argument specifies the number of elements in *alTable*. If you just want to reset the color table, however, both *clTable* and *alTable* should be set to NULL. Otherwise specify a count in *clTable* and the starting address of the application data in *alTable*. If you do use *alTable*, each color value is a 4-byte integer. The actual RGB values are based on the following formula:

```
(red * 65536) + (green * 256) + blue
```

In the formula, the initial values for *red*, *green*, and *blue* are intensity values that range up to 255. (Note that the primary 16 colors are always supported; creating additional colors depends on your system needs).

After setting the color table, the program example calls GpiAssociate to disassociate the specified presentation space from its current device context. The reason for this should be obvious: a presentation space can only be associated with a single device context at any given moment. The reverse is also true: a device context can only be associated with a single presentation space at any given moment.

The key step after disassociating the presentation space is to obtain a handle to a metafile. This is accomplished by actually closing the current device content via the DevCloseDC call:

```
hmf = DevCloseDC(hdcMeta);
```

If you fail to disassociate the active presentation space, you find out when you attempt to call DevCloseDC. It returns a system-defined error, namely PMERR_DC_IS_ASSOCIATED. Otherwise, a successful call to DevCloseDC returns a metafile handle, if OD_METAFILE was specified in the original call to DevOpenDC. When you use DevCloseDC for devices other than a metafile, it returns DEV_OK upon successful completion.

After restoring the presentation space with GpiDestroy, and then deleting the disk file containing the metafile (if one exists), the program finally gets around to calling a metafile function. This function is GpiSave-MetaFile, which does as its name announces. It simply takes the handle to the metafile and writes it to disk.

The GpiLoadMetaFile acts similarly in retrieving the metafile from disk. When it comes to the GpiPlayMetaFile function, however, a lot more is happening behind the scenes. Here's its definition:

```
LONG GpiPlayMetaFile(hps, hmf, cOptions, alOptions,
                                pcSegments, cchDesc, pszDesc)
HPS hps;
HMF hmf;
LONG cOptions;
PLONG alOptions;
PLONG pcSegments;
LONG cchDesc;
PSZ pszDesc;
```

The first and second arguments to GpiPlayMetaFile should be obvious. The third argument, *cOptions*, supplies a count of the number of elements contained in the fourth argument, *alOptions*. The latter is an array specifying loading options.

The next argument, *cSegments*, is of little concern in release 1.1 of OS/2, but you still need to supply it an address of a LONG value (the return is always zero and indicates the number of renumbered segments in the metafile). The sixth argument, *cchDesc*, simply specifies the number of bytes in the buffer referenced by the final argument, *pszDesc*, which contains the actual metafile data.

Much more needs to be said about the fourth argument, *alOptions*. To refresh your memory, here's what *alOptions* looked like in the example:

```
static LONG alOptions[10] = {
                        0L,
                        LT_ORIGINALVIEW,
                        RS_DEFAULT,
                        LC_LOADDISC,
                        RES_DEFAULT,
                        SUP_DEFAULT,
                        CTAB_DEFAULT,
                        CREA_DEFAULT,
                        0L,
                        RSP_DEFAULT   };
```

The Presentation Manager defines 10 system constants (denoted by a PMF prefix) that correspond to each element in the *alOptions* array. Each constant represents a loading option category. Several of the categories themselves consists of system identifiers such as RES_DEFAULT and SUP_DEFAULT, which are used in the example. Table 9-13 lists and describes the PMF constants.

Table 9-13: GpiPlayMetaFile Loading Options

ARRAY CONSTANT	DESCRIPTION
PMF_SEGBASE	Reserved and must be set to zero.
PMF_LOADTYPE	Specifies metafile transformations. Identifiers are LT_NOMODIFY and LT_DEFAULT, which use the current viewing transform; and LT_ORIGINAL-VIEW, which uses the original viewing transform.
PMF_RESOLVE	Reserved and must be RS_DEFAULT or RS_NODIS-CARD.
PMF_LCIDS	Specifies the loading action. LC_NOLOAD and LC_NOLOAD do not load the object; and LC_LOAD-DISC loads the object.
PMF_RESET	Specifies whether the presentation space is reset. Identifiers are RES_NORESET and RES_DEFAULT, which do not reset the presentation space; and RES_RESET, which resets the presentation space.
PMF_SUPPRESS	Specifies whether the metafile is played. Identifiers are SUP_NOSUPRESS and SUP_DEFAULT, which do not suppress part of the metafile; and SUP_SU-PRESS, which suppresses part of the metafile based on the PMF_RESET option.
PMF_COLORTABLES	Specifies the color table action. Identifiers are CTAB_NOMODIFY and CTAB_DEFAULT, which uses the currently specified color table; and CTAB_REPLACE, which places a new color table in the presentation space.
PMF_COLORREALIZABLE	Specifies whether to use the LCOL_REALIZABLE option (see Table 9-11). Identifiers are CREA_DE-FAULT, which use the LCOL_REALIZABLE option; and CREA_NOREALIZE and CREA_DEFAULT, which leave the color table alone.

CHAPTER 10

BITMAPPED RESOURCES

Bitmap images play an important role in the Presentation Manager. Because you can store them in dynamic link libraries, or in disk files, they serve as a resource-efficient way to enhance both the appearance and functionality of applications. The Presentation Manager supports three types of bitmapped images: general purpose bitmaps, icons, and pointers.

This chapter explains the necessary steps for incorporating pointers and icons into your application by using the *Icon Editor* and *Resource Compiler*. The chapter also includes a section on implementing icons in an application, but a lengthy description of pointers is deferred until Chapter 13. Here, the main thrust is general purpose bitmaps, which serve as an adjunct to the Presentation Manager's graphic capabilities. General purpose bitmaps can be put to the following uses:

- Attractive displays.
- Special menus that can be displayed rapidly.
- Instructional and warning symbols.
- Common format for storing graphic data.
- Rapid window repainting.
- Real-time animation.

A bitmap is a graphic image stored in memory. Usually, you create a bitmap and then save it to a disk file, although you can create a bitmap on-the-fly, store it in memory, and then redisplay it when you want. The Presentation Manager supports both monochrome and color bitmaps. A monochrome bitmap is the more fundamental of the two types, in that each bit directly corresponds to a video pixel. For color bitmaps, at least one additional bit is required to describe the color of the pixel. Figure 10-1 shows the conceptual difference between monochrome and color bitmaps.

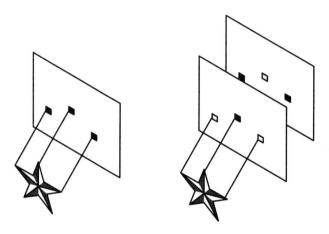

Figure 10-1: Monochrome and Color Bitmaps

At the user-interface level, bitmapped images are extremely important components of the Presentation Manager. In the form of icons, bitmaps not only provide the user with easy access to a task such as loading an application, but also symbolize (excuse the pun) the object oriented logic behind the Presentation Manager. That is, while the methods of object oriented programming encapsulate large amounts of data into a single object, so too do icons.

True, this analogy might be more meaningful to the programmer than the user, but it is the user who benefits from the icon-driven desktop. For example, in a desktop environment in which word processing files and directories correspond to icons, users can organize files by drawing upon their everyday spatial reasoning skills, instead of their computer knowledge. It is up to you, the creative programmer, to provide this real-world interface if you want to fully exploit the iconic capabilities of the Presentation Manager.

Canned Graphics

You can create a bitmap in one of two ways. The most widely used method is with the Presentation Manager's *Icon Editor*, which lets you design a bitmap in *wysiwyg* fashion. The other method requires you to hard-code bitmaps and use several Gpi functions. This section looks at the *Icon Editor* utility, which also serves as your primary tool for creating icons and pointers. Additionally, this section explains the resource compiler requirements for incorporating bitmaps, icons, and pointers into an application.

The *Icon Editor* provides a *wysiwyg* screen in which you design and create bitmaps by selecting individual pixels within a given matrix. The most critical point to note before using the *Icon Editor* is it handles bitmaps differently than it does icons and pointers. One reason for this is it allows you to create icons and pointers for a specific type of video display device. Here's the supported resolutions for icons and pointers:

- Low resolution — designed for CGA display monitors and other monitors that use a 640 by 200 pixel matrix. Icons and pointers are stored in a format of 32 by 15 pixels.

- Medium resolution — designed for EGA display monitors with a 640 by 350 pixel matrix; VGA monitors with a 640 by 480 pixel matrix; and Hercules compatible monitors with a 720 by 348 pixel matrix. Icons and pointers are stored in a format of 32 by 32 pixels.

- High resolution — designed for monitors that support a pixel matrix greater than medium resolution such as the the IBM 8514/A. Icons and pointers are stored in a format of 64 by 64 pixels.

When you use the *Icon Editor*, you can manipulate four color variations for icons and pointers. These are black, white, screen, and inverse screen. Screen color means that the associated pixel is always the same color as the screen. Inverse screen means that the associated pixel is always the opposite color of the screen. For example, if the screen is blue, an inverse pixel is red; or if the screen is green, the inverse pixel is magenta. The *Icon Editor* handles these color variations by maintaining two bitmaps for each pointer and icon. It then applies AND and XOR masks to the icon or pointer matrix. The AND mask produces the screen and inverse screen information. The XOR mask applies any inversions you have requested. At first, taking advantage of the *Icon Editor*'s coloring method is difficult. You should note that you must emphasize the screen color in order to create irregularly shaped icons and pointers. You should also use the inverse screen color sparingly, but do not avoid it altogether because it produces a pleasing contrast against a color background. For example, inverse coloring is invaluable when you need to create a pointer that acts as a cross-hair device.

When it comes to general purpose bitmaps, the *Icon Editor* does not give you as much color flexibility, but it lets you create larger bitmaps. The allowable pixel matrix range for general purpose bitmaps (hereafter referred to as bitmaps) is 1 * 1 to 99 * 99. A bitmap created anywhere in this range can be used on CGA, EGA, VGA, Hercules, or higher resolution displays. In the *Icon Editor*, you are limited to creating black and white bitmaps. When you display the bitmap using WinDrawBitmap, you can specify foreground and background colors, effectively changing the two colors of the bitmap. (With the GpiBitBlt function, you can create more complex bitmaps with multiple colors as explained later in the chapter.)

Another difference between a bitmap and an icon or a pointer is a bitmap does not have a hotspot. A hotspot is a single pixel within the icon or pointer matrix. Icons and pointers use hotspots as reference points. An icon's hotspot defines it screen location for the Presentation Manager. A pointer's hotspot defines its screen location for your application. Only one hotspot is allowed per icon or pointer. Bitmaps, icons and pointers are also given different filename extensions. These are:

- .BMP — Bitmap resource filename extension.

- .ICO — Icon resource filename extension.

- .PTR — Pointer resource filename extension.

Bitmaps are stored in an application's .EXE file with a resource type of RT_BITMAP; icons and pointers are stored in the .EXE file with a resource type of RT_POINTER. You should also note that you use many of the same functions for icons and pointers. For example, WinLoadPointer loads either an icon or a pointer. Alternatively, you can load a pointer by specifying the FS_ICON style as part of the frame window style argument when calling WinCreateStdWindow and specifying the icon's ID in the ID resource argument.

Resource Compiler Details

Specifying a bitmap, icon, or pointer in a resource (.RC) script is a relatively simple procedure. Before you specify any of the bitmap types in the script, you should defines IDs for each instance of each type in the application's header file. For example, the following lines define IDs for a bitmap, icon, and pointer, respectively.

```
#define IDB_BITMAP  300
#define IDI_ICON    400
#define IDP_POINTER 500
```

Each bitmap type has an associated resource compiler key word: BITMAP, ICON, and POINTER. Typically, you place the line defining your bitmapped resource at the beginning of the script file. Here are example lines for each of the three types:

```
BITMAP IDB_BITMAP APPBMAP1.BMP
ICON IDI_ICON APPICON.ICO
POINTER IDP_POINTER APPPTR.PTR
```

In your resource script, you can also replace one or more menu items with bitmaps. To do this, you can specify MIS_BITMAP in the SUBMENU statement to tell the *Resource Compiler* to use the bitmap referenced in the *string* argument. Note that you must specify the bitmap in *string*. One way to do this is to use the decimal number, preceded by the pound sign (#) and followed by a null-terminator. Here's an example that loads a bitmap defined as having a value of 10.

```
SUBMENU "#10\0", IDM_EDITMENU, MIS_BITMAP
```

Much can be accomplished with bitmaps in menus. For example, you can provide the user top-level menus comprised entirely of bitmaps. In turn, these menus can reference submenus. For best results, use the maximum width of 99 pels when you create a bitmap in the *Icon Editor*. The following program demonstrates how to create a top-level bitmap menu.

```
/* BMMENU.H (Header file) */

#define ID_RESOURCE     1
```

```
#define IDB_CUT          10
#define IDB_COPY         11
#define IDB_PASTE        12
#define IDB_ABOUT        13
#define IDM_EDIT         100
#define IDM_CUT          101
#define IDM_COPY         102
#define IDM_PASTE        103
#define IDM_ABOUT        104
#define IDM_SELECT       200
#define IDM_SELECTGROUP 201
#define IDM_SELECTALL    202


/* BMMENU.RC (Resource script) */

#include <os2.h>
#include "bmmenu.h"

BITMAP IDB_CUT cut.bmp
BITMAP IDB_COPY copy.bmp
BITMAP IDB_PASTE paste.bmp
BITMAP IDB_ABOUT about.bmp

MENU ID_RESOURCE
{
  SUBMENU "~Edit", IDM_EDIT
    {
      MENUITEM "#10\0", IDM_CUT, MIS_BITMAP | MIS_SUBMENU
        {
          MENUITEM "~Select", IDM_SELECT
          MENUITEM "~Select Group", IDM_SELECTGROUP
          MENUITEM "~Select All", IDM_SELECTALL
        }
      MENUITEM "#11\0", IDM_COPY, MIS_BITMAP
      MENUITEM "#12\0", IDM_PASTE, MIS_BITMAP
      MENUITEM "#13\0", IDM_ABOUT, MIS_BITMAP
    }
}

/* BMMENU.C (Bitmap menu example) */

#define INCL_PM
#include <os2.h>
#include "bmmenu.h"

MRESULT EXPENTRY ApplicationProc(HWND,USHORT,MPARAM,MPARAM);
HAB     hab;
```

```
HMQ     hmq;
HWND    hwndFrame, hwndClient;

int main(void)
{
QMSG qmsg;
static CHAR szClass[] = "bm-menu";

ULONG ctldata = FCF_TITLEBAR | FCF_SYSMENU | FCF_MINMAX
                | FCF_SIZEBORDER | FCF_SHELLPOSITION
                | FCF_TASKLIST | FCF_MENU;

hab = WinInitialize(NULL);
hmq = WinCreateMsgQueue(hab, 0);
WinRegisterClass(hab, szClass, ApplicationProc, 0L, 0);

hwndFrame = WinCreateStdWindow(HWND_DESKTOP, WS_VISIBLE,
                        &ctldata, szClass, NULL,
                        0L, NULL, ID_RESOURCE, &hwndClient);

while(WinGetMsg(hab, &qmsg, NULL, 0, 0))
                WinDispatchMsg(hab, &qmsg);

WinDestroyWindow(hwndFrame);
WinDestroyMsgQueue(hmq);
WinTerminate(hab);
return(0);
}

MRESULT EXPENTRY ApplicationProc(hwnd, msg, mp1, mp2)
HWND  hwnd;
USHORT msg;
MPARAM mp1;
MPARAM mp2;
{
    HPS   hps;
    RECTL rcl;
    static CHAR szMessage[20] = "Bitmap Menu Example";

    switch(msg)
      {
        case WM_CLOSE:
            WinPostMsg(hwnd, WM_QUIT, 0L, 0L);
            break;

        case WM_PAINT:
            hps = WinBeginPaint(hwnd, NULL, NULL);
```

```
                WinQueryWindowRect(hwnd, &rcl);
                WinFillRect(hps, &rcl, CLR_DEFAULT);

                WinDrawText(hps, -1, szMessage, &rcl,
                            CLR_NEUTRAL, CLR_BACKGROUND,
                            DT_CENTER | DT_VCENTER);

                WinEndPaint(hps);
                break;

        case WM_ERASEBACKGROUND:
                return(TRUE);
                break;

        default:
                return(WinDefWindowProc(hwnd, msg, mp1, mp2));
                break;
    }

    return(0L);
}
```

All of the work occurs within the resource script in the example program. The source code is merely presented for you convenience. Figure 10-2 illustrates what the output of the program can look like (given you create the bitmaps in the *Icon Editor*).

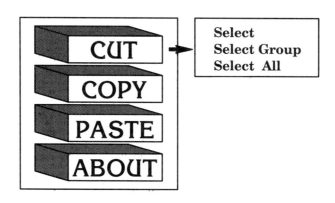

Figure 10-2: Bitmap Menu Example

Icons

As already noted, icons and pointers have much in common. The two resources are so similar that you can interchange them in an application by merely respecifying filenames in the resource script file. Pointers do have special relevance for mouse issues, however, and these are detailed in Chapter 13. For now, remember that almost anything you learn about icons also applies to pointers.

Every Presentation Manager application should have an icon associated with it — the icon that represents the application when the user minimizes it. Accordingly, you should take care in designing the minimize icon — it represents your application as much as the first screen or the front cover of your documentation.

One of the first things you must do in order to incorporate an icon into your application is to modify your make file. The following make file upgrades the make file from Chapter 4. This version compiles an icon as well as a bitmap (for use elsewhere in the program). If you do not want to use a bitmap, simply remove the reference to "template.bmp" in the file.

```
# TEMPL (Make File)

templ.obj : templ.c
    cl -c -W3 -As -G2sw -Oas -Zpei templ.c

templ.res : templ.rc templ.h templ.bmp templ.ico
    rc -r bitmap1

templ.exe : templ.obj templ.def templ.res
    link templ, /align:16, NUL, os2, templ
```

As noted, you must also define an ID for an icon in the application's header file, and then reference the pointer in the resource script. You define an icon by using the Resource Compiler's POINTER statement and matching it to a filename representing the icon. Here's the appropriate code:

```
POINTER ID_RESOURCE TEMPL.ICO
```

At this step, you can incorporate the icon into your source code. To add a minimize icon to the application, specify FCF_ICON in the second argument of WinCreateStdWindow, and the icon ID in the resource argument. Here's a call to WinCreateStdWindow that creates a minimize icon:

```
hwndFrame = WinCreateStdWindow(
                              HWND_DESKTOP,
                              WS_VISIBLE,
                              &ctlData,
                              szClass,
                              NULL,
                              0L,
                              NULL,
                              ID_RESOURCE,
                              &hwndClient);
```

Because menus and accelerator tables also require resource IDs, you will likely never create an ID called ID_ICON. Instead, the common practice is to define an ID called ID_RESOURCE (as used in the example call). This naming methodology applies only to the resource ID that you supply to the WinCreateStdWindow call. When you specify other IDs, you should use the first letter of the resource name in the third character position of the ID name. Here are some typical examples:

- ID_RESOURCE — Used in WinCreateStdWindow.

- IDMMENU1 — Typical menu item identifier.

- IDB_BITMAP1 — Typical bitmap identifier.

- IDD_DIALOG1 — Typical dialog box, or dialog item, identifier.

- IDP_POINTER1 — Typical pointer identifier.

More Icons

You can use icons inside a standard window to aid the user in various ways. For example, icons in a child window can offer the user an image-based selection method (somewhat similar to the previous menu example, but without the menu structure). You can also use icons with text to call attention to given sections of text. This implementation is similar to static bitmaps, which you might prefer. The HPOINTER data type references icons inside an application. Note that this is the same data type used for pointers. Before you can load an icon, you must declare an icon handle:

```
HPOINTER hicon;
```

The next step is to load the icon. You accomplish this with the WinLoad-Pointer function, which is defined as follows:

```
HPOINTER WinLoadPointer(hwndDesktop, hmod, idres)
HWND hwndDesktop;
HMODULE hmod;
USHORT idres;
```

The return value from WinLoadPointer is the handle to the icon, or *hicon* from the previous example. The first argument to WinLoadPointer, *hwndDesktop*, must be HWND_DESKTOP. The *hmod* argument specifies the source of the icon resource. If the argument is set to NULL, the Presentation Manager loads the icon from the application's .EXE file; otherwise, *hmod* must reference a dynamic link library. The last argument, *idres*, is simply the icon ID as defined in the application's header file. A good place to call WinLoadPointer is in the WM_CREATE message block. Here's a typical call:

```
hicon = WinLoadPointer(HWND_DESKTOP, NULL, IDI_ICON1);
```

The next step, drawing the icon, should occur in the WM_PAINT message handler, or within a function called from the WM_PAINT message handler. You use the WinDrawPointer function to draw an icon. Here's the definition for WinDrawPointer:

```
BOOL WinDrawPointer(hps, x, y, hptr, fs)
HPS hps;
SHORT x, y;
HPOINTER hptr;
USHORT fs;
```

Because WinDrawPointer is a drawing function (even though it is not a GPI function), it requires a handle to a presentation space as its first argument. You can set *hps* to either a micro or normal presentation space. The second and third arguments, *x* and *y*, specify the horizontal and vertical window coordinates of the lower left corner of the icon. The *hptr* argument is the icon handle, or *hicon* from the previous examples. The *fs* argument specifies a flag that tells the Presentation Manager how to draw the icon. Table 10-1 lists the valid flags.

The DP_HALFTONED and DP_INVERTED flags are convenient for indicating the occurrence of an icon-related event. For example, in a file manager application, you could use the DP_INVERTED flag to darken icons corresponding to selected files. Meanwhile, you could use the DP_HALFTONED flag to indicate some event in progress — say, once the user selected several files for printing, an icon drawn with the DP_HALFTONED flag might indicate that the file is being printed.

Table 10-1: Icon/Pointer Flags

FLAG	BIT	DESCRIPTION
DP_NORMAL	0x0000	Specifies that the icon/pointer be drawn as created.
DP_HALFTONED	0x0001	Specifies that black pixels in the icon/pointer be drawn in halftone shade.
DP_INVERTED	0x0002	Specifies inversion for all black and white pixels in the icon/pointer matrix.

You can select an icon by tracking the mouse. The Presentation Manager provides several mouse messages (explained in Chapter 13) that can be adapted for this purpose. By trapping the appropriate messages, you can activate the selection state of an icon by merely having the user click on it.

Simple Bitmaps

For simple general purpose bitmaps, you can use a combination of Win and Gpi functions. The overhead involved is much less than in using only Gpi functions, but the results are not as spectacular — especially in the areas of color and size.

The initial steps for implementing a simple bitmap are similar to those for loading and displaying an icon or pointer. After defining a bitmap ID in the application's header file, you specify the bitmap in the resource script. Recall that the Resource Compiler creates a resource of type RT_BITMAP for all bitmaps specified in the resource script. In your program code, create a handle for a bitmap as follows:

```
HBITMAP hbm;
```

Now you can load the bitmap. The WM_CREATE message handler is a convenient place to do so. If the size of the bitmap will vary, you must load it after obtaining and setting the associated window coordinates. You can use the WinCalcFrameRect function to obtain either the frame or client window coordinates during the WM_CREATE message. The function for loading a bitmap is WinLoadBitmap, which is defined as follows:

```
HBM GpiLoadBitmap(hps, hmod, idBitmap, lWidth, lHeight)
HPS hps;
USHORT hmod, idBitmap;
LONG lWidth, lHeight;
```

As with all Gpi functions, the first argument is a handle to a micro or a normal presentation space. The *hmod* argument specifies the source of the icon resource. If the argument is set to NULL, the Presentation Manager loads the icon from the application's .EXE file; otherwise, *hmod* must reference a dynamic link library. The next argument, *idBitmap*, contains the bitmap ID from the application header file. The final two arguments, *lWidth* and *lHeight*, specify the bitmap's length and height in pixels. You can use these arguments to stretch or to shrink the bitmap; or, to recreate the bitmap as it appeared in the *Icon Editor*, specify zero for both *lWidth* and *lHeight*.

Next you must prepare to call the WinDrawBitmap function. You do so by setting up either a RECTL or POINTL structure to establish the window coordinates for the bitmap. If you choose RECTL, use WinQueryWindowRect to obtain the current window dimensions. To fill the window with the bitmap, you do not have to modify the RECTL structure as long as you have set the *lWidth* and *lHeight* to zero in the call to WinLoadBitmap. To specify a given size relative to the window dimensions, you must modify the *xLeft*, *yBottom*, *xRight*, and *yTop* fields of RECTL. If you use this method, you need to trap the WM_ERASEBACKGROUND message so the

Presentation Manager repaints the full window rectangle. The following settings place the bitmap in the center of the current window:

```
rcl.xLeft = rcl.xRight / 4;
rcl.yBottom = rcl.yTop / 4;
rcl.xRight = rcl.xRight / 4 * 3;
rcl.yTop = rcl.yTop / 4 * 3;
```

This gives you variable control over the placement of the bitmap in the current window, but not much control over how much — or more to the point, how little — of the bitmap is displayed. To extract part of a bitmap, you can reference a second instance of RECTL and set its fields to the section of the bitmap you want to display. You are responsible for maintaining the original size of the bitmap. There is no Win function that returns a bitmap's size; there is a Gpi function that does so, but not as efficiently as tracking the pixel dimensions of the bitmap yourself.

You can use the POINTL structure to place the bitmap in a given area of a window. This method requires you to set the *x* and *y* fields of POINTL to the bitmap's starting position, If you want to manipulate the size of the bitmap later, set the *x* and *y* fields of POINTL to zero.

Now you can draw the bitmap. The WinDrawBitmap function makes this process relatively easy. Here's the definition for WinDrawBitmap:

```
BOOL WinDrawBitmap (hps, idBitmap, pwrcSrc, ptl,
                    clrFore, clrBack, fs)
HPS hps;
Hbm idBitmap;
PRECTL pwrcSrc;
PPOINT ptl;
LONG clrFore, clrBack;
USHORT fs;
```

The first two arguments to WinDrawBitmap are familiar ones. The *pwrcSrc* argument points to a RECTL structure that defines the source dimensions of the bitmap. The *ptl* defines the target rectangle for the bitmap. Note that if you reference RECTL here, you must cast it to type PPOINTL. The *clrFore* and *clrBack* arguments set the foreground and background color for the bitmap. The final argument, *fs*, specifies one or more flags that inform the Presentation Manager how to draw the bitmap. Table 10-2 lists the valid flags.

Table 10-2: Bitmap Style Flags

FLAG	BIT	DESCRIPTION
DBM_NORMAL	0x0000	Specifies that the bitmap be drawn as created.
DBM_INVERT	0x0001	Specifies inversion for all black and white pixels in the bitmap.
DBM_HALFTONE	0x0002	Specifies halftone shading of the bitmap and can be ORed with DBM_NORMAL and DBM_INVERT.
DBM_STRETCH	0x0004	Specifies that the bitmap should be stretched to the rectangle specified by ptl.
DBM_IMAGEATTRS	0x0008	Specifies that color conversion be performed by using the image attributes.

The final step in dealing with simple bitmaps is to remove all bitmaps from memory. You accomplish this with a call to GpiDeleteBitmap:

```
GpiDeleteBitmap(hbm);
```

The following program example uses some of the methods described in this section. The program loads a bitmap into the lower left-hand corner of the client window and allows you to increase or decrease the size of the bitmap via two menu controls.

```
/* BITMAP1.H (Header file) */

#define DIV 20
#define MUL 5

#define IDD_NULL  -1
#define ID_RESOURCE 1
#define IDB_EXAMPLE 2
#define IDD_ABOUT  3

#define IDM_BMMENU      100
#define IDM_BMLARGER    101
#define IDM_BMSMALLER   102
#define IDM_ABOUT       103
```

```
/*  BITMAP1.RC (resource script) */

#include <os2.h>
#include "bitmap1.h"

BITMAP IDB_EXAMPLE bitmap1.bmp

MENU ID_RESOURCE
{
SUBMENU "~Bitmap",  IDM_BMMENU
  {
      MENUITEM "~Larger\t^L", IDM_BMLARGER
      MENUITEM "~Smaller\t^S", IDM_BMSMALLER
      MENUITEM "~About...", IDM_ABOUT
  }
}

ACCELTABLE ID_RESOURCE
{
   "^L", IDM_BMLARGER
   "^S", IDM_BMSMALLER
}

DLGTEMPLATE IDD_ABOUT
{
  DIALOG "", 1, 10, 10, 150, 80, FS_DLGBORDER
  {
    CTEXT "This program lets you adjust", IDD_NULL,  0, 70, 150, 8

    CTEXT "the size of a bitmap once", IDD_NULL, 0, 55, 150, 8
    CTEXT "it is loaded into memory.", IDD_NULL, 0, 40, 150, 8
    DEFPUSHBUTTON "Ok", DID_OK, 6, 4, 40, 12,
                     WS_TABSTOP | WS_GROUP
  }
}


/* BITMAP1.C (Bitmap program example) */

#define INCL_WIN
#define INCL_GPI

#include <os2.h>
#include <stddef.h>
#include "bitmap1.h"
```

```
MRESULT EXPENTRY BitmapWndProc(HWND, USHORT, MPARAM, MPARAM);
MRESULT EXPENTRY AboutDlgBoxProc(HWND,USHORT,MPARAM,MPARAM);


int main(void)
{

HAB hab;
HMQ hmq;
QMSG qmsg;
HWND hwndFrame, hwndClient;
static CHAR szClass [] = "Bitmapper";
ULONG ctlData = FCF_TITLEBAR | FCF_SYSMENU | FCF_MINMAX
                | FCF_SIZEBORDER | FCF_SHELLPOSITION
                | FCF_TASKLIST | FCF_MENU |FCF_ACCELTABLE;


hab = WinInitialize(0);
hmq = WinCreateMsgQueue(hab, 0);

WinRegisterClass(hab, szClass, BitmapWndProc,
                CS_SIZEREDRAW, 0);

hwndFrame = WinCreateStdWindow(
                        HWND_DESKTOP,
                        WS_VISIBLE,
                        &ctlData,
                        szClass,
                        NULL,
                        0L,
                        NULL,
                        ID_RESOURCE,
                        &hwndClient);

while(WinGetMsg(hab, &qmsg, NULL, 0, 0))
            WinDispatchMsg(hab, &qmsg);

WinDestroyWindow(hwndFrame);
WinDestroyMsgQueue(hmq);
WinTerminate(hab);

return(0);
}
```

```
MRESULT EXPENTRY BitmapWndProc(hwnd, msg, mp1, mp2)
HWND hwnd;
USHORT msg;
MPARAM mp1, mp2;
{

    HPS hps;
    RECTL rcl, rclBmp;
    static SHORT usFactor = 1;
    static SHORT cx, cy;
    static HBITMAP hbm;


    switch(msg)
        {
        case WM_CREATE:
                hps = WinGetPS(hwnd);
                hbm = GpiLoadBitmap(hps, NULL,
                                    IDB_EXAMPLE, 0L, 0L);
                WinReleasePS(hps);
                return(FALSE);

        case WM_SIZE:
                cx = SHORT1FROMMP(mp2);
                cy = SHORT2FROMMP(mp2);

        case WM_COMMAND:
                switch((COMMANDMSG(&msg)->cmd))
                    {
                    case IDM_BMLARGER:
                        if(usFactor != DIV - 1)
                            usFactor++;
                        WinInvalidateRect(hwnd, NULL, NULL);
                        return(NULL);

                    case IDM_BMSMALLER:
                        if(usFactor != DIV - (DIV + 1))
                            usFactor--;
                        WinInvalidateRect(hwnd, NULL, NULL);
                        return(NULL);

                    case IDM_ABOUT:
                        WinDlgBox(HWND_DESKTOP, hwnd,
                                    AboutDlgBoxProc,
                                    NULL, IDD_ABOUT, NULL);
                        break;
                    }
```

```
        case WM_PAINT:
           hps = WinBeginPaint(hwnd, NULL, NULL);
           WinQueryWindowRect(hwnd, &rcl);
           GpiErase(hps);

           rclBmp.xLeft = (rcl.xLeft / DIV) * (MUL + usFactor);
           rclBmp.yBottom =
                       (rcl.yBottom / DIV) * (MUL + usFactor);
           rclBmp.xRight =
                       (rcl.xRight / DIV) * (2 * (MUL + usFactor));

           rclBmp.yTop = (rcl.yTop / DIV) * (2 * (MUL + usFactor));

           if(hbm)
           WinDrawBitmap(hps, hbm, NULL,
                       (PPOINTL) &rclBmp,
                       CLR_NEUTRAL,
                       CLR_BACKGROUND,
                       DBM_STRETCH);

           WinEndPaint(hps);
           return(NULL);


        case WM_DESTROY:
           if(hbm)
                GpiDeleteBitmap(hbm);
           return(NULL);

        }

    return WinDefWindowProc(hwnd, msg, mp1, mp2);
}



MRESULT EXPENTRY AboutDlgBoxProc(hwndDlg, msg, mp1, mp2)
HWND hwndDlg;
USHORT msg;
MPARAM mp1, mp2;
{

    return(WinDefDlgProc(hwndDlg, msg, mp1, mp2));

}
```

Gpi Bitmaps

Using the Gpi functions to manipulate bitmaps gives you extensive control over the bitmapped image. Not only can you manipulate colors more effectively using the Gpi functions, you can use these functions to manipulate bitmaps in device memory, save bitmaps to disk, create TIFF-formatted files, and integrate bitmaps with drawing functions.

When you load a bitmap using the Gpi functions, the Presentation Manager requires that it be transferred to a device context. The combined Win and Gpi method does not appear to require this step because the Presentation Manager internally places the bitmap data in its default presentation space, the cached micro-PS. The sequence of events associated with the loading a bitmap is relatively straightforward. The main reason for this is the bitmap already exists on disk. Here is a step-by-step summary for loading and displaying a bitmap using the Gpi bitmap functions:

1. Create a device context, using DevOpenDC.

2. Create a presentation space, using GpiCreatePS.

3. Set the bitmap to the device context, using GpiSetBitmap.

4. Copy the bitmap from the presentation space associated with the device context to the specified window, using GpiBitBlt.

Things get more involved when you create a bitmap in a device context. Doing so opens up a world of possibilities such as creating drawings in separate threads of execution. Here are the basic steps for creating and then displaying a bitmap image.

1. Create a device context, using DevOpenDC.

2. Create a presentation space, using GpiCreatePS.

3. Create a bitmap, using GpiCreateBitmap.

4. Associate the presentation space with the device context, using the GpiAssociate function.

5. Associate the bitmap to the device context, using GpiSetBitmap.

6. Use a given set of Gpi drawing functions to create an image, specifying the presentation space from Step 2.

7. Copy the bitmap from the presentation space associated with the device context to the specified window, using the GpiBitBlt call.

What you can accomplish with bitmaps seems endless. Be forewarned, however, that fully exploiting the Gpi bitmap functions means your code will become heavily reliant on a given device. Nevertheless, bitmaps greatly enhance an application, if used wisely. Table 10-3 lists the complete set of Gpi bitmap functions and describes the purpose of each.

Table 10-3: Gpi Library Bitmap Functions

FUNCTION	DESCRIPTION
GpiBitBlt	Copies all or part of a bitmap image from a presentation space associated with a device context to a second presentation space.
GpiCreateBitmap	Creates a bitmap in a presentation space and uses device memory, if possible. Returns the bitmap handle.
GpiDeleteBitmap	Deletes a bitmap from a presentation space. If the bitmap is set at the time of the call, the bitmap is not deleted.
GpiLoadBitmap	Loads a bitmap into a presentation space and uses device memory, if possible. Returns the bitmap handle.
GpiQueryBitmapBits	Transfers a bitmap from a presentation space to a specified storage medium.
GpiQueryBitmapDimension	Returns the width and height of a bitmap. Must follow a call to GpiSetBitmapDimension.
GpiQueryBitmapHandle	Returns the handle of a bitmap set in a presentation space.
GpiQueryBitmapParameters	Fills a copy of BITMAPINFOHEADER for the specified bitmap.
GpiQueryDeviceBitmapFormats	Returns bitcount and plane information describing the bitmap's device format.

(continued)

347

Table 10-3: Continued

FUNCTION	DESCRIPTION
GpiSetBitmap	Sets the bitmap as the current bitmap associated with a device context.
GpiSetBitmapBits	Transfers a bitmap data from a specified storage medium to an already defined bitmap in a presentation space.
GpiSetBitmapDimension	Specifies a width and height for a bitmap in a presentation space. The unit of measure is millimeters.
GpiSetBitmapId	Associates a local identifier with a bitmap in a presentation space.

Bitmap Device Format

The Presentation Manager supports four external bitmap formats that you can use to manipulate data for a given device. These formats are common to many raster-based devices. You will likely want to use these formats for anything but the most specialized tasks. Once a bitmap is transferred to a device context, you can readily convert it to device-dependent formats as necessary. Each of the four supported formats is linear, based on an established bit-count that represents a single display pixel. Table 10-4 lists the formats.

Table 10-4: Raster-Based Bitmap Formats

BITCOUNT	PLANES
1	1
4	1
8	1
24	1

The Presentation Manager processes a bitmap one scan-line at a time in the order that each pixel appears in the target window. This means that the pixel representing the lower left corner of the bitmap is the first pixel processed. The crucial display information for each pixel is stored in the most significant bits of the first byte of each bitcount. Each scan-line, in turn, is padded at the end so that each scan-line begins on a ULONG boundary. As a result, the input buffer need only be a scan-line in height.

Bitmap Structures

This type of setup is necessary to copy the bitmap image from the device context to the display screen when you use the GpiBitBlt function to display a bitmap. If the bitmap does not already exist on disk, additional format information is required. For example, if you create an image using GPI drawing functions and want to save the image as a bitmap, you must define the bitmap's structure for both the device context and the GpiCreateBitmap function. At this point, the BITMAPINFO and BITMAPINFOHEADER structures become relevant. Here are their definitions:

```
typedef struct _BITMAPINFO {
        ULONG  cbFix;
        USHORT cx;
        USHORT cy;
        USHORT cPlanes;
        USHORT cBitCount;
        RGB    argbColor[1];
} BITMAPINFO;


typedef struct _BITMAPINFOHEADER {
        ULONG  cbFix;
        USHORT cx;
        USHORT cy;
        USHORT cPlanes;
        USHORT cBitCount;
} BITMAPINFOHEADER;
```

As you can see, the BITMAPINFOHEADER structure is a subset of the BITMAPINFO structure. The only difference between the two structures is the *argbColor* field in BITMAPINFO. This field is an array of 24 bit RGB values that you set according to the current bitmap format. You only need to set *argbColor* if you are not using the 24-bit format. The fields common to both structures are straightforward. The *cbFix* field is the size of the structure. You should use the **sizeof** operator to obtain the size of the structure (a technique that also ensures compatibility with later releases of the Presentation Manager). The *cx* and *cy* fields represent the width and height of the bitmap. The remaining two fields, *cPlanes* and *cBitCount*, define the bitplane format. The *cPlanes* argument contains the number of planes and the *cBitCount* argument contains the associated bitcount. Here's an example definition of BITMAPINFOHEADER:

```
bmp.cbFix = (ULONG) sizeof(BITMAPINFOHEADER);
bmp.cx = (USHORT) (rcl.xRight - rcl.xLeft);
bmp.cy = (USHORT) (rcl.yTop - yBottom);
bmp.cPlanes = 1L;
bmp.cBitCount = 24L;
```

Loading and Displaying a Bitmap

Before loading a bitmap from disk to a device context, you must set it using the GpiSetBitmap function. GpiSetBitmap requires that the specified presentation space already be associated with the device context. The physical device associated with the device context does not have to be the same device on which you created the bitmap. For example, you will likely want to create a bitmap on screen, store it, and later associate it with a device context for a printer.

GpiSetBitmap simply takes two arguments: the handle to the presentation space, represented by *hps*; and the handle to bitmap to be set, represented by *hbm*. If GpiSetBitmap finds a bitmap already current in the device context, it returns the handle to this bitmap before setting the new bitmap. The following fragment shows the necessary code leading up to the GpiSetBitmap call (excluding basic definitions).

```
/* Set data block for device context. */

static PSZ szData[9] = { 0, "DISPLAY", 0, 0, 0, 0, 0, 0, 0 };

/* Set the maximum possible size of the window. */
```

```
    size.cx = WinQuerySysValue(HWND_DESKTOP,SV_CXFULLSCREEN);
    size.cy = WinQuerySysValue(HWND_DESKTOP,SV_CYFULLSCREEN);

/* Set the device context for the memory device and create
the associated presentation space for the full screen.  */

    hdc=DevOpenDC(hab, OD_MEMORY, (PSZ) "*", 8L,
            (PDEVOPENDATA) datablock, (HDC) NULL);
    hpsDC=GpiCreatePS(hab, hdc, (PSIZEL) &size,
            (LONG) PU_PELS | GPIT_NORMAL | GPIA_ASSOC);

/* Load the bitmap and associate it. */

    hbitmap = GpiLoadBitmap(hpsDC, NULL, ID_BITMAP, 0L, 0L);
    GpiSetBitmap(hpsDC, hbm);
```

Although these setup procedures primarily apply to loading bitmaps from disk, you can use them with bit block transfers — commonly known as bit blitting. Simply put, bit blitting is a RAM to RAM transfer, moving bitmap data from device context memory to the current display memory. This makes drawing a bitmap a much faster process, especially if you delegate much of the setup work to a secondary thread. Indeed, bit blitting easily lends itself to real-time animation routines, including ones involving multiple objects (if multiple threads are employed). Here's the definition for the GpiBitBlt function:

```
LONG GpiBitBlt(hpsDst, hpsSrc, cPoints, paptlPoints,
                    lRop, flOptions)
HPS hpsDst, hpsSrc;
LONG cPoints;
PPOINTL paptlPoints;
LONG lRop, flOptions;
```

GpiBitBlt's six arguments pack a lot of information. The function starts off simply enough, with *hpsDst* and *hpsSrc* naming the destination and source presentation spaces. The *cPoints* argument specifies the number of points in each *paptlPoints* array. In turn, *paptlPoints* orders these points in the form:

```
xDst1, yDst1, xDst2, yDst2, xSrc1, ySrc1, xSrc2, ySrc2
```

The array information is interpreted in pairs. For example, *xDst* and *yDst* represent the bottom left corner of the destination rectangle in coordinates understood by the device context; and *xSrc2* and *ySrc2* represent the source rectangle in coordinates understood by the source device.

With the *lRop* argument, you can create some nifty effects by manipulating the three possible bitmaps. Through a logic operation, you can essentially create a fourth bitmap from the three described by *lRop*. For example, by ANDing the initial setting of the destination bitmap with the source bitmap, you create an entirely new bitmap. Similarly, you can choose to include the active pattern when combining destination and source, although it is not necessary to do so. Table 10-5 lists the various operations that you can specify through the *lRop* argument.

Table 10-5: Identifiers for GpiBitBlt Logical Operations

IDENTIFIER	BIT	DESCRIPTION
ROP_SRCCOPY	0x00CCL	Copies source to destination.
ROP_SRCPAINT	0x00EEL	ORs source with destination.
ROP_SRCAND	0x0088L	ANDs source with destination.
ROP_SRCINVERT	0x0066L	XORs source with destination.
ROP_SRCERASE	0x0044L	ANDs source with inverted destination.
ROP_NOTSRCCOPY	0x0033L	Copies inverted source.
ROP_NOTSRCERASE	0x0011L	ANDs inverted source with the instance of the inverted destination.
ROP_MERGECOPY	0x00C0L	ANDs source with active pattern.
ROP_MERGEPAINT	0x00BBL	ORs destination with inverted source.
ROP_PATCOPY	0x00F0L	Copies the active pattern.
ROP_PATPAINT	0x00FBL	ORs the active pattern with destination and inverted source.
ROP_PATINVERT	0x005AL	XORs the destination and active pattern.
ROP_DSTINVERT	0x0055L	Copies inverted destination.
ROP_ZERO	0x0000L	Set to zero.
ROP_ONE	0x00FFL	Set to one.

The final argument to GpiBitBlt lets you specify stretching and compression characteristics for the destination image. A set of BBO identifiers indicate exactly how to handle lines and columns for stretched and compressed images. Table 10-6 lists these identifiers.

In addition to the BBO identifiers, you can create your own identifiers to indicate how a bitmap should be stretched or compressed for a particular device. Values 15 through 31 are reserved for this purpose, but values 32 through 32,767 are reserved for system use.

When you use GpiBitBlt, you should ensure that the entire source rectangle is visible. If part of the rectangle is not visible (that is, it has been moved off-screen), the Presentation Manager places undefined values in the equivalent area in the destination rectangle.

Table 10-6: GpiBitBlt Compression Identifiers

IDENTIFIER	BIT	DESCRIPTION
BBO_NOSCALE	0x0001	Indicates that the bitmap should neither be stretched or compressed.
BBO_OR	0x0002	Indicates that the bitmap should be stretched or compressed as necessary by ORing eliminated rows and columns.
BBO_AND	0x0003	Indicates that the bitmap should be stretched or compressed as necessary by ANDing eliminated rows and columns. Used in monochrome mode.
BBO_IGNORE	0x0004	Indicates that the bitmap should be stretched or compressed as necessary. Eliminated rows and columns are ignored. Used in color modes.

The following program draws a bitmap with the GpiBitBlt function. It uses the ROP_SRCCOPY identifier to copy the source bitmap from the presentation space associated with a secondary device context. The destination is the presentation space associated with the device context created in the call to the WinBeginPaint function. The BBO_OR identifier is also used to size the bitplane to the destination rectangle.

```
/* Header file for BMBLT.C */

#define ID_BITMAP  1
```

353

```
#define ID_BMBLT    4

/* Resource file for BMAP */

#include <os2.h>
#include "bmap.h"

POINTER ID_RESOURCE bmap.ico
BITMAP  ID_BITMAP3  bmap3.bmp


/* Example (BMBLT.C) Bitmap Using GpiBitBlt */

#define INCL_WIN
#define INCL_GPI

#include <os2.h>
#include "bmblt.h"

MRESULT EXPENTRY BitmapWndProc(HWND,USHORT,MPARAM,MPARAM);
VOID InitializeDevice(HWND);
VOID InitializeBitmap(HWND);

HAB    hab;
HDC    hdc;
HPS    hpsDC;
POINTL bmap[5];
HBITMAP hbitmap = (HBITMAP) NULL;
PSZ szData[9] = { 0, "DISPLAY", 0, 0, 0, 0, 0, 0, 0 };

int main(void)
{

HMQ     hmq;
HWND    hwndFrame, hwndApp;
QMSG    qmsg;
static CHAR szTitleBar[40];
static CHAR szClass[] = "GPI BITMAPS";
ULONG   ctlData = FCF_STANDARD
                    & ~FCF_MENU & ~FCF_ACCELTABLE;

hab = WinInitialize(NULL);
hmq = WinCreateMsgQueue(hab, 0);
WinRegisterClass(hab, szClass,
                    BitmapWndProc, CS_SIZEREDRAW, 0);
```

```
hwndFrame = WinCreateStdWindow(
                        HWND_DESKTOP,
                        WS_VISIBLE | FS_ICON,
                        &ctlData,
                        szClass,
                        NULL,
                        0L,
                        NULL,
                        ID_RESOURCE,
                        &hwndApp);

InitializeDevice(hwndFrame);

while(WinGetMsg(hab, &qmsg, NULL, 0, 0))
    WinDispatchMsg(hab, &qmsg);

WinDestroyWindow(hwndFrame);
WinDestroyMsgQueue(hmq);
WinTerminate(hab);
return(0);
}


MRESULT EXPENTRY BitmapWndProc(hwnd, msg, mp1, mp2)
HWND   hwnd;
USHORT  msg;
MPARAM  mp1, mp2;
{

    HPS  hps;
    RECTL rcl;

    switch (msg)
        {
        case WM_PAINT:
            hps = WinBeginPaint(hwnd, NULL, &rcl);
            WinFillRect(hps, &rcl, SYSCLR_WINDOW);
            WinQueryWindowRect(hwnd, &rcl);
            bmap[0].x = 0;
            bmap[0].y = 0;
            bmap[1].x = rcl.xRight - rcl.xLeft;
            bmap[2].x = 0;
            bmap[2].y = 0;

            GpiBitBlt(hps, hpsDC, 3L, (PPOINTL) bmap,
                    (LONG) ROP_SRCCOPY, (LONG) BBO_OR);
            WinEndPaint(hps);
```

```
                return(0);

        case WM_DESTROY:
                GpiAssociate(hpsDC, (HDC) NULL);
                GpiDestroyPS(hpsDC);
                DevCloseDC(hdc);
                break;

        default:
                return(WinDefWindowProc(hwnd, msg, mp1, mp2));
    }
    return(0L);
}


VOID InitializeDevice(hwnd)
HWND hwnd;
{
SIZEL size;

size.cx = WinQuerySysValue(HWND_DESKTOP, SV_CXFULLSCREEN);
size.cy = WinQuerySysValue(HWND_DESKTOP, SV_CYFULLSCREEN);

hdc=DevOpenDC(hab, OD_MEMORY,
            (PSZ) "*", 8L,
            (PDEVOPENDATA) datablock,
            (HDC) NULL);

hpsDC=GpiCreatePS(hab, hdc, (PSIZEL) &size,
            (LONG) PU_PELS | GPIT_NORMAL | GPIA_ASSOC);
}


VOID InitializeBitmap(hwnd)
HWND hwnd;
{

    if(hbitmap == NULL) {
        hbitmap = GpiLoadBitmap(hpsDC, NULL,
                            ID_BMBLT, 0L, 0L);
        GpiSetBitmap(hpsDC, hbitmap);
}
```

CHAPTER 11

TEXT PROCESSING AND FONTS

Handling text in the Presentation Manager is a singular experience. In most programming environments, learning text display is a straightforward. Usually, it involves using some function named print or write (or some variation thereof) that prints the specified string or numeric variable. And while the C language's **printf** statement might beguile newcomers, it does not necessarily require as much formatting intervention as do the Presentation Manager's Gpi text display functions.

Intervention might not be quite the right word: there are built-in Gpi text display aids at your disposal, but these require substantial preliminary setup — much as if you were programming your own BIOS text routines in DOS. In the Presentation Manager, you are frequently responsible for maintaining current window coordinates, cursor positioning, and obtaining the length of text strings. Additionally, because the Presentation Manager uses proportional fonts, you are responsible for a host of concerns that traditionally fall in the province of typesetting, not programming. As a result, this chapter addresses three major subjects:

- Text resources — System resources contained in resource scripts and specially referenced ASCII files.

- Text display — Functions and methods used in Presentation Manager programs that display graphically composed text.

- Fonts — System or programmer-defined resources that allow you to change the appearance of text.

This chapter interweaves these three subjects — as does the Presentation Manager itself — and attempts to be as comprehensive as possible. The information on fonts is limited to introductory material, however. Additionally, you should refer to Chapter 6 for a more generalized description of resources. For now, take a look at Table 11-1, which provides a beginner's lexicon of some key terms.

Table 11-1: Typography Lexicon

TERM	DEFINITION
baseline	The imaginary line on which letters without descenders seem to rest.
descender	The portion of a letter below the baseline.
fixed width	Monospaced type.
kerning	Amount of spacing between two or more letters.
leading	Amount of spacing between text lines.
letterform	A single letter.
point	A unit of typographic measure equal to 1/72.77 of an inch.
point size	The height of the font expressed in points.
serif	A small stroke ending a main stroke of a letterform.
typeface	A unique design of the alphanumeric character set.
type size	The size of a typeface, measured from line to line, with no interline space added.

String Resources

Typically, string resources consist of text and IDs that identify the text. String resource scripts are similar to other resource scripts used by the Presentation Manager. They are different only in the sense that they incorporate text into the binary resource, instead of a bitmapped image, dialog box, or menu definition.

The precise definition of a string resource is it is any null-terminated character string with a unique string identifier. String resources are stored in an expanded segment in the application's .EXE file. This expanded space lets you store multiple string resources under one ID. The resource compiler formats the binary resource so that the first byte in each string specifies the length of the string in bytes. If the first byte is zero, the Presentation Manager knows it has reached the end of the resource table. A single resource segment can contain up to 16 null-terminated strings. Each string has an associated string ID, but more conveniently, the entire segment can be referenced with the ID of the first string in the segment.

The resource compiler statement that defines strings is called STRINGTABLE. It allows you to define segments between with the BEGIN and END key words, or alternatively, by using French brackets. No individual string can be longer than 256 characters. The following statement defines some strings associated with EREWHON.C, which appears later in this chapter.

```
STRINGTABLE
{
    ID_TITLE, "Erewhon Revisited"
    ID_AUTHOR, "ID_AUTHOR"
    ID_PUBLISHER, "Everyman's Library"
    ID_PUBDATE, "1932"
    ID_CHAPTER, "Professor Hanky and Panky"
}
```

You can also define strings by simply using the RESOURCE statement to reference an ASCII file. Using this technique falls into the realm of programmer-defined resources, which can reference a binary or an ASCII file. The following example defines a programmer-defined string resource having a type ID of IDS_TXTFILE and a resource ID of IDS_PARAGRAPH.

```
/* Resource script file that loads erewhon.h text file. */

#include "EREWHON.H"

RESOURCE IDS_TXTFILE IDS_PARAGRAPH EREWHON.TXT

/* EREWHON.TXT — separate text file. */

        It was Panky, not Hanky, who had given him the Musical
        Bank money. Panky was the greater humbug of the two,
        for he would humbug even himself — a thing, by the way,
        not very hard to do; and yet he was the less successful
```

```
humbug, for he could humbug no one who was worth hum-
bugging — not for long. Hanky's occasional frankness
put people off their guard. He being a professor, would
of course profess, but would not lie more than was in
the bond; he was log-rolled and log-rolling, but
still, in a robust wolfish fashion, human.
```

The header file for the previous two examples necessarily defines several IDs. Recall that IDs directly associated with the RESOURCE are known as type IDs. These IDs need not differ from one another, but the ID that follows (the resource ID, which must be set to a value between 0 and 65,535) must be unique. Subsequent IDs, if any, are related to the STRINGTABLE statement. Here's the header file for the EREWHON.C program listed later in the chapter:

```
/* Header file for EREWHON.TXT and associated resources. */

#define IDS_TXTFILE     256
#define IDS_PARAGRAPH   1
#define IDS_TITLE       1
#define IDS_AUTHOR      2
#define IDS_PUBLISHER   3
#define IDS_PUBDATE     4
#define IDS_CHAPTER     5
```

Numerous STRINGTABLE statements can be defined in a header file. The resource compiler, however, processes all strings from the various STRINGTABLE statements as if they were a single statement. No two STRINGTABLE strings can have the same ID. In practice, it is common to sequentially number IDs associated with STRINGTABLE statements. In fact, failure to observe this practice results in an unnecessarily large .EXE file as well as the unnecessary use of RAM while running the application.

Loading a String Resource

You can load a string resource when your application requires it. As with other resources, you have the choice of loading a resource from the application's .EXE file, or from a dynamic link library. The WinLoadString function loads string resources that you define using the STRINGTABLE statement. Here's its definition:

```
SHORT WinLoadString(hab, hmod, id,cchMax, pchBuffer)
HAB hab;
HMODULE hmod;
USHORT id;
SHORT cchMax;
PSZ pchBuffer;
```

After specifying the anchor block handle, you can tell WinLoadString where the resource resides. If the resource is in the .EXE file, set *hmod* to NULL; if the resource is in a dynamic link library, obtain a resource module handle by calling DosLoadModule. The *id* argument is the resource ID, not the type ID. For example, if you wanted to load the IDS_TXTFILE resource, you would specify IDS_PARAGRAPH to satisfy the *id* argument. The next argument, *cchMax*, specifies the size of the buffer to hold the string resource. To load a paragraph of text, you could define an array and then satisfy *cchMax* as follows:

```
sizeof(TextLines)
```

The final argument, *pchBuffer*, specifies a temporary buffer for the string. In practice, the *pchBuffer* argument is the variable name for the string that you want to manipulate. A common practice in Presentation Manager programs is to define the titlebar text as a string resource, load this text using WinLoadString, then reference *pchBuffer* in WinRegisterClass and WinCreateStdWindow.

To load a programmer-defined string resource such as the EREWHON.TXT file, you need to use the DosGetResource function. For intensive use of string resources, DosGetResource is convenient because it loads the string resource into a section of memory, which you can access using a segment selector. The following call to DosGetResource loads IDS_TXTFILE from the previous examples.

```
DosGetResource(NULL, IDS_TXTFILE, ID_PARAGRAPH, &psel);
```

The first argument to DosGetResource specifies the resource module handle; setting it to NULL tells the function to load the resource from the .EXE file. As should be clear, the next two arguments specify the type ID and resource ID, respectively. The final argument, *psel*, is a far pointer that references the variable to receive the segment selector from the function call. DosGetResource returns zero if the call is successful; otherwise, it returns:

- ERROR_INVALID_MODULE (190)
- ERROR_INVALID_SELECTOR (490)

After you obtain the segment selector from DosGetResource, you need to retrieve the size of the segment. You do this with a call to DosSizeSeg as in the following:

```
DosSizeSeg(psel, &pulSize);
```

Next, you must ensure that you can reference the text resource. You can quickly accomplish this by using the MAKEP macro, which combines the segment selector and an address offset to create a 32-bit pointer to the text resource.

```
lpTxtRes = MAKEP(psel, 0);
```

The zero argument in MAKEP specifies the offset from the beginning of the resource segment to the desired byte within the segment. After using MAKEP, you will likely want to set a second variable of type PUCHAR equal to *lpTxtRes* (in order to have a base reference to *lpTextRes*).

You are now ready to begin manipulating the strings from the text resource. For example, the following fragment establishes the number of text lines from the EREWHON.TXT file:

```
while (lpText - lpTxtRes < (USHORT) pulSize)
{

    if (*lpText == '\0' || *lpText == EOF)
        break;

    if (*lpText == '\r')
        TextLines ++;

    lpText++;

}
```

When you have no further need for the resource segment, free the associated memory with a call to the DosFreeSeg function. DosFreeSeg takes *psel* as its only argument. If, for some reason an error results from the call, the function returns a value of 5, or symbolically:

- ERROR_ACCESS_DENIED

Gpi Text Display

Up until now, program examples have used the WinDrawText function to display text in a window. While WinDrawText is a useful function, it carries with it too much overhead to blend in efficiently with the Gpi functions handling other output. In the following sections, you will be introduced to more efficient text management functions from the Gpi library.

Using the Gpi functions for text output requires an understanding of typography mechanics. Don't let this scare you. If you want, you can get by with a minimum of new terms and concepts. On the other hand, learning one of the oldest crafts from the electronic perspective can be quite rewarding. It will give you a deeper understanding of how text characters are formatted, as well a new topic of conversation with your desktop publishing friends.

Before you can use Gpi functions, you must obtain a handle to a presentation space. You can use either the WinGetPS function or use the Gpi functions directly (see Chapter 9). The Gpi functions represent a more versatile approach to presentation spaces. For example, you can call GpiCreatePS from any point in the program, including **main()**. In fact, you must call GpiCreatePS if you want to use a normal-PS or micro-PS. If you stick with the cached micro-PS, you do not have to call GpiCreatePS. Instead, you simply call WinGetPS from the point in the program at which you want to access the presentation space. WinGetPS takes *hwnd* as its only argument.

Font Basics

Most of the Gpi text functions access a structure called FONTMETRICS. This structure contains more than 45 fields for controlling such typographic elements as proportional spacing, kerning, and leading. More often than not, you only need to manipulate a few of the more common fields for text display. (When it comes to creating fonts, you need to get more intimately involved with FONTMETRICS, as you will see later in the chapter.) Table 11-2 describes the FONTMETRICS fields.

Table 11-2: Fields in FONTMETRICS

FIELD	TYPE	DESCRIPTION
szFamilyname;	CHAR	Name of the type family, including Courier (monospaced), Helvetica, and Roman.
szFacename;	CHAR	Name specifying the typeface.
idRegistry;	SHORT	ID used by the Presentation Manager to register the font as a resource.
usCodePage;	SHORT	Registered code page (1 to 999).
lEmHeight;	LONG	Average height above the baseline of the uppercase characters in a font.
lXHeight;	LONG	Average height above the baseline of the lowercase characters in a font.
lMaxAscender;	LONG	Maximum height above the baseline of any character in a font.
lMaxDescender;	LONG	Maximum depth below the baseline of any character in a font.
lLowerCaseAscent;	LONG	Maximum height above the baseline of any lowercase character in a font.
lLowerCaseDescent;	LONG	Maximum distance below the baseline of any character in a font.
lInternalLeading;	LONG	The height of a character, including accent marks.
lExternalLeading;	LONG	Distance from the bottom of one character to the top of the character below it.
lAveCharWidth;	LONG	Average distance from the left side of a character to the left side of the next character.
lMaxCharInc;	LONG	Maximum horizontal distance from the left edge of one character to the left edge of the next.
lEmInc;	LONG	Space corresponding to an uppercase M.

(continued)

Table 11-2: Continued

FIELD	TYPE	DESCRIPTION
lMaxBaselineExt;	LONG	Maximum vertical distance from one character baseline to the next character baseline.
sCharSlope;	LONG	Slant of each character, increasing clockwise from the right angle of the character.
sInlineDir;	SHORT	Angle of a line of type, increasing clockwise from the base of the character.
sCharRot;	SHORT	Angle for character rotation, increasing clockwise from the right angle of the character.
usWeightClass;	USHORT	Controls the line thickness of a character relative to its size.
usWidthClass;	USHORT	Controls the width of a character relative to its size.
sXDeviceRes;	USHORT	Number of pixels per inch in the horizontal axis of the output display device.
sYDeviceRes;	SHORT	Number of pixels per inch in the vertical axis of the output display device.
sFirstChar;	SHORT	Code point for the first character in a font.
sLastChar;	SHORT	Code point for the last character in a font.
sDefaultChar;	SHORT	Default code point (used when an invalid code point is passed to the application).
sBreakChar;	SHORT	Code point for character (usually a white space) that defines word breaks for text justification.
sNominalPointSize;	SHORT	Normal size of the font.
sMinimumPointSize;	SHORT	Minimum size of the font.
sMaximumPointSize;	SHORT	Maximum size of the font.
fsType;	USHORT	Indicates fixed/proportional spacing (bit 15); protected or licensed font (bit 14); kerning flag (bit 13); and single, double, or mixed byte (bits 12 and 11).

(continued)

Table 11-2: Continued

FIELD	TYPE	DESCRIPTION
fsDefn;	USHORT	Indicates image/vector font (bit 15); and device or physical font (bit 0).
fsSelection;	USHORT	Indicates normal/italic characters (bit 15); normal/ underscored characters (bit 14); and normal/over-strike characters (bit 11).
fsCapabilities;	USHORT	Indicates whether font can be mixed with graphics (bit 15).
lSubscriptXSize;	LONG	Point width of subscript characters.
lSubscriptYSize;	LONG	Point height of subscript characters.
lSubscriptXOffset;	LONG	Horizontal offset of subscript characters.
lSubscriptYOffset;	LONG	Vertical offset of subscript characters.
lSuperscriptXSize;	LONG	Point width of superscript characters.
lSuperscriptYSize;	LONG	Point height of superscript characters.
lSuperscriptXOffset;	LONG	Horizontal offset of subscript characters.
lSuperscriptYOffset;	LONG	Vertical offset of subscript characters.
lUnderscoreSize;	LONG	Size of the underscore stoke. Size is measured in number of character strokes.
lUnderscorePosition;	LONG	Distance in pixels of the first underscore stroke below the baseline.
lStrikeoutSize;	LONG	Point size of the overstrike stroke.
lStrikeoutPosition;	LONG	Distance in pixels of the first overstrike stroke above the baseline.
sKerningPairs;	SHORT	Number of kerning pairs.
sReserved;	SHORT	Reserved.
lMatch;	LONG	Font match identifier. A positive match indicates a physical font and a negative match indicates a device-specific font.

Obviously, unless you become heavily involved in the graphic aspects of text display, you will not need to use many of the fields in FONTMETRICS. Some of the more important ones, however, are illustrated in Figure 11-1.

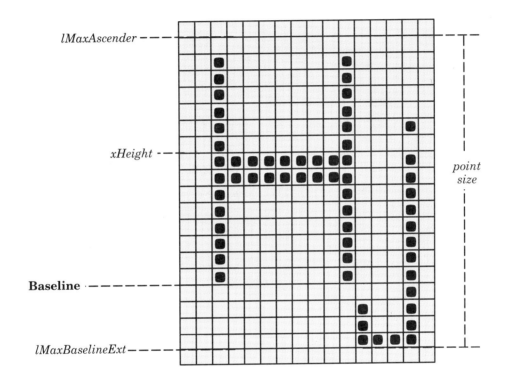

Figure 11-1: Character Components

Before you can display text, you need to access FONTMETRICS. On first glance, the WM_CREATE message block seems to be an ideal place for the required code (however, because the FONTMETRICS structure is quite large, you should call a separate procedure to get its values). To access FONTMETRICS, you need to define a structure variable (usually *fm*) and then call the GpiQueryFontMetrics function. Here's the definition for GpiQueryFontMetrics:

```
GpiQueryFontMetrics(hps, cbMetrics, pfmMetrics)
HPS hps
LONG cbMetrics
FONTMETRICS pfmMetrics
```

The first argument is a handle to a presentation space. The next argument, *cbMetrics*, is the size of the FONTMETRICS structure. Use the **sizeof** operator here to obtain the structure size. The last argument, *pfmMetrics*, is a pointer to the FONTMETRICS structure — in essence, opening the door to the store of font knowledge contained in FONT-METRICS.

After calling GpiQueryFontMetrics, you can readily refer to any field in the structure. If you use the system font, however, the only values you typically need to retrieve from FONTMETRICS are *lAveCharWidth*, *lMaxBaselineExt*, and *lMaxDescender*. When you obtain these values, you should cast them as SHORT integers. The following example shows a typical function you could call from the WM_CREATE message block.

```
GetFontInfo(AveChar, MaxBase, MaxDesc)
SHORT *AveChar, *MaxBase, *MaxDesc;
{

    FONTMETRICS fm;
    HPS hps;
    HWND hwnd;

    hps=WinGetPs(hwnd);
    GpiQueryFontMetrics(hps, (LONG) sizeof(fm), &fm);

    AveChar = (SHORT) fm.lAveCharWidth;
    MaxBase = (SHORT) fm.MaxBaselineExt;
    MaxDesc = (SHORT) fm.MaxDescender;

    WinReleasePS(hps);

}
```

Gpi Text Functions

The Gpi functions that you use in drawing text are few compared to the total number of Gpi functions. In this section, the functions of major concern are ones you need to display text for normal input/output operations.

Additionally, this section details functions that allow you to manipulate the graphic box associated with text elements. Table 11-3 lists these functions.

Table 11-3: Gpi Text Functions

FUNCTION	DESCRIPTION
GpiMove	Advances screen coordinates.
GpiQueryFontMetrics	Retrieves font information.
GpiCharString	Draws a character string at the current position.
GpiCharStringAt	Draws a character string from specified position.
GpiCharStringPos	Draws a character string with controls at current position.
GpiCharStringPosAt	Draws a character string with controls at specified position.
GpiQueryCharStringPosAt	Processes a character string and returns the coordinates of each character.

The GpiCharStringAt Function

The GpiCharStringAt is the **printf** of the Presentation Manager. It is not as easy to use, however. You have to control the current cursor position at all times. This explains the "At" in GpiCharStringAt; it simply means at the specified screen coordinates. Here's the definition for the GpiCharStringAt function:

```
LONG GpiCharStringAt(hps, ptl, lTotal, pchStr)
HPS hps;
PPOINTL ptl;
LONG lTotal;
PCH pchStr;
```

As with most Gpi functions, the first argument is the handle to the presentation space. The name argument is a far pointer to the POINTL structure, which controls the x and y screen coordinates. The *lTotal* argument specifies the number of characters in the string to be displayed. The *pchStr* argument is a pointer to the actual character string.

By referencing the POINTL fields within the same routine in which you call GpiCharStringAt, you can easily control screen coordinates. A common way of accomplishing this is with a **for** loop, as shown in the following fragment:

```
for(i=0; i<lines; lines++)
{
    linelen = 0 ;
    while(pchStr[linelen] != '\r')
        linelen++;

    ptl.x = 0;
    ptl.y = cx - MaxBase * (i + 1) + MaxDesc;
    GpiCharStringAt(hps, &ptl, (LONG) linelen, pchStr);
    pchStr += linelen + 2;
}
```

This routine is not too different to one that you might use in a standard C program (assuming you have written a function that acted similarly to GpiCharStringAt). Each character in *pchStr* is printed at the current *ptl.x* and *ptl.y* position. After each character is printed, GpiCharStringAt advances the current POINTL coordinates. Thus, the next character can be printed without resolving the coordinates on a character-by-character basis. The major difference to a standard C string handling routine is the way the *ptl.y* field is set. The following breakdown shows the calculation for the *ptl.y* field.

1. Obtain the *cx* value in the WM_SIZE handler.

2. Obtain *lMaxBaselineExt* and *lMaxDescender* values by calling the GpiQueryFontMetrics function.

3. Set *ptl.y* by multiplying *lMaxBaselineExt* times the current line value (in the example, $i + 1$), and add *lMaxDescender* to the product. Then subtract the result from *cx*.

When GpiCharStringAt returns, the screen coordinates are set to the end of the character string just printed. Essentially, using GpiCharStringAt combines calls to GpiMove and GpiCharString. The following two calls have the same effect as the single call to GpiCharStringAt in the previous example:

```
GpiMove(hps, ptl);
GpiCharString(hps,
            lTotal, pchStr);
```

As shown in earlier chapters with the WinDrawText function, you can use **sprintf** with the GpiCharStringAt function. Because standard C function allows you to format and store its output in a character buffer, you can reference the buffer directly in GpiCharStringAt. Using **sprintf**, you can confine the Gpi character display code to a separate function. Here's how to do it:

```
linelen = sprintf(szBuf, "%s", szAnyString);

GpiCharStringAt(
            hps,
            &ptl,
            (LONG) linelen,
            szBuf);
```

The **sprintf** function works identically to the **printf** function. Note that **sprintf** returns the numbers of characters in the buffer, not including the terminating NULL character.

DISPLAYING TEXT FROM A THREAD

When you want to write to screen from a thread that does not have control over the current window, you must create a separate stack area for the call to GpiCreateStringAt. To do this, the thread must call WinInitialize. This creates an output stack for the given thread. Internally, the Presentation Manager associates this output stack only with this thread. You must also call WinTerminate before the thread returns control to the thread in which it was created. Typically, you should call WinTerminate after you have exhausted the need for GpiCreateStringAt. If you use any Presentation Manager functions that require an anchor block handle before calling WinTerminate, ensure that you supply the anchor block handle returned from the most recent call to WinInitialize.

The following program example (EREWHON.C) illustrates some of the text functions described so far. The purpose of the program is to display resource-based text to the display monitor.

```
/* EREWHON.C ( Main Program) */

#define INCL_PM
#define INCL_DOS

#include <os2.h>
#include <stddef.h>
#include <stdlib.h>
#include <stdio.h>
#include "erewhon.h"


MRESULT EXPENTRY StringWndProc(HWND, USHORT, MPARAM, MPARAM);
VOID GetFontData(SHORT *, SHORT *, SHORT *);
VOID DisplayHeader(SHORT, SHORT);
VOID DisplayText(PUCHAR, SHORT, SHORT, SHORT);

HAB hab;
HPS hps;
POINTL ptl;
SHORT xPos, yPos, cx, cy, sLine;
USHORT id[6] = { ID_TITLE,
                 ID_AUTHOR,
                 ID_PUBLISHER,
                 ID_PUBDATE,
                 ID_CHAPTER,
                 ID_PAGEREF };

int main (void)
{

HMQ hmq;
HWND hwndFrame, hwndClient;
QMSG qmsg;
ULONG ctlData = FCF_TITLEBAR | FCF_SYSMENU | FCF_MINMAX
                | FCF_SIZEBORDER | FCF_SHELLPOSITION

static CHAR szTitleBar[40];
static CHAR szClass[] = "erewhon";


hab = WinInitialize(0);
hmq = WinCreateMsgQueue(hab, 0);
```

```
WinLoadString(hab, NULL, ID_TITLE,
            sizeof szTitleBar, szTitleBar);

WinRegisterClass(hab, szClass,
            StringWndProc, CS_SIZEREDRAW, 0);

hwndFrame = WinCreateStdWindow(
                        HWND_DESKTOP,
                        WS_VISIBLE,
                        &ctlData,
                        szClass,
                        szTitleBar,
                        0L,
                        NULL,
                        ID_RESOURCE,
                        &hwndClient);

while(WinGetMsg(hab, &qmsg, NULL, 0, 0))
            WinDispatchMsg(hab, &qmsg);

WinDestroyWindow(hwndFrame);
WinDestroyMsgQueue(hmq);
WinTerminate(hab);
return(0);
}


MRESULT EXPENTRY StringWndProc(hwnd, msg, mp1, mp2)
HWND hwnd;
USHORT msg;
MPARAM mp1, mp2;
{

    PUCHAR lpTxt;
    ULONG ulSize;
    static PUCHAR lpTxtRes;
    static SEL psel;
    static SHORT AveChar, MaxBase, MaxDesc, TxtLines;

    switch (msg)
      {
        case WM_CREATE:
            DosGetResource(NULL, ID_TXTFILE,
                            ID_PARAGRAPH, &psel);
            DosSizeSeg (psel, &ulSize);
            lpTxtRes = MAKEP (psel, 0);
            lpTxt = lpTxtRes;
```

```
                     while (lpTxt - lpTxtRes < (USHORT) ulSize)
                       {
                         if (*lpTxt == '\0' || *lpTxt == EOF) break;
                         if (*lpTxt == '\r') TxtLines ++;
                         lpTxt++;
                       }
                  hps=WinGetPS(hwnd);
                  GetFontData(&AveChar, &MaxBase, &MaxDesc);
                  WinReleasePS (hps);
                  return(FALSE);

              case WM_SIZE:
                  cx = SHORT1FROMMP (mp2);
                  cy = SHORT2FROMMP (mp2);
                  ptl.x = AveChar * 4;       /* 4 character indent. */
                  xPos = cx;
                  yPos = cy;
                  return(NULL);

              case WM_PAINT:
                  hps = WinBeginPaint(hwnd, NULL, NULL);
                  GpiErase(hps);
                  DisplayHeader(MaxBase, MaxDesc);
                  DisplayText(lpTxtRes, TxtLines,
                                       MaxBase, MaxDesc);
                  WinEndPaint(hps);
                  return(NULL);

              case WM_DESTROY:
                  DosFreeSeg(psel);
                  return(0);

              default:
                  return(WinDefWindowProc (hwnd, msg, mp1, mp2));
           }

       return(0L);
   }



VOID GetFontData(AveChar, *MaxBase, *MaxDesc)
SHORT *AveChar, *MaxBase, *MaxDesc
{

   FONTMETRICS  fm;
```

```
    GpiQueryFontMetrics (hps, (LONG) sizeof(fm), &fm);
    *AveChar = (SHORT) fm.lAveCharWidth;
    *MaxBase = (SHORT) fm.lMaxBaselineExt;
    *MaxDesc = (SHORT) fm.lMaxDescender;
}


VOID DisplayHeader(MaxBase, MaxDesc)
SHORT MaxBase, MaxDesc
{
    SHORT   linelen, i;
    CHAR    item[50];

    sLine = 0;
    for(i=0; i<6; i++)
        {
        WinLoadString(hab, NULL, id[i], sizeof item, item);
        linelen = 0;
        while (item[linelen] != '\0')
              linelen++;

        ptl.y = cy - MaxBase * (i + 1) + MaxDesc;
        GpiCharStringAt(hps, &ptl, (LONG) linelen, item);
        }
    sLine = i;
}


VOID DisplayText(lpTxt, TxtLines, MaxBase, MaxDesc)
PUCHAR lpTxt;
SHORT TxtLines, MaxBase, MaxDesc
{

    SHORT i, linelen;

    sLine++;
    for(i=sLine; i < sLine + TxtLines; i++)
        {
        linelen = 0;
        while(lpTxt[linelen] != '\r')
              linelen++;
        ptl.y = cy - MaxBase * (i + 1) + MaxDesc;
        GpiCharStringAt(hps, &ptl, (LONG) linelen, lpTxt);
        lpTxt += linelen + 2;
        }
    sLine = i;
}
```

For demonstration purposes, EREWHON.C isolates the different uses of text resources and the GpiCharStringAt function in three local functions. In order to service these functions, the program obtains font information in the WM_CREATE message. Additionally, the program obtains the current dimensions of the window in the WM_SIZE message. The WinBeginPaint function is invoked in the WM_PAINT message. This compensates for the fact that the Presentation Manager does not automatically validate the current window when the presentation space is released.

The program also eliminates the need to invalidate the current window in order to refresh the window's contents. Instead of using invalidation techniques, it uses the GpiErase function, which you will recall from Chapter 9. All-in-all, the text display methods in the program example represent a more elegant approach to text output than using WinDrawText. Accordingly, here is a revamped version of the file display program from Chapter 5. Besides better text output routines, it includes a more elaborate scrollbar routine.

```
/* SCROLL2.H (Header file) */

#define ATTRIBUTE 0
#define OPENFLAG 0x01
#define OPENMODE 0x040
#define BUFLENGTH 80


/* SCROLL2.C (Program file) */

#define INCL_PM
#define INCL_DOS

#include <os2.h>
#include <string.h>
#include "scroll2.h"

MRESULT EXPENTRY ScrollWndProc(HWND,USHORT,MPARAM,MPARAM);
VOID GetFontData(HWND,SHORT *,SHORT *,SHORT *);
VOID  ReadTextFile(VOID);
SHORT GetScrollBar(SHORT,SHORT,SHORT,SHORT,SHORT);
VOID DisplayText(HPS,SHORT,SHORT,SHORT,SHORT,SHORT);
CHAR szDisplay[50][81];
SHORT TotalLines = 0;
```

```
int main(void)
{

static CHAR szClass [] = "Scroll2";
HAB hab;
HMQ hmq;
HWND hwndClient, hwndFrame;
QMSG qmsg;
ULONG ctlData = FCF_TITLEBAR | FCF_SYSMENU
               | FCF_SIZEBORDER | FCF_MINMAX | FCF_VERTSCROLL
               | FCF_SHELLPOSITION | FCF_TASKLIST;


hab = WinInitialize(NULL);
hmq = WinCreateMsgQueue(hab, 0);

WinRegisterClass(hab, szClass,
                 ScrollWndProc, CS_SIZEREDRAW, 0);

hwndFrame = WinCreateStdWindow(
                              HWND_DESKTOP,
                              WS_VISIBLE,
                              &ctlData,
                              szClass,
                              NULL,
                              0L,
                              NULL,
                              0,
                              &hwndClient);

while(WinGetMsg(hab, &qmsg, NULL, 0, 0))
                WinDispatchMsg(hab, &qmsg);

WinDestroyWindow(hwndFrame);
WinDestroyMsgQueue(hmq);
WinTerminate(hab);

return(0);
}


MRESULT EXPENTRY ScrollWndProc(hwnd, msg, mp1, mp2)
HWND hwnd;
USHORT msg;
MPARAM mp1, mp2;
{
```

```
HPS hps;
SHORT i=0;
static HWND  hwndVscroll;
static SHORT sVscroll=0, cx, cy;
static SHORT AveChar, MaxBase, MaxDesc;

switch(msg)
   {
      case WM_CREATE:
           GetFontData(hwnd, &AveChar, &MaxBase, &MaxDesc);
           ReadTextFile();
           hwndVscroll = WinWindowFromID(
                           WinQueryWindow(hwnd,
                                 QW_PARENT, FALSE),
                           FID_VERTSCROLL);

           WinSendMsg(hwndVscroll, SBM_SETSCROLLBAR,
           MPFROM2SHORT(sVscroll, 0),
           MPFROM2SHORT(0, TotalLines - 1));
           return(NULL);

      case WM_SIZE:
           cx = SHORT1FROMMP(mp2);
           cy = SHORT2FROMMP(mp2);
           return(NULL);

      case WM_VSCROLL:
           sVscroll = GetScrollBar(sVscroll,
                           SHORT2FROMMP(mp2),
                           SHORT1FROMMP(mp2),
                           cx, AveChar);

           WinSendMsg(hwndVscroll, SBM_SETPOS,
                      MPFROM2SHORT(sVscroll, 0), NULL);

           WinInvalidateRect(hwnd, NULL, FALSE);
           return(NULL);

      case WM_PAINT:
           hps = WinBeginPaint(hwnd, NULL, NULL);
           GpiErase(hps);
           DisplayText(hps, cy, sVscroll,
                      AveChar, MaxBase, MaxDesc);

           WinEndPaint(hps);
           return(NULL);
   }
```

```
    return(WinDefWindowProc(hwnd, msg, mp1, mp2));
}


VOID GetFontData(hwnd, AveChar, MaxBase, MaxDesc)
HWND hwnd;
SHORT *AveChar, *MaxBase, *MaxDesc;
{

    HPS hps;
    FONTMETRICS  fm;

    hps = WinGetPS(hwnd);
    GpiQueryFontMetrics(hps,(LONG) sizeof(fm), &fm);
    *AveChar =(SHORT) fm.lAveCharWidth;
    *MaxBase =(SHORT) fm.lMaxBaselineExt;
    *MaxDesc =(SHORT) fm.lMaxDescender;
    WinReleasePS(hps);
}


SHORT GetScrollBar(sVscroll, sScroll, sSlider, cy, AveChar)
SHORT sVscroll, sScroll, sSlider, cy, AveChar;
{

    switch(sScroll)
      {
        case SB_SLIDERPOSITION:
            sVscroll = sSlider;
            break;

        case SB_PAGEDOWN:
            sVscroll += cy / AveChar;
            break;

        case SB_PAGEUP:
            sVscroll -= cy / AveChar;
            break;

        case SB_LINEUP:
            sVscroll--;
            break;

        case SB_LINEDOWN:
            sVscroll++;
            break;
```

```
        }

    return(sVscroll);
}


VOID ReadTextFile()
{

    CHAR    szText[50][BUFLENGTH+1];
    USHORT  usAction, usBytes;
    HFILE   hf;
    ULONG   ulSize = 0;
    SHORT   i=0, j=0, k=0, n=0;

    DosOpen("TESTFILE", &hf, &usAction, ulSize,
               ATTRIBUTE, OPENFLAG, OPENMODE, 0L);

    do {
         DosRead(hf, szText[i], BUFLENGTH, &usBytes);
         szText[i][usBytes] = 0;
         i++;
    } while(usBytes == BUFLENGTH);

    TotalLines = i;
    i=0;

    while(j <= TotalLines )
       switch(szText[j][i])
          {
                 case 10:
                    szDisplay[k][n] = 0;
                    k++; n=0; i++;
                    break;

                 case 13:
                    i++;
                    break;

                 case 0:
                    j++; i=0;
                    break;

                 default:
                    szDisplay[k][n] = szText[j][i];
                    i++; n++;
          }
```

```
    TotalLines = k;
    DosClose(hf);
}

VOID DisplayText(hps, cy, sVscroll,
                        AveChar, MaxBase, MaxDesc)
HPS hps;
SHORT cy, sVscroll;
SHORT AveChar, MaxBase, MaxDesc;
{

    SHORT i, sNewPos;
    POINTL ptl;

    sNewPos = (sVscroll < 0) ? 0 : sVscroll;
    for(i=0; i < TotalLines; i++)
      {
        ptl.x = AveChar;
        ptl.y = cy - MaxBase * (i + 1 - sNewPos) + MaxDesc;
        GpiCharStringAt(hps, &ptl,
                        (LONG) strlen(szDisplay[i]),
                        szDisplay[i]);
      }
}
```

The GpiCharStringPosAt Function

The GpiCharStringPosAt function is similar to GpiCharStringAt, but gives you added features, including controls for character boxes and string attributes. For example, you can specify a background rectangle for a character string and vary the color of the rectangle. The function also gives you independent kerning control over each character in a string by correlating the string to a specified spacing array. Here's the definition for GpiCharStringPosAt:

```
LONG GpiCharStringPosAt(hps, ptl, prcl, flOptions,
                        lTotal, pchStr, adx)
HPS hps;
PPOINTL ptl;
PRECTL prcl;
ULONG flOptions;
LONG lTotal;
PCH pchStr;
PLONG adx;
```

The first two arguments are familiar ones; *hps* identifies the presentation space and *ptl*, which is used identically to its equivalent in GpiCharStringAt, references the POINTL structure. It is the next argument, *prcl*, that begins to make GpiCharStringPosAt a unique animal; *prcl* points to the RECTL structure, through which you can specify the four boundary points for a background rectangle.

To specify coordinates for *prcl*, you must create a copy of the RECTL structure, then set each field to an appropriate value. If you set *prcl* to NULL, the function ignores the argument. Doing this, however, affects some of the options available through the *flOptions* argument — in particular, the function ignores the CHS_OPAQUE and CHS_CLIP options if *prcl* is set to NULL. Table 11-4 lists the system defined constants for *flOptions*.

Table 11-4: Formatting Options for GpiCharStringPosAt

OPTION	BIT	DESCRIPTION
CHS_OPAQUE	0x0001L	Defines the color for the string background rectangle set by *prcl*.
CHS_VECTOR	0x0002L	Increments the *adx* vector. This option must be set for vector spacing to occur.
CHS_LEAVEPOS	0x0008L	Leaves the value of the current position intact. If this option is not set, the current position is set to the end of the string.
CHS_CLIP	0x0010L	Clips the string to the specified rectangle.

The next two arguments to GpiCharStringPosAt — *lTotal* and *pchStr* — fulfill the same purpose as in GpiCharStringAt. The final argument, *adx*, allows you to set a vector of increments that control character spacing in the *pchStr* string. A vector of increments can be specified, allowing control over the position of each character after the first. This vector consists of distances measured in world coordinates (along the baseline for left-to-right and right-to-left character directions, and along the shearline for top-to-bottom and bottom-to-top directions). The *ith* increment is the distance of the reference point (for example, bottom left corner) of the $(i + 1)th$ character from the reference point of the *ith*. The last increment can be used to update the current position. The following example uses *adx* to display several strings with increased horizontal spacing.

```
VOID AdjustCharSpace (MaxBase, MaxDesc)
SHORT MaxBase, MaxDesc;
{
SHORT   linelen, i, adx[16];
CHAR    item[50];
RECTL   rcl;

for(i=0; i<16; i++) adx[i] = i + 1;
  for(i=0; i<2; i++)
    {
        WinLoadString(hab, NULL, id[i], sizeof item, item);
        linelen = 0;
        while (item[linelen] != '\0')
             linelen++;
        ptl.y = cx - MaxBase * (i + 1) + MaxDesc;
        rcl.xLeft = ptl.x;
        rcl.yBottom = ptl.y + MaxBase;
        rcl.xRight = (LONG) 400;
        rcl.yTop = (LONG) ptl.y + MaxDesc;
        GpiCharStringPosAt(hps, &ptl, &rcl, CHS_VECTOR,
                          (LONG) linelen, item, (PLONG) adx);
    }
}
```

This example simulates the GpiCharStringAt function, but defines a rectangle for each character string and increases the spacing between characters.

The *rcl.yBottom* and *rcl.yTop* values are calculated from the current POINTL coordinates and *lMaxBaselineExt* and *lMaxDescender*, respectively. In essence, this creates normal spacing between lines. The *adx* value, which controls spacing between characters, is set through the **for** loop at the beginning of the function.

More Positioning

As with the GpiCharStringAt function, you can use a lesser form of the GpiCharStringPosAt function if you want to exert your own control over the current position. Normally, GpiCharStringPosAt sets the current position to the end of the current string. The following two calls have the same effect as the single call to GpiCharStringAt in the previous example:

```
GpiMove(hps, ptl);
GpiCharString(hps, lTotal, pchStr);
```

Before using either GpiCharStringPos or GpiCharStringPosAt, you can query the character positioning that results from each function. This is accomplished through the GpiQueryCharStringPos and GpiQueryCharStringPosAt. As is the case with their namesakes, GpiQueryCharStringPos does not reset the current position. On the other hand, the current position is reset by GpiQuerCharStringPosAt. Here's the definition for the latter.

```
LONG GpiQueryCharStringPosAt(hps, ptl, flOptions,
                             lTotal, pchStr, dx, ptlPos)
HPS hps;
PPOINTL ptl;
ULONG flOptions,
LONG lTotal
PCH pchStr;
PLONG adx;
PPOINTL ptlPos;
```

Unlike GPiCharStringPosAt, the GpiQueryCharStringPosAt function does not reference the RECTL structure, nor does it allow you to specify a value in *flOptions* other than CHS_VECTOR and zero, which specifies that *adx* is to be ignored. Additionally, GpiQueryCharStringPosAt includes a second POINTL argument, *ptlPos*, which returns an array of points (in world coordinates) that describe the positioning of the current string. The first point in the array corresponds to the initial current position. The last point in the array corresponds to the new current position as if the string had been drawn.

Fonts

You have already been introduced to the Presentation Manager's controlling structure for its font system, namely FONTMETRICS. As Table 11-2 shows, this structure contains all the font data you could ever need in order to create, manipulate, and change fonts in an application.

The peculiar thing is that you don't actually use FONTMETRICS to specify a new font. You do, however, use its values to create your own *logi-*

cal font. A logical font only exists in the currently specified presentation space: you can modify it, or not, and expect to get the same results every time you print a text string. This is especially critical when you use a font in a presentation space associated with a device context for a printer or other external device. The logical font, in essence, assumes the characteristics dictated by the specified device context.

This is not the case with a *physical font*. A physical font exists in memory, not a presentation space. You can access a physical font from several presentation spaces within the same application, or you can merely load and use a physical font instead of the system default font. In all, the Presentation Manager supports three physical font families:

- Roman — Distinguished by its upright style and is the most common type used for normal text. Usually associated with the Times typeface and is often called Times Roman. The most unique feature of Times Roman is its *serif* style, which means it has small strokes adorning the end of character lines.

- Swiss — Distinguished by a large x-height (the nominal height above the baseline of the font's lowercase characters). The Presentation Manager uses the Helvetica typeface for its Swiss fonts. Unlike Times Roman, the Helvetica typeface does not have serifs. The term for this is *sans serif*.

- Courier — A monospaced font that duplicates the appearance of typewritten text. In this book, program examples are set in Courier.

In addition to supporting these type families, the Presentation Manager supports numerous typefaces and styles. The styles supported include italics, bold italics, underlining, and strikethrough. The default Presentation Manager font is referred to as "System Proportional," which is 12-point typeface from the Swiss family and is stored in the DISPLAY.DLL file (a dynamic link library file). Table 11-5 lists the point sizes available for the three font families.

Loading a Font

If you haven't changed the default directory structure of your OS/2 files, take a look in the \OS/2\DLL subdirectory. You will find three files with a .FON filename extension. This is an important fact to know because you

Table 11-5: Point Sizes

FONT	8	10	12	14	18	14
Courier	●	●	●	○	○	○
Roman	●	●	●	●	●	●
Swiss	●	●	●	●	●	●

have to reference the path as well as the filenames of the font files when you want to load one or more physical fonts. The following routine loads all three font families:

```
VOID LoadFonts()
{
    static CHAR *filespec[] = { "\\OS2\\DLL"COURIER.FON"
                                "\\OS2\\DLL"HELV.FON
                                "\\OS2\\DLL"TIMES.FON" }

    GpiLoadFonts(hab, filespec);

}
```

The GpiLoadFonts function in the example is largely self-explanatory. You merely supply it an anchor block handle plus the appropriate file specification. When the function is successful, all of the fonts contained in the specified file become available to the application. The actual disk format of the font is determined by two structures. The first is FONTSIGNA-TURE, which is defined as follows:

```
typedef struct _FONTSIGNATURE {
        ULONG      ulIdentity
        ULONG      ulSize
        CHAR       achSignature
} FONTSIGNATURE
```

The first field, *ulIdentity*, is defined to the value of 0xFFFFFFFE. The second field, *ulSize*, is defined to the value of 20. The final field, *achSignature*, is the text string containing the following characters:

```
"OS/2 FONT "
```

The second structure is similar in form. The structure is called ENDFONT and it is defined as follows:

```
typedef struct _FONTEND {
        ULONG      ulIdentity
        ULONG      ulSize
} FONTEND
```

The first field, *ulIdentity* is defined to the same value as in signature structure. The second field, *ulSize*, is defined to the value of 8. In the font file itself, three other structures fall between these two structures. You already know FONTMETRICS, which is the first of these three structures. The next two are:

- FONTDEFINITIONHEADER
- KERNINGPAIRTABLE

Further description of these structures is beyond the scope of this book. Suffice it to say that both structures detail the specific definitions of characters within a font. This said, it should be noted that you do not need to manipulate these structures in order to change fonts and font styles in the Presentation Manager. More than likely, you would only begin to study these structures if you wanted to modify the actual file definition of a font.

One other step is involved in font loading: unloading the fonts when you are through with them. The function that handles this is GpiUnloadFonts. It takes the same arguments as GpiLoadFonts and is straightforward enough. Ensure, however, that you do not unload the current font.

Setting Font Attributes

When you create a logical font, you are primarily concerned with the attributes that the font uses. Similarly, before you display text using the GpiCharStringAt function, you need to know some information about the attributes of the current font. The structure that controls the setting of font attributes is FATTRS. Through it, you can ultimately change all characteristics about a font, but only if you combine your manipulation of FATTRS with information from the FONTMETRICS structure. If you make a global copy of FATTRS, you can reference the fields when you need the baseline and ascender values for text display. Here's the definition for FATTRS:

```
typedef struct _FATTRS {
        USHORT    usRecordLength;
        USHORT    fsSelection;
        LONG      lMatch;
        CHAR      szFacename[FACESIZE];
        USHORT    idRegistry;
        USHORT    usCodePage;
        LONG      lMaxBaselineExt;
        LONG      lAveCharWidth;
        USHORT    fsType;
        USHORT    fsFontUse;
} FATTRS
```

Why is FATTRS crucial? As you can see, it appears to be a reduced version of the FONTMETRICS structure. It is, but with two exceptions: the *fsSelection* field allows you to specify a system-defined value for different types styles; and the *fsFontUse*, which is unique to FATTRS, allows you to specify a system-defined value that controls the way in which the presentation space displays the specified font. Tables 11-6 and 11-7 describe the identifiers for the *fsSelection* and *fsFontUse* fields.

Table 11-6: Font Style Identifiers (*fsSelection*)

OPTION	BIT	DESCRIPTION
FATTR_SEL_ITALIC	0x0001	Italic characters.
FATTR_SEL_UNDERSCORE	0x0002	Underscored characters.
FATTR_SEL_STRIKEOUT	0x0010	Requests strikeout characters.
FATTR_SEL_BOLD	0x0020	Bold characters.

Table 11-7: Font Use Identifiers (*fsFontUse*)

OPTION	BIT	DESCRIPTION
FATTR_FONTUSE_NOMIX	0x0002	Displays text without specifically mixing it with graphic objects.
FATTR_FONTUSE_OUTLINE	0x0004	Selects a vector font.
FATTR_FONTUSE_TRANSFORMABLE	0x0008	Modifies characters, including scaling, shearing, and rotation.

You can directly set either of the *fsSelection* or *fsFontUse* fields in the FATTRS structure to an appropriate identifier. In a program that frequently changes font characteristics, you will likely create variables equal to the FATTR* identifiers and set the *fsSelection* and *fsFontUse* via these variables. The following example sets the two fields using the system identifiers:

```
fat.fsSelection = FATTR_SEL_ITALIC;
fat.fsFontUse = FATTR_FONTUSE_TRANSFORMABLE;
```

Creating a Logical Font

It's time to get down to the business of creating a logical font. The function that you use to create a logical font is appropriately named GpiCreateLog-Font. In order to use GpiCreateLogFont successfully, follow these steps:

1. Load one or more font files using the GpiLoadFonts function.

2. Query the physical fonts from the font files in order to obtain the necessary attributes with which to create the logical font.

3. Zero the attributes of any previous logical font using the GpiCharSet function.

4. Ensure that no outstanding font ID is associated with the specified presentation. Use the GpiDeleteSetId function to do this.

5. Reference the FATTRS structure and set the fields equal to fields of the queried font (with any changes you want to make).

6. Call the GpiCreateLogFont function and specify the current copy of the FATTRS structure (among other values).

7. Set the attributes of the logical font using the GpiCharSet function.

You already know how to load physical fonts. Using these as your basis for creating a logical font is an easy way to obtain appropriate data for the FATTRS structure and the GpiCreateLogFont function. If you do not go through this process, the Presentation Manager attempts to match the specified logical font with any other currently available physical font. For now, take a look at the definition for GpiQueryFonts:

```
LONG GpiQueryFonts(hps, flOptions, pszFacename,
                   pcFonts, cbMetrics, pfmMetrics)
HPS hps;
ULONG flOptions;
PSZ pszFacename;
PLONG pcFonts;
LONG cbMetrics;
PFONTMETRICS pfmMetrics;
```

As usual the first field is the handle to a presentation space. Depending on how you structure you program, however, this presentation space should be created especially for the display of fonts and/or other graphic data. The following routine initializes such a presentation space:

```
VOID InitializePS(hwnd)
HWND hwnd;
{
    SIZEL size;
    HDC hdcInit;

    hdcInit = WinOpenWindowDC(hwnd);
    size.cx = 0;
    size.cy = 0;
    hpsInit = GpiCreatePS(hab, hdcInit, &size,
                   PU_PELS | GPIF_DEFAULT
                   | GPIT_NORMAL | GPIA_ASSOC);

}
```

The presentation space satisfied, the next argument in GpiQueryFonts is *flOptions*, which should tip you off to the fact that you need to supply some system identifiers. And indeed you do, but unlike other functions that require options, you only have two identifiers from which to choose:

- QF_PUBLIC — Specifies that you want to query the publicly available system fonts. The related bit value is 0x0001.

- QF_PRIVATE — Specifies that you want to query the private fonts (that is, ones you have created or purchased). The related bit value is 0x0002.

The next argument in GpiQueryFonts points to the typeface that you want to query. This argument, *pszFaceName*, reduces the query only to those fonts having the specified typeface. If you specify NULL, the function only queries available physical fonts. The final two arguments — *cbMetrics* and *pfmMetrics* — are identical to the similarly named arguments used in GpiQueryFonts. You simply specify the size and address of the FONTMETRICS structure, respectively.

The next two functions that you can call are GpiSetCharSet and GpiDeleteSetID. Both functions take two arguments: the necessary presentation space handle, and a value that allows the function to clear the current font. The second argument in GpiSetChar is 0L. The second argument to GpiDeleteSetId is the logical font ID. Typically, the logical font ID is the index to an array that you use in subsequently setting the FATTR structure. The function tells the Presentation Manager to delete the currently set font from the presentation space and make the associated ID — referred to as *lcid* — available for reuse.

To complete the step-by-step process of creating a logical font, you must set the FATTRS structure, call GpiCreateLogFont, and then call GpiSetCharSet again. The following routine puts all these elements together and displays a sample text string formatted in each of the system's physical fonts. The routine makes some assumptions, including that a copy of the FATTRS structure has been initialized as shown in the previous example. It also assumes a global array of type FONTMETRICS.

```
BOOL ListAllFonts()
{

    BOOL fValue;
    SHORT i, j;
    static LONG lOldFont = 0;
    LONG lFonts = 60L;
    static CHAR *filespec[] = { "\\OS2\\DLL"COURIER.FON"
                                "\\OS2\\DLL"HELV.FON
                                "\\OS2\\DLL"TIMES.FON" }


    GpiLoadFonts(hab, filespec);
    GpiQueryFonts(hpsInit,
                (ULONG) QF_PUBLIC | QF_PRIVATE,
                NULL, (LONG) MAXFONTS,
                (LONG) sizeof(FONTMETRICS), fm);

    for(j=0; j < MAXFONTS; j++)
```

```
GpiSetCharSet (hpsInit, 0L);
GpiDeleteSetId (hpsInit, lOldFont);
lOldFont = i;

fat.usRecordLength = sizeof (FATTRS);
fat.lMatch = 0;
fat.fsSelection = usStyleSelected;
strcpy(fat.szFacename, fm[i].szFacename);
fat.idRegistry = fm[i].idRegistry;
fat.usCodePage = 850;
fat.lMaxBaselineExt = fm[i].lMaxBaselineExt;
fat.lAveCharWidth = fm[i].lAveCharWidth;
fat.fsType = FATTR_TYPE_FIXED;
fat.fsFontUse = 0;

GpiCreateLogFont (hpsInit, (PSTR8) szApplication,
                (LONG)i, &fat);

GpiSetCharSet (hpsInit, (LONG)i);

ptl.y = cy - fmCur.lMaxBaselineExt * (j + 1)
                        + fmCur.lMaxDescender;

GpiCharStringAt (hpsInit, &ptl,
                (LONG) strlen(text),
                text);
        return(fValue);
}
```

Until now, the GpiCreateLogFont function has been mentioned, but not described. When the call to GpiCreateLogFont is registered with the Presentation Manager, it examines the requirements for the specified logical font and surveys all physical fonts currently in memory. In the example routine, the Presentation Manager gains access to all of its disk-based physical fonts. Thus, it finds an exact match for the specified logical font. Here's the definition for GpiCreateLogFont:

```
BOOL GpiCreateLogFont (hps, pchName, lcid, pfat)
HPS hps;
PSTR8 pchName;
LONG lcid;
PFATTRS pfat;
```

The first argument you know. The second argument, *pchName*, is a pointer to the logical font name, an eight-character name as indicated by the special PSTR8 data type. The next argument, *lcid*, specifies the ID used to refer to the font. The ID value must be in the range of 1 to 254. The final argument, *pfat*, is simply a pointer to the FATTRS structure.

The following program example brings together the different elements in creating logical fonts. It uses the system's physical fonts as the basis to create a logical font. When you run the program and select a font from the Select dialog box, the program looks up the specified physical font and creates a corresponding logical font.

```
/* SHOWFONT.H (Header file) */

#define MAXFONTS 60

#define ID_RESOURCE      1
#define IDD_NULL         -1

#define IDS_FAMILY       0
#define IDS_TYPEFACE     1
#define IDS_TYPEWIDTH    2
#define IDS_TYPESIZE     3
#define IDS_BLANK        4
#define IDS_NUMBERS      5
#define IDS_ALPHASMALL   6
#define IDS_ALPHABIG     7

#define IDM_FONTMENU     100
#define IDM_FONTSELECT   101
#define IDM_ABOUT        102

#define IDD_FONT         600
#define IDD_COURIER      601
#define IDD_HELVETICA    602
#define IDD_SYSTEM       603
#define IDD_TIMES        604
#define IDD_8POINT       605

#define SIZEOFFSET       700    /* Use this in source code. */
#define IDD_10POINT      710
#define IDD_12POINT      712
#define IDD_14POINT      714
#define IDD_18POINT      718
#define IDD_24POINT      724

#define IDD_NORMALSTYLE  800
#define IDD_ITALICSTYLE  801
```

```
#define IDD_BOLDSTYLE    802

#define IDD_ABOUT        900



/* SHOWFONT.RC (Resource file) */

#include <os2.h>
#include "showfont.h"

STRINGTABLE
{
    IDS_FAMILY,    "Font family: "
    IDS_TYPEFACE,  "Typeface: "
    IDS_TYPEWIDTH  "Type width: "
    IDS_TYPESIZE   "Type size: "
    IDS_BLANK      " "
    IDS_NUMBERS,   "1234567890"
    IDS_ALPHASMALL, "abcdefghijklmnopqrstuvwxyz"
    IDS_ALPHABIG,  "ABCDEFGHIJKLMNOPQRSTUVWXYZ"
}

MENU ID_RESOURCE
{
    SUBMENU "~Font",  IDM_FONTMENU
    {
        MENUITEM "~Select...\t^S",  IDM_FONTSELECT,
                                        MIA_CHECKED
        MENUITEM "~About...",  IDM_ABOUT
    }
}

ACCELTABLE ID_RESOURCE
{
    "^S",  IDM_FONTSELECT
}

DLGTEMPLATE IDD_ABOUT
{
    DIALOG "", 1, 20, 20, 150, 130, FS_DLGBORDER
    {
        CTEXT "Font View Program"    IDD_NULL 0, 100, 150, 8
        CTEXT "This program lets you," IDD_NULL 0, 70, 150, 8
        CTEXT "look at the different" IDD_NULL, 0, 55, 150, 8
        CTEXT "fonts on your system." IDD_NULL, 0, 40, 150, 8
        DEFPUSHBUTTON "Ok", DID_OK, 6, 4, 40, 12,
```

```
                                            WS_TABSTOP | WS_GROUP
    }
}

DLGTEMPLATE IDD_FONT
{
    DIALOG "", 2, 15, 5, 220, 140, FS_DLGBORDER
    {
        CTEXT "Font Selection", IDD_NULL, 20, 127, 160, 8
        GROUPBOX "Typeface", IDD_NULL, 5, 70, 80, 55
        CHECKBOX "Courier", IDD_COURIER, 8, 102, 75, 12,
                            WS_GROUP
        CHECKBOX "Helvetica", IDD_HELVETICA, 8, 92, 75, 12
        CHECKBOX "System", IDD_SYSTEM, 8, 82, 75, 12
        CHECKBOX "Times", IDD_TIMES, 8, 72, 75, 12

        GROUPBOX "Point size", IDD_NULL, 105, 70, 90, 55
        CHECKBOX " 8", IDD_8POINT, 112, 102, 30, 12, WS_GROUP
        CHECKBOX "10", IDD_10POINT, 112, 92, 30, 12
        CHECKBOX "12", IDD_12POINT, 112, 82, 30, 12
        CHECKBOX "14", IDD_14POINT, 146, 102, 30, 12
        CHECKBOX "18", IDD_18POINT, 146, 92, 30, 12
        CHECKBOX "24", IDD_24POINT, 146, 82, 30, 12

        GROUPBOX "", IDD_NULL, 5, 40, 190, 25
        CHECKBOX "Normal" IDD_NORMALSTYLE, 15, 45, 45, 12
        CHECKBOX "Italic", IDD_ITALICSTYLE, 70, 45, 45, 12
        CHECKBOX "Bold", IDD_BOLDSTYLE, 120, 45, 45, 12

        DEFPUSHBUTTON  "Ok", MBID_OK,  15, 6, 70, 20,
                            WS_TABSTOP | WS_GROUP
        PUSHBUTTON    "Cancel", MBID_CANCEL, 115, 6, 70, 20,
                            WS_TABSTOP | WS_GROUP
    }
}


/* SHOWFONT.C (Program file) */

#define INCL_PM

#include <os2.h>
#include <stdio.h>
#include <stdlib.h>
#include <string.h>
#include <stddef.h>
#include "showfont.h"
```

```
MRESULT EXPENTRY FontWndProc(HWND,USHORT,MPARAM, MPARAM);
MRESULT EXPENTRY FontDlgBoxProc(HWND,USHORT,MPARAM,MPARAM);
MRESULT EXPENTRY AboutDlgBoxProc(HWND,USHORT,MPARAM,MPARAM);

VOID InitializePS(HWND);
BOOL ChangeFont(VOID);
VOID DisplayFont(HPS,SHORT,SHORT);

HAB hab;
HPS hpsInit;
CHAR szApplication[8];
CHAR szFontSelected[80] = "Tms Rmn\0";

USHORT usSizeSelected = 14;
USHORT usStyleSelected = 0;
FATTRS fat;
FONTMETRICS fmCur;
FONTMETRICS fm[60];

int main(void)
{
HMQ hmq;
QMSG qmsg;
HWND hwndFrame, hwndClient;
static CHAR szClass[] = "Fonts";
ULONG ctlData = FCF_TITLEBAR | FCF_SYSMENU | FCF_MENU
                | FCF_ACCELTABLE | FCF_MINMAX | FCF_SIZEBORDER
                | FCF_SHELLPOSITION | FCF_TASKLIST;

hab = WinInitialize(NULL);
hmq = WinCreateMsgQueue(hab, 0);
WinRegisterClass(hab,szClass,
                FontWndProc, CS_SIZEREDRAW, 0);

hwndFrame = WinCreateStdWindow(
                            HWND_DESKTOP,
                            WS_VISIBLE,
                            &ctlData,
                            szClass,
                            NULL,
                            0L,
                            NULL,
                            ID_RESOURCE,
                            &hwndClient);

while(WinGetMsg(hab, &qmsg, NULL, 0, 0))
```

```
                    WinDispatchMsg(hab, &qmsg);

WinDestroyWindow(hwndFrame);
WinDestroyMsgQueue(hmq);
WinTerminate(hab);
return(0);
}

MRESULT EXPENTRY FontWndProc(hwnd, msg, mp1, mp2)
HWND  hwnd;
USHORT msg;
MPARAM mp1, mp2;
{

    RECTL rcl;
    static SHORT cx, cy;

    switch (msg)
       {

        case WM_CREATE:
             InitializePS(hwnd);
             return(FALSE);

        case WM_SIZE:
             cx = SHORT1FROMMP(mp2);
             cy = SHORT2FROMMP(mp2);
             return(NULL);

        case WM_COMMAND:
             switch((COMMANDMSG(&msg)->cmd))
                {
                 case IDM_FONTSELECT:
                     WinDlgBox(HWND_DESKTOP, hwnd,
                             FontDlgBoxProc,
                             NULL, IDD_FONT, NULL);

                     WinInvalidateRect(hwnd, NULL, NULL);
                     break;

                 case IDM_ABOUT:
                     WinDlgBox(HWND_DESKTOP, hwnd,
                             AboutDlgBoxProc,
                             NULL, IDD_ABOUT, NULL);
                     break;
                }
             break;
```

```
        case WM_PAINT:
            WinBeginPaint(hwnd, hpsInit, (PWRECT)NULL);
            WinQueryWindowRect(hwnd,&rcl);
            WinFillRect(hpsInit, &rcl, CLR_DEFAULT);
            DisplayFont(hpsInit, cx, cy);
            WinEndPaint(hpsInit);
            return(NULL);

        case WM_ERASEBACKGROUND:
            return(TRUE);

        case WM_CLOSE:
            WinPostMsg(hwnd, WM_QUIT, 0L, 0L);
            break;

        case WM_DESTROY:
            GpiAssociate(hpsInit,NULL);
            GpiDestroyPS(hpsInit);
            return(NULL);

        default:
            return(WinDefWindowProc(hwnd, msg, mp1, mp2));
    }

    return(0L);
}



VOID InitializePS(hwnd)
HWND hwnd;
{

    SIZEL size;
    HDC hdcInit;

    hdcInit = WinOpenWindowDC(hwnd);
    size.cx = 0;
    size.cy = 0;
    hpsInit = GpiCreatePS(hab, hdcInit, &size,
                    PU_PELS | GPIF_DEFAULT
                    | GPIT_NORMAL | GPIA_ASSOC);

}
```

```
MRESULT EXPENTRY FontDlgBoxProc(hwndDlg, msg, mp1, mp2)
HWND hwndDlg;
USHORT msg;
MPARAM mp1, mp2;
{
    USHORT id;

    switch(msg)
      {

        case WM_CONTROL:
              id = SHORT1FROMMP(mp1);
              if(id >= IDD_COURIER && id <= IDD_TIMES)
                 {
                     WinSendDlgItemMsg(hwndDlg, id,
                            BM_SETCHECK,
                            MPFROM2SHORT(FALSE, 0), NULL);

                     switch(id)
                        {
                          case IDD_COURIER:
                                  strcpy(szFontSelected,
                                          "Courier");
                                  break;

                          case IDD_HELVETICA:
                                  strcpy(szFontSelected,
                                          "Helv");
                                  break;

                          case IDD_SYSTEM:
                                  strcpy(szFontSelected,
                                      "System Proportional");
                                  break;

                          case IDD_TIMES:
                                  strcpy(szFontSelected,
                                          "Tms Rmn");
                                  break;
                        }

                     WinSendDlgItemMsg(hwndDlg, id,
                            BM_SETCHECK,
                            MPFROM2SHORT(TRUE, 0), NULL);
                 }
```

```
if(id >= IDD_NORMALSTYLE && id <= IDD_BOLDSTYLE)
    {
    WinSendDlgItemMsg(hwndDlg, id,
            BM_SETCHECK,
            MPFROM2SHORT(FALSE, 0), NULL);

        switch(id)
            {
            case IDD_NORMALSTYLE:
                    usStyleSelected = 0;
                    break;

            case IDD_ITALICSTYLE:
                    usStyleSelected =
                            FATTR_SEL_ITALIC;
                    break;

            case IDD_BOLDSTYLE:
                    usStyleSelected =
                            FATTR_SEL_BOLD;
                    break;
            }

    WinSendDlgItemMsg(hwndDlg, id,
            BM_SETCHECK,
            MPFROM2SHORT (TRUE, 0), NULL);
    }

if(id >= IDD_8POINT && id <= IDD_24POINT)
    {
    WinSendDlgItemMsg(hwndDlg, id,
            BM_SETCHECK,
            MPFROM2SHORT(FALSE, 0), NULL);

    usSizeSelected = id - SIZEOFFSET;

    WinSendDlgItemMsg(hwndDlg, id,
            BM_SETCHECK,
            MPFROM2SHORT (TRUE, 0), NULL);
    break;
    }

case WM_COMMAND:
    switch(COMMANDMSG(&msg)->cmd)
        {
        case DID_OK:
            if(!ChangeFont())
```

```
                    WinMessageBox(HWND_DESKTOP, hwndDlg,
                        "Font not available as specified.\n"
                        "Try different point size or style.",
                        "Font Not Found",
                        0, MB_OK | MB_ICONEXCLAMATION);
                    break;
                }
        }

    return(WinDefDlgProc(hwndDlg, msg, mp1, mp2));
}


MRESULT EXPENTRY AboutDlgBoxProc(hwndDlg, msg, mp1, mp2)
HWND hwndDlg;
USHORT msg;
MPARAM mp1, mp2;
{

    return(WinDefDlgProc(hwndDlg, msg, mp1, mp2));
}


BOOL ChangeFont()
{

    BOOL fValue;
    SHORT i, j;
    LONG lMaxFonts = 60L;
    static LONG lOldFont = 0;
    static CHAR *pszFilespec[] =
                    { "C:\\OS2\\DLL\\COURIER.FON",
                      "C:\\OS2\\DLL\\HELV.FON",
                      "C:\\OS2\\DLL\\TIMES.FON" };

    for(j=0; j < 3; j++)
        GpiLoadFonts(hab, pszFilespec[j]);

    GpiQueryFonts(hpsInit,
                (ULONG) QF_PUBLIC | QF_PRIVATE,
                NULL, &lMaxFonts,
                (LONG) sizeof(FONTMETRICS), fm);

    for(j=0; j < MAXFONTS; j++)
        if(strcmp(szFontSelected, fm[j].szFacename) == 0
        && usSizeSelected == fm[j].sNominalPointSize / 10)
            {
```

```
                    i = j;
                    fValue = TRUE;
                    break;
                }
            else
                {
                    i = 0;                        /* Accept system font. */
                    fValue = FALSE;
                }

    GpiSetCharSet(hpsInit, 0L);
    GpiDeleteSetId(hpsInit, lOldFont);
    lOldFont = i;

    fat.usRecordLength = sizeof(FATTRS);
    fat.lMatch = 0;
    fat.fsSelection = usStyleSelected;
    strcpy(fat.szFacename, fm[i].szFacename);
    fat.idRegistry = fm[i].idRegistry;
    fat.usCodePage = 850;
    fat.lMaxBaselineExt = fm[i].lMaxBaselineExt;
    fat.lAveCharWidth = fm[i].lAveCharWidth;
    fat.fsType = FATTR_TYPE_FIXED;
    fat.fsFontUse = 0;

    GpiCreateLogFont(hpsInit,
                    (PSTR8) szApplication,
                    (LONG)i, &fat);

    GpiSetCharSet(hpsInit, (LONG)i);
    return(fValue);
    }

VOID DisplayFont(hps, cx, cy)
HPS hps;
SHORT cx, cy;
    {

    RECTL rcl;
    SHORT i, j;
    POINTL ptl;
    CHAR line [8][80], szBuffer[80];

    for(i=0; i<8; i++)
        WinLoadString(hab, NULL, i, sizeof line[i], line[i]);
```

```
    WinFillRect(hps, &rcl, CLR_WHITE);
    GpiQueryFontMetrics(hps,
                        (LONG)sizeof(FONTMETRICS), &fmCur);

    strcat(line[0], fmCur.szFamilyname);
    strcat(line[1], fmCur.szFacename);
    if(fmCur.fsType == 1)
        strcat(line[2],"Fixed");
    else
        strcat(line[2],"Proportional");

    sprintf(szBuffer, "%d pt.\0",
                fmCur.sNominalPointSize / 10 );
    strcat(line[3], szBuffer);
    cy -= cy / 10;
    ptl.x = (LONG) cx / 14;
    for(j=0; j<8; j++)
        {
        ptl.y = cy - fmCur.lMaxBaselineExt * (j + 1)
                    + fmCur.lMaxDescender;

        GpiCharStringAt(hps, &ptl,
                    (LONG)strlen(line[j]), line[j]);
        }  .
    }
```

Vector Fonts

Sometimes, if the Presentation Manager can't find a close match between the specified logical font and the available physical fonts, it simulate the logical font with a vector-based font. A vector-based font is one constructed of line segments. The Presentation Manager can create a vector font because, minimally, it knows what all characters, numbers, and other symbols look like. All it has to do is evaluate the system default font — or any other immediately available font — to determine how it should draw the line segments in order to create the specified logical font. Figure 11-2 shows the difference between a vectored font, and a physical, bitmapped, font.

If you are concerned that the GpiCreateLogFont will create a vector-based font (and you want this to happen, given no physical fonts are available), you should ensure that the Presentation Manager can create the vector rendition correctly. To do this, you need to set the character angle,

Bitmapped Font   Vector Font

Figure 11-2: Bitmapped vs. Vector Font

and character box values. This requires that you call the following functions:

- GpiSetCharAngle — Specifies the relative vector for the characters in a text string. The function takes two arguments, *hps* and *pgradlAngle*. The latter argument is a pointer to a GRADIENTL structure that contains a point that defines the baseline angle by its relative coordinates. When both *x* and *y* are zero, the character angle is reset to the default value.

- GpiSetCharBox — Sets the current character-box attribute to the specified value. The function takes two arguments, *hps* and *psizfxBox*. The latter is a pointer to a SIZEF structure that contains the character box size. Note that the width and height of the character box are long signed integers. For example, a width of 8 world coordinate units equals 8 * 65,536.

- GpiSetCharShear — Specifies the character shear attribute, which transforms characters by changing upright lines to a normal angle (resembling italics). The function takes two arguments, *hps* and *pptlShear*. The latter is a pointer to a POINTL structure that contains a point identifying the shear angle coordinates. When *aptl.x* is 1, upright characters are created. When *aptl.x* and *aptl.y* are both positive or both negative, the characters slope from bottom to top, left to right.

CHAPTER 12

INPUT FOCUS AND THE KEYBOARD

Input focus is a simple, yet important, concept in the Presentation Manager. Managing input focus is akin to making sure that you have removed the lens cap from your camera before you take a photograph — or have turned on the computer before you run a program. Without the correct input focus, your application draws a blank and acts indifferently in an otherwise robust world.

Defined, input focus means a window is currently active and ready to receive character input from the keyboard. In practice, the Presentation Manager uses its own logic to establish input focus, so you need to know the rules of this logic to ensure that a given window has the input focus when you expect it. Once you become familiar with the rules, processing keyboard input is a matter of tracking the cursor (if you want) and collecting, storing, and retrieving individual characters.

Internally, the Presentation Manager uses a device monitor to capture keyboard input. In OS/2, a device monitor retrieves and decodes device-related data. For a Vio-based program, you install your own device monitor using the DosMonOpen and DosMonRead functions, among others. This is not the case with the Presentation Manager, which installs its own keyboard monitor. If you have the correct input focus, all you need to do to capture keyboard input in a Presentation Manager application is process the WM_CHAR message. The following sequence summarizes the events leading up to the WM_CHAR message.

1. The user presses a key.
2. The Presentation Manager decodes the key.
3. The decoded key sequence enters the system message queue.
4. A WM_CHAR message is generated.
5. The user releases the key.

6. The Presentation Manager decodes the key.

7. The decoded key sequence enters the system message queue.

8. A WM_CHAR message is generated.

Note the redundancy in this sequence; it emphasizes the fact that the Presentation Manager generates a WM_CHAR message for each press and release of a key. If you are familiar with keyboard scancode processing through the BIOS, the similarity to a scancode's make/break values is obvious.

The similarity is only surface deep, however. The Presentation Manager uses it own coding for processing keyboard input — coding that splits the keyboard into virtual keys, code keys, and dead keys. Loosely translated, these keys are the set of function keys, the set of alphanumeric keys, and special two-press key sequences that create characters specific to some foreign languages such as the umlaut character.

The Presentation Manager achieves a great deal of flexibility with its keyboard decoding system. Notably, no source code changes are required to port an application to a foreign language, or to EBCDIC from ASCII, or vice versa. All keyboard device driver considerations are handled by a dynamic link library. OS/2 also offers several Kbd functions to create custom translation tables that you can use with Presentation Manager applications. For additional information on these functions, refer to the Microsoft *OS/2 Programmer's Reference Manual*.

Input Focus

The Presentation Manager automatically monitors keyboard input and routes it to its own message queue. It does so because — being the top dog it is — it needs to evaluate keyboard input in case the user presses a system key sequence such as Ctrl-Esc to invoke the *Task Manager*. As a result, an application must tell the Presentation Manager where to route a WM_CHAR message — or, in other words, you must ensure that some window (and particularly, the window you want) has the input focus.

Input focus has ramifications for both concurrently running applications as well as an application running concurrent windows. If you do not specify input focus, the Presentation Manager routes WM_CHAR messages to the currently active application's frame window, where they sit until the user clicks the mouse on the frame window. This represents a default route for WM_CHAR messages, but not a default means of specifying a input focus. For example, if an application had a second standard window, clicking in this window would not shift the input focus. Instead, it would make this window the active window. Once the second window became the active window, however, clicking on it again would shift the input focus.

As you can see, input focus is associated with the active status of a window: in order for a window to receive the input focus, it must first be the active window. The user recognizes the window with the input focus by noting the following:

- The window is on top of all other windows.
- The window border is a different color.
- The window's titlebar stands out from other titlebars (that is, it is displayed in the default color for an active titlebar).

When a window receives or loses the input focus, the Presentation Manager sends it a WM_SETFOCUS message. This affords the application an opportunity to perform window specific initialization or exit processing. It also gives you a place in the main application window where you can track input focus. To obtain the current input focus, you extract the *mp2* value from WM_SETFOCUS and retain it in a static variable of type BOOL. To track the previous window with the input focus, you extract the *mp1* value from WM_SETFOCUS and retain it in a static variable of type HWND.

Alternatively, you can use the WinQueryFocus function to obtain the window with the current input focus. A typical call to WinQueryFocus looks like this:

```
hwndSave = WinQueryFocus(hwnd, fLock);
```

WinQueryFocus is defined as a function of type HWND and returns the handle to the window having the input focus. You can replace the hwnd argument with HWND_DESKTOP when appropriate. The *fLock* argument lets you lock the window if you want (see box).

In addition to querying the current focus, you can set the input focus using the WinSetFocus function. Invoking WinSetFocus generates a

WM_SETFOCUS message and toggles the input focus of the specified window. Here's a typical call to WinSetFocus:

```
fSuccess = WinSetFocus(hwnd, hwndSetFocus);
```

As usual, *hwnd* identifies the desktop window and can be set to HWND_DESKTOP if you like. The *hwndSetFocus* argument is almost as straightforward: it identifies the window that receives the focus and must either be *hwnd* or a descendent of *hwnd*. If you set *hwndSetFocus* to HWND_DESKTOP, or NULL, the Presentation Manager removes the input focus from the current window and does not reassign it. This lull in input focus is useful for allowing the user to re-establish the input focus by clicking on a window of choice.

LOCKING A WINDOW

In a multi-threaded application, it is often advisable to lock a window to guarantee it is not destroyed. This is especially important to prevent the owner from destroying the window and creating a second window with the same handle. For example, if the destroyed window contained a WM_CHAR processing block, and the new window also contained a WM_CHAR processing block, you might not realize the destroyed window had been replaced with the new window. A locked window cannot be destroyed. You can lock a window through most functions that return window handles such as WinQueryFocus. You can also lock a window by calling the WinLockWindow, which locks the specified window, or WinLockWindowUpdate, which locks a parent window as well as any of its children. To find out whether a window is locked, you can again use most functions that return a window handle, or call WinQueryWindowLockCount, which returns a zero value if the window is not locked. Once your need to lock a window has passed, you should ensure that the application unlocks the window. Attempting to destroy a locked window can lead to unpredictable results. You can unlock a window using most functions that return a window handle, or by calling WinLockWindow.

The WM_ACTIVATE Message

When the input focus changes, so can the active window. If changing the input focus does change the active window, the Presentation Manager sends a WM_ACTIVATE message to the application's previously active window. Similarly, if a new application receives active status, a WM_ACTIVATE message is sent to the previous application to notify it of the loss of active status.

The *mp1* parameter of WM_ACTIVATE (of type BOOL) specifies the active status of the window. If *mp1* is TRUE, WM_ACTIVATE gives the active status to a window; if *mp1* is FALSE, the window loses the active status. The *mp2* parameter of WM_ACTIVATE (of type HWND) identifies the window targeted for the change in active status — that is, if *mp1* is TRUE, *mp2* identifies the window losing the active status; and if *mp1* is FALSE, *mp2* identifies the window acquiring the active status.

During changes in input focus and active status, the Presentation Manager processes WM_ACTIVATE and WM_SETFOCUS messages in a strict order. Here's the sequence when both input focus and active status changes apply:

1. A WM_ACTIVATE message with *mp1* set to FALSE occurs, removing the active status from the previous window.

2. A WM_SETFOCUS message with *hwndSetFocus* set to FALSE occurs, removing input status from the previous window.

3. A WM_SETFOCUS message with *hwndSetFocus* set to TRUE occurs, assigning input status to the new window.

4. A WM_ACTIVATE message with *mp1* set to TRUE occurs, assigning the active status to the new window.

Some precautions are necessary when processing the WM_ACTIVATE message. For one thing, you should not create modeless windows or dialog boxes if *mp1* is set to FALSE. Doing so could cause the same window or dialog box to receive conflicting WM_ACTIVATE messages, which would likely cause the application to fail. Another area of concern is if you call the WinSetFocus function during a WM_ACTIVATE message, do not expect a WM_SETFOCUS message with *hwndSetFocus* set to FALSE to occur. The obvious reason for this is if no window currently has input focus, there is no purpose in attempting to remove the input focus.

The WM_FOCUSCHANGE Message

The WM_FOCUSCHANGE message is a powerful message, but one you will not use in most applications. Nevertheless, WM_FOCUSCHANGE provides a good insight into the way the Presentation Manager handles input focus, active status, selection setting, and z-ordering.

Both the WinSetFocus and WinFocusChange functions generate the WM_FOCUSCHANGE message. In each case, WM_FOCUSCHANGE occurs before associated WM_SETFOCUS and WM_ACTIVATE messages and is sent to both the window acquiring the input focus and the window losing the input focus. The default window procedure, WinDefWindowProc, processes WM_FOCUSCHANGE by sending it to each window in a hierarchy of windows until it reaches the owner window. If the message reaches a main application window (a frame window) before it reaches the owner window, the main application window sends it directly to the owner window or the parent of the owner window (whichever is closer in the hierarchy). At this point, WM_SETFOCUS, WM_ACTIVATE, and WM_SETSELECTION messages are generated.

In case you do want to process the WM_FOCUSCHANGE message, you should do so by subclassing the main application window. You do this by trapping WM_FOCUSCHANGE and then calling the WinSubclassWindow function. This is an effective way to add processing punch to your main application window, without including otherwise burdensome code. The following example demonstrates a simple hook into a subclassed function:

```
case WM_FOCUSCHANGE:
        WinSubclassWindow(hwnd, subMainAppWindow);
        break;
```

Once control passes to the subclassed function, you can perform whatever operation you need. If you intend to process any additional messages in the subclassed function, you need to set up **switch-case** messages blocks. To exit the subclassed function, call the main application window (or whichever frame window that invoked the subclass) at the end of your case statement. In effect, this replaces WinDefWindowProc.

To actually process WM_FOCUSCHANGE, you need to extract the $mp1$ and $mp2$ values from the message. The $mp1$ parameter (of type HWND) identifies the window associated with the current input focus. The $mp2$ parameter of WM_FOCUSCHANGE contains two values. The low word of $mp2$ specifies the status of the input focus associated with $mp1$: a TRUE value indicates the window specified by *mp1* is losing the input focus; and FALSE value indicates the window is acquiring the input focus. Meantime, the high word value of *mp2* (of type USHORT) specifies boolean flags that qualify the changing input focus. Table 12-1 lists these flags.

Table 12-1: WM_FOCUSCHANGE Flags

FLAG	BIT	DESCRIPTION
FC_NOLOSEFOCUS	0x0002	Window losing the focus does not receive WM_SETFOCUS.
FC_NOSETACTIVE	0x0004	Window receiving active status does not receive WM_ACTIVATE.
FC_NOLOSEACTIVE	0x0008	Window losing active status does not receive WM_ACTIVATE.
FC_NOSETSELECTION	0x0010	Window receiving selection status does not receive WM_SETSELECTION.
FC_NOLOSESELECTION	0x0020	Window losing the selection status does not receive WM_SETSELECTION.
FC_NOBRINGTOTOP	0x0040	No windows are brought to the top as a result of the new input focus.
FC_NOBRINGTOTOPFIRSTWINDOW	0x0080	The main application is not brought to the top as a result of the new input focus.
FC_SETACTIVEFOCUS	0x0100	The first child window of the first frame window in the window hierarchy receives the input focus.
FC_QUERYACTIVE	0x0200	The active window is returned.
FC_QUERYTASK	0x0400	The task window is returned.

An application can control the various states of a window through careful manipulation of the WM_FOCUSCHANGE flags. Note again, however, that it is likely you will not need to use the WM_FOCUSCHANGE message. On the other hand, by studying how the message works, you will gain a greater understanding of how the Presentation Manager manipulates one or more hierarchies of windows.

Moving the Cursor

What is a window without a cursor? Not much, if the purpose of the window is to prompt the user for text input. On the other hand, if the window is designed for graphics display and has a mouse pointer, you will not need to use a cursor. The choice is yours.

In the Presentation Manager, a cursor should be associated with a given window. For this reason, it is good practice to create a cursor when the window gets the input focus. This way a window rectangle remains unchanged until the user actually clicks on it — or the application code internally assigns the input focus to it.

Conversely, you should destroy a cursor when the window loses the input focus. The Presentation Manager provides three functions to create, display, and remove a cursor. Here's the definition for WinCreateCursor, which creates a cursor, but does not display it:

```
BOOL WinCreateCursor(hwnd, x, y, cx,cy, fs, prclClip)
HWND hwnd;
SHORT x, y, cx,cy;
USHORT fs;
PRECTL prclClip;
```

As is typical, *hwnd* can be the desktop window or HWND_DESKTOP. The *x* and *y* arguments specify the horizontal and vertical cursor coordinates. The *cx* and *cy* arguments specify the horizontal and vertical dimensions of the cursor. If either of these is zero, the Presentation Manager uses the normal system dimensions contained in SV_CXBORDER and SV_CYBORDER. The *fs* argument specifies a system-defined style for the cursor. Table 12-2 lists the available cursor styles, which can be ORed with one another to create additional styles.

Table 12-2: System-Defined Cursor Styles

STYLE	BIT	DESCRIPTION
CURSOR_SOLID	0x0000	Specifies a solid cursor.
CURSOR_HALFTONE	0x0001	Specifies a halftone cursor.
CURSOR_FRAME	0x0002	Specifies a framed cursor.
CURSOR_FLASH	0x0004	Specifies a flashing cursor.
CURSOR_SETPOS	0x8000	Specifies new cursor location is in effect.

The final argument to WinCreateCursor is *prclClip*, which points to a RECTL structure containing the dimensions to a rectangle in which the cursor is visible. The cursor must stay in this rectangle to remain visible. You can clip the cursor to the current window rectangle by setting *prclClip* to NULL. If you choose to do this, ensure that you destroy the cursor immediately before the WM_SIZE message, and call WinCreateCursor after obtaining the new window dimensions from WM_SIZE. If you omit this step, the clipping region associated with the cursor is not updated.

To create a cursor based on current character dimensions, use the *lAveCharWidth* and *lMaxBaselineExt* fields from the FONTMETRICS structure (refer to Chapter 11). Setting *cx* to *lAveCharWidth* and *cy* to *lMaxBaselineExt* creates a block cursor equivalent to the full dimensions of a character; setting *cx* to *lAveCharWidth* and *cy* to zero creates an underline cursor; and setting *cx* to zero and *cy* to *lMaxBaselineExt* creates a vertical line cursor. A vertical line cursor, combined with the CURSOR_FLASH option, is the standard Presentation Manager cursor for text processing applications.

To actually display the cursor, you must call the WinShowCursor function. WinShowCursor takes *hwnd* and *fShow*, a boolean value that shows the cursor when set to TRUE, and hides the cursor when set to FALSE. To destroy the cursor, you simply call WinDestroyCursor, specifying *hwnd* as the only argument. Note that the WinDestroyCursor function returns a FALSE boolean value if the cursor does not belong to the specified window.

Processing Character Input

Interpreting keyboard codes means interpreting the WM_CHAR message. When you trap a WM_CHAR message, you do whatever you like with the resultant code. For example, you should use WM_CHAR processing to trap special keys such as PageUp and PageDn so you can build an interface that otherwise would only be available through the mouse. This, not too incidentally, is both a good idea and strongly recommended by the *Application Style Guide*. Note, however, that you can duplicate much of what a mouse does by using keyboard accelerators (see Chapter 6).

The WM_CHAR Message

The WM_CHAR message is slightly more powerful than some other Presentation Manager messages. Altogether, you can obtain five distinct values by processing the *mp1* and *mp2* parameters. Table 12-3 lists these values.

Table 12-3: Values Contained in the WM_CHAR Message

FUNCTION	PARAM	BITS	DESCRIPTION
Key control flags	mp1	0-15	Presentation Manager keyboard flags for additional processing.
Repeat count	mp1	16-23	Key press repeat count.
Scan code	mp1	24-31	Hardware specific make/break keyboard scan codes.
Character code	mp2	0-15	Presentation Manager codes for letter, number, and standard symbol keys.
Virtual code	mp2	16-31	Presentation Manager codes for special keys such as PageUp, Tab, and Spacebar.

To extract the *mp1* and *mp2* values, you can use several different macros, including HIUCHAR and LOUCHAR macros, which are specifically designed for the WM_CHAR message. Alternatively, you can use CHAR-MSG, a stack macro that is also designed for WM_CHAR (see Chapter 3). The CHARMSG macro is based on a similarly named structure, which contains fields for each of the five values that you can obtain from a WM_CHAR messages. Here's the CHARMSG structure:

```
struct _CHARMSG {
            USHORT chr;          /* mp2 */
            USHORT vkey;
            USHORT fs;           /* mp1 */
            UCHAR cRepeat;
            UCHAR scancode;
};
```

Of the five fields in this structure, the *fs* field (which corresponds to the keyboard control flags entry in Table 12-3) has the widest impact. Because it tells you what type of key event has occurred, you can use it to distinguish which of the other four fields applies. Additionally, it allows you to determine shifted-key status. Recall, that the *fs* naming convention indicates an array of flags of type SHORT. Knowing this, you can expect an array of identifiers that you can combine using the logical OR operator. Table 12-4 lists these identifiers, which are prefixed with KC (for keyboard control).

Table 12-4: Keyboard Control Flags

FLAG	BIT	DESCRIPTION
KC_CHAR	0x0001	Character code (letter, number, symbol).
KC_VIRTUALKEY	0x0002	Dedicated keys (Tab, Spacebar, Shift).
KC_SCANCODE	0x0004	Hardware make/break scan code.
KC_SHIFT	0x0008	Right and left Shift keys.
KC_CTRL	0x0010	Dedicated Ctrl key.

(continued)

Table 12-4: Continued

FLAG	BIT	DESCRIPTION
KC_ALT	0x0020	Dedicated Alt key.
KC_KEYUP	0x0040	Indicates press/release status. A zero equals a key press; a one indicates a key release.
KC_PREVDOWN	0x0080	Indicates the key state before WM_CHAR.
KC_LONEKEY	0x0100	Used by the accelerator decoding system to determine if a keystroke is a character or an accelerator.
KC_DEADKEY	0x0200	Indicates the key press does not advance the cursor.
KC_COMPOSITE	0x0400	Indicates that the key code is a combination of the current key and the previous dead key.
KC_INVALIDCOMP	0x0800	Indicates the key code is not a valid combination with the previous dead key. In this case, the application should alert the user of the improper key.
KC_TOGGLE	0x1000	Set if the key is toggled. Note that the Num Lock key toggles the numeric keypad.
KC_INVALIDCHAR	0x2000	Indicates that a virtual key did not translate to a character.

Character Keys

Processing the standard alphanumeric keys is relatively simple compared to processing some of the virtual keys and other special keys. The primary reason for this is character keys have less code associated with them.

Before you start, you will want to specify the window boundaries for character input. Basically, you should establish minimum and maximum x and y positions for any given line of typed input. If you skip this step, the Presentation Manager allows the user to continue typing, right off the left side of the window. The characters do not shift left, but if you resize the window, previously typed characters appear (assuming the application has the appropriate logic to display the characters after resizing the window).

The best way to establish the boundary conditions for a line of typed input is to do it during WM_SIZE processing, then test the boundaries before your code processes a given character. For example, for a line width of approximately 62 characters, you can use 200 as the value against which to compare the current character position. Alternatively, if you incorporate cursor logic into the character processing routine, you can compare the current cursor position. A simple **if** statement lets you set up the comparison value. Here's a minimal WM_SIZE message block designed for character and cursor processing:

```
case WM_SIZE:
        xApp = SHORT1FROMMP(mp2);
        yApp = SHORT2FROMMP(mp2);
        if(XSIZE < xApp / yApp)
              xSize = XSIZE;
        else
              xSize = xApp / yApp;

        if(hwnd == WinQueryFocus(HWND_DESKTOP, FALSE))
              {
              WinDestroyCursor(hwnd);
              WinCreateCursor(hwnd, 0, yApp - MaxBase,
                              AveChar,MaxBase,
                              CURSOR_SOLID,
                              NULL);
              WinShowCursor(hwnd, TRUE);
              return(0);
              }
        }
```

The example assumes that XSIZE is defined as a line width value such as 200. Using this value, a value for XSIZE is then determined. Subsequently, the example establishes whether the window currently has the input focus. If it does, the cursor is destroyed, re-initialized, and displayed anew. This sequence ensures that the cursor is clipped to the current window. Note that setting the cursor in the WM_SIZE message block does not obviate the need to tend to the cursor while processing the WM_SET-FOCUS message.

The next step in processing a character is to test for the KC_CHAR flag. This is simple enough: you merely use the CHARMSG macro in an **if** statement to see whether KC_CHAR is set to TRUE. The following WM_CHAR message block tests for KC_CHAR, calls a function to store characters, and handles associated cursor logic.

```
case WM_CHAR:
        if (CHARMSG(&msg)->fs & KC_CHAR)
            {
            WinShowCursor(hwnd, FALSE);

            ProcessCharInput(hwnd, CHAR1FROMMP(mp2));

            WinCreateCursor(hwnd, AveChar * xCur,
                            yApp - MaxBase * (1 + yCur),
                            0, 0. CURSOR_SETPOS,
                            NULL);

            WinShowCursor(hwnd, TRUE);
            }
        break;
```

By processing character input in a function called from the WM_CHAR message block, you need to invalidate with the current window so WM_PAINT processing can redraw the window. The following program uses this technique and also controls the cursor as it processes character input.

```
/* TYPERITE.C (Program file) */

#define INCL_PM

#include <os2.h>
#include <stddef.h>
#include <string.h>

MRESULT EXPENTRY TypeWndProc(HWND, USHORT, MPARAM, MPARAM);
VOID GetFontData(HWND, SHORT *, SHORT *, SHORT *);
VOID DisplayKeyInput(HWND, CHAR, SHORT, SHORT, SHORT, SHORT);

CHAR szDisplay[40][100];
SHORT sLine = 1;
SHORT xCur = 0, yCur = 1;

int main(void)
{

static CHAR szClass[] = "TypeRite";
HAB hab;
```

```
HMQ hmq;
HWND hwndFrame, hwndClient;
QMSG qmsg;
ULONG ctlData = FCF_TITLEBAR | FCF_SYSMENU | FCF_MINMAX
                | FCF_SIZEBORDER | FCF_SHELLPOSITION
                | FCF_TASKLIST;


hab = WinInitialize(NULL);
hmq = WinCreateMsgQueue(hab, 0);

WinRegisterClass(hab, szClass,
                TypeWndProc, CS_SIZEREDRAW, 0);

hwndFrame = WinCreateStdWindow(
                        HWND_DESKTOP,
                        WS_VISIBLE,
                        &ctlData,
                        szClass,
                        NULL,
                        0L,
                        NULL,
                        0,
                        &hwndClient);

while(WinGetMsg(hab, &qmsg, NULL, 0, 0))
                WinDispatchMsg(hab, &qmsg);

WinDestroyWindow(hwndFrame);
WinDestroyMsgQueue(hmq);
WinTerminate(hab);

return(0);
}


MRESULT EXPENTRY TypeWndProc(hwnd, msg, mp1, mp2)
HWND hwnd;
USHORT msg;
MPARAM mp1, mp2;
{

    HPS hps;
    BOOL fSize = FALSE;
    CHAR key;
    SHORT i, ySizeCur, TotalLines;
    POINTL ptl;
```

```
static SHORT cx, cy;
static SHORT AveChar, MaxBase, MaxDesc;

switch(msg)
    {
    case WM_CREATE :
         GetFontData(hwnd, &AveChar, &MaxBase, &MaxDesc);
         return(FALSE);

    case WM_SIZE:
         cx = SHORT1FROMMP(mp2);
         cy = SHORT2FROMMP(mp2);
         WinShowCursor(hwnd, TRUE);

         if(xCur == 0)
              ySizeCur == yCur;
         else
            {
              ySizeCur = yCur -1;
              fSize = TRUE;
            }

         ySizeCur = (xCur > 0) ? yCur -1 : yCur;
         WinCreateCursor(hwnd,
                         AveChar * xCur + 1,
                         cy - MaxBase * yCur,
                         0, 0, CURSOR_SETPOS, NULL);
         break;

    case WM_SETFOCUS:
         if(SHORT1FROMMP(mp2))
            {
              WinCreateCursor(hwnd,
                         AveChar * xCur,
                         cy - MaxBase * yCur,
                         AveChar, MaxBase,
                         CURSOR_SOLID
                         | CURSOR_FLASH, NULL);

              WinShowCursor(hwnd, TRUE);
            }

         else
            {
              WinShowCursor(hwnd, FALSE);
              WinDestroyCursor(hwnd);
            }
```

```
        break;

case WM_CHAR:
    if(CHARMSG(&msg) -> fs & KC_CHAR)
        {
        switch(CHARMSG(&msg) -> chr)

        /* Other key handlers can go here! */

        default:
            WinShowCursor(hwnd, FALSE);

            key = CHAR1FROMMP(mp2);

            DisplayKeyInput(hwnd, key, cy,
            AveChar, MaxBase, MaxDesc);

            WinShowCursor(hwnd, TRUE);

            WinCreateCursor(hwnd, AveChar * xCur,
                            cy - MaxBase * yCur,
                            0, 0, CURSOR_SETPOS,
                            NULL);
        }

    return(TRUE);

case WM_PAINT:
    hps = WinBeginPaint(hwnd, NULL, NULL);
    GpiErase(hps);

    TotalLines = (fSize = TRUE) ? sLine + 1 : sLine;

    for(i=0; i < TotalLines; i++)
        {
        ptl.x = 0;
        ptl.y = cy - MaxBase * i + MaxDesc;

        GpiCharStringAt(hps, &ptl,
                    (LONG) strlen(szDisplay[i]),
                    szDisplay[i]);
        }
    WinEndPaint(hps);
    fSize = FALSE;
    return(NULL);
```

```
            }

        return WinDefWindowProc(hwnd, msg, mp1, mp2);
}


VOID GetFontData(hwnd, AveChar, MaxBase, MaxDesc)
HWND hwnd;
SHORT *AveChar, *MaxBase, *MaxDesc;
{

    HPS hps;
    FONTMETRICS  fm;

    hps = WinGetPS(hwnd);
    GpiQueryFontMetrics(hps,(LONG) sizeof fm, &fm);

    *AveChar = (SHORT) fm.lAveCharWidth;
    *MaxBase = (SHORT) fm.lMaxBaselineExt;
    *MaxDesc = (SHORT) fm.lMaxDescender;

    WinReleasePS(hps);
}


VOID DisplayKeyInput(hwnd, key, cy,
                            AveChar, MaxBase, MaxDesc)
HWND hwnd;
CHAR key;
SHORT cy, AveChar, MaxBase, MaxDesc;
{

    HPS hps;
    static SHORT i=0;
    POINTL ptl;

    hps = WinGetPS(hwnd);
    GpiSetBackMix(hps, BM_OVERPAINT);

    if(key == '\r' || i == 99)
       {
          szDisplay[sLine][i] = 0;
          i = 0;
          yCur++;
          xCur = 0;
          sLine++;
       }
```

```
    else
      {
        ptl.y = cy - MaxBase * yCur + MaxDesc;
        ptl.x = i * AveChar;
        szDisplay[sLine][i] = key;
        szDisplay[sLine][i+1] = 0;

        GpiCharStringAt(hps, &ptl, 1L, &key);

        xCur++;
        i++;
      }

    WinReleasePS(hps);
  }
```

Virtual Keys

Virtual keys represent a slightly different problem for processing keyboard input. Unlike alphanumeric keys, virtual keys cannot be lumped into one category, so you must test for each key that is expected by your application. All virtual key identifiers begin with VK. Table 12-5 lists the virtual key identifiers associated with the IBM 101-keyboard.

Table 12-5: Virtual Key Identifiers for 101-Keyboard

IDENTIFIER	BIT	KEY/KEY SEQUENCE
VK_BREAK	0x04	Ctrl-Break
VK_BACKSPACE	0x05	Backspace
VK_TAB	0x06	Tab
VK_BACKTAB	0x07	Shift-Tab
VK_SHIFT	0x09	Right/Left Shift
VK_CTRL	0x0A	Ctrl
VK_ALT	0x0B	Alt
VK_PAUSE	0x0D	Pause

(continued)

Table 12-5: Continued

IDENTIFIER	BIT	KEY/KEY SEQUENCE
VK_CAPSLOCK	0x0E	Caps Lock
VK_ESC	0x0F	Escape
VK_SPACE	0x10	Spacebar
VK_PAGEUP	0x11	Page Up
VK_PAGEDOWN	0x12	Page Down
VK_END	0x13	End
VK_HOME	0x14	Home
VK_LEFT	0x15	Left Cursor
VK_UP	0x16	Up Cursor
VK_RIGHT	0x17	Right Cursor
VK_DOWN	0x18	Down Cursor
VK_PRINTSCRN	0x19	Print Screen
VK_INSERT	0x1A	Insert
VK_DELETE	0x1B	Delete
VK_SCRLLOCK	0x1C	Scroll Lock
VK_NUMLOCK	0x1D	Num Lock
VK_ENTER	0x1E	Enter (Return)
VK_SYSRQ	0x1F	System Request
VK_F1 - VK_F12	0x20-0x2B	Standard Function Key
VK_F13 - VK_F24	0x2C-0x37	Shifted Function Key

The function keys listed in Table 12-5 apply to all keyboards modeled after the IBM 101-keyboard. To ensure compatibility with different keyboards, especially the old PC-style keyboard, do not use the F21 through F24 function keys. Also note that to shift function keys with Alt and Ctrl, you must first process the Alt or Ctrl key, then the appropriate function key.

Most of the cursor keys affect cursor movement in some way. As with programming any C application, you must make adjustments to cursor values in response to these keys. For example, to have the Home key move the cursor to the beginning of the current line, you modify the *xSize* value in response to VK_HOME. The following code fragment demonstrates this:

```
case VK_HOME:
        xSize = 0;
        break;
```

Similarly, to have the End key move the cursor to the end of the current line, you modify the *xSize* value in response to VK_END. Here's an appropriate example:

```
case VK_END:
        xCur = xSize - 1;
        break;
```

Processing the PageUp and PageDown keys requires a little bit more code. For both, you must set up a variable for the maximum length of the current window, the vertical equivalent to *xSize* (assume this variable is also set to 200 and is named *ySize*). The following code processes the VK_PAGEUP and VK_PAGEDOWN identifiers:

```
case VK_PAGEUP:
        yCur = 0;
        break;

case VK_PAGEDOWN:
        yCur = ySize - 1;
        break;
```

The arrow keys are not as straightforward as some of the other cursor movement keys. For the VK_LEFT and VK_UP identifiers, for instance, you must reset the *xCur* and *yCur* values, respectively. Then you must test whether the cursor has reached a boundary condition. Here's the code for the VK_LEFT and VK_UP identifiers:

```
case VK_LEFT:
        xCur = (xCur - 1 + xSize) % xSize;
        if (xCur == xSize - 1)
                yCur = (yCur - 1 + ySize) % ySize;
        break;

case VK_UP:
        yCur = (yCur - 1 + ySize) % ySize;
        if (yCur == ySize -1)
                xCur = (xCur - 1 + xSize) % xSize;
        break;
```

Handling the right arrow and down arrow keys is similar, but you must test for the zero boundary condition. Here's the code for the VK_RIGHT and VK_DOWN identifiers:

```
case VK_RIGHT:
        xCur = (xCur + 1) % xSize;
        if (xCur == 0)
                yCur = (yCur + 1) % ySize;
        break;

case VK_DOWN:
        yCur = (yCur + 1 ) % ySize;
        if (yCur == 0)
                xCur = (xCur + 1) % xSize;
        break;
```

Controlling the Insert and Delete keys is a little different because you need to modify the string into which you have accumulated characters from the WM_CHAR message. You can use a pointer (of type PUCHAR) to reference the character string. The following example shows how to handle VK_INSERT and VK_DELETE keys:

```
case VK_INSERT:
        for (i = xSize - 1; i > xCur; i--)
            {
                *lpString + yCur * xSize + i =
                  *lpString + yCur * xSize + i - 1;
                .
                .
                .
            }
        break;
```

```
case VK_DELETE:
      for(i = xSize - 1; i > xCur; i--)
           {
              *lpString + yCur * xSize + i =
                   *lpString + yCur * xSize + i - 1;
              .
              .
              .
      break;
```

Of the other virtual key identifiers, you should note that you do not have to process the identifiers associated with common keys such as VK_BACK, VK_ESCAPE, VK_SPACE, and VK_TAB. Instead of processing these identifiers, you can obtain the equivalent key press information from KC_CHAR.

Shift States

Although you can obtain the status of a shift key from its associated VK identifier, most keyboard processing should be oriented toward the KC flags that indicate shift status. The three KC shift states are KC_SHIFT, KC_ALT, and KC_CTRL.

You have a choice in the way you obtain the status of the shift state. You can either use the CHARMSG macro or call the WinGetKeyState function. Here's one way to test the shift state using the CHARMSG macro:

```
if(CHARMSG(&msg)->fs & (KC_CHAR & KC_SHIFT))
   ProcessText(UpperCase);      /* Example function. */
else
   ProcessText(LowerCase);
```

In some instances, you might want to test whether a key has been shifted, but not incorporate a lot of testing logic in your code. The WinGetKeyState function is handy for a quick test. It returns the shift status of the WM_CHAR key code you are currently processing — versus the shift status of the most recent key press. In other words, WinGetKeyState is synchronized to the last message obtained from the queue. Here's an example call:

```
stat = WinGetKeyState(HWND_DESKTOP, VK_SHIFT);
```

You should call this function after obtaining the character in which you are interested. If the key is set, the return value is a negative SHORT integer, corresponding to the high bit of the return value (0x8000). The high bit in the return value (0x0001) is set if the key has been toggled. A key is considered to have been toggled when it has been depressed an odd number of times since system boot.

To obtain the current shift state, you can use the WinGetPhysicalKeyState function. The current shift state is the last possible shift state, not necessarily the shift state associated with the key code currently in the queue. WinGetPhysicalKeyState works identically to WinGetKeyState. If you only want to obtain the shift state status, test whether WinGetPhysicalKeyState returns a negative SHORT integer.

Make/Break Codes

Determining between a key press and a key release — or make and break code — is a matter of processing the KC_KEYUP and KC_PREVDOWN identifiers. The Presentation Manager generates two WM_CHAR messages for each key press and release. These identifiers indicate the status of each of these messages for the current and previous keys, respectively.

The KC_KEYUP identifier tells you the status of the current key's make/break sequence. When KC_KEYUP is set to one, it indicates a key press; when it is set to zero, it indicates a key release. The KC_PREVDOWN identifier tells you the status of the previous key's make/break sequence. When KC_PREVDOWN is set to zero, it indicates a key press; when it is set to one, it indicates a key release.

For most applications, you will not want to know the status of the make/break code. You can dispense with make/break sequences altogether by including the following line of code near the beginning of the WM_CHAR message block.

```
if(CHARMSG(&msg)->fs & KC_KEYUP)
    break;
```

To process make/break sequences, test the values of KC_KEYUP and KC_PREVDOWN. If you want to determine whether a key is held down (indicating typematic action), KC_KEYUP is set to zero and KC_PREV-

DOWN is set to one. Otherwise, both identifiers are set to zero for a normal key press, or set to one for a normal key release.

If you choose to process shift states by testing the VK_SHIFT, VK_CTRL, or VK_ALT identifiers, you should note that these keys affect the order in which the Presentation Manager queues make/break sequences. The rule of thumb is a WM_CHAR message is generated to indicate a shift key press, followed by the two WM_CHAR messages for a character's make/break sequence. For example, a Ctrl-X key combination would generate a WM_CHAR message containing VK_CTRL, with both KC_KEYUP and KC_PREVDOWN set to zero. In turn, two WM_CHAR messages containing the make/break codes would follow. Finally, another WM_CHAR message containing VK_CTRL would occur, with KC_KEYUP and KC_PREVDOWN set to one.

It is also possible to use shift keys with other virtual keys, but you should avoid the F1 and F10 keys, which the Presentation Manager uses as system keys (F1 invokes help and F10 simulates the Alt key). If you do need to process these keys, you must subclass the frame window using the WinSubClassWindow function. Your subclassing function must trap the F10 and F1 WM_CHAR messages and pass the WM_CHAR messages to the client window, without passing the message to the old frame window function.

CHAPTER 13

MICE AND POINTERS

For many users who adopt the Presentation Manager, the mouse will be the single most different experience for them. Fortunately, using a mouse is not intrinsically difficult; but perhaps more than in any other interface area, it is important that your application adhere to accepted mouse and pointer techniques. These, of course, have largely evolved from Microsoft *Windows* as well as some notable mouse-driven graphics programs.

The one sacred rule of mouse programming is you must include a robust mouse interface for your application. Almost as sacred, but not universally observed, you must provide keyboard equivalents for as many mouse-based commands as possible.

This is often difficult, and sometimes next to impossible, but you should give it your best effort. Just think of the poor user whose mouse breaks and who must wait a day or two before getting a new one. Some users also prefer the keyboard whenever possible, so you do not want to alienate a class of individuals even before you compile your application.

The Presentation Manager comes equipped with a fully implemented mouse interface. By now, you are more than familiar with the mouse interface for accessing an application's menus, and moving, sizing, and closing windows, among other things.

The remaining mouse adventure ahead of you is to process the messages that occur within a window. Additionally, if you want to create your own mouse pointers, you need to learn how to include pointer bitmaps in your code.

Before you go any further, however, you should get used to mouse lingo. Table 13-1 lists a sampling of common mouse terms.

Table 13-1: Mouse Lexicon

TERM	DEFINITION
Arrow	The default system pointer.
Button	The clicking mechanism on the mouse. A mouse can have one, two, or three buttons.
Click	The act of depressing a mouse button. To "click" on an item means clicking the left button.
Double-Click	The act of depressing the mouse button twice in quick succession. This typically executes a program or command.
Drag	The act of depressing the mouse button and keeping it held down until a series of items, or a range of text, is highlighted.
Hotspot	The area of the pointer that retrieves a single pixel address from the screen for processing.
Hourglass	A pointer that tells the user that the CPU is occupied with the specified operation.
I-Beam	A pointer that tells the user to insert data.
Pointer	The cursor associated with mouse movement.
Point	Movement of the pointer until its hotspot is on the target area.

The Presentation Manager's mouse interface supports one-, two-, or three-button mice as well as various other pointing devices such as pucks or cross hair readers. In developing your application, you should take into consideration the type of pointing device that the user will likely have. Most *Windows* applications use only one mouse button, thus ensuring compatibility with any type of pointing device. For Presentation Manager applications, it is likely safe to assume that most users have a two-button mouse — given the rise in popularity of the two- and three-button mouse.

Is There A Mouse?

If you are the generous type, you might want to include a comprehensive keyboard interface in your application. Even so, you probably would prefer to have your users choose the mouse in certain cases such as in a drawing program. Thus, there is little reason to include keyboard controls for moving the cursor in the drawing area — but, for those few users who do not have a mouse, you do not want to totally omit the keyboard interface.

The solution is to query the system to find out whether it has a mouse. You do this with the WinQuerySysValue function. The following call does the trick:

```
lMouse = WinQuerySysValue(HWND_DESKTOP,
                    SV_CMOUSEBUTTONS);
```

This call returns zero if the a mouse is not present. Otherwise, the call returns the number of buttons that the mouse supports. The latter piece of information is also useful (and will be explained in a later section).

Mouse Processing

The Presentation Manager considers the mouse a priority item. When it first creates a window, it immediately places a mouse-related message in the message queue. By now, you can probably guess the name of this message: it is WM_MOUSEMOVE, the most important of the three mouse messages that the Presentation Manager generates. (Note that some reference materials combine the mouse messages with the mouse button messages, but this book refers to the two sets of messages as distinct sets.)

Controlling the mouse means controlling WM_MOUSEMOVE. Whenever the mouse moves onscreen, the Presentation Manager generates a WM_MOUSEMOVE message. This message notifies the window function of the mouse's whereabouts. When you trap WM_MOUSEMOVE, you can obtain the coordinates of the mouse pointer, then do with them what you want such as draw a line, move the insertion pointer, or begin highlighting a section of text. The pointer coordinates are relative to the current window, not the screen. Figure 13-1 shows the mouse x and y coordinates in relation to the message values you use to obtain window positioning data.

The high and low words of the *mp1* parameter of the WM_MOUSE-MOVE message contain the pointer coordinates for the mouse. As with other message parameter values, you can use the SHORT1FROMMP and SHORT2FROMMP macros to obtain the pointer coordinates. Or, as with the WM_COMMAND parameter values, you can use a stack macro to ex-

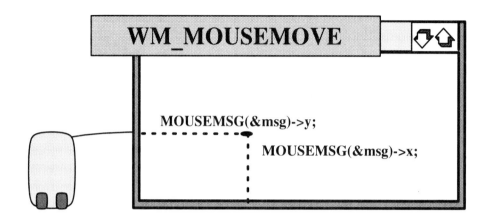

Figure 13-1: Obtaining Pointer Coordinates

tract the coordinates — namely, the MOUSEMSG macro, which is explained in Chapter 3.

The MOUSEMSG macro references the _MOUSEMSG struct, which contains x and y fields corresponding to the pointer coordinates. It also contains a field called *codeHitTest*, which you use when you want to reference a given object onscreen.

To extract the two *mp1* values from WM_MOUSEMOVE, you typically declare two pointer position variables of type POINTL, which maintain the current coordinates for Gpi text and graphic functions. After declaring these variables, you use the MOUSEMSG macro to extract the *mp1* values:

```
ptlPos.x = MOUSEMSG(&msg)->x;
ptlPos.y = MOUSEMSG(&msg)->y;
```

Alternatively, here is the code using the SHORT1FROMMP and SHORT2FROMMP macros:

```
xPos = SHORT1FROMMP(mp1);
yPos = SHORT2FROMMP(mp2);
```

The combination of obtaining the x and y coordinates, creating a presentation space, and calls to GpiMove and GpiLine will yield immediate results. Try the following program to see exactly what these results are:

```
#define INCL_WIN
#define INCL_GPI
#include <os2.h>
#include <stddef.h>

MRESULT EXPENTRY AppWindowFunc(HWND, USHORT, MPARAM, MPARAM);

int main (void)
{

HAB      hab;
HMQ      hab;
HWND     hwndFrame, hwndClient;
static CHAR szClass [] = "Line Fill";
QMSG     qmsg;
ULONG ctlData = FCF_TITLEBAR | FCF_SYSMENU | FCF_MENU
                | FCF_SIZEBORDER | FCF_MINMAX | FCF_TASKLIST
                | FCF_SHELLPOSITION | FCF_ACCELTABLE;

hab = WinInitialize(NULL) ;
hmq = WinCreateMsgQueue(hab, 0) ;
WinRegisterClass(hab, szClass,
                    AppWindowFunc, CS_SIZEREDRAW, 0);

hwndFrame = WinCreateStdWindow(
                    HWND_DESKTOP,
                    WS_VISIBLE,
                    &ctlData
                    szClass,
                    NULL,
                    0L,
                    NULL,
                    0,
                    &hwndClient);

while (WinGetMsg (hab, &qmsg, NULL, 0, 0))
          WinDispatchMsg (hab, &qmsg);

WinDestroyWindow(hwndFrame);
WinDestroyMsgQueue(hmq);
WinTerminate(hab);
return(0);
}
```

```
MRESULT EXPENTRY AppWindowFunc(hwnd, msg, mp1, mp2)
HWND hwnd;
USHORT msg;
MPARAM mp1, mp2;
{
POINTL ptl;
HPS hps;

switch (msg)
  {
    case WM_MOUSEMOVE:
         hps = WinGetPS (hwnd) ;
         ptl.x = MOUSEMSG(&msg)->x ;
         ptl.y = MOUSEMSG(&msg)->y ;
         GpiMove(hps, &ptl);
         GpiLine(hps, &ptlPos);
         WinReleasePS (hps) ;
         return(TRUE);

    case WM_PAINT:
         hps = WinBeginPaint(hwnd, NULL, NULL);
         GpiErase(hps);
         WinEndPaint(hps);
         return(NULL);
  }
return(WinDefWindowProc(hwnd, msg, mp1, mp2));
}
```

This program shows how a line is drawn. The only problem is it does not refresh the line after you the move the pointer. Instead, the beginning of the line remains anchored at the initial mouse coordinates and continues to fill in the area from these coordinates to the current position of the mouse pointer. (You could actually adapt this type of routine for a fill or paint function in a graphics program, if you wanted the user to be able to fill an area on-the-fly.)

How do you control where the line begins? You probably would prefer that the beginning of the line match the current pointer position. One way of doing this would be to duplicate the use of the MOUSEMSG macros to establish the position of the pointer and call GpiMove to set the initial position. This is fine, but you also want to give the user the ability to set the initial position. Inevitably, your code must act upon some signal from the mouse.

In addition to the WM_MOUSEMOVE message, you can process the WM_MOUSEFIRST and WM_MOUSELAST messages. At times, it is important that you distinguish the first and last mouse messages to set entry and exit conditions. Table 13-2 lists the three mouse messages.

Table 13-2: Mouse Messages

MESSAGE	BIT	DESCRIPTION
WM_MOUSEMOVE	0x0070	General mouse message.
WM_MOUSEFIRST	0x0070	First mouse message.
WM_MOUSELAST	0x0079	Last mouse message.

On the Button

The Presentation Manager supports several messages that signify a given press or release of a mouse button. Each button has its own set of messages. Before you begin writing code for the mouse button, you should decide how many buttons you want your application to support.

If you decide to support less than the maximum of three buttons, you can still put the unused buttons to work. For example, an application that supports only the first button can duplicate the first button's functionality for the second and third buttons. Conversely, you can give added functionality to a two- or three-button mouse. This technique does not necessarily offend the one-button mouse user (the few that exist), and could give two- and three-button users a useful feature or two.

Your first step in writing code for the mouse buttons is to find out how many buttons a given mouse has. As already mentioned, you do this by calling WinQuerySysValue and supplying it the SV_CMOUSEBUTTONS identifier. The return value is the number of buttons. What you do with the result depends on your application. One common technique is to enable routines for two- and three-button mouses, depending on the result. So as not to use executable file resources, these routines can be stored in a dynamic link library.

Buttons send three different types of signals to the Presentation Manager. The two most common signals result from a single click on a mouse button. Internally, a single click equals two distinct signals: one indicating the user has pressed the button; and the other indicating the user has released the button. The third type of signal results from a double-click, which occurs when the user quickly presses and releases a button in quick succession. Table 13-3 lists the various button messages.

Table 13-3: Button Messages

MESSAGE	VALUE	DESCRIPTION
WM_BUTTONCLICKFIRST	0x0071	First button click.
WM_BUTTONCLICKLAST	0x0079	Last button click.
WM_BUTTON1DOWN	0x0071	Button one pressed.
WM_BUTTON1UP	0x0072	Button one released.
WM_BUTTON1DBLCLK	0x0073	Double-click from button one.
WM_BUTTON2DOWN	0x0074	Button two pressed.
WM_BUTTON2UP	0x0075	Button two released.
WM_BUTTON2DBLCLK	0x0076	Double-click from button two.
WM_BUTTON3DOWN	0x0077	Button three pressed.
WM_BUTTON3UP	0x0078	Button three released.
WM_BUTTON3DBLCLK	0x0079	Double-click from button three.

With the exception of WM_BUTTONCLICKFIRST and WM_BUTTONCLICKLAST (both of which are used for filtering purposes), the button messages contain the pointer coordinates in the *mp1* parameter. For some applications, this means you could ignore the WM_MOUSEMOVE message altogether. For example, if you wanted to draw a line, you could simply have the user click on the beginning and end of the line. Then, after the second click, you call GpiLine to draw the line. Some drawing applications prefer this method; others do not.

You can also combine button messages with WM_MOUSEMOVE. The most common example of this is dragging the pointer, a technique that highlights the associated area as the user moves the mouse. In order to do this, you must set a static flag to retain the state of the left button, then evaluate the flag whenever the application generates a WM_MOUSE-MOVE message. The following code fragment illustrates this technique for drawing a user-defined line:

```
MRESULT EXPENTRY AppWindowFunc(hwnd, msg, mp1,mp2)
HWND hwnd;
USHORT msg;
MPARAM mp1, mp2;
{

static POINTL ptl;
HPS     hps;
BOOL    fButton = FALSE;

switch (msg)
  {
  case WM_BUTTON1DOWN:
        ptl.x = MOUSEMSG(&msg)->x ;
        ptl.y = MOUSEMSG(&msg)->y ;
        GpiMove(hps, &ptl);
        fButton = TRUE;
        return(TRUE);

  case WM_MOUSEMOVE:
        if(fButton)
          {
            ptl.x = MOUSEMSG(&msg)->x;
            ptl.y = MOUSEMSG(&msg)->y;
            GpiLine(hps, &ptl);
          }
        return(TRUE);

  case WM_BUTTON1UP:
        fButton = FALSE;
        return(TRUE);

  case WM_PAINT:
        hps = WinBeginPaint(hwnd, NULL, NULL) ;
```

```
        GpiErase(hps);
        WinEndPaint(hps);
        return(NULL);
    }

return WinDefWindowProc (hwnd, msg, mp1, mp2) ;
}
```

This bare bone windows procedure shows the logic needed to draw a line based on the pointer movement. First, it retrieves the current pointer coordinates in the WM_BUTTON1DOWN block and then calls GpiMove to reset the current drawing position. After this, the *fButton* variable is set to TRUE. The code in WM_MOUSEMOVE then retrieves the new pointer position and draws the line. When the user finishes, the button is released and the *fButton* variable is reset to FALSE in the WM_BUTTON1UP block. The following program example gives you a more complete idea of how to process mouse messages:

```
/* MOUSER.H (Header file) */

#define IDD_NULL   -1
#define IDM_MENURES 1
#define IDD_DLGMIX  2
#define IDD_DLGPAT  3
#define IDM_HELP    4

#define IDM_DRAW    100
#define IDM_SCREEN  101
#define IDM_BOXES   102
#define IDM_CIRCLES 104
#define IDM_LINES   105


/* MOUSER.RC (Resource Script) */

#include <os2.h>
#include "mouser.h"

MENU IDM_MENURES
  {
    SUBMENU "~Draw",  IDM_DRAW
    {
      MENUITEM "~Clear (reset)\t^S", IDM_SCREEN
      MENUITEM "~Box\t^B", IDM_BOXES, MIA_CHECKED
      MENUITEM "~Circle\t^C", IDM_CIRCLES
```

```
        MENUITEM "~Line\t^L", IDM_LINES
     }
}

ACCELTABLE IDM_MENURES
  {
    "^S",  IDM_SCREEN
    "^B",  IDM_BOXES
    "^C",  IDM_CIRCLES
    "^L",  IDM_LINES
  }



/* MOUSER.C (Program file) */

#define INCL_WIN
#define INCL_GPI

#include <os2.h>
#include <stddef.h>
#include <stdlib.h>
#include "mouser.h"

MRESULT EXPENTRY MouseWndProc(HWND,USHORT,MPARAM,MPARAM);

VOID RouteTheMouse(HWND, BOOL, SHORT, SHORT, SHORT);
VOID DrawBox(HPS,BOOL,SHORT,SHORT);
VOID DrawCircle(HPS,BOOL,SHORT,SHORT);
VOID DrawLine(HPS,BOOL,SHORT,SHORT);

HAB hab;

int main(void)
{

HMQ hmq;
HWND hwndClient, hwndFrame;
QMSG qmsg;
static CHAR szClass[] = "Mouse Move";
ULONG ctlData = FCF_TITLEBAR | FCF_SYSMENU | FCF_SIZEBORDER
                | FCF_MINMAX | FCF_TASKLIST | FCF_MENU
                | FCF_SHELLPOSITION | FCF_ACCELTABLE;

hab = WinInitialize(0);
hmq = WinCreateMsgQueue(hab, 0);
WinRegisterClass(hab, szClass,
```

```
                            MouseWndProc,
                            CS_SIZEREDRAW | CS_SYNCPAINT, 0);

hwndFrame = WinCreateStdWindow(
                                HWND_DESKTOP,
                                WS_VISIBLE,
                                &ctlData,
                                szClass,
                                NULL,
                                0L,
                                NULL,
                                IDM_MENURES,
                                &hwndClient);
while(WinGetMsg(hab, &qmsg, NULL, 0, 0))
            WinDispatchMsg(hab, &qmsg);

WinDestroyWindow(hwndFrame);
WinDestroyMsgQueue(hmq);
WinTerminate(hab);
return(0);
}


MRESULT EXPENTRY MouseWndProc(hwnd, msg, mp1, mp2)
HWND hwnd;
USHORT msg;
MPARAM mp1, mp2;
{

    HPS  hps;
    static SHORT sDraw;
    static BOOL fStart = FALSE, fMouse = FALSE;

    switch(msg)
      {
        case WM_COMMAND:
            switch((COMMANDMSG(&msg)->cmd))
              {
                case IDM_SCREEN:
                    hps = WinGetPS(hwnd);
                    GpiErase(hps);
                    WinReleasePS(hps);
                    return(NULL);

                case IDM_BOXES:
                    sDraw = 1;
                    return(NULL);
```

```
                    case IDM_CIRCLES:
                         sDraw = 2;
                         return(NULL);

                    case IDM_LINES:
                         sDraw = 3;
                         return(NULL);

                 }
              break;

       case WM_BUTTON1DOWN:
              fStart = TRUE;
              fMouse = TRUE;
              RouteTheMouse(hwnd, fStart, sDraw,
                          SHORT1FROMMP(mp1),
                          SHORT2FROMMP(mp1));
              return(TRUE);

       case WM_MOUSEMOVE:
              if(fMouse == FALSE)
                    break;

              fStart = FALSE;
              RouteTheMouse(hwnd, fStart, sDraw,
                          SHORT1FROMMP(mp1),
                          SHORT2FROMMP(mp1));
              return(TRUE);

       case WM_BUTTON1UP:
              sDraw = 0;
              fMouse = FALSE;
              return(TRUE);

       case WM_PAINT:
              hps = WinBeginPaint(hwnd, NULL, NULL);
              GpiErase(hps);
              WinEndPaint(hps);
              return(NULL);
       }

    return WinDefWindowProc(hwnd, msg, mp1, mp2);
}

VOID RouteTheMouse(hwnd, fStart, sDraw, x, y)
HWND hwnd;
```

```
BOOL fStart;
SHORT sDraw, x, y;
{

    HPS hps;

    hps = WinGetPS(hwnd);

    switch(sDraw)
        {
            case 1:
                DrawBox(hps, fStart, x, y);
                break;

            case 2:
                DrawCircle(hps, fStart, x, y);
                break;

            case 3:
                DrawLine(hps, fStart, x, y);
                break;

            default:
                break;
        }

    WinReleasePS(hps);
}


VOID DrawBox(hps, fStart, x, y)
HPS hps;
BOOL fStart;
SHORT x, y;
{

    LONG  c = 1;
    POINTL ptl;
    static SHORT xStart, yStart;

    if(fStart)
        {
            xStart = x;
            yStart = y;
        }

    GpiErase(hps);
```

```
    GpiSetColor(hps, CLR_BLUE);
    ptl.x = xStart;
    ptl.y = yStart;
    GpiMove(hps, &ptl);
    ptl.x = x;
    ptl.y = y;
    GpiBox(hps, DRO_OUTLINE, &ptl, 0L, 0L);
}


VOID DrawCircle(hps, fStart, x, y)
HPS hps;
BOOL fStart;
SHORT x, y;
{

    LONG lIncrement;
    POINTL ptl;
    static SHORT xStart;

    if(fStart)
        xStart = x;

    lIncrement = abs(x - xStart);
    GpiErase(hps);
    GpiSetColor(hps, CLR_BLUE);
    ptl.x = x;
    ptl.y = y;
    GpiMove(hps, &ptl);
    GpiFullArc(hps, DRO_OUTLINE, lIncrement * 65536L);
}


VOID DrawLine(hps, fStart, x, y)
HPS hps;
BOOL fStart;
SHORT x, y;
{

    SHORT  i=0;
    POINTL ptl;
    static SHORT xStart, yStart;

    if(fStart)
      {
        xStart = x;
        yStart = y;
```

```
    }

    GpiErase(hps);
    GpiSetColor(hps, CLR_BLUE);
    ptl.x = xStart;
    ptl.y = yStart;
    GpiMove(hps, &ptl);
    ptl.x = x;
    ptl.y = y;
    GpiLine(hps, &ptl);
}
```

This program example lets you create and size either a box, circle, or line. Using some boolean flags, the program begins a drawing routine when it receives a WM_BUTTON1DOWN message. It then sizes the specified object, erasing the screen with each change in size. To make the erasing process cleaner, you could scale down the size of the redraw area by using the WinQueryWindowRect and WinFillRect functions. To do this, you would need to set the size of the current rectangle to the previous size of the object being drawn.

More Tracking

Another way of tracking a button is with the WinQueryKeyState function. The following call obtains the state of the left mouse button:

```
fButton = WinQueryKeyState(HWND_DESKTOP, VK_BUTTON1);
```

This call uses a VK identifier to reference the left button. As you might guess, there are three VK identifiers associated with the mouse. These are listed in Table 13-4.

Table 13-4: Button Identifiers

IDENTIFIER	BIT	DESCRIPTION
VK_BUTTON1	0x01	Button one.
VK_BUTTON2	0x02	Button two.
VK_BUTTON3	0x03	Button three.

Yet another, even faster, method of obtaining the next button message uses the WinQueryQueueStatus message. WinQueryQueueStatus returns the status of the message queue. The high word of the return value contains the types of messages in the queue. The low word contains the types of messages added to the queue since the last call to WinQuery-QueueStatus. If no messages are in the queue, WinQueryQueueStatus returns a zero value.

By testing for zero, you can put WinQueryQueueStatus to work without extracting the high and low words from the return value. The following code fragment illustrates the technique:

```
case WM_MOUSEMOVE:
        while(stat = (USHORT) WinQueryQueueStatus
                                (HWND_DESKTOP))
            {
            WinPeekMsg(hab, &qmsg, NULL,
                    0, 0, PM_NOREMOVE);

            if(qmsg.msg == WM_BUTTON1DOWN)
                {
                    ptlPos.x = MOUSEMSG(&msg)->x ;
                    ptlPos.y = MOUSEMSG(&msg)->y ;
                    GpiLine(hps, &ptl);
                }

            WinGetMsg(hab, &qmsg, NULL, 0, 0);
            WinDispatchMsg(hab, &qmsg);
            }
```

This fragment polls the message queue until WinQueryQueueStatus returns a zero value. In turn, the WinPeekMsg function obtains the current message and puts it in the local copy of the *qmsg* struct. The fragment then tests whether the current message is WM_BUTTON1DOWN. If it is WM_BUTTON1DOWN, the call to GpiLine is made. Otherwise, WinGetMsg gets the next message in the queue.

Because WinQueryQueueStatus has established the presence of messages in the queue, there is no chance that WinGetMsg will unnecessarily hang until a message arrives. Finally, WinDispatchMsg extracts the message from the queue and sends it to the application window function. Accordingly, you should not process the WM_BUTTON1DOWN message anywhere but inside the WM_MOUSEMOVE block.

Position Functions

The Presentation Manager supports two additional functions that report pointer coordinates. These are the WinQueryPointerPos and WinQuery-MsgPos functions, both of which return the pointer position in terms of screen coordinates, not window coordinates. Both functions have legitimate applications, but neither is as dynamic as mouse/button message processing.

If you know that the pointer is going to be relatively static, you can effectively use WinQueryPointerPos. It returns the pointer position at the exact time the function is called, no sooner, no later. The call to WinQueryPointerPos looks like this:

```
WinQueryPointerPos(HWND_DESKTOP, &ptl);
```

As with the MOUSEMSG macro, WinQueryPointerPos references the POINTL structure and fills its x and y fields with the current screen coordinates of the pointer.

One necessary use of WinQueryPointerPos is its role in determining the current keyboard shift state when a mouse button is pressed. (Note that you cannot obtain this information from processing button messages.) The applicable shift state keys are Ctrl and Shift. To retrieve the shift state, call WinGetKeyState with the appropriate VK identifier as in the following:

```
WinGetKeyState(HWND_DESKTOP, VK_CTRL);
```

This call returns the value of the 0x8000 bit. If the value is less than zero, the key has been pressed; otherwise, the bit is not set. After making this call, incorporate your results from WinQueryPointerPos and you will know whether the mouse button was clicked during a shifted state.

The WinQueryMsgPos function is a little more powerful than Win-QueryPointerPos. It returns the pointer position corresponding to the time that the message entered the message queue. This being the case, you can use WinQueryMsgPos with both the WinPeekMsg and WinGetMsg calls. Here's a typical call to WinQueryMsgPos:

```
WinQueryMsgPos(hab, &ptl);
```

This call also fills the x and y fields of the POINTL structure. And as is the case with WinQueryPointerPos, the call to WinQueryMsgPos uses screen coordinates, not window coordinates. Note that to obtain valid results using WinQueryMsgPos, you must use it for queued messages only.

Capturing the Mouse

At times, you will want to process mouse messages in a window function other than the one in which they occur. The Presentation Manager provides two functions for this purpose — WinSetCapture and WinQueryCapture.

The WinSetCapture function captures all mouse messages that occur in any window, at any given time. In the call to WinSetCapture, you specify the window to receive the mouse and button message. Here is a typical call:

```
fLock = WinSetCapture(HWND_DESKTOP, hwnd);
```

WinSetCapture returns an unlocked window handle. If you need to perform some operation in the window where a mouse message originated, use *fLock* to obtain the window handle from the function call. In the *hwnd* argument to WinSetCapture, you can specify any of the following:

- The window that you want to receive the mouse and button messages.

- A special window handle called HWND_THREADCAPTURE, which captures the mouse and button messages to the current thread, instead of a specified window.

- A NULL value, which releases the capture process and causes the mouse and button messages to have NULL handles. Additionally, a NULL value causes all coordinates to be screen-based.

After you invoke WinSetCapture, you can process mouse messages with the same code that handles them for the current window. To release the capture process, you must call WinSetCapture a second time and set *hwnd* to either a different window or NULL. When you release the capture process, the Presentation Manager posts a WM_MOUSEMOVE message. The reason for this is to allow the newly specified window — or the previous window if *hwnd* is NULL — to display its associated mouse pointer.

The WinQueryCapture function simply lets you obtain the handle of the window controlling the capture process. You call WinQueryCapture as follows:

```
hwndCapture = WinQueryCapture(HWND_DESKTOP, flock);
```

This call returns the handle to the window that owns the capture process. Note that you must specify HWND_DESKTOP as the first argument, and not merely a parent window handle. For the *fLock* argument, you can use TRUE, FALSE, or the value returned from WinSetCapture call. If you set *fLock* to TRUE, WinQueryCapture returns a locked window handle. A FALSE value ensures that an unlocked handle is returned.

Pointers

A pointer is the tail that wags the mouse — that is, the icon that actually lets you know the location of the mouse.

Either way you look at it, controlling the mouse pointer involves serious planning. For one thing, you need to follow guidelines in the *Application Style Guide*. Three of the most relevant guidelines are:

- Use the appropriate system default pointers when the need arises. For example, when you perform a time-consuming operation, use the hourglass pointer.

- Use custom pointers within an application when child control windows are implemented. For example, if you had a panel of icon-based child control windows, the mouse pointer should change to indicate the selected icon.

- When a pointer moves between windows, use different pointers to indicate input focus. For example, if your client window coexists with several child windows, use one pointer design for the client window, and a different design for the child windows.

Usually, a pointer is displayed only if a mouse is attached to the system. In some cases, it is also displayed if there is no mouse. An example case is when the hourglass pops up during a CPU-intensive operation. Additionally, whenever an insertion is necessary, the Presentation Manager displays the I-beam pointer by default. It is the programmer's obligation to be consistent with these and other system practices. For example, in a text processing application, you should use the I-beam pointer to indicate insert mode.

Pointer design is also an issue. You create pointers the same way that you create icons — using the *Icon Editor*. Basically, the mouse pointer design should reflect the operation or the window associated with the pointer. You should also design the pointer so the hotspot area is obvious to the user.

Pointer Basics

As with other resources, you must define a mouse pointer in the application's resource script (the .RC file). The necessary steps are similar to those required for an icon. To summarize, you define a pointer ID in the resource script, but you do not need to modify the call to the WinCreate-StdWindow function.

After the initial setup, you can load your custom mouse pointer using the WinLoadPointer function. Here's a typical call to WinLoadPointer:

```
WinLoadPointer(HWND_DESKTOP, hmod, idRes);
```

The return value from WinLoadPointer is a handle to the pointer. You need this handle for later reference. The return value is usually stored in a variable named *hptr*. The first argument, *hwndDesktop*, must be the handle to the desktop window, or HWND_DESKTOP. The *hmod* argument specifies the source of the pointer resource. If the argument is set to NULL, the Presentation Manager loads the pointer from the applications .EXE file; otherwise, *hmod* must reference a dynamic link library. The last argument, *idres*, is simply the pointer ID as defined in the resource script.

Where you call WinLoadPointer is up to you. Inside **main()** is as good a place as any if you do not intend on destroying and then reloading the pointer. Actually, you can load as many pointers as you require in **main()** and change pointers upon receiving the WM_CONTROLPOINTER message (explained in the next section). Alternatively, you can wait until a particular need arises to load a pointer, thus minimizing system overhead. A good conditional location for the WinLoadPointer function is in the WM_CREATE message block — particularly if your application uses a series of windows. Note that when you replace a system pointer such as the hourglass with a custom pointer, you cannot destroy the system pointer, even if you never intend to use it.

The next step in pointer setup is to call the WinSetPointer function. This function activates the pointer. Here is the call:

```
WinSetPointer(HWND_DESKTOP, hptr);
```

A convenient place to call the WinSetPointer function is in the handler for the WM_MOUSEMOVE message. This way, the pointer changes when a given application window function receives the WM_MOUSE message. You can simply insert the call to WinSetPointer, without conditional logic; Microsoft claims the speed of the function is sufficiently fast not to make a difference in performance. In cases where you want to temporarily remove the pointer, you should use conditional logic. You remove the pointer by setting *hptr* in WinSetPointer to NULL.

Finally, you call the WinDestroyPointer function to destroy a pointer. WinDestroyPointer takes *hptr* as its only argument. If you merely replace the system pointer with a custom pointer, you do not have to worry about destroying the pointer. When using multiple pointers, however, the need to destroy one or more will arise. Note that only the thread that creates a pointer can destroy it.

Replacing the system pointer with a custom pointer is a straightforward process. The following program changes the system arrow pointer when it enters the application window, then restores it to the system pointer when it enters the desktop window. Figure 13-2 illustrates the pointer used in the program.

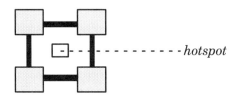

Figure 13-2: Pointer Isolating Hotspot

```
/* MOUSER.H (Header file) */

#define ID_POINTER 255

/* MOUSER.RC (Resource script) */

POINTER 255 mouser.ptr

/* MOUSER.C (Program file) */

#define INCL_WIN
#define INCL_GPI
#include <os2.h>
#include <stddef.h>
#include "mouser.h"

MRESULT EXPENTRY AppWindowFunc(HWND, USHORT, MPARAM, MPARAM);

HPOINTER hptr;

int main(void)
{
HAB     hab;
HMQ     hmq;
HWND    hwndFrame, hwndClient;
static CHAR szAppClass[] = "MoveTarg";
QMSG    qmsg;
ULONG ctlData = FCF_TITLEBAR | FCF_SYSMENU | FCF_SIZEBORDER
                | FCF_MINMAX | FCF_TASKLIST | FCF_MENU
                | FCF_SHELLPOSITION | FCF_ACCELTABLE;

hab = WinInitialize(NULL);
hmq = WinCreateMsgQueue(hab, 0);
WinRegisterClass(hab, szAppClass,
                 AppWindowFunc, CS_SIZEREDRAW, 0);

hwndFrame = WinCreateStdWindow(
                                HWND_DESKTOP,
                                WS_VISIBLE,
                                &ctlData,
                                szAppClass,
                                NULL,
                                0L,
                                NULL,
                                0,
                                &hwndClient);
```

```
hptr = WinLoadPointer(HWND_DESKTOP, NULL, ID_POINTER);

while(WinGetMsg(hab, &qmsg, NULL, 0, 0))
            WinDispatchMsg(hab, &qmsg);
WinDestroyWindow(hwndFrame);
WinDestroyMsgQueue(hmq);
return(0);
}


MRESULT EXPENTRY AppWindowFunc(hwnd, msg, mp1,mp2)
HWND hwnd;
USHORT msg;
MPARAM mp1, mp2;
{

HPS     hps;
RECTL   rcl;
POINTERINFO ptr;
static CHAR szText[] = "Watch the Pointer Change Shape!";

switch(msg)
  {
    case WM_MOUSEMOVE:
        WinSetPointer(HWND_DESKTOP,hptr);
        WinQueryPointerInfo(hptr, &ptr);
        DosBeep(100+ptr.xHotSpot, ptr.xHotSpot);
        DosBeep(400+ptr.yHotSpot, ptr.yHotSpot);
        break;

    case WM_PAINT:
        hps = WinBeginPaint(hwnd, NULL, NULL);
        WinQueryWindowRect(hwnd, &rcl);

        WinDrawText(hps, -1, szText, &rcl,
                    CLR_NEUTRAL, CLR_BACKGROUND,
                    DT_CENTER | DT_VCENTER
                    | DT_ERASERECT);

        WinEndPaint(hps);
        return 0 ;

    default:
        return(WinDefWindowProc(hwnd, msg, mp1, mp2));
  }

return(0L);
}
```

This program changes the system arrow pointer to a custom pointer when the application window has the input focus. The program also calls the WinQueryPointerInfo function to obtain the current x and y coordinates of the pointer's hotspot. It then uses these coordinates in two calls to DosBeep to produce sound effects that last as long as the pointer remains in the application window.

More Pointer Functions

The Presentation Manager supports several functions that give you ready-made flexibility in handling pointers. In combination with these functions, the Presentation Manager also makes available the POINTERINFO structure. As demonstrated in the previous example, you can use Win-QueryPointerInfo to reference the POINTERINFO structure. Here's how POINTERINFO is defined:

```
typedef struct _POINTERINFO {
        BOOL   fPointer;
        SHORT  xHotSpot;
        SHORT  yHotSpot;
        HBITMAP hbmPointer;
} POINTERINFO;
```

As you have seen, the *xHotSpot* and *yHotSpot* fields define the pointer's hotspot. The *fPointer* field specifies the size of the pointer. You can choose between standard pointer size (TRUE) and system icon size (FALSE). When necessary, the bitmap associated with the pointer is stretched to accommodate the specified pointer size. The last field, *hbmPointer*, identifies a bitmap that you want to associate with the pointer.

The *hbmPointer* is used primarily by the WinCreatePointer function. The sole purpose of WinCreatePointer is to create a pointer from an icon-sized bitmap. You can use these larger pointers in conjunction with icons located in control windows as previously described. A typical call to WinCreatePointer looks like this:

```
hptr = WinCreatePointer(HWND_DESKTOP, hbmPointer,
             fPointer, xHotSpot, yHotSpot);
```

The return value from WinCreatePointer is the handle of the new pointer. Note that the first argument must be HWND_DESKTOP or the handle to the desktop window.

Another handy pointer function is WinShowPointer, which shows or hides a pointer. WinShowPointer takes two arguments: HWND_DESKTOP and *fShow*. The latter represents the SV_MOUSEPRESENT system value. The following code sets the visibility state of the pointer, based on SV_MOUSEPRESENT.

```
fShow = WinQuerySysValue(HWND_DESKTOP, SV_MOUSEPRESENT);
fSuccess = WinShowPointer(HWND_DESKTOP, fShow);
```

When *fShow* equals one (that is, when a mouse is present), WinShowPointer makes the pointer visible. A zero value indicates that no mouse is present.

SHOW FUNCTIONS

The WinShowPointer function is one of four functions (of type BOOL) that show or hide a given component in the Presentation Manager. Here is the complete set:

> WinShowCursor(HWND hwnd, BOOL fShow)
> WinShowPointer(HWND hwndDesktop, BOOL fShow)
> WinShowTrackRect(HWND hwnd, BOOL fShow)
> WinShowWindow(HWND hwnd, BOOL fShow)

Pointer Messages

Melding the use of pointers, icons, and child control windows can be a powerful feature in an application. The Presentation Manager conveniently provides two messages to assist you in associating unique pointers with child control windows. These messages are WM_CONTROLPOINTER and WM_HITTEST.

The WM_CONTROLPOINTER message is sent to the owner of the child control window whenever the pointer passes over the child control window. WM_CONTROLPOINTER contains a handle (of type HPOINTER) to the current pointer in its *mp2* parameter. The handle to the corresponding window is contained in *mp1*. The following code extracts the pointer handle from the WM_CONTROLPOINTER message, then resets the pointer.

```
case WM_CONTROLPOINTER:
        hptr = PVOIDFROMMP(mp2);
        if(hptr != new_hptr)
                WinSetPointer(HWND_DESKTOP, new_hptr);
        break;
```

After you extract the pointer handle, the simplest way to reset the pointer is by calling WinSetPointer. Alternatively, you can post a modified WM_CONTROLPOINTER message. This method, however, requires more conditional logic.

You will find the WM_HITTEST message handy when you use the Win-PeekMsg and WinGetMsg functions. The WM_HITTEST message precedes all messages in the queue that are related to the pointer.

The primary purpose of WM_HITTEST is to allow you to determine the target window of a given mouse message. If the WM_HITTEST determines the target window is valid, you can extract the pointer coordinates from the *mp1* parameter in WM_HITTEST.

You can respond to a WM_HITTEST message by sending it a return value. Table 13-5 lists the valid returns values for WM_HITTEST.

Table 13-5: WM_HITTEST Return Values

IDENTIFIER	VALUE	DESCRIPTION
HT_NORMAL	0	Indicates that a message should be processed as normal, unless the message is WM_BUTTON1DOWN or WM_MOUSEMOVE. These messages should be posted to the window.
HT_TRANSPARENT	(-1)	Indicates that hit testing should continue on windows beneath the current window.
HT_DISCARD	(-2)	Indicates the message should be discarded.
HT_ERROR	(-3)	Identical to HT_DISCARD, unless a button-down message is in the queue. If this is the case, an alarm sounds.

The System Pointer

The WinQuerySystemPointer function allows you to obtain a handle to one of several system pointers. You can access these pointers for your own use, but must ensure that no other thread is currently using the pointer you want to access. If you do attempt to use a system pointer currently in use by another thread, unpredictable results can occur. Here's the definition for WinQuerySystemPointer:

```
HPOINTER WinQuerySysPointer(hwndDesktop, iptr, fLoad)
HWND hwndDesktop;
SHORT iptr;
BOOL fLoad;
```

The first argument is simply the handle to the desktop window. You can specify a specific variable or HWND_DESKTOP. The second and third arguments are the keys to this function. Particularly, the third argument, *fLoad*, which lets you create a copy of the system pointer if you specify TRUE; or merely obtain a handle to the current version of this pointer if you specify FALSE. What kind of system pointer do you want to use? The second argument takes care of this for you: *iptr* specifies one of 14 system pointers available. Table 13-6 lists and defines the system identifiers (prefixed with SPTR) associated with the system pointers.

Table 13-6: System Pointers

IDENTIFIER	VALUE	DESCRIPTION
SPTR_ARROW	1	Arrow pointer.
SPTR_TEXT	2	I-beam pointer.
SPTR_WAIT	3	Hourglass pointer.
SPTR_SIZE	4	Size pointer.
SPTR_MOVE	5	Move pointer.
SPTR_SIZENWSE	6	Downward double-headed arrow.
SPTR_SIZENESW	7	Upward double-headed arrow.

(continued)

Table 13-6: Continued

IDENTIFIER	VALUE	DESCRIPTION
SPTR_SIZEWE	8	Horizontal double-headed arrow
SPTR_SIZENS	9	Vertical double-headed arrow
SPTR_APPICON	10	Standard application icon
SPTR_HANDICON	11	Hand icon
SPTR_QUESICON	12	Question mark icon
SPTR_BANGICON	13	Exclamation mark icon
SPTR_NOTEICON	14	Note icon

The Tracking Rectangle

The WinTrackRect function draws a tracking rectangle. Interestingly, the internal frame control procedure uses the WinTrackRect function itself to manage window resizing. WinTrackRect provides a general method of mouse tracking by illuminating the current position via the tracking rectangle outline — allowing the user to position the entire rectangle or size a specific side or corner.

Only one tracking rectangle can be used at any given time. The rectangle that results from the user's manipulation is returned in the *ti* argument of the WinTrackRect, which is defined as follows:

```
BOOL WinTrackRect(hwnd, hps, pti)
HWND hwnd;
HPS hps;
PTRACKINFO pti;
```

The *hwnd* argument identifies the window where you want the tracking to occur. When *hwnd* is the desktop window or HWND_DESKTOP, tracking occurs over the entire screen. The *hps* argument identifies the presentation space. Setting the *hps* argument to NULL indicates that *hwnd* defines the presentation space associated with the tracking activity. The third and critical argument, *pti*, is a pointer to the TRACKINFO structure, which is defined as follows:

```
typedef struct _TRACKINFO {
        SHORT cxBorder;
        SHORT cyBorder;
        SHORT cxGrid;
        SHORT cyGrid;
        SHORT cxKeyboard;
        SHORT cyKeyboard;
        RECTL rclTrack;
        RECTL rclBoundary;
        POINTL ptlMinTrackSize;
        POINTL ptlMaxTrackSize;
        USHORT fs;
        USHORT cxLeft;
        USHORT cyBottom;
        USHORT cxRight;
        USHORT cyTop;
} TRACKINFO;
```

The first two fields in TRACKINFO — *cxBorder* and *cyBorder* — specify the border width and height. The next two fields, *cxGrid* and *cyGrid*, specify the horizontal and vertical bounds of the tracking movements. The next two fields, *cxKeyboard* and *cyKeyboard*, specify the position as indicated by certain keys. Table 13-7 lists the associated keys.

Table 13-7: Tracking Rectangle Key Values

KEY	DESCRIPTION
Enter	Accepts the new tracking position or tracking size.
Left-arrow	Moves the tracking rectangle, along with the mouse pointer, to the left of the previously obtained current position.
Up-arrow	Moves the tracking rectangle, along with the mouse pointer, up relative to the previously obtained current position.
Right-arrow	Moves the tracking rectangle, along with the mouse pointer, to the right of the previously obtained current position.
Up-arrow	Moves the tracking rectangle, along with the mouse pointer, down relative to the previously obtained current position.
Esc	Cancels the current operation and causes the value of the tracking rectangle to be undefined.

The next field in the TRACKINFO structure specifies the start of the tracking rectangle. If *rclTrack* is modified while the rectangle is being tracked, it indicates that tracking is complete. The next argument, *rclBoundary,* specifies an absolute boundary that the tracking rectangle cannot leave. The next two fields, *ptlMinTrackSize* and *ptlMaxTrackSize,* specify the minimum and maximum tracking size, respectively. The eleventh field, *fs*, specifies various tracking options. These options are described in Table 13-8.

Table 13-8: Tracking Options

KEY	BIT	DESCRIPTION
TF_LEFT	0x0001	Tracks the left side of the rectangle.
TF_TOP	0x0002	Tracks the top side of the rectangle.
TF_RIGHT	0x0004	Tracks the right side of the rectangle.
TF_BOTTOM	0x0008	Tracks the bottom side of the rectangle.
TF_MOVE	0x000F	Tracks all sides of the rectangle.
TF_POINTERPOS	0x0010	If no other options are specified, the pointer is centered in the rectangle. If one of the other positioning options are specified, the pointer is centered along the specified side of the rectangle.
TF_GRID	0x0020	Restricts tracking to the grid defined by the *cxGrid* and *cyGrid* arguments.
TF_STANDARD	0x0040	Specifies that the width, height, grid width, and grid height are multiples of border width and border height.
TF_ALINBOUNDARY	0x0080	Restricts tracking to the bounding rectangle.
TF_ALINBOUNDARY	0x0200	Restricts tracking to the opposite edge of the bounding rectangle.

The final four fields in TRACKINFO specify the rectangle's relationship to the bounding rectangle. These fields are only used when the TF_PARTINBOUNDARY option is set for the *fs* field. The *cxLeft* field specifies the amount that the rectangle can move beyond the left side of the bounding rectangle. The field *cyBottom* specifies the amount that the rectangle can move beyond the bottom of bounding rectangle. The field *cxRight* specifies the amount the rectangle can move beyond the right side of the bounding rectangle. The *cyTop* field specifies the amount the rectangle can move beyond the top of the bounding rectangle.

CHAPTER 14

HOOKS AND HELP

The Presentation Manager provides an alternative message processing method that lets you bypass both the system and application message queues. The method, called hook processing, comprises a built-in scheme of filtering messages and re-routing them to programmer-defined functions. Within this scheme, you have the choice of using queue hooks, which filter messages for the current application; or system hooks, which filter messages for multiple applications. Additionally, with system hooks, you can build comprehensive hook chains that pass messages from application to application.

Hooks serve various purposes. You can use them to debug a program by placing them at critical points in your code and having an associated routine display relevant information on the progress of the program. You can also use them to monitor various application events such as keyboard input, window movement, the presence of dialog boxes, and whether a message has been removed from the system message queue. You can even use them to record all the keystrokes associated with an entire session (such as during a tutorial) and then playback the keystrokes.

By using the various default hooks, you can process hook-related messages for application-specific or system-wide purposes. For example, you can install a hook to handle all WM_HELP messages and then return control to the main message loop when the message has been appropriately processed. At the other extreme, you can seize a message before it enters the main message loop, handle it in a specially designed hook function, and then redirect program control to the message queue. At this point, you have the option of processing the message, or rejecting it in favor of the next message in the queue.

In terms of the interface, hooks can be used as device monitors to create keyboard macros or activate pop-up utilities to supplement some other aspect of an application. While this type of implementation could possibly be contrary to a tenet or two in the *Application Style Guide,* it is a snappy way to provide the user with unrelated, but often-used utilities such as a calculator or calendar. Additionally, a hook can be used to invoke a pop-up utility stored in dynamic link library, meaning you can use hooks to share the same utilities between applications.

The most significant use of hooks is to incorporate an extensive, yet unobtrusive, help system in an application. If you have used the *Dialog Box Editor* or the system *File Manager*, you are likely familiar with the Presentation Manager's help windows. The primary method of building such a help system is through hooks. As with pop-up utilities, a help system can be either local to an application or shared by several applications. In both cases, you use a hook chain to administer the help system. Here's a summary of the two types of hook chains:

- Queue Chain — A local chain, pertaining only to the thread that controls the message queue identified when installing the hook.

- System Chain — A shared chain, pertaining to all active Presentation Manager applications.

Experimenting with queue hooks is a good way to get the flavor of the hook system. In a queue hook, you can place any associated routines directly in the application. System hooks, however, require that you place the associated routines in a dynamic link library.

Installing A Hook

From a coding viewpoint, installing a hook is similar to creating a message queue. Once installed, a hook automatically calls a function that you have previously associated with this hook.

The arguments for the associated function are predetermined and obtained internally; you supply the function definition as you do with the function for the client window. Instead of using the PFNWP data type as the client window function does, hooks use the PFN data type. Arguments for each hook function vary depending on the type of hook.

Installing a hook is simple. Typically, you call the WinSetHook function as part of an application's initialization. The call must not precede the call to WinCreateMsgQueue, because you must supply WinSetHook with a handle to a message queue. If you want, you can call WinSetHook immediately after WinCreateMsgQueue. Here's the definition for WinSetHook:

```
BOOL WinSetHook(hab, hmq, iHook, pfnHook, hmod)
HAB hab;
HMQ hmq;
SHORT iHook;
PFN pfnHook;
HMODULE hmod;
```

The *hab* and *hmq* arguments represent anchor block and queue handles, respectively. To set *hmq* to the queue associated with the current thread, you can specify the HMQ_CURRENT identifier. Otherwise, if you have not tracked the queue handle associated with a given window, you should call WinQueryWindowULong to obtain the queue handle. If you want to create a system hook, you must set *hmq* to NULL. The *iHook* argument specifies the type of hook that you want to install. The Presentation Manager provides several hook types as described in Table 14-1.

Table 14-1: Hook Type Identifiers

IDENTIFIER	VALUE	DESCRIPTION
HK_SENDMSG	0	Calls the hook function with each occurrence of WinSendMsg or WinDispatchMsg.
HK_INPUT	1	Calls the hook function when a message is removed from the queue.
HK_MSGFILTER	2	Called within a system mode loop during system-assisted events such as the display of a dialog box.
HK_JOURNALRECORD	3	Called after the Presentation Manager receives keyboard or mouse input.
HK_JOURNALPLAYBACK	4	Called when the message recorded by HK_JOURNALRECORD is ready.
HK_HELP	5	Called routinely by WinDefWindowProc as a result of a help request.

The final two arguments to WinSetHook are clear cut: *pfnHook* is the name of the function you want to associate with the hook; and *hmod* specifies the module that contains the hook function. For queue-based hooks, set *hmod* to NULL if the hook function is contained in the application's .EXE file. Here is a typical call to WinSetHook:

```
WinSetHook(hAB, HMQ_CURRENT, HK_HELP, (PFN)HelpHook, NULL);
```

Note the shorthand method of specifying the address of the HelpHook function set by this example. Casting the hook function name to type PFN is the most convenient way of providing WiSetHook the associated address. Alternatively, you could declare a variable of type PFN and set it to the function name, before calling WinSetHook.

Other Hook Functions

The Presentation Manager has two other functions designed for use with hooks and hook chains. These are the WinReleaseHook function, which frees an application's hook from its associated chain; and the Win-CallMsgFilter function, which calls a hook function to process system window messages. The WinReleaseHook function requires little explanation: it takes the same arguments as WinSetHook. You can call Win-ReleaseHook whenever you need to release the current hook from the hook chain.

The WinCallMsgFilter function is more interesting. You can use it from any practical location within an application to filter system messages that control window movement, resizing, scrollbars, and menus. Here's how it is defined:

```
BOOL WinCallMsgFilter(hab, pqmsg, msgf)
HAB hab;
PQMSG pqmsg;
SHORT msgf;
```

As usual, *hab* specifies the anchor block handle. More distinctively, the *pqmsg* argument makes WinCallMsgFilter one of the few functions in the Presentation Manager that actually point to the message queue structure. In essence, this gives you arbitrary control to transfer message processing outside the main message loop. One result of this is you cannot use Win-

CallMsgFilter to call all of the various hooks. Instead, you are limited to calling hooks initiated by HK_MSGFILTER, which filters messages from inside the system-mode loop. (Note that the WM_QUIT message is passed to HK_MSGFILTER when it occurs during the system-mode loop.)

The final argument to WinCallMsgFilter specifies the message filter code, which can be an application specific value, or one of the system MSGF identifiers. The MSGF values, which correspond to the context in which the hook is called, are described in Table 14-2.

Table 14-2: System-Defined Message Code Identifiers

IDENTIFIER	VALUE	DESCRIPTION
MSGF_DIALOGBOX	1	Handles dialog box messages.
MSGF_MESSAGEBOX	2	Handles message box messages.
MSGF_TRACK	8	Handles system messages for menus, window movement, window sizing, and scrollbars. Additionally, this hook causes the *rclTrack* and *fs* fields of the TRACKINFO structure to be updated.

The return value from WinCallMsgFilter is important. It reflects the status of the function that processes the HK_MSGFILTER hook. A typical call to WinCallMsgFilter looks like this:

```
if(WinCallMsgFilter(hab, pqmsg, MSGF_DIALOGBOX))
    return(TRUE);
```

If WinCallMsgFilter returns TRUE, the hook has successfully processed the message, meaning it should not be processed in the main message loop of the application window function. Conversely, if it returns FALSE, the main message loop should process the message.

Hook Processing

After installation, processing a hook is a matter of writing a function to perform the filter operations that you require. Each HK type that initiates a hook has its own specific function definition. As with the function definition for the main window application, you cannot modify the function definition for a hook. To supply a hook function with additional values, you must use global variables.

Four of the six types of hooks reference the QMSG structure. Inside the hook function, you can obtain the current message value and its parameters by directly referencing QMSG. Refer to Chapter 5 for complete information on QMSG. For convenience, here's the definition for QMSG:

```
typedef struct _QMSG {
            HWND  hwnd;
            USHORT msg;
            MPARAM mp1;
            MPARAM mp2;
            ULONG time;
            POINTL ptl;
} QMSG;
```

Because a hook function might have to coexist in a hook chain, ensure that your hook functions service the chain (even though you have no intention of creating a chain yourself). Typically, control flow passes from the first hook function in a chain to the next function in the chain until either a TRUE value is returned, or no more functions exist in the chain.

To coexist in the hook chain, the hook function merely needs to return a TRUE value upon successful completion. Otherwise, it must return a FALSE value. The Presentation Manager monitors the return values from the hook chain and passes control to subsequent hooks in the chain whenever a FALSE value is returned. For any given hook chain, control passes from function to function based on the order in which the hooks were installed.

The Input Hook

The input hook (initiated by the HK_INPUT identifier) intercepts messages immediately after they emerge from the application message queue. The interception occurs before either the WinPeekMsg or WinGetMsg functions obtain the value of the message.

The input hook is highly adaptable and can be used to create keyboard macros and monitors for pop-up utilities. The Presentation Manager requires that you define the input hook function in the following manner:

```
BOOL EXPENTRY InputHook(hab, pqmsg, fs)
HAB hab;
PQMSG qmsg;
USHORT fs;
```

You can specify any name you like for the input hook function, but In-putHook is the name suggested by Microsoft. The input hook function takes *hab* as its first argument, *qmsg* as its second argument, and one of two system-defined options as its third argument. The options are:

- PM_NOREMOVE — Indicates that the message has not been re-moved from the queue. The associated bit value is 0x0000.

- PM_REMOVE — Indicates that the message has been removed from the queue. The associated bit value is 0x0001.

Perhaps the most suggestive use of the input hook function is to estab-lish a keyboard monitor. This is possible because the mouse and keyboard device drivers each call an entry point in the PMDD.SYS device driver. The call to the entry point occurs at the time of the associated interrupt and informs the PMDD.SYS driver that an event has occurred. In re-sponse, the PMDD.SYS driver places the event on the system message queue. The product is a WM_CHAR message or a mouse messages.

Before the message even reaches the queue, you can trap it with the HK_INPUT hook, thereby preventing a message from reaching the client window procedure — or other window queue, depending on the type of hook you have installed. As stated, you can set up a system-wide hook, or one specifically targeted for a given window procedure. The following ex-ample sets up a hook function to respond to a hot key sequence.

```
BOOL EXPENTRY InputHook(hab, pqmsg, fs)
HAB hab;
PQMSG pqmsg;
USHORT fs;
{
    static BOOL fStatus = FALSE;

    if(CHAR3FROMMP(pmsg.mp2 == VK_HOME) && fStatus == TRUE)
      {
        PopupUtility(pqmsg.hwnd, pqmsg.ptl);
```

```
            fStatus = FALSE;
            return(TRUE);
       }

    if(CHAR3FROMMP(pqmsg.mp2) == VK_ALT)
            fStatus = TRUE;
    else
            fStatus = FALSE;

    return(FALSE);
}
```

In the example, the InputHook function tests for the Alt-Home sequence by referencing the *mp2* field of the QMSG structure. Until it finds the sequence, the function continues to return a FALSE value, thereby allowing normal processing of the message. When it does find the Alt-Home sequence, it calls the PopupUtility function. Ultimately, when control returns to the InputHook function, it returns a TRUE value, thereby obviating the need to process the message in the client window's message loop.

The Message Filter Hook

The message filter hook (initiated by the HK_MSGFILTER identifier) lets you monitor several system-controlled events as they occur. Depending on the situation, the message filter hook gives you a way to obtain message and coordinate information on menus, windows, dialog boxes, scrollbars, and message boxes. Recall, too, that you can arbitrarily invoke the message filter using the WinCallMsgFilter function. In general, the message filter hook gives you a way to process messages not accessible through the application's own message loop.

Although apparently redundant with some message based processing, the message filter hooks can be used for debugging and intercepting messages in a system hook chain. The Presentation Manager requires that you define the message hook function in the following manner:

```
BOOL EXPENTRY MsgFilterHook(hab, pqmsg, fs)
HAB hab;
PQMSG pqmsg;
USHORT fs;
```

Again, the function name is that suggested by Microsoft. The *hab* and *pqmsg* arguments reference the anchor block and message queue, respectively. The *fs* argument references one of the MSGF identifiers. The following example intercepts the WM_SIZE message before it can be processed by the client window's message loop.

```
BOOL EXPENTRY MsgFilterHook(hab, pqmsg, fs)
HAB hab;
PQMSG pqmsg;
USHORT fs;
{

    SHORT x, y;

    if(pqmsg.msg == WM_SIZE)
      {
        x = SHORT1FROMMP(pqmsg.mp1);
        y = SHORT2FROMMP(pqmsg.mp2);

        if(!ValidWindowSize(x, y))
          {
            WinMessageBox(HWND_DESKTOP, NULL,
                         "Invalid Window Size Requested!",
                         "Try a different direction.",
                         0, MB_OK | MB_ICONQUESTION
                         | MB_MOVEABLE);
            return(TRUE);
          }
      }

    return(FALSE);
}
```

After intercepting the WM_SIZE message, the example function calls a function to validate the window's pending size. If the size is invalid, a message box appears and informs the user. The MsgFilterHook function then returns a TRUE value, which prevents further processing of the message. Otherwise, a FALSE value is returned and the message is processed normally in the main application window's message loop.

The Send Message Hook

The send message hook (initiated by the HK_SENDMSG identifier) can be used as a safeguard against messages that are not processed in the system queue. That is, messages generated by the WinSendMessage and Win-DispatchMessage functions.

The send message hook is one of the two supported hooks that does not reference the QMSG structure. Instead, it references SMHSTRUCT, a reduced version of the QMSG structure:

```
typedef struct _SMHSTRUCT {
          MPARAM mp2;
          MPARAM mp1;
          USHORT msg;
          HWND  hwnd;
} SMHSTRUCT;
```

As you can see, SMHSTRUCT contains enough information to evaluate those messages not directly processed by the Presentation Manager. In addition to SMHSTRUCT, the definition for the send message hook function references the thread status of the associated message. Here's the definition for the send message function:

```
BOOL EXPENTRY SendMsgHook(hab, smhs, fThread)
HAB hab;
PSMHSTRUCT smhs;
BOOL fThread;
```

The *fThread* argument is TRUE if the message is generated by another thread. It is FALSE if it is generated within the current thread. Unless you merely wanted to safeguard against application-generated messages, you would likely use the send message hook in conjunction with the filter message hook. The following example links the two hooks:

```
BOOL EXPENTRY SendMsgHook(hab, smhs, fThread)
HAB hab;
PSMHSTRUCT smhs;
BOOL fThread;
{

if(smhs.msg == WM_INITDLG)
    {
```

```
            if(WinCallMsgFilter(qmsg, MSGF_DIALOGBOX))
                  return(TRUE);
            else
                  return(FALSE);
      }
  else
      return(FALSE);
  }
```

This example simply tests for the WM_INITDLG message and if it receives it, the WinCallMsgFilter function passes it along to the message filter hook. The SendMsgHook function then returns the value returned to it by WinCallMsgFilter.

The Journal Hooks

The journal hooks give you the capability of recording and replaying keyboard-based messages. They are ideal for recording tutorial sessions in which it is necessary to replay a student's keyboard input.

The recording hook (initiated by the HK_JOURNALRECORD identifier) sends raw WM_CHAR and button messages to the journal record function before these messages can be processed by the system queue or accelerator table. The playback hook (initiated by the HK_JOURNALPLAYBACK identifier) replays the recorded messages at a chronological time that you specify in the record hook function.

The journal hooks are suited to debugging purposes as well as transferring messages to one or more windows in a system hook chain. Both journal functions reference the QMSG structures. Here are the definitions for the two functions:

```
BOOL EXPENTRY JournalRecordHook(hab, pqmsg)
HAB hab;
PQMSG pqmsg;


BOOL EXPENTRY JournalPlaybackHook(hab, pqmsg, fSkip)
HAB hab;
PQMSG qmsg;
BOOL fSkip;
```

The playback time is determined by the *pqmsg.time* field, which you can set to the current system time or any chronological time following the current system time. If *fSkip* in the playback function is FALSE, the function returns the next available message. The function continues to return this message until *fSkip* is TRUE.

In general, handling the WM_CHAR and button messages in a journal hook function is identical to handling these messages elsewhere. The exception occurs when you process mouse double click messages, which are interpreted as single click messages. If you must replay double click messages, you should save and restore the state of the system timing variables and cursor flash rate to avoid timing problems. Note that you cannot call the WinGetMsg and WinPeekMsg functions from a journal hook function.

The Presentation Manager also supplies a journal message to assist you in processing journal hooks. The WM_JOURNALNOTIFY message lets you use the WinQueryQueueStatus and WinGetPhysKeyState functions with journal hook functions. When a journal hook is installed, the Presentation Manager generates a WM_JOURNALNOTIFY message if either the WinQueryQueueStatus or WinGetPhysKeyState function has new data to return.

The *mp1* parameter of WM_JOURNALNOTIFY is of type ULONG and specifies which of the two functions were called. JRN_QUEUESTATUS (0x00000001L) represents the WinQueryQueueStatus function and JRN_PHYSKEYSTATE (0x00000002L) represents the WinGetPhys-KeyState function.

The *mp2* parameter specifies the value for the *mp1* parameter. For JRN_QUEUESTATUS, which is of type ULONG, it merely reports the result of the queue status. For JRN_PHYSKEYSTATE, the low word of *mp2* specifies the virtual key value in the low byte. The high word of *mp2* specifies the physical key state. When the key is depressed, the 0x8000 bit is set. When the key is released, the 0x0001 bit is set.

Getting Help

The Presentation Manager's help interface is one area in which you should acquiesce to the *Application Style Guide*. For the most part, the interface is a good one — and it is quite likely that every Presentation Manager user will already know how to use it. What is more, you can create a common help system for several applications by using the system hook chain.

A user requests help by pressing the F1 key or by clicking on the help box in the titlebar of the main application window. Both actions invoke a help window that contains information on the current topic. This initial window, which can be moved and sized, is often the only help window that the user needs to access. For example, selecting help immediately after starting the *File Manager* utility displays a help window with general program information. Selecting help later — say, after choosing the option to create a directory — displays a help window with information on the selected option. Note that the user cannot click on the titlebar help box when the current selection is a modal dialog box. As a result, you should include a help button within the modal dialog box. The F1 key works with both modal and modeless dialog boxes.

No matter when the user invokes it, the initial help window should always contains pushbuttons to exit the help window, summon a help topics index, and display a window that defines key sequences recognized by the application. These pushbuttons are arranged at the bottom of the window and comprise the *common actions area*. If necessary, the initial help window should also contain a vertical scrollbar. Additionally, the name of the application should appear in the help window's titlebar.

The help index window is an important component of a Presentation Manager help system. Because the index window is a listbox control, you can easily incorporate any number of index topics without burdening your code with cursor tracking logic. Like the initial help window, the index window is moveable and resizable. It also has a common actions area, and in many cases, a vertical scrollbar. Index items are arranged one item per screen line. In extensive applications, it is a good idea to indent subtopics.

In a typical index window, the user can select a topic from the list by double clicking on the topic. Alternatively, the user can press the Enter key or click on the Enter pushbutton. The latter appears with the display of the index window, but appears as the index pushbutton in the initial help window.

The behavior of a help window resembles that of other top-level windows. Because of a help window's narrower functionality, you do not have to build-in quite as many controls. Here are some important facts about help windows:

- The user can move between a help window and any other frame or control window, including the desktop window.

- Help windows are not clipped to the main application window.

- When a user minimizes an application, the help window is removed from the screen as well, but its reappears when the application is restored.

- Standard Z-axis ordering does not apply to help windows.

- The user can obtain help on an application when it is minimized. For this to occur, the minimize icon must have the input focus and the user must press F1.

The Help Hook

The Presentation Manager use the help hook to provide a built-in method of developing comprehensive help systems. Not only does the help hook give you more flexibility than other hooks, it simplifies the code necessary to create a professional help system.

Whenever a help request is generated from any system component such as a menu or message box, the Presentation Manager automatically invokes the help hook function. The way this occurs, however, is more like traditional message processing. Here is the sequence of events:

1. The user requests help via the F1 key, a menu option, a dialog box option, or a message box option.

2. The Presentation Manager receives the help request and generates a WM_HELP message.

3. The WM_HELP message transits the client window's message loop, giving you the opportunity to modify or to divert the message.

4. If the WM_HELP message is not diverted, the default window procedure processes it by invoking the help hook function.

In some cases, such as when you divert the WM_HELP message, you might like to call the help hook function directly. Unlike the other supported hooks, this is possible: you can either call the WinDefWindowProc function and specify WM_HELP as its second argument; or you can call the help hook function by name and supply the proper arguments, which are explained later.

WM_HELP

The Presentation Manager generates a WM_HELP message as a result of the user requesting help. The source of the help request can be a keyboard accelerator, menu, dialog box, or a source specific to an application. All WM_HELP messages enter the application window's message queue. If WM_HELP is not filtered in the application's message loop, or if a help hook is not installed, the Presentation Manager does not process WM_HELP.

The *mp1* and *mp2* parameters of WM_HELP are both USHORT values. The *mp1* parameter contains the ID associated with the source of the WM_HELP message. The *mp2* parameter specifies the control type. Table 14-3 lists the valid identifiers for the *mp2* parameter.

Table 14-3: Help Source Identifiers

IDENTIFIER	VALUE	DESCRIPTION
CMDSRC_OTHER	0	Application specific source. The *mp1* parameter specifies additional control information.
CMDSRC_PUSHBUTTON	1	Pushbutton source. The *mp1* parameter identifies the window that contains the pushbutton.
CMDSRC_MENU	2	Menu source. In this case, the *mp1* parameter identifies the menu item.
CMDSRC_ACCELERATOR	3	Keyboard accelerator source. In this case, the *mp1* parameter contains the accelerator command value.

The Help Hook Function

The help hook function is the most versatile function associated with one of the Presentation Manager's default hooks. When you set the help hook by specifying the HK_HELP identifier in the call to WinSetHook, the Presentation Manager passes all WM_HELP messages to the help hook function. If necessary, you can also call the help hook function directly.

Unlike most other hook functions, the help hook function does not reference the QSMG structure. Instead, it uses a unique set of arguments that, among other things, specify whether a help window should be displayed. Here's the definition of the help hook function:

```
BOOL EXPENTRY HelpHook(hab, usContext, idTopic,
                       idSubTopic, prcRectl)
HAB hab;
USHORT usContext, idTopic, idSubTopic;
PRECTL prcRectl;
```

HelpHook is the name suggested by Microsoft. The *hab* argument, as usual, references the anchor block handle. The *usContext* argument specifies whether the help request originated from a menu, dialog box, message box, or custom source. The remaining arguments to HelpHook vary, depending on the value of context. Table 14-4 lists the different possible values for *idTopic*, *idSubTopic*, and *prcRectl*.

Table 14-4: HelpHook Argument Values

CONTEXT	*idtopic*	*idsubtopic*	*prcrectl*
Menu	Submenu ID	Menu item ID	Bounding rectangle of the selected item.
Dialog Box	Dialog box ID	Control ID	Bounding rectangle of the control.
Message Box	Messagebox ID	Button ID	Bounding rectangle of the control.

If the WM_HELP message originates from a programmer-defined source, *idTopic* specifies the ID of the window that sent the message; *idSubTopic* specifies the ID of the window with the input focus; and *prcRectl* specifies the screen coordinates of the window with the input focus. Note, however, that if *idSubTopic* is NULL, *prcRectl* specifies the window coordinates of the window that sent the message.

The following example sets an HK_HELP initiated hook and includes a HelpHook function. The function contains a message box, but could contain the code necessary to initiate a help system.

```
/* HELP.C (Example program that uses help hook.) */

#define INCL_WIN
#define INCL_GPI
#define INCL_DOS

#include <os2.h>

MRESULT EXPENTRY ClientWndProc(HWND, USHORT, MPARAM, MPARAM);
BOOL EXPENTRY HelpHook(HAB, USHORT, USHORT, USHORT, PRCRECTL)

int main (void)
{


HMQ      hmq;
HWND     hwndFrame, hwndApp;
QMSG     qmsg;
static CHAR szTitleBar[40];
static CHAR szAppClass[13] = "Help Program";
ULONG   ctlData = FCF_STANDARD & ~FCF_MENU & ~FCF_ACCELTABLE;

hab = WinInitialize(0);
hmq = WinCreateMsgQueue(hab, 0);
WinRegisterClass(hab,  szAppClass,
                       ClientWndProc,  CS_SIZEREDRAW, 0);


WinSetHook(hAB, HMQ_CURRENT, HK_HELP, (PFN)HelpHook, NULL);

hwndFrame = WinCreateStdWindow(
                     HWND_DESKTOP,
                     WS_VISIBLE | FS_ICON,
                     &ctlData,
                     szAppClass,
                     NULL,,
                     0L,
                     NULL,
                     ID_RESOURCE,
                     &hwndApp);

while(WinGetMsg(hab, &qmsg, NULL, 0, 0))
        WinDispatchMsg(hab, &qmsg);
```

```
WinDestroyWindow(hwndFrame);
WinDestroyMsgQueue(hmq);
WinTerminate(hab);
return(0);
}

MRESULT EXPENTRY ClientWndProc(hwnd, msg, mp1, mp2)
HWND hwnd;
USHORT msg;
MPARAM mp1, mp2
{

switch (msg)
    {
        case WM_ERASEBACKGROUND:
            return (TRUE);

        case WM_PAINT:
            hps = WinBeginPaint(hwnd, NULL, NULL);
            WinEndPaint(hps);
            break;

        default:
            return(WinDefWindowProc (hwnd, msg, mp1, mp2));
    }

return(0L);
}

BOOL EXPENTRY HelpHook(hAb, Context, idTopic, idSubTopic,
                        prcRectl)
HAB hab;
USHORT usContext, idTopic, idSubTopic;
PRECTL prcRectl;


{
WinMessageBox(HWND_DESKTOP, NULL,
                (PSZ)"Help Window, called from",
                (PSZ)"HelpHook() goes here.",
                0, MB_OK | MB_ICONQUESTION | MB_MOVEABLE);
return(TRUE);
}
```

CHAPTER 15

CLIPBOARD CONTROL

One of the most confounding experiences for a DOS user is data exchange. No matter how foolproof, DOS data exchange methods usually require the user to perform an undue amount of work. Not so in the Presentation Manager, which lets the user move data from one program to another with just a few clicks of the mouse.

The clipboard is central to data exchange in the Presentation Manager. It is a system-defined way of transferring shared memory between applications. In essence, the clipboard acts as a staging area for data that you extract from one application by receiving *cut* or *copied* data, and then relinquishing the data when you *paste* it into another application.

As a rule, data remains in the clipboard until you paste it, or until you extract more data, at which point the Presentation Manager overwrites any data already in the clipboard.

It is your responsibility to incorporate cut, copy, and paste commands in an application. Usually, these are placed in a top-level menu. It is also good practice to use Shift-Delete, Ctrl-Insert, and Shift-Insert as the accelerator keys associated with the cut, copy, and paste commands. These are the accelerators recommended by the Microsoft *Application Style Guide*. Figure 15-1 shows a menu with cut, copy, and paste commands. These commands are available in most applications that use the clipboard.

Cutting or copying a range of data requires the user to highlight a range by dragging the cursor and then invoking the cut or copy command. Pasting data requires the user to enter a new window, place the cursor or pointer at the location where data is to be pasted, and then invoke the paste command.

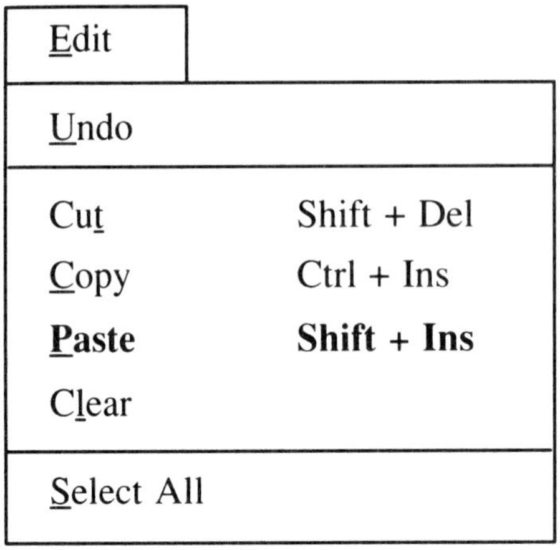

```
┌──────────────┐
│ Edit         │
├──────────────┴─────────────────────┐
│ Undo                               │
├────────────────────────────────────┤
│ Cut              Shift + Del        │
│ Copy             Ctrl + Ins         │
│ Paste            Shift + Ins        │
│ Clear                              │
├────────────────────────────────────┤
│ Select All                         │
└────────────────────────────────────┘
```

Figure 15-1: Edit Menu Found in Many Applications

The clipboard can accept various types of data, including text, bit-mapped images, metafiles, and custom-formatted data. Obviously, to transfer all of these various types of data to the clipboard would be a wasteful process — copying a text string to the clipboard is one thing, but a bitmap image is another. To avoid this overhead, the Presentation Manager lets you reference a data object through the clipboard, then transfer the data only upon demand. This technique is called *delayed rendering*.

Sophisticated applications can use several clipboard formats at the same time. For example, a word processor can support ASCII text, bitmaps, and metafiles. The cycle and rendering impact of rendering data in all these formats can be high, especially for large amounts of data.

Delayed rendering, however, allows the application to make a private copy of the relevant data, tell the clipboard all the formats it can display in it, and then continue. When there is a request for the data, it is sent in the given format at the time of the request.

You can view the contents of the clipboard by using the clipboard viewer functions. These functions open a window and display the contents of the clipboard. You will see how to write such a program using the functions in this chapter.

Setting Up the Clipboard

The first step in setting up the clipboard is opening it. To open the clipboard, call the WinOpenClipbrd function, which takes a handle to the specified anchor block as its only argument.

Only one thread or process can open the clipboard at a given time. The following call opens the clipboard:

```
fSuccess = WinOpenClipbrd(hab);
```

The function returns a TRUE value if the operation was successful; otherwise, it returns a FALSE value. You should also note that if another thread or process has the clipboard open when you call WinOpenClipbrd, the function does not return until the clipboard is closed.

Before you access any additional clipboard functions, you need to set up a memory segment in which to store the data destined for the clipboard. You do this with a call to DosAllocSeg:

```
usCode = DosAllocSeg(length + 1, &sel, SEG_GIVEABLE);
```

The DosAllocSeg function allocates storage for the extracted data, based on *length* (number of bytes), and *sel* (the address of the segment selector). The SEG_GIVEABLE flag indicates that the owner process can release the segment to other processes. To reference the data segment, use the MAKEP macro:

```
pszPaste = MAKEP(sel, 0);
```

Before you actually transfer the data to the clipboard, it's a good idea to ensure that the clipboard is empty. You do this with a call to the WinEmptyClipbrd function:

```
fSuccess = WinEmptyClipbrd(hab);
```

The WinEmptyClipbrd call frees all handles previously associated with the clipboard. The function returns a TRUE value if the operation was successful; otherwise, it returns a FALSE value.

Transferring Data

The Presentation Manager provides one basic function for transferring data to the clipboard. This function is WinSetClipbrdData and it handles both system-formatted data as well as custom-formatted data. As a rule, WinSetClipbrdData should only be invoked as a result of a user-request to cut or copy data.

Using WinSetClipbrdData to move data for reasons internal to an application is not a good idea. At all times, the user should be able to assume that cut or copied data is safe in the clipboard, unless another user-invoked operation overwrites it. In order to transfer data, the WinSetClipbrdData function references the selector that you derive from the DosAllocSeg call. WinSetClipbrd also defines the selector as well as the type of data involved in the transfer. Here's how WinSetClipbrd is defined:

```
BOOL WinSetClipbrdData(hab, ulData, fmt, rgfFmtInfo)
HAB hab;
ULONG ulData;
USHORT fmt, rgfFmtInfo;
```

The first argument is the anchor block handle. The second argument, *ulData*, specifies the data object that is destined for the clipboard. Typically, you set *ulData* to the selector derived from DosAllocSeg. Setting *ulData* to NULL, however, generates a WM_RENDERFMT message, which postpones the actual data transfer process. The next argument, *fmt*, specifies the data type. All available data types are prefixed by CF. Table 15-1 lists the CF data types.

Table 15-1: Clipboard Data Types

IDENTIFIER	VALUE	DESCRIPTION
CF_TEXT	1	Specifies one or more lines of ASCII text. Each line must be terminated by a carriage return and a linefeed. The entire block is NULL-terminated.
CF_BITMAP	2	Specifies a system-formatted bitmap as defined by the bitmap structures.

(continued)

Table 15-1: Continued

IDENTIFIER	VALUE	DESCRIPTION
CF_DSPTEXT	3	Specifies custom-formatted text such as a document file or non-standard ASCII file.
CF_DSPBITMAP	4	Specifies a custom-formatted bitmap.
CF_METAFILE	5	Specifies a Gpi-formatted metafile.
CF_DSPMETAFILE	6	Specifies a custom-formatted metafile.

In addition to the type of clipboard data, the WinSetClipbrdData function specifies the memory model format of the data. This information is contained in the *rgfFmtInfo* argument, which can be one to five constants prefixed with CFI. To supply extended format information, you can OR these constants together. Table 15-2 describes the CFI constants.

Table 15-2: Extended Information for Clipboard Data

IDENTIFIER	BIT	DESCRIPTION
CFI_OWNERFREE	0x0001	Indicates the WinEmptyClipbrd function does not free the supplied handle. It is the application's responsibility to free the data.
CFI_OWNERDISPLAY	0x0002	Indicates the format is drawn by the clipboard owner in the clipboard-viewer window, using the WM_PAINTCLIPBOARD message. The *ulData* argument should be NULL.
CFI_SELECTOR	0x0100	Indicates the supplied handle references a selector plus zero offset to a segment in storage.
CFI_HANDLE	0x0200	Indicates the supplied handle references a bitmap or metafile.

You can combine any number of the CFI constants in order to properly describe custom data formats. For system formats, you need only use the

485

CFI_SELECTOR. This is the minimal allotment. You must specify at least one CFI constant in order for WinSetClipbrdData to process the clipboard data.

After the call to WinSetClipbrdData, ensure that you close the clipboard by calling WinCloseClipbrd. This function, which takes *hab* as its only argument, frees the clipboard so other processes can access it. The following program demonstrates how to place data in the clipboard window:

```
#define INCL_PM
#define INCL_GPI
#define INCL_DOS
#include <os2.h>

VOID GetMenuItem(HWND, USHORT);

CHAR   szClipMsg[256] = "";
HWND   hwndEdit;

int main (void)
{

HMQ     hmq;
HWND    hwndFrame, hwndClient;
QMSG    qmsg;
static CHAR szTitleBar[40];
static CHAR szClass[] = "clipbrd1";
ULONG   ctlData = FCF_STANDARD
                    & ~FCF_MENU & ~FCF_ACCELTABLE;


hab = WinInitialize(0);
hmq = WinCreateMsgQueue(hab, 0);

WinLoadString(hab, NULL, ID_TITLE, sizeof szTitleBar,
              szTitleBar);

WinRegisterClass(hab, szClass,
                 ClientWndProc, CS_SIZEREDRAW, 0);


hwndFrame = WinCreateStdWindow(
                 HWND_DESKTOP,
                 WS_VISIBLE | FS_ICON,
                 &ctlData,
                 szClass,
```

```
                         NULL,
                         0L,
                         NULL,
                         ID_RESOURCE,
                         &hwndClient);
}

MRESULT EXPENTRY MainAppFunc(hwnd, msg, mp1, mp2)
HWND hwnd;
USHORT msg;
MPARAM mp1, mp2;
{

HPS     hps;
RECTL   rcl;
FONTMETRICS fm;
USHORT  cxChar,cyChar;

switch (msg)
    {
        case WM_SIZE:
            WinQueryWindowrcl(hwndFrame,&rcl);

            hwndEdit = WinCreateWindow(hwndClient,
                        WC_ENTRYFIELD,
                        NULL,
                        WS_VISIBLE | ES_AUTOSCROLL
                            | ES_MARGIN,
                        5 * cxChar,
                        ((rcl.yTop - rcl.yBottom)
                        / 2) - cyChar,
                        cxChar * 27,
                        cyChar,
                        hwndClient,
                        HWND_TOP,
                        WID_EDIT,
                        NULL,
                        NULL);

            WinSetFocus(HWND_DESKTOP,hwndEdit);
            break;

        case WM_CREATE:
            hps = WinGetPS(hwnd);

            GpiQueryFontMetrics(hps,
                        (ULONG)sizeof(FONTMETRICS), &fm);
```

```
                WinReleasePS(hps);
                cxChar = fm.lAveCharWidth;
                cyChar = fm.lMaxBaselineExt - fm.lMaxDescender;
                break;

        case WM_PAINT:
                hps = WinBeginPaint(hwnd,NULL,&rcl);
                WinFillrcl(hps,&rcl,CLR_WHITE);
                WinEndPaint(hps);
                break;

        case WM_COMMAND:
                GetMenuItem(hwnd,LOUSHORT (mp1));
                break;

        default:
                return( WinDefWindowProc( hwnd, msg, mp1, mp2 ) );
    }

return(0L);
}

VOID GetMenuItem(hwnd, usMenuID)
HWND hwnd;
USHORT usMenuID;
{

SEL     sel;
PSZ     pszDest,pszSrc;
BOOL    fSuccess;
USHORT usSuccess, usLen;

switch (usMenuID)
    {
        case IDM_COPY:
                if(WinOpenClipbrd(hab))
                    {
                        usLen = WinQueryWindowText (
                                hwndEdit,80,szClipMsg);
                        usSuccess =DosAllocSeg(usLen + 1,
                                &sel,  SEG_GIVEABLE);
                        pszDest = MAKEP(sel,0);
                        pszSrc = &szClipMsg[0];
                        while (*pszDest++ = *pszSrc++);
                        WinEmptyClipbrd(hab);
                        fSuccess = WinSetClipbrdData(hab,
```

```
                            (ULONG)sel, CF_TEXT,
                              CFI_SELECTOR);
                    WinCloseClipbrd(hab);
            }
        break;

    case IDM_QUIT:
        WinPostMsg(hwnd,WM_CLOSE,0L,0L);
        break;

    default:
        break;

    }
}
```

Viewing The Clipboard

How you design your clipboard window depends on its role in your application. In most cases, there is little reason to deprive a clipboard window of frame window capabilities, especially for text applications. On the other hand, you might want to fix the size and position of the clipboard and therefore would specify a limited frame style.

The only limits on the number of clipboards that can exist at the same time are those imposed by system resources. Because of the likelihood of multiple clipboards, an application must not monopolize clipboard data. Instead, an application should work in concert with the clipboard viewer chain. In general, this means any clipboard messages received by one clipboard window should be passed along to the next clipboard window. Note that even though multiple clipboard windows can exist, the same anchor block handle is used to reference each clipboard.

In order to display data in a clipboard window, the window must receive the WM_DRAWCLIPBOARD message with both *mp1* and *mp2* set to 0L. The Presentation Manager generates WM_DRAWCLIPBOARD whenever the contents of the clipboard change. Thus, if your clipboard window is constantly visible, its contents are automatically updated. If the visibility is in question, the controlling process must generate the WM_DRAW-CLIPBOARD message. This is accomplished by calling WinSendMsg as in the following example:

```
WinSendMsg(hwnd, WM_DRAWCLIPBOARD, (MPARAM)0L, (MPARAM)0L);
```

Recall that WinSendMsg does not return until the associated message has been processed. Because of this, you can place the call to WinSendMsg in the WM_PAINT message block. The following WM_PAINT message block is a typical way of sending a WM_DRAWCLIPBOARD message.

```
case WM_PAINT:
        hps = WinBeginPaint(hwnd,NULL,&rcl);
        WinFillrcl(hps,&rcl,CLR_WHITE);
        WinSendMsg(hwnd,WM_DRAWCLIPBOARD,
                      (MPARAM)0L, (MPARAM)0L);
        WinEndPaint(hps);
        return(0L);
```

After ensuring that the **WM_DRAWCLIPBOARD** message is generated, you can begin processing the message. This involves opening the clipboard, querying its contents, and getting a valid selector if the clipboard contains data. To open the clipboard, you use WinOpenClipbrd as you did for placing data in the clipboard. To query the clipboard, you use the WinQueryClipbrdData function as in the following call:

```
hwndClip = WinQueryClipbrdData(hab, fmt);
```

WinQueryClipbrdData returns a handle to clipboard data in the format specified by *fmt*. If *fmt* does not match the format of the clipboard data, WinQueryClipbrdData returns NULL. A more efficient way of calling WinQueryClipbrdData is to include the call in a test and specify a CF data format. The following fragment, which assumes that the memory supplied to the clipboard is giveable, demonstrates this.

```
if(!(hData = (SEL)WinQueryClipbrdData(HABX, CF_TEXT)))
    {
        WinCloseClipbrd(HABX);
        return(FALSE);
    }

lpchClip = MAKEP((SEL)hData, 0);
```

At this point, the only additional processing required is to display the data in the clipboard window. For text data, you can use a Gpi character function, or for less significant needs, WinDrawText. Similarly, you can

use Gpi bitmap functions or WinDrawBitmap. For metafiles, you must use
the metafile functions. The following program example displays text after
it has been copied to the clipboard.

```
#define INCL_PM
#define INCL_DOS
#include <os2.h>


int main (void)
{

HMQ     hmq;
HWND    hwndFrame, hwndClient;
QMSG    qmsg;
static CHAR szTitleBar[40];
ULONG   ctlData = FCF_STANDARD & ~FCF_MENU & ~FCF_ACCELTABLE;
static CHAR szClass[] = "clipbrd2";

hab = WinInitialize(0);
hmq = WinCreateMsgQueue(hab, 0);

WinLoadString(hab, NULL, ID_TITLE, sizeof szTitleBar,
            szTitleBar);

WinRegisterClass(hab, szClass,
                    ClientWndProc,CS_SIZEREDRAW, 0);

hwndFrame = WinCreateStdWindow(
                    HWND_DESKTOP,
                    WS_VISIBLE | FS_ICON,
                    &ctlData,
                    szClass,
                    NULL,
                    0L,
                    NULL,
                    ID_RESOURCE,
                    &hwndClient);

while (WinGetMsg (hab, &qmsg, NULL, 0, 0))
            WinDispatchMsg (hab, &qmsg);

WinDestroyWindow(hwndFrame);
WinDestroyMsgQueue(hmq);
WinTerminate(hab);
return(0);
}
```

```
MRESULT EXPENTRY MainAppFunc(hwnd, msg, mp1, mp2)
HWND hwnd;
USHORT msg;
MPARAM mp1, mp2;
{

HPS hps;
RECTL rcl;
HBITMAP hbitmap;
ULONG hText;
PSZ pszText;
POINTL ptlDest;

switch (msg)
    {
        case WM_PAINT:
            hps = WinBeginPaint(hwnd, NULL, &rcl);
            WinFillrcl(hps, &rcl, CLR_WHITE);

            WinSendMsg(hwnd, WM_DRAWCLIPBOARD,
                    (MPARAM)0L, (MPARAM)0L);

            WinEndPaint(hps);
            return(0L);

        case WM_DRAWCLIPBOARD:
            if(!WinOpenClipbrd(hab))
                return(0L);

            if(hText = WinQueryClipbrdData(hab, CF_TEXT))
                {
                    pszText = MAKEP((SEL)hText, 0);
                    hps = WinGetPS(hwnd);
                    WinQueryWindowrcl(hwnd, &rcl);

                    WinDrawText(hps, 0xFFFF, pszText, &rcl,
                            CLR_BLACK, CLR_WHITE,
                            DT_CENTER | DT_VCENTER
                            | DT_ERASErcl);

                    WinValidatercl(hwnd, NULL, FALSE);
                    WinReleasePS(hps);
                    WinCloseClipbrd(hab);

                    return(0L);
                }
```

```
            WinCloseClipbrd(hab);
            return(0L);

        default:
            return(WinDefWindowProc(hwnd, msg, mp1, mp2));

    }
    return(0L);
}
```

This program provides a succinct way of displaying clipboard data. It works fine as an example, but it would be unacceptable in a real Presentation Manager environment. Its major shortcoming is it does not test whether another clipboard window needs to receive the WM_DRAWCLIPBOARD message. In other words, it does not service the clipboard viewer chain. The most straightforward way to correct this is by querying the clipboard viewer with the WinQueryClipboardViewer function. The following call returns a handle to the current clipboard window:

```
hwndNextClip = WinQueryClipbrdViewer(hab, fLock);
```

Although WinQueryClipbrdViewer returns the handle to the current clipboard window, the program making the call will likely become the current clipboard window. Hence the name, *hwndNextClip*. In keeping with this logic, you should call WinQueryClipbrdViewer before calling any other clipboard functions — thereby maintaining the correct perspective on the current clipboard window. A good place for the call is in **main()**.

Subsequently, as one of the last actions in your WM_DRAWCLIPBOARD message block, you must send *hwndNextClip* a WM_DRAWCLIPBOARD message. If no other clipboard windows exist in the viewer chain, the WinQueryClipbrdViewer function returns a NULL value.

Another way to tackle the viewer chain is by letting all other clipboard windows in the chain process WM_DRAWCLIPBOARD before the current application. This method requires that you test for previously existing clipboard windows as your first action in the WM_DRAWCLIPBOARD message block. The following example accomplishes this:

```
case WM_DRAWCLIPBOARD:
        if(hwndPrevClip = WinQueryClipbrdViewer(hab, fLock))
```

```
        WinSendMsg(hwndClip, WM_DRAWCLIPBOARD,
                            (MPARAM)0L, (MPARAM)0L);
    WinSetClipbrdViewer(hab, hwnd);
    .
    .
    .
    break;
```

In either of the previous approaches, you ultimately call Win-SetClipbrdViewer. This function passes full control of the clipboard viewer chain to the current application. Once this step is achieved, your application is fully integrated within the chain. To remove the current application from the chain, you merely work backward by resetting the clipboard viewer to the next or previous clipboard window in the chain as shown in the following call:

```
    WinSetClipbrdViewer(hab, hwndPrevClip);
```

In most cases, you should test whether *hwndPrevClip* or any other clipboard viewer still exists before assigning it the status of current clipboard viewer. Ensure, however, that you do reset the chain, either at the end of the **WM_DRAWCLIPBOARD** message block or in the **WM_DESTROY** message block.

Delayed Rendering

Displaying bitmaps and metafiles every time an application transfers one to the clipboard can take its toll on system resources. Because of this, the Presentation Manager offers a technique called delayed rendering, which lets you postpone displaying clipboard data until another application requests it as a result of a paste operation.

The first two steps for delayed rendering are the same as those for a standard clipboard transfer of data: you call the WinOpenClipbrd and WinEmptyClipbrd functions to initialize the clipboard for use by your application. Next you specify the clipboard owner with the WinSetClipbrdOwner function. Calling WinSetClipbrdOwner is simple enough:

```
    WinSetClipbrdOwner(hab, hwnd);
```

Once the clipboard owner is set, the Presentation Manager routes several additional clipboard messages to the owner — additional, that is, to

WM_DRAWCLIPBOARD, which the Presentation Manager automatically routes through the clipboard viewer chain. These owner-oriented messages are:

- WM_RENDERFMT

- WM_DESTROYCLIPBOARD

- WM_PAINTCLIPBOARD

- WM_SIZECLIPBOARD

- WM_HSCROLLCLIPBOARD

- WM_VSCROLLCLIPBOARD

Importantly, the WinSetClipbrdOwner function makes the WM_RENDERFMT message available to the application controlling the clipboard. Of course, before you can process WM_RENDERFMT, you need to call WinSetClipbrdData. Instead of referencing the current anchor block handle (as you do for immediate rendering), you set the *hab* argument to NULL. Here is an example call:

```
WinSetClipbrdData(NULL, sel, CF_BITMAP, CFI_SELECTOR);
```

After calling WinSetClipbrdData, you close the clipboard in the ordinary manner. Thereafter, control of the clipboard (from the owner window perspective) is via the WM_RENDERFMT message block. A WM_RENDERFMT message is generated when the application performing the paste operation calls WinQueryClipbrdData. The *mp1* parameter of the WM_RENDERFMT message contains the requested data format (equal to one of the CF identifiers). Upon receiving the WM_RENDERFMT message, the owner application processes it as follows:

```
case WM_RENDERFMT:
        if(SHORT1FROMMP(mp1) == CF_BITMAP)
        WinSetClipbrdData(hab, sel, CF_BITMAP, CFI_SELECTOR);
```

When you receive the WM_RENDERFMT message, call WinSetClipbrdData as you would have done if you had intended to immediately render the associated data. If you specify CFI_OWNERFREE as the memory model, an additional step is required: you must process the WM_DESTROYCLIPBOARD message. Doing so merely requires another call to WinSetClipbordData in order to release any data slated for delayed rendering.

A message that takes WM_RENDERFMT one step further is WM_RENDERALLFMTS. This message occurs when the application that owns the clipboard is about to be destroyed. As with WM_RENDERFMT, you should release all unrendered data to the clipboard viewer chain by calling WinSetClipbrdData. This call ensures that the chain has access to the data even after the application no longer exists.

As for other messages that the owner window can receive, you process these similarly to routine frame window messages. In effect, clipboard message processing requires you to build a secondary **switch-case** block, somewhat equivalent to the application's main processing block. Here's a summary of the window-related clipboard messages:

- WM_PAINTCLIPBOARD — This message occurs if CFI_OWNER-
  DISPLAY is part of the memory model for the clipboard data, and the clipboard needs repainting. The *mp1* parameter of WM_PAINTCLIP-
  BOARD contains the handle to the clipboard application window.

- WM_SIZECLIPBOARD — This message occurs if CFI_OWNER-
  DISPLAY is part of the memory model for the clipboard data, and the clipboard application window has changed size. The *mp1* parameter contains the handle to the clipboard application window. The *mp2* parameter references the RECTL structure, which specifies the window area to paint. A WM_SIZECLIPBOARD message zeroes all fields in the RECTL structure when the clipboard application window is about to be destroyed or made iconic. This affords the application an opportunity to free any display resources related to clipboard data.

- WM_HSCROLLCLIPBOARD — This message occurs if CFI_OWN-
  ERDISPLAY is part of the memory model for the clipboard data, and the user accesses the horizontal scrollbar. The *mp1* parameter contains the handle to the clipboard application window. The high word of *mp2* contains a valid scrollbar control such as SB_LINELEFT and SB_PAGELEFT. The low word of *mp2* is set to 0, unless it describes SB_THUMBPOSITION.

- WM_VSCROLLCLIPBOARD — This message occurs if CFI_OWNER-DISPLAY is part of the memory model for the clipboard data, and the user accesses the horizontal scrollbar. The *mp1* parameter contains the handle to the clipboard application window. The high word of *mp2* contains a valid scrollbar control such as SB_LINEUP and SB_PAGE-DOWN. Unless *mp2* descibes SB_THUMBPOSITION, it is set to zero.

Enumerating Data Formats

Although the clipboard is designed for synchronous data transfer, you can use the WinEnumClipbrdFmts function to transfer one instance of each valid CF data type to the clipboard. WindEnumClipbrdFmts obtains a list of all data formats available in the clipboard. For each data format it obtains, or enumerates, you can use WinSetClipbrdData to transfer the data to the clipboard. A call to WinEnumClipbrdFmts looks like this:

```
index = WinEnumClipbrdFmts(hab, fmt);
```

Importantly, the value returned by WinEnumClipbrdFmts is the index to the next available clipboard data format. When there are no available formats, the function returns zero. Recall that each format was defined as an integer — ranging from one for CF_TEXT, to seven for CF_DSPMETA-FILE. With this in mind, note how the following routine places each available format in the clipboard:

```
WinOpenClipbrd(hwnd);
WinEmptyClipbrd(hab);

while(i = WinEnumClipbrdFmts(hab, fmt[i])
    {
        WinSetClipbrdData(hab, sel[i], CF[i], CFI[i]);
            i++;
        WinCloseClipbrd(hwnd);
    }
```

Of course, you do not have to use WinEnumClipbrdFmts to transfer more than one data format to the clipboard. Instead, you can use separate calls to WinSetClipbrdData.

CHAPTER 16

MULTITASKING

It's a new age: if window objects are the heart of the Presentation Manager, multitasking is its soul. Without the ability to handle multiple tasks at the same time, the Presentation Manager would be little more than Microsoft *Windows* in OS/2 form. Of course, this is not the case. The Presentation Manager offers full multitasking capabilities that let you create programs with simultaneously executing threads. Among other things, this means an application can display the results of one task while readying the next task's output; or better yet, read and write to disk while continuing to process keyboard and mouse input.

In addition to multitasking, this chapter details the use of the system timer. The timer is not used in strict multitasking programming methods; however, it does give you a way to execute a process based on an elapsed amount of time. In the Presentation Manager, the timer is best suited to coordinating non-critical events. Importantly, the timer also provides you a method of control over an application's message queue. That is, in the likelihood that the queue does not receive any user or system messages, you can rely on the presence of a timer message.

Using The Timer

The timer is one of the most straightforward elements of the Presentation Manager. Based on the actual timer chip in your 80286- or 80386-based machine, the Presentation Manager timer generates an interrupt 32 times per second. In milliseconds, which is how you specify time when dealing with the timer, this represents an interrupt about every 31.5 milliseconds. In a full minute, there are some 65,536 interrupts generated, with 1 second roughly equivalent to 1,000 milliseconds. You can set the timer anywhere in the range of 0 to 65,536 milliseconds. Setting it to zero causes the timer to time out immediately, which translates into about 1/18 of a second.

The Presentation Manager supports the timer through two functions and one message. Simply enough, the two functions are WinStartTimer and WinStopTimer. The message is WM_TIMER, which carries only one relevant piece of information: the ID of the timer that generates the message. This is contained in the lower word of the *mp1* parameter. The *mp2* parameter is reserved and set to NULL. You can extract the timer ID from the WM_TIMER message with the following code:

```
idTimer = SHORT1FROMMP(mp1);
```

How the Presentation Manager handles the WM_TIMER message is unique. What makes it so is the fact that the Presentation Manager does not normally route WM_TIMER messages through the application message queue. Instead, it checks all active timers each time you call Win-GetMsg or WinPeekMsg. When it finds that a timer has been triggered, it generates a WM_TIMER message and routes it directly to the application message queue. The reason for this method is to ensure that the application message loop does not receive multiple WM_TIMER messages from the same timer.

The meaningful word in the previous description is "normally." The Presentation Manager does route WM_TIMER through the application message queue if the message is not associated with a window. In this case, the WM_TIMER message is identified by a unique value assigned by the Presentation Manager and then posted to the message queue. In order to take advantage of this method, do not specify a window handle when activating a timer with the call to WinStartTimer. Here's the definition of WinStartTimer:

```
USHORT WinStartTimer(hab, hwnd, idTimer, dtTimeout)
HAB     hab;
HWND    hwnd;
USHORT  idTimer;
USHORT  dtTimeout;
```

The *hab* argument is the anchor block handle. The *hwnd* argument specifies the window handle associated with the message queue that processes the WM_TIMER messages. Setting *hwnd* to NULL causes the Presentation Manager to assign a unique value to *idTimer*. As a result, the WM_TIMER message is posted to the application's message queue (as previously described). In other cases, *idTimer* represents the ID that you assign to the timer. The *dtTimeout* specifies the interval, in milliseconds, to wait before triggering the timer. For example, setting *dtTimeout* to 10,000 triggers the timer and generates a WM_TIMER message every 10 seconds.

Before you activate a timer, ensure that the Presentation Manager can allocate resources for it. The Presentation Manager supports a maximum of 40 timers. If no other timers exist in your application, you might be tempted to activate a timer without checking for the existence of other timers. Doing so, however, is not a good idea: timers could be in use by other applications with which your application must coexist. The following example ensures that the Presentation Manager creates the specified timer, or notifies the user in the event that it cannot:

```
if(WinStartTimer(hab, hwndClient, ID_TIMER5, 2000))
    {
        while(WinGetMsg(hab, &qsmg, NULL, 0, 0))
            WinDispatchMsg(hab, &qsmg);
    }
else
        WinMessageBox(HWND_DESKTOP, hwndClient,
            "The Presentation Manager cannot",
            "create a timer at the moment.",
            NULL, 0, MB_OK | MB_ICONEXCLAMATION);
```

You can also find out the number of active timers by using WinQuerySysValue. The following call returns the number of timers:

```
lTimers = WinQuerySysValue(hwndDesktop, SV_CTIMERS);
```

Under normal circumstances, the Presentation Manager feeds timer messages to an application until you deactivate the timer. Even so, you cannot depend on receiving a WM_TIMER message for each instance of *idTimeout*. The reason for this is the Presentation Manager does not stockpile timer messages. At any given moment, you can expect to receive only the last generated WM_TIMER message for any given timer. Thus, if a user takes 30 seconds to resize a window and the application has a 1 second timer, the first 29 WM_TIMER messages would not be processed. One implication of this is you cannot reliably track chronological time using the WM_TIMER message.

The following program example activates a timer and processes the WM_TIMER message. Each time the application message loop receives a WM_TIMER message — approximately once per second — the window position is reset.

```c
/* TMFLASH.C (Timer causes window to flash.) */

#define INCL_WIN
#define ID_TIMER 1

#include <os2.h>
#include <stddef.h>
#include <stdlib.h>
#include <stdio.h>

MRESULT EXPENTRY AppWndProc(HWND, USHORT, MPARAM, MPARAM);

int main (void)
{

HMQ     hmq;
HWND    hwndFrame, hwndClient;
QMSG    qmsg;
static CHAR szClass[] = "timer";
ULONG   ctlData = FCF_STANDARD
                    & ~FCF_MENU ~FCF_ACCELTABLE;

hab = WinInitialize(0);
hmq = WinCreateMsgQueue(hab, 0);
WinRegisterClass(hab, szClass,
                    AppWndProc, CS_SIZEREDRAW, 0);

hwndFrame = WinCreateStdWindow(
                    HWND_DESKTOP,
                    WS_VISIBLE | FS_ICON,
                    &ctlData,
                    szClass,
                    NULL,
                    0L,
                    NULL,
                    ID_RESOURCE,
                    &hwndClient);

if(WinStartTimer(hab, hwndClient, ID_TIMER, 2000))
```

```
    {
        while(WinGetMsg(hab, &qsmg, NULL, 0, 0))
            WinDispatchMsg(hab, &qsmg);
    }
else
        WinMessageBox(HWND_DESKTOP, hwndClient,
                "The Presentation Manager cannot",
                "create a timer at the moment.",
                NULL, 0, MB_OK | MB_ICONEXCLAMATION);

WinStopTimer(hab, hwndClient, ID_TIMER);
WinDestroyWindow(hwndFrame);
WinDestroyMsgQueue(hmq);
WinTerminate(hab);
return(0);
}


MRESULT EXPENTRY AppWndProc(hwnd, msg, mp1, mp2)
HWND hwnd;
USHORT msg;
MPARAM mp1, mp2;
{

switch (msg)
  {
    case WM_TIMER:
        if(ID_TIMER == SHORT1FROMMP(mp1))
            WinFlashWindow(hwnd,  TRUE);
        else
            return(WinDefWindowProc (hwnd, msg, mp1, mp2));

    default:
        return(WinDefWindowProc (hwnd, msg, mp1, mp2));
  }

return(0L);
}
```

After the application message loop processes the WM_CLOSE message, the timer is deactivated with a call to the WinStopTimer function. WinStopTimer takes three arguments: *hab*, the anchor block handle; *hwnd*, the window handle; and *idTimer*, the ID for the timer. You should note that WinStopTimer aborts all timer messages, even those that have occurred since the last call to WinGetMsg.

Internal Timers

The Presentation Manager uses different timers to control some of its own internal events. As a result, you need to filter your WM_TIMER messages from the system-generated timer messages. This is why the previous example calls WinDefWindowProc in the WM_TIMER block: the internal timer messages must be processed, and the best way to accomplish this is through the default processing of WinDefWindowProc. Table 16-1 lists the identifiers associated with the Presentation Manager's internal timers.

Table 16-1: Internal Timers

IDENTIFIER	BIT	DESCRIPTION
TID_CURSOR	0xFFFF	Cursor timer.
TID_SCROLL	0xFFFE	Scrollbar timer.
TID_FLASHWINDOW	0xFFFD	Window flashing timer.

Timer Tasking

As *Windows'* programmers know, you can simulate multitasking by using the WM_TIMER message. This is accomplished by having your code perform a given task with each occurrence of the WM_TIMER message. Because the user can interrupt the frequency of WM_TIMER, it is not the most reliable method.

You likely could find some appropriate uses of WM_TIMER tasking. For instance, you could track the amount of time a user spends actually working in an application by manipulating WM_TIMER and a static variable associated with keyboard and mouse input. The following program example uses this technique:

```
/* WORKMUCH.C (Timer tracks amount of work.) */

#define INCL_WIN
```

```
#define ID_TIMER 1

#include <os2.h>
#include <stddef.h>
#include <stdlib.h>
#include <stdio.h>

MRESULT EXPENTRY AppWndProc(HWND, USHORT, MPARAM, MPARAM);

int main (void)
{

HMQ     hmq;
HWND    hwndFrame, hwndClient;
QMSG    qmsg;
static CHAR szClass[] = "working";
ULONG   ctlData = FCF_STANDARD
                      & ~FCF_MENU & ~FCF_ACCELTABLE;

hab = WinInitialize(0);
hmq = WinCreateMsgQueue(hab, 0);

WinRegisterClass(hab, szClass,
                      AppWndProc, CS_SIZEREDRAW, 0);

hwndFrame = WinCreateStdWindow(
                      HWND_DESKTOP,
                      WS_VISIBLE | FS_ICON,
                      &ctlData,
                      szClass,
                      NULL,
                      0L,
                      NULL,
                      ID_RESOURCE,
                      &hwndClient);

if(WinStartTimer(hab, hwndClient, ID_TIMER, 65000))
    while(WinGetMsg(hab, &qsmg, NULL, 0, 0))
            WinDispatchMsg(hab, &qsmg);
else
    WinMessageBox(HWND_DESKTOP, hwndClient,
                "The Presentation Manager cannot",
                "create a timer at the moment.",
                NULL, 0, MB_OK | MB_ICONEXCLAMATION);

WinStopTimer(hab, hwndClient, ID_TIMER);
WinDestroyWindow(hwndFrame);
```

```
WinDestroyMsgQueue(hmq);
WinTerminate(hab);
return(0);
}

MRESULT EXPENTRY AppWndProc(hwnd, msg, mp1, mp2)
HWND hwnd;
USHORT msg;
MPARAM mp1, mp2;
{

static BOOL  fWork = FALSE;
static SHORT  sMin;

switch (msg)
   {
        case WM_CHAR:
             ProcessCharInput(hwnd);
             fWork = TRUE;
             break;

        case WM_MOUSE:
             ProcessMouseInput(hwnd);
             fWork = TRUE;
             break;

        case WM_TIMER:
             if(ID_TIMER == SHORT1FROMMP(mp1) && work == TRUE)
                sMin++;
             else
                return(WinDefWindowProc(hwnd, msg, mp1, mp2);
             fWork = FALSE;
             break;
        default:
             return(WinDefWindowProc (hwnd, msg, mp1, mp2));
   }
   return(0);
   }
```

The example uses a one-minute timer. It calls programmer-defined functions for processing keyboard and mouse input, then sets the *fWork* variable to TRUE. In the WM_TIMER message handler, the *sMin* variable is incremented whenever the timer ID equals ID_TIMER and work equals TRUE. The *work* variable is then reset to FALSE. The bottom line is the user receives credit for a minute's worth of work only if a key or mouse message has been processed in the current minute.

Multitasking

The cleanest way to execute multiple tasks in the Presentation Manager is to make use of the multitasking functions available in the Dos library. You can freely use these functions, but when you do, you must realize that your code cannot interact with an application's message queue. In essence, using the Dos functions allows you to program an independent function that performs a given task, but does so with minimum knowledge of messages in the application's message queue.

The mechanism that controls threads in OS/2 is the system scheduler. The scheduler assigns CPU time to a thread based on its priority. The thread with the highest priority always gets preferential treatment and generally receives all the CPU time it needs to complete execution. Thread priorities fall into three categories: time-critical, regular, and idle-time. Typically, all threads within the same application — which is the main concern of the Presentation Manager programmer — receive the same priority. At times, however, you might want to boost the priority of a given thread, and the Dos library functions accommodate this. Table 16-2 lists selected Dos multitasking functions and summarizes what they do.

Table 16-2: Dos Library Multitasking Functions

FUNCTION	DESCRIPTION
DosCreateThread	Creates a thread to execute a programmer-specified function.
DosCWait	Causes a thread to wait until another thread completes.
DosExit	Ends a thread. Frequently used to end the **main**() function.
DosGetPID	Obtains the identification code of the thread, process, and parent process of the current process.
DosGetPrty	Obtains the scheduling priority of specified thread.
DosResumeThread	Restarts a thread halted by the DosSuspendThread function.
DosSetPrty	Sets the scheduling priority for a specified thread.
DosSuspendThread	Halts thread execution until a call toDosResumeThread.

Programming threads in the Presentation Manager is much easier than the topic implies. From a coding viewpoint, a secondary thread is merely a function that performs some task. Some trigger mechanism — which can be a RAM semaphore or merely the call to DosCreateThread — activates the thread function. In turn, the thread function can call other functions, if necessary, or simply perform its task. As noted, the thread function cannot directly interact with the application's message queue. When the thread finishes executing, it can post a programmer-defined message informing the application that it has completed its work, and pass some data to the application via the message. Alternatively, the thread can merely call DosExit and cease to exist. Presumably, in this case, the thread performed some standalone operation or modified one or more global variables. Figure 16-1 shows a typical relationship between a thread and the main body of code in a Presentation Manager application.

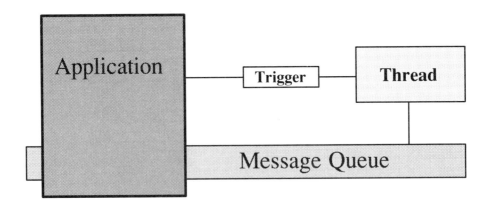

Figure 16-1: Application/Thread Relationship

Besides using global variables and the WinPostMessage function, threads can signal with one another, or with their parent process, by using semaphores. OS/2 supports two kinds of semaphores:

- System semaphores — created using the DosCreateSem function and used to protect a process' resources from inappropriate access.

- RAM semaphores — which is a global variable of type ULONG. This type of semaphore is used for signaling between threads, but is also used to safeguard resources within the same process.

The Dos library provides several semaphore functions. In addition to functions to create, clear, and close a semaphore, these functions give you tools to wait for an active semaphore to clear. Table 16-3 lists the Dos library semaphore functions.

Table 16-3: Dos Library Semaphore Functions

FUNCTION	DESCRIPTION
DosCloseSem	Closes a system semaphore.
DosCreateSem	Creates a system semaphore and returns a handle to the semaphore.
DosMuxSemWait	Waits a specified length of time for one of several semaphores to clear.
DosOpenSem	Opens a system semaphore and returns a handle to the semaphore.
DosSemClear	Clears a system or RAM semaphore and allows you to set a new semaphore owner.
DosSemRequest	Requests that a system or RAM semaphore be set. If the semaphore is not clear, DosSemRequest waits a specified period for the semaphore to clear.
DosSemSet	Sets a system or RAM semaphore. The DosSemWait or DosMuxSemWait functions must be used if you need to wait for the semaphore to clear.
DosSemSetWait	Sets a system or RAM semaphore and waits for the semaphore to clear.
DosSemWait	Waits for the specified system or RAM semaphore to clear.

Presentation Manager Threads

In general, the Presentation Manager follows the same rules for creating threads that apply to OS/2 kernel programming. Because of its message-based structure, the Presentation Manager also implements its own thread — the message queue thread, which results from your call to WinCreateMsgQueue. This distinguishes the Presentation Manager from OS/2: when you execute a Presentation Manager program, at least one thread is immediately active. Additionally, whenever you create a second message queue, a second message queue thread results, and so on.

Typical OS/2 threads are called queueless threads in the Presentation Manager. A queueless thread is useful because it can perform a task without interfering with other events in the application. With a queueless thread, you need not be concerned with the time that it takes to execute its task. A queueless thread has its limitations, however. They are:

- Windows cannot be created by queueless threads, but a queueless thread can obtain a handle to a presentation space and draw in the associated window.

- Messages must be posted by queueless threads, not sent via the WinSendMsg function. Nor can a queueless thread invoke another function that sends a message to a message queue.

- WM_TIMER messages are posted to the message queue belonging to the thread that created the timer.

As the last caveat might indicate, there is more to a queueless thread than meets the eye. Although a queueless thread begins its existence without a message queue, you can create a message queue within a queueless thread. This type of thread is typically referred to as an object window, which has fewer restrictions than a queueless thread — it cannot create its own window display or process keyboard and mouse input — but it is still not a full-blown message queue thread. Additionally, you must always return an object window thread to a queueless state in order to dispose of it.

Under release 1.1 of the Presentation Manager, functions that can be accessed in a separate thread of execution fall into the following categories:

- Heap manager functions.

- Atom manager functions.

- System information functions.

- Resource functions.

- Dos support functions.

- Gpi functions.

Creating a Thread

There are two fundamental ways to create a second thread of execution. One way is to create it when the need arises and then dispose of it when it finishes executing. Another way is to create the thread early in the program, typically in the WM_CREATE message block, and use a RAM semaphore to activate the thread in response to a given situation.

The first method is simple enough. Say you had a menu option to recalculate all values in your application. When the user selects the menu option, the Presentation Manager generates a WM_COMMAND message with the associated menu option ID. The logical place to execute the recalculation thread is in the **case** statement for the option ID. A call to DosCreateThread would accomplish this nicely by activating the thread function, and then return control to the **case** statement. Eventually, the thread function would complete its task and post a message notifying the message queue thread of the fact.

In practice, this is not a flawless method. What, for instance, would happen if other threads wanted to use the active thread? Clearly you need some blocking method. True, you could block access to the thread by toggling a boolean variable, but boolean blocking tactics could get sticky.

Enter RAM semaphores. Through the use of a RAM semaphore and a function such as DosSemWait, you can guarantee that a thread executes only when appropriate. RAM semaphores also allow you to easily build complex conditions as the basis of executing a thread.

Calling DosCreateThread

Assuming your thread function is intact, the first step in executing a thread is to call the DosCreateThread function. Although it takes only three arguments, DosCreateThread comes packed with complex niceties. Here's the definition for DosCreateThread:

```
USHORT DosCreateThread(pfnFunction, ptidThread, pbThrdStack)
VOID (FAR *) pfnFunction(VOID);
PTID ptidThread;
PBYTE pbThrdStack;
```

The first argument to DosCreateThread is the name of the thread function. The function can contain no arguments itself and must be declared as
type VOID FAR, which represents the physical address of the function.
The *ptidThread* function is a variable into which the Presentation Manager returns the thread ID. The thread ID is required by various Dos
thread and semaphore functions.

The third argument, *pbThrdStack*, is somewhat unusual. Normally, a
function's stack space is created automatically, but this is not the case
with a thread function. The programmer must define the stack space,
which is often allocated from the heap. In so doing, note that stacks begin
at the highest addresses in memory and expand in the direction of the
lower memory. As a result, *pbThrdStack* must point to the last word in the
stack.

THE THREAD REGISTERS

The thread function has its own stack. In the stack, OS/2 maintains a virtual copy of
the thread's CPU registers. When the thread receives processing time from the system scheduler, its CPU register values are copied to the system's CPU registers.
When its execution time elapses, the thread's virtual registers are updated. The
relevant registers are the local descriptor table (LDT), which defines the address
space of the owner process; the Code Segment (CS) and Instruction Pointer (IP) registers, which define the thread's next instruction; and the Stack Segment (SS) and
Stack Pointer (SP) registers, which define the call stack. The remaining CPU registers are used for the thread function's variables.

When you create a stack, you must add the size of stack already requested stack memory to *pbThrdStack*. The following code, which assumes a stack variable of type UCHAR, uses this technique:

```
pbThrdStack = pStack + sizeof(pStack);
DosCreateThread(ThreadFunction, ptidThread, pbThrdStack);
```

An alternative method to this approach uses the C **malloc** function. You can use **malloc** to obtain a pointer to the lowest address in the memory space created for the thread function stack. For example, you can define the size of the stack as a constant (say, STACK) and use the following code to satisfy *pbThrdStack*:

```
pbThrdStack = (CHAR FAR *) malloc(STACK) + STACK;
DosCreateThread(ThreadFunction, ptidThread, pbThrdStack);
```

In these routines, you should check whether memory allocation was successful. You should also check the value that DosCreateThread returns, as in the following example:

```
iError = DosCreateThread(ThreadFunction,
            ptidThread, pbThrdStack);
if(iError == ERROR_NOT_ENOUGH_MEMORY)
    WinMessageBox(HWND_DESKTOP, hwndClient,
            "A memory or process error has",
            "occurred. Thread not created.",
            NULL, 0, MB_OK | MB_ICONEXCLAMATION);
```

A return value of zero from DosCreateThread indicates success. If there is not enough memory to create the thread, the system returns a system-defined error code announcing this fact.

Setting a RAM Semaphore

RAM semaphores are your gateway to effective control over threads. Two preliminary steps are necessary when using RAM semaphores: always initialize the RAM semaphore to zero before using it; and, whenever possible, make the actual call to set the semaphore immediately before the call to DosCreateThread. This last measure is not mandatory, but certainly makes for more readable code.

A RAM semaphore is actually a global variable of type LONG. Setting a RAM semaphore to zero tells any polling threads that the semaphore is clear, and that the thread can go ahead and execute. If a RAM semaphore is any other value than zero, the thread must wait before it can execute. This is a convenient way of blocking one thread from accessing resources currently in use by another thread. It is also a convenient way to trigger a thread, even though no other threads are competing for the same resources.

The most common way to set a semaphore is to use the DosSemSet function. DosSemSet simply creates a handle for the semaphore. It takes a single argument — the address of a variable of type HSEM, the OS/2 data type for semaphore handles. (Note that if you use DosSemSet with system semaphores, the semaphore handle must be opened using either DosCreateSem or DosOpenSem.) Names given to RAM semaphores often relate to the name of the associated thread or the thread's task — a variation of other Presentation Manager naming schemes. A typical call to DosSemSet looks like this:

```
DosSemSet(&DiskOpSem);
```

An alternative way to set a semaphore is with the DosSemRequest function. DosSemRequest is typically used for a semaphore that has been previously set. Its distinguishes itself from DosSemSet by waiting for a semaphore to clear, which occurs when the controlling thread calls DosSemClear. Here's the definition for DosSemRequest:

```
USHORT DosSemRequest(hsem, lTimeOut)
HSEM hsem;
LONG lTimeOut;
```

As with the DosSemSet function, DosSemRequest sets a semaphore handle, represented in the function definition by *hsem*. The second argument, *lTimeOut*, specifies the time that the function should wait for the semaphore to clear. Table 16-5 describes the possible values for *lTimeOut*.

Table 16-5: Wait Values for DosSemRequest

TIME-OUT VALUE	DESCRIPTION
-1	DosSemRequest waits for the semaphore to clear.
Zero	DosSemRequest returns immediately if the semaphore is not clear.
More than zero	DosSemRequest waits the time specified (in milliseconds) for the semaphore to clear.

The Thread Function

Despite its bare appearance, the thread function is a powerful tool in Presentation Manager programs. And although you cannot directly pass arguments to a thread function, it operates almost identically to a standard C function. For example, it inherits any resources that the calling process owns, even if one or more of those resources are opened by a different thread.

Thread functions also use variables the same way C functions do. Automatic variables such as loop counters exist for the duration of the thread function. Static variables also act as they normally do. The only variables you should treat differently are global variables, because a competing thread can unexpectedly modify a global variable — although this, too, is mitigated by the correct use of semaphores.

You can also exchange values with a thread via the stack itself. When you initialize the thread function's stack, you can pass arguments to it by placing values in its memory locations. The following example illustrates this technique:

```
pbThrdStack = cStack + sizeof(cStack);
*--pbThrdStack = arg1;
*--pbThrdStack = arg2;
DosCreateThread(ThreadFunction, ptidThread,
                (UCHAR *) pbThrdStack);
```

Passing values back to the application is another matter. You can use addressing similar to that in the example, which is efficient, but will likely leave you some work to do elsewhere. A better way to pass a limited number of values back to the application is via the WinPostMessage function.

Talking about WinPostMessage is putting the message before the means. The first thing you must address in a thread function is the semaphore state. For example, assume you used DosCreateThread to create a thread and called DosSemSet to set a semaphore. Here's a template thread function that would operate under these circumstances:

```
VOID FAR ThreadFunction()
    {
        while(!bExitThread)
        {
                DosSemWait(&lTrigger);
```

```
            .
            .
            .
         /* Perform some task here. */
            .
            .
            .
         DosSemSet(&lTrigger);
         WinPostMsg(hwndClient, WM_USER_1, 0L, 0L);
      }
   }
```

   With this template, you can program almost any type of task you would program in a normal C function (that is, if you observe the Presentation Manager's restrictions on queueless threads). For this template to work, you need to include the following calls in your application program:

1. During initialization of the application (preferably in the WM_CRE-ATE message block), call DosSemSet to set *lTrigger*.

2. Immediately after calling DosSemSet, call DosCreateThread to activate the thread function. Remember that you must size the thread function's stack before calling DosCreateThread.

3. At some point in the application, call DosSemClear to change the status of *lTrigger*. This will cause the thread function to begin executing immediately .

4. After the WinGetMsg loop, include a call to DosSuspendThread so the thread does not impede normal termination of the application.

   Some new material is covered here as well as in the template. First, the DosSemWait function is necessary to complete the thread's trigger mechanism. It operates identically to the waiting mechanism described for Dos-RequestSem. Its single argument is *lTimeOut*, which specifies the waiting period. Refer to Table 16-4 for the valid *lTimeOut* values.
   Conceptually, you might pair DosSemWait with DosSemClear. In cause and effect terms, this is accurate because DosSemClear actually causes DosSemWait to return a zero value which, in turn, allows the thread to execute. In fact, however, DosSemClear is the antithesis of DosSetSem: it merely reverses the state of the semaphore put into effect by DosSetSem. Figure 16-2 shows the relationship between the three semaphore functions.

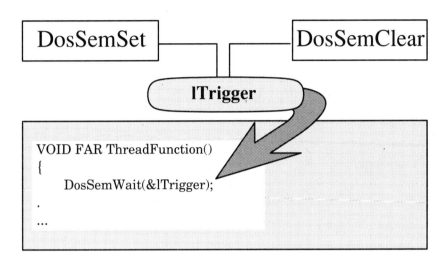

Figure 16-2: Semaphore Trigger Process

In this model, you must call DosSemSet from the thread function after it has performed its task. This sets the stage anew for the application to use DosSemClear to restart the thread, either from the same location in the program or a different one.

The last step in the thread function is to call WinPostMessage. The first argument to WinPostMsg, the window handle, must be set to the window handle that represents the window where you want the message posted. The next argument, the message identifier, must be set to a user-defined message such as WM_USER_1 in the template. The final two arguments — the message parameters — can contain data that you want to pass back to the window. For example, to post two variables representing the total and subtotal of a calculation (both of type LONG), you would make the following call:

```
WinPostMsg(hwndClient, WM_USR_1, ltotal, lsubtotal);
```

Because WinPostMsg expects LONG values in its *mp1* and *mp2* arguments, these are naturally easier to pass back to the window. But you can also pass other types using the macros that construct MPARAM values. The following thread function uses this technique:

```
VOID FAR ThreadFunction()
{
MPARAM mp1, mp2
SHORT  i, randnum[4];

while(!bExitThread)
    {
        DosSemWait(&lTrigger);
        for(i=0; i <= 4; i++)
            randnum[i] = rand();
        mp1 = MPFROM2SHORT(randnum[0], randnum[1]);
        mp2 = MPFROM2SHORT(randnum[2], randnum[3]);
        DosSemSet(&lTrigger);
        WinPostMsg(hwndClient, WM_USER_1, mp1, mp2);
    }
}
```

In both the template and the previous example, the variable *bExit-Thread* appeared. What is this? It is simply a global BOOLEAN variable that gives you another way to block a thread. For each thread function you use in an application, you can define a unique global variable for this purpose. One benefit of this strategy is you can ensure that a thread is shut down when you terminate the application.

Another way to accomplish this same effect is to use the Dos-SuspendThread function. DosSuspendThread takes the thread ID as its only argument and immediately halts the execution of the specified thread. Here's a typical call:

```
DosSuspendThread(ptidThread);
```

A thread that calls DosSuspendThread can only suspend threads within the same process from which you invoke it. To resume the execution of a suspended thread, use DosResumeThread.

The following program example uses some of the techniques discussed in this and previous sections. It uses a separate thread of execution to obtain coordinates for placement of "stars" in the client window. The example posts user messages to draw the starts and clear the window:

```
/* UNIV.H (Header file) */

#define STACKSIZE 32000

#define WM_USER1 WM_USER+1
#define WM_USER2 WM_USER+2


#define ID_RESOURCE 1

#define IDM_UNIV     100
#define IDM_START    101
#define IDM_ZOOMIN   102
#define IDM_ZOOMOUT 103
#define IDM_END      104

/* UNIV.RC (Resource script) */

#include <os2.h>
#include "univ.h"


MENU ID_RESOURCE
{
    SUBMENU "~Universe", IDM_UNIV
      {
        MENUITEM "~Start\t^S", IDM_START
        MENUITEM "~Zoom in\t^I", IDM_ZOOMIN
        MENUITEM "~Zoom out\t^O", IDM_ZOOMOUT
        MENUITEM "~End\t^E",  IDM_END
      }
}


ACCELTABLE ID_RESOURCE
{
    "^S",  IDM_START
    "^I",  IDM_ZOOMIN
    "^O",  IDM_ZOOMOUT
    "^E",  IDM_END
}


/* UNIV.C (Program file) */

#define INCL_PM
```

```
#define INCL_DOS

#include <os2.h>
#include <stddef.h>
#include <stdlib.h>
#include "univ.h"


MRESULT EXPENTRY AppWndProc(HWND,USHORT,MPARAM,MPARAM);
VOID FAR ThreadProc(VOID);
VOID InitializePS(HWND);


HMQ hmq;
HAB hab;
CHAR szClass[] = "chaos";
HWND hwndFrame, hwndClient;
HPS hpsInit;
BOOL fContinue = FALSE, fSizeUp = FALSE;
LONG lTrigger;
TID idThread;
UCHAR pbThread[STACKSIZE];


int main(void)
{

QMSG qmsg;
ULONG  ctlData = FCF_STANDARD & ~FCF_ICON;


hab = WinInitialize(NULL);
hmq = WinCreateMsgQueue(hab, 0);

WinRegisterClass(hab, szClass,
                 AppWndProc, CS_SIZEREDRAW, 0);

hwndFrame = WinCreateStdWindow(
                      HWND_DESKTOP,
                      WS_VISIBLE,
                      &ctlData,
                      szClass,
                      NULL,
                      0L,
                      NULL,
                      ID_RESOURCE,
                      &hwndClient);
```

```
while(WinGetMsg(NULL, &qmsg, NULL, 0, 0 ))
            WinDispatchMsg(NULL, &qmsg);

DosSuspendThread(idThread);

WinDestroyWindow( hwndFrame );
WinDestroyMsgQueue( hmq );
WinTerminate( hab );
return(0);
}


MRESULT EXPENTRY AppWndProc(hwnd, msg, mp1, mp2)
HWND hwnd;
USHORT msg;
MPARAM mp1, mp2;
{

    HPS hps;
    RECTL rcl;
    POINTL ptl;
    static SHORT sZoom = 1;

    switch(msg)
      {
        case WM_CREATE:
              InitializePS(hwnd);
              DosSemSet(&lTrigger);

              DosCreateThread((PFNTHREAD)ThreadProc,
                          &idThread,
                          pbThread+STACKSIZE-2);

              return 0L;

        case WM_SIZE:
              fSizeUp = TRUE;
              break;


        case WM_PAINT:
              hps = WinBeginPaint(hwnd,NULL,&rcl);
              WinFillRect(hps,&rcl,CLR_BLACK);
              WinEndPaint(hps);
              return(NULL);
```

```
case WM_COMMAND:
     switch ((COMMANDMSG(&msg)->cmd))
       {
          case IDM_START:
              fContinue = TRUE;
              DosSemClear(&lTrigger);
              break;

          case IDM_END:
              fContinue = FALSE;
              break;

          case IDM_ZOOMIN:
              sZoom++;
              break;

          case IDM_ZOOMOUT:
              sZoom--;
              break;

          default:
              break;

       }

case WM_USER1:
     WinQueryWindowRect(hwnd,&rcl);
     WinFillRect(hpsInit,&rcl,CLR_BLACK);
     return(0L);

case WM_USER2:
     WinQueryWindowRect(hwnd,&rcl);
     ptl.x = SHORT1FROMMP(mp1);
     ptl.y = SHORT1FROMMP(mp2);
     GpiSetColor(hpsInit, (LONG) (rand() % 16));
     GpiMove(hpsInit,&point);
     GpiFullArc(hpsInit,
                    DRO_OUTLINEFILL,
                    (LONG) sZoom * 65536);
     return(0L);

case WM_ERASEBACKGROUND:
     return(TRUE);
```

```
        case WM_CLOSE:
            WinReleasePS(hpsInit);
            break;
    }

    return(WinDefWindowProc(hwnd, msg, mp1, mp2));
}


VOID FAR ThreadProc()
{

    RECTL  rcl;
    SHORT sX, sY, i;

    DosSetPrty(PRTYS_THREAD, PRTYC_IDLETIME, 0, 0);

    while(1)
      {
        DosSemWait(&lTrigger,-1L);
        WinPostMsg(hwndClient, WM_USER1, 0L, 0L);

        for(i = 0; i <= 2000; i++)
          {
            if(!fContinue)
              break;

            if(fSizeUp)
              {
                WinQueryWindowRect(hwndClient,&rcl);
                fSizeUp = FALSE;
              }

            sX = (SHORT)(rand() % rcl.xRight);
            sY = (SHORT)(rand() % rcl.yTop);

            WinPostMsg(hwndClient,
                    WM_USER2,
                    MPFROMSHORT(sX),
                    MPFROMSHORT(sY));
          }

        if(!fContinue)
            DosSemSet(&lTrigger);
        DosSleep(100L);
      }
}
```

```
VOID InitializePS(hwnd)
HWND hwnd;
{

    SIZEL size;
    HDC hdcInit;

    hdcInit = WinOpenWindowDC(hwnd);
    size.cx = 0;
    size.cy = 0;

    hpsInit = GpiCreatePS(hab, hdcInit, &size,
                          PU_PELS | GPIF_DEFAULT
                          | GPIT_NORMAL | GPIA_ASSOC);
}
```

Object Windows

Recall that is it possible for a queueless thread to be a message queue thread. Thankfully, you can simply refer to this special thread as an object window. What distinguishes an object window from a standard window is an object window cannot display windows or process keyboard and mouse input. Additionally, only two system-defined messages are available to an object window, WM_CREATE and WM_DESTROY.

What does this stripped-down window do? Just about anything you would want a queueless thread to do and a little more. For one thing, it can let you implement your own set of objects in the form of user-defined messages. Each message could then invoke its own thread to perform the processing necessary to create the object. And except for this type of subsequent thread processing, object window processing is limited to the initial thread function and an object window function.

You do not use semaphores to activate an object window, even though an object window runs in a second thread of execution. Instead, you can activate the object window's thread function even before you create the application message queue. The actual call to DosCreateThread activates the thread function. No special steps are necessary to invoke the DosCreate-Thread function. Call it as if you were creating a thread that used semaphores.

An object window communicates with the frame window via the Win-PostMsg function. Because an object window's message queue is always active, a call to WinPostMsg delivers the message to the object window in express fashion. The handles for both the frame and object windows should be defined as global variables, because you will likely need to access both in the thread function as well as the object window function. Minimally, you will need the client window handle available to the object window function if you intend to post messages to the client window from the object window function.

The thread function for an object window bears a striking resemblance to the **main()** function in a Presentation Manager program. The major difference is you do not have to initialize an object window with WinInitialize. Nor do you have to use WinCreateStdWindow to create the object window. Instead, you can use WinCreateWindow. Additionally, it is not necessary to supply live values to all of WinCreateWindow arguments. Here's an example call:

```
hwndObject = WinCreateWindow(
            HWND_OBJECT,        /* Parent window. */
            szObjClass,         /* Window class. */
            NULL,               /* Text string. */
            0L,                 /* Window style. */
            0,                  /* Horizontal axis. */
            0,                  /* Vertical axis. */
            0,                  /* Width. */
            0,                  /* Height. */
            NULL,               /* Owner window. */
            HWND_TOP,           /* Screen location. */
            0,                  /* Child ID. */
            NULL,               /* Control data. */
            NULL);              /* PM parameters. */
```

By looking at this call, you can get an idea of what an object window is all about. Notice the parent window handle is set to HWND_OBJECT, the only special identifier needed to create an object window. Also notice what is missing from the call to WinCreateWindow. For example, no owner handle is supplied, because an object window needs no owner (in fact, object windows are sometimes referred to as orphan windows). Nor do you need to supply WinCreateWindow with control data for scrollbars or other system controls. The reason, simply enough, is an object window is not visible.

On the other hand, if you do want to make an object window visible —
which you can do by using the WinSetParent function — you should call
WinCreateWindow with a full range of arguments.

The rest of the thread function should look familiar. Here's a template
you can use for most applications:

```
VOID PASCAL FAR ObjectWindowThread(VOID)
{

HMQ     hmq;
QMSG    qmsg;
static CHAR szObjClass[] = "Object Thread";

hmq = WinCreateMsgQueue(hab, 0);

WinRegisterClass(hab, szObjClass, ObjectWndFunc, OL, NULL);

hwndObject = WinCreateWindow(
                HWND_OBJECT,
                szObjClass,
                NULL,
                OL,
                0,
                0,
                0,
                0,
                NULL,
                HWND_TOP,
                0,
                NULL,
                NULL);

WinPostMsg(hwndFrame, WM_OBJCREATE, OL, OL);

while(WinGetMsg(hab, &qmsg, NULL, 0, 0))
        WinDispatchMsg(hab, &qmsg);

WinDestroyWindow(hwndObject);
WinDestroyMsgQueue(hmq);
WinPostMsg(hwndFrame, WM_OBJDESTROY, OL, OL);
DosExit(0, 0);
}
```

The thread function also differs to **main()** in that it makes two calls to
WinPostMsg — one before creating the object window message queue, and

the other after it destroys the queue. The first call to WinPostMsg posts a user-defined WM_OBJCREATE message. You can use this message to take care of any initial processing that the client window must perform for the benefit of the object window. In addition, if you create the object window thread from **main()**, you can be sure that WM_OBJCREATE precedes most system messages in the client window message queue. Therefore, you could perform some other initialization odds-and-ends in the WM_OBJCREATE block.

The second call to WinPostMsg posts a WM_OBJDESTROY message to the client window message queue. The intention here is to synchronize the closing of both the object window and the client window. To do this, follow these steps:

1. Post a WM_QUIT message to the object window from the WM_CLOSE block in the client window.

2. Abort any processing in the object window.

3. Post a WM_OBJDESTROY message to the client window.

4. Process the WM_OBJDESTROY message by posting a WM_QUIT message to the client window's message queue.

Note that if you intend to have WM_OBJDESTROY signal the end of the application, you must post a WM_QUIT message from the WM_OBJDESTROY message block. Otherwise, there is no way for the client window message queue to get the word that the user wants to quit.

The Object Window Function

The object window function shares some traits with other message queue functions. On the surface, its structure is identical to the client window's **switch-case** construction. The object window function definition is also the same as that used for the client window function. As stated, however, the only familiar messages that it processes are WM_CREATE and WM_DESTROY. Any other messages are user-defined messages. Messages not trapped by the object window function are processed by WinDefWindowProc. Here's a sample object window function:

```
MRESULT FAR PASCAL ObjectWndProc(hwnd, msg, mp1, mp2)
HWND    hwnd;
USHORT msg;
MPARAM mp1, mp2);
{

SHORT   randnumber;

switch(msg)
    {
        case WM_GET_RAND:
                randnumber = LOUSHORT(mp1);
                while(!randnumber)
                    {
                        randnumber = rand(32);
                        mp1 = MPFROMSHORT(randnumber);
                        WinPostMsg(hwndClient, WM_PUT_RAND,
                                    mp1, 0L);
                    }
                break;

        case WM_QUIT_OK:
                WinPostMsg(hwndClient, WM_QUIT_NOW, 0L, 0L);
                break;

        default:
                return(WinDefWindowProc(hwnd, msg, mp1, mp2);
    }

return(0L);
}
```

The example processes two messages forwarded to it from the client window application queue (via the thread function, of course). There is no problem processing the second message. It simply alerts the object window function of the user's desire to quit. The WM_QUIT_OK block responds by posting its own user-defined quit message. The first message, WM_GET_RAND, is a different story. Its message routine continues looping until the **rand()** function returns the number equal to *randnumber*, which is derived from *mp1*. The problem is the random number processing could take a very long time. What happens if the user wants to quit?

In the example, if the user wanted to quit a WM_QUIT_OK message would be placed in the object window message queue. If this occurred, it would change the status of the queue. You can detect this change in status by calling the WinQueryQueueStatus function. The following example, which assumes a LONG variable of *lQueue*, shows the WM_GET_RAND message block with the call to WinQueryQueueStatus:

```
case WM_GET_RAND:
        randnumber = LOUSHORT(mp1);
        while(!randnumber)
            {
            if(!WinQueryQueueStatus)
                break;
            randnumber = rand(32);
            mp1 = MPFROMSHORT(randnumber);
            WinPostMsg(hwndClient, WM_PUT_RAND, mp1, 0L);
            }
        break;
```

The use of object windows does not obviate the need for queueless threads. During some CPU-intensive operations, an object window cannot call WinQueryQueueStatus. If you performed a disk-based operation through an object window, for instance, the user would have to wait until the operation concluded before being able to abort the program. On the other hand, object windows do let you take care of many multitasking needs — and the major benefit in using them is consistency in message processing.

A Word About WinSetParent

As mentioned, the WinSetParent function lets you transform an object window into a normal window. You can also use WinSetParent to convert a normal window into an object window. This is convenient if your window needs to get initialization input from the user, but thereafter has no reason to be displayed. Here's the definition for WinSetParent:

```
BOOL WinSetParent(hwnd, hwndNewParent, fRedraw)
HWND hwnd;
HWND hwndNewParent;
BOOL fRedraw;
```

The *hwnd* argument identifies the window that you want to transform. The *hwndNewParent* argument is the key argument. It allows you to specify the new owner, either HWND_OBJECT, HWND_DESKTOP, or a descendent of the desktop. Note that if you choose to specify a descendent of HWND_DESKTOP, ensure that the descendent is not related to *hwnd*. The *fRedraw* argument specifies an indicator that controls window redrawing. Specifying TRUE for *fRedraw* ensures that the window is redrawn under all circumstances.

CHAPTER 17

MESSAGE LIBRARY

Learning the Presentation Manager's extensive set of messages is just as important as learning its function calls. There is no easy way to become familiar with the message set. Using the Presentation Manager's various messages — and determining which categories suit your needs — is the best way to approach this undertaking.

A message always carries at least one value that acts as a selection mechanism. A selection mechanism is the parameter that distinguishes it from other messages and consequently tells an object such as a window to perform a certain operation. A message does not reference memory. Instead, it tells an object to address memory. In the Presentation Manager, messages are distinguished by the values contained in the *mp1* and *mp2* parameters.

This chapter serves as a reference to all of the Presentation Manager's messages. Keep in mind that the Presentation Manager supports two types of messages: the type that you must handle in the client window procedure and/or subclassed window functions; and the type that you send to control windows. Both types of messages are cataloged here. A brief summary of how you use a given class of message precedes each section.

There are eight sets of messages defined by the Presentation Manager. Tables 17-1 through 17-8 list these sets. Individual message descriptions begin after these tables.

In the descriptions contained in this chapter, note that when either *mp1* or *mp2* contain more than one value, your attention is drawn to both the low and high word values. If either *mp1* or *mp2* contains a single value, no distinction between the low and high word is necessary. Also, if a description omits either or both *mp1* and *mp2*, the values for these parameters are reserved and set to NULL.

Table 17-1: Button Messages

MESSAGE	DESCRIPTION
BM_CLICK	Simulates a button click.
BM_QUERYCHECK	Retrieves button check state.
BM_QUERYCHECKINDEX	Retrieves index of checked radio button.
BM_QUERYHILITE	Retrieves highlighted state.
BM_SETCHECK	Sets button's check state.
BM_SETDEFAULT	Sets button's default state.
BM_SETHILITE	Sets button's highlighted state.

Table 17-2: Entry Field Messages

MESSAGE	DESCRIPTION
EM_CLEAR	Deletes selection in entry field control.
EM_COPY	Pastes selection in entry field control.
EM_CUT	Deletes selection in entry field control.
EM_PASTE	Pastes from the clipboard.
EM_QUERYCHANGED	Checks if contents have changed.
EM_QUERYFIRSTCHAR	Retrieves offset of first visible character.
EM_QUERYSEL	Retrieves offsets of first and last character.
EM_SETFIRSTCHAR	Sets first character on left.
EM_SETSEL	Sets selection range.
EM_SETTEXTLIMIT	Sets maximum characters in entry field.

Table 17-3: Listbox Messages

MESSAGE	DESCRIPTION
LM_DELETEALL	Deletes all items in listbox control.
LM_DELETEITEM	Deletes a specified item from the list.
LM_INSERTITEM	Inserts item text.
LM_QUERYITEMCOUNT	Retrieves number of items in list.
LM_QUERYITEMHANDLE	Retrieves item's handle.
LM_QUERYITEMTEXT	Copies text from item.
LM_QUERYITEMTEXTLENGTH	Retrieves item's text length.
LM_QUERYSELECTION	Retrieves index of selected item.
LM_QUERYTOPINDEX	Retrieves index of top item.
LM_SEARCHSTRING	Searches list for a match.
LM_SELECTITEM	Sets an item's selection state.
LM_SETITEMHANDLE	Sets an item's handle.
LM_SETITEMHEIGHT	Sets height of items.
LM_SETITEMTEXT	Sets item text.
LM_SETTOPINDEX	Sets item to top of listbox.

Table 17-4: Menu Messages

MESSAGE	DESCRIPTION
MM_DELETEITEM	Deletes menu item.
MM_DISMISSMENU	Removes the menu display.
MM_ENDMENUMODE	Terminates menu selection.
MM_INSERTITEM	Inserts menu item.
MM_ISITEMVALID	Queries if item is valid.
MM_ITEMIDFROMPOSITION	Retrieves item's identity.
MM_ITEMPOSITIONFROMID	Retrieves position of menu item.
MM_QUERYITEM	Retrieves information about menu item.
MM_QUERYITEMATTR	Retrieves attributes and style bits.
MM_QUERYITEMCOUNT	Retrieves the number of menu items.

(continued)

Table 17-4: Continued

MESSAGE	DESCRIPTION
MM_QUERYITEMTEXT	Copies menu string to a buffer.
MM_QUERYITEMTEXTLENGTH	Retrieves text length.
MM_QUERYSELITEMID	Retrieves identity of selected menu item.
MM_REMOVEITEM	Removes a menu item.
MM_SELECTITEM	Selects an item.
MM_SETITEM	Sets item definition.
MM_SETITEMATTR	Sets an item's attributes.
MM_SETITEMHANDLE	Sets the item handle.
MM_SETITEMTEXT	Sets item text.
MM_STARTMENUMODE	Starts menu selection.

Table 17-5: Scrollbar Messages

MESSAGE	DESCRIPTION
SBM_QUERYHILITE	Obtains highlight state of scrollbar.
SBM_QUERYPOS	Retrieves slider position.
SBM_QUERYRANGE	Retrieves slider's boundary values.
SBM_SETHILITE	Sets highlight state of scrollbar.
SBM_SETPOS	Sets slider position.
SBM_SETSCROLLBAR	Sets slider range.

Table 17-6: Static Control Messages

MESSAGE	DESCRIPTION
SM_QUERYHANDLE	Retrieves the handle of a display object.
SM_SETHANDLE	Sets the display object handle.

Table 17-7: Titlebar Messages

MESSAGE	DESCRIPTION
TBM_QUERYHILITE	Retrieves the titlebar highlight state.
TBM_SETHILITE	Sets the titlebar highlight state.
TBM_TRACKMOVE	Moves the titlebar's owner window.

Table 17-8: Window Messages

MESSAGE	DESCRIPTION
WM_ACTIVATE	Toggles a window's active state.
WM_ACTIVATETHREAD	Announces activation of another thread's window.
WM_ADJUSTWINDOWPOS	Announces intention to adjust window position.
WM_BUTTON1DBLCLK	Indicates click on the left mouse button.
WM_BUTTON1DOWN	Indicates the left mouse button is depressed.
WM_BUTTON1UP	Indicates the left mouse button is released.
WM_BUTTON2DBLCLK	Indicates click on the center mouse button.
WM_BUTTON2DOWN	Indicates the center mouse button is depressed.
WM_BUTTON2UP	Indicates the center mouse button is released.
WM_BUTTON3DBLCLK	Indicates click on the right mouse button.
WM_BUTTON3DOWN	Indicates the right mouse button is depressed.
WM_BUTTON3UP	Indicates the right mouse button is released.
WM_BUTTONCLICKFIRST	Tracks relation of first to second button click.
WM_BUTTONCLICKLAST	Tracks relation of second to first button click.
WM_CALCFRAMERECT	Allows preservation of resized window areas.
WM_CALCVALIDRECTS	Allows complex repositioning of windows.
WM_CANCELMODE	Cancels existing modal dialog box.
WM_CHAR	Contains the most recent key press in the queue.
WM_CLOSE	Announces that a window is about to close.

(continued)

Table 17-8: Continued

MESSAGE	DESCRIPTION
WM_COMMAND	Carries data for control windows/accelerators.
WM_CONTROL	Carries control data for child windows.
WM_CONTROLHEAP	Requests a heap handle for a child window.
WM_CONTROLPOINTER	Announces mouse pointer is on a child window.
WM_CREATE	Announces that a window has just been created.
WM_DDE_ACK	Acknowledges receipt of various DDE messages.
WM_DDE_ADVISE	Requests update for window posting the message.
WM_DDE_DATA	Notifies second application of impending data.
WM_DDE_EXECUTE	Contains a command string for server application.
WM_DDE_FIRST	Announces the first message in DDE exchange.
WM_DDE_INITIATE	Requests DDE conversation of another application.
WM_DDE_INITIATEACK	Acknowledges DDE request for conversation.
WM_DDE_POKE	Asks another application to accept DDE message.
WM_DDE_REQUEST	Request for DDE message from client application.
WM_DDE_TERMINATE	Request to terminate DDE conversation.
WM_DDE_UNADVISE	Announces server application should not update.
WM_DESTROY	Announces that window is about to be destroyed.
WM_DESTROYCLIPBOARD	Announces that the clipboard has been emptied.
WM_DRAWCLIPBOARD	Notification that clipboard contents have changed.
WM_DRAWITEM	Tells owners that a listbox item needs redrawing.
WM_ENABLE	Occurs when a window's enable state is changing.
WM_ERASEBACKGROUND	Tells the frame window to redraw itself.
WM_ERROR	Allows detection of error condition.
WM_FLASHWINDOW	Tells the current window to flash.
WM_FOCUSCHANGE	Announces that the focus window is changing.
WM_FORMATFRAME	Tells frame window to recalculate the controls.
WM_HELP	Announces request from user for help.
WM_HITTEST	Carries mouse pointer position data.
WM_HSCROLL	Announces request to scroll window.
WM_HSCROLLCLIPBOARD	Command to scroll clipboard horizontally.

(continued)

Table 17-8: Continued

MESSAGE	DESCRIPTION
WM_INITDLG	Occurs when a dialog box window is created.
WM_INITMENU	Occurs when a menu is being initialized.
WM_JOURNALNOTIFY	Allows complete scan of message queue.
WM_MATCHMNEMONIC	Tells owner if mnemonic has been found.
WM_MEASUREITEM	Command to calculate height of items.
WM_MENUEND	Notification that menu is terminating.
WM_MENUSELECT	Announces a menu item has been selected by user.
WM_MOUSELAST	Announces the last mouse message in a series.
WM_MOUSEMOVE	Occurs whenever the mouse pointer is moved.
WM_MINMAXFRAME	Indicates minimize, maximize, or restore operation.
WM_MOUSEFIRST	Announces the first mouse message in a series.
WM_MOVE	Occurs when a window moves.
WM_NEXTMENU	Allows you to obtain next/previous menu handle.
WM_NULL	Occurs when a WM_CHAR message is translated into a keyboard accelerator.
WM_OTHERWINDOWDESTROYED	Announces a registered window is being destroyed.
WM_PAINT	Announces that a window needs to be repainted.
WM_PAINTCLIPBOARD	Command to paint the clipboard.
WM_QUERYACCELTABLE	Request for handle to accelerator table.
WM_QUERYBORDERSIZE	Contains the window border dimensions.
WM_QUERYCONVERTPOS	Retrieves a conversion code.
WM_QUERYDLGCODE	Queries dialog box control window capabilities.
WM_QUERYFOCUSCHAIN	Queries the current input focus chain.
WM_QUERYFRAMECTLCOUNT	Allows you to obtain the count of frame controls.
WM_QUERYFRAMEINFO	Queries window to find out its configuration.
WM_QUERYICON	Retrieves icon handle from frame window.
WM_QUERYTRACKINFO	Occurs at start of a TBM_TRACKMOVE message.
WM_QUERYWINDOWPARAMS	Retrieves parameters from window data structure.
WM_QUEUESTATUS	Returns queue status for hook processing.
WM_QUIT	Announces that application is terminating.

(continued)

Table 17-8: Continued

MESSAGE	DESCRIPTION
WM_RENDERALLFMTS	Contains available clipboard data formats
WM_RENDERFMT	Specifies the clipboard data format.
WM_SEM1	Contains message for a separate thread.
WM_SEM2	Contains an inter-thread message.
WM_SEM3	Contains an inter-thread message.
WM_SEM4	Contains an inter-thread message.
WM_SETACCELTABLE	Specifies a handle for an accelerator table.
WM_SETBORDERSIZE	Changes the window border size control.
WM_SETFOCUS	Announces a change of input focus.
WM_SETICON	Contains icon handle to set application icon.
WM_SETSELECTION	Announces selection state of a window.
WM_SETWINDOWPARAMS	Occurs when window configuration changes.
WM_SHOW	Occurs when visible state of window changes.
WM_SIZE	Occurs when size of window changes.
WM_SIZECLIPBOARD	Announces clipboard has changed size.
WM_SUBSTITUTESTRING	Requests string substitution.
WM_SYSCOLORCHANGE	Announces color change to top-level windows.
WM_SYSCOMMAND	Contains command message from a control window.
WM_SYSVALUECHANGED	Occurs when an application posts a system value change.
WM_TIMER	Occurs when the timer has timed out.
WM_TRACKFRAME	Notification that tracking operation is beginning.
WM_TRANSLATEACCEL	Allows accelerator translation of WM_CHAR.
WM_UPDATEFRAME	Occurs after format change to window.
WM_USER	Defines beginning of user messages.
WM_VSCROLL	Announces request to scroll window.
WM_VSCROLLCLIPBOARD	Command to scroll clipboard vertically.

Button Control Messages

Button messages give you an efficient way to exchange data with button controls, including pushbuttons, radio buttons, and checkboxes, among others. Button controls can be any of 13 different styles, ranging from BS_PUSHBUTTON to BS_HELP (see Chapter 8 for complete information).

Data sent by a button control to your application is contained in the WM_CONTROL message. Commands are sent in the WM_COMMAND, WM_SYSCOMMAND, and WM_HELP messages. As with other controls, it is the WM_CONTROL message that is most important. Here is a code fragment that tests whether a button has been clicked:

```
case WM_CONTROL:
    if(SHORT2FROMMP(mp1) == BN_CLICKED)
      {
            .
            .
            .
      }
    break;
```

The BN_CLICKED identifier in the code fragment is a button notification code. The WM_CONTROL message identifies a button control in *mp1 (low)*. It also sends any of three BN (button notification) codes in *mp1 (high)*:

- BN_CLICKED — Button has been clicked.

- BN_DBLCLICKED — Button has been double-clicked.

- BN_PAINT — Button needs repainting.

You can also use the button messages to send data to a button control. This is accomplished with the WinSendMsg or the WinSendDlgItemMsg function. The following function call sends a message to a button control:

```
WinSendDlgItemMsg(hwndDlg,SHORT1FROMMP(mp1), BM_SETCHECK,
                 MPFROM2SHORT(TRUE, 0), NULL);
```

You will notice in the WinSendDlgItemMsg function that the SHORT1FROMMP and MPFROM2SHORT macros are used. The first macro identifies the checkbox control while the latter sets the high word of *mp1* for the BM_SETCHECK message. The following listings describe all the button messages.

BM_CLICK

This message simulates a button click and causes the same effect on a button control as if the user had clicked on the mouse button, producing a WM_CONTROL message and a BN_CLICKED notification message.

PARAMETER	TYPE	DESCRIPTION
mp1	BOOL	Specifies whether the button is up or down. A TRUE value specifies that the default release of the mouse button occurs.

No **return value** is used for this message.

BM_QUERYCHECK

This message is application generated and has no parameter values. The message is sent to a control window to access the checked state of a button control. The button control must be one of the following styles:

- BS_AUTORADIOBUTTON
- BS_AUTOCHECKBOX
- BS_AUTO3STATE
- BS_CHECKBOX
- BS_RADIOBUTTON
- BS_3STATE

The **return value** is 1 if the button is unchecked, 2 if the button is checked, and 3 if it is an indeterminate state.

BM_QUERYCHECKINDEX

This message is application generated and has no parameter values. The message is sent to assess the zero-based index of a checked radio button. It can be sent to any radio button or auto radio button within a group.

The **return value** is the zero-based index of the checked radio button if the operation succeeds. If it fails, the return value is -1.

BM_QUERYHILITE

This message is application generated and has no parameter values. The message is sent to assess the highlighting state of a button control. The message applies only to buttons with a style of BS_PUSHBUTTON.

The **return value** is TRUE when the button is highlighted. It is FALSE when it is not highlighted or if the button is not of style BS_PUSHBUT-TON.

BM_SETCHECK

This message is application generated. It is sent to set the checked state of a button control. When *fCheck* is TRUE, the button is displayed as checked. If it is FALSE, the button is displayed as unchecked. When the button style is BS_USERBUTTON, a WM_CONTROL message is sent to the owner with a notification code of BN_PAINT. Otherwise, the message operates as described for the following button styles:

- BS_AUTOCHECKBOX

- BS_AUTORADIOBUTTON

- BS_AUTO3STATE

- BS_CHECKBOX

- BS_RADIOBUTTON

- BS_3STATE

PARAMETER	TYPE	DESCRIPTION
mp1	USHORT	Specifies the check state of the button. A value of FALSE displays the button as unchecked. A value of TRUE displays the button as checked. A value of 2 also displays a three-state button in its indeterminate state.

The **return value** is the prior check state of the button.

BM_SETDEFAULT

This message is application generated. It is sent to set the default state of a button control. When the button is of style BS_PUSHBUTTON or BS_USERBUTTON, and *fDefault* is TRUE, the button is displayed in its default state. If *fDefault* is FALSE, it is displayed in its non-default state.

PARAMETER	TYPE	DESCRIPTION
mp1	USHORT	A TRUE value sets the default state. A FALSE value sets the non-default state.

The **return value** is TRUE when the operation succeeds. It is FALSE when an error occurs.

BM_SETHILITE

This message is application generated. It is sent to set the highlight state of a button control. The button is displayed as highlighted if it is of style BS_PUSHBUTTON and *fHighlight* is TRUE. If *fHighlight* is FALSE, the button is not highlighted. Buttons of style BS_USERBUTTON receive a WM_CONTROL message as a result of BM_SETHILITE. This WM_CONTROL message contains a notification code of BN_HILITE or BN_UNHILITE.

PARAMETER	TYPE	DESCRIPTION
mp1	BOOL	Specifies the highlight state. A TRUE value sets the button's highlighted state. A FALSE value sets the non-highlighted state.

The **return value** is TRUE when the prior button state was set to highlight mode. It is FALSE when it was not set to highlight mode.

Entry Field Control Messages

This section lists the messages designed for entry field controls. The EM messages allow you to specify various default states for entry field text as well as to paste, copy, and delete text contained in an entry field. Most frequently, entry field controls appear in dialog boxes, but you can include them elsewhere in an application if you want. Entry field controls can be any of the following four styles:

- ES_CENTER — Entry field text is centered.
- ES_MARGIN — Entry field text includes margin border.
- ES_LEFT — Entry field text is left justified.
- ES_RIGHT — Entry field text is right justified.

As with other controls, the WM_CONTROL message conveys specific information related to entry field controls. The WM_CONTROL message identifies an entry control in *mp1 (low)*. Additionally, the following EN (entry notification) codes are contained in *mp1 (high)*:

- EN_CHANGE — Entry field contents have changed.
- EN_KILLFOCUS — Entry is losing focus.
- EN_MEMERROR — Entry field lacks enough allocated memory.
- EN_SCROLL — Entry field is about to scroll.
- EN_SETFOCUS — Entry field is gaining focus.

The following code fragment sets the maximum number of characters for the entry field control:

```
WinSendDlgItemMsg(hwnd, IDD_SOMEDIALOG, EM_SETTEXTLIMIT,
                MPFROM2SHORT(80, 0), NULL);
```

The example sends a message to a dialog box and uses the EM_SET-TEXTLIMIT message to specify a text length of 80 characters. The key to this function call is the MPFROM2SHORT macro. Note how the macro not only constructs the expected *mp1 (low)* value, but also combines the zero, or NULL, value that the message requires in *mp1 (high)*. The following listings describe all the entry field control messages.

EM_CLEAR

This message is application generated and has no parameter values. The message is sent to delete the current selection in an entry field control.

The **return value** is TRUE when the operation succeeds. It is FALSE when an error occurs.

EM_COPY

This message is application generated and has no parameter values. The message is sent to paste the current selection in an entry field control. The selection is pasted to the clipboard in CF_TEXT format. This message does not affect the selection state of the control.

The **return value** is TRUE when the operation succeeds. It is FALSE when an error occurs.

EM_CUT

This message is application generated and has no parameter values. The message is sent to delete the current selection in an entry field control. The selection is pasted to the clipboard in CF_TEXT format.

The **return value** is TRUE when the operation succeeds. It is FALSE when an error occurs.

EM_PASTE

This message is application generated and has no parameter values. The message is sent to replace the current selection in an entry field control. The replacement selection, which is of the CF_TEXT format, is obtained from the clipboard.

The **return value** is TRUE when the operation succeeds. It is FALSE when an error occurs.

EM_QUERYCHANGED

This message is application generated and has no parameter values. The message is sent to assess whether the contents of the entry field control have been modified since the last occurrence of a WM_QUERYWINDOW-PARAMS or EM_QUERYCHANGED message.

The **return value** is TRUE when the contents have been modified. It is FALSE when this is not the case, or when an error occurs.

EM_QUERYFIRSTCHAR

This message is application generated and has no parameter values. The message is sent to obtain the index of the character in the first position of the edit control.

The **return value** is the zero-based offset of the first character.

EM_QUERYSEL

This message is application generated and has no parameter values. The message is sent to obtain the offsets of the current selection in an entry field control.

The **return value** (in its low word) contains the byte offset of the first character of the selection. The byte offset of the last character is contained in the high word of the return value.

EM_SETFIRSTCHAR

This message is application generated. It is sent to set the character that is displayed in the first position of an entry field. The contents of the field are scrolled if necessary.

PARAMETER	TYPE	DESCRIPTION
mp1	SHORT	Specifies the offset to the character to place in the first position of the entry field control.

The **return value** is TRUE when the operation succeeds. It is FALSE when an error occurs.

EM_SETSEL

This message is application generated. It is sent to set the selection range in an entry field. The entire section of text is selected when the first character position is zero and the last character position is greater than or equal to the total characters in the entry field.

PARAMETER	TYPE	DESCRIPTION
mp1 (low)	USHORT	Specifies the first character offset.
mp1 (high)	USHORT	Specifies the last character offset.

The **return value** is TRUE when the operation succeeds. It is FALSE when an error occurs.

EM_SETTEXTLIMIT

This message is application generated. It is sent to set the maximum number of characters for an entry field control. This message causes the system to allocate memory from the control heap for the specified maximum number of characters.

PARAMETER	TYPE	DESCRIPTION
mp1	SHORT	Specifies the maximum number of characters for an entry field control.

The **return value** is TRUE when the operation succeeds. It is FALSE when not enough memory exists to hold the specified number of characters.

Listbox Control Messages

Listboxes contain a series of text strings (one per line) from which the user can select a string and initiate a related action. A listbox always incorporates a scrollbar so the user can scroll through the contents. If the number of text strings in the listbox does not exceed the height of the listbox, the scrollbar is automatically disabled. Each string in a listbox has an associated index value. The index begins with the system identifier, LIT_FIRST. A listbox can be any of the following three styles:

- LS_MULTIPLESEL — Listbox supports multiple selection.
- LS_NOADJUSTPOS — Listbox is confined to specified dimensions.
- LS_OWNERDRAW — Listbox supports bitmaps as well as text strings.

Listboxes send three window messages: WM_CONTROL, WM_DRAW-
ITEM, and WM_MEASUREITEM. The latter two messages cause an application to do exactly what their names indicate — that is, to draw or
measure an item. The WM_CONTROL message identifies the listbox in
the low word of its *mp1* parameter. In *mp2 (high)*, it can send any of the
following LN (listbox notification) codes:

- LN_ENTER — Listbox has received an Enter or Return key press.

- LN_KILLFOCUS — Listbox has relinquished input focus.

- LN_SCROLL — Listbox is about to scroll.

- LN_SELECT — Listbox item is being selected.

- LN_SETFOCUS — Listbox has gained the focus.

You can use the WinSendMsg or WinSendDlgItemMsg to send listbox
messages. The following code fragment uses one of the LM messages to delete an item from a listbox:

```
WinSendDlgItemMsg(hdlg,id,
                  LM_DELETEITEM,
                  MPFROM2SHORT(index,0),0l);
```

This call to WinSendDlgItemMsg simply tells the listbox control to delete the item specified by *index*. The *mp1 (high)* parameter of
LM_DELETEITEM is reserved as NULL so the MPFROM@SHORT
macro requires 0 or NULL in this corresponding position. The following
listings describe all the listbox control messages.

LM_DELETEALL

This message is application generated and has no parameter values. The
message is sent to delete all items in a listbox control.

The **return value** is TRUE when the operation succeeds. It is FALSE
when an error occurs.

LM_DELETEITEM

This message is application generated. It is sent to delete a listbox item.

PARAMETER	TYPE	DESCRIPTION
mp1	SHORT	Specifies the index of the item.

The **return value** is the number of items that remain in the list.

LM_INSERTITEM

This message is application generated. It is sent to insert an item into a listbox control. The *iItem* parameter determines placement of the item.

PARAMETER	TYPE	DESCRIPTION
mp1	SHORT	Specifies the item's index. The index must be zero-based or one of the following identifiers:
		LIT_END
		LIT_SORTASCENDING
		LIT_SORTDESCENDING
mp2	PSZ	Specifies the text to insert.

The **return value** is the text item position if the operation succeeds. If the listbox cannot allocate space to insert the item, the return value is LIT_MEMERROR. Other errors are returned as LIT_ERROR.

LM_QUERYITEMCOUNT

This message is application generated and has no parameter values. The message is sent to obtain the number of items in a listbox control.

The **return value** contains the item count.

LM_QUERYITEMHANDLE

This message is application generated. It is sent to obtain the handle of the specified item in a listbox.

PARAMETER	TYPE	DESCRIPTION
mp1	USHORT	Specifies the item's index.

The **return value** is the handle to the item if the operation succeeds. If the operation fails, the return value is zero.

LM_QUERYITEMTEXT

This message is application generated. It is sent to copy the text for a listbox item. The text is copied into a buffer that the application must provide. The buffer size can be established by sending a LM_QUERYITEM-TEXTLENGTH message for the item.

PARAMETER	TYPE	DESCRIPTION
mp1 (low)	USHORT	Specifies the item's index.
mp1 (high)	SHORT	Specifies the maximum character count.
mp2	PSZ	Pointer to the text buffer.

The **return value** is the length of the text, excluding the null terminator.

LM_QUERYITEMTEXTLENGTH

This message is application generated. It is sent to obtain the length of the text in a listbox item.

PARAMETER	TYPE	DESCRIPTION
mp1	USHORT	Specifies the index of the item.

The **return value** is the character length of the text. If the item does not exist, or an error occurs, the operation returns zero.

LM_QUERYSELECTION

This message is application generated. It is sent to enumerate the selected listbox item(s).

PARAMETER	TYPE	DESCRIPTION
mp1	SHORT	Specifies the index of the previous item. Setting *mp1* to LIT_FIRST selects the first item in a multiple listbox control.

The **return value** is the selected item's index for a single selection listbox; it is the next item's index for a multiple listbox. If no items are selected, or no item's index is greater than *iItem* (in the case of a multiple listbox), the operation returns LIT_NONE.

LM_QUERYTOPINDEX

This message is application generated and has no parameter values. The message is sent to obtain the index of the item at the top of the listbox.

The **return value** is the item's index. If the listbox is empty, the operation returns LIT_NONE.

LM_SEARCHSTRING

This message is application generated. It is sent to search the list for a match string. The message operation returns the first string that matches the specified string. Case sensitive (LSS_CASESENSITVE), leading character (LSS_PREFIX), and substring matching (LSS_SUBSTRING) are supported.

PARAMETER	TYPE	DESCRIPTION
mp1 (low)	USHORT	Specifies one of the following identifiers: LSS_CASESENSITIVE. LSS_PREFIX LSS_SUBSTRING
mp1 (high)	USHORT	Specifies the index of the item to search first. Specifying LIT_FIRST initiates the search with the first item. All searches wrap to the beginning and continue until the return to the first item searched.
mp2	PSZ	Pointer to the search string.

The **return value** is the index of the next item meeting the search criteria. The operation returns LIT_NONE if no match is found. It returns LIT_ERROR if an error occurs.

LM_SELECTITEM

This message is application generated. It is sent to set the selection state of a listbox item. When sending this message to a single selection listbox, the selection state of the previously selected item is toggled.

PARAMETER	TYPE	DESCRIPTION
mp1	SHORT	Specifies the index of the item to select/ deselect.
mp2	BOOL	Specifies whether the item should be selected/ deselected. Setting this to TRUE selects the item. Setting it to FALSE deselects the item.

The **return value** is TRUE when the operation succeeds. It is FALSE when an error occurs.

LM_SETITEMHANDLE

This message is application generated. It is sent to set the handle of a listbox item.

PARAMETER	TYPE	DESCRIPTION
mp1	USHORT	Specifies an index to an item.
mp2	ULONG	Specifies a handle to an item.

The **return value** is TRUE when the item exists. The operation returns FALSE if the item does not exist.

LM_SETITEMHEIGHT

This message is application generated. It is sent to set the height of the items in a listbox

PARAMETER	TYPE	DESCRIPTION
mp1	ULONG	Specifies the height of each listbox item.

The **return value** is TRUE when the operation succeeds. It is FALSE when an error occurs.

LM_SETITEMTEXT

This message is application generated. It is sent to copy text from a specified buffer to an item in a listbox.

PARAMETER	TYPE	DESCRIPTION
mp1	SHORT	Specifies the item's index.
mp2	PSZ	Pointer to the buffer that contains the text to copy to the item specified by *mp1*.

The **return value** is TRUE when the operation succeeds. It is FALSE when an error occurs.

LM_SETTOPINDEX

This message is application generated. It is sent to scroll an item to the top of a listbox.

PARAMETER	TYPE	DESCRIPTION
mp1	SHORT	Specifies the index of the item to place at the top of the listbox.

The **return value** is TRUE when the operation succeeds. It is FALSE when an error occurs.

Menu Control Messages

The menu control messages allow you to interact with both the system and application menus. Menus exist throughout the complex infrastructure of the Presentation Manager and its messages can be used for purposes ranging from checking or unchecking a menu item to modifying system menus.

When you program menus, you need to specify a menu style (denoted by an MS identifier). The MS style dictates various default actions of a menu and is detailed in Chapter 7. Menus also require you to specify menu item styles (denoted by MIS identifiers) and menu item attributes (denoted by MIA identifiers). These menu components are also described in Chapter 7.

Menus send several window messages, but generally, you need to be the most concerned with the WM_COMMAND message, which conveys the user's selection in the form of a command.

You can use the COMMANDMSG macro to obtain the command. Alternatively, you can use the Presentation Manager's standard extraction macros if you want. Here is the complete list of window messages that you use with menus:

- WM_COMMAND

- WM_DRAWITEM

- WM_HELP

- WM_INITMENU

- WM_MEASUREITEM

- WM_MENUSELECT

- WM_NEXTMENU

- WM_SYSCOMMAND

To pass data to a menu, you use the WinSendMsg function. In doing so, be aware of these concerns: the correct handle to the menu, the message's parameters, and whether you want to check or uncheck the menu item. If, say, you want to both query and check a menu item, you would need two separate calls to WinSendMsg. The following code fragment is the appropriate call to check a menu item:

```
WinSendMsg (hwndMenu,
            MM_SETITEMATTR,
            MPFROM2SHORT (sItem, TRUE),
            MPFROM2SHORT (MIA_CHECKED, MIA_CHECKED));
```

In the example, the first use of the MPFROM2SHORT macro specifies the menu item and also tells the menu control to search submenus and/or resultant dialog boxes until it finds the item. The second use of the macro tells the menu control to check the item (as indicated by the MIA_CHECKED identifier). The following listings describe all the menu control messages.

MM_DELETEITEM

This message is application generated. It is sent to delete a menu item.

PARAMETER	TYPE	DESCRIPTION
mp1 (low)	USHORT	Specifies the menu item ID.
mp1 (high)	BOOL	Specifies submenus in the search. A value of TRUE specifies submenus. A FALSE value does not.

The **return value** is the count of menu items that remain if the operation succeeds. If it fails, the return value is FALSE.

MM_DISMISSMENU

This message is application generated. It is sent to dismiss a menu. The menu control receives the message and responds by making the menu invisible.

The **return value** is TRUE when the operation succeeds. It is FALSE when an error occurs.

MM_ENDMENUMODE

This message is application generated. It is sent to a menu to dismiss a menu selection.

PARAMETER	TYPE	DESCRIPTION
mp1	BOOL	Specifies whether a submenu window is dismissed. Setting this to TRUE dismisses the submenu. Setting it to FALSE retains the submenu.

No **return value** is supplied by this message.

MM_INSERTITEM

This message is application generated. It is sent to insert a menu item. The *pmi* parameter, which points to the item to be inserted, references the MENUITEM structure. If the index's item is MIT_END, the item is added to the end of the list. If the item style is MIS_TEXT, the text of the item is pointed to by *mp2*.

PARAMETER	TYPE	DESCRIPTION
mp1	PMENUITEM	Pointer to a MENUITEM structure.
mp2	PSZ	Pointer to the menu item text.

The **return value** is the insert position of the menu item if the operation succeeds. If the operation cannot allocate space to insert the item, it returns MIT_MEMERROR. If any other error occurs, the operation returns MIT_ERROR when the *iPosition* field of MENUITEM is invalid.

MM_ISITEMVALID

This message is application generated. It is sent to establish whether a menu item can be selected.

PARAMETER	TYPE	DESCRIPTION
mp1 (low)	USHORT	Specifies a menu item ID.
mp1 (high)	BOOL	Specifies submenus in the search. A value of TRUE specifies submenus. A value of FALSE does not.

The **return value** is TRUE when the operation succeeds. It is FALSE when an error occurs.

MM_ITEMIDFROMPOSITION

This message is application generated. It is sent to obtain the menu item ID.

PARAMETER	TYPE	DESCRIPTION
mp1	SHORT	Specifies the menu item index.

The **return value** is the menu item ID. If the operation results in an error, it returns MID_ERROR.

MM_ITEMPOSITIONFROMID

This message is application generated. It is sent to obtain the menu item position.

PARAMETER	TYPE	DESCRIPTION
mp1 (low)	USHORT	Specifies a menu item ID.
mp1 (high)	BOOL	Specifies submenus in the search. A value of TRUE specifies submenus. A value of FALSE ignores submenus.

The **return value** is the menu item index. If no item is found, the operation returns MIT_NONE.

MM_QUERYITEM

This message is application generated. It is sent to copy information about the menu item to a MENUITEM structure. Note that this message does not obtain text for MIS_TEXT menu items. Use the MM_QUERYITEM-TEXT message to do this.

PARAMETER	TYPE	DESCRIPTION
mp1 (low)	USHORT	Specifies a menu item ID.
mp1 (high)	BOOL	Specifies submenus in the search. A value of TRUE specifies submenus. A value of FALSE ignores submenus.
mp2	PMENUITEM	Pointer to a MENUITEM structure.

The **return value** is TRUE when the operation succeeds. It is FALSE when an error occurs.

MM_QUERYITEMATTR

This message is application generated. It is sent to obtain the attribute state of the menu item.

PARAMETER	TYPE	DESCRIPTION
mp1 (low)	USHORT	Specifies a menu item ID.
mp1 (high)	BOOL	Specifies submenus in the search. A value of TRUE specifies submenus. A FALSE value does not.
mp2	USHORT	Specifies the attribute state, which can be any combination of the following identifiers:

> MIA_FRAMED
>
> MIA_CHECKED
>
> MIA_DISABLED
>
> MIA_HILITED

The **return value** is the attribute state of the menu item.

MM_QUERYITEMCOUNT

This message is application generated and has no parameter values. The message is sent to find out how many items a menu contains. Submenus are counted as a single item when the message is sent to the menu bar.

The **return value** is the number of menu items.

MM_QUERYITEMTEXT

This message is application generated. It is sent to obtain the text of a menu item. This message only applies to menu items of style MIS_TEXT. Before using this message, you can obtain the length of the menu item text by using the MM_QUERYITEMTEXTLENGTH message.

PARAMETER	TYPE	DESCRIPTION
mp1 (low)	USHORT	Specifies a menu item ID.
mp1 (high)	SHORT	Specifies the maximum number of characters to copy from the menu item.
mp2	PSZ	Pointer to a buffer to hold the copied text.

The **return value** is the string length of the menu item. The operation returns zero if no text is copied due to an error.

MM_QUERYITEMTEXTLENGTH

This message is application generated. It is sent to obtain the length of a menu item. This message only applies to menu items of style MIS_TEXT.

PARAMETER	TYPE	DESCRIPTION
mp1	USHORT	Specifies the menu item ID.

The **return value** is the string length of the menu item.

MM_QUERYSELITEMID

This message is application generated and has no parameter values. The message is sent to obtain the identifier of the selected menu item.

The **return value** is the menu item ID. If no item is selected, the operation returns MIT_NONE. If an error occurs, MID_ERROR is returned.

MM_REMOVEITEM

This message is application generated. It is sent to remove a menu item.

PARAMETER	TYPE	DESCRIPTION
mp1 (low)	USHORT	Specifies a menu item ID.
mp1 (high)	BOOL	Specifies submenus in the search. A value of TRUE specifies submenus. A value of FALSE ignores submenus.

The **return value** is the number of items that remain in the menu. If the operation encounters an error, it returns FALSE.

MM_SELECTITEM

This message is application generated. It is sent to select or deselect a menu item.

PARAMETER	TYPE	DESCRIPTION
mp1 (low)	USHORT	Specifies a menu item ID. Setting this parameter to MIT_NONE specifies that all items in the menu are deselected.
mp1 (high)	BOOL	Specifies submenus in the search. A value of TRUE specifies submenus. A value of FALSE ignores submenus.
mp1 (low)	BOOL	Specifies whether the menu is selected. Setting this parameter to TRUE selects the item. Setting it to FALSE deselects the item.
mp1 (high)	BOOL	Specifies whether the menu is dismissed. Setting this parameter to TRUE posts a WM_COMMAND, WM_SYSCOMMAND, or WM_HELP message before the item is actually dismissed.

The **return value** is TRUE when the operation succeeds. It is FALSE when an error occurs.

MM_SETITEM

This message is application generated. It is sent to set a menu item and copy the item definition into a copy of the MENUITEM structure. When *fInclSubMenus* is TRUE and the menu does not include an item that corresponds to *id* field in MENUITEM, the operation searches the submenus and dialog boxes associated with the menu.

PARAMETER	TYPE	DESCRIPTION
mp1	BOOL	Specifies submenus in the search. A value of TRUE specifies submenus. A value of FALSE ignores submenus.
mp2	PMENUITEM	Pointer to a MENUITEM structure.

The **return value** is TRUE when the operation succeeds. It is FALSE when an error occurs.

MM_SETITEMATTR

This message is application generated and has no parameter values. The message is sent to change the attributes of a menu item.

PARAMETER	TYPE	DESCRIPTION
mp1 (low)	USHORT	Specifies a menu item ID.
mp1 (high)	BOOL	Specifies submenus in the search. A value of TRUE specifies submenus. A value of FALSE ignores submenus.
mp2 (low)	USHORT	Specifies an attribute mask. It can be any combination of the following identifiers:

MIA_FRAMED

MIA_CHECKED

MIA_DISABLED

MIA_HILITED

mp2 (high)	USHORT	Specifies new attributes for a menu item.

The **return value** is TRUE when the operation succeeds. It is FALSE when an error occurs.

MM_SETITEMHANDLE

This message is application generated. It is sent to set the handle to a menu item. You can use this message to display a bitmap for a menu item.

PARAMETER	TYPE	DESCRIPTION
mp1	BOOL	Specifies a menu item ID.
mp2l	HWND	Specifies a handle to the menu item.

The **return value** is TRUE when the operation succeeds. It is FALSE when an error occurs.

MM_SETITEMTEXT

This message is application generated. It is sent to copy buffered text to a menu item. The style of menu item must be MIS_TEXT.

PARAMETER	TYPE	DESCRIPTION
mp1	BOOL	Specifies a menu item ID.
mp2	PSZ	Pointer to a text buffer.

The **return value** is TRUE when the operation succeeds. It is FALSE when an error occurs.

MM_STARTMENUMODE

This message is application generated. It is sent to begin menu selection.

PARAMETER	TYPE	DESCRIPTION
mp1 (low)	BOOL	Specifies whether the selected menu should show the associated submenu. Setting this parameter to TRUE displays the submenu.
mp2 (high)	BOOL	Specifies whether the menu should be resumed. Setting this parameter to TRUE resumes the menu.

The **return value** is TRUE when the operation succeeds. It is FALSE when an error occurs.

Scrollbar Messages

Scrollbar controls give the user a common way to page through different types of windows in the Presentation Manager. Additionally, you can incorporate horizontal scrollbars into a window, thus allowing the user to scroll the window sideways. Scrollbars have two window styles that specify how the scrollbar is created. The SBS_HORZ specifies a horizontal scrollbar and the SBS_VERT specifies a vertical scrollbar.

Processing scrollbar messages means handling the WM_HSCROLL and WM_VSCROLL window messages to determine what action to take. These window messages identify the scrollbar in *mp1 (low)* and supply SB (scrollbar notification) codes in *mp1 (high)*. The WM_HSCROLL message supplies the following SB codes:

- SB_LINELEFT — Scroll left.
- SB_LINERIGHT — Scroll right.

- SB_PAGELEFT — Scroll left one full page.

- SB_PAGERIGHT — Scroll right one full page.

- SB_SLIDERPOSITION — Scroll to final slider position.

- SB_SLIDERTRACK — Scroll as slider moves.

- SB_ENDSCROLL — Scrolling has finished.

The WM_VSCROLL message supplies the following SB codes:

- SB_LINEUP — Scroll up one line.

- SB_LINEDOWN — Scroll down one line.

- SB_PAGEUP — Scroll up one full page.

- SB_PAGEDOWN — Scroll down one full page.

- SB_SLIDERPOSITION — Scroll to final slider position.

- SB_SLIDERTRACK — Scroll as slider moves.

- SB_ENDSCROLL — Scrolling has finished.

To pass data to a scrollbar, you can use the WinSendMsg or WinSendDlgItemMsg, depending on the scrollbar's orientation. The following code fragment sets a scrollbar's range and slider position:

```
WinSendMsg(hwndHscroll, SBM_SETSCROLLBAR,
            MPFROM2SHORT (sHpos, 0),
            MPFROM2SHORT (0, sHmax)) ;
```

In the example, the SBM_SCROLLBAR message requires three values. The only reserved value is *mp1 (high)*. The *mp1 (low)* value specifies the position of the slider. The two *mp2* values specify the range. The following listings describe all the scrollbar control messages.

SBM_QUERYHILITE

This message is application generated and has no parameter values. The message is sent to obtain the current highlight state of the scrollbar. The message returns one of the following identifiers, which indicates the area that currently is highlighted:

- SB_LINEUP
- SB_LINEDOWN
- SB_PAGEUP
- SB_PAGEDOWN
- SB_SLIDERTRACK

The **return value** is one of the SB identifiers.

SBM_QUERYPOS

This message is application generated and has no parameter values. The message is sent to obtain the current position of the slider in a scrollbar window.

The **return value** is the slider position.

SBM_QUERYRANGE

This message is application generated and has no parameter values. The message is sent to obtain the bounding values of a scrollbar.

The **return value** contains the bounding values for the scrollbar. The low word contains the first bounding value. The high word contains the last bounding value.

SBM_SETHILITE

This message is application generated. Its purpose is to set the highlight state of the scrollbar. You should set the *mp1* parameter to an SB identifier that specifies the area of the scrollbar that you want highlighted. The following SB identifiers are valid:

- SB_LINEUP
- SB_LINEDOWN
- SB_PAGEUP
- SB_PAGEDOWN
- SB_SLIDERTRACK

PARAMETER	TYPE	DESCRIPTION
mp1	SHORT	Specifies an SB identifier.

The **return value** is TRUE when the operation succeeds. It is FALSE when an error occurs.

SBM_SETPOS

This message is application generated. It is sent to set a scrollbar's slider position. The slider moves to the nearest valid position when the *usPos* does not fall within the valid position range.

PARAMETER	TYPE	DESCRIPTION
mp1	USHORT	Specifies the slider position.

The **return value** is TRUE in all cases.

SBM_SETSCROLLBAR

This message is application generated. It is sent to set the scrollbar range and slider position.

PARAMETER	TYPE	DESCRIPTION
mp1	USHORT	Specifies the slider position.
mp2 (low)	USHORT	Specifies the first possible slider position.
mp2 (high)	USHORT	Specifies the last possible slider position.

The **return value** is TRUE in all cases.

Static Control Messages

Static controls allow you to enhance a standard control window. Specified by one of system SS style identifiers (see Chapter 8), static controls are best used to gain precision over the labels for button controls as well as text fields in listbox controls. Alternatively, when you want to spruce up a control with a bitmap or icon, static controls provide the means to do so. The static control messages are designed to handle bitmap and icon data.

Static controls accept no input, nor do they send any WM_COMMAND messages to the parent window. They do return information to an application via the following window messages:

- WM_MATCHMNEMONIC

- WM_QUERYWINDOWPARAMS

- WM_SETWINDOWPARAMS

To send a scrollbar message, you can use either the WinSendMsg or WinSendDlgItemMsg function. The following code queries a bitmap handle:

```
WinSendMsg(hwndControl,
            SM_QUERYHANDLE,
            MPFROMLONG(hwndBmap),NULL);
```

The function call simply queries the bitmap handle with the SM_QUERYHANDLE message. The queried handle is actually returned in the WM_QUERYWINDOWPARAMS message. The following listings describe the static control messages.

SM_QUERYHANDLE

This message is application generated and has no parameter values. The message is sent to obtain the handle to a static control (icon or bitmap).

The **return value** is the handle to a static control.

SM_SETHANDLE

This message is application generated. It is sent to set the handle to a static control (icon or bitmap).

PARAMETER	TYPE	DESCRIPTION
mp1	HWND	Specifies a handle to a bitmap or icon.

The **return value** is a handle to a static control object.

Titlebar Messages

The titlebar messages allow you to manipulate the highlight state of a titlebar and move the owner window of a titlebar. Titlebars pass data to an application via two window messages:

- WM_QUERYWINDOWPARAMS

- WM_SETWINDOWPARAMS

You can use the WinSendMsg function to pass a message to a titlebar. The following code fragment queries a titlebar's highlight state:

```
WinSendMsg(hwnd, SM_QUERYHANDLE, NULL, NULL);
```

This call tells the titlebar control to return the value of the highlight state to the application. Accordingly, the titlebars sends a WM_QUERY-WINDOWPARAMS message. The following listings describe the titlebar control messages.

TBM_QUERYHILITE

This message is application generated and has no parameter values. The message is sent to obtain the highlight state of a titlebar.

The **return value** is TRUE when the titlebar is highlighted. It is false when the titlebar is not highlighted.

TBM_SETHILITE

This message is application generated. It is sent to toggle the titlebar highlight .

PARAMETER	TYPE	DESCRIPTION
mp1	BOOL	Specifies the highlight state. Setting this parameter to TRUE activates the highlight. Setting it to FALSE deactivates the highlight.

The **return value** is TRUE when the operation succeeds. It is FALSE when an error occurs.

TBM_TRACKMOVE

This message is application generated. It is sent to the titlebar control window, which moves its owner as a result of receiving this message. Because it affects a frame control, this message internally generates a WM_QUERYTRACKINFO message, which is sent to the owner of the size control. If the return value from this latter message is TRUE, the sizing operation is performed by accessing the TRACKINFO structure. If the return value if FALSE, the operation terminates.

PARAMETER	TYPE	DESCRIPTION
mp1	USHORT	Specifies a TF (tracking flag) identifier.

The **return value** is TRUE upon success. Otherwise, it is FALSE.

Window Messages

The WM (window messages) encompass all aspects of the Presentation Manager. Some messages have specific responsibilities and only arise at certain times. Other messages are more general such as WM_PAINT and WM_SIZE and are used in most applications. Still other messages are designed primarily for the internal frame control procedure (see Chapter 5), but can be handled through a subclassed window procedure, thus enabling an application full access to them.

A window message is always defined by the current value of the QMSG structure. You can actually derive a message's values from the QMSG structure, but in most cases, you should adhere to standard message processing and handle messages in a **switch-case** routine. The QMSG structure tells you that a message contains four basic values. First, it contains a handle to the window to which the message is addressed. The handle is referred to as *hwnd* of type HWND. The next value in a message is the message name. This is referred to as *msg* of type USHORT. The next two values are a message's real muscle. Known as message parameters, these values are 32-bits long and are referred to as *mp1* and *mp2* of type MPARAM. (In addition to the basic message values referenced in QMSG, the structure also contains fields that specify the time of the message and mouse position at the time of the message.)

When you decipher a message inside a message handler — the term adopted to describe the routines associated with each **case** statement — you'll find much more than the four basic values. You'll find that the *mp1* and *mp2* parameters contain more than one just one piece of data each. In many cases, both *mp1* and *mp2* contain two distinct 16-bit values: high and low word values of type USHORT, but they can also contains other values, ranging from pointers to four distinct values of type UCHAR.

In many cases, the *mp1* parameter contains a command associated with the current message, or it identifies a window or other object on which some action should be performed. In some cases, the *mp2* parameter contains information that further describes the data contained in *mp1*.

The Presentation Manager makes several macros available to extract as well as create message parameter values. Additionally, it supports macros to obtain a message result from a function return value. These various macros are described in detail in Chapter 3. Note, too, that the OS/2 API toolkit offers numerous macros for converting different data types. The following listings describe the WM messages.

WM_ACTIVATE

This message occurs when a window is being activated or deactivated. It can be initiated either by the system or by a call to WinSetFocus. Both the window losing the active status and the window gaining the activate status receive the WM_ACTIVATE message. Note that the message is sent to a window losing its active status before it is sent to the window receiving the active status.

PARAMETER	TYPE	DESCRIPTION
mp1	BOOL	Specifies the active state. When *mp1* is TRUE, the window identified by *mp2* is activated; when it is FALSE, the window is deactivated.
mp2	HWND	Handle to the window changing state.

The **return value** is TRUE when the operation succeeds. It is FALSE when an error occurs.

WM_ACTIVATETHREAD

This function-driven message occurs when a window that is owned by another thread becomes active. When *mp1* is TRUE, this message identifies the process and thread (the low and high words of *mp2*, respectively) associated with the previously active window. When *mp1* is FALSE, the message identifies the process and thread associated with the window about to become active. The functions that initiate the WM_ACTIVATETHREAD message are:

- WinSetActiveWindow
- WinSetFocus
- WinCreateWindow
- WinShowWindow
- WinSetWindowPos
- WinSetMultiWindowPos

PARAMETER	TYPE	DESCRIPTION
mp1	BOOL	Specifies the thread activation state. A TRUE value indicates a window is being activated. A FALSE value indicates a window is being deactivated.
mp2 (low)	USHORT	Process ID.
mp2 (high)	USHORT	Thread ID.

The **return value** is NULL in all cases.

WM_ADJUSTWINDOWPOS

This system message occurs when a window is about to be moved or resized as a result of a call to WinSetWindowPos or WinSetMultiWindow-Pos. Additionally, the message occurs when a window — from a frame window to a menu or dialog box control — is first created. You can use WM_ADJUSTWINDOWPOS to modify the location or size of the window before the calling process carries out the move or resize operation. Size and position data is stored in SWP structure.

PARAMETER	TYPE	DESCRIPTION
mp1	PSWP	Pointer to a SWP data structure.

The **return value** is TRUE if the SWP structure is modified. It is FALSE if no modifications have been made.

WM_BUTTON1DBLCLK

This system message occurs when the user double-clicks on button one of the mouse. As a result of the WM_BUTTON1DBLCLK message, the menu control selects an item.

PARAMETER	TYPE	DESCRIPTION
mp1 (low)	SHORT	Horizontal pointer location in window coordinates.
mp1 (high)	SHORT	Vertical pointer location in window coordinates.
mp2	ULONG	The hit-test result.

The **return value** is TRUE if the message was processed. It is FALSE if the message was ignored.

WM_BUTTON2DBLCLK

This system message occurs when the user double-clicks on button two of the mouse. As a result of the WM_BUTTON2DBLCLK message, the menu control selects an item.

PARAMETER	TYPE	DESCRIPTION
mp1 (low)	SHORT	Horizontal pointer location in window coordinates.
mp1 (high)	SHORT	Vertical pointer location in window coordinates.
mp2	ULONG	The hit-test result.

The **return value** is TRUE if the message was processed. It is FALSE if the message was ignored.

WM_BUTTON3DBLCLK

This system message occurs when the user double-clicks on button three of the mouse. As a result of the WM_BUTTON3DBLCLK message, the menu control selects an item.

PARAMETER	TYPE	DESCRIPTION
mp1 (low)	SHORT	Horizontal pointer location in window coordinates.
mp1 (high)	SHORT	Vertical pointer location in window coordinates.
mp2	ULONG	The hit-test result.

The **return value** is TRUE if the message was processed. It is FALSE if the message was ignored.

WM_BUTTON1DOWN

This system message occurs when the user clicks on button one of the mouse. As a result of the WM_BUTTON1DOWN message, the menu control highlights the associated menu item. A WM_CONTROL is also posted to its owner with a notification code of LN_SELECT.

PARAMETER	TYPE	DESCRIPTION
mp1 (low)	SHORT	Horizontal pointer location.
mp1 (high)	SHORT	Vertical pointer location.
mp2	ULONG	The hit-test result.

The **return value** is TRUE when the operation succeeds. It is FALSE when an error occurs.

WM_BUTTON2DOWN

This system message occurs when the user clicks on button two of the mouse. As a result of the WM_BUTTON2DOWN message, the menu control highlights the associated menu item. A WM_CONTROL message is also posted to its owner with a notification code of LN_SELECT.

PARAMETER	TYPE	DESCRIPTION
mpl (low)	SHORT	Horizontal pointer location.
mpl (high)	SHORT	Vertical pointer location.
mp2	ULONG	The hit-test result.

The **return value** is TRUE when the operation succeeds. It is FALSE when an error occurs.

WM_BUTTON3DOWN

This system message occurs when the user clicks on button three of the mouse. There is no predefined response to this button press.

PARAMETER	TYPE	DESCRIPTION
mpl (low)	SHORT	Horizontal pointer location.
mpl (high)	SHORT	Vertical pointer location.
mp2	ULONG	The hit-test result.

The **return value** is TRUE when the operation succeeds. It is FALSE when an error occurs.

WM_BUTTON1UP

This system message occurs when the user releases button one of the mouse.

PARAMETER	TYPE	DESCRIPTION
mpl (low)	SHORT	Horizontal pointer location.
mpl (high)	SHORT	Vertical pointer location.
mp2	ULONG	The hit-test result.

The **return value** is TRUE when the operation succeeds. It is FALSE when an error occurs.

WM_BUTTON2UP

This system message occurs when the user releases button two of the mouse. Coinciding with this message, a WM_CONTROL message is posted to its owner with a notification code of LN_SELECT.

PARAMETER	TYPE	DESCRIPTION
mp1 (low)	SHORT	Horizontal pointer location.
mp1 (high)	SHORT	Vertical pointer location.
mp2	ULONG	The hit-test result.

The **return value** is TRUE when the operation succeeds. It is FALSE when an error occurs.

WM_BUTTON3UP

This system message occurs when the user releases button three of the mouse. The listbox window control takes no action.

PARAMETER	TYPE	DESCRIPTION
mp1 (low)	SHORT	Horizontal pointer location.
mp1 (high)	SHORT	Vertical pointer location.
mp2	ULONG	The hit-test result.

The **return value** is TRUE when the operation succeeds. It is FALSE when an error occurs.

WM_BUTTONCLICKFIRST

This system message occurs when the first in a series of mouse messages occurs. It is a constant that is set equal to the first mouse button click and it is used with WM_BUTTONCLICKLAST to test for mouse messages. The message has no parameter values.

WM_BUTTONCLICKLAST

This system message occurs when the first in a series of mouse messages occurs. It is a constant that is set equal to the first mouse button click and it is used with WM_BUTTONCLICKFIRST to test for mouse messages. The message has no parameter values.

WM_CALCFRAMERECT

This function-driven message occurs when a window calculates a rectangle within its boundaries. The message results from a call to the WinCalcFrameRect function.

PARAMETER	TYPE	DESCRIPTION
mp1	RECTL	Pointer to a rectangle in window coordinates.
mp2	BOOL	Flag indicating whether the window is a frame window. A TRUE value indicates the window is a frame window. A FALSE value indicates that the window is not a frame window.

The **return value** is TRUE when the operation succeeds. It is FALSE when an error occurs.

WM_CALCVALIDRECTS

This function-driven message occurs when a window is about to be resized. The message results from calls to WinSetWindowPos and WinSetMultiWindowPos, both of which attempt to establish the integrity of the valid rectangle. Processing this message allows you to set the coordinates of the rectangle that must be preserved as a result of the resizing operation. You can also specify where the rectangle is placed within the resized window. For example, the WinDefWindowProc function handles this message by relocating the rectangle in the top left corner of the window. This default processing returns the following:

```
(CVR_ALIGNTOP | CVR_ALIGNLEFT)
```

Areas of the window outside the valid rectangle are also redrawn to best suit the relocated rectangle. This message does not occur, however, if the window is of style CS_SIZEREDRAW, which requires that windows be completely redrawn when resized.

574

PARAMETER	TYPE	DESCRIPTION
mp1	PRECTL	Pointer to a source rectangle in coordinates relative to the parent window.
mp2	PRECTL	Pointer to a destination rectangle in coordinates relative to the parent window.

The **return value** specifies if a valid rectangle exists. The message processes predefined identifiers, which you can OR to produce combined effects. The identifiers are the following:

IDENTIFIER	DESCRIPTION
CVR_ALIGNLEFT	Rectangle aligned with window's left edge.
CVR_ALIGNBOTTOM	Rectangle aligned with window's bottom edge.
CVR_ALIGNTOP	Rectangle aligned with window's top edge.
CVR_ALIGNRIGHT	Rectangle aligned with window's right edge.

WM_CANCELMODE

This function-driven message occurs when an application assumes control of the pointer. The message is generated by the WinSetCapture function. The purpose of the message is to terminate any existing modal dialog box once the application has assumed control of the pointer. This allows the application to establish its own pointer routines. The system performs no default processing for WM_CANCELMODE, which has no parameter values.

The **return value** is NULL.

WM_CHAR

This system message results from a user key press. The message is posted to the queue for the window that has the current input focus. The parameters contain various key codes, which give you full keyboard processing capabilities. Refer to Chapter 12 for complete information.

575

PARAMETER	TYPE	DESCRIPTION
mp1	USHORT	Specifies the keyboard control codes.
mp2	USHORT	Specifies the character code.

The **return value** is TRUE if the message has been processed. It is FALSE in all other cases.

WM_CLOSE

This system message occurs when the application is about to terminate. The message has no parameter values. It purely serves as a signal. You can use this message to add routines to the termination process, or abort if you find that necessary. Refer to Chapter 5 for additional details.

The **return value** is NULL in all cases.

WM_COMMAND

This system message occurs in response to an application-based event such as when a control window has data it must pass to its owner window. It also occurs when a keystroke is translated into a command accelerator. The system posts the message to owner's window message queue. No default processing occurs for this message.

PARAMETER	TYPE	DESCRIPTION
mp1	USHORT	The command value .
mp2	USHORT	The source of the command, which corresponds with a window control and is one of the following:
		CMDSRC_PUSHBUTTON
		CMDSRC_MENU
		CMDSRC_ACCELERATOR
		CMDSRC_OTHER

The **return value** is NULL.

WM_CONTROL

This system message occurs in response to an application-based event such as when a control window passes data to its owner window via the

WinSendMsg function. This is the standard message for processing values obtained from dialog boxes. No default processing occurs for this message.

PARAMETER	TYPE	DESCRIPTION
mp1	USHORT	The control window ID.
mp2	ULONG	Control data, which is control dependent.

The **return value** is NULL.

WM_CONTROLHEAP

This system message occurs when a control window needs a handle to a heap, because some event (for which the control is responsible) requires allocated memory. Relevant controls are menus, listboxes, and other dialog boxes that have edit controls. The default window procedure does process this message by returning the owner window's message queue heap handle. The WM_CONTROLHEAP message has no parameter values.

The **return value** is a handle to a heap.

WM_CONTROLPOINTER

This system message occurs when the mouse pointer moves over a control window. The message is sent to the owner of the control window, affording it an opportunity to set the mouse pointer to a new shape. The *mp2* parameter of this message contains the handle to the mouse pointer. You can return the message directly, substituting a new handle, or call WinDefWindowProc and substitute the new handle for that call. The default procedure handles the rest of the processing.

PARAMETER	TYPE	DESCRIPTION
mp1	USHORT	The control window ID.
mp2	HPOINTER	Handle to the mouse pointer.

The **return value** is a handle to a pointer.

WM_CREATE

This system message occurs when an application creates a window. The window procedure receives this message after the window has been created, but before it becomes visible.You can trap this message in order to process initialization routines. There is no default processing of this message.

PARAMETER	TYPE	DESCRIPTION
mp1	FAR *	Pointer to control data.
mp2	FAR *	Pointer to a CREATESTRUCT structure.

The **return value** is FALSE if the Presentation Manager should continue with the process of creating the window. It is TRUE if the process should aborted.

WM_DDE_ACK

This message should be posted by an application after it receives one of several dynamic data exchange messages from another application (see each DDE message). The WM_DDE_ACK message contains a pointer to the DDESTRUCT. The *offszItenName* field of the structure identifies the item with which the incoming message is concerned. The message handler should modify the *fsStatus* field of this structure so that the messages process one of the following system-defined responses:

- DDE_FACK — Should be set to 0 (not accepted) or 1 (accepted).
- DDE_FBUSY — Should be set to 0 (not busy) or 1 (busy).
- DDE_NOTPROCESSED — Returns application specific return codes.
- DDE_FAPPSTATUS — Message not understood and thus ignored.

PARAMETER	TYPE	DESCRIPTION
mp1	HWND	Handle to the sender window.
mp2	PDDESTRUCT	Pointer to a DDESTRUCT structure.

The **return value** is NULL.

WM_DDE_ADVISE

This message is posted by a client application. It asks the receiving application to forward updated information whenever the specified data item changes. The update is expected to be forwarded in a WM_DDE_ACK message. Data particulars are contained in the DDESTRUCT structure. The update item is specified in the *offszItemName* field of this structure; and the format of the update item is specified in the *usFormat* field. The message handler in the receiving application should modify the *fsStatus* field of DDESTRUCT to one of the following:

- DDE_FACKREQ — Setting this bit to 1 requests the server application to send it a WM_DDE_DATA message (which should also have DDE_FACKREQ set to 1).

- DDE_FNODATA — Setting this bit to 1 requests the server to send a data alert in the form of a WM_DDE_DATA. This message tells the client that the data item has change. In turn, the client can issue a WM_DDE_REQUEST message.

PARAMETER	TYPE	DESCRIPTION
mp1	HWND	Handle to the sender window.
mp2	PDDESTRUCT	Pointer to a DDESTRUCT structure.

The **return value** is NULL.

WM_DDE_DATA

This message should be posted by an application. It is designed to inform a client application of available exchange data. The WM_DDE_DATA message expects a WM_DDE_ACK message in return. The exchange data is identified in the *offszItemName* field of the DDESTRUCT structure; its format is contained in the *usFormat* field; and the data itself is contained in the *offabData* field.

The WM_DDE_DATA handler in the receiving application should modify the *fsStatus* field of DDESTRUCT to one of the following:

- DDE_FACKREQ —Setting this bit to 1 places the burden of sending a WM_DDE_ACK message on the client application. Setting it to 0 relieves the client application of having to acknowledge.

- DDE_FRESPONSE — Setting this bit to 1 indicates that the data results from receiving a WM_DDE_REQUEST message. Setting it to 0 indicates the data results from receiving a WM_DDE_ADVISE message.

PARAMETER	TYPE	DESCRIPTION
mp1	HWND	Handle to the sender window.
mp2	PDDESTRUCT	Pointer to a DDESTRUCT structure.

The **return value** is NULL.

WM_DDE_EXECUTE

This message should be posted by a client application. It contains a command string for a server application. The client application expects the server to generate a WM_DDE_ACK message. The command string is contained in the *offabData* field of the DDESTRUCT structure.

PARAMETER	TYPE	DESCRIPTION
mp1	HWND	Handle to the sender window.
mp2	PDDESTRUCT	Pointer to a DDESTRUCT structure.

The **return value** is NULL.

WM_DDE_INITIATE

This message should be sent by an application to one or more applications in order to initiate a conversation. This initiating application does not require a WM_DDE_ACK message. Instead, it expects the receiving applications to call the WinDdeRespond function. In turn, this function sends a WM_DDE_INITIATEACK message. The initiating application references a topic of conversation in the DDEINIT structure. The *pszTopic* field contains the topic. The referenced copy of the DDEINIT structure must be in shared memory.

PARAMETER	TYPE	DESCRIPTION
mp1	HWND	Handle to the sender window.
mp2	DDEINIT	Pointer to a DDEINIT structure.

The **return value** is NULL.

WM_DDE_INITIATEACK

This message results from a call to WinDdeRespond. An application calls WinDdeRespond for the explicit purpose of responding to a WM_DDE_INITATE message. The application calling WinDdeRespond names itself in the *pszAppName* field of the DDEINIT structure. The referenced copy of the DDEINIT structure must be in shared memory.

PARAMETER	TYPE	DESCRIPTION
mp1	HWND	Handle to the sender window.
mp2	DDEINIT	Pointer to a DDEINIT structure.

The **return value** is NULL.

WM_DDE_POKE

This message should be posted by an application. It asks the receiving application to accept unsolicited data. In response to receiving this message, an application should send a WM_DDE_ACK message. The unsolicited data is referenced in the DDESTRUCT structure. The data is identified in *offszItemName* field of this structure; the format of the data is contained in the *usFormat* field; and the data itself is contained in the *offabData* field.

PARAMETER	TYPE	DESCRIPTION
mp1	HWND	Handle to the sender window.
mp2	PDDESTRUCT	Pointer to a DDESTRUCT structure.

The **return value** is NULL.

WM_DDE_REQUEST

This message is posted by a client application to a server application. The message requests that the server supply a specified data item. The data is referenced in the DDESTRUCT structure. The data is identified in the *ofszItemName* field of this structure; and the format of the data is contained in the *usFormat* field.

PARAMETER	TYPE	DESCRIPTION
mp1	HWND	Handle to the sender window.
mp2	PDDESTRUCT	Pointer to a DDESTRUCT structure.

The **return value** is NULL.

WM_DDE_TERMINATE

This message is posted by an application involved in an DDE conversation. The purpose of the message is to terminate the conversation. The receiving application should also post a WM_DDE_TERMINATE message to confirm that the conversation has concluded.

PARAMETER	TYPE	DESCRIPTION
mp1	HWND	Handle to the sender window.

The **return value** is NULL.

WM_DDE_UNADVISE

This message is posted by a client application to a server application. The message informs the server that the previously specified data item needs

no additional updating. The data is referenced in the DDESTRUCT structure. The data is identified in the *offszItemName* field of this structure.

PARAMETER	TYPE	DESCRIPTION
mp1	HWND	Handle to the sender window.
mp2	PDDESTRUCT	Pointer to a DDESTRUCT structure.

The **return value** is NULL.

WM_DESTROY

This system message occurs when an application wants to destroy a window. The window that is about to be destroyed receives this message. You
can trap WM_DESTROY to perform window termination routines. This
message has no parameter values and there is no default processing.

The **return value** is NULL in all cases.

WM_DRAWITEM

This system message occurs when a control window requires redrawing.
The owner of the control receives the message. You can take advantage of
this message if you need to modify the appearance of a control before it is
redrawn. Using this message, you can target specific controls for modifica-
tion. There is no default processing of this message.

PARAMETER	TYPE	DESCRIPTION
mp1	SHORT	The window ID.
mp2	POWNERITEM	Pointer to an OWNERITEM structure.

The **return value** is TRUE if the owner modifies the item. It is FALSE if
processing occurs normally.

WM_ENABLE

This system message occurs when an application changes the enable state
of a window. The message is sent to the window undergoing the change in

enable state. One cause of the message is the WinEnableWindow function. A change to the WS_DISABLE style bit also initiates the WM_ENABLE message. There is no default processing for this message.

PARAMETER	TYPE	DESCRIPTION
mp1	BOOL	Flag specifying the enable state. A TRUE value indicates a previously disabled window has been enabled. A FALSE value indicates a previously enabled window has been disabled.

The **return value** is NULL in all cases.

WM_ERASEBACKGROUND

This system message repaints the client area of the frame window with the system background color. You must trap this message and return TRUE in order to have the repainting take effect. Refer to Chapter 5 for complete details on this message.

PARAMETER	TYPE	DESCRIPTION
mp1	HPS	Identifies for the frame window.
mp2	PWRECT	Points to a WRECT structure that contains the rectangle to be painted.

The **return value** is TRUE if the message is processed. It is FALSE if the message is not processed.

WM_ERROR

This function-driven message results from when either the WinGetMsg or WinPeekMsg functions encounters an error condition. An effective place to anticipate this message is immediately before it is dispatched via the WinDispatchMsg function. The system performs no default processing on the WM_ERROR message.

PARAMETER	TYPE	DESCRIPTION
mp1	USHORT	System error code.

The **return value** is NULL.

WM_FLASHWINDOW

This system message occurs after a call to the WinFlashWindow function. The message is processed by the internal frame window procedure (WC_FRAME).

PARAMETER	TYPE	DESCRIPTION
mp1	BOOL	Flag indicating whether the window flashes. A TRUE value indicates the window is about to flash. A FALSE value indicates it is about to stop flashing.

The **return value** is TRUE when the operation succeeds. It is FALSE when an error occurs.

WM_FOCUSCHANGE

This system message is handled by the Presentation Manager's internal frame window procedure. The message occurs as a result of user manipulation of various windows or as a result of calls to the WinSetFocus or WinFocusChange functions. In most cases, you should avoid processing this message. Instead, you are afforded an opportunity to qualify changes to a windows focus state (as well as its active and enabled state) by processing the following messages, which occur in the order of their appearance here:

- WM_SETFOCUS — received by the window losing the focus.
- WM_SETSELECTION — received by the window being deselected.
- WM_ACTIVATE — received by the window being deactivated.
- WM_ACTIVATE — received by the window being activated.
- WM_SETSELECTION — received by the window being selected.
- WM_SETFOCUS — received by the window receiving the focus.

PARAMETER	TYPE	DESCRIPTION
mp1	HWND	Handle to a window that is undergoing a change in focus.
mp2 (low)	BOOL	Flag indicating the status of *mp1*. A TRUE value indicates the window identified in *mp1* is losing focus. A FALSE value indicates the window is gaining focus.
mp2	USHORT	Flag bits modifying the change in focus. These bits can be any combination of the following:

> FC_NOSETFOCUS
>
> FC_NOLOSEFOCUS
>
> FC_NOSETACTIVE
>
> FC_NOLOSEACTIVE
>
> FC_NOSETSELECTION
>
> FC_NOLOSESELECTION
>
> FC_NOBRINGTOTOP
>
> FC_SETACTIVEFOCUS
>
> FC_QUERYACTIVE
>
> FC_QUERYTASK

The **return value** is a handle to the active window when FC_QUERYAC-TIVE is used. It is the handle to the task window when FC_QUERYTASK is used. In all other cases, it is NULL.

WM_FORMATFRAME

This system message occurs when the frame window controls require positioning. The purpose of the message is to let the internal frame window procedure calculate the dimensions for frame window controls. The message is initiated when a frame window is first created, resized, repositioning, or after a call to WinFormatFrame function.

The Presentation Manager gives the client window procedure the opportunity to affect processing of this message. By trapping the message and returning TRUE, you can effectively block the internal frame window procedure from processing the message. If you return FALSE, the internal frame window procedure calls the WinFormatFrame and WinSetMultWindowPos functions. The WM_FORMATFRAME message is generally applicable if your program subclasses frame controls. This message — as well as the WM_QUERYFRAMECTLCOUNT message — must be subclassed by calling the previous window procedure and modifying the result of that procedure. WM_FORMATFRAME has no parameter values.

The **return value** is TRUE for modified processing. It is FALSE for normal processing.

WM_HELP

This system message occurs as a result of a control window or accelerator reporting a user request for help. An application should trap the WM_HELP message and display a help routine based on the contents of its parameter values. With the exception of this provision, the WM_HELP message is identical to the WM_COMMAND message. There is no default processing of WM_HELP.

PARAMETER	TYPE	DESCRIPTION
mp1	USHORT	The command value .
mp2	USHORT	The command source, which corresponds with a window control and is one of the following:

> CMDSRC_PUSHBUTTON
> CMDSRC_MENU
> CMDSRC_ACCELERATOR
> CMDSRC_OTHER

The **return value** is NULL.

WM_HITTEST

This system message results from an application request for a message via the WinPeekMsg or WinGetMsg functions. The purpose of the message is to obtain data related to the pointer (specifically, in conjunction with a mouse click).

The window associated with the hit–testing routine must be of style CS_HITTEST in order for this message to occur. If this is the case, the message can occur as a result of any of the following messages:

- WM_MOUSEMOVE

- WM_BUTTON1DOWN

- WM_BUTTON2DOWN

- WM_BUTTON3DOWN

If the window to receive the pointer-related message is disabled, the WinDefWindowProc reports this with a HT_ERROR value. Otherwise, no default processing is performed. Refer to Chapter 13 for additional information on this message and its HT identifiers.

PARAMETER	TYPE	DESCRIPTION
mp1 (low)	SHORT	Horizontal pointer location in window coordinates.
mp1 (high)	SHORT	Vertical pointer location in window coordinates.

The **return value** is an HT identifier.

WM_HSCROLL

This system message occurs as the result of a horizontal scrollbar command. The message is posted to the message queue procedure for the owner window of the scrollbar control. There is no default processing of this message. For additional information on this message and scrollbar processing, refer to Chapter 5.

PARAMETER	TYPE	DESCRIPTION
mp1	USHORT	Scrollbar window ID.
mp2 (low)	SHORT	Slider position. If this value is FALSE, it means the slider is not being moved.
mp2 (high)	USHORT	One of the scrollbar window identifiers:

SB_LINELEFT

SB_LINERIGHT

SB_PAGELEFT

SB_PAGERIGHT

SB_SLIDERPOSITION

SB_SLIDERTRACK

SB_ENDSCROLL

The **return value** is NULL.

WM_INITDLG

This system message occurs when a dialog box is created. It affords you an opportunity to perform any required initialization for the dialog box. There is no default processing of this message.

PARAMETER	TYPE	DESCRIPTION
mp1	HWND	Handle to the dialog box control that is about to receive the input focus.
mp2	FAR *	Pointer to the CREATEPARAMS structure.

The **return value** is TRUE if the dialog box procedure changes the window receiving the input focus. It is FALSE if this window is not changed.

WM_INITMENU

This system message occurs immediately prior to initialization of a menu control. The message affords you an opportunity to execute any program initialization required for the menu control. The WM_INITMENU message occurs when a menu control is about to be initialized. There is no default processing for this message.

PARAMETER	TYPE	DESCRIPTION
mp1	SHORT	The menu control ID.
mp2	HWND	Handle to the menu.

The **return value** is NULL.

WM_JOURNALNOTIFY

This system message occurs during a hook operation that supports journal processing. The message allows WinQueryQueueStatus and WinGet-PhysKeyState functions to work properly during journal playback. There is no default processing for this message. For additional information on hook processing, refer to Chapter 14.

PARAMETER	TYPE	DESCRIPTION
mp1	ULONG	Command specifying the invoked function. A value of JRN_QUEUESTATUS indicates that WinQueryQueueStatus was called. A value of JRN_PHYSKEYSTATE indicates that WinGetPhysKeyState was called.
mp2	ULONG	If this value is JRN_QUEUESTATUS, the high word of this parameter is one of the QS identifiers (see WinQueryQueueStatus).

The **return value** is 0L.

WM_MATCHMNEMONIC

This system message occurs when a mnemonic match results from a comparison of a dialog box control item and a user key press. There is no default processing of this message.

PARAMETER	TYPE	DESCRIPTION
mp1	USHORT	The character to match.

The **return value** is TRUE when the mnemonic is found. It is false if the mnemonic is not found.

WM_MENUSELECT

This system message occurs after the user selects a menu item. The message is sent to the owner window procedure of the menu control. There is no default processing for this message.

PARAMETER	TYPE	DESCRIPTION
mp1	USHORT	Menu item ID.
mp2	HWND	Handle to the menu window.

The **return value** is TRUE for normal processing. The return value is FALSE when it is necessary to retain the menu display and not post a message.

WM_MEASUREITEM

This system message occurs when a control window is created. It gives you an opportunity to specify the size for items that the control uses. For example, you can specify the height of text items for a listbox that is of style LS_OWNERDRAW. Similarly, you can trap this message to establish the height of a menu item.

PARAMETER	TYPE	DESCRIPTION
mp1	PSWP	Pointer to a SWP structure.
mp2	PSZ	Pointer to a text string representing an item for the specified control.

The **return value** is the height of the text item.

WM_MINMAXFRAME

This system message occurs immediately before a frame window is minimized, maximized, or restored. The internal frame window procedure passes this message to the client window procedure, where you can trap the message if necessary. The system initializes the following window data words before generating this message.

- QWS_XRESTORE
- QWS_YRESTORE
- QWS_CXRESTORE
- QWS_CYRESTORE

If you need to retain the previous size and position information of the frame window, you can invoke WinQueryWindowPos while processing the WM_MINMAXFRAME message. The frame window size and position values are not modified until the message returns to the internal frame window procedure.

PARAMETER	TYPE	DESCRIPTION
mp1	PSWP	Pointer to a SWP structure.

The **return value** is TRUE if the internal frame procedure should not process the message. It is FALSE if normal processing should occur.

WM_MOUSEFIRST

This system message is a constant that alerts the client window procedure of the first in a series of mouse messages. WM_MOUSEFIRST has no parameter values. You typically pair this message with WM_MOUSELAST if you use it at all. There is no default processing for this message.

No **return value** is used by this message.

WM_MOUSELAST

This system message is a constant that alerts the client window procedure of the first message in a series of mouse messages. WM_MOUSELAST has no parameter values. You typically pair this message with WM_MOUSE-FIRST, if you use it at all. There is no default processing for this message.

No **return value** is used by this message.

WM_MOUSEMOVE

The WM_MOUSEMOVE message is sent to a window when the mouse pointer moves. If the mouse is not captured, the message goes to the window beneath the mouse pointer. Otherwise, the message goes to the mouse capture window. A WM_MOUSEMOVE handler should return TRUE if it processes the message; otherwise, it should return FALSE.

PARAMETER	TYPE	DESCRIPTION
mp1 (low)	SHORT	Horizontal pointer location in window coordinates.
mp1 (high)	SHORT	Vertical pointer location in window coordinates.
mp2	ULONG	The hit-test result.

The **return value** is TRUE when the window procedure processes the message and the operation succeeds. It is FALSE when it does not.

WM_MOVE

This message occurs when a window of style CS_MOVENOTIFY changes its screen location. The message is also generated by the WinSetWindow-Pos, WinSetMultWindowPos, and WinScrollWindow functions. You can obtain the new window position by trapping this message and calling the WinQueryWindowRect function. You can also make the associated window rectangle coordinates relative to any window by calling the Win-MapWindowPoints function. The WM_MOVE message has no parameter values. It is simply a signal message. There is no default processing of this message

The **return value** is NULL is in all cases.

WM_NEXTMENU

This system message occurs when the user moves the menu selector bar to either the beginning or the end of a menu. The message is routed to the owner of a menu window. This affords you the opportunity to switch control to the previous or next menu by passing the appropriate menu ID in the return value of WM_NEXTMENU. The default window procedure does not process this message.

PARAMETER	TYPE	DESCRIPTION
mp1	HWND	Handle to the current menu.
mp2	BOOL	Flag indicating the next or previous menu. A TRUE value indicates the previous menu. A FALSE value indicates the next menu.

The **return value** is a handle to the next or previous menu. If a valid handle cannot be obtained, this message should return NULL.

WM_NULL

This message has no predefined purpose. It is not sent by the system. The message has no parameter values. It is merely a predefined message that you can use as a signal. It is intended to do nothing. The system does use the message, however, when it translates a WM_CHAR message into a keyboard accelerator. When the translation occurs, the system converts the WM_CHAR message into a WM_NULL message. The default window procedure performs no processing of this message.

The **return value** is NULL.

WM_OTHERWINDOWDESTROYED

The system message occurs when a registered window is destroyed. It is sent to all top-level windows. The system performs no default processing for this message.

The **return value** is NULL.

WM_PAINT

The system message occurs when the client area window requires repainting. This can occur when the application has called the WinUpdateWindow function, or just as a natural result of a message being retrieved from the queue. The latter, however, requires the client area window to have an update region specified. The WM_PAINT message has no parameter values. It is purely a signal message. The system performs no default processing of the message.

The **return value** is NULL.

WM_PAINTCLIPBOARD

The system message occurs when the client area of the clipboard needs repainting. The message contains a handle to the clipboard. The handle has the CFI_OWNERSHIP flag set. The application must determine whether an entire client area of the clipboard needs repainting. To do this, the application must compare the dimensions of the drawing area to the dimensions obtained through the WM_SIZECLIPBOARD message. The system performs no default processing of this message.

PARAMETER	TYPE	DESCRIPTION
mp1	HWND	Handle to the clipboard.

The **return value** is NULL.

WM_QUERYACCELTABLE

The system message occurs after the user presses an accelerator key. The message returns the handle of the accelerator table that you want to associate with the current window. No parameter values are used with this message. Nor does the system perform default processing for the message.

The **return value** is NULL.

WM_QUERYBORDERSIZE

This system messages occurs so the application can determine the size of the current window's border. The message references the WPOINT structure, which contains the border's dimensions. The internal frame window procedure processes this message by initializing the border to a width and height of zero; setting the border dimensions to the available dimensions; and adding the default style of a dialog box border (when appropriate). The internal frame window's default processing varies its treatment according to the following:

- WC_SIZE — dimensions are calculated as a result of available values.

- SV_CX/CYDLGBORDER — dimension affected by FS_DLGBORDER.

- SV_CX/CYBORDER — dimensions affect by FS_BORDER.

PARAMETER	TYPE	DESCRIPTION
mp1	PWPOINT	Pointer to a WPOINT structure, which contains the horizontal and vertical dimensions of the border.

The **return value** is TRUE when the operation succeeds. It is FALSE when an error occurs.

WM_QUERYDLGCODE

This system message is processed by the dialog box procedure. The message allows the application to determine the type of dialog box control that is currently active. It also provides a way for you to know what types of input messages the dialog box control uses. There is not default processing for this message, but its return value is critical: it tells the system the control's capabilities by setting a DLG flag. The following flags are used:

- DLGC_BUTTON — Button (uses BM_CLICK message).

- DLGC_CHECKBOX — Checkbox button.

- DLGC_DEFAULT — Default pushbutton.

- DLGC_ENTRYFIELD — Edit control (uses EM_SETSEL message).
- DLGC_MENU — Menu control.
- DLGC_PUSHBUTTON — Standard pushbutton.
- DLGC_RADIOBUTTON — Radio button (used with DLGC_BUTTON).
- DLGC_SCROLLBAR — Scrollbar control
- DLGC_STATIC — Static control (no cursor key enumeration).

PARAMETER	TYPE	DESCRIPTION
mp1	PQMSG	Pointer to QMSG structure.

The **return value** is a DLGC code.

WM_QUERYFRAMEINFO

This message occurs when the system requires information about the frame window. There are no parameter values for this message. Default processing simply returns a value. The value is one of the following system identifiers that specify information about the frame window:

- FI_FRAME — Standard frame window.
- FI_OWNERHIDE — Owner window dictates display state.
- FI_ACTIVATEOK — The window may be activated if it isn't disabled.
- FI_NOMOVEWITHOWNER — Owner movement is ignored.

The **return value** is an FI identifier.

WM_QUERYICON

This system message allows an application to query a frame window for a handle to the icon it uses to represent itself in minimized form. The message has no parameter values. The system performs no default processing on the message.

The **return value** is a handle to an icon.

WM_QUERYTRACKINFO

This system message occurs as a result of the titlebar receiving a WM_TRACKFRAME or TBM_TRACKMOVE message. The message is sent to the window procedure for the titlebar control and occurs when the system processes TBM_TRACKMOVE. There is no default processing for WM_QUERYTRACKINFO.

PARAMETER	TYPE	DESCRIPTION
mp1	USHORT	Specifies tracking flags containing a combination of one or more TF flags.
mp2	FAR *	Points to the TRACKINFO data structure.

The **return value** is TRUE to continue sizing or moving. It is FALSE to terminate sizing or moving.

WM_QUERYWINDOWPARAMS

This system message occurs when an application queries the window parameters. The default window procedure queries the appropriate window parameters, placing the results in *mp1*, according to the value of the status flags in *mp1*. If another window or process receives this message, its associated data areas must be in memory shared by both processes.

PARAMETER	TYPE	DESCRIPTION
mp1	FAR *	Points to a WNDPARAMS data structure that defines the data to be returned. The window text, window text length, control data, and control data length are selectively returned according to which WNDPARAMS flags are set.

The **return value** is TRUE upon success. Otherwise, it is FALSE.

WM_QUEUESTATUS

This message occurs as result of a call to the WinQueryQueueStatus function during a journal recording or playback hook. The system performs no default processing on this message.

PARAMETER	TYPE	DESCRIPTION
mp1	USHORT	Queue status (one of the system-defined QS identifiers).

The **return value** is NULL.

WM_QUIT

The WM_QUIT message is posted to terminate the application. Typically, this message is posted by the application when the application quit command is selected from the menu bar. It causes the WinGetMsg function to return FALSE, rather than TRUE as for all other messages. Applications that call WinPeekMsg rather than WinGetMsg should test explicitly for WM_QUIT. The default window procedure takes no action on this message.This message should not be dispatched to the default window procedure. The purpose of this message is to cause the WinGetMsg loop to terminate.

The **return value** is NULL.

WM_SEM1

This system-defined message is a high priority message designed for an application's inter-thread communication. A thread can send or post this message.When the message is posted, the system ORs it with previous WM_SEM1 messages still in the queue. The WM_SEM1 message has priority over other system-defined semaphore messages, the WM_TIMER message, and the WM_PAINT message. The system clears the *mp1* parameter of WM_SEM1 after it is retrieved from the queue. The 32-bit value contained in *mp1* is application specific. For example, an application can set a flag via *mp1* to initiate some action by the receiving routine. The system performs no default processing on this message.

PARAMETER	TYPE	DESCRIPTION
mp1	ULONG	Application specific.

The **return value** is NULL.

WM_SEM2

This message operates identically to the WM_SEM1 message. The only difference between the two messages is WM_SEM2 has a lower priority than WM_SEM1. The system performs no default processing on this message.

PARAMETER	TYPE	DESCRIPTION
mp1	ULONG	Application specific.

The **return value** is NULL.

WM_SEM3

This message operates identically to the WM_SEM1 and WM_SEM2 messages. It has a lower priority than these two messages, however. It also has a lower priority than the WM_TIMER message. No system default processing occurs for the WM_SEM3 message.

PARAMETER	TYPE	DESCRIPTION
mp1	ULONG	Application specific.

The **return value** is NULL.

WM_SEM4

This message operates identically to the other semaphore messages, but has the lowest priority of the group. Additionally, it has a lower priority than both the WM_TIMER and WM_PAINT messages. No system default processing occurs for the WM_SEM4 message.

PARAMETER	TYPE	DESCRIPTION
mp1	ULONG	Application specific.

The **return value** is NULL.

WM_SETFOCUS

This system message occurs when a window is about to lose or gain the input focus. You should exercise restraint when processing this message. Unless you determine that the window is also becoming active (see WM_ACTIVATE), you should not change the focus/active window when processing WM_SETFOCUS. If you do, the focus/active window must be restored before the application completes the WM_SETFOCUS message block. Note that dialog boxes invoked during processing of the WM_SET-FOCUS and WM_ACTIVATE messages should be system modal. There is no default processing for this message.

PARAMETER	TYPE	DESCRIPTION
mp1	HWND	Handle to the window losing the focus. If no window previously had the focus, this parameter is NULL.
mp2	BOOL	Flag indicating whether the window is losing or gaining the focus. A TRUE value indicates the window is gaining the focus. A FALSE value indicates the window is losing the focus.

The **return value** is NULL.

WM_SETICON

This system message occurs when a frame window is minimized. The message is used by the internal frame window procedure to set the application's minimize icon.

PARAMETER	TYPE	DESCRIPTION
mp1	HPOINTER	Handle to an icon.

The **return value** is TRUE when the operation succeeds. It is FALSE when an error occurs.

WM_SETWINDOWPARAMS

This system message occurs when an application sets or changes the window parameters. The message allows you access to the WNDPARAMS structure, which contains a record of the window parameters specified when the window was created. If a window belonging to another thread accesses the window parameter data, the data must be in shared memory. There is no default processing of this message.

PARAMETER	TYPE	DESCRIPTION
mp1	FAR *	Pointer to a WNDPARAMS structure.

The **return value** is TRUE when the operation succeeds. It is FALSE when an error occurs.

WM_SHOW

This system message occurs after a window changes its visibility state. The visibility state is dictated by the window's WS_VISIBLE style bit. There is no system default processing of this message.

PARAMETER	TYPE	DESCRIPTION
mp1	BOOL	Flag indicating whether the window is shown or hidden. A TRUE value indicates the window is shown. A FALSE value indicates it is hidden.

The **return value** is NULL.

WM_SIZE

This system message occurs when a window changes its size, but is not generated when a window is created. In point of time, the WM_SIZE message occurs before a window is repainted. This affords you an opportunity to get the size of the current client area and set up your painting routine accordingly. WM_SIZE also occurs before a window is repositioned. Because of this fact, you should not call any paint routines directly from the

WM_SIZE message block — if you do, any window repositioning will invalidate the coordinates you obtain from WM_SIZE. The system performs no default processing for this message.

PARAMETER	TYPE	DESCRIPTION
mp1 (low)	SHORT	The previous width of the client area.
mp1 (high)	SHORT	The previous height of the client area.
mp2 (low)	SHORT	The new width of the client area.
mp2 (high)	SHORT	The new height of the client area.

The **return value** is NULL.

WM_SUBSTITUTESTRING

This function-driven message occurs when a string substitution is imminent in a control window. The message results from any call to the WinSubstituteStrings function. The system itself calls this function when it creates child controls in a dialog box. By processing the WM_SUBSTITUTESTRING message, you can change the index values of the strings to be substituted. The system performs no default processing for this message. For additional information, refer to the WinSubstituteStrings function.

PARAMETER	TYPE	DESCRIPTION
mp1	SHORT	Index value that represents the decimal character in the substitution string.

The **return value** is the substitution string, or NULL if there is no substitution string.

WM_SYSCOLORCHANGE

This function-driven message occurs as a result of a change to any of the system colors. It is generated by the WinSetSysColors function. As a result of this message, all windows are invalidated and redrawn with the new system colors. Processing WM_SYSCOLORCHANGE affords you an opportunity to call WinQuerySysColor to obtain the new color values. The system performs no default processing for this message, which has no parameter values.

The **return value** is NULL.

WM_SYSCOMMAND

This system message occurs in response to an application-based event such as when a control window has data it must pass to its owner window. It also occurs when a keystroke is translated into a command accelerator. The system posts the message to owner's window message queue. No default processing occurs for this message.

PARAMETER	TYPE	DESCRIPTION
mp1	USHORT	The command value .
mp2	USHORT	The source of the command, which corresponds with a window control and is one of the following predefined codes:

CMDSRC_PUSHBUTTON
CMDSRC_MENU
CMDSRC_ACCELERATOR
CMDSRC_OTHER

The **return value** is NULL.

WM_SYSVALUECHANGED

This is an application-driven message that alerts the system of a change to a system value. Whenever an application changes a system value, it should post this message to all top-level windows. There is no default processing of this message.

PARAMETER	TYPE	DESCRIPTION
mp1	USHORT	First in an unbroken series of system values.
mp2	USHORT	Last in an unbroken series of system values. Note that if only one system is being changed, the contents of *mp2* are the same as *mp1*.

The **return value** is NULL.

WM_TIMER

This system message occurs when the system timer times out. Timer messages are polled by the WinGetMsg and/or WinPeekMsg functions. When these functions are used to retrieve a message from the queue, they automatically check whether the system timer has timed out. If it has, they return a WM_TIMER message to the message queue. This design prevents timer messages from overloading a message queue. WM_TIMER messages are queued at a lower priority than all other system messages, excepting WM_SEM3, WM_PAINT, and WM_SEM4. The system performs no default processing of WM_TIMER messages.

PARAMETER	TYPE	DESCRIPTION
mp1	USHORT	A timer ID.

The **return value** is zero.

WM_TRACKFRAME

This system message occurs when a window is moved or resized (assuming the window is not of style CS_CLIPCHILDREN). The message references the *fs* options field in the TRACKINFO structure, which controls the system's tracking rectangle. The WM_TRACKFRAME message affords you an opportunity to modify the characteristics of the tracking rectangle before the WinTrackRect function completes the tracking operation. The system performs no default processing for this message. For additional information on the TRACKINFO structure, refer to Chapter 13.

PARAMETER	TYPE	DESCRIPTION
mp1	USHORT	References the *fs* options field of the TRACKINFO structure. This field contains an ORed combination of TF identifiers.

The **return value** is TRUE when the operation succeeds. You should return FALSE in the event of an error.

WM_TRANSLATEACCEL

This system message coincides with each occurrence of a WM_CHAR message. The WM_TRANSLATEACCEL message is sent to the focus window to permit accelerator key translation, if necessary. If the translation occurs, the systems converts the WM_CHAR to a WM_NULL message. Note that if the focus window is not the frame window, this message is normally passed up the window lineage to the frame window. In turn, the frame control procedure processes the WM_TRANSLATEACCEL message by invoking the WinTranslateAccel function. There is no default processing of the WM_TRANSLATEACCEL message.

PARAMETER	TYPE	DESCRIPTION
mp1	PQMSG	Pointer to a QMSG structure.

The **return value** is TRUE when the WM_CHAR message is successfully translated. It is FALSE if it has not been translated or the focus window (or the top-level window in the lineage) does not have an accelerator table.

WM_UPDATEFRAME

This application-driven message occurs when an application modifies the frame controls. The application sends the WM_UPDATEFRAME message after it adds or removes a frame control. The message is processed by the frame control procedure, which updates the appearance of the frame window. The WM_UPDATEFRAME handler in the client window procedure should return FALSE to allow the frame control procedure to process the message. When it does so, the frame control procedure sends a WM_FOR-MATFRAME message to itself. Additionally, if the window style specified FCF_STYLEBORDER, the frame control procedure invalidates the border. Note that the WM_UPDATEFRAME message repaints the contents of the frame window, including the client area. You can avoid this by calling WinSetParent and setting its *fRedraw* argument to FALSE.

PARAMETER	TYPE	DESCRIPTION
mp1	ULONG	References the ORed combination of frame style bits (that is, the FCF identifiers).

The **return value** is TRUE.

WM_USER

The WM_USER message is the base message from which you define custom messages for the application. You do not use the WM_USER message itself in an application. The following is a typical definition of two user messages:

```
#define WM_USER1   (WM_USER + 0)
#define WM_USER2   (WM_USER + 1)
```

WM_VSCROLL

This system message occurs as the result of a vertical scrollbar command. The message is posted to the message queue procedure for the owner window of the scrollbar control. There is no default processing of this message. For additional information on this message and scrollbar processing, refer to Chapter 5.

PARAMETER	TYPE	DESCRIPTION
mp1	USHORT	Scrollbar window ID.
mp2 (low)	SHORT	Slider position. If this value is FALSE, it means the slider is not being moved.

mp2 (high)   USHORT   One of the scrollbar window identifiers:

                                        SB_LINELEFT
                                        SB_LINERIGHT
                                        SB_PAGELEFT
                                        SB_PAGERIGHT
                                        SB_SLIDERPOSITION
                                        SB_SLIDERTRACK
                                        SB_ENDSCROLL

The **return value** is NULL.

CHAPTER 18

WIN LIBRARY FUNCTIONS

The Win library of functions is a large set of functions that give you control over most aspects of the Presentation Manager. Except for graphics output, which is handled by the Gpi library, the Win library gives you most of the tools you need to manage frame windows, child windows, dialog boxes, menus, and much more. This chapter summarizes the the complete library of Win functions. The first section of the chapter presents the Win functions according to their functional grouping. The second section presents each function, with a brief description, its arguments, and return value.

Functional Categories

In this section, the Win functions are presented by functional category. Note that categories correspond to the larger, conceptual differentiations between functionality. Some of the categories can be divided into a series of smaller categories, especially the Window Management category. Refer to Chapter 2 for additional information on more functional groupings.

Table 18-1: Accelerators   **(INCL_WINACCELERATORS)**

FUNCTION	DESCRIPTION
WinCopyAccelTable	Copies an accelerator table.
WinCreateAccelTable	Creates an accelerator table.
WinDestroyAccelTable	Destroys an accelerator table.
WinLoadAccelTable	Loads an accelerator table.
WinQueryAccelTable	Queries the accelerator table.
WinSetAccelTable	Sets an accelerator table.
WinTranslateAccel	Translates a WM_CHAR message.

Table 18-2: Atom Management   (INCL_WINATOM)

FUNCTION	DESCRIPTION
WinAddAtom	Adds an atom to an atom table.
WinCreateAtomTable	Creates an empty atom table.
WinDestroyAtomTable	Destroys an atom table.
WinDeleteAtom	Deletes an atom from an atom table.
WinFindAtom	Finds an atom in the atom table.
WinQueryAtomLength	Queries atom length.
WinQueryAtomName	Queries atom name.
WinQueryAtomUsage	Queries atom usage count.
WinQuerySystemAtomTable	Returns handle of the system atom table.

Table 18-3: Catch/Throw   (INCL_WINCATCHTHROW)

FUNCTION	DESCRIPTION
WinCatch	Captures the current execution environment.
WinThrow	Restores the execution environment.

Table 18-4: Clipboard   (INCL_WINCLIPBOARD)

FUNCTION	DESCRIPTION
WinCloseClipbrd	Closes the clipboard.
WinEmptyClipbrd	Empties the clipboard.
WinEnumClipbrdFmts	Enumerates the list of clipboard data formats.
WinOpenClipbrd	Opens the Clipboard.
WinQueryClipbrdData	Obtains a handle to the current clipboard.
WinQueryClipbrdFmtInfo	Determines format of data in the clipboard.
WinQueryClipbrdOwner	Obtains the current clipboard owner window.
WinQueryClipbrdViewer	Obtains the current clipboard viewer window.
WinSetClipbrdData	Puts data into the Clipboard.
WinSetClipbrdOwner	Sets the current Clipboard Owner Window.
WinSetClipbrdViewer	Sets the current Clipboard Viewer Window.

Table 18-5: Cursor (INCL_WINCURSORS)

FUNCTION	DESCRIPTION
WinCreateCursor	Creates a cursor for a specified window.
WinDestroyCursor	Destroys the current cursor.
WinQueryCursorInfo	Obtains information about the current cursor.
WinShowCursor	Displays or hides the cursor.

Table 18-6: Dialog Boxes (INCL_WINDIALOGS)

FUNCTION	DESCRIPTION
WinAlarm	Generates an audible alarm.
WinCreateDlg	Creates a dialog window.
WinDefDlgProc	Calls the default dialog procedure.
WinDismissDlg	Hides the dialog window.
WinDlgBox	Loads and processes a modal dialog box.
WinEnumDlgItem	Returns the window handle of a dialog item.
WinLoadDlg	Creates a dialog window.
WinMapDlgPoints	Maps dialog points to window coordinates.
WinMessageBox	Creates, displays and operates a message box.
WinProcessDlg	Processes modal dialog messages.
WinQueryDlgItemShort	Translates the text of a dialog item.
WinQueryDlgItemText	Retrieves the text of a dialog item.
WinSendDlgItemMsg	Sends message to dialog item.
WinSetDlgItemShort	Sets dialog text to an integer.
WinSetDlgItemText	Sets text in a dialog item.
WinSubstituteStrings	Performs string substitution.

Table 18-7: Dynamic Data Exchange (INCL_WINDDE)

FUNCTION	DESCRIPTION
WinDdeInitiate	Sends initiate message to all windows.
WinDdeRespond	Responds to sender of initiate message.
WinDdePostMsg	Post's a message to a message queue.

Table 18-8: Error Control   (INCL_WINERRORS)

FUNCTION	DESCRIPTION
WinGetLastError	Gets last error state.
WinGetErrorInfo	Gets error information.
WinFreeErrorInfo	Frees memory allocation for error information.

Table 18-9: Frame Window   (INCL_WINFRAMEMGR)

FUNCTION	DESCRIPTION
WinCalcFrameRect	Calculates client rectangle from frame rectangle.
WinCreateFrameControls	Creates the standard frame controls.
WinCreateStdWindow	Creates a standard window.
WinCopyRect	Copies a rectangle.
WinEqualRect	Compares two rectangles for equality.
WinFormatFrame	Calculates size and position of frame controls.
WinFlashWindow	Starts or stops flashing a window.
WinGetMinPosition	Sets the minimized window position.
WinGetMaxPosition	Sets maximized window position.
WinInflateRect	Expands a rectangle.
WinIntersectRect	Calculates intersection of two source rectangles.
WinIsRectEmpty	Checks whether a rectangle is empty.
WinMakePoints	Converts points to graphics points.
WinMakeRect	Converts a rectangle to a graphics rectangle.
WinOffsetRect	Offsets a rectangle.
WinPtInRect	Queries whether a point lies within a rectangle.
WinSetRect	Sets rectangle coordinates.
WinSetRectEmpty	Sets a rectangle empty.
WinSetRectEmpty	Sets a rectangle empty.
WinSubtractRect	Subtracts rectangles.
WinUnionRect	Calculates a union rectangle.

Table 18-10: Hooks   **(INCL_WINHOOKS)**

FUNCTION	DESCRIPTION
WinCallMsgFilter	Calls a message-filter hook.
WinReleaseHook	Releases an application hook.
WinSetHook	Installs a hook.

Table 18-11: Input   **(INCL_WININPUT)**

FUNCTION	DESCRIPTION
WinEnablePhysInput	Enables or disables queuing of physical input.
WinFocusChange	Changes the focus.
WinGetKeyState	Gets key state.
WinGetPhysKeyState	Gets physical key state.
WinIsPhysInputEnabled	Determines if physical input is enabled.
WinQueryCapture	Queries mouse capture.
WinQueryFocus	Returns the focus window.
WinSetFocus	Sets the focus window.
WinSetCapture	Captures all mouse messages.
WinSetKeyboardStateTable	Gets or sets the keyboard state.

Table 18-12: Memory   **(INCL_WINHEAP)**

FUNCTION	DESCRIPTION
WinAllocMem	Allocates memory from the heap space.
WinAvailMem	Returns size of largest free block on heap.
WinCreateHeap	Creates a heap.
WinFreeMem	Frees memory from the heap.
WinLockHeap	Locks a heap.
WinDestroyHeap	Destroys a heap.
WinReallocMem	Reallocates memory in the heap.

Table 18-13: Menus   (INCL_WINMENUS)

FUNCTION	DESCRIPTION
WinCreateMenu	Creates a menu window.
WinLoadMenu	Creates a menu window.

Table 18-14: Messages   (INCL_WINMESSAGEMGR)

FUNCTION	DESCRIPTION
WinBroadcastMsg	Broadcasts a message to multiple windows.
WinCancelShutdown	Continue processing after WM_QUIT message.
WinCreateMsgQueue	Creates a message queue.
WinDestroyMsgQueue	Destroys the message queue.
WinDispatchMsg	Dispatches message.
WinGetMsg	Gets a message from message queue.
WinInSendMsg	Determines if thread is processing a message.
WinMsgMuxSemWait	Waits for one or more semaphores.
WinMsgSemWait	Waits until a semaphore is cleared.
WinPeekMsg	Inspects the thread's message queue.
WinPostMsg	Posts a message.
WinPostQueueMsg	Posts a message to a message queue.
WinQueryMsgPos	Queries message position.
WinQueryMsgTime	Queries message time.
WinQueryQueueInfo	Retrieves information about the queue.
WinQueryQueueStatus	Retrieves the message queue status.
WinSendMsg	Sends a message.
WinSetMsgInterest	Sets a window's message interest.
WinWaitMsg	Waits for a filtered message.

Table 18-15: Pointers   (INCL_WINPOINTERS)

FUNCTION	DESCRIPTION
WinSetPointer	Sets the desktop pointer handle.
WinSetPointerPos	Sets the pointer position.
WinShowPointer	Shows or hides a pointer.
WinQuerySysPointer	Returns the system pointer handle.
WinLoadPointer	Loads a pointer resource.
WinDestroyPointer	Destroys a pointer or Icon.
WinCreatePointer	Creates a pointer from a bitmap.
WinQueryPointer	Returns a handle to the desktop pointer.
WinQueryPointerInfo	Queries pointer information.
WinQueryPointerPos	Retrieves the pointer position.
WinSetPointerPos	Sets the pointer position.
WinQueryPointerPos	Retrieves the pointer position.
WinQueryPointerInfo	Queries pointer information.
WinDrawPointer	Draws a pointer.
WinGetSysBitmap	Returns handle to standard system bitmap.

Table 18-16: Rectangles   (INCL_WINTRACKRECT)

FUNCTION	DESCRIPTION
WinShowTrackRect	Shows/displays a tracking rectangle.
WinTrackRect	Draws a tracking rectangle.

Table 18-17: Shell API   (INCL_WINCOUNTRY)

FUNCTION	DESCRIPTION
WinCompareStrings	Compares two strings.
WinCpTranslateChar	Translates a character between code pages.
WinNextChar	Move to next character in a string.
WinPrevChar	Moves to previous character in a string.
WinQueryCp	Returns the queue code page.
WinQueryCpList	Queries available code pages.
WinSetCp	Sets the code page.
WinUpper	Converts a string to upper case.
WinUpperChar	Converts a character to upper case.

Table 18-18: Shell Data   (INCL_WINSHELLDATA)

FUNCTION	DESCRIPTION
WinQueryProfileData	Obtains information from OS2.INI.
WinQueryProfileSize	Obtains size of keyname in OS2.INI.
WinQueryProfileString	Retrieves a text string from OS2.INI.
WinWriteProfileData	Places data into OS2.INI.
WinWriteProfileString	Places a keyname into OS2.INI.

Table 18-19: Start Programs   (INCL_WINPROGRAMLIST)

FUNCTION	DESCRIPTION
WinAddProgram	Adds a program entry to Start Programs.
WinCreateGroup	Creates a group entry in Start Programs.
WinQueryDefinition	Gets a copy of the program information block..
WinQueryProgramTitles	Obtains data about a program or program group.

Table 18-20: System Values   (INCL_WINSYS)

FUNCTION	DESCRIPTION
WinGetCurrentTime	Gets the current time.
WinQuerySysValue	Returns the system value.
WinQuerySysColor	Returns the system color.
WinStartTimer	Starts a timer.
WinSetSysColors	Sets system colors.
WinSetSysValue	Sets system value.
WinStopTimer	Stops a timer.

Table 18-21: Task Manager   (INCL_WINSWITCHLIST)

FUNCTION	DESCRIPTION
WinAddSwitchEntry	Adds an entry to the switch list.
WinChangeSwitchEntry	Changes information in the switch list.
WinQueryProfileInt	Retrieves integer from OS2.INI.
WinQueryTaskTitle	Obtains application title.
WinRemoveSwitchEntry	Removes entry from the switch list.

Table 18-22: Windows   (INCL_WINWINDOWMGR)

FUNCTION	DESCRIPTION
WinBeginPaint	Obtains a presentation space ready for drawing.
WinBeginEnumWindows	Begins an enumeration process.
WinCreateWindow	Creates a window.
WinDefWindowProc	Calls the default window procedure.
WinDestroyWindow	Destroys a window.
WinDrawBitmap	Draws a bitmap.
WinDrawText	Draws a single line of formatted text.
WinDrawBorder	Draws a border.
WinEnableWindow	Sets the window enabled state.
WinEnableWindowUpdate	Enables window updating.
WinEndEnumWindows	Ends the enumeration process.
WinEndPaint	Indicates redrawing of a window is complete.
WinExcludeUpdateRegion	Excludes an update region.
WinFillRect	Draws a filled rectangular area.
WinGetClipPS	Retrieves a clipped presentation space.
WinGetNextWindow	Obtains next window handle from enumeration list.
WinGetPS	Obtains a cache presentation space.
WinGetScreenPS	Returns a screen-based presentation space.
WinInitialize	Initialize presentation manager facilities.
WinInvertRect	Inverts a rectangular area.
WinIsChild	Tests if one window is a descendant of another.

(continued)

Table 18-22: Continued

FUNCTION	DESCRIPTION
WinIsWindow	Tests if window handle is valid.
WinIsWindowEnabled	Returns the enabled state of the window.
WinIsWindowVisible	Returns the visibility of a window.
WinInvalidateRect	Adds a rectangle to a window's update region.
WinInvalidateRegion	Adds a region to a window's update region.
WinIsThreadActive	Determines thread ownership.
WinIsWindowEnabled	Returns the enabled state of the window.
WinIsWindowVisible	Returns the visibility of a window.
WinLoadMessage	Loads a message from a resource.
WinLoadString	Loads a string from a resource.
WinLockWindow	Locks or unlocks a window.
WinLockWindowUpdate	Locks a window and children from updating.
WinLockVisRegions	Locks/unlocks visible regions of all windows.
WinMapWindowPoints	Maps a set of points between coordinate spaces.
WinMultWindowFromIDs	Finds the handles of child windows.
WinQueryActiveWindow	Returns the active window handle.
WinQueryClassInfo	Queries class information.
WinQueryDesktopWindow	Returns the desktop window handle.
WinQueryClassName	Query class name.
WinQueryObjectWindow	Returns the desktop object-window handle.
WinQuerySysModalWindow	Returns the current system modal window.
WinQueryUpdateRect	Returns the update rectangle.
WinQueryUpdateRegion	Obtains the update region of a window.
WinQueryVersion	Returns version and revision number.
WinQueryWindowLockCount	Returns the window lock count.
WinQueryWindow	Returns the handle of a window.
WinOpenWindowDC	Opens a device context for a window.
WinQueryWindowLockCount	Returns the window lock count.
WinQueryWindowPos	Retrieves the window size and position.

(continued)

Table 18-22: Continued

FUNCTION	DESCRIPTION
WinQueryWindowProcess	Obtains process and thread identifier.
WinQueryWindowPtr	Retrieves a pointer from reserved window words.
WinQueryWindowRect	Returns a window rectangle.
WinQueryWindowText	Copies window text into a buffer.
WinQueryWindowTextLength	Returns window text length.
WinQueryWindowULong	Obtains ULONG value from reserved memory.
WinQueryWindowUShort	Obtains integer from reserved window words.
WinReleasePS	Releases a cache presentation space.
WinRegisterClass	Registers a window class.
WinScrollWindow	Scrolls the contents of a window rectangle.
WinSetActiveWindow	Sets active window.
WinSetParent	Changes the parent window handle.
WinSetMultWindowPos	Sets multiple window positions.
WinSetOwner	Changes the owner window.
WinSetWindowPos	Sets window position.
WinSetWindowText	Sets the window text.
WinShowWindow	Sets the window visibility state.
WinSubclassWindow	Creates a subclass of the window.
WinRegisterWindowDestroy	Registers window destroy notification.
WinTerminate	Terminates an application.
WinUpdateWindow	Updates a window.
WinSetWindowBits	Writes into a bit field.
WinSetWindowPtr	Places a pointer value into reserved window words.
WinSetWindowUShort	Places an integer into reserved window words.
WinSetSysModalWindow	Makes a window system modal.
WinSetWindowULong	Places long value into reserved window words.
WinValidateRect	Validates a rectangle.
WinValidateRegion	Validates a region..
WinWindowFromDC	Retrieves window handle from DC.
WinWindowFromID	Returns a child window handle.
WinWindowFromPoint	Finds a window below a point.

Function Descriptions

The Win library makes for quite an extensive programming environment in and of itself. Likely, it will take you more than a few evenings to master the some 235 functions included in the library. Even after you have a good idea what a function does, you need a quick reference. This section is designed to serve that purpose. For detailed information on a function, when appropriate, individual function descriptions refer you to other parts of this book.

ATOM WinAddAtom(*hAtomTbl, pszAtomName*)

HATOMTBL hAtomTbl;
PSZ pszAtomName;

WinAddAtom adds a new atom to an atom table. You can use this function to create custom messages for inter-application purposes.

ARGUMENT	DESCRIPTION
hAtomTbl	The atom table ID, which is returned from a prior call to the WinCreateAtomTable function.
pszAtomName	Pointer to a null-terminated character string that comprises the atom to be added to the table. A string that begins with the # character is converted into a 16-bit integer. The function returns the atom without making changes to the atom table when the integer is a valid integer atom. A string that begins with a ! character causes denotes that the next two bytes should be interpreted as an atom.

The **return value** is the atom corresponding to the passed string. A zero return value indicates that the specified atom or atom table was invalid.

HPROGRAM WinAddProgram(*hab, pProgInfo, hProg-Group*)

HAB hab;
PIBSTRUCT pProgInfo;
HPROGRAM hprog;

620

WinAddProgram adds a program entry to the *Start Programs* window. A program title must be unique within the same group.

ARGUMENT	DESCRIPTION
hab	Handle to the anchor block.
pProgInfo	Pointer to a PIBSTRUCT, which contains the program information.
hProgGroup	Handle to the program group.

The **return value** is the handle to the program added to *Start Programs*. If the function fails, it returns NULL.

HSWITCH WinAddSwitchEntry(*pswctl*)
PSWCNTRL pswctl;

The WinAddSwitchEntry function appends the *Task Manager's* switch list with the specified entry. If the entry exceeds 60 characters, the entry is truncated. Leading and trailing spaces are also removed.

ARGUMENT	DESCRIPTION
pswctl	Pointer to a SWCNTRL structure that describes the entry to be appended to the switch list.

The **return value** is the handle to the new switch list entry. Otherwise, the return value is NULL.

BOOL WinAlarm(*hwndDesktop, rgfType*)
HWND hwndDesktop;
USHORT rgfType;

The WinAlarm function sounds an alarm. It is similar to the DosBeep function, but the duration and frequency of the beep must be set using the WinSetSysValue function.

ARGUMENT	DESCRIPTION
hwndDesktop	The desktop window ID, which is usually represented as HWND_DESKTOP.
rgfType	Specifies the alarm style. The *rgfType* parameter is used to signify different situations to the operator. Different alarms are selected by using the following values: WA_WARNING, WA_NOTE WA_ERROR The alarm is not generated if SV_ALARM is set to FALSE.

The **return value** is TRUE if the function is successful or FALSE if an error occurs.

NPBYTE WinAllocMem(*hHeap, cb*)

HHEAP hHeap;
USHORT cb;

The WinAllocMem function returns the 16-bit offset from the beginning of the memory segment for a heap containing an allocated object. The lower two bits in the returned pointer are always zero. If WinAllocMem cannot allocate the memory object, it returns NULL.

ARGUMENT	DESCRIPTION
hHeap	A handle specifying a heap. The handle must be obtained by calling the WinCreateHeap function.
cb	Specifies the total number of bytes to allocate.

The **return value** is a near pointer to the allocated memory object. If the function is unsuccessful, it returns NULL.

USHORT WinAvailMem(*hHeap, fCompact, cbMinFree*)

HHEAP hHeap;
BOOL fCompact;
USHORT cbMinFree;

WinAvailMem returns the size of the largest free block on the heap. This function does not grow the segment so as to meet the specified minimum free block size.

ARGUMENT	DESCRIPTION
hHeap	A handle specifying a heap. The handle must be obtained by calling WinCreateHeap.
fCompact	A flag that indicates how memory is compacted. Specifying TRUE reorganizes the heap. Specifying FALSE disallows reorganization. Refer to HM_MOVEABLE in the listing for WinCreateHeap.
cbMinFree	Ignored.

The **return value** is the largest available memory block available . If the function is unsuccessful, it returns 0xFFFF, which indicates an error.

HENUM WinBeginEnumWindows(*hwnd*)
HWND hwnd;

WinBeginEnumWindows supplies an enumeration handle for the immediate child windows of a given window. The z-order of the enumerated windows is based on the time the function is called. The topmost window is listed first. Child windows of the immediate child windows are not included in the enumeration process. When you are through with the enumeration handle, you must destroy it using WinEndEnumWindows.

ARGUMENT	DESCRIPTION
hwnd	The handle specifying the window for which you want an enumeration of immediate child windows.

The **return value** is the enumeration handle. You can use it in calls to WinGetNextWindow in order to obtain the handle of a given child window.

HPS WinBeginPaint(*hwnd, hps, prclPaint*)
HWND hwnd;
HPS hps;
PRECTL prclPaint;

WinBeginPaint automatically provides a presentation space and allows you to draw in a window. The associated update region is also automatically set.

ARGUMENT	DESCRIPTION
hwnd	Handle to the window in which you want to draw.
hps	Handle to an existing presentation space (optional). Setting this argument to NULL automatically obtains a cached presentation space.
prclPaint	Pointer to a RECTL structure set to the smallest rectangle bounding the update region.

The **return value** is a handle to a presentation space.

BOOL WinBroadcastMsg(*hwnd, msg, mp1, mp2, rgf*)
HWND hwnd;
USHORT msg;
MPARAM mp1, mp2;
BOOL rgf;

WinBroadcastMsg broadcasts a message to more than one window. Whether the message is sent or posted depends on the thread status of each recipient window. If *hwnd* is NULL, all main windows on the screen receive the message.

ARGUMENT	DESCRIPTION
hwnd	Handle to the window whose descendants are the recipient windows.
msg	Message ID.
mp1	First message parameter.
mp2	Second message parameter.
rgf	Specifies recipient windows through one of the following identifiers:

BMSG_POST	Immediate child windows.
BMSG_SEND	Immediate child windows.
BMSG_POSTQUEUE	Meesage queue threads.
BMSG_DESCENDANTS	All descendants of *hwnd*.
BMSG_FRAMEONLY	Only CS_FRAME style windows.

The **return value** is TRUE if the function succeeds. It is FALSE if an error occurs.

BOOL WinCalcFrameRect(*hwndFrame, prcl, fClient*)
HWND hwndFrame;
PRECTL prcl;
BOOL fClient;

WinCalcFrameRect calculates a client rectangle from a frame rectangle or a frame rectangle from a client rectangle. Importantly, this function works even if the frame window is hidden.

ARGUMENT	DESCRIPTION
hwndFrame	Handle to a frame window.
prcl	Pointer to a RECTL structure that specifies the window rectangle.
fClient	Flag specifying the provided rectangle. Setting this to TRUE specifies that the rectangle is provided for the frame window. Setting it to FALSE specifies that the rectangle is provided for the client area.

The **return value** is TRUE if the function succeeds. It is FALSE if an error occurs.

BOOL WinCallMsgFilter(*hab, pqmsg, msgf*)
HAB hab;
PQMSG pqmsg;
SHORT msgf;

WinCallMsgFilter invokes a message filter hook, thereby establishing hook processing.

ARGUMENT	DESCRIPTION
hab	Handle to anchor block.
pqmsg	Pointer to a QMSG structure that holds the message to be passed to the message filter hook.
msgf	Code for the message filter hook. It is either an MSGF identifier, or a programmer-defined value.

The **return value** is TRUE when the message filter hook returns TRUE. It is FALSE when all message filter hooks return FALSE, or when no message filter hooks have been defined.

BOOL WinCancelShutdown(*hmq, fCancelAlways*);

HMQ hmq;
BOOL fCancelAlways;

WinCancelShutdown permits a thread to continue working after it receives a WM_QUIT message. In order to accomplish this, you must call WinCanCancelShutdown while processing WM_QUIT in the thread's message queue. If the active window belongs to the thread issuing the WinCancelShutdown call, the window is deactivated and goes to the bottom of the z-order.

ARGUMENT	DESCRIPTION
hmq	Handle to a message queue thread.
fCancelAlways	Flag specifying whether the thread receives the WM_QUIT messages during system shutdown. A TRUE value specifies that the thread does not receive a WM_QUIT message during system shutdown. A FALSE value specifies that the thread ignores the WM_QUIT message.

The **return value** is TRUE if the function succeeds. It is FALSE if an error occurs.

SHORT WinCatch(*pCatchBuf*)

PCATCHBUF pCatchBuf;

WinCatch obtains the current execution environment (including system registers and instruction counter) and copies it to a specified buffer. You can later access the buffer and restore the environment by using the the WinThrow function.

ARGUMENT	DESCRIPTION
pCatchBuf	Pointer to a CATCHBUF structure that contains the execution environment.

The **return value** is zero if the function succeeds. It is non-zero if an error occurs.

USHORT WinChangeSwitchEntry(*hSwitch, pswctl*)

HSWITCH hSwitch;
PSWCNTRL pswctl;

WinChangeSwitchEntry modifies switchlist data, including a title of up to 60 characters. Any blank spaces before or after the title are removed by WinChangeSwitchEntry.

ARGUMENT	DESCRIPTION
hSwitch	Handle to the switchlist entry.
pswctl	Pointer to a SWCNTRL data structure that contains the entry's switchlist data.

The **return value** is zero if the function succeeds. It is non-zero if an error occurs.

BOOL WinCloseClipbrd(*hab*)

HAB hab;

WinCloseClipbrd closes the clipboard. If the clipboard viewer is active at the time of this call, the contents of the clipboard are drawn. Note that the clipboard must be active in order for this function to work.

ARGUMENT	DESCRIPTION
hab	Handle to the anchor block.

The **return value** is TRUE if the function succeeds. It is FALSE if an error occurs.

USHORT WinCompareStrings(*hab, idcp, idcc, psz1, psz2, reserved*)

HAB hab;
USHORT idcp, idcc;
PSZ psz1, psz2;
USHORT reserved;

WinCompareStrings compares two specified strings.

ARGUMENT	DESCRIPTION
hab	Handle to the anchor block.
idcp	Code page ID.
idcc	Country-code ID.
psz1	Pointer to the first string.
psz2	Pointer to the second string.
reserved	Reserved value, which must be zero.

The **return value** is the result of the comparison. It is one of the following values: WCS_EQ, strings are equal; WCS_LT, first string is less than second string; WCS_GT, second string is greater than first string; and WCS_ERROR, invalid country code or code page ID.

USHORT WinCopyAccelTable(*haccel, pacct, cbCopyMax*)
HACCEL haccel;
PACCELTABLE pacct;
USHORT cbCopyMax;

WinCopyAccelTable copies an accelerator table. You can use this function to get the accelerator table data for a given accelerator table handle. The data is copied as an instance of the ACCELTABLE structure. Additionally, you can use the function to obtain the size of the accelerator table data.

ARGUMENT	DESCRIPTION
haccel	Handle to an accelerator table.
pacct	Pointer to a memory area to hold the accelerator table data. Setting this argument to NULL copies only the number of ACCELTABLE bytes corresponding to *cbCopyMax*.
cbCopyMax	The maximum number of bytes for the copied instance of the ACCELTABLE structure.

The **return value** indicates the amount of data copied. If unsuccessful, the function returns zero.

BOOL WinCopyRect(*hab, prclDst, prclSrc*)
HAB hab;
PRECTL prclDst, prclSrc;

WinCopyRect copies a rectangle.

ARGUMENT	DESCRIPTION
hab	Handle to the anchor block.
prclDst	Pointer to a RECTL structure that specifies the destination.
prclSrc	Pointer to a RECTL structure that specifies the source.

The **return value** is TRUE if the function is successful or FALSE if an error occurs.

UCHAR WinCpTranslateChar(*hab, cpSrc, chSrc, cpDst*)
HAB hab;
USHORT cpSrc;
UCHAR chSrc;
USHORT cpDst;

WinCpTranslateChar translates a character between code pages.

ARGUMENT	DESCRIPTION
hab	Handle to the anchor block.
cpSrc	Code page containing the source character.
chSrc	Character to be translated.
cpDst	Code page of the translated character.

The **return value** is the translation. If a translation is impossible, the result is a standard character.

BOOL WinCpTranslateString(*hab, cpSrc, pszSrc, cpDst, cchDestMax, pchDest*)

HAB hab;
USHORT cpSrc;
PSZ pszSrc;
USHORT cpDst, cchDestMax;
PSZ pchDest;

WinCpTranslateString translates null-terminated strings between code pages.

ARGUMENT	DESCRIPTION
hab	Handle to the anchor block.
cpSrc	Code page of the source string.
pszSrc	Pointer to the string to be translated.
cpDst	Code page of the translated string.
cchDestMax	Maximum length of the output string.
pchDest	Pointer to the buffer for the translated string.

The **return value** is TRUE if the function succeeds. It is FALSE if an error occurs.

HACCEL WinCreateAccelTable(*hab, pacct*)

HAB hab;
PACCELTABLE pacct;

WinCreateAccelTable creates an accelerator table. The accelerator table definition must already be in memory for the function to work.

ARGUMENT	DESCRIPTION
hab	Handle to the anchor block.
pacct	Pointer to an ACCELTABLE data structure that contains an accelerator table.

The **return value** is an accelerator table handle.

HATOMTBL WinCreateAtomTable(*cbInitial, cbBuckets*)
USHORT cbInitial, cbBuckets;

WinCreateAtomTable creates an empty atom

ARGUMENT	DESCRIPTION
cbInitial	Number of initial bytes for the atom table.
cbBuckets	The size of the hash table used to access atoms. Typically, this argument should be set to a prime number or zero, which specifies the default size of 37.

The **return value** is a handle to the atom table. The function returns NULL if an error occurs.

BOOL WinCreateCursor(*hwnd, x, y, cx, cy, fs, prclClip*)
HWND hwnd;
SHORT x, y, cx, cy;
USHORT fs;
PRECTL prclClip;

WinCreateCursor creates a cursor in a window.

ARGUMENT	DESCRIPTION
hwnd	Handle to the window that will display the cursor.
x	The base horizontal position of the cursor.
y	The base vertical position of the cursor.
cx	The width of the cursor. Setting this argument to zero specifies the system nominal border width of SV_CXBORDER.
cy	The height of the cursor. Setting this argument to zero specifies the system nominal border width of SY_CXBORDER.

(continued)

ARGUMENT	DESCRIPTION
fs	The cursor appearance, which is one of the following:

CURSOR_SOLID	Solid cursor.
CURSOR_HALFTONE	Halftone cursor.
CURSOR_FRAME	Rectangular frame cursor.
CURSOR_FLASH	Flashing cursor.
CURSOR_SETPOS	Other flags ignored.

prclClip	Pointer to a RECTL structure that specifies a cursor rectangle. When the cursor extends beyond the rectangle, it is no longer visible.

The **return value** is TRUE if the function succeeds. It is FALSE if an error occurs.

HWND WinCreateDlg(*hwndParent, hwndOwner, pfnDlgProc, pdlgt, pCreateParams*)

HWND hwndParent, hwndOwner;
PFNWP pfnDlgProc;
PDLGTEMPLATE pdlgt;
PVOID pCreateParams;

WinCreateDlg creates a dialog box. Note that this function creates a dialog box as specified by a resource-based template, not a memory-based template (as is the case with the WinLoadDlg function).

ARGUMENT	DESCRIPTION
hwndParent	Handle to the parent window.
hwndOwner	Handle to the owner window.
pfnDlgProc	Pointer to the dialog box procedure.
pdlgt	Pointer to a DLGTEMPLATE structure.
pCreateParams	Reserved value, which must be NULL.

The **return value** is a handle to a dialog box.

BOOL WinCreateFrameControls(*hwndFrame, flStyle, pszTitle, hmod*)

HWND hwndFrame;
ULONG flStyle;
PSZ pszTitle;
HMODULE hmod;

WinCreateFrameControls creates frame controls for a specified window.

ARGUMENT	DESCRIPTION
hwndFrame	Handle to a frame window. This frame window becomes the owner and parent of the created frame controls.
flStyle	Frame style values that specify the frame controls.
pszTitle	Pointer to a null-terminated string that becomes the titlebar string.
hmod	Resource file, from which a menu resource template is loaded, if FS_MENU is specified.

The **return value** is TRUE if the function succeeds. It is FALSE if an error occurs.

HPROGRAM WinCreateGroup(hab, pszTitle, chVisibility, reserved1, reserved2);

HAB hab;;
PSZ pszTitle;
UCHAR chVisibility;
ULONG reserved1, reserved2;

WinCreateGroup creates an entry for the specified program group in *Start Programs* utility. The new group is always created empty. To add programs to the group, use the WinAddProgram function.

ARGUMENT	DESCRIPTION
hab	Handle to the anchor block.
pszTitle	Pointer to the title of the group (a null-terminated string).
chVisibility	Specifies the visibility of the group. Setting this to SHE_VISIBLE makes the group visible. Setting it to SHE_INVISIBLE makes the group invisible.
reserved1	Reserved and must be set to zero.
reserved2	Reserved and must be set to zero.

The **return value** is a handle to a *Start Programs* group. If the function fails, it returns NULL.

HEAP WinCreateHeap(*selHeapBase, cbHeap, cbGrow, cbMinDed, cbMaxDed, fsOptions*)

USHORT selHeapBase, cbHeap, cbGrow;
USHORT cbMinDed, cbMaxDed, fsOptions;

WinCreateHeap creates a heap.

ARGUMENT	DESCRIPTION
selHeapBase	Segment address for the local heap.
cbHeap	Initial heap size in bytes.
cbGrow	Minimum number of bytes to increase the heap when it is necessary to comply with a memory allocation request. Setting this argument to zero specifies the default size of 512 bytes.
cbMinDed	Minimum number of dedicated free lists.
cbMaxDed	Maximum number of dedicated free lists.
fsOptions	Optional heap characteristics. In release 1.1, the only option supported is HM_MOVEABLE, which provides moveable object support.

The **return value** is a handle to a heap. A non-zero heap handle indicates the heap has been initialized. A zero heap handle indicates it has not been initialized.

HWND WinCreateMenu(*hwndOwner, pMenuTmp*)
HWND hwndOwner;
PVOID pMenuTmp;

WinCreateMenu creates a menu based on the associated menu template.

ARGUMENT	DESCRIPTION
hwndOwner	Handle to the owner window (which is also the parent window in this case).
pMenuTmp	Pointer to a menu template.

The **return value** is the menu-window handle.

HMQ WinCreateMsgQueue(*hab, cmsg*)
HAB hab;
SHORT cmsg;

WinCreateMsgQueue creates a message queue for the currently executing thread. It must be called immediately after the WinInitialize function.

ARGUMENT	DESCRIPTION
hab	Handle to the anchor block.
cmsg	Maximum queue size. Setting this argument to zero specifies the default queue size.

The **return value** is a handle to a message queue. If the message queue cannot be created, the function returns NULL.

HPOINTER WinCreatePointer(*hwndDesktop, hbmPointer, fPointer, xHotspot, yHotspot*)
HWND hwndDesktop;
HBITMAP hbmPointer;
BOOL fPointer;
SHORT xHotspot;
SHORT yHotspot;

WinCreatePointer creates a mouse pointer or an icon, both of which are bitmaps. The bitmap must be an even vertical size. It must also be logically divided into two vertical-based sections. Each section must represent one of the two images corresponding to the bitmap's XOR and AND drawing masks. The result permits four colors: black, white, background, and inverted background.

ARGUMENT	DESCRIPTION
hwndDesktop	Handle to the desktop window.
hbmPointer	Handle to the source bitmap.
fPointer	Flag specifying whether the resultant bitmap is a pointer or an icon. Specifying TRUE causes the source bitmap to be sized to the system-pointer dimensions. Specifying FALSE causes the source bitmap to be sized to system-icon dimensions.
xHotspot	The horizontal position of the pointer hotspot.
yHotspot	The vertical position of the pointer hotspot.

The **return value** is the handle to the resultant pointer or icon.

HWND WinCreateStdWindow(*hwndParent, flStyle, pCtlData, pszClientClass, pszTitle, styleClient, hmod, idResources, phwndClient*);

```
HWND hwndParent;
ULONG flStyle;
PVOID pCtlData;
PSZ pszClientClass;, pszTitle;
ULONG styleClient;
HMODULE hmod;
USHORT idResources;
PHWND phwndClient;
```

636

The WinCreateStdWindow function creates a frame window, or a standard window used for special purposes. For the latter, you should use WinSetWindowPos to size and position the window on the desktop. Note that when you OR different control data identifiers (represented by the FCF identifier), not all combinations are valid. (Refer to Chapter 4 for detailed information on the system identifiers used with this function.)

ARGUMENT	DESCRIPTION
hwndParent	Handle to the parent window. Setting this argument to NULL or HWND_DESKTOP creates a standard window. Setting the argument to HWND_OBJECT creates an object window, which is typically used in multi-threaded applications.
flStyle	The frame window style, which is specified by ORing the WS and FS identifiers .
pCtlData	Pointer to a 32-bit value that is specified by ORing the FCF identifiers.
pszClientClass	Pointer to the class name. The class name is either a null terminated string first specified through WinRegisterClass, or an integer (up to five digits) that corresponds to one of the WC identifiers.
pszTitle	Pointer to the titlebar text string.
styleClient	The style of the client window.
hmod	An icon, accelerator table, or menu resource. Specifying NULL causes the function to obtain the resource from the application's .EXE file. Specifying NULL causes the application to load the resource from a dynamic link library.
idResources	The resource ID.
phwndClient	Pointer to the client window handle.

The **return value** is a handle to the frame window handle, or it is NULL if an error occurred.

HWND WinCreateWindow(*hwndParent, pszClass, pszName, flStyle, x, y, cx, cy, hwndOwner, hwndInsBehind, id, pCtlData, pPresParams*)

HWND hwndParent;
PSZ pszClass, pszName;
ULONG flStyle;
SHORT x, y, cx, cy;
HWND hwndOwner, hwndInsBehind;
USHORT id;
PVOID pCtlData, pPresParams;

WinCreateWindow creates a new child window. It is to be distinguished from WinCreateStdWindow, which creates a frame window.

ARGUMENT	DESCRIPTION
hwndParent	The parent window for the new window.
pszClass	Pointer to a null-terminated string that contains the registered class name.
pszName	Pointer to window text or other class-specific data.
flStyle	Flag specifying the window style.
x	Horizontal window position relative to the parent window.
y	Vertical window position relative to the parent window.
cx	Width of the window.
cy	Depth of the window.
hwndOwner	Handle to the owner window.
hwndInsBehind	Handle to the sibling window. The specified window is placed behind this window.
id	The window ID, which is a programmer-defined value.
pCtlData	Pointer to a buffer with class-specific information.
pPresParams	Pointer to the presentation parameters, a reserved field that must be set to zero.

The **return value** is a handle to the window. If an error occurs, or the window cannot be created, the return value is NULL.

BOOL WinDdeInitiate(*hwndClient, pszAppName, psz-TopicName*)

HWND hwndClient;
PSZ pszAppName; pszTopicName;

WinDdeIntiate is issued to other applications to request the beginning of dynamic data exchange.

ARGUMENT	DESCRIPTION
hwndClient	Handle to the client window.
pszAppName	Pointer to the application name.
pszTopicName	Pointer to the topic name.

The **return value** is TRUE if the function succeeds. Otherwise, it is FALSE.

BOOL WinDdePostMsg(*hwndTo, hwndFrom, wm, pddes, fRetry*)

HWND hwndTo, hwndFrom;
USHORT wm;
PDDESTRUCT pddes;
BOOL fRetry;

WinDdePostMsg posts a message to another application's message queue.

ARGUMENT	DESCRIPTION
hwndTo	Handle to the window receiving the message.
hwndFrom	Handle to the window posting the message.
wm	The message number.
pddes	Pointer to a DDESTRUCT structure.
fRetry	Flag specifying number of retry times to post the message.

The **return value** is TRUE if the function succeeds. Otherwise, it is FALSE.

MRESULT WinDdeRespond(*hwndClient, hwndServer, pszAppName, pszTopicName*)

HWND hwndClient;, hwndServer;
PSZ pszAppName; pszTopicName;

WinDdeRespond answers the initiate acknowledgment message by sending it back to the initiate application. The function concatenates two DDE strings into a shared memory buffer.

ARGUMENT	DESCRIPTION
hwndClient	Handle to the client window.
hwndServer	Handle to the server window.
pszAppName	Pointer to the application name.
pszTopicName	Pointer to the topic name.

The **return value** is derived from sending the WM_DDE_INITIATEACK message to the client window.

MRESULT WinDefDlgProc(*hwndDlg, msg, mp1, mp2*)

HWND hwndDlg;
USHORT msg;
MPARAM mp1, mp2;

WinDefDlgProc calls the default dialog procedure, which handles defaults dialog window processing. It is similar in practice to WinDefWindowProc.

ARGUMENT	DESCRIPTION
hwndDlg	Handle to the dialog window.
msg	The message ID.
mp1	Message parameter one.
mp2	Message parameter two.

The **return value** is the message return data.

MRESULT WinDefWindowProc(*hwnd, msg, mp1, mp2*)

HWND hwnd;
USHORT msg;
MPARAM mp1, mp2;

WinDefWindowProc calls the default window procedure, which provides default processing for a window with a message queue. If you need to ensure that your application processes all messages, you must use this function.

ARGUMENT	DESCRIPTION
hwnd	Handle to a message queue window.
msg	The message ID.
mp1	Message parameter one.
mp2	Message parameter two.

The **return value** is the message return data.

ATOM WinDeleteAtom(*hAtomTbl, atom*)

HATOMTBL hAtomTbl;
ATOM atom;

WinDeleteAtom deletes an atom from the atom table. You obtain a handle to atom table when you call the WinCreateAtomTable function.

ARGUMENT	DESCRIPTION
hAtomTbl	Handle to an atom table.
atom	An atom to be deleted.

The **return value** is NULL if the function succeeds. It is equal to the value of the atom if it fails without deleting the atom.

BOOL WinDestroyAccelTable(*haccel*)

HACCEL haccel;

WinDestroyAccelTable destroys an accelerator table.

ARGUMENT	DESCRIPTION
haccel	Handle to the accelerator table to be destroyed.

The **return value** is TRUE if the function succeeds. It is FALSE if an error occurs.

HATOMTBL WinDestroyAtomTable(*hAtomTbl*)

HATOMTBL hAtomTbl;

WinDestroyAtomTable destroys an atom table created by the WinCreateAtomTable function.

ARGUMENT	DESCRIPTION
hAtomTbl	Handle to the atom table to be destroyed.

The **return value** is NULL if the function succeeds. It is *hAtomTbl* if an error occurs.

BOOL WinDestroyCursor(*hwnd*)

HWND hwnd;

WinDestroyCursor erases and destroys the current cursor when, and only when, it belongs to the specified window.

ARGUMENT	DESCRIPTION
hwnd	Handle to the window owning the cursor.

The **return value** is TRUE if the function succeeds. It is FALSE if an error occurs.

HHEAP WinDestroyHeap(*hHeap*)
HHEAP hHeap;

WinDestroyHeap destroys a heap created by the WinCreateHeap function.

ARGUMENT	DESCRIPTION
hHeap	Handle to the heap to be destroyed. You obtain the handle to the heap by calling WinCreateHeap.

The **return value** is zero if the function succeeds. It is non-zero if an error occurs.

BOOL WinDestroyMsgQueue(*hmq*)
HMQ hmq;

WinDestroyMsgQueue destroys a message queue. You must call this function for each message queue in an application before terminating the application.

ARGUMENT	DESCRIPTION
hmq	Handle to the message queue to destroy.

The **return value** is TRUE if the function succeeds. It is FALSE if an error occurs.

BOOL WinDestroyPointer(*hptr*)
HPOINTER hptr;

WinDestroyPointer destroys a pointer or icon

ARGUMENT	DESCRIPTION
hptr	Handle to a pointer or icon to destroy.

The **return value** is TRUE if the function succeeds. It is FALSE if an error occurs.

BOOL WinDestroyWindow(*hwnd*)

HWND hwnd;

WinDestroyWindow destroys a window and any of its child windows.

ARGUMENT	DESCRIPTION
hwnd	Handle to the window to destroy.

The **return value** is TRUE if the function succeeds. It is FALSE if an error occurs.

BOOL WinDismissDlg(*hwndDlg, usResult*)

HWND hwndDlg;
USHORT usResult;

WinDismissDlg hides a dialog window. It also causes the WinProcessDlg or WinDlgBox function to return.

ARGUMENT	DESCRIPTION
hwndDlg	Handle to the dialog window to hide.
usResult	The value returned as a result of the call to WinProcessDlg or WinDlgBox.

The **return value** is TRUE if the function succeeds. It is FALSE if an error occurs.

ULONG WinDispatchMsg(*hab, pqmsg*)

HAB hab;
PQMSG pqmsg;

WinDispatchMsg causes the Presentation Manager to call a window procedure and pass the current message from the specified message queue.

ARGUMENT	DESCRIPTION
hab	Handle to the anchor block.
pqmsg	Pointer to a QMSG structure containing the message.

The **return value** is that from the associated window procedure.

USHORT WinDlgBox(*hwndParent, hwndOwner, pfnDlgProc, hmod, idDlg, pCreateParams*)

HWND hwndParent, hwndOwner;
PFNWP pfnDlgProc;
HMODULE hmod;
USHORT idDlg;
PVOID pCreateParams;

WinDlgBox loads and executes a modal dialog box.

ARGUMENT	DESCRIPTION
hwndParent	Handle to the parent window.
hwndOwner	Handle to the owner window.
pfnDlgProc	Pointer to the dialog box procedure.
hmod	Handle to the dialog box resource. You must specify NULL or a handle obtained from DosLoadModule function.
idDlg	The ID of the dialog box as specified in the resource file.
pCreateParams	Pointer to the dialog procedure data.

The **return value** results from the dismissed dialog window. In the event of an error, the return value is DID_ERROR.

BOOL WinDrawBitmap(*hpsDst, hbm, pwrcSrc, pptlDst, clrFore, clrBack, fs*)

HPS hpsDst;
HBITMAP hbm;
PRECTL pwrcSrc;
PPOINTL pptlDst;
LONG clrFore, clrBack;
USHORT fs;

WinDrawBitmap draws a bitmap. To do so, it uses the current image colors and mixes. In order to use this function, DM_DRAW must be active.

ARGUMENT	DESCRIPTION
hpsDst	Handle to the presentation space that will display the bitmap.
hbm	Handle to the bitmap.
pwrcSrc	Pointer to the RECTL a structure. Specifying NULL redraws the entire bitmap.
pptlDst	Pointer to lower left position of the bitmap in the presentation space.
clrFore	Foreground color.
clrBack	Background color.
fs	Flags specifying the characteristics of the bitmap. Refer to Chapter 10 for details on the DBM identifiers.

The **return value** is TRUE if the function succeeds. It is FALSE if an error occurs.

BOOL WinDrawBorder(*hps, prcl, cx, cy, clrFore, clrBack, rgfCmd*)

HPS hps;
PRECTL prcl;
SHORT cx, cy;
LONG clrFore;, clrBack;
USHORT rgfCmd;

WinDrawBorder creates a rectangular frame with the specified window. In order to use this function, DM_DRAW must be active.

ARGUMENT	DESCRIPTION
hps	Handle to the presentation space in which the border is drawn.
prcl	Pointer to a RECTL structure.
cx	Width of the left and right sides of the border rectangle.

(continued)

ARGUMENT	DESCRIPTION
cy	Height of the top and bottom sides of the border rectangle.
clrFore	Foreground color.
clrBack	Background color.
rgfCmd	Flags specifying the characteristics of the border rectangle. Refer to Chapter 4 for details on the DB identifiers.

The **return value** is TRUE if the function succeeds. It is FALSE if an error occurs.

BOOL WinDrawPointer(*hps, x, y, hptr, fs*)
HPS hps;
SHORT x, y;
HPOINTER hptr;
USHORT fs;

WinDrawPointer draws a pointer. In order to use this function, DM_DRAW must be active.

ARGUMENT	DESCRIPTION
hps	Handle to the presentation space to draw the bitmap.
x	The horizontal position to locate the pointer.
y	The vertical position to locate the pointer.
hptr	Handle to the pointer.
fs	Flags specifying the characteristics of the border rectangle. Refer to Chapter 13 for details on the identifiers.

The **return value** is TRUE if the function succeeds. It is FALSE if an error occurs.

SHORT WinDrawText(*hps, cchText, pchText, pcrl, clrFore, clrBack, rgfCmd*)
HPS hps;
SHORT cchText;
PSZ pchText;
PRECTL prcl;
LONG clrFore, clrBack;
USHORT rgfCmd;

WinDrawText draws a single line text string. In order to use this function, DM_DRAW must be active.

ARGUMENT	DESCRIPTION
hps	Handle to the presentation space for the text string.
cchText	Number of characters in the string to draw. Setting this to to 0xFFFF indicates the string is null-terminated and its length should be is calculated by the function.
pchText	Pointer to the character string to draw.
pcrl	Pointer to a RECTL structure.
clrFore	Foreground color.
clrBack	Background color.
rgfCmd	Flags specifying the characteristics of the border rectangle. Refer to Chapter 4 for details on the identifiers.

The **return value** is the number of characters that the function draws.

BOOL WinEmptyClipbrd(*hab*)
HAB hab;

WinEmptyClipbrd empties the clipboard. It also removes and frees all handles related to data in the clipboard.

ARGUMENT	DESCRIPTION
hab	Handle to the anchor block.

The **return value** is TRUE if the function succeeds. It is FALSE if an error occurs.

BOOL WinEnablePhysInput(*hwndDesktop, fEnable*)
HWND hwndDesktop;
BOOL fEnable;

WinEnablePhysInput controls the state of physical input. The function can both enable and disable physical input.

ARGUMENT	DESCRIPTION
hwndDesktop	Handle to the desktop window.
fEnable	Flag specifying whether input is queued or disabled. Specifying TRUE enables mouse and keyboard input. Specifying FALSE disables mouse and keyboard input.

The **return value** is TRUE if the function succeeds. It is FALSE if an error occurs.

BOOL WinEnableWindow(*hwnd, fEnable*)
HWND hwnd;
BOOL fEnable;

WinEnableWindow sets a window's enabled state. When the enable state of a window is changing, a WM_ENABLE message is sent before this function returns.

ARGUMENT	DESCRIPTION
hwnd	Handle to a window.
fEnable	The new enabled state. Setting this to TRUE enables the window state. Setting this to FALSE disables the window state.

The **return value** is TRUE if the function succeeds. It is FALSE if an error occurs.

BOOL WinEnableWindowUpdate(*hwnd, fEnable*)

HWND hwnd;
BOOL fEnable;

WinEnableWindowUpdate sets the visibility state of a window. The visibility state is critical to redrawing activities in the window. For example, you can use this function to postpone drawing when making other changes to the window.

ARGUMENT	DESCRIPTION
hwnd	Handle to a window.
fEnable	Visibility state. Specifying TRUE sets the visibility state to visible. Specifying FALSE sets the visibility state to invisible.

The **return value** is TRUE if the function succeeds. It is FALSE if an error occurs.

BOOL WinEndEnumWindows(*henum*)

HENUM henum;

WinEndEnumWindow terminates the window enumeration process.

ARGUMENT	DESCRIPTION
henum	Handle to the enumeration obtained with WinBeginEnumWindow.

The **return value** is TRUE if the function succeeds. It is FALSE if an error occurs.

BOOL WinEndPaint(*hps*)

HPS hps;

WinEndPaint restores the active presentation space to its inactive mode. This function should always be paired with the WinBeginPaint function.

ARGUMENT	DESCRIPTION
hps	Handle to the active presentation space.

The **return value** is TRUE if the function succeeds. It is FALSE if an error occurs.

USHORT WinEnumClipbrdFmts(*hab, fmt*)
HAB hab;
USHORT fmt;

WindEnumClipbrdFmts enumerates the available clipboard data formats.

ARGUMENT	DESCRIPTION
hab	Handle to the anchor block.
fmt	The index of the last clipboard data format enumerated. The index should start at zero

The **return value** is the index of the next available clipboard data format. A zero return value indicates that the enumeration process is complete.

HWND WinEnumDlgItem(*hwndDlg, hwnd, code, fLock*)
HWND hwndDlg, hwnd;
USHORT code;
BOOL fLock;

WinEnumDlgItem returns the handle to the window that consists of a dialog item within a dialog box.

ARGUMENT	DESCRIPTION
hwndDlg	Handle to a dialog box window.
hwnd	A child window of the dialog box window. This window can either be an immediate child window or a window with a lower ranking in the z-order.
code	The dialog box item to return, denoted by an EDI identifier.
fLock	Specifies whether to lock the item window before the function returns.

The **return value** is the handle to the window that consists of the dialog box item.

BOOL WinEqualRect(*hab, pcrl1, pcrl2*)
HAB hab;
PRECTL pcrl1, pcrl2;

WinEqualRect compares the equality of two rectangles.

ARGUMENT	DESCRIPTION
hab	Handle to the anchor block.
pcrl1	Pointer to a RECTL structure.
pcrl2	Pointer to a RECTL structure.

The **return value** is TRUE when the rectangles are equal. It is FALSE when they are not equal or in the event of an error.

SHORT WinExcludeUpdateRegion(*hps, hwnd*)
HPS hps;
HWND hwnd;

WinExcludeUpdateRegion subtracts the update region of a window from the clipping region of a presentation space.

ARGUMENT	DESCRIPTION
hps	Handle to the presentation space associated with the updated clipping region.
hwnd	Handle to the window associated with the subtracted clipping region.

The **return value** indicates the result form of the clipping area. Refer to GpiCombineRegion for the meanings of the valid return values.

BOOL WinFillRect(*hps, pcrl, clr*)
USHORT fmt;
HPS hps;
PRECTL pcrl;
LONG clr;

WinFillRect fills the specified rectangle with the color specified by *clr*.

ARGUMENT	DESCRIPTION
hps	Handle to the active presentation space.
pcrl	Pointer to a RECTL structure.
clr	The color with which to paint the rectangle. Refer to Chapter 4 for additional information on colors.

The **return value** is TRUE if the function succeeds. It is FALSE if an error occurs.

ATOM WinFindAtom(*hAtomTbl, pszAtomName*)
HATOMTBL hAtomTbl;
PSZ pszAtomName;

WinFindAtom function finds an atom in the atom table.

ARGUMENT	DESCRIPTION
hAtomTbl	Handle to the atom table.
pszAtomName	Pointer s to a null-terminated character string for inclusion in the atom table.

The **return value** is the new associated atom, or if the string is not located in the table, it is NULL.

BOOL WinFlashWindow(*hwndFrame, fFlash*)
HWND hwndFrame;
BOOL fFlash;

WinFlashWindow causes the specified window to flash.

ARGUMENT	DESCRIPTION
hwndFrame	Handle to the window to flash.
fFlash	Flag specifying whether to start or stop flashing. Specifying TRUE causes the window to flash; specifying FALSE cause the window to stop flashing.

The **return value** is TRUE upon success. Otherwise it is FALSE.

BOOL WinFocusChange(*hwndDesktop, hwndSetFocus, fsFocusChange*)
HWND hwndDesktop, hwndSetFocus;
USHORT fsFocusChange;

WinFocusChange sets the focus to the specified window.

ARGUMENT	DESCRIPTION
hwndDesktop	Handle to the desktop window for which the focus is changing.
hwndSetFocus	Handle to the window receiving the focus.
fsFocusChange	One of the FC identifiers, which control how the focus changes:

FC_NOSETFOCUS	Inhibit WM_SETFOCUS for the window receiving the focus.
FC_NOLOSEFOCUS	Inhibit WM_SETFOCUS for the the window losing the focus.
FC_NOSETACTIVE	Inhibit WM_ACTIVATE for the window becoming active.
FC_NOLOSEACTIVE	Inhibit WM_ACTIVATE for the window being deactivated.
FC_NOSETSELECTION	Inhibit WM_SETFOCUS for the window receiving the selection.
FC_NOLOSESELECTION	Inhibit WM_SETSELECTION for the window losing the selection.
FC_NOBRINGTOTOP	Inhibit any change in z-order.
FC_SETACTIVEFOCUS	Set the focus to the child window (which previously had the focus) of the first frame window encountered in the z-order.

The **return value** is TRUE if the function succeeds. If an error occurs, the return value is FALSE.

SHORT WinFormatFrame(*hwndFrame, prclFrame, pswp, cswpMax, prclClient*)

HWND hwndFrame;
PRECTL prclFrame;
PSWP pswp;
SHORT cswpMax;
PRECTL prclClient;

WinFormatFrame calculates the size and position of all frame window controls.

ARGUMENT	DESCRIPTION
hwndFrame	Handle to a frame window.
prclFrame	Pointer to a RECTL structure, which is typically the window rectangle identified by the *hwndFrame*.
pswp	Pointer to an array of SWP structures. The array should have a minimum of 12 elements, filled in the order of the FID values of the frame controls. The FID _CLIENT window should be the last array element.
cswpMax	The count of the number of array elements.
prclClient	Pointer to the FID_CLIENT window rectangle (after the window has been formatted). When *prclClient* is NULL, the function does not return a client window rectangle.

The **return value** is number of SWP structures returned in the *pswp* array.

BOOL WinFreeErrorInfo(*perri*)

PERRINFO perri;

WinFreeErrorInfo frees error information block memory.

ARGUMENT	DESCRIPTION
perri	Pointer to an ERRINFO structure.

The **return value** is TRUE if the function succeeds. It is FALSE if an error occurs.

NPBYTE WinFreeMem(*hHeap, npMem, cbMem*)
HHEAP hHeap;
NPBYTE npMem;
USHORT cbMem;

WinFreeMemory frees heap memory previously allocated by the WinAllocMem function.

ARGUMENT	DESCRIPTION
hHeap	Handle to the heap.
npMem	Pointer to the memory block to be freed.
cbMem	The size of the memory to freed. This size must equal the allocated size of the block.

The **return value** is NULL if the function succeeds. Otherwise, the function returns the *npMem* argument.

HPS WinGetClipPS(*hwnd, hwndClip, fs*)
HWND hwnd, hwndClip;
USHORT fs;

WinGetClipPS returns a clipped presentation space.

ARGUMENT	DESCRIPTION
hwnd	Handle to the parent window.
hwndClip	Identifies the type of clipping (refer to Chapter 9).
fs	Flag specifying clipping method (refer to Chapter 9).

The **return value** is a presentation space. If the function fails, it returns NULL.

ULONG WinGetCurrentTime(*hab*)
HAB hab;

WinGetCurrentTime returns the current time.

ARGUMENT	DESCRIPTION
hab	Handle to the anchor block.

The **return value** is the system timer count (in milliseconds) from the restart time.

PERRINFO WinGetErrorInfo(*hab*)
HAB hab;

WinGetErrorInfo returns error information.

ARGUMENT	DESCRIPTION
hab	Handle to the anchor block.

The **return value** is a pointer to an ERRINFO structure. If no error data is available, the function returns NULL.

SHORT WinGetKeyState(*hwndDesktop, vkey*)
HWND hwndDesktop;
SHORT vkey;

WinGetKeyState returns the key state coinciding with the last queue message posted.

ARGUMENT	DESCRIPTION
hwndDesktop	Handle to the desktop window.
vkey	The virtual key value in the low byte (zero in the high byte).

The **return value** is the relevant key bit. When the key is pressed, the value is 0x8000. When the key is toggled, the value is 0x0001 bit is set.

ERRORID WinGetLastError(*hab*)
HAB hab;

WinGetLastError returns the error associated with a failed function call.

ARGUMENT	DESCRIPTION
hab	Handle to the anchor block.

The **return value** is the previous non-zero error code.

BOOL WinGetMaxPosition(*hwnd, pswp*)
HWND hwnd;
PSWP pswp;

WinGetMaxPosition places the size and position of a maximized window in the SWP structure

ARGUMENT	DESCRIPTION
hwnd	Handle to a frame window.
pswp	Pointer to a SWP structure.

The **return value** is TRUE if the function succeeds. It is FALSE if an error occurs.

BOOL WinGetMinPosition(*hwnd, pswp, pptl*)
HWND hwnd;
PSWP pswp;
PPOINTL pptl;

WinGetMinPosition allows you to determine where to position a minimized frame window. The relevant size and position information is place in the SWP structure.

ARGUMENT	DESCRIPTION
hwnd	Handle to a frame window.
pswp	Pointer to a SWP structure.
pptl	Pointer to a POINTL structure.

The **return value** is TRUE if the function succeeds. It is FALSE if an error occurs.

BOOL WinGetMsg(*hab, pqmsg, hwndFilter, msgFirst, msgLast*)

HAB hab;
PQMSG pqmsg;
HWND hwndFilter;
USHORT msgFirst, msgLast;

WinGetMsg function processes a message from the message queue of the specified thread. The function also provides filtering capabilities (refer to Chapter 3).

ARGUMENT	DESCRIPTION
hab	Handle to the anchor block.
pqmsg	Pointer to a QMSG structure.
hwndFilter	Handle to a window filter.
msgFirst	The first message in the filter sequence.
msgLast	The last message in the filter sequence.

The **return value** is TRUE unless the message received from the message queue is WM_QUIT, in which case it is FALSE.

HWND WinGetNextWindow(*henum*)

HENUM henum;

WinGetNextWindow obtains the handle of the next window in the enumeration list, which is a z-order listing of a window lineage based on the time of the function call. Enumeration always begins with the topmost child window. As a precursor to this function, you must call Win-BeginEnumWindows.

ARGUMENT	DESCRIPTION
henum	Handle to enumeration list.

The **return value** is the handle to the next window in the enumeration list. In the event of an error, the function returns NULL.

SHORT WinGetPhysKeyState(*hwndDesktop, sc*)
HWND hwndDesktop;
SHORT sc;

WinGetPhysKeyState returns the physical key state.

ARGUMENT	DESCRIPTION
hwndDesktop	Handle to the desktop window.
sc	The virtual key value (low byte) and zero (high byte).

The **return value** is the relevant key bit. When the key is pressed, the value is 0x8000. When the key is toggled, the value is 0x0001 bit is set.

HPS WinGetPS(*hwnd*)
HWND hwnd;

WinGetPS obtains a cache presentation space. This type of presentation space is particularly suitable for drawing objects that do not have to be stored. In point of fact, this function closely approximates the GpiCreatePS function. (Refer to Chapter 9 for additional information.)

ARGUMENT	DESCRIPTION
hwnd	Handle to the window in which to set up the presentation space.

The **return value** is the handle to the presentation space.

HPS WinGetScreenPS(*hwndDesktop*)
HWND hwndDesktop;

WinGetScreenPS function establishes a presentation space that lets you draw to any window and/or the desktop window. The call to Win-GetScreenPS establishes a micro presentation space. (Refer to Chapter 9 for additional information.)

ARGUMENT	DESCRIPTION
hwndDesktop	Handle to the desktop window.

The **return value** is a handle to a micro presentation space.

HBITMAP WinGetSysBitmap(*hwndDesktop, ibm*)
HWND hwndDesktop;
USHORT ibm;

WinGetSysBitmap returns a handle to a system bitmap.

ARGUMENT	DESCRIPTION
hwndDesktop	Handle to the desktop window.
ibm	One of the following system bitmap identifiers:

SBMP_SYSMENU	System menu
SBMP_SBUPARROW	scroll bar up arrow
SBMP_SBDNARROW	scroll bar down arrow
SBMP_SBRGARROW	scroll bar right arrow
SBMP_SBLFARROW	scroll bar left arrow
SBMP_MENUCHECK	Menu check mark
SBMP_CHECKBOXES	Dialog box check mark
SBMP_BTNCORNERS	Push button corner
SBMP_MINBUTTON	Minimize button
SBMP_MAXBUTTON	Maximize button
SBMP_RESTOREBUTTON	Restore button

The **return value** is the bitmap handle, or NULL in the event of an error.

BOOL WinInflateRect(*hab, prcl, cx, cy*)
HAB hab;
PRECTL prcl;
SHORT cx, cy;

WinInflateRect function creates an expanded

ARGUMENT	DESCRIPTION
hab	Handle to the anchor block.
prcl	Pointer to a RECTL structure.
cx	The horizontal expansion.
cy	The vertical expansion.

The **return value** is TRUE if the function succeeds. It is FALSE if an error occurs.

HAB WinInitialize(*fsOptions*)
USHORT fsOptions;

WinInitialize sets up the Presentation Manager so that you can create a frame window and run an application. (Refer to Chapter 4 for additional information.)

ARGUMENT	DESCRIPTION
fsOptions	Initialization options.

The **return value** is an anchor-block handle.

BOOL WinInSendMsg(*hab*)
HAB hab;

WinInSendMsg determines whether a thread is currently processing a message initiated by a different thread. This function is quite frequently used to determine how to proceed when errors occur in other threads.

ARGUMENT	DESCRIPTION
hab	Handle to the anchor block.

The **return value** is TRUE when the current thread is processing a message initiated by another thread. It is FALSE if this is not the case, of if an error occurred.

BOOL WinIntersectRect(*hab, prclDst, prclSrc1, prclSrc2*)
HAB hab;
PRECTL prclDst, prclSrc1, prclSrc2;

WinIntersectRect calculates the intersection of the two source rectangles. It then returns the result as the destination rectangle.

ARGUMENT	DESCRIPTION
hab	Handle to the anchor block.
prclDst	Pointer to a RECTL structure.
prclSrc1	Pointer to a RECTL structure.
prclSrc2	Pointer to a RECTL structure.

The **return value** is TRUE when the source rectangles intersect. It is FALSE if they do not intersect or if an error occurs.

BOOL WinInvalidateRect(*hwnd, prcl, fInclChildren*)
HWND hwnd;
PRECTL prcl;
BOOL fInclChildren;

WinInvalidateRect adds a rectangle to the update region of the specified window. The update region is a subregion of a window that is invalid or requires redrawing. A window of style CS_SYNCPAINT is redrawn as a result of calling WinInvalidateRect. The function also affects windows of style WS_CLIPCHILDREN, in that they are updated when they overlap a window of style CS_SYNCPAINT.

ARGUMENT	DESCRIPTION
hwnd	Handle to the window that requires updating.
prcl	Pointer to a RECTL structure.
fInclChildren	Flags specifying the affected lineage. Specifying TRUE causes the descendants of *hwnd* to be included in the invalid rectangle. Specifying FALSE causes the descendants to be included only if style of the parent is not WS_CLIPCHILDREN.

The **return value** is TRUE if the function succeeds. It is FALSE if an error occurs.

BOOL WinInvalidateRegion(*hwnd, hrgn, fInclChildren*)
HWND hwnd;
HRGN hrgn;
BOOL fInclChildren;

WinInvalidateRegion adds a region to the update region of the specified window. This function operates similarly to WinInvalidateRect. (See WinInvalidateRect for specific information.)

ARGUMENT	DESCRIPTION
hwnd	Handle to a window with a region that requires updating.
hrgn	Handle to a region to be added to the window's update region. When this argument is NULL, the entire window is placed into the update region.
fInclChildren	Flag specifying the affected lineage.Specifying TRUE causes the descendants of *hwnd* to be included in the invalid region. Specifying FALSE causes the descendants to be included only if style of the parent is not WS_CLIPCHILDREN.

The **return value** is TRUE if the function succeeds. It is FALSE if an error occurs.

BOOL WinInvertRect(*hps, prcl*)

HPS hps;
PRECTL prcl;

WinInvertRect function causes a rectangle area to be inverted.

ARGUMENT	DESCRIPTION
hps	Handle to a presentation space.
prcl	Pointer to a RECTL structure.

The **return value** is TRUE if the function succeeds. It is FALSE if an error occurs.

BOOL WinIsChild(*hwnd, hwndParent*)

HWND hwnd, hwndParent;

WinIsChild determines whether one window is the child of another window.

ARGUMENT	DESCRIPTION
hwnd	Handle to the child window.
hwndParent	Handle to the parent window.

The **return value** is TRUE when the child window is a descendant of the specified parent. It is FALSE when it is not a child window, or when it is an object window.

BOOL WinIsPhysInputEnabled(*hwndDesktop*)

HWND hwndDesktop;

WinIsPhysInputEnabled reports on the status of a hardware interrupt.

ARGUMENT	DESCRIPTION
hwndDesktop	Identifies the desktop.

The **return value** is TRUE when the hardware interrupt is enabled. It is FALSE if the interrupt is disabled.

BOOL WinIsRectEmpty(*hab, prcl*)
HAB hab;
PRECTL prcl;

WinIsRectEmpty establishes whether a rectangle is empty — that is, whether the rectangle has no established area. If this is the case, the right boundary of the rectangle is less than or equal to the left boundary, and the bottom boundary is less than or equal to the top boundary.

ARGUMENT	DESCRIPTION
hab	Handle to the anchor block.
prcl	Pointer to a RECTL structure.

The **return value** is TRUE when the rectangle is empty, or when an error occurs. When the rectangle is not empty, the return value is FALSE.

BOOL WinIsThreadActive(*hab*)
HAB hab;

WinIsThreadActive establishes whether the calling thread of execution owns the active window.

ARGUMENT	DESCRIPTION
hab	Handle to the anchor block of the calling thread.

The **return value** is TRUE when the calling thread of execution owns the active window. It is FALSE when the thread does not own the active window.

BOOL WinIsWindow(*hab, hwnd*)
HAB hab;
HWND hwnd;

WinIsWindow establishes the validity of a supplied window handle.

ARGUMENT	DESCRIPTION
hab	Handle to the anchor block.
hwnd	Handle to the window to test.

The **return value** is TRUE when the function identifies a valid window handle. It is FALSE when the converse is true.

BOOL WinIsWindowEnabled(*hwnd*)
HWND hwnd;

WinIsWindowEnabled returns the enabled state of the specified window.

ARGUMENT	DESCRIPTION
hwnd	Handle to a window.

The **return value** is TRUE when the window is enabled. It is FALSE when the window is not enabled.

BOOL WinIsWindowVisible(*hwnd*)
HWND hwnd;

WinIsWindowVisible returns a window's visibility state .

ARGUMENT	DESCRIPTION
hwnd	Handle to a window.

The **return value** is TRUE when the specified window and its parents have the WS_VISIBLE style bit set. It is FALSE when the window is not visible.

HACCEL WinLoadAccelTable(*hab, hmod, idAccelTable*)
HAB hab;
HMODULE hmod;
USHORT idAccelTable;

WinLoadAccelTable loads an accelerator table.

ARGUMENT	DESCRIPTION
hab	Handle to the anchor block.
hmod	Handle to a module returned by the DosLoadModule function.
idAccelTable	An accelerator table.

The **return value** is the accelerator table handle. If you call this function twice in succession and specify identical arguments to the function, a different value is returned.

HWND WinLoadDlg(*hwndParent, hwndOwner, pfnDlgProc, hmod, idDlg, pCreateParams*)

HWND hwndParent, hwndOwner;
PFNWP pfnDlgProc;
HMODULE hmod;
USHORT idDlg;
PVOID pCreateParams;

WinLoadDlg creates a dialog window from the dialog template. (For additional information, refer to Chapter 8.)

ARGUMENT	DESCRIPTION
hwndParent	Handle to the parent window of the dialog box.
hwndOwner	Handle to the owner window of the dialog box.
pfnDlgProc	Pointer to a dialog box procedure.
hmod	Handle to the resource containing the dialog box. Specifying NULL indicates the resource is present in the .EXE file of the application. Alternatively, you must specify the handle returned by the DosLoadModule function.
idDlg	The dialog box window as specified in the resource file.
pCreateParams	Pointer to the dialog box procedure data, if any.

The **return value** is the dialog box handle. NULL is returned if the function fails.

HWND WinLoadMenu(*owner, hmod, menuid*)

HWND owner;
HMODULE hmod;
USHORT menuid;

WinLoadMenu function creates a menu window from the menu template. (Refer to Chapter 7 for additional information on WinLoadMenu.)

ARGUMENT	DESCRIPTION
owner	Handle to the owner and parent window.
hmod	Handle to the resource containing the menu. Specifying NULL indicates the resource is present in the .EXE file of the application. Alternatively, you must specify the handle returned by the DosLoadModule function.
menuid	The menu ID as it occurs in the resource template.

The **return value** is the menu window handle.

SHORT WinLoadMessage(*hab, hmod, id, cchMax, pchBuf*)

HAB hab;
HMODULE hmod;
USHORT id;
SHORT cchMax;
PSZ pchBuf;

WinLoadMessage loads a message from a resource.

ARGUMENT	DESCRIPTION
hab	Handle to the anchor block.
hmod	Handle to a module returned by DosLoadModule.
id	A message ID.
cchMax	Size of the supplied buffer.
pchBuf	Pointer to the buffer receiving the message.

The **return value** is the message length, excluding the null-terminating character. The function returns zero if an error occurs.

HPOINTER WinLoadPointer(*hwndDesktop, hmod, idres*)

HWND hwndDesktop;
HMODULE hmod;
USHORT idres;

WinLoadPointer loads a pointer resource from a resource file.

ARGUMENT	DESCRIPTION
hwndDesktop	Handle to the desktop window.
hmod	Handle to the pointer resource is loaded. This handle is returned by the DosLoadModule function. When NULL, this argument indicates that the resource should be loaded from the .EXE file of the application. Alternatively, it is loaded from a dynamic link library.
idres	The resource identifier as specified in the resource file.

The **return value** is the handle to the pointer. It is NULL if an error occurs.

SHORT WinLoadString(*hab, hmod, id, cchMax, pchBuffer*)

HAB hab;
HMODULE hmod;
USHORT id;
SHORT cchMax;
PSZ pchBuffer;

WinLoadString function loads a string from a resource.

ARGUMENT	DESCRIPTION
hab	Handle to the anchor block.
hmod	A module returned by the DosLoadModule function.
id	A string ID.
cchMax	Size of the supplied buffer.
pchBuffer	Pointer to the buffer receiving the string.

The **return value** is the string length, not including the null-termination character. If an error occurs, the return value is zero.

PVOID WinLockHeap(*hHeap*)
HHEAP hHeap;

WinLockHeap locks a heap and returns the address of the start of a segment that contains the heap. For memory allocated from an application's data segment, the returned short pointers can be used as offsets relative to DS register address. Memory allocated from other segments causes the short pointers to be returned as relative to the beginning of the segment containing the heap.

ARGUMENT	DESCRIPTION
hHeap	Handle to the heap. You obtain this handle by calling the WinCreateHeap function.

The **return value** is a far pointer to the start of the segment that contains the passed heap.

SHORT WinLockVisRegions(*hwndDesktop, fLock*)
HWND hwndDesktop;
BOOL fLock;

WinLockVisRegions locks/unlocks the visible regions of all windows currently on the screen. It also prevents any of the visible regions from changing.

ARGUMENT	DESCRIPTION
hwndDesktop	Handle to the desktop window.
fLock	Flag specifying the lock state of the visible regions. Specifying TRUE causes the visible regions to be locked. Specifying FALSE causes the visible regions to be unlocked.

The **return value** is TRUE if the function succeeds. It is FALSE if an error occurs.

HWND WinLockWindow(*hwnd, fLock*)
HWND hwnd;
BOOL fLock;

WinLockWindow function locks/ unlocks a specified window.

ARGUMENT	DESCRIPTION
hwnd	Handle to a window.
fLock	Flag specifying whether to lock or unlock the window. Specifying TRUE locks the window. Specifying FALSE unlocks the window.

The **return value** is the window handle if the function succeeds. If it is NULL if an error occurs.

BOOL WinLockWindowUpdate(*hwndDesktop, hwndUpdate*)
HWND hwndDesktop, hwndUpdate;

WinLockWindowUpdate locks a window and its child windows. As a result, it prevents them from being updated, but allows all threads to continue running.

ARGUMENT	DESCRIPTION
hwndDesktop	Handle to the desktop.
hwndUpdate	Handle to the window lock.

The **return value** is TRUE if the function succeeds. It is FALSE if an error occurs.

BOOL WinMakePoints(*hab, pwpt, cwpt*)
HAB hab;
PWPOINT pwpt;
SHORT cwpt;

WinMakePoints converts points to graphics points.

ARGUMENT	DESCRIPTION
hab	Handle to the anchor block.
pwpt	Pointer to a WPOINT structure.
cwpt	Number of points to be converted.

The **return value** is TRUE if the function succeeds. It is FALSE if an error occurs.

BOOL WinMakeRect(*hab, pwrc*)
IIAB hab;
PWRECT pwrc;

WinMakeRect converts a rectangle to a graphics rectangle by converting the argument that references the WRECT structure to a reference to the RECTL structure.

ARGUMENT	DESCRIPTION
hab	Handle to the anchor block.
pwrc	Pointer to a WRECT structure.

The **return value** is TRUE if the function succeeds. It is FALSE if an error occurs.

BOOL WinMapDlgPoints(*hwndDlg, pptl, cwpt, fCalcCoords*)
HWND hwndDlg;
PPOINTL pptl;
USHORT cwpt;
BOOL fCalcCoords;

WinMapDlgPoints maps points of a dialog window from dialog coordinates to window coordinates. Alternatively, it maps points from window coordinates to dialog coordinates. The mapping direction depends on the *fCalcWindowCoords* argument. The mapped coordinates are specified by the array pointed to by the *pptl* argument. Ultimately, the mapped points are substituted into the array.

ARGUMENT	DESCRIPTION
hwndDlg	Handle to a dialog window.
pptl	Pointer to an array of POINTL structures.
cwpt	The number of coordinate points.
fCalcCoords	Flag specifying the mapping calculation. Specifying TRUE indicates the points are in dialog coordinates, and consequently are mapped to window coordinates. Specifying FALSE indicates the points are in window coordinates relative to the dialog window, and consequently are mapped to dialog coordinates.

The **return value** is TRUE if the function succeeds. It is FALSE if an error occurs.

BOOL WinMapWindowPoints(*hwndFrom, hwndTo, pptl, cwpt*)

HWND hwndFrom, hwndTo;
PPOINTL pptl;
SHORT cwpt;

WinMapWindowPoints maps a set of points from one window into a another window.

ARGUMENT	DESCRIPTION
hwndFrom	Handle to source window. A value of NULL or HWND_DESKTOP specifies screen coordinates.
hwndTo	Handle to the destination window. A value of NULL or HWND_DESKTOP specifies screen coordinates.
pptl	Pointer to a POINTL or RECTL structure.
cwpt	Number of POINTL structures in the *pptl* array, or the value of 2 if a RECTL structure is used.

The **return value** is TRUE if the function succeeds. It is FALSE if an error occurs.

USHORT WinMessageBox(*hwndParent, hwndOwner, pszText, pszCaption, idWindow, flStyle*)
HWND hwndParent, hwndOwner;
PSZ pszText, pszCaption;
USHORT idWindow, flStyle;

WinMessageBox displays a message box.

ARGUMENT	DESCRIPTION
hwndParent	Handle to the parent window.
hwndOwner	Handle to the owner window.
pszText	Pointer to the message text.
pszCaption	Pointer to the message title.
idWindow	The window identifier of the message box window.
flStyle	Flag denoted by an MB identifier, which specifies the type of message box (refer to Chapter 8).

The **return value** for a message box is an MBID identifier such as MBID_CANCEL. (Refer to Chapter 8 for a complete listing.)

USHORT WinMsgMuxSemWait(*pisemCleared, pmxsl, dtTimeout*)
PUSHORT pisemCleared;
PVOID pmxsl;
LONG dtTimeout;

WinMsgMuxSemWait waits for a semaphore to clear.

ARGUMENT	DESCRIPTION
pisemCleared	Pointer to the index value of the most recently cleared semaphore.
pmxsl	Pointer to a MUXSEMLIST structure, which can contain a list of up to 15 semaphores that require clearing.
dtTimeout	Elapsed time in milliseconds to wait for the semaphores to clear.

The **return value** is zero if the function succeeds. It is non-zero if an error occurs.

USHORT WinMsgSemWait(*hsem, dtTimeout*)

HSEM hsem;
LONG dtTimeOut;

WinMsgSemWait function waits for a semaphore to clear. The function returns immediately if no previous thread has set the semaphore.

ARGUMENT	DESCRIPTION
hsem	Handle to the semaphore.
dtTimeout	The time period, in milliseconds, to wait for the semaphore to clear.

The **return value** is zero if the function succeeds. It is non-zero if an error occurs.

SHORT WinMultWindowFromIDs(*hwndParent, phwnd, idFirst, idLast*)

HWND hwndParent;
PHWND phwnd;
USHORT idFirst, idLast;

WinMultWindowFromIDs obtains the handles of child windows with IDs in a specified range. The function is primarily used to enumerate controls within a group of child window controls.

ARGUMENT	DESCRIPTION
hwndParent	Handle to the parent window.
phwnd	Pointer to an array of handles to child window controls.
idFirst	First child window control ID.
idLast	Last child window control ID.

The **return value** is the number of window handles. It is zero if no window handles are returned.

PSZ WinNextChar(*hab, idcp, idcc, psz*)
HAB hab;
USHORT idcp, idcc;
PSZ psz;

WinNextChar moves to the next character in a string, including double-byte character set strings.

ARGUMENT	DESCRIPTION
hab	Handle to the anchor block.
idcp	Code page.
idcc	Country code.
psz	Pointer to a character in a null-terminated string.

The **return value** is the next character in the string. When the function reaches the end of the string, it returns NULL.

BOOL WinOffsetRect(*hab, prcl, cx, cy*)
HAB hab;
PRECTL prcl;
SHORT cx, cy;

WinOffsetRect offsets the coordinates of a rectangle by adding the current *cx* value to the left and right coordinates, as well as adding the current *cy* value to the top and bottom coordinates.

ARGUMENT	DESCRIPTION
hab	Handle to the anchor block.
prcl	Pointer to a RECTL structure.
cx	The horizontal offset.
cy	The vertical offset.

The **return value** is TRUE if the function succeeds. It is FALSE if an error occurs.

BOOL WinOpenClipbrd(*hab*)
HAB hab;

WinOpenClipbrd opens the clipboard and disallows other threads and processes from accessing the clipboard. When the clipboard has been previously opened, the function waits until it is closed.

ARGUMENT	DESCRIPTION
hab	Handle to the anchor block.

The **return value** is TRUE if the function succeeds. It is FALSE if an error occurs.

HDC WinOpenWindowDC(*hwnd*)
HWND hwnd;

WinOpenWindowDC opens a window-based device context. This function can be used to associate a device context with a presentation space, using the GpiCreatePS function. You can open only one device per window and the visible region of the specified window is automatically updated. Note that you cannot close the device context using the DevCloseDC function.

ARGUMENT	DESCRIPTION
hwnd	Identifies a window.

The **return value** is a handle to a window-based device context.

BOOL WinPeekMsg(*hab, pqmsg, hwndFilter, msgFirst, msgLast, fs*)
HAB hab;
PQMSG pqmsg;
HWND hwndFilter;
USHORT msgFirst, msgLast, fs;

WinPeekMsg examines the contents of a message queue. The function does not wait for message to arrive in the queue, nor does it necessarily remove messages from the queue.

ARGUMENT	DESCRIPTION
hab	Handle to the anchor block.
pqmsg	Pointer to a QMSG structure.
hwndFilter	Handle to the window filter.
msgFirst	The first message.
msgLast	The last message.
fs	Flag specifying whether to remove the message from the queue. Setting this flag to PM_REMOVE removes the message from the queue. Setting it to PM_NOREMOVE leaves the message in the queue.

The **return value** is TRUE if the specified message exists. It is FALSE if the message does not exist.

BOOL WinPostMsg(*hwnd, msg, mp1, mp2*)
HWND hwnd;
USHORT msg;
MPARAM mp1, mp2;

WinPostMsg posts a message to a message queue.

ARGUMENT	DESCRIPTION
hwnd	Handle to the window that owns the message queue. Specifying NULL causes the function to post the message to the queue associated with the current thread.
msg	The message identity.
mp1	First message parameter.
mp2	Second message parameter.

The **return value** is TRUE if the function succeeds. It is FALSE if an error occurs.

BOOL WinPostQueueMsg(*hmq, msg, mp1, mp2*)
HMQ hmq;
USHORT msg;
MPARAM mp1, mp2;

WinPostQueueMsg can post a message to any message queue in the system. In order to post the message and it parameters, however, you must access the QMSG structure and set its fields accordingly. The *qmsg.hwnd* field is automatically set to NULL, and the *qmsg.time* and *qmsg.pt* fields are automatically set based on the system time and mouse position at the time of the call to WinPostQueueMsg.

ARGUMENT	DESCRIPTION
hmq	Handle to a message queue.
msg	The message identity.
mp1	First message parameter.
mp2	Second message parameter.

The **return value** is TRUE upon success. Otherwise, it is FALSE.

PSZ WinPrevChar(*hab, idcp, idcc, pszStart, psz*)
HAB hab;
USHORT idcp, idcc;
PSZ pszStart, psz;

WinPrevChar moves to the previous character in a string.

ARGUMENT	DESCRIPTION
hab	Handle to the anchor block.
idcp	Code page.
idcc	Country code.
pszStart	Pointer to a character string.
psz	Pointer to a character in *pszStart*.

The **return value** is the previous character in the string. If the function reaches the beginning of the string, the return value is *pszStart*.

USHORT WinProcessDlg(*hwndDlg*)
HWND hwndDlg;

WinProcessDlg processes messages destined for a modal dialog box. Processed messages are typically dispatched to a window or dialog procedure until the application message queue is empty. In order for this function to return, the dialog box procedure must first call WinDismissDlg.

ARGUMENT	DESCRIPTION
hwndDlg	Handle to a dialog window.

The **return value** reflects the value returned by WinDismissDlg.

BOOL WinPtInRect(*hab, prcl, pptl*)
HAB hab;
PRECTL prcl;
PPOINTL pptl;

WinPtInRect tests whether a point lies within a rectangle.

ARGUMENT	DESCRIPTION
hab	Handle to the anchor block.
prcl	Pointer to a RECTL structure referencing the rectangle.
pptl	Pointer to a POINTL structure referencing the point.

The **return value** is TRUE when the point lies in the rectangle. It is FALSE when this is not the case.

HACCEL WinQueryAccelTable(*hab, hwndFrame*)
HAB hab;
HWND hwndFrame;

WinQueryAccelTable queries an accelerator table associated with either a window or a queue. The function generates a WM_QUERYACCELTABLE message when it finds a valid window-based accelerator table. This message contains the handle to the accelerator table.

ARGUMENT	DESCRIPTION
hab	Handle to the anchor block.
hwndFrame	Handle to the frame window. Setting this argument to NULL causes the function to query the queue accelerator table. Setting it to a valid window handle causes the function to query the accelerator table for the window.

The **return value** is a handle to an accelerator table if the function succeeds. A return value of NULL indicates an error.

HWND WinQueryActiveWindow(*hwnd, fLock*)
HWND hwnd;
BOOL fLock;

WinQueryActiveWindow enumerates a parent window's child windows and returns the currently active window.

ARGUMENT	DESCRIPTION
hwnd	Handle to the parent window.
fLock	Flag specifying the window lock state. Setting this argument to TRUE locks the window. Setting it to FALSE unlocks it.

The **return value** is the currently active window handle, in the lock state specified by *fLock*. If the function found that no window was active, it returns NULL.

USHORT WinQueryAtomLength(*hAtomTbl, atom*)
HATOMTBL hAtomTbl;
ATOM atom;

WinQueryAtomLength queries the length of an atom. You can use this function to establish the buffer size required by the WinQueryAtomName function.

ARGUMENT	DESCRIPTION
hAtomTbl	Handle to an atom table.
atom	Either a string-based or integer-based atom.

The **return value** is the atom length, excluding the null termination character. For an integer atom, the function consistently returns a value of 6. If the specified atom is invalid, the function returns zero.

USHORT WinQueryAtomName(*hAtomTbl, atom, pchBuffer, cchBufferMax*)

HATOMTBL hAtomTbl;
ATOM atom;
PSZ pchBuffer;
USHORT cchBufferMax;

WinQueryAtomName returns an atom name for a given atom.

ARGUMENT	DESCRIPTION
hAtomTbl	Handle to an atom table.
atom	Either a string-based or integer-based atom.
pchBuffer	Pointer to the buffer for the character string.
cchBufferMax	Maximum buffer size, in bytes.

The **return value** is the actual number of bytes copied to the buffer, excluding the null terminating byte. If the specified atom or the atom table is invalid, the return value is zero.

USHORT WinQueryAtomUsage(*hAtomTbl, atom*)

HATOMTBL hAtomTbl;
ATOM atom;

WinQueryAtomUsage returns the use count for the specified atom. The use count is simply the number of times that atom has been used.

ARGUMENT	DESCRIPTION
hAtomTbl	Handle to an atom table handle.
atom	A string-based or integer-based atom.
atom	Specifies the atom whose use count is to be returned.

The **return value** is the atom's use count. It is 0xFFFF if the atom is an integer atom, or zero if the atom or atom table is invalid.

HWND WinQueryCapture(hwndDesktop, fLock)
HWND hwndDesktop;
BOOL fLock;

WinQueryCapture returns the handle to the window that currently controls mouse capture.

ARGUMENT	DESCRIPTION
hwndDesktop	Handle to the desktop window.
fLock	Flag specifying the lock request. Setting this argument to TRUE causes the function to return the a locked window handle. Setting it to FALSE causes it to return an unlocked window handle.

The **return value** is the handle to the window that currently controls mouse capture. If no window has control of mouse capture, the function returns NULL.

BOOL WinQueryClassInfo(*hab, pszClass, pclsi*)
HAB hab;
PSZ pszClass;
PCLASSINFO pclsi;

WinQueryClassInfo returns information on a window's class. You should use this function to create subclasses based on a existing class.

ARGUMENT	DESCRIPTION
hab	Handle to the anchor block.
pszClass	Pointer to a null-terminated string that contains the class name.
pclsi	Pointer to a CLASSINFO structure.

The **return value** is TRUE if the function succeeds. It is FALSE if an error occurs.

SHORT WinQueryClassName(*hwnd, cchMax, pch*)
HWND hwnd;
SHORT cchMax;
PSZ pch;

WinQueryClassName copies the window class name into a buffer. The function allows you to specify a null-terminated string up to the length of *cchMax*. Longer strings are truncated to the length of *cchMax*.

ARGUMENT	DESCRIPTION
hwnd	Identifies a window.
cchMax	The length of the *pch* buffer.
pch	Pointer to a buffer to hold the class name.

The **return value** is the class name string, excluding the null-terminator.

ULONG WinQueryClipbrdData(*hab, fmt*)
HAB hab;
USHORT fmt;

WinQueryClipbrdData obtains a handle to the current clipboard data.

ARGUMENT	DESCRIPTION
hab	Handle to the anchor block.
fmt	The format of the clipboard data.

The **return value** is a handle to the clipboard. In the event that the specified format is not applicable to the data, the function returns NULL.

BOOL WinQueryClipbrdFmtInfo(*hab, fmt, pfFmtInfo*)
HAB hab;
USHORT fmt;
PUSHORT pfFmtInfo;

WinQueryClipbrdFmtInfo tests whether the specified data format is in the clipboard. If the format is present, the function returns information about the format.

ARGUMENT	DESCRIPTION
hab	Handle to the anchor block.
fmt	The data format sought by the function.
pfFmtInfo	Pointer to a variable for the clipboard memory model and the clipboard CFI usage identifiers. (Refer to Chapter 15 for additional information on the CFI identifiers.)

The **return value** is TRUE if the function finds the specified format . It is FALSE if it does not find the format.

HWND WinQueryClipbrdOwner(*hab, fLock*)
HAB hab;
BOOL fLock;

WinQueryClipbrdOwner obtains the handle to the window that currently owns the clipboard.

ARGUMENT	DESCRIPTION
hab	Handle to the anchor block.
fLock	Flag indicating whether the clipboard owner window should be locked during this function call. Specifying TRUE locks the window. Specifying FALSE leaves the window unlocked.

The **return value** is the handle to the window that currently owns the clipboard. In the event that no window owns the clipboard, the function returns NULL.

HWND WinQueryClipbrdViewer(*hab, fLock*)
HAB hab;
BOOL fLock;

WinQueryClipbrdViewer obtains the handle to the window that currently is the clipboard viewer window.

ARGUMENT	DESCRIPTION
hab	Handle to the anchor block.
fLock	Flag indicating whether the clipboard owner window should be locked during this function call. Specifying TRUE locks the window. Specifying FALSE leaves the window unlocked.

The **return value** is the handle to the clipboard viewer. In the clipboard viewer does not exist, the function returns NULL.

USHORT WinQueryCp(*hmq*)
HMQ hmq;

WinQueryCp returns the code page to the message queue window requesting it.

ARGUMENT	DESCRIPTION
hmq	Identifies a message queue.

The **return value** is the queue code page for the specified message queue. If the function fails, it returns zero to denote an error.

USHORT WinQueryCpList(*hab, ccpMax, pacp*)
HAB hab;
USHORT ccpMax;
PUSHORT pacp;

WinQueryCpList obtains the number of available code pages.

ARGUMENT	DESCRIPTION
hab	Handle to the anchor block.
ccpMax	The maximum number of code pages to be returned.
pacp	Pointer to an array of the code pages available.

The **return value** is the number of code pages. In the event of an error, the function returns NULL.

BOOL WinQueryCursorInfo(*hwndDesktop, pcsri*)
HWND hwndDesktop;
PCURSORINFO pcsri;

WinQueryCursorInfo obtains information describing the current cursor.

ARGUMENT	DESCRIPTION
hwndDesktop	Identifies an anchor block.
pcsri	Pointer to a CURSORINFO structure. The structure contains data on the cursor, including the cursor's size and position in window coordinates.

The **return value** is TRUE if the function succeeds. It is FALSE if an error occurs.

HWND WinQueryDesktopWindow(*hab, hdc*)
HAB hab;
HDC hdc;

WinQueryDesktopWindow returns the desktop window handle.

ARGUMENT	DESCRIPTION
hab	Handle to the anchor block.
hdc	Handle to a device context. Setting this argument to NULL indicates that the device is the screen.

The **return value** is the desktop window handle. The function returns NULL if the queried device cannot support windowing.

BOOL WinQueryDlgItemShort(*hwndDlg, idItem, pResult, fSigned*)

HWND hwndDlg;
USHORT idItem;
PSHORT pResult;
BOOL fSigned;

WinQueryDlgItemShort translates a dialog box string into an integer value. You should use this function when you want to translate numeric dialog box input (in the form of a text string) into a binary number.

ARGUMENT	DESCRIPTION
hwndDlg	Handle to a dialog box.
idItem	The dialog box string to be translated.
pResult	Pointer to the resultant integer value.
fSigned	Flag specifying whether the dialog box string should be converted as a signed or unsigned SHORT. Setting this argument to TRUE indicates the input is signed. Setting it to FALSE indicates the input is unsigned.

The **return value** is TRUE if the function succeeds. It is FALSE if an error occurs.

SHORT WinQueryDlgItemText(*hwndDlg, idItem, cchBufferMax, pchBuffer*)

HWND hwndDlg;
USHORT idItem, cchBufferMax;
PSZ pchBuffer;

WinQueryDlgItemText obtains a string from a dialog box as the result of the user entering text in response to a dialog box item.

ARGUMENT	DESCRIPTION
hwndDlg	Handle to a dialog box.
idItem	The dialog box item associated with the text string.
cchBufferMax	Maximum number of characters for the *pchBuffer* argument.
pchBuffer	Pointer to a buffer for the the dialog box text.

The **return value** is the length the text string associated with a given dialog box item. If an error occurs, the function returns zero.

HWND WinQueryFocus(*hwndDesktop, fLock*)
HWND hwndDesktop;
BOOL fLock;

WinQueryFocus returns the handle of the focus window.

ARGUMENT	DESCRIPTION
hwndDesktop	Handle to the desktop window.
fLock	Flag indicating the lock state of the window. Setting this to TRUE locks the window. It is the responsibility of the calling routine to unlock it. Setting this argument to FALSE returns an unlocked window handle.

The **return value** is a handle to the focus window. If there is no focus window, the function returns NULL.

BOOL WinQueryMsgPos(*hab, pptl*)
HAB hab;
PPOINTL pptl;

WinQueryMsgPos returns the pointer position at the time the last message was posted from the current message queue. The pointer position is returned in screen coordinates.

ARGUMENT	DESCRIPTION
hab	Handle to the anchor block.
pptl	Pointer to a POINTL structure.

The **return value** is TRUE if the function succeeds. It is FALSE if an error occurs.

ULONG WinQueryMsgTime(*hab*)
HAB hab;

WinQueryMsgTime returns the system time (in milliseconds) corresponding to the last time that the WinGetMsg or WinPeekMsg functions retrieved a message from the queue.

ARGUMENT	DESCRIPTION
hab	Handle to the anchor block.

The **return value** is the time that WinGetMsg or WinPeekMsg last retrieved a message from the queue.

HWND WinQueryObjectWindow(*hwndDesktop*)
HWND hwndDesktop;

WinQueryObjectWindow returns a handle to the desktop object window.

ARGUMENT	DESCRIPTION
hwndDesktop	Handle to a desktop window.

The **return value** is the handle to the desktop object window.

HPOINTER WinQueryPointer(*hwndDesktop*)
HWND hwndDesktop;

WinQueryPointer returns the handle to the pointer associated with the desktop window.

ARGUMENT	DESCRIPTION
hwndDesktop	Handle to the desktop window.

The **return value** is a handle to the desktop pointer. In the event of an error, the function returns NULL.

BOOL WinQueryPointerInfo(*hptr, pptri*)
HPOINTER hptr;
PPOINTERINFO pptri;

WinQueryPointerInfo allows you to obtain pointer information by referencing the POINTERINFO structure.

ARGUMENT	DESCRIPTION
hptr	Identifies a pointer.
pptri	Pointer to a POINTERINFO structure.

The **return value** is TRUE if the function succeeds. It is FALSE if an error occurs.

BOOL WinQueryPointerPos(*hwndDesktop, pptl*)
HWND hwndDesktop;
PPOINTL pptl;

WinQueryPointerPos obtains the pointer coordinates at the time of the last successful call to WinQueryPointerPos. The pointer coordinates are contained in the POINTL structure.

ARGUMENT	DESCRIPTION
hwndDesktop	Handle to the desktop window.
pptl	Pointer to a POINTL structure.

The **return value** is TRUE if the function succeeds. It is FALSE if an error occurs.

USHORT WinQueryProfileData(*hab, pszAppName, pszKeyName, pchBinaryData, pcchData*)
HAB hab;
PSZ pszAppName, pszKeyName;
PVOID pchBinaryData;
PUSHORT pcchData;

WinQueryProfileData performs a search of the OS2.INI file and obtains relevant data. The format of the data is binary. The *pszAppName* and *pszKeyName* values must exactly match the names as they appear in the corresponding fields of the OS2.INI file. As a precursor to this function, call WinQueryProfileSize to establish how much space you need to allocate for the returned data.

ARGUMENT	DESCRIPTION
hab	Handle to the anchor block.
pszAppName	Pointer to a null-terminated text string containing the name of the application requiring the initialization data.The string can be no longer than 1,024 bytes (including the null terminator).
pszKeyName	Pointer to a null-terminated text string containing the name of the keyname/value pair for which the value is returned. The string can be no longer than 1,024 bytes (including the null terminator).
pchBinaryData	Pointer to an array of bytes for the binary data.
pcchData	Pointer specifying the maximum length of *pchBinaryData*. The length is in bytes. A successful call places the actual number of bytes returned in *pchBinaryData*.

The **return value** is TRUE if the function succeeds. It is FALSE if an error occurs.

SHORT WinQueryProfileInt(*hab, pszAppName, pszKeyName, sDefault*)
HAB hab;
PSZ pszAppName, pszKeyName;
SHORT sDefault;

WinQueryProfileInt performs a case sensitive search of the OS2.INI file and retrieves a specified integer value. A default value is returned if the application name/keyname pair is not found.

ARGUMENT	DESCRIPTION
hab	Handle to the anchor block.
pszAppName	Pointer to a null-terminated text string containing the name of the application requiring the initialization data. The string can be no longer than 1,024 bytes (including the null terminator).
pszKeyName	Pointer to a null-terminated text string containing the name of the keyname/value pair for which the value is returned. The string can be no longer than 1,024 bytes (including the null terminator).
sDefault	The default value if *pszKeyName* does not yield a name.

The **return value** is the value specified in OS2.INI.

USHORT WinQueryProfileSize(*hab, pszAppName, pszKeyName, pcchValue*)

HAB hab;
PSZ pszAppName, pszKeyName;
PUSHORT pcchValue;

WinQueryProfileSize performs a case search of the OS2.INI file and obtains the size of an application's keyname entry from the OS2.INI file. The size is in bytes. Use this function to allocate space for data returned by WinQueryProfileString.

ARGUMENT	DESCRIPTION
hab	Handle to the anchor block.
pszAppName	Pointer to a null-terminated text string containing the name of the application requiring the initialization data.The string can be no longer than 1,024 bytes (including the null terminator).
pszKeyName	Pointer to a null-terminated text string containing the name of the keyname/value pair for which the value is returned. The string can be no longer than 1,024 bytes (including the null terminator).

(continued)

ARGUMENT	DESCRIPTION
pcchValue	Pointer to a variable that holds the length of *pszKeyName parameter*

The **return value** is zero when the function succeeds. If it fails, the return value is zero.

USHORT WinQueryProfileString(*hab, pAppName, pKeyName, pDef, pProfileString, cchMaxPstring*)
HAB hab;
PVOID pAppName, pKeyName, pDef, pProfileString;
USHORT cchMaxPstring;

WinQueryProfileString obtains a text string from the OS2.INI file. You should use WinUpper on the string.

ARGUMENT	DESCRIPTION
hab	Handle to the anchor block.
pszAppName	Pointer to a null-terminated text string containing the name of the application requiring the initialization data. The string can be no longer than 1,024 bytes (including the null terminator). Setting this argument to NULL causes the function to enumerate all application names in OS2.INI.
pszKeyName	Pointer to a null-terminated text string containing the name of the keyname/value pair for which the value is returned. The string can be no longer than 1,024 bytes (including the null terminator). Setting this argument to NULL causes the function to enumerate all keynames in OS2.INI.
pDef	Pointer to the *pProfileString* text string.
pProfileString	Pointer to the *pKeyName* text string.
cchMaxPstring	Maximum number of characters for *pProfileString* .

The **return value** is the byte length of *pProfileString*. Otherwise, the function returns a predefined system error code.

695

BOOL WinQueryQueueInfo(*hmq, pmqi, cbCopy*)
HMQ hmq;
PMQINFO pmqi;
USHORT cbCopy;

WinQueryQueueInfo queries queue information, including the process and thread ID, the message capacity of the queue, and the address of the queue.

ARGUMENT	DESCRIPTION
hmq	Handle to a message queue.
pmqi	Pointer to an MQINFO structure.
cbCopy	The number of bytes of data for the MQINFO structure.

The **return value** is TRUE if the function succeeds. It is FALSE if an error occurs.

ULONG WinQueryQueueStatus(*hwndDesktop*)
HWND hwndDesktop;

WinQueryQueueStatus returns a status code for the message queue associated with the current queue. You can use this function to predetermine whether a message exists in the queue by incorporating it in a routine with WinGetMsg or WinPeekMsg. Note that the function returns a two-part value: the high word indicates the types of messages in the queue; the low word indicates the types of message added to the queue since the last call to WinQueryQueueStatus. Available messages are denoted by QS, or queue status, bits. (For additional information, refer to Chapter 3.)

ARGUMENT	DESCRIPTION
hwndDesktop	Handle to the desktop window.

The **return value** reflects the type of message and the QS bits. When there are no messages in the queue, the low word of return value is zero.

LONG WinQuerySysColor(*hwndDesktop, clr, lReserved*)

HWND hwndDesktop;
LONG clr, lReserved;

WinQuerySysColor returns the system color.

ARGUMENT	DESCRIPTION
hwndDesktop	Handle to the desktop window.
clr	The system color index, which must be one of the SYSCLR (see the WinSetSysColors function).
lReserved	Must be zero.

The **return value** is an RGB value.

HWND WinQuerySysModalWindow(*hwndDesktop, fLock*)

HWND hwndDesktop;
BOOL fLock;

WinQuerySysModalWindow returns the current system modal window.

ARGUMENT	DESCRIPTION
hwndDesktop	Handle to the desktop window.
fLock	Flag indicating whether the system modal window should be locked. Setting this flag to TRUE locks the window. Setting it to FALSE unlocks the window.

The **return value** is the handle to the current system modal window. If no system modal window exists, the return value is NULL.

HPOINTER WinQuerySysPointer(*hwndDesktop, iptr, fLoad*)

HWND hwndDesktop;
SHORT iptr;
BOOL fLoad;

WinQuerySysPointer function returns the system pointer handle. (Refer to Chapter 13 for additional information on this function.)

ARGUMENT	DESCRIPTION
hwndDesktop	Handle to the desktop window.
iptr	One of the SPTR system identifiers, which specify the type of pointer.
fLoad	Flag indicating whether to copy the system pointer. Setting the flag to TRUE causes the pointer to be copied. Setting it to FALSE returns a handle to the pointer.

The **return value** is a handle to a system pointer. If the function fails, it returns a predefined system error code.

HATOMTBL WinQuerySystemAtomTable(*void*)

WinQuerySystemAtomTable returns the handle to the system atom table. When using the atom management functions, you should call this function before calling any other atom function.

The **return value** is the handle to the system atom table.

LONG WinQuerySysValue(*hwndDesktop, iSysValue*)
HWND hwndDesktop;
SHORT iSysValue;

WinQuerySysValue returns the system value.

ARGUMENT	DESCRIPTION
hwndDesktop	Identifies the desktop window.
iSysValue	The system value.

The **return value** is the system value if the function succeeds. If it fails, the function returns zero.

USHORT WinQueryTaskTitle(*idProcess, pszTitle, cbTitle*)
USHORT idProcess;
PSZ pszTitle;
USHORT cbTitle;

WinQueryTaskTitle obtains the application's title from the switch list.

ARGUMENT	DESCRIPTION
idProcess	Application ID.
pszTitle	Pointer to the application title.
cbTitle	Maximum byte length of *pszTitle*. The function truncates the length of the string if is longer than specified.

The **return value** is zero if the function succeeds. It is non-zero if an error occurs.

BOOL WinQueryUpdateRect(*hwnd, prcl*)
HWND hwnd;
PRECTL prcl;

WinQueryUpdateRect obtains the dimensions of the rectangle that bounds the update region of a window.

ARGUMENT	DESCRIPTION
hwnd	Handle to a window.
prcl	Pointer to a RECTL structure.

The **return value** is TRUE if the function succeeds. It is FALSE if an error occurs.

SHORT WinQueryUpdateRegion(*hwnd, hrgn*)
HWND hwnd;
HRGN hrgn;

WinQueryUpdateRegion obtains the update region of a window.

ARGUMENT	DESCRIPTION
hwnd	Handle to a window.
hrgn	Handle to a window update region.

The **return value** is the type of update region (see GpiCombineRegion).

ULONG WinQueryVersion(*hab*)
HAB hab;

WinQueryVersion obtains the OS/2 version number. As part of the return value, the function also obtains any major and minor revision numbers.

ARGUMENT	DESCRIPTION
hab	Handle to the anchor block.

The **return value** is the OS/2 version number and revision level.

HWND WinQueryWindow(*hwnd, cmd, fLock*)
HWND hwnd;
SHORT cmd;
BOOL fLock;

WinQueryWindow obtains the handle to a window related to the specified window. The relationship is based on the position of the window in the z-order and is specified by using one of the system defined QW (query window) identifiers. Refer to Chapter 5 for additional information.

ARGUMENT	DESCRIPTION
hwnd	Handle to a window.
cmd	System defined QW identifier.
fLock	Flag indicating whether the window specified by the return value is locked. Setting this argument to TRUE locks the window. Setting it to FALSE unlocks the window.

The **return value** is the handle to the related window.

HDC WinQueryWindowDC(*hwnd*)
HWND hwnd;

WinQueryWindowDC obtains a device context specifically created by the WinOpenWindowDC function. The device context is always associated with a given window.

ARGUMENT	DESCRIPTION
hwnd	Handle to a window.

The **return value** is a handle to a screen device context. If an error occurs, or the device context was not created with WinOpenWinDC, the function returns NULL.

SHORT WinQueryWindowLockCount(*hwnd*)
HWND hwnd;

WinQueryWindowLockCount obtains the window lock count.

ARGUMENT	DESCRIPTION
hwnd	Handle to a window.

The **return value** is the lock count for a locked window. If a window is not locked, of if an error occurred, the return value is zero.

BOOL WinQueryWindowPos(*hwnd, pswp*)
HWND hwnd;
PSWP pswp;

WinQueryWindowPos obtains the size and position of a window. Refer to Chapter 5 for additional information on the SWP structure, which this function references in order to pass size and position information.

ARGUMENT	DESCRIPTION
hwnd	Handle to a window.
pswp	Pointer to an SWP structure.

The **return value** is TRUE if the function succeeds. It is FALSE if an error occurs.

BOOL WinQueryWindowProcess(*hwnd, ppid, ptid*)
HWND hwnd;
PPID ppid;
PTID ptid;

WinQueryWindowProcess obtains the process and thread identifiers associated with the thread that created a window.

ARGUMENT	DESCRIPTION
hwnd	Handle to a window.
ppid	The process identifier.
ptid	The thread identifier.

The **return value** is TRUE if the function succeeds. It is FALSE if an error occurs.

PVOID WinQueryWindowPtr(*hwnd, index*)
HWND hwnd;
SHORT index;

WinQueryWindowPtr obtains a pointer value from a window's reserved memory.

ARGUMENT	DESCRIPTION
hwnd	Handle to a window.
index	Index of the pointer value. Valid values are in the range of zero to the number of bytes reserved for window data.

The **return value** is a pointer value. If the function fails, it returns a predefined error message such as PMERR_INVALID_HWND.

BOOL WinQueryWindowRect(*hwnd, prclDest*)
HWND hwnd;
PRECTL prclDest;

WinQueryWindowRect obtains a window rectangle. The dimensions of the rectangle are in window coordinates.

ARGUMENT	DESCRIPTION
hwnd	Handle to a window.
prclDest	Pointer to a RECTL structure.

The **return value** is TRUE if the function succeeds. It is FALSE if an error occurs.

SHORT WinQueryWindowText(*hwnd, cchBufferMax, pszBuffer*)
HWND hwnd;
SHORT cchBufferMax;
PSZ pszBuffer;

WinQueryWindowText obtains a text string from a window and copies it into a buffer. For frame windows, the string copied is the titlebar text. If the string is longer than *cchBufferMax*, the function truncates it. As a result of this function, a WM_QUERYFRAMEINFO message is generated.

ARGUMENT	DESCRIPTION
hwnd	Handle to a window.
cchBufferMax	Length of the text buffer.
pszBuffer	Pointer to a text buffer for the window text.

The **return value** is the string length.

SHORT WinQueryWindowTextLength(*hwnd*)
HWND hwnd;

The WinQueryWindowTextLength function returns the length of the window text, not including any null termination character. This function sends a WM_QUERYFRAMEINFO message to the window identified by the hwnd parameter.

ARGUMENT	DESCRIPTION
hwnd	Identifies a window.

The **return value** is the length of the window text. If the function fails, it returns a predefined error message such as PMERR_INVALID_HWND.

ULONG WinQueryWindowULong(*hwnd, index*)
HWND hwnd;
SHORT index;

WinQueryWindowULong obtains a ULONG value from reserved window memory. You can use this function to query window memory for the current window or that associated with a different thread. Note that this is a convenient, shorthand method for windows of different threads to exchange data.

ARGUMENT	DESCRIPTION
hwnd	Handle to the window to query.
index	Index into the window memory containing the ULONG value that is the object of the query. A valid value falls in the range of zero to the number of ULONG items in window memory. You can use any of the QWL identifiers to satisfy this argument (refer to Chapter 5).

The **return value** is the ULONG value from window memory.

USHORT WinQueryWindowUShort(*hwnd, index*)
HWND hwnd;
SHORT index;

WinQueryWindowUShort obtains a USHORT value from reserved window memory. You can use this function to query window memory for the current window or that associated with a different thread. Note that this is a convenient, shorthand method for windows of different threads to exchange data.

ARGUMENT	DESCRIPTION
hwnd	Handle to the window to query.
index	Index into the window memory containing the USHORT value that is the object of the query. A valid value falls in the range of zero to the number of USHORT items in window memory. You can use any of the QWS identifiers to satisfy this argument (refer to Chapter 5).

The **return value** is the USHORT value from window memory.

NPBYTE WinReallocMem(*hHeap, npMem, cbOld, cbNew*)
HHEAP hHeap;
NPBYTE npMem;
USHORT cbOld, cbNew;

WinReallocMem reallocates the size of a memory block on the heap. When the new size of the object is larger than the old size, the WinAllocMem function is called automatically to allocate additional memory.

ARGUMENT	DESCRIPTION
hHeap	Handle to a heap.
npMem	Pointer to a memory block.The function ignores the two lower bits of this argument, which must be obtained with a call to either WinAllocMem or WinReallocMem.
cbOld	The old byte size of the memory block.
cbNew	The new byte size of the memory block.

The **return value** is a pointer to the reallocated memory block if the function succeeds. If it fails, the return value is NULL.

BOOL WinRegisterClass(*hab, pszClass, pfnWndProc, flStyle, cbWindowData*)

HAB hab;
PSZ pszClass;
PFNWP pfnWndProc;
ULONG flStyle;
USHORT cbWindowData;

WinRegisterClass registers a window class. Refer to Chapter 4 for a complete explanation of this function.

ARGUMENT	DESCRIPTION
hab	Handle to the anchor block.
pszClassName	Pointer to the window class name.
pfnWndProc	Pointer to the window procedure. Specifying NULL indicates the application lacks its own window procedure.
flStyle	Flag specifying the default window style, which can be a system-defined CS style, or a class-specific style. Note that you must specify CS_PUBLIC to create a public window class.
cbWindowData	The number of bytes for reserved window memory storage.

The **return value** is TRUE if the function succeeds. It is FALSE if an error occurs.

USHORT WinRegisterWindowDestroy(*hwnd, fRegister*)

HWND hwnd;
BOOL fRegister;

WinRegisterWindowDestroy informs other applications that a window has been destroyed.

706

ARGUMENT	DESCRIPTION
hwnd	Handle to a window.
fRegister	Flag specifying whether the window requires registration. Setting this to TRUE registers the window, causing a WM_OTHERWIN-DOWDESTROYED message to be broadcast. The function does not register the window if you specify FALSE for this argument.

The **return value** is TRUE if the function succeeds. It is FALSE if an error occurs.

BOOL WinReleaseHook(*hab, hmq, iHook, pfnHook, hmod*)
HAB hab;
HMQ hmq;
SHORT iHook;
PFN pfnHook;
HMODULE hmod;

WinReleaseHook releases a hook from a hook chain.

ARGUMENT	DESCRIPTION
hab	Handle to the anchor block.
hmq	Handle to the message queue associated with the hook. Setting this argument to NULL releases the hook from the hook chain. Setting it to HMQ_CURRENT releases the hook from the message queue of the calling thread.
iHook	Type of hook chain.
pfnHook	Pointer to the hook routine.
hmod	Handle to the module containing the application procedure.

The **return value** is TRUE if the function succeeds. It is FALSE if an error occurs.

BOOL WinReleasePS(*hps*)
HPS hps;

WinReleasePS releases a cached presentation space

ARGUMENT	DESCRIPTION
hps	Handle to the cached presentation space.

The **return value** is TRUE if the function succeeds. It is FALSE if an error occurs.

USHORT WinRemoveSwitchEntry(*hSwitch*)
HSWITCH hSwitch;

WinRemoveSwitchEntry removes an entry from the switchlist.

ARGUMENT	DESCRIPTION
hSwitch	Handle to the switchlist entry.

The **return value** is zero if the function succeeds. If it fails, it is non-zero.

SHORT WinScrollWindow(*hwnd, dx, dy, prclScroll, prclClip, hrgnUpdate, prclUpdate, rgfsw*)
HWND hwnd;
SHORT dx, dy;
PRECTL prclScroll, prclClip;
HRGN hrgnUpdate;
PRECTL prclUpdate;
USHORT rgfsw;

WinScrollWindow function scrolls the contents of a window . This function uses device units to manage both vertical and horizontal scrolling. Be advised this is the only recommended method of scrolling the contents of a window.

ARGUMENT	DESCRIPTION
hwnd	Handle to a window.
dx	Horizontal distance to scroll.
dy	Vertical distance to scroll.
prclScroll	Pointer to a RECTL structure defining the window rectangle to scroll. Setting *prclScroll* to NULL causes the entire window to be scrolled.
prclClip	Pointer to a RECTL structure defining the clipping rectangle.
hrgnUpdate	Handle to the update region. If you do not set this handle to NULL, it must reference the region that is uncovered by the scroll.
prclUpdate	Pointer to a RECTL structure that contains the boundaries of the rectangle that the scroll invalidates.
rgfsw	Array specifying the characteristics of the scroll. You satisfy this argument with one of the system SW identifiers, which are explained in Chapter 5.

The **return value** is one of the the following special error codes: RGN_ER-ROR, indicating an error that you should obtain via WinGetLastError; RGN_NULL, indicating a no invalid rectangle; RGN_RECT, indicating a simple invalid rectangle; and RGN_COMPLEX, indicating a complex invalid rectangle.

MRESULT WinSendDlgItemMsg(*hwndDlg, idItem, msg, mp1, mp2*)
HWND hwndDlg;
USHORT idItem, msg;
MPARAM mp1, mp2;

WinSendDlgItemMsg sends a message to an item in a dialog box.

ARGUMENT	DESCRIPTION
hwndDlg	Handle to a dialog box window.
idItem	The dialog item receiving the message.
msg	The message identity.
mp1	First message parameter.
mp2	Second message parameter.

The **return value** is the result from the item in the dialog box.

MRESULT WinSendMsg(*hwnd, msg, mp1, mp2*)

HWND hwnd;
USHORT msg;
MPARAM mp1, mp2;

WinSendMsg function sends a window. The call does not return until the window processes the message.

ARGUMENT	DESCRIPTION
hwnd	Handle to the window receiving the message.
msg	The message identity.
mp1	First message parameter.
mp2	Second message parameter.

The **return value** is the result from the specified message queue procedure in the specified window.

BOOL WinSetAccelTable(*hab, haccel, hwndFrame*)

HAB hab;
HACCEL haccel;
HWND hwndFrame;

WinSetAccelTable sets the accelerator for a window or queue.

ARGUMENT	DESCRIPTION
hab	Handle to the anchor block.
haccel	The accelerator table. If set to NULL, the function removes the accelerator table from the window or queue.
hwndFrame	Handle to the frame window. If set to NULL, the accelerator table is set.

The **return value** is TRUE if the function succeeds. It is FALSE if an error occurs.

BOOL WinSetActiveWindow(*hwndDesktop, hwnd*)
HWND hwndDesktop, hwnd;

WinSetActiveWindow gives the specified window the active status. This call accomplishes the same as WinFocusChange when its *fsFocusChange* argument is set to FC_SETACTIVEFOCUS.

ARGUMENT	DESCRIPTION
hwndDesktop	Handle to the desktop window.
hwnd	Handle to the window receiving the active status.

The **return value** is TRUE if the function succeeds. It is FALSE if an error occurs.

BOOL WinSetCapture(*hwndDesktop, hwnd*)
HWND hwndDesktop, hwnd;

WinSetCapture captures all mouse messages.

ARGUMENT	DESCRIPTION
hwndDesktop	Handle to the desktop window.
hwnd	Handle to the window receiving the mouse messages. Setting this argument to HWND_THREADCAPTURE causes the function to capture all mouse messages for the current thread.

The **return value** is TRUE if the function succeeds. It is FALSE if an error occurs.

BOOL WinSetClipbrdData(*hab, ulData, fmt, rgfFmtInfo*)
HAB hab;
ULONG ulData;
USHORT fmt, rgfFmtInfo;

WinSetClipbrdData copies data to the clipboard and frees any data (of the specified format) already in the clipboard.

ARGUMENT	DESCRIPTION
hab	Handle to the anchor block.
ulData	The data placed in the clipboard. Setting this argument to NULL causes a WM_RENDERFMT message to be set to the clipboard owner window.
fmt	Format of the data.
pfFmtInfo	Pointer to a variable for the clipboard memory model and the clipboard CFI usage identifiers. (Refer to Chapter 15 for additional information on the CFI identifiers.)

The **return value** is TRUE if the function succeeds. It is FALSE if an error occurs.

BOOL WinSetClipbrdOwner(*hab, hwnd*)
HAB hab;
HWND hwnd;

WinSetClipbrdOwner sets the clipboard owner window.

ARGUMENT	DESCRIPTION
hab	Handle to the anchor block.
hwnd	Handle to the new clipboard owner window. Setting this argument to NULL releases the current owner of the clipboard, but does not assign a new one.

The **return value** is TRUE when a new clipboard owner is designated. It is FALSE when there is no owner.

BOOL WinSetClipbrdViewer(*hab, hwnd*)
HAB hab;
HWND hwnd;

WinSetClipbrdViewer designates a window as the clipboard-viewer. Ensure that the clipboard is open before calling this function.

ARGUMENT	DESCRIPTION
hab	Handle to the anchor block.
hwnd	Handle to a window that will become the clipboard-viewer. Setting this argument to NULL releases the current owner of the clipboard-viewer, but does not assign a new one.

The **return value** is TRUE when a new clipboard-viewer owner is designated. It is FALSE when there is no owner.

BOOL WinSetCp(*hmq, CodePage*)
HMQ hmq;
USHORT CodePage;

WinSetCp sets the queue code page for the message queue.

ARGUMENT	DESCRIPTION
hmq	Handle to a message queue.
CodePage	The code page, which must be one of the ASCII code pages defined in the system's CONFIG.SYS file.

The **return value** is TRUE if the function succeeds. It is FALSE if an error occurs.

BOOL WinSetDlgItemShort(*hwndDlg, idItem, usValue, fSigned*)
HWND hwndDlg;
USHORT idItem, usValue;
BOOL fSigned;

713

WinSetDlgItemShort converts an integer into a text string that comprises a dialog box item.

ARGUMENT	DESCRIPTION
hwndDlg	Handle to the dialog box.
idItem	The dialog item.
usValue	The integer value.
fSigned	Flag indicating whether the integer is signed or unsigned. Setting this to TRUE specifies unsigned. Setting it to FALSE specifies signed.

The **return value** is TRUE if the function succeeds. It is FALSE if an error occurs.

SHORT WinSetDlgItemText(*hwndDlg, idItem, pszText*)
HWND hwndDlg;
USHORT idItem;
PSZ pszText;

WinSetDlgItemText sets the text comprising a dialog box item.

ARGUMENT	DESCRIPTION
hwndDlg	Handle to a dialog box.
idItem	Dialog box item ID.
pszText	Pointer to the dialog box item text string, which is null-terminated.

The **return value** is TRUE if the function succeeds. It is FALSE if an error occurs.

BOOL WinSetFocus(*hwndDesktop, hwndSetFocus*)
HWND hwndDesktop, hwndSetFocus;

WinSetFocus sets the system focus to the specified window.

ARGUMENT	DESCRIPTION
hwndDesktop	Handle to the desktop window.
hwndSetFocus	Handle to the window receiving the focus.

The **return value** is TRUE if the function succeeds. It is FALSE if an error occurs.

BOOL WinSetHook(*hab, hmq, iHook, pfnHook, hmod*)
HAB hab;
HMQ hmq;
SHORT iHook;
PFN pfnHook;
HMODULE hmod;

WinSetHook sets a hook into a hook chain for an application. The function enables system hooks that are defined by HK identifiers.

ARGUMENT	DESCRIPTION
hab	Handle to the anchor block.
hmq	Handle to a message queue to which the hook is linked. Setting this to NULL installs the hook into the system hook chain. Setting it to HMQ_CURRENT links the hook to the message queue belonging to the calling thread.
iHook	Type of hook chain, which is specified by one of the system HK identifiers (see Chapter 14).
pfnHook	Pointer to the application's hook procedure.
hmod	Handle to the module containing the hook procedure.

The **return value** is TRUE if the function succeeds. It is FALSE if an error occurs.

BOOL WinSetKeyboardStateTable(*hwndDesktop, pKeyStateTable, fSet*)

HWND hwndDesktop;
BYTE pKeyStateTable;
BOOL fSet;

WinSetKeyboardStateTable sets the keyboard state, or alternatively, obtains information about the keyboard state. As a result of using this function, the value returned by WinGetKeyState is modified.

ARGUMENT	DESCRIPTION
hwndDesktop	Handle to the desktop window.
pKeyStateTable	Pointer to a 256-byte table indexed by the value of the virtual keys.
fSet	Flag indicating whether the function sets the keyboard state or obtains a copy of it. Setting it to TRUE sets the keyboard state. Setting it to FALSE obtains the keyboard state.

The **return value** is TRUE upon success. Otherwise, it is FALSE.

BOOL WinSctMsgInterest(*hwnd, msgclass, control*)

HWND hwnd;
USHORT msgclass;
SHORT control;

WinSetMsgInterest sets the message interest of a window.

ARGUMENT	DESCRIPTION
hwnd	Handle to a window.
msgclass	The message class, which is either a message class identifier such as WM_SHOW; or system-defined SMI_ALL identifier, which signifies this function should process all messages.
control	Specifies the message interest. It is either SMI_INTEREST, which signifies an interest in the message; or SMI_NOINTEREST, which signifies no interest in the message.

The **return value** is TRUE if the function succeeds. It is FALSE if an error occurs.

BOOL WinSetMultWindowPos(*hab, pswp, cswp*)
HAB hab;
PSWP pswp;
SHORT cswp;

WinSetMultWindowPos sets the window position for multiple windows of the same parent. It acts the same as the WinSetWindowPos function, but is more efficient than successive WinSetWindowPos calls. Both WinSet-MultWindowPos and WinSetWindowPos reference the SWP structure in order to obtain window coordinate data.

ARGUMENT	DESCRIPTION
hab	Handle to the anchor block.
pswp	Pointer to an array of SWP structures.
cswp	The number of SWP structures.

The **return value** is TRUE if the function succeeds. It is FALSE if an error occurs.

BOOL WinSetOwner(*hwnd, hwndOwner*)
HWND hwnd, hwndOwner;

WinSetOwner changes a window's owner.

ARGUMENT	DESCRIPTION
hwnd	Handle to the window having its owner changed.
hwndOwner	Handle to the window that will be the new owner of *hwnd*. Setting this to NULL gives *hwnd* a NULL owner — or no owner.

The **return value** is TRUE if the function succeeds. It is FALSE if an error occurs.

BOOL WinSetParent(*hwnd, hwndParent, fRedraw*)
HWND hwnd, hwndParent;
BOOL fRedraw;

WinSetParent changes a window's parent.

ARGUMENT	DESCRIPTION
hwnd	Handle to the window having its parent changed.
hwndParent	Handle to the window that will be the new parent of *hwnd*. Setting this argument to HWND_DESKTOP causes *hwnd* to become a main window.
fRedraw	Flag specifying a redraw indicator. Setting this to TRUE redraws the old and new parent when *hwnd* is a visible window. Setting this to FALSE prevents redrawing.

The **return value** is TRUE if the function succeeds. It is FALSE if an error occurs.

BOOL WinSetPointer(*hwndDesktop, hptrNew*)
HWND hwndDesktop;
HPOINTER hptrNew;

WinSetPointer sets the desktop pointer.

ARGUMENT	DESCRIPTION
hwndDesktop	Handle to the desktop window.
hptrNew	Handle to the new pointer. Setting this handle to NULL removes the pointer from the screen.

The **return value** is TRUE if the function succeeds. It is FALSE if an error occurs.

BOOL WinSetPointerPos(*hwndDesktop, x, y*)
HWND hwndDesktop;
SHORT x, y;

WinSetPointerPos sets the pointer position.

ARGUMENT	DESCRIPTION
hwndDesktop	Handle to the desktop window.
x	Horizontal pointer position in screen coordinates.
y	Vertical pointer position in screen coordinates.

The **return value** is TRUE upon success. Otherwise, it is FALSE.

BOOL WinSetRect(*hab, prcl, xLeft, yBottom, xRight, yTop*)
HAB hab;
PRECTL prcl;
SHORT xLeft, yBottom. xRight, yTop;

WinSetRect function sets the coordinates of a rectangle.

ARGUMENT	DESCRIPTION
hab	Handle to the anchor block.
prcl	Pointer to a RECTL structure.
xLeft	Lower left corner of the rectangle.
yBottom	Bottom edge of the rectangle.
xRight	Right corner of the rectangle.
yTop	Top edge of the rectangle.

The **return value** is TRUE upon success. Otherwise, it is FALSE.

BOOL WinSetRectEmpty(*hab, prcl*)
HAB hab;
PRECTL prcl;

WinSetRectEmpty sets a rectangle's dimensions to zero.

ARGUMENT	DESCRIPTION
hab	Handle to the anchor block.
prcl	Pointer to a RECTL structure.

The **return value** is TRUE if the function succeeds. It is FALSE if an error occurs.

BOOL WinSetSysColors(*hwndDesktop, flOptions, flFormat, clrFirst, cclr, pclr*)

HWND hwndDesktop;
ULONG flOptions, flFormat;
LONG clrFirst;
ULONG cclr;
PLONG pclr;

WinSetSysColors sets the value of the system color. As a result, a WM_SYSCOLORCHANGE message is sent to all frame windows. In response to this message, you should call WinQuerySysColor to query the new color values. (Refer to Chapter 5 for complete details on this function, including the system identifiers used in the call.)

ARGUMENT	DESCRIPTION
hwndDesktop	Handle to a desktop window.
flOptions	Either LCOL_RESET or LCOL_PURECOLOR.
flFormat	Either LCOLF_INDRGB or LCOLF_CONSECRGB.
clrFirst	The starting color index when LCOLF_CONSECRGB applies. If this is the case, specify one of the SYSCLR identifiers.
cclr	The number of *pclr* elements, or zero to reset the color table . When *flFormat* is LCOLF_INDRGB, set this argument to an even number.
pclr	The starting address of the application data area that contains the color-table definition data. Format is determined by *flFormat*. Color values are four-byte integers. The applicable formula is: (*Red* x 65536) + (*Green* x 256) + *Blue*. The *Red*, *Green*, and *Blue* values represent intensities. The maximum intensity is 255.

The **return value** is TRUE if the function succeeds. It is FALSE if an error occurs.

BOOL WinSetSysModalWindow(*hwndDesktop, hwnd*)

HWND hwndDesktop, hwnd;

WinSetSysModalWindow designates as the system modal window. Alternatively, it terminates the system modal state of a window.

ARGUMENT	DESCRIPTION
hwndDesktop	Handle to the desktop window.
hwnd	Handle to the window to receive system modal status. Setting this argument to NULL ends the system modal state.

The **return value** is TRUE if the function succeeds. It is FALSE if an error occurs.

BOOL WinSetSysValue(*hwndDesktop, iSysValue, lValue*)

HWND hwndDesktop;
SHORT iSysValue;
LONG lValue;

WinSetSysValue sets a system value associated with one of SV identifiers.

ARGUMENT	DESCRIPTION
hwndDesktop	Handle to the desktop window.
iSysValue	One of the SV identifiers.
lValue	The system value, which accepts durations in milliseconds and frequencies ranging from 25H to 7FFFH.

The **return value** is TRUE if the function succeeds. It is FALSE if an error occurs.

BOOL WinSetWindowBits(*hwnd, index, flData, flMask*)

HWND hwnd;
SHORT index;
ULONG flData, flMask;

WinSetWindowBits is used to set the ULONG bits that define a window's characteristics. This duplicates the functionality of setting the ULONG bits in an initial call to a function such as WinCreateStdWindow. In other words, it lets you modify your original FCF settings after calling WinCreateStdWindow (as well as similar functions).

ARGUMENT	DESCRIPTION
hwnd	Handle to the window.
index	Bytes used. Values fall between zero and number of extra window bytes. The QWL or QWS identifiers can also be specified.
flData	The new window data.
flMask	Flag specifying a mask value. Set this to 1 to write new data to *flData*. Set it to 0 to leave the existing ULONG value intact.

The **return value** is TRUE if the function succeeds. It is FALSE if an error occurs.

BOOL WinSetWindowPos(*hwnd, hwndInsBehind, x, y, cx, cy, fs*)
HWND hwnd, hwndInsBehind;
SHORT x, y, cx, cy, fs;

The WinSetWindowPos sets the screen position of a window. Refer to Chapters 4 and 5 for additional information on this function.

ARGUMENT	DESCRIPTION
hwnd	Handle to a window.
hwndInsBehind	Handle to the window that specifies the relative position of *hwnd*.
x	Horizontal position of the window.
y	Vertical position of the window.
cx	Height of the window.
cy	Width of the window.
fs	Flag specifying one of SWP identifiers.

The **return value** is TRUE if the function succeeds. It is FALSE if an error occurs.

BOOL WinSetWindowPtr(*hwnd, index, p*)
HWND hwnd;
SHORT index;
PVOID p;

WinSetWindowPtr sets a pointer value into reserved window memory.

ARGUMENT	DESCRIPTION
hwnd	Handle to a window.
index	Index of the pointer value. Valid values are in the range of zero to the number of bytes reserved for window data.
p	Pointer to the window word value.

The **return value** is TRUE if the function succeeds. It is FALSE if an error occurs.

BOOL WinSetWindowText(*hwnd, pszText*)
HWND hwnd;
PSZ pszText;

WinSetWindowText sends a WM_SETWINDOWPARAMS message to the specified window. You can use this message to change to titlebar text.

ARGUMENT	DESCRIPTION
hwnd	Handle to a window.
pszText	Pointer to a text string.

The **return value** is TRUE if the function succeeds. It is FALSE if an error occurs.

BOOL WinSetWindowULong(*hwnd, index, ul*)
HWND hwnd;
SHORT index;
ULONG ul;

WinSetWindowULong sets a ULONG into reserved window memory.

ARGUMENT	DESCRIPTION
hwnd	Handle to a window.
index	Zero-based index of the ULONG value. Valid values fall in the range of zero to the number of ULONGs of window data , or any of the system-defined QWL values.
ul	A ULONG to store in the window words.

The **return value** is TRUE if the function succeeds. It is FALSE if an error occurs.

BOOL WinSetWindowUShort(*hwnd, index, us*)
HWND hwnd;
SHORT index;
USHORT us;

WinSetWindowUShort sets a USHORT into reserved window memory.

ARGUMENT	DESCRIPTION
hwnd	Handle to a window.
index	Zero-based index of the USHORT value. Valid values fall in the range of zero to the number of USHORTs of window data , or any of the system-defined QWS values.
ul	A USHORT to store in the window words.

The **return value** is TRUE if the function succeeds. It is FALSE if an error occurs.

BOOL WinShowCursor(*hwnd, fShow*)
HWND hwnd;
BOOL fShow;

WinShowCursor displays or hides the cursor.

ARGUMENT	DESCRIPTION
hwnd	Handle to the window that owns the cursor.
fShow	Flag specifying whether the function displays or hides the cursor. Setting this to TRUE displays the cursor. Setting it to FALSE hides the cursor.

The **return value** is TRUE if the function succeeds. It is FALSE if an error occurs.

BOOL WinShowPointer(*hwndDesktop, fShow*)
HWND hwndDesktop;
BOOL fShow;

WinShowPointer displays or hides a pointer.

ARGUMENT	DESCRIPTION
hwndDesktop	Handle to the desktop window.
fShow	Flag specifying the pointer update level.

The **return value** is TRUE if the function succeeds. It is FALSE if an error occurs.

BOOL WinShowTrackRect(*hwnd, fShow*)
HWND hwnd;
BOOL fShow;

WinShowTrackRect displays or hides the tracking rectangle.

ARGUMENT	DESCRIPTION
hwnd	Handle to the window passed to the function.
fShow	Flag specifying the visible state of the rectangle. Setting this to TRUE shows the rectangle. Setting it to FALSE hides the rectangle.

The **return value** is TRUE if the function succeeds. It is FALSE if an error occurs.

BOOL WinShowWindow(*hwnd, fShow*)

HWND hwnd;
BOOL fShow;

WinShowWindow function sets the window's visibility state. You initially set the visibility state of a window — in WinCreateStdWindow and WinCreateWindow — by setting the WS_VISIBLE style bit.

ARGUMENT	DESCRIPTION
hwnd	Handle to a window.
fShow	Flag indicating the new visibility state. Setting this to TRUE makes the window visible. Setting it to FALSE makes the window invisible.

The **return value** is TRUE if the function succeeds. It is FALSE if an error occurs.

USHORT WinStartTimer(*hab, hwnd, idTimer, dtTimeout*)

HAB hab;
HWND hwnd;
USHORT idTimer, dtTimeout;

WinStartTimer starts a timer. The function generates a WM_TIMER message, when executed in normal fashion, and posts the message to the queue associated with the current thread.

ARGUMENT	DESCRIPTION
hab	Handle to the anchor block.
hwnd	Handle to the window that comprises part of the timer ID. Setting this to NULL causes *idTimer* to be ignored. As a result the function returns a unique timer ID.
idTimer	The timer ID.
dtTimeout	The timer delay in milliseconds. Specifying this to zero causes the timer to time out as fast as possible (after about 1/18 of a second).

The **return value** is TRUE if the function succeeds when *hwnd* is not Null. If hwnd is NULL, the return value is a unique non-zero value, or zero in the event of an error occurs. If the function fails, it returns FALSE.

BOOL WinStopTimer(*hab, hwnd, idTimer*)

HAB hab;
HWND hwnd;
USHORT idTimer;

WinStopTimer stops a timer and halts all WM_TIMER messages.

ARGUMENT	DESCRIPTION
hab	Handle to the anchor block.
hwnd	Handle to a window.
idTimer	Timer ID.

The **return value** is TRUE if the function succeeds. It is FALSE if an error occurs.

PFNWP WinSubclassWindow(*hwnd, pfnwp*)

HWND hwnd;
PFNWP pfnwp;

WinSubclassWindow subclasses a window.

ARGUMENT	DESCRIPTION
hwnd	Handle to the window to subclass.
pfnwp	Pointer to the address of the window procedure.

The **return value** is the address of the previous window procedure belonging to the window specified by the *hwnd* parameter. If the function fails, it is NULL.

SHORT WinSubstituteStrings(*hwnd, pszSrc, cchDstMax, pszDst*)

HWND hwnd;
PSZ pszSrc;
SHORT cchDstMax;
PSZ pszDst;

WinSubstituteStrings searches a text string and allows you to dynamically replace dummy characters. You can use this function to manipulate information in interface controls such as dialog boxes. The dummy characters are always denoted by a percent character (%) and followed by a number from 0 to 9.

ARGUMENT	DESCRIPTION
hwnd	Handle to the window processing the function.
pszSrc	Pointer to the null-terminated text string.
cchDstMax	Maximum number of characters in *pszDst*.
pszDst	Pointer to the null-terminated text string that results from the replacement of its dummy characters. If the string is too long, it is truncated (but the null terminator is preserved).

The **return value** is the number of returned characters. If the function fails, it returns zero.

BOOL WinSubtractRect(*hab, prclDst, prclSrc1, prclSrc2*)
HAB hab;
PRECTL prclDst, prclSrc1, prclSrc2;

WinSubtractRect subtracts one rectangle from another rectangle.

ARGUMENT	DESCRIPTION
hab	Handle to the anchor block.
prclDst	Pointer to a RECTL structure set to the new rectangle.
prclSrc1	Pointer to a RECTL structure set to the source rectangle.
prclSrc2	Pointer to a RECTL structure set to the destination rectangle.

The **return value** is TRUE when *prclDst* references a non-empty rectangle. If *prclDst* references an empty rectangle, the function returns FALSE.

BOOL WinTerminate(*hab*)
HAB hab;

WinTerminate terminates an application and properly shuts down the associated Presentation Manager resources. If you do not make this call, the Presentation Manager itself performs the necessary shut down operations. It is strongly recommended that you make this call near the end of your application.

ARGUMENT	DESCRIPTION
hab	Handle to the anchor block.

The **return value** is TRUE if the function succeeds. It is FALSE if an error occurs.

VOID WinThrow(*pctchbf, sThrowBack*)
PCTCHBF pctchbf;
SHORT sThrowBack;

WinThrow restores the execution environment. Previously, the environment must have been saved in a buffer by using the WinCatch function.

ARGUMENT	DESCRIPTION
pctchbf	Pointer to a CATCHBUF structure containing the execution environment.
sThrowBack	The SHORT value returned to the WinCatch function.

No **return value** results from this function.

BOOL WinTrackRect(*hwnd, hps, pti*)
HWND hwnd;
HPS hps;
PTRACKINFO pti;

WinTrackRect draws a tracking rectangle that you use in conjunction with the mouse pointer to position objects on the screen. Only one tracking rectangle rectangle can be active at any given time. For additional information, refer to Chapter 13.

ARGUMENT	DESCRIPTION
hwnd	Handle to the window receiving the tracking rectangle.
hps	Handle to the presentation space used for drawing the clipping rectangle. Setting *hps* to NULL causes *hwnd* to be used to calculate a presentation space for tracking.
pti	Pointer to a TRACKINFO structure.

The **return value** is TRUE if the function succeeds. If it fails, the return value is FALSE.

BOOL WinTranslateAccel(*hab, hwnd, haccel, pqmsg*)

HAB hab;
HWND hwnd;
HACCEL haccel;
PQMSG pqmsg;

WinTranslateAccel translates a WM_CHAR message into either a WM_COMMAND, WM_SYSCOMMAND, or WM_HELP message.

ARGUMENT	DESCRIPTION
hab	Handle to the anchor block.
hwnd	Handle to the destination window.
haccel	Handle to the accelerator table. A NULL value causes the function to reference the current accelerator table.
pqmsg	Pointer to a QMSG structure.

The **return value** is TRUE if the function succeeds. It is FALSE if an error occurs.

BOOL WinUnionRect(*hab, prclDst, prclSrc1, prclSrc2*)

HAB hab;
PRECTL prclDst, prclSrc1, prclSrc2;

WinUnionRect calculates the rectangle bounding two source rectangles.

ARGUMENT	DESCRIPTION
hab	Handle to the anchor block.
prclDst	Pointer to a RECTL structure set to the new rectangle.
prclSrc1	Pointer to a RECTL structure set to the source rectangle.
prclSrc2	Pointer to a RECTL structure set to the destination rectangle.

The **return value** is TRUE when *prclDst* references a non-empty rectangle. If *prclDst* references an empty rectangle, the function returns FALSE.

BOOL WinUpdateWindow(*hwnd*)
HWND hwnd;

WinUpdateWindow forces a window update. All child windows of the specified window are also updated.

ARGUMENT	DESCRIPTION
hwnd	Handle to a window.

The **return value** is TRUE upon success. Otherwise, it is FALSE.

USHORT WinUpper(*hab, idcp, idcc, psz*)
HAB hab;
USHORT idcp, idcc;
PSZ psz;

WinUpper converts a string into an uppercase string.

ARGUMENT	DESCRIPTION
hab	Handle to the anchor block.
idcp	Specifies the code page. A NULL value causes the function to reference the current code page.
idcc	Specifies the country code. A NULL value causes the function to reference the default country.
psz	Pointer to a string.

The **return value** is the converted string's length.

USHORT WinUpperChar(*hab, idcp, idcc, c*)

HAB hab;
USHORT idcp, idcc, c;

WinUpperChar converts a character to its uppercase equivalent.

ARGUMENT	DESCRIPTION
hab	Handle to the anchor block.
idcp	Specifies the code page. A NULL value causes the function to reference the current code page.
idcc	Specifies the country code. A NULL value causes the function to reference the default country.
c	A character.

The **return value** is the converted character if the function succeeds. If it fails, it returns zero.

BOOL WinValidateRect(*hwnd, prcl, fIncludeChildren*)

HWND hwnd;
PRECTL prcl;
BOOL fIncludeChildren;

WinValidateRect subtracts a rectangle from the update region of an asynchronous paint window.

ARGUMENT	DESCRIPTION
hwnd	Handle to a window.
prcl	Pointer to a RECTL structure containing the rectangle to be subtracted.
fIncludeChildren	Flag indicating the validation scope. Setting this to TRUE sets the scope to all descendants of *hwnd* in the valid rectangle. Setting it to FALSE sets the scope to all descendants of *hwnd* in the valid rectangle (if the parent window is not WS_CLIPCHILDREN).

The **return value** is TRUE if the function succeeds. It is FALSE if an error occurs.

BOOL WinValidateRegion(*hwnd, hrgn, fIncludeChildren*)
HWND hwnd;
HRGN hrgn;
BOOL fIncludeChildren;

WinValidateRegion subtracts a region from the update region of an asynchronous paint window. If any part of the window has become invalid since the last call to WinBeginPaint, WinQueryUpdateRect, or WinQueryUpdateRegion, the function has no effect. Do not use this function on CS_SYNCPAINT windows.

ARGUMENT	DESCRIPTION
hwnd	Handle to a window.
hrgn	Handle to the region to be subtracted.
fIncludeChildren	Flag indicating the validation scope. Setting this to TRUE sets the scope to all descendants of *hwnd* in the valid rectangle. Setting it to FALSE sets the scope to all descendants of *hwnd* in the valid rectangle (if the parent window is not WS_CLIPCHILDREN).

The **return value** is TRUE if the function succeeds. It is FALSE if an error occurs.

BOOL WinWaitMsg(*hab, msgFirst, msgLast*)
HAB hab;
USHORT msgFirst, msgLast;

WinWaitMsg waits for the next message that meets the filtering conditions set by *msgFirst* and *msgLast*. The function filters all messages that have occurred since the last call to WinGetMsg or WinPeekMsg .

ARGUMENT	DESCRIPTION
hab	Handle to the anchor block.
msgFirst	The first message in the filter sequence.
msgLast	The last message in the filter sequence.

The **return value** is TRUE if the function succeeds. It is FALSE if an error occurs.

HWND WinWindowFromDC(*hdc*)
HDC hdc;

WinWindowFromDC determines the window associated with a window device context.

ARGUMENT	DESCRIPTION
hdc	Handle to a window device context.

The **return value** is a handle to a window if the function succeeds. If the device context is not a window device context, the return value is NULL. If an error occurs, the return value is also NULL.

HWND WinWindowFromID(*hwndParent, id*)
HWND hwndParent;
USHORT id;

WinWindowFromID obtains a handle to a child window.

ARGUMENT	DESCRIPTION
hwndParent	Handle to the parent window.
id	A child window.

The **return value** is a handle to a handle to a child window. If the function does not find a child window, it returns NULL.

HWND WinWindowFromPoint(*hwnd, pptl, fChildren, fLock*)
HWND hwnd;
PPOINTL pptl;
BOOL fChildren, fLock;

WinWindowFromPoint finds the window on the basis of both screen location and lineage. Specifically, it finds a window that lies beneath a specified point and is also a descendant of a specified window. The usual purpose of this function is to find a given child window.

ARGUMENT	DESCRIPTION
hwnd	Handle to a window.
pptl	Pointer to a POINTL structure that contains the test point. If *hwnd* is NULL or HWND_DESKTOP, *pptl* must be set to screen coordinates.
fChildren	Flag specifying which child windows to test. Setting this to TRUE tests all descendants of *hwnd*. Setting it to FALSE tests only the immediate descendants of *hwnd*.
fLock	Flag specifying whether to lock the window. Setting this to TRUE locks the descendant of *hwnd*. Setting it to FALSE specifies no locks.

The **return value** is the handle to the window beneath *pptl*. When no child window corresponds to *pptl*, the function returns *hwnd*. When *pptl* does not correspond to any window in the *hwnd* lineage, the function returns NULL.

USHORT WinWriteProfileData(*hab, pszAppName, pszKeyName, pchBinaryData, cchData*)
HAB hab;
PSZ pszAppName, pszKeyName;
PVOID pchBinaryData;
USHORT cchData;

The WinWriteProfileData places binary data into a keyname/value pair in OS2.INI. The data entered into OS2.INI is not terminated with a null character.

ARGUMENT	DESCRIPTION
hab	Handle to the anchor block.
pszAppName	Pointer to a null-terminated text string containing the name of the application requiring the initialization data.The string can be no longer than 1,024 bytes (including the null terminator).
pszKeyName	Pointer to a null-terminated text string containing the name of the keyname/value pair for which the value is returned. The string can be no longer than 1,024 bytes (including the null terminator).
pchBinaryData	Pointer to an array of bytes for the binary data.
cchData	Size of *pchBinaryData* in bytes.

The **return value** is zero upon success. Otherwise, it is non-zero

BOOL WinWriteProfileString(*hab, pszAppName, pszKeyName, pszValue*)

HAB hab;
PSZ pszAppName;
PVOID pszKeyName, pszValue;

WinWriteProfileString enters a keyname/value pair into the OS2.INI file.

ARGUMENT	DESCRIPTION
hab	Handle to the anchor block.
pszAppName	Pointer to a null-terminated text string containing the name of the application requiring the initialization data.The string can be no longer than 1,024 bytes (including the null terminator).
pszKeyName	Pointer to a null-terminated text string containing the name of the keyname/value pair for which the value is returned. The string can be no longer than 1,024 bytes (including the null terminator).
pszValue	Pointer to a null-terminated ASCII text string containing the value of the keyname/value. When *pszValue* is NULL, the function deletes the string referenced by *pszKeyName*. When *pszValue* is not NULL, the function uses the value of the keyname/value (even if the string is a zero-length string).

The **return value** is TRUE if the function succeeds. It is FALSE if an error occurs.

736

INDEX

X

Z

PROGRAMMER'S GUIDE TO
PRESENTATION MANAGER

Example Programs
Order Form

Please send me a disk containing the programs from this
book. I understand that the programs may vary slightly,
and I have enclosed a check for $14.95 for the disk.

_____
Name

_____
Address

_____   _____   _____
City   State   Zip

☐   3.5-inch disk

☐   5.25-inch disk

Please make your check payable to Alan Southerton and
send it along with this order form to:
        P.O. Box 373, Broadway, NC 27505